this series of companions to major philosophers
lly commissioned essays by an international team of
ther with a substantial bibliography, and will serve as
work for students and nonspecialists. One aim of the
dispel the intimidation such readers often feel when
the work of a difficult and challenging thinker.

art Mill (1806–73) ranks among the very greatest thinkers
eteenth century. Through his books, journalism, corre-
and political activity, his impact on modern culture and
s been immense, and his continuing importance for con-
philosophy and social thought is widely recognized.

npanion furnishes the reader with a systematic and fully
e account of the many facets of Mill's thought and influ-
enc e volume also illuminates the many connections between
Mi losophy and contemporary work in epistemology, ethics,
soc nd political philosophy, and economics. It will be of special
inte t to all philosophers as well as a broad range of students and
rea of political science, economics, and the history of ideas.

N readers will find this the most convenient and accessible
guid o Mill currently available. Advanced students and specialists
will d a conspectus of recent developments in the interpretation
of Mi .

THE CAMBRIDGE COMPANION TO

MILL

The Cambridge Companion to
MILL

Edited by John Skorupski
University of St Andrews

PUBLISHED BY THE PRESS SYNDICATE OF THE UNIVERSITY OF CAMBRIDGE
The Pitt Building, Trumpington Street Cambridge CB2 1RP, United Kingdom

CAMBRIDGE UNIVERSITY PRESS
The Edinburgh Building, Cambridge CB2, 2RU, United Kingdom
40 West 20th Street, New York, NY 10011-4211, USA
10 Stamford Road, Oakleigh, Melbourne 3166, Australia

First published 1998

Printed in the United States of America

Typeset in Trump Medieval

Library of Congress Cataloging-in-Publication Data
The Cambridge companion to Mill / [edited by] John Skorupski.
p.   cm.
Includes bibliographical references and index.
ISBN 0-521-41987-5 (hard). – ISBN 0-521-42211-6 (pbk.)
1. Mill, John Stuart, 1806–1873. I. Skorupski, John, 1946–   .
B1607.C25   1997
192–dc21   97-2968
                                                               CIP

*A catalog record for this book is available from
the British Library*

ISBN 0 521 41987 5 hardback
ISBN 0 521 42211 6 paperback

In Memory of
John M. Robson
1927–1995
to whom all admirers of John Stuart Mill are indebted

Contents

vii

viii   Contents

Contributors

WENDY DONNER is an associate professor of philosophy at Carleton University, Ottawa. She is the author of *The Liberal Self: John Stuart Mill's Moral and Political Philosophy* (1991) and has published articles in political philosophy, environmental ethics, and feminist ethics. Currently she is co-editing an anthology on selfhood and identity politics.

ANDY HAMILTON is a lecturer in philosophy at Durham University. He has published articles on self-knowledge and personal identity, on Mach and the Vienna Circle, and on aesthetics.

T. H. IRWIN is Susan Linn Sage Professor of Philosophy at Cornell University. His books include *Plato's Gorgias* (translation with notes, 1979), *Aristotle's Nicomachean Ethics* (translation with notes, 1985), *Aristotle's First Principles* (1988), *Classical Thought* (1988), and *Plato's Ethics* (1995).

PHILIP KITCHER is Presidential Professor of Philosophy at the University of California at San Diego. He is the author of *Abusing Science: The Case Against Creationism* (1982), *The Nature of Mathematical Knowledge* (1983), *Vaulting Ambition: Sociobiology and the Quest for Human Nature* (1985), *The Advancement of Science* (1993), and *Lives to Come: The Genetic Revolution and Human Possibilities* (1996). He has also written articles in the philosophy of science, the philosophy of mathematics, and the philosophy of biology, and on figures in the history of philosophy.

ALAN MILLAR is a professor of philosophy at the University of Stirling. He is the author of *Reasons and Experience* (1991) and various articles on perceptual experience. His works also include articles which explore links between Joseph Butler's theology and his moral philosophy.

PETER P. NICHOLSON is a reader in politics at the University of York. He is the author of *The Political Philosophy of the British Idealists: Selected Studies* (1990).

JONATHAN RILEY is a professor at the Murphy Institute of Political Economy, Tulane University. He is the author of *Liberal Utilitarianism* (1966) and *Mill's On Liberty* (Routledge, forthcoming), and the editor of *J. S. Mill: Principles of Political Economy and Chapters on Socialism* (1994).

JOHN ROBSON was a university professor and professor of English at the University of Toronto. He wrote extensively on nineteenth-century thought and literature. He was General and Textual Editor of *The Collected Works of John Stuart Mill* (1963–91) and author of *The Improvement of Mankind: The Social and Political Thought of John Stuart Mill* (1968).

ALAN RYAN is Warden of New College, Oxford. He is the author of *The Philosophy of John Stuart Mill* (1970) and *J. S. Mill* (1974), and editor of *Mill* in the Norton Critical Edition series (1996).

GEOFFREY SCARRE is a lecturer in philosophy at the University of Durham. His publications include *Logic and Reality in the Philosophy of John Stuart Mill* (1989) and *Utilitarianism* (1996).

MARY LYNDON SHANLEY is the Margaret Stiles Halleck Professor of Political Science at Vassar College. She is the author of *Feminism, Marriage and the Law in Victorian England* (1989). She edited, with Carole Pateman, *Feminist Interpretations and Political Theory* (1990), and with Uma Narayan, *Contested Concepts: Essays in Feminist Political Theory* (forthcoming). Her current work explores theoretical issues in contemporary family law.

JOHN SKORUPSKI is Professor of Moral Philosophy at the University of St Andrews. He is the author of *Symbol and Theory* (1975), *John Stuart Mill* (1989), and *English-Language Philosophy 1750–1945* (1993). His current interests are in ethics, metaphysics, and political philosophy.

C. L. TEN was educated at the former University of Singapore (now National University of Singapore) and at the London School of Economics. He is a professor of philosophy at Monash University, Australia. He is the author of *Mill on Liberty* (1980) and *Crime, Guilt and Punishment* (1987), and editor of *The Nineteenth Century* (Routledge History of Philosophy, vol. VII).

FRED WILSON is a professor of philosophy at the University of Toronto. He has published extensively in the philosophy of science and in the early history of modern philosophy. Among his publications are *Psychological Analysis and the Philosophy of John Stuart Mill* (1990) and *Empiricism and Darwin's Science* (1991). In 1994 Professor Wilson was elected a fellow of the Royal Society of Canada; he has also served as president of the Canadian Association of University Teachers.

Method of citation

All page references to the writings of Mill are to *The Collected Works of John Stuart Mill* (33 volumes), John M. Robson, General Editor (Toronto: University of Toronto Press, 1963–91). They are given as follows: *CW* I:15, for *Collected Works*, Volume I, page 15.

Introduction: The fortunes of liberal naturalism

I. THE FALL AND RISE OF A REPUTATION: MILL AND MODERNISM

> I cannot go on – Mill is dead! I wonder if this news will have affected you as it does me. . . .

So Henry Sidgwick wrote after John Stuart Mill's death on 7 May 1873. Several days later he continued:

> Mill's prestige has been declining lately: partly from the cause to which most people attribute it – the public exhibition of his radicalism: but partly to the natural termination of his philosophical reign – which was of the kind to be naturally early and brief. . . . I should say that from about 1860–65 or thereabouts he ruled England in the region of thought as very few men ever did. I do not expect to see anything like it again.[1]

This indicates Mill's influence at its peak as well as presaging its decline. Four decades later, Balfour wrote that Mill's authority in the English Universities had been "comparable to that wielded . . . by Hegel in Germany and in the middle ages by Aristotle", and Dicey noted that "John Mill was between 1860 and 1870 at the height of his power. His authority among the educated youth of England was greater than may appear credible to the present generation".[2] It was already becoming necessary to explain how influential Mill had been.

The vicissitudes of Mill's reputation – as epistemologist, moral philosopher, political and cultural critic – connect with much else in the philosophy and history of our century, not least with the rise

I am grateful to Andy Hamilton for his helpful comments on a draft of this introduction.

I

and fall of European modernism and European socialism. By 'modernism' I mean the culture of the period which stretches roughly from the 1890s to the 1960s or thereabouts. This was also the period in which Mill's stock stood relatively low. His reputation as a philosopher fell rapidly from his death to the First World War.[3] In the renewed surge of modernism that came after the war and continued to the 1950s and 1960s it remained low. Mill was remembered as a personally noble figure and ancestral liberal voice. In politics and social morality one could argue that his influence had lapsed just because his ideas had been assimilated – though it was only one side of Mill, the social egalitarian side, of which that could be said. On the curricula of university philosophy departments, however, *Utilitarianism* received a regular roasting for its 'logical errors' while Mill's empiricism about logic and mathematics was mentioned as an awful warning of what defensible empiricism must find a way to avoid. Nor was it only the Vienna Circle which took the idea that logic and mathematics are 'analytic' to be "an important advance in the development of empiricism" (Carnap 1963, 47). The doctrine became orthodox – a dogma one might say of analytic modernism – until the assault on the notion of analyticity which began in the 1950s, led by Quine, and eventually itself became a dogma of the new naturalism.

From about the 1960s or early 1970s the situation has been changing. Current trends in philosophy make it easier to appreciate Mill, to rethink his work and put it to use, than it has been for a hundred years or more. Revaluation began with Mill's ethics, moved to his social and political theory, and has eventually widened to his general philosophy.[4] It has again become possible to recognise Mill's true stature. He gave his country's empiricist and liberal traditions a formulation as important as John Locke's. As an ethical thinker, Mill's significance is matched in the nineteenth century only by Hegel and Nietzsche. The three of them speak in sequence from successive thirds of the century; they close an equilateral triangle of possibilities. Hegel sublimates the yearning for self-transcendence into absolute idealism. Mill and Nietzsche present alternatives for those who have that yearning but reject idealism and cleave to a naturalistic view of man – a view of human beings as natural entities, in a natural world to which there is, in Nietzsche's word, no 'beyond'. Both, in very different ways, seek a way to affirm human transcendence or self-making within such a world. They define the anti-poles of modern (as against ancient) naturalism. The question 'Mill or Nietzsche?' has a special resonance today.[5]

But to go back to the flight from Mill. Naturally, one of its causes was simply the revolt of generations. Consider this, from a review of Mill's posthumously published *Three Essays on Religion*:

> we are conscious of increased admiration for the fine intellectual faculty, the beautiful moral nature, the docility, the patience, the moderation, and the aesthetic or romantic enthusiasm of their lamented author. With wonderful caution in investigation are united prodigious boldness of thought, punctual emphasis of expression, careful analysis, lucid order, logical sobriety, and unabated mental vigour; while a noble Schiller-like tone of sentiment pervades, as a subtle perfume of the soul, the serener air of the author's loftiest speculation. (Call 1875, 2)

How must such effusions have affected younger thinkers who needed to find their own way! Would one wish to contend with an older figure who was seen as (let us say) a sort of Keynes, Popper, Rawls and Solzhenitsyn rolled into one? Mill's apotheosis was a barrier to new thinking. Even Sidgwick wrote in another letter that "Mill will have to be destroyed, as he is becoming as intolerable as Aristeides" – though with the balance one expects from him he added, "when he is destroyed, we shall have to build him a mausoleum as big as his present temple of fame".[6]

Call is absurdly high-flown – but not merely fanciful.[7] 'Aesthetic and romantic enthusiasm' and 'mental vigour', combined with 'caution', 'order', 'punctual emphasis' and 'logical sobriety' – that captures Mill's attractive qualities. 'Docility', 'patience', and 'moderation' (as against balance) do so less well. More like it are scornfulness and impatience with the mediocre, and priggishness in relation to the average sensual human being. Still, these less attractive qualities are the obverse of the 'noble Schiller-like tone of sentiment', a phrase which well places Mill's outlook and identity in the early, romantic and revolutionary nineteenth century. Yet this tone of sentiment, and the ethical and aesthetic outlook from which it arose, or to which it gave rise, was probably the quality in Mill which the subsequent century found hardest to come to terms with. It connects Mill with Hegel's German contemporaries. It remains a difficulty, perhaps the greatest remaining difficulty, in our own understanding of Mill. We shall come back to it in section IV.

Generational revolt aside, the last forty years of the nineteenth century saw major changes in logic, psychology and economics. Insofar as Mill defended obsolete positions in these disciplines, however intelligently, he had to be thrust aside. It was more difficult then than it is now, when Mill is no longer a figure of influence in them, to disentangle his philosophy of logic from his adherence to syllogistic theory, his moral psychology from his associationism, his social philosophy from his classical economics. But those years saw much more than a generational revolt and a set of paradigm-changes in the disciplines which interested Mill. They saw a great philosophical sea-change, whose ground-swell was a reaction against precisely the liberal naturalism of the nineteenth century which Mill classically represents.

This was as true in epistemology as in ethics. In Britain the first, brief, aspect of the reaction was the rise of British idealism. The idealists, led by the Oxford philosopher T. H. Green, rejected the very coherence of Mill's naturalistic empiricism. The philosophy they sought to replace it with did not survive – but their criticism of the coherence of naturalistic empiricism was in the spirit of the times. That same naturalism was rejected just as firmly by realists from Frege to Moore, and then later by Wittgenstein and the Vienna Circle, who introduced the new conception of the a priori as 'analytic' which I referred to earlier.

Not only was the philosophical tide racing against Mill, so, though less obviously, was the political tide. Liberalism in those *fin-de-siècle* years was moving in a collectivist direction. T. H. Green was a significant British leader of this *fin-de-siècle* constructive liberalism, just as he was a leader of *fin-de-siècle* idealism. But the transitional phase of idealism and constructive liberalism was, from 1900, rapidly eclipsed in politics by socialism and social democracy and in epistemology (within 'analytic philosophy') by realism and then logical positivism and ordinary-language philosophy.

These changes around 1900 were the really decisive ones. The shift from Mill's ethical and political concerns to Green's is, in comparison, not so clearcut. Mill operates with a 'positive' notion of moral freedom as well as a 'negative' notion of civil liberty. By the end of his life he thought of himself as a kind of socialist; but the posthumously published 'Chapters on Socialism' (*CW* V) show very clearly how his socialism develops from his concern with the ethical stature of the individual just as Green's liberal interventionism does, and he rejects centralist and revolutionary or class-based kinds of socialism just as much as Green would. Mill's concern with the development of the individual was less moralistic and more in the early nineteenth century's spirit of romantic hellenism than Green's – an important difference which one should not obscure. Nonetheless a very much bigger change of ethical vision comes between both Mill and Green and this century's political ideas. Mill's and Green's concern with individual development – with notions like responsibility, moral freedom, the elevation and ennoblement of the feelings, all of which require an objective philosophical anthropology – was replaced on the political plane with questions of social justice and national efficiency, on the moral plane with a denial of the determinacy of human nature and hence of the possibility of philosophical anthropology, and finally, on the epistemological plane, with an eventual denial of the objectivity of values. The picture is complex in its details but the direction of the change is clear and momentous.[8]

As one contemplates these trends it becomes apparent that more recently a further instalment of philosophical and political changes has occurred. It has not yet lost its momentum in philosophy and it is gradually working its way through the broader culture. The keynote in philosophy is the resurgence of naturalism; but as ever, the pattern of change is complex. As before, an epistemological shift is central to it: of which the Quinean criticism of analyticity which was noted above is a major part. Yet Quine's naturalism continues to maintain a view of the relation of language and thought which developed in the 1930s – a conception in which the mental has to be characterised in terms of physics and speech-dispositions or rejected. It is already much easier for a Quinean naturalist to find value in Mill's naturalistic epistemology than it would have been for a logical empiricist or an Oxford language analyst. But it is even easier if one does not reject the very viability, from a strictly philosophical point of view, of the world of human understanding: of intentionality, normativity, synonymy. There is here a very important difference between the nineteenth-century naturalism of Mill and the post-modernist naturalism of Quine.[9] There is no suggestion in Mill that a naturalistic philosophy must eschew intentional states – beliefs, purposes, sentiments, etc. Rather, Mill is a naturalist in the sense that he thinks (i) that beliefs, purposes, sentiments are genuine properties of the human being seen as a natural entity and (ii) that the normative can be grounded in them – nothing *beyond* them is required.

In moral and political philosophy there has been a much-remarked resurgence of substantive ethical and political inquiry, often recovering Millian concerns. No less remarkable is how strongly the return of naturalism and the revival of substantive ethical and political inquiry has been accompanied by a reassertion of ethical objectivity. That is the kind of naturalism found in Mill, which I have just contrasted with Quine's. Not that naturalistic reassertion of objectivity is the only thing happening in current philosophy; with the resurgence of naturalism there also comes an intensified assault on objectivity. This is one reason why the antipoles of Mill and Nietzsche now seem so relevant. The growth of interest in these two philosophers follows from a revival of naturalism and of interest in its consequence for ethics.

II. NATURALISM IN EPISTEMOLOGY: MILL, HUME AND REID

The central questions about the coherence of naturalism are firmly back on the agenda. In assessing them, however, it is important to bear in mind that the history of philosophical naturalism contains more than one way of doing epistemology in a naturalistic spirit. In particular there is the tradition, one might say, to which Hume belongs, and the tradition to which Reid belongs. If Nietzsche stands loosely in the tradition of Hume, Mill stands loosely in the tradition of Reid.

Critics of naturalism highlight the tradition of Hume. Hume's philosophy seems to show that a naturalistic science of the mind leaves no space for our notion of ourselves as persons acting, thinking and feeling from reasons. Just because it seems to show this, it is surprising neither that Hume should have been in eclipse in Britain in the first two-thirds of the nineteenth century, nor that he should then have been revived in the last third, by a variety of philosophers whose common theme was a renewed reaction against naturalism. For in Britain there was always an influential alternative to Hume – the non-sceptical naturalistic tradition to which Reid belongs. It remained the dominant philosophy in the first part of the century. Only when naturalism came squarely into focus as the main threat to religion did Hume come back into play. He was presented by Green as the most intelligent naturalist, the one who clearly saw where naturalism led: to a complete scepticism or nihilism about reason. In Green's version of the philosophical canon, Kant then found a way to avoid that terminus by providing an alternative to naturalism. After Hume and Kant we must conclude either that the mind in some way constructs nature, or that epistemological and ethical nihilism is forced.[10]

The epistemological standpoints of modernism are continuous with those of Hume, rather than those of Reid and Mill. That is true whether one looks at the Nietzschean or at the Viennese side of modernist philosophy. However, in modernism Hume's counterweight to nihilism – that fine enlightenment item, the irresistible power of human nature – has disappeared. It is replaced by a Nietzschean notion of the transvaluing power of the strong individual, or an existential notion of authentic choice or by Vienna Circle conventionalism. Hume's distinction between factual propositions and normative claims becomes a distinction between factual propositions within language-frameworks and *choices* – about language-frameworks or about ethical stances.

What then of the other naturalist tradition, that of Mill and Reid? It may seem strange to link these names. Philosophic radicalism, the philosophy and politics associated with Bentham from which Mill sprang, shares important doctrines with Hume. Bentham generously acknowledged Hume's influence in leading him to a clear distinction between the normative and the factual. Bentham, James Mill, and John Stuart Mill all share with Hume an adherence to associationism. Moreover, Mill placed followers of Reid, together with Kantians, in what he variously called the 'intuitional', 'transcendental', and 'a priori school' – to which he opposed his own school of 'experience and association'.

On the other hand the Mills took a rather hostile attitude to Hume. They saw him as a littérateur whose sceptical arguments were an aspect of his literary pretensions, a diversion from the sober science of the mind. They were also not beyond seeing scepticism as a comfort-blanket for Tories.[11]

It is in fact Mill's view of scepticism as unserious or unreal that most clearly places him, as an epistemologist, with Reid rather than with Hume. Mill agrees with Reid and disagrees with Hume on a fundamental point of epistemological method. He thinks that if we can show that a cognitive disposition plays what I will call a *primitively normative* role in our thinking that can vindicate its normative legitimacy.

The most scientific proceeding can be no more than an improved form of that which was primitively pursued by the human understanding, while undirected by science. . . . (*CW* VII:318–19)

Principles of Evidence and Theories of Method are not to be constructed *à priori*. The laws of our rational faculty, like those of every other natural agency, are only learnt by seeing the agent at work. (*CW* VIII:833)

The construction is not a priori in that it involves no Platonic intuiting or transcendental deducing. We discover and codify our primitive normative responses by critical reflection on our practice. The responses are normative in content, in that they are responses about what, in a given context, there is reason to believe (or do or feel). What it is for them to be primitive is something we must consider further. At any rate *that* they are primitive is apparently a sufficient basis for accepting them as sound.

The method does not differ from Reid's philosophy of common sense, though the conclusions do. Mill had no reason to highlight his agreement with Reid, since at the time he wrote the underlying point of method was not in dispute. Instead he highlighted his very substantial disagreement. In his view various principles of Reidian common sense – that is, principles which according to Reid are primitively normative – are not primitive or 'original' but can be explained away. So his portfolio of primitively normative dispositions is much slimmer than Reid's. He holds that the only primitive form of reasoning is enumerative induction. He further recognises as normative a primitive disposition to accept past-tense propositions on the basis of memory. On this austere basis Mill develops his science of inductive logic and his account of logic and mathematics as inductive sciences.

What then is it to recognise a disposition as primitively normative? And why does Mill end up with a much shorter list than Reid's?

In the *System of Logic* the disposition taken as primitively normative is the disposition to generalise from experience. Methods of induction other than enumerative induction are not, Mill thinks, independent sources of new truth. Hypothetical inference – inference to a hypothesis which explains the data and is simpler than any other available hypothesis – does not on its own warrant assertion that the hypothesis is true, though it may be heuristically valuable. His (and Reid's) case against it is that more than one hypothesis might explain the data. The eliminative methods of induction which Mill identifies are underpinned by enumerative induction. Deductive principles of reasoning are justified inductively. The fabric of belief which emerges from what he calls the "inductive process" is self-stabilising in that it confirms, extends and refines, rather than undermining, the primitively warranted norm of enumerative induction.

Here the method stands out clearly. In the *Examination of Sir William Hamilton's Philosophy*, however, it is harder to get it into focus. Now Mill distinguishes an "introspective" and a "psychological" method in what he calls the "interpretation of consciousness". The introspective method is that of Reid and his followers. It inspects consciousness to establish what our "intuitive beliefs" are – those beliefs, or those dispositions to believe in the presence of non-cognitive states of consciousness, which we find we cannot reject. It undertakes a process of scrutiny to get at the ones which are authentically "ultimate" and to screen out those which are not. Having done that it assumes that the remaining beliefs and dispositions to believe are not further explicable – and that they are true or sound.

Though the introspective method "interprets consciousness" rather than "seeing the agent at work", it is otherwise not unlike Mill's own epistemological method in the *System of Logic*. So why does Mill reject it in favour of his "psychological method"? It turns out that he wants to emphasise the need to inquire into the *origin* of our beliefs. He finds the common-sensists insufficiently critical on this score. His preferred psychological method reduces the "data of consciousness" to the minimal number of elements which can, by associationist principles, be shown capable of generating the rest. Mill thinks the psychological method shows that some belief-forming dispositions which the introspective method takes to be ultimate are in fact explicable. In particular he argues that the formation of our perceptual judgements is explicable on associationist principles *without assuming that we perceive anything external to the mind*. It is this that leads him to his phenomenalism.

Memory, in contrast, must be acknowledged as a mode of "intuitive knowledge" – for neither our perceptual judgements nor our judgements of memory are explicable *without assuming that we really do remember things*:

> as all the explanations of mental phenomena presuppose Memory, Memory itself cannot admit of being explained. Whenever this is shown to be true of any other part of our knowledge, I shall admit that part to be intuitive. (*CW* IX:165, footnote)

In broad terms one may say that both Mill and Reid hold that a belief-forming disposition which is in certain ways 'explicable' is not primitively normative. The difference is about how many are so 'explicable'. But what is this connexion between inexplicability and normative authority? Surely not every explanation of why we have a belief-forming disposition undermines its normative authority. Let us call explanations which do, 'subversive'. When if ever is an explanation subversive? A *strong* view would say that an explanation is subversive when its truth fails to imply that beliefs formed by the disposition it explains are (by and large, in normal cases) true; that is, when it fails to imply that the disposition to form them is reliable. Let us say that an explanation which does imply that the explained disposition is reliable is 'confirming'. An example of a confirming explanation would be an evolutionary explanation which explained the survival value of our disposition to generalise from experience in terms of its tendency to generate true expectations. Then the strong view says that an explanation is subversive if it is not confirming. A *weak* view is that an explanation subverts a belief-forming disposition only if it implies either that that disposition is unreliable or that we cannot know whether or not it is reliable. On the weak view an explanation may be neither subversive nor confirming.

The strong view becomes very strong if we add to it the claim that any primitively normative disposition must be confirmingly explained *before* its authority is vindicated. We then have a short route to scepticism, since to explain any primitive disposition confirmingly we must accept the authority of some primitive dispositions. There is no reason to attribute to Mill the very strong view. In fact what he says about memory in the passage quoted above, and what he says elsewhere about induction, is incompatible with attributing it to him. On the other hand his argument for phenomenalism does seem to depend on the *strong* view.

Mill thinks that his explanation of the disposition to form perceptual beliefs is subversive when those beliefs are taken to be about "external causes of sensation" rather than about "permanent possibilities of sensation". For when those beliefs are understood in the realist as against the phenomenalist way then Mill's explanation implies, he thinks, that we cannot know whether the disposition to form them is reliable. It is not clear that he is right. What actually implies that we cannot know whether the disposition is reliable – if anything – is not Mill's associationist explanation of the disposition but his inductivism. And if inductivism has that consequence in the case of perception (understood as knowledge of external causes of sensation), it also has that consequence in the case of memory. In *this* respect there is no asymmetry between the two faculties.

Mill does also say, of the tie between a sensation and a memory of it, that

there is something real in this tie, real as the sensations themselves, and not a mere product of the laws of thought without any fact corresponding to it. (*CW* IX:207)

But we can ask how Mill knows this, given that he denies that hypothetical reasoning is primitively normative. He could only respond that his knowledge of the "real tie" relies on the authority of the faculty of memory. There would be no fallacy in this response, contrary to proponents of the very strong view. However, it would still generate no asymmetry with perception, since we could argue similarly that there is a real tie in the case of perception – relying on the authority of the faculty of perception.

Apparently the asymmetry Mill sees is this. In the case of perception we can explain the belief that there is a real tie, or causal linkage, between a perceptual experience and a physical object external to that experience by the associationist laws of thought – without assuming the existence of physical objects external to experience. But in the case of memory there is no analogous way of explaining our belief in a causal linkage between a remembering experience and the experience remembered as "a mere product of the laws of thought". For the associationist laws of thought already assume that memory is an effective causal mechanism. This then is the disanalogy with perception. The point is that the explanation of perception is not a confirming explanation. If Mill takes that alone as showing it to be subversive, he is taking the strong (though not the very strong) view.

Whether Mill is justified in taking the strong view in this case is a question we need not pursue. There is certainly danger in taking the strong as against the weak view overall; that is, for all our belief-forming dispositions – including dispositions to form normative as against factual beliefs. Perhaps Mill could say that the strong view is justified in the case of perception precisely because we are dealing with a disposition to form factual beliefs. But the point to note for present purposes is rather this: Mill produces no confirming explanation of our primitive disposition to take an apparent remembering that p as warranting the belief that p. He simply says that "as all the explanations of mental phenomena presuppose Memory, Memory itself cannot admit of being explained".

At first glance this is a *non sequitur*. Why should it follow from the fact that all our explanations presuppose memory that (the reliability of) memory itself cannot be explained? What does follow is that it cannot be a precondition of the *authority* of memory that a confirming explanation of its *reliability* should first be supplied. In other words memory is 'intuitive' in that first, its authority has to be accepted without any such confirming explanation, and second, no subversive explanation which would defeat its authority is available. Reflection on our practice shows that the tendency to fix beliefs on the basis of memory plays a normative role in our thought. It also shows that our tendency to generalise from experience plays a normative role. And in neither case is there a subversive explanation of that role.

Overall we can apparently extract three criteria of the primitively normative from Mill. Primitively normative dispositions are those which

(a) are discovered by careful examination of our consciousness and practice to play a normative role in our thinking;
(b) cannot be derived from, and can be reflectively harmonised with, other such dispositions; and
(c) are *not* subversively explicable.

These criteria operate in Mill's moral philosophy as well as in his treatment of memory, perception and science. Thus he argues in the spirit of (a) and (b) that happiness is the one thing desirable because we only desire a thing when we take it to be enjoyable. We treat the fact that a thing is enjoyable as a reason for desiring it; we do not derive this reason from any other reason, and we treat nothing else as an underived reason for desiring. Against intuitionist views in ethics Mill deploys arguments based on (b) and (c) – such 'intuitions' cannot be harmonised and are subversively explicable. Crucially, he fails to provide a systematic justification, based on (a), (b) and (c), of the normative authority of the utility principle itself. He takes it to be the ultimate principle of "Teleology" or "Practical Reason" (*System of Logic, CW* VIII:950–51), and he discusses what psychological factors will make it stable and capable of commanding allegiance (*Utilitarianism*, ch. 3). The points he makes in this latter discussion might also serve to show that our adherence to the principle is not subversively explicable. Moreover he often suggests that our moral practices are best systematised by the utility principle. But the explicit case he makes for it in chapter 4 of *Utilitarianism* is famously, indeed disastrously, rudimentary.

More generally, he never provides a clear and explicit discussion of his epistemological method. This leaves his minimalist argument against the Reidian long-list of primitively normative principles pretty unclear. Suppose, however, that we had some clear statement of the epistemological method to which Reid and Mill both seem to subscribe – a comprehensive account, say, of some such criteria as (a), (b) and (c). That might well help to resolve the disagreement between them. But even if it did, another, more abstract, challenge to the method *as such* comes from the Critical direction; that is, from Kantians, or naturalists in the tradition not of Reid but of Hume.

How, a philosopher in these traditions might ask, can Mill dismiss scepticism? Mill makes a distinction between verbal and real propositions which plays a role in his epistemology as fundamental as that played in Hume's epistemology by the distinction between relations of ideas and matters of fact and existence. He holds that no real proposition is a priori. On this basis, together with a semantic analysis of logic and mathematics which shows that these sciences have real content, he denies that logic and mathematics themselves are a priori. Why then is he not led to a scepticism even more thoroughgoing than Hume's?

Enumerative induction and memory (and any other principles which the criterion of the primitively normative endorses as legitimate) are not merely verbal principles. So neither, on Mill's own account, can be a priori. It appears to follow that if they are propositions – judgeable contents – at all they can be known only on the basis of evidence. Mill's idea of the 'evidence' for them seems to consist of evidence that they are primitively normative. But this is evidence of the wrong kind. What is needed is evidence that they are likely to preserve truth. And now we have a vicious circle, since nothing can be inferred from any evidence unless we accept some inferential principles as primitively legitimate, without evidence.

Unless empiricism is to collapse into the conclusion that no knowledge is possible, we must either conclude that some propositions are assertible irrespective of empirical evidence or deny that normative claims are propositions – judgeable contents – at all. The latter, expressivist, path belongs in the naturalistic tradition of Hume and the Vienna Circle and still has powerful exponents. There is, however, a naturalistic alternative. It accepts that normative claims have genuine propositional content but it does not take a realist view of that content. It distinguishes the respective epistemologies appropriate to normative and factual propositions. The epistemology we adhere to, in assessing the tenability of a normative claim, is an epistemology of critical self-examination and discussion as modelled by some version of (a)–(c). Factual propositions on the other hand must ultimately be grounded on empirical evidence – because they are true or not according to whether they picture facts which can only be known empirically.

To make this distinction is to reject the view that all content is factual content, in that sense of fact which goes with a correspondence conception of truth and a matching epistemology. But the thesis that all propositional content is factual content is perhaps the deepest doctrine of modernism in philosophy. It was endorsed in both the realist and the positivist phases of analytical modernism. To make sense of the naturalism of Reid and Mill one must therefore defend a naturalism which is neither realist nor positivist: which does not hold that all informative content is factual. Normative propositions are genuine propositions, judgeable contents. But they make no ontological claim about any domain, natural or non-natural.

Such a conclusion cannot be attributed either to Reid or to Mill. The nearest we find to a discussion of these issues in Mill is in the final chapter of the *System of Logic*, where he draws a distinction between Science and Art. He says that "sciences in the only proper sense of the term" are "inquiries into the course of nature". However, "moral knowledge" results from "an inquiry the results of which do not express themselves in the indicative, but in the imperative mood, or in periphrases equivalent to it" (*CW* VIII:943). This at least makes it clear that Mill does distinguish between the normative and the factual. But it may also seem that he here endorses an expressivist view of normative claims, as expressing commands *rather* than propounding propositions. In my view, this interpretation would go beyond the textual evidence. In talking of the imperative mood Mill probably meant no more than Kant meant in talking of categorical and hypothetical imperatives. After all, he accepts that the term "moral knowledge" is *not* "improper" and also accepts, "borrowing the language of the German metaphysicians", that its ultimate principles "may also be termed, not improperly, the principles of Practical Reason" (*CW* VIII:949–50). So he seems to accept that these imperatives are objects of knowledge cognisable by reason.

An even bigger question for the interpretation of Mill's epistemology is whether he would have applied a similarly framed distinction between the indicative and the imperative across the board, that is, in epistemology as well as in ethics – as the defence here offered of his epistemological method requires. The chapter of the *System of Logic* which has just been mentioned, 'Of the Logic of Practice, or Art' treats only of practical, not of theoretical, reason. Would Mill agree that there are imperatives of theoretical as well as of practical reason? Does he take enumerative induction and a principle concerning the authority of memory to be such imperatives? The issue is crucial and Mill's silence on the point is perhaps the greatest lacuna in his philosophy.

III. UTILITARIANISM: SOCIAL CONSTRUCTION, HISTORY AND UTOPIA

The resurgence of naturalism and the decline (at least in analytic philosophy) of modernist epistemologies which follow the spirit of Hume and Nietzsche have made it easier to sympathise with Mill's epistemology – to see how it might be developed and given defences which he did not give. The decline of another important ingredient in modernism makes it easier to recapture the underlying spirit of his ethics and politics.

The ingredient in question is a constructivist vision of the social. It sees society as a machine for living together, a machine which can be constructed and reconstructed according to a rational design. We need clear vision, technical knowledge provided by social science, and the good will to work together – collective planning rather than uncoordinated individual initiative. 'We are building a new society.'

Social constructivism can be traced to nineteenth-century progressive thought and further back to the Enlightenment; indeed it is a permanently possible attitude. I call it an ingredient of modernism because it achieved an unparalleled influence in modernist political culture – say in the period from the Russian Revolution and its aftermath in the 1920s to the 1960s or 1970s. We are now going through a (possibly over-sharp) reaction against it. One powerful cause is the decline and eventual dramatic collapse of what East Europeans called 'actually existing socialism'. Those particular experiments in construction were not products of social constructivism alone; they drew on aspects of Marxism which did not have the same influence in Western Europe – the vision of a 'scientifically' necessary evolutionary process to communism, and the vision of communism as emancipated communal life unmediated by any disciplinary institutions at all. In other words, their ideology combined constructivism with certain specific forms of historicism and utopianism. Constructivism does not have to go with these. It could provide legitimating sustenance to political and administrative elites without them. What has put it in disrepute is the failure of systems of planning and control which it requires – the systemic failure most dramatically seen in Eastern Europe.

Now utilitarianism is easily taken as an expression of this constructivist attitude; it is probably no accident that the association between the two ideas should have gained a particularly strong grip in this period. F. R. Leavis's "technologico-Benthamite" springs to mind as does Bernard Williams's "government-house utilitarianism". The latter phrase neatly evokes an administrative elite, self-legitimated by abstract ideals of benevolence, managing a social reality from which it is emotionally detached. 'Government House', it is true, is not where one would expect to find the typical utilitarian; 'Ministry of Supply utilitarianism' would be more like it. In that respect Leavis hits it better.[12] But certainly many who are attracted to utilitarianism as an ethic are also attracted to constructivism as a political and social attitude. This has been particularly true in our century and it had already proved true in Mill's time.

That time was also one of strong reaction against constructivism – and Mill was one of its most potent critics. It is hard to put his thinking on this in a nutshell. Some of his programmatic statements about psychology and social science and their role in policy certainly smack of the scientistic prejudice that there is nothing between science and prejudice. That is characteristic of social constructivism – but these statements fade when Mill deals with the moral sciences and their limitations in detail; and in his ethical writing he freely draws on a humanistic and historical moral psychology.

A good starting point for appreciating this side of his thought is his criticism of Bentham and Comte, the former in the essay on 'Bentham' and its companion piece on 'Coleridge', and the latter in the extended two-part essay on 'Auguste Comte and Positivism' (all three are in *CW* X).

Mill was no simple critic of either thinker. He rightly thought he had learned valuable things from both of them. Bentham gave him materials for an analysis of justice, moral rights and moral obligation, and a theory of their connexion with the interest of security. These became the backbone of Mill's ethics. Comte had also been an important influence on Mill. He did not convince Mill that psychology and economics, the strong points of the philosophic radicals, were pseudo-sciences – but he did convince him that the leading role in social science would be played by a historical sociology which pictured society as a functional organic 'consensus' of all its aspects, continuously evolving through time.

Comte represented, in a "scientific" format, the criticism of Enlightenment social thought as abstract and unhistorical which was very widespread in the early nineteenth century. But Mill's feeling for the historicity of society and human nature also came from elsewhere – from Coleridge and Carlyle and through them from German romanticism. It was from here that he drew a conception of character and culture which informed his moral psychology, and a romantic hellenism which informed his ethical ideal. These lay at the heart of his liberal anti-constructivism.

What history and moral psychology teach ethics is this: that responsibility, trust and civil association knit together only when they are maintained by a functioning cultural tradition and practice. The error of Enlightenment *philosophes* was to trust too much in the invariance and resilience of ethical sentiments. They

believed them to be more deeply rooted in human nature than they are; to be not so dependent, as in fact they are, upon collateral influences. They thought them the natural and spontaneous growth of the human heart; so firmly fixed in it, that they would subsist unimpaired, nay invigorated, when the whole system of opinions and observances with which they were habitually intertwined was violently torn away. ('Coleridge', *CW* X:131)

Constructivists in spirit, they did not grasp the conditions necessary for such a system of opinions and observances – namely, education of personal impulses to a restraining discipline, shared allegiance to some enduring and unquestioned values, and "a strong and active principle of cohesion" among "members of the same community or state".

They threw away the shell without preserving the kernel; and attempting to new-model society without the binding forces which hold society together, met with such success as might have been anticipated. ('Coleridge', *CW* X:138)

Moral education, the formation of character, was Mill's particular concern. Without it there can be no development of humanity to its highest powers. Character is formed by the evolution of purpose, will and conscience from primitive feelings and desires; this evolution requires a favourable and stable social setting. Here Mill had new things to say, which went beyond Benthamism and on the other hand often show an affinity with Hegel on *sittlichkeit* and the development of the will.

His criticism of Comte in 'Auguste Comte and Positivism' is also scathing. He had, it is true, found in the teaching of Comte and the Saint-Simonians a valuable corrective to "the common doctrines of Liberalism" (*CW* I:173). Comte saw the need for discipline and allegiance which Enlightenment *philosophes* and simple-minded liberals failed to see. Understanding as he did the historical evolution of society, he had much to teach about conditions for stability. But he had little to teach about the conditions for moral progress. If Bentham was "a boy to the last", untouched by self-consciousness and impervious to the influence of other times and nations ('Bentham', *CW* X:92), Comte was finally a liberticide, obsessed with consensus. His utopian vision of an organic society would stamp out independence and individuality, impose a central hierarchy and guarantee moral stagnation. Comte did not neglect the cultivation of character as Bentham did – but he neglected the importance of providing for it a diversity of situations and of ensuring that the culture of the individual should be largely self-culture.

In contrast Mill agreed with French liberals of the stamp of Guizot and Tocqueville, who argued that conflict and opposition of ideas and social forces was a precondition of moral as well as material progress: "No one of the ancient forms of society contained in itself that systematic antagonism, which we believe to be the only condition under which stability and progressiveness can be permanently reconciled to one another" ('Guizot's Essays and Lectures on History', *CW* XX:269). It was this that had made "the European family of nations an improving, instead of a stationary portion of mankind" – "Not any superior excellence in them, which, when it exists, exists as the effect, not the cause; but their remarkable diversity of character and culture" ('On Liberty', *CW* XVIII:274).

These criticisms of Comte's utopianism blended with another. Comte committed the error which is often, but falsely, charged against the whole class of utilitarian moralists; he required that the test of conduct should also be the exclusive motive of it. . . . The golden rule of morality, in M. Comte's religion, is to live for others, "vivre pour autrui". . . . M. Comte is a morality-intoxicated man. Every question with him is one of morality, and no motive but that of morality is permitted. ('Auguste Comte and Positivism', *CW* X:335–36)

With such a view Mill could not more vehemently disagree:

Why is it necessary that all human life should point but to one object, and be cultivated into a system of means to a single end? May it not be the fact that mankind, who after all are made up of single human beings, obtain a greater sum of happiness when each pursues his own, under the rules and conditions required by the good of the rest, than when each makes the good of the rest his only object, and allows himself no personal pleasures not indispensable to the preservation of his faculties? The regimen of a block-aded town should be cheerfully submitted to when high purposes require it, but is it the ideal perfection of human existence? (*CW* X:337)

If we criticise some varieties of utilitarianism for being ahistorical, or naively constructivist – or for their authoritarian flavour, or for an abstract utopianism which propounds universal altruism or a single duty of optimising well-being, then we make exactly the objections Mill made against the utilitarianisms of Bentham and Comte. He cannot be accused of making utilitarianism abstract – but one might in retrospect make an opposite criticism. There was abundant human insight and caution in his sense of how utilitarianism could be applied as a source of political and social guidance; but he gave too little philosophical attention to abstract analysis of thesis itself.

Utilitarianism as such *is* an abstract ethical thesis about what has intrinsic ethical value. Mill did not think hard enough about its content. He did think hard about the claim that happiness is the only thing that has ethical value, and he said wise things about it. One may nevertheless think he did not think hard enough, and was too attached to hedonism. But about the distributive content of the utilitarian thesis he hardly thought at all. I do not have in mind the question of what 'middle principles' of justice might be grounded on the thesis, a question which he discussed in various places at length. I am thinking about the content of the thesis itself: about how it proposes to measure overall ethical value, or general good, as a function of the good of individuals. Here Mill's weakness is not merely that he failed to analyse the arguments available to the egoist (as Sidgwick saw). Let us allow that he was not interested in that issue and simply took for granted a principle of impartiality. Even so, he did not think about what constraints a principle of impartiality could plausibly put on functions from individual happiness to general good, or even about the implications, for that question, of his own distinction between quantity and quality of pleasure. At this level of analysis of utilitarianism his contribution is slim.

These are live ethical questions which can only be pursued abstractly and analytically. What Mill offers in moral and political philosophy is something else – balance and wholeness of vision. He wanted to propound a fuller vision of human well-being than Bentham's, a vision which included a substantive ideal of life, and to show that a utilitarianism inspired by these things would produce a liberal society which encompassed many "experiments of living" but did not lack sources of permanence or stability. Bentham hammers the utilitarian nail more single-mindedly, Sidgwick pays greater attention to analytic detail, but neither has this inspiring breadth of vision and imaginative sympathy.

In fact Balfour's comparison of Mill with Aristotle and Hegel is apt at least in this way: all these three philosophers were synthesisers whose influence depended on their wholeness and many-sidedness. What Aristotle did for Athenian aristocrats and Hegel for Prussian constitutionalists, Mill did for humanist European liberals.

This is Mill's greatest quality. In many ways Mill stands in relation to Enlightenment thought and the French Revolution as we stand in relation to modernist thought and the socialist revolutions. The balanced critical attitude he took to those, we need to take to these. But there is one big difference. The standpoint from which Mill revalued the ideas of the Enlightenment and the politics of the French Revolution was a romantic-hellenic ideal of human life – the 'noble Schiller-like tone of sentiment'. It is not clear whether we have that or any substitute for it to bring to our revaluation of modernism and social democracy.

IV. THE LIBERAL AND THE DEMOCRATIC ETHOS

Can a liberal and utilitarian naturalism inspire? Or does it somehow turn its face from the sorrow and grandeur of life? Is it even coherent?

Those who experience the thought-world of liberal naturalism as a diminution of life are also apt to argue for its incoherence. To show up the iron cage as an impossible object would be a great relief. Therein lies the personal significance – for philosophers as different as Green the religious moralist and Nietzsche the anti-liberal anti-moralist – of the critique of naturalism which we discussed above. They could readily have agreed that the outlook of liberal naturalism assumes a vindication of the objectivity of its liberal values which it simply cannot provide. Hence their disdain for Mill.

Certainly this is a fundamental objection to Mill's philosophical project; the prospects for answering it turn on the issues about naturalism and epistemology which were noted in section II. There it was suggested that the naturalistic method followed (in their very different ways) by Mill and Reid is not fundamentally incoherent, as its critics suggest. It can affirm the objectivity of the normative: it simply needs to exhibit in a perspicuous way the relevant differences between normative and factual propositions, and the epistemologies appropriate to them.

But this objection often overlaps with another, which contains a greater variety of strands: that whatever Mill's good intentions, liberal naturalism inevitably declines into instrumental individualism, populist destruction of high culture and conformist mediocrity.

The epistemological part of this further objection lies in the thought that a naturalistic framework can make no sense of the strong valuations, or qualitative distinctions, which a high ideal of life like Mill's requires. The feeling that it cannot do so – often experienced, and recently argued most powerfully by Charles Taylor (Taylor 1989) – is part of what makes people think liberal naturalism diminishes life. However, there is no *special* epistemological problem about the objectivity of such distinctions. If a naturalistic account of objectivity can be given at all, then it can apply to these distinctions as to others. Clearly the possibility of acknowledging the higher is central to Mill's ethical vision. He tells us, in rough but serviceable terms, what the criterion of higher forms of well-being is. It is what "human beings with highly developed faculties can care to have" (*System of Logic*, *CW* VIII:952), or in the well-known discussion in chapter 2 of *Utilitarianism*, what "competent judges" would prefer. This should be no surprise: it is simply an application of the epistemology of self-examination and discussion which we noted in section II. Mill's appeal to "competent judges" acknowledges the obvious point that in any such self-examination and discussion certain voices emerge as more authoritative than others, for example because they win acceptance as being more penetrating and dispassionate. Further defence of Mill's liberal naturalism on this point – its acknowledgement of higher goods – therefore resolves into further defence of the epistemology of reflection and discussion (which does not, incidentally, differ in essence from Taylor's own dialogical conception of reason).

At this point we must keep in mind some large and significant differences between liberalisms in this century and the philosophical liberalism of Mill's time – the period from the end of the Napoleonic wars to the 1860s – in which Mill's thought formed and developed. One could argue that in that period liberal thought achieved its maturest form to date. Mill was only one of the thinkers who shaped this classical liberalism. To all of them the proposition that modern – 'bourgeois' or 'democratic' – society has atomising and diminishing effects would have been no surprise. But the idea that *liberalism* has these effects would certainly have surprised them. They would have distinguished a liberal ethos which they defended from a democratic ethos which they feared.

Their thinking was shaped by those two earthquakes in European politics and culture, the French Revolution and German romanticism. Revolutionary terror and its Bonapartist sequel taught them that there was something to fear on the left, from Jacobinism, popular sovereignty, the leadership of a great individual, as well as on the right from aristocratic and clerical reaction. They maintained the defining liberal doctrine of rule of law and equality of rights under law, but rejected as 'abstract' earlier foundations for it, from social contract and natural right to the general will. In place of these they affirmed a teleological criterion of human flourishing. They filled out this notion by a romantic hellenism which owed most to German romantic philosophy. It differed from earlier forms of humanism, among other things by its recognition of the historicity of human nature and morality and by its emphasis on the educative importance of negative liberty and diversity of life in developing and empowering human beings.[13]

The ideal of realised human power is central to this liberal ethic: specifically, the ideal of an interactive balance of moral freedom and individual spontaneity.[14] Moral freedom means the capacity of self-government – the capability of ordering one's actions by what one is oneself able to recognise as good reasons. Spontaneity is not the simple expression of feeling. It assumes the culture of the feelings as moral freedom assumes the culture of reason and will. So it assumes that there is something to be cultivated, something to be got right; it involves the idea of right, appropriate feeling – the overcoming of immaturity, stuntedness, repression, as also of distorting limitations, delusions, enslaving emotional needs, and then beyond that, the development of insight. Here, in its notions of freedom and spontaneity, is one important point at which classical liberalism assumes the objectivity of valuations – and in that way differs from modernist notions of authenticity, expression, radical choice and the like.

The ideal inspires Mill's *Liberty*:

> There is a Greek ideal of self-development, which the Platonic and Christian ideal of self-government blends with, but does not supersede. It may be better to be a John Knox than an Alcibiades, but it is better to be a Pericles than either; nor would a Pericles, if we had one in these days, be without anything good which belonged to John Knox. (*CW* XVIII:265–66)

This romantic-hellenic ideal is the source of classical liberals' intense anxieties about democratic mass culture. On their view, the cultivation of moral freedom requires civil and political liberty, and the cultivation of spontaneity requires tolerance of diversity, since different human natures achieve spontaneity in very different ways. *If* democracy provides these conditions and gives rise to a society of developed human beings, it is good. And according to Mill at least (who was the most democratically inclined of the classical liberals), it is in a democracy that they can best be provided. Yet although such a type of democracy is possible, it is not a proximate or certain prospect. Forms of democracy which drift into "collective despotism" can become a positive threat to human development by restricting liberty or threatening the toleration of diversity. This was a danger to which Mill thought America had already succumbed. His advice for warding it off was not less democracy but more liberty:

> if the American form of democracy overtakes us first, the majority will no more relax their despotism than a single despot would. But our only chance is to come forward as Liberals, carrying out the Democratic idea, not as Conservatives, resisting it.[15]

Hence the essay *On Liberty*, with its defence of liberty of thought and discussion and its exposition of individuality as one of the elements of well-being. Nor were these the only instruments by which Mill hoped to steer from bad forms of democracy towards good. Some of his recommendations – plural voting, a public ballot, a franchise restricted by educational qualification – may now seem misguided or simply quaint. Others, including proportional representation of minorities and – not least – his life-long advocacy of equal rights for women, may seem ahead of his time. Either way the reasons he gives for them are invariably interesting. Mill was always a democrat. But his criterion of democracy was the good of the people, not the will of the people.

So liberalism must carry out the democratic idea, but it must be on its guard against a form of democracy which is inimical to the liberal ideal, a certain democratic ethos which is more or less subtly opposed to the (classical) liberal ethos. And by now we too must surely agree that whether or not Mill's fears were exaggerated, they were not misplaced. Much of the political culture of this century – including its rather faded liberal strands – reacted against the classical liberal ethos on behalf of exactly that democratic ethos. It very specifically rejected every element in the epistemology and ethics of classical liberalism: the objectivism about the normative, the hellenic-romantic moral psychology and the acknowledgement of historicity.

Of particular importance was the rejection of objectivity. Modernist liberalism holds that you cannot appraise ends and values. It is precisely here that it replaces the liberal ethos by the democratic ethos. The difference is a subtle one, lying in the understanding of 'equal respect'. The liberal ethos affirms equal rights and rejects inherited status. The democratic ethos says that the *ends and values* of all individuals deserve equal respect. They deserve equal respect *because* there can be no ground for giving them unequal respect: the ultimate ends and values of individuals are simply unappraisable. Attempts to evaluate ends become dangerous fanaticism, bigotry or snobbery.

This syndrome is hugely formative. The classical liberals' objective affirmation of freely developed diversity is replaced by a tolerance of diversity based on *epistemological* neutrality. Thus, from the classical liberal's point of view, to acknowledge that there is a rank-order of ends and of ways of living is not incompatible with the affirmation of diversity: at each rank in the order there can be an indefinite plurality of ways of living. In contrast, the modernist liberal thinks his liberalism is superior precisely by its recognition of the meaninglessness of such ranking. Modernist liberalism tries to base political tolerance on an epistemology of subjectivism – it even conflates political tolerance with that epistemology, so that the rejection of subjectivism is itself taken as intolerance.

What I have just been sketching is populist doctrine. More philosophical versions of modernist liberalism reject the fallacy of inferring to tolerance in politics from subjectivism about ethics. Yet it is striking how much they still attempt to derive defences of liberty from theses in epistemology rather than from a substantive ethical ideal. Consider three of this century's most influential liberal philosophers: Popper, Berlin and Rawls. Popper's liberalism, with its emphasis on the moral and political significance of an epistemological 'dualism of facts and decisions' (Popper 1950) and its tilting with the windmills of 'historicism' (Popper 1961) is closest to the populist version. In contrast, Berlin's 'value-pluralism' is apparently not a form of subjectivism – and he does not confuse the nineteenth century's sense of the shaping significance of history for individuals and collectivities with a doctrine of historical inevitability. Nonetheless, 'value-pluralism' is an epistemological doctrine about 'values' and the argument from it to liberalism is supposed to rest on a standpoint of epistemological detachment from any one system of values rather than on the endorsement of a specifically liberal ethos.[16]

Rawls distinguishes between 'comprehensive' and 'political' liberalism (Rawls 1993a). Comprehensive liberalism is one of a number of philosophical and ethical positions, liberal and non-liberal – Rawls cites Mill and Kant as developing comprehensive forms of liberalism. 'Political liberalism' refrains from endorsing any one comprehensive position, liberal or other. It does not even take a view on meta-ethical questions about the existence and nature of truth in ethics, questions on which, as Rawls says, comprehensive positions will have a view.[17] It restricts itself to assessing which comprehensive positions are 'reasonable' (so it is committed to the objectivity at least of this question) and then arguing to constitutional proposals from an 'overlapping consensus' of such reasonable positions.

Berlin rejects populist subjectivism and Rawls refrains from affirming it, but in both cases there is a structural similarity with the populist argument to liberalism. An argument for tolerance is developed from a standpoint of epistemological detachment, rather than from a 'comprehensive' ethical ideal. The similarity is evident in the role played by 'the fact of reasonable pluralism' in Rawls's argument:

Once we accept the fact that reasonable pluralism is a permanent condition of public culture under free institutions, the idea of the reasonable is more suitable as part of the basis of public justification for a constitutional regime than the idea of moral truth. Holding a political conception as true, and for that reason alone the one suitable basis of public reason, is *exclusive, even sectarian. and so likely to foster public division.*[18]

A related feature of recent American liberal theory which further distinguishes it from classical liberalism is its insistence that the state must not favour any conception of the good. It must not do so either (1) by prohibiting any individual from pursuing his or her conception (within just limits) or (2) by acting as a persuader in favour of some conception. But while (1), permissive neutrality, is clearly continuous with classical liberal theory, (2), persuasive neutrality, is not. The classical liberal does have a conception of the good – the hellenic-romantic ideal with its notion of a balance of moral freedom and expressive spontaneity. And it is no part of classical liberalism to deny the state or society a role in fostering, as against enforcing, that ideal through its educational and cultural policies.[19]

On the other hand, how realistic is it to invoke that hellenic-romantic ideal of balance now? It is far from being the only ideal we encounter in contemporary societies. It is not even particularly influential compared to others. Taken overall, it was never even very influential in the nineteenth century, and in this century it has faced a long period of hostility and decline. Given these uncertain fortunes, and the great diversity of ideals in contemporary societies, it is inevitable that liberals should ask how close the connexion is or should be between classical liberal ideals and the arguments for a liberal social and political order. The question is powerfully raised by Rawls, and anyone sympathetic to classical liberalism must face up to it.

One may suspect that the objective tendency of Rawlsian liberalism, as more generally with modernist liberalism, is not simply neutralist but away from the classical liberal ethos and towards endorsement of a democratic ethos which classical liberals would have seen as inimical to their ideal. It is striking, for example, that recent American liberal philosophy has returned to notions of contract, natural right and general will which liberals of Mill's time found both metaphysical and dangerous. There is indeed a similar debate about these notions in contemporary philosophy, but it has come to be characterised as a debate between liberals and 'communitarians' – as though one could *equate* liberalism with endorsement of these notions, or endorsement of strong doctrines of state neutrality such as those mentioned above. This characterises liberalism in a way which leaves out classical liberalism: it shows how far the terms of the debate about 'liberalism' have shifted.

I believe that there is a real historical crux for liberal thought here. What should it take from its two legacies – that of classical liberalism (which changes in philosophy and politics have once again rendered accessible), and that of modernism, with its varieties of epistemological and political neutralism or detachment? Should liberal thought now endorse its contemporary American and modernist strands and relinquish its classical liberal inheritance, or should it seek to regenerate the inheritance and reject those contemporary American and modernist elements as a democratic ideology alien to its essential spirit? Revaluing Mill will form a part, though no more than a part, of any serious answer to that question.

To endorse current neutralist varieties of liberal theory risks promoting bad forms of democracy under a liberal mask. The state is debarred from seeking to maintain allegiance to the liberal ethos; yet public discussion (Rawls's 'public reason') is handed the dangerous tool of disqualifying from the agenda comprehensive positions which are deemed to be 'unreasonable'. Of course a careful Rawlsian will have answers to these worries. But as with any political prescription, what one must consider is how it will be used in political fact.

Certainly the same point can be made about classical liberalism. Just as one can ask whether the objective effect of Rawls's political liberalism is entrenchment of conformist political correctness and mediocrity, so one can ask whether the objective effect of classical liberalism is an unacceptable or even dangerous elitism.

It is no easy question. Mill was an elitist in the sense that he believed that there are individuals of higher intellectual and moral powers and that they have an obligation to exercise moral and intellectual influence. But he was emphatically not an authoritarian. His was a liberal elitism and he took pains to distinguish it from that of hero worshippers like Carlyle and 'liberticides' like Comte.[20] Yet even if Mill's high conception of human powers poses, in his hands at least, no threat to liberty, may it not pose dangers of a different kind? Suppose we take the existence of higher goods with real seriousness, rather than merely paying lip service to it. And suppose we are committed to an impartial standard of general well-being as a political as well as an ethical criterion. How then are qualitative judgements about the good life to be entered into an overall assessment of the general good? In requiring utilitarianism to take them into account Mill makes a move of political as well as ethical significance. For what rank do we give to the achievement of higher forms of well-being in our social ordering, the rank which highly developed human natures attach to them or that which less developed human natures attach to them? Mill's answer is unambiguous: it is the verdict of 'competent judges' which stands.

The strain this could place on democratic and egalitarian convictions is easy to see.[21] One can reply that we are fortunate enough (or more accurately some of us are fortunate enough) to live in a world of great affluence. It does not lack hard choices; but it simply is not the case that providing access to higher goods in the degree which 'competent judges' would call for requires immiserating great numbers of people – let alone a despotism of spiritual aristocrats in the manner envisaged by Nietzsche. It *might* have required it. Perhaps even in the past it has required it – on what did Athenian culture or that of mediaeval monasteries stand? But to acknowledge this is simply to see what any teleological liberal must see anyway:

that liberal politics rests on empirical circumstance and not self-evident natural rights.

Acknowledging the higher in the shape of the classical liberal's romantic-hellenic ideal threatens (as we stand) neither enslavement nor immiseration. The problem to which it gives rise (as we stand) is rather less dramatic, but still insidious. It is an ideal which can seem (to borrow Rawls's words) "exclusive, even sectarian, and so likely to foster public division". To some extent this is peculiar to it. Unlike various great religious ideals, it is this-worldly and involves no salvific and redemptive 'beyond' to which all of us have a possible access lying in our own hands. This is its hard edge on which feelings are bruised. So even if we acknowledge the higher should we perhaps depoliticise or privatise it, as neutralist liberalism suggests? Relegate it to 'comprehensive liberalism' but give it no role in political priorities or questions of resource allocation?

Surely not. That would cut off ethical ideals from the most important debates of the polis – a drastic solution, a kind of political lobotomy. On the contrary. Those who are inspired by a great ethic have a responsibility to seek to influence and persuade – to find a public language in which they can do so. This is not to say that the classical liberal ethic can ever give rise to personal inspiration, as against more or less notional respect, in a great majority. One should be a realist about that. However, the stability of liberal order does not require it to do so. Social solidarity is made up of an amalgam of things and the liberal ideal can be a vitalising element in the amalgam. There are, in any society, people who hunger for a great ethic and more or less controversy about what ethical vision is best. The character of the society is set in the longest run by which great ethical ideas acquire the greatest authority (not hegemony). It is for that reason that a liberal society cannot afford to be neutralist but must continually sustain the prestige of the liberal ideal. This may be something that classical liberals like Mill can help us relearn.

NOTES

1 Henry Sidgwick to C. H Pearson, 10/15 May 1873; quoted in Collini 1991, 178.
2 Balfour 1915, 138; Dicey 1914, 386.

3 His influence on liberal thought was more resilient. Hayek (writing in 1962) assessed it thus:

> During the forty years after his death he governed liberal thought as did no other man, and as late as 1914 he was still the chief source of inspiration of the progressive part of the intellectuals of the West – of the men whose dream of an indefinitely peaceful progress and expansion of Western civilisation was shattered by the cataclysms of war and revolution. . . . His reputation declined with the confidence in the steady advance of civilisation in which he believed, and for a time the kind of minds who had believed in him were attracted by more revolutionary thinkers. (F. A. Hayek, 'Introduction', *CW* XII:xvi)

But if this is right, it only shows how liberal thought had got beached by ebbing philosophical tides. The philosophical sea-change is not explicable by the collapse of liberal confidence; one might rather say that it contributed to it, by providing radical alternatives to the Millian philosophical synthesis.

4 An important contribution has been the Toronto edition of Mill's *Collected Works*, the first volumes of which (*The Earlier Letters of John Stuart Mill, 1812–1848, CW* XII–XIII) were published in 1963. In his introduction to these volumes, which I have already quoted in note 3, Hayek says that interest in Mill among intellectual historians and political theorists had been gradually but steadily reviving for twenty years. The revival of interest in Mill among philosophers came later, just as the decline had come earlier.

5 Alasdair MacIntyre's question was 'Nietzsche or Aristotle'? (MacIntyre 1981, chs. 9 & 18). From MacIntyre's standpoint, it turns out that Nietzsche and Mill are on the same side:

> in the end the Nietzschean stance is only one more facet of that very moral culture of which Nietzsche took himself to be an implacable critic. . . . the crucial moral opposition is between liberal individualism in some version or other and the Aristotelian tradition in some version or other. (MacIntyre 1981, 241)

This seems to me to combine a distortion of 'liberal individualism' with an impossible dream. To take Mill as the alternative to Nietzsche is, however, still to make the alternative a liberalism based on a notion of human well-being – and one which contains as much Aristotelianism as is viable for us now (perhaps rather more than is viable for us now). See section IV.

6 Sidgwick and Sidgwick 1906, 33–34.

7 He does not extend his 'eulogistic estimate' to the essay on theism, which he thinks suffers from stylistic 'imperfections' and philosophical 'infirmities'.

8 I have tried to trace these various developments in more detail in Skorupski 1993a. See also Skorupski 1990–91.

9 I mean a naturalism which follows the modernist phase in twentieth-century philosophy, rejecting some of its most salient tendencies but nevertheless continuing some others.

10 These options were already being actively canvassed in Germany in the 1780s – from the publication of Kant's first Critique (see Beiser 1987). One crucial difference lying behind subsequent developments in Britain and Germany is the presence in Britain of an influential naturalistic alternative to Hume, in the shape of the epistemology discussed in this section.

11 In 'Bentham' Mill acknowledges Hume as "the profoundest negative thinker on record" but describes him as

the prince of *dilettanti*, from whose writings one will hardly learn that there is such a thing as truth, far less that it is attainable; but only that the *pro* and *con* of everything may be argued with infinite ingenuity, and furnishes a fine intellectual exercise. This absolute scepticism in speculation very naturally brought him round to Toryism in practice; for if no faith can be had in the operations of human intellect, and one side of every question is about as likely as another to be true, a man will commonly prefer that order of things which, being no more wrong than every other, he has hitherto found compatible with his private comforts. (*CW* X:80)

This was written when Mill was twenty-two and was struck out in the 1838 edition. Compare the eighteen-year-old Mill's comments on Hume as quoted by Alexander Bain (1882, 34): "the object of his reasonings was not to attain truth, but to show that it was unattainable. His mind, too, was completely enslaved by a taste for literature. . . ."

No doubt Mill here reflects the views of his father. By the time of his *Examination of Sir William Hamilton's Philosophy* (published 1865) he takes a very different view. He now disagrees with the account of Hume as a thinker who drew sceptical conclusions from the received premises of British empiricism. His impression now is that "Hume's scepticism, or rather his professed admiration for scepticism" was a "disguise" for the radical science of the mind which Hume thought would follow "if we put complete confidence in the trustworthiness of our rational faculty" (*CW* IX:498–99, footnote). Only "a few detached expressions in a single essay (that 'on the Academical or Sceptical Philosophy,')" count, Mill thinks, against this reading. In effect Mill anticipates Kemp-Smith's (1940) rejoinder to Green, treating Hume as a scientific naturalist *rather* than a sceptic. However, this underplays the fact that Hume *uses* sceptical arguments to show that our beliefs do not result from the application of reason. His "sceptical solution" of "sceptical doubts

about the understanding" affirms, of general beliefs formed by induction, that we cannot help believing them – but denies that we have
reason to believe them.

12 Victorian utilitarians and imperialists were mostly opposed. However,
James and John Stuart Mill played an important part – from London – in
the governance of India: one could say they were 'India House utilitarians'. In principle they both took a robustly progressivist attitude to the
morality of traditional societies. But their policy ideas came to differ
strongly as Mill veered towards anti-constructivism. The influence on
him of the French and German ideas about historicity of culture and
character discussed in this section dovetailed with those of a historically
minded group of officials in the East India Company. See Zastoupil 1994.

13 Three of these 'classical liberals' – Burckhardt, J. S. Mill and Tocqueville
– are examined under the illuminating title of 'Aristocratic Liberalism'
by Kahan (1992). Chapter 4 of this book valuably compares their ethical
vision with that of earlier civic or republican humanism. Wilhelm von
Humboldt, whose *Sphere and Duties of Government* (Humboldt 1996)
was written in 1791 though not published till 1852, also belongs here.

14 I take the terms 'moral freedom' and 'individual spontaneity' from Mill.
Another version of the contrast I have in mind is Matthew Arnold's
'strictness of conscience' and 'spontaneity of consciousness' (*Culture
and Anarchy*, Arnold 1993). However, 'strictness of conscience' is too
narrow for the Millian notion of moral freedom; it fits the Kantian
notion of autonomy better.

15 This is from a letter to Henry Fawcett of 5 February 1860 (*CW* XV:672)
in which Mill is concerned with ways to promote a plan for proportional
representation.

16 Here I follow John Gray's interpretation of Berlin (Gray 1993 and 1995).
However, both Berlin and Popper show a much stronger continuity with
classical European liberalism than does Rawls. Thus on another view it
is not clear how far 'value-pluralism' differs from classical liberals'
affirmation of the objective value of a diversity of way of living, and it is
arguable that Gray's interpretation pushes it further than does Berlin.
In practice, at any rate, Berlin's liberal sentiment differs little from
Humboldt's or Mill's – it amounts to classical liberalism with a dash of
modernist bitters. As for Popper, the historical story he tells of tribalism,
the open and closed society and 'the strains of civilisation' has a strong
affinity to the French liberals' historical sociology. The connexion he
makes between fallibilism and the value of liberty of discussion was
made by Mill (though without the modernist epistemology). And (from
many examples) his description of Pericles is positively Millian: "a
democrat who well understands that democracy cannot be exhausted by

the meaningless principle that 'the people should rule', but that it must be based on faith in reason, and on humanitarianism" (Popper 1950, 187).

17 See Rawls 1993a, Lecture III, 'Political Constructivism'.

18 Rawls 1993a, 129; my emphasis.

19 I argue this point with reference to Mill in Skorupski 1997.

20 "The initiation of all wise or noble things, comes and must come from individuals; generally at first from some one individual. The honour and glory of the average man is that he is capable of following that initiative; that he can respond internally to wise and noble things, and be led to them with his eyes open. I am not countenancing the sort of 'hero-worship' which applauds the strong man of genius for forcibly seizing on the government of the world and making it do his bidding in spite of itself. All he can claim, is freedom to point out the way. The power of compelling others into it, is not only inconsistent with the freedom and development of all the rest, but corrupting to the strong man himself" ('On Liberty', *CW* XVIII:269).

21 For Mill this strain was mitigated by his conviction that human beings are in the long run all equally capable of developing higher powers. Bain thought this to be one of his "greatest theoretical errors" as a scientific thinker; it is hard to disagree. Mill's other error was disregard of the physiological conditions of mentality – in both cases, Bain thought, "his feelings operated in giving his mind a bias" (Bain 1882, 146–47).

1 Mill on language and logic

I. INTRODUCTORY

Mill's theory of meaning[1] is couched in the syntax of syllogism rather than that of modern, post-Fregean logic, whereas the advance of logic has been a pivotal element in the story of twentieth-century philosophy. But this should not blind us. A Millian semantics and epistemology of logic can be stated as well in a modern as in a syllogistic framework; in fact the modern framework allows it to be stated more perspicuously. Mill's doctrine of connotation and denotation and his thoroughgoing empiricism remain robust. And it was as a defender of empiricism in the epistemology of science – including logic and mathematics – rather than as a contributor to logic or science as such that he wrote.[2]

The real criticism of Mill remains much the same as that made by his nineteenth-century critics. He does not reflect enough about the content of his empiricism and its overall coherence. The same criticism, it is true, can be made of many contemporary naturalists. We shall come back to it in section VI. But first the outlines of Mill's position must be set down and some influential misconceptions set aside.

Mill is an empiricist in that he holds that no *informative assertion about the world is a priori*. In the *System of Logic* he distinguishes between 'verbal' and 'real' propositions, and between 'merely apparent' and 'real' inferences. The assertion of a purely verbal proposition conveys no information about the world, though it can convey information about the language in which the assertion itself is couched. Similarly, a merely apparent inference moves to no new assertion – its conclusion has been literally asserted in its premises. There is hence no problem about justifying a verbal assertion or a merely apparent inference – there is nothing to justify. In contrast, no real proposition or inference is a priori. All such propositions and inferences must in the end be grounded on data and methods of induction. As to the status of data, the *System of Logic* is supposedly neutral between subjectivists and direct realists. Its professed aim is to codify fully the methods of induction, whatever may be the data to which induction is applied.

This is reasonably familiar territory to a twentieth-century empiricist. What makes empiricism distinctive in Mill's hands – and quite different from twentieth-century varieties before Quine – is his demonstration that mathematics and logic itself contain real propositions. It follows, if empiricism is sound, that the justification of logic and mathematics must in the end be inductive.

II. VERBAL AND REAL – CONNOTATION AND DENOTATION

Let us go into a little more detail. Mill's distinction between verbal and real propositions relies on his doctrine of denotation and connotation. Singular and general terms, or as he calls them, 'names', denote things and connote attributes of things. 'Propositions', in Mill's use of the term, are sentences which have a meaning (an 'import'). His concern is to explain how the connotation and denotation of names contributes to the import of propositions. On this point, that the meaning of terms is their contribution to the meaning of sentences, he is as emphatic as one could wish – unsurprisingly, given the stress Bentham had already laid on the sentence as the integer of meaning.

A general name connotes attributes and denotes each object which has those attributes. Attributes are properties of things, not ideas of those properties (see section V). Most singular names also connote attributes; proper names, however – 'Dartmouth', 'Tully', 'Cicero', etc. – do not. They denote an object but connote no attribute. Their meaning, that is, their contribution to the import of propositions, is determined by their denotation. A language can also contain non-connotative names of attributes – 'abstract' names such as 'whiteness', or 'white' used abstractly – and in this case also meaning is determined by denotation.

Mill's account of verbal propositions and inferences is developed within this framework.[3] He envisages two types of verbal proposition.

The first type is made up of connotative names only: in verbal propositions of this kind the attributes connoted by the predicate are a subset of the attributes connoted by the subject. Mill intends this to cover particular and singular as well as universal propositions: 'Some fathers are parents' and 'My father is a parent' as well as 'All fathers are parents'. The standard modern assumption is that the last of these has no existential implication while the former two entail the existence of fathers. Mill's position is less crisp. Apparently he thinks that assertion of *any* proposition normally carries an "implied assertion" or "tacit assumption" that there exist objects denoted by the subject name (*CW* VII:113). The speaker implicitly or tacitly asserts that there are objects denoted by the subject name and explicitly asserts that they have attributes connoted by the predicate name – if there are no such objects he has failed to make any assertion (about objects).

However, when someone assertively utters a proposition like 'All fathers are parents' he makes no real assertion about *fathers* and should rather be understood as making a semantic assertion about the name 'father' – giving a partial definition of its meaning. So this is a 'verbal proposition'. The point of asserting a verbal proposition is to define or elucidate the meaning of the subject name and hence the existence of objects denoted by the subject name is not implied; it is not a precondition of the assertion achieving its object. Nevertheless there often remains an *apparent* implication of existence. It "arises", Mill thinks, "from the ambiguity of the copula" which apart from indicating predication is also "a concrete word connoting existence". The implication is no part of the point of the utterance, which is to explain the meaning of the subject-name: "we may say, A ghost is a disembodied spirit, without believing in ghosts" (*CW* VII:113). It is not, therefore, "really" implied by the assertive utterance of the proposition. But Mill thinks that it is usually conveyed, even when a definition is explicitly given in metalinguistic form. This becomes important in Mill's discussion of 'definitions' in geometry, where he is concerned to rebut the view that geometrical reasoning is purely verbal. A definition such as 'A triangle is a rectilinear figure with three sides', taken in the strict sense, cannot be a premise – cannot "be made the foundation of a train of reasoning" (*CW* VII:149). But the implied assumption of (possible) existence is real and not merely verbal; and is indeed implicitly assumed in trains of geometrical reasoning.

Verbal propositions, then,

do not relate to any matter of fact, in the proper sense of the term, at all, but to the meaning of names. Since names and their signification are entirely arbitrary, such propositions are not, strictly speaking, susceptible of truth or falsity, but only of conformity or disconformity to usage or convention; and all the proof they are capable of, is proof of usage; proof that the words have been employed by others in the acceptation in which the speaker or writer desires to use them. (*CW* VII:109)

Real propositions, on the other hand,

predicate of a thing some fact not involved in the signification of the name by which the proposition speaks of it; some attribute not connoted by name. . . . When I am told that all, or even that some objects, which have certain qualities, or which stand in certain relations, have also certain other qualities, or stand in certain other relations, I learn from this proposition a new fact; a fact not included in my knowledge of the meaning of the words, nor even of the existence of things answering to the signification of those words. It is this class of propositions only which are in themselves instructive, or from which any instructive propositions can be inferred. (*CW* VII:115–16)

Mill also thinks that there is a second class of verbal propositions: identity propositions in which the copula is flanked by connotationless proper names, such as 'Cicero is Tully'. They are verbal in that, according to Mill, the only information conveyed is about the names themselves: 'Cicero' denotes the same object as 'Tully' does. Putting this another way: he thinks that there is no extra-linguistic fact in the world to which 'Cicero is Tully' corresponds – understanding such a proposition is not a matter of grasping how the world must be for it to be true. The difficulty, which Mill fails to note, is that knowledge that Cicero is Tully is *not* a priori. We cannot know the proposition to be true just by reflecting on the meaning of the names – whereas Mill says that verbal propositions can be so understood. His overall intention in introducing the distinction between verbal and real propositions was to show that the apparent 'aprioricity' of verbal propositions is innocuous *because* such propositions are empty of content. Treating proper-name identities as verbal obscures this aim.

Not that this is mere oversight on Mill's part; what one should say about proper-name identities is of course a fundamental issue in semantics. And a radical Millian empiricist owes some account of the epistemology of the logic of identity – for example of the transitivity of identity, or of the indiscernability of identicals. He must either show how the apriority of such principles arises from their purely verbal status or deny their apriority. Mill does not deal with these issues, but the thought that a proper-name identity such as 'Cicero is Tully' conveys no fact about the world would clearly be central to what he would have said about them. Because it conveys no fact about the world the inference 'Cicero is a Roman, Cicero is Tully, therefore Tully is a Roman' is merely apparent. It advances to no proposition whose truth depends on any facts other than those on which the truth of the premises depends.

But Mill provides no characterisation of 'verbal' which *shows* these inferences involving the logic of identity to be verbal – merely apparent. Perhaps his best route would have been that later attempted by Wittgenstein in the *Tractatus*: showing how a language could be constructed containing no sign of identity, and arguing that in it any information content expressible in our language (and not metalinguistic – *about* our language) could be expressed.

In such a reconstructed language, identity propositions would drop out, and the distinction between real and verbal propositions and inferences would successfully pick out as real Mill's intended class of propositions and inferences – those which are genuinely 'instructive'.[4] Suppose we do think of the matter in this way. Then the most useful approach to characterising the distinction between verbal and real is provided by Mill in his remarks about real and merely apparent inference. He says that an inference is "apparent, not real" when "the proposition ostensibly inferred from another, appears on analysis to be merely a repetition of the same, or part of the same, assertion, which was contained in the first" (CW VII:158).

In such cases there is not really any inference; there is in the conclusion no new truth, nothing but what was already asserted in the premises, and obvious to whoever apprehends them. The fact asserted in the conclusion is either the very same fact, or part of the fact, asserted in the original proposition. (CW VII:160)

We can use this characterisation of an apparent or verbal inference to characterise a verbal proposition. Consider the inference $P, \ldots,$ P_n, therefore C; and the conditional If P_1 & &, $\ldots,$ & P_n then C. Call the conditional the *corresponding conditional* of the inference. Taking the notion of a verbal inference as basic, we define a verbal proposition as the corresponding conditional of a verbal inference. An inference is verbal if and only if the set of propositions constituting the conclusion is a subset of the set of propositions constituting the premises. This is in line with two important features of Mill's understanding of the logical connectives. He assumes that to assert a conjunction A *and* B is simply to assert A and to assert B. And he takes If A then B to mean *The proposition B is a legitimate inference from the proposition A.*[5]

Consider the proposition 'If Tom is a father, then Tom is a parent'. The corresponding inference is 'Tom is a father, therefore Tom is a parent'. Analysis of the connotation of 'father' reduces 'Tom is a father' to the conjunction 'Tom is male and Tom is a parent'. Thus, by Mill's account of conjunction, the propositions constituting the premise are: 'Tom is male', 'Tom is a parent'. The inference is revealed as verbal, hence also the corresponding conditional. In general, determining whether an inference is verbal or real will call for an analysis of connotations, and an analysis of "compound propositions" in terms of Mill's definitions of the connectives.

But what about general propositions, like 'All fathers are parents'? Mill does not have a consistent view of general statements. However, it is compatible with one of the lines he takes to treat 'All fathers are male parents' as meaning 'Any proposition of the form 'x is a parent' is inferable from the corresponding proposition of the form 'x is a father'. 'The proposition "Tom is a parent" is inferable from the proposition "Tom is a father"' is a substitution-instance of this schema. We can now stipulate that a universal proposition is verbal if and only if all its substitution instances are verbal.[6]

III. LOGIC CONTAINS REAL INFERENCES

Mill argues that logic itself contains real inferences and propositions. Of course, on his definitions of the connectives certain deductive inferences, for example from a conjunction to one of its conjuncts, will be verbal. But, Mill holds, the laws of contradiction and excluded middle are real – and therefore a posteriori – propositions. He takes it that *not P* is equivalent in meaning to *It is false that P*; if we further assume the equivalence in meaning of *P* and *It is true that P*, the principle of contradiction becomes the principle of exclusion – as he puts it, "the same proposition cannot at the same time be false and true". "I cannot look upon this", he says, "as a merely verbal proposition. I consider it to be . . . one of our first and most familiar generalizations from experience" (*CW* VII:277). He makes analogous remarks about excluded middle, which turns – on these definitions – into the principle of bivalence, 'Either it is true that *P* or it is false that *P*'. The principles of bivalence and exclusion are real – "instructive" – propositions.

To this semantic analysis Mill adds an epistemological argument. If logic did not contain real inferences, all deductive reasoning would be a *petitio principii*, a begging of the question – it could produce no new knowledge. If valid deductions are all verbal, then the conclusion of any valid deduction is asserted in the premises. To know the truth of the premises is to know that each proposition asserted in the premises is true. Hence, since the conclusion is one of those propositions, it is to know the truth of the conclusion. Yet deduction clearly produces new knowledge. So logic must contain real inferences.

Logicians have persisted in representing the syllogism as a process of inference or proof; though none of them has cleared up the difficulty which arises from the inconsistency between that assertion, and the principle, that if there be anything in the conclusion which was not already in the premises, the argument is vicious. (*CW* VII:185)

This difficulty, which may seem factitious, is in fact deep. Recognising the full depth of the issue (an issue which remained central to analytic philosophy) is one of the merits of the *System of Logic*. Throwing up dust will not help, as Mill rightly insists:

It is impossible to attach any serious scientific value to such a mere salvo, as the distinction drawn between being involved by *implication* in the premises and being directly asserted in them. (*CW* VII:185)

Sadly, however, Mill's discussion loses concentration and direction at just this point. For he also has another objective. It is interesting, but it is quite distinct and prevents him from giving a clear explanation of his own of why the syllogism is not a *petitio principii*.

He wants to demystify the role universal propositions play in thought by arguing that "all inference is from particulars to particulars". In principle universal propositions add nothing to the force of an argument; singular conclusions could always be derived inductively direct from singular premises. The value of universal propositions is psychological. They play the role of "memoranda", summary records of the inductive potential of all that we have observed, and they facilitate "trains of reasoning" (as e.g. in 'This is *A*, All *A*s are *B*s No *B*s are *C*s, so this is not *C*'). Psychologically they greatly increase our memory and reasoning power, but epistemologically they are dispensable.

This thesis depends on Mill's rejection of "intuitive" knowledge of universal truths and, further, on his inductivism. If universal propositions could be introduced into reasoning either by a priori insight into their truth or by inferences to the best explanation, they would have sources other than direct generalisation on experience. There would be principles governing their introduction other than the principle of enumerative induction and hence they would not be eliminable from our reasoning to previously unknown singular propositions. But whether Mill is right in his empiricism and inductivism about universal propositions is an issue separate from the deep question he raises about whether deduction can be both a verbal process and a discovery of new truth.

However, the connexion between this question, Mill's empiricism and his thesis that all inference is from particulars to particulars can also be made in a different way. Consider the inference from 'Everything is *F*' to '*a* is *F*'. Is it a real or verbal inference? A rationalist could hold that it is a real inference requiring a priori insight. But it is impossible to hold it real if one also wishes to argue that real inferences are a posteriori. A way of treating it as verbal which is open to Mill, given his analysis of conjunction, is to treat the premise as a conjunction: '*a* is *F* and *b* is *F* and . . .'. At a number of points in his discussion Mill comes close to this view of generality. Another approach is to deny that 'Everything is *F*' is propositional at all – to hold instead that it expresses a rule: to accept, of any given object, that it is *F*. On this view the relation between 'Everything is *F*' and '*a* is *F*' is not that of inference from premise to conclusion. Similarily, 'Everything which is F is G' will express a rule: to hold, of any object, that its being G is inferable from its being F. In this sense all inference will be from particulars to particulars – a universal 'proposition' is in fact the expression of a rule of inference and does not feature in the syllogism as a *premise*.

Sometimes Mill talks as if there was really no such thing as syllogistic reasoning at all, only inductive inference from singular premises to a singular conclusion. But this is evidently not what happens as a matter of psychological fact, and Mill realises that. Syllogistic reasoning is a distinct and separate process from inductive reasoning. When he is concentrating on the distinctness of syllogistic reasoning, Mill emphasizes that a universal proposition is "a memorandum of the nature of the conclusions which we are prepared to prove" (*CW* VII:207). It is then that he comes closest to the second approach which we have mentioned here.

On this second approach there will still be an inference involved in any piece of syllogistic reasoning over and above that licensed by the universal proposition. For example, where the reasoning is of the form '*a* is *F*, all *F*s are *G*s, so *a* is *G*', the inference involved is a case of modus ponens: *a* is *F*, '*a* is *G*' is inferable from '*a* is *F*', so *a* is *G*. Once again we can ask whether this is a verbal or a real inference. Surely, if I have the premise that *p* and the premise that the proposition that *q* is inferable from the proposition that *p*, then my inference that *q* is merely verbal. But on the characterisation of verbal inference which he gives it looks as though Mill must deny that it is verbal. For the proposition that *a* is *G* is asserted neither in the premise that *a* is *F*, nor in the premise that *a* is *G* is inferable from *a* is *F*. The set of propositions asserted in the premises simply does not include the proposition that *a* is *G*.

A rationalist can say that modus ponens is a form of real inference known to be valid by a priori insight. But what should Mill say? He does not consider the question. But he could have taken exactly the same line about conditionality that he tends to take about generality. He could have said that 'The proposition that *q* is inferable from the proposition that *p*' is not itself to be understood as a proposition but expresses a rule. So the *inference* in modus ponens is a real inference: from *p* to *q*. On this view we must allow that rules of inference as well as inferences can be said to be verbal or real. A rule of inference is verbal if it corresponds to a verbal inference. Thus 'If

p then p' is a verbal rule of inference, while 'Everything is F' or 'If p then q' are (for most instances) real rules of inference. All real rules of inference are a posteriori. And we also have Mill's claim that exclusion and bivalence are a posteriori. So these express real, a posteriori rules of inference. Exclusion licences inference from assertion of the truth of a proposition to denial of its falsehood (and from assertion of its falsehood to denial of its truth). Bivalence licenses inference from denial of the truth of a proposition to assertion of its falsehood (and from denial of its falsehood to assertion of its truth). Logic turns out to be concerned with the universal laws of negation, or given Mill's view that negation and falsehood are the same concept, one might say with the universal laws of falsehood and truth. Mill was a universalist about logic in exactly the way Frege was. He believed that the laws of logic are simply the most general laws of truth. The difference between them, of course, is that according to Mill these laws are a posteriori.[7]

IV. THE EPISTEMOLOGY OF LOGIC

Mill's demonstration that logic contains real propositions and inferences would not suit a twentieth-century Viennese empiricist, but it need not shock an intuitionist or a Kantian. A Kantian, it is true, would have to revise his view of logic as a purely formal discipline. He would have to concede that logic itself is synthetic a priori; specifically, that bivalence and exclusion are not purely formal principles but themselves rest on intuition. Within the Kantian framework that in turn would force the conclusion that logical truths, like other synthetic a priori truths, are restricted to the domain of phenomena.[8]

Thinkers of an intuitionist-cum-Kantian stamp were the opposition Mill had to deal with. So how does he establish his crucial empiricist thesis, that all real inferences and propositions are a posteriori, against them?

He thinks that arguments for the opposing view, that there are real propositions whose truth is nevertheless "perceived *a priori*" (*CW* VII:231), are "reducible to two" (*CW* VII:233).

The first simply points to the fact that we consider ourselves to have grounds for accepting certain propositions, in mathematics and (as we now also see) in logic, not on the basis of inductions from experience but by appeal to 'intuition'; that is to say, to our perceptual imagination – to what we can imagine as perceptible. Since we are prepared to endorse them on this basis alone it seems that they must rest on a priori properties of pure perceptual imagination, and not on facts discovered by actual perception. Mill replies that while we are indeed often justified in basing geometrical claims, for example, on intuition, the fact that that *is* a justifiable mode of reasoning in geometry is a posteriori. The reliability of perceptual imagination as a guide to real possibilities is itself an empirical question.

The second argument Mill considers turns on the Kantian point that "Experience tells us, indeed, what is, but not that it must necessarily be so, and not otherwise" – though Mill considers it in a formulation offered by Whewell:

experience cannot offer the smallest ground for the necessity of a proposition. She can observe and record what has happened; but she cannot find, in any case, or in any accumulation of cases, any reason for what *must* happen. . . . To learn a proposition by experience, and to see it to be necessarily true, are two altogether different processes of thought. (Whewell 1858a, 1:65–67; quoted by Mill at CW VII:237)

Since we do have insight into the necessary truth of certain propositions, that insight cannot be based on experience and must be a priori.

Mill rejects any metaphysical distinction between necessary and contingent truth; like Quine he thinks the highest kind of necessity is natural necessity. The only other sense of 'necessary truth' he is prepared to concede to Whewell is 'proposition the negation of which is not only false but inconceivable'.

This, therefore, is the principle asserted: that propositions, the negation of which is inconceivable, or in other words, which we cannot figure to ourselves as being false, must rest on evidence of a higher and more cogent description than any which experience can afford. (CW VII:237–38)

In response Mill dwells at length on associationist explanations of inconceivability. But elsewhere he makes the epistemological basis of his reply clear:

even assuming that inconceivability is not solely the consequence of limited experience, but that some incapacities of conceiving are inherent in the mind, and inseparable from it; this would not entitle us to infer, that what we are thus incapable of conceiving cannot exist. Such an inference would only be warrantable, if we could know *a priori* that we must have been created capable of conceiving whatever is capable of existing: that the universe of thought and that of reality, the Microcosm and the Macrocosm (as they once were called) must have been framed in complete correspondence with one another.... That this is really the case has been laid down expressly in some systems of philosophy, by implication in more, and is the foundation (among others) of the systems of Schelling and Hegel: but an assumption more destitute of evidence could scarcely be made.... (*CW* IX:68)

It needs to be shown that what we are "incapable of conceiving cannot exist". And it must be shown to be true a priori: not internally and a posteriori. That is the real force of Mill's case. It lies in the impossibility of providing any model of a priori knowledge about the world which is consistent with the view that such knowledge is in every case distinct from what is known and must conform to it. Denying that knowledge must in every case conform to its object was Kant's 'Copernican revolution' – there are, rather, framework features of our knowledge to which every object must conform. But Kant's transcendental-idealist interpretation of those features is inconsistent with naturalism, whereas naturalism is Mill's most fundamental commitment. On this point at least, that naturalism is incompatible with the possibility of a priori knowledge about the world, Mill and Kantian idealists could agree. The disagreement of course is about whether without synthetic a priori knowledge any knowledge is possible at all. Mill's critics would urge that it is not.

V. IS MILL'S VIEW PSYCHOLOGISTIC? CONCEPTUALISM, NOMINALISM AND REALISM

But before coming to this fundamental criticism it will be useful to examine a more recent accusation (it seems to stem from Husserl). It is that Mill's treatment of logic is 'psychologistic'. 'Psychologism' is a loose term but we may take it to consist in one or both of two views:

(1) that laws of logic are simply psychological laws concerning our mental processes; or

(2) that 'meanings' are mental entities, and that 'judgements' assert relationships among these entities.

Neither of these views can be attributed to Mill. On the other hand, behind the accusation of psychologism there lurks the more fundamental issue, which does indeed distinguish nineteenth-century naturalism, epitomised in its high form by Mill, from the Kantian Critical tradition. But first we must establish that Mill endorsed neither (1) nor (2) and take stock of three epistemologies of logic which he contrasted with his own.

Mill holds that logic is the most general empirical science, "universally true of all phaenomena" (*CW* IX:380–81). This already stands in clear contrast to (1). Since logic's laws are "laws of all phaenomena" and phaenomena are all we know, "we are quite safe in looking upon them as laws of Existence" (*CW* IX:382). The laws of logic are, Mill accepts, also laws of thought, in the sense that they are principles in terms of which we cannot but think. We violate them often enough in our thinking, of course, but we never do so knowingly, for "knowingly to violate them is impossible" (*CW* IX:373). But we have already seen that Mill denies that their standing as laws of existence can be deduced from the fact that they codify laws of thought. To prove that "a contradiction is unthinkable" is not to prove it "impossible in point of fact" (*CW* IX:382). And it is the latter claim, not the former, which is required to vindicate "the thinking process". "Our thoughts are true when they are made to correspond with Phaenomena" (*CW* IX:384); if

there were any law necessitating us to think a relation between *phaenomena* which does not in fact exist between the phaenomena, then certainly the thinking process would be proved invalid, because we should be compelled by it to think true something which would really be false. (*CW* IX:383)

What then of (2) – the view that meanings are mental entities and that 'judgements' assert relationships among these entities? Fierce criticism of precisely this view is a central feature of the *System of Logic*. Mill calls it 'Conceptualism'. It was propagated, according to Mill, by Descartes and became especially popular in the era of Leibniz and Locke. He considers it "one of the most fatal errors ever introduced into the philosophy of logic; and the principal cause why the theory of the science has made such inconsiderable progress during the last two centuries" (*CW* VII:89). Conceptualists confused judgements with the contents of judgement, that is, with propositions.

They considered a Proposition, or a Judgement, for they used the two words indiscriminately, to consist in affirming or denying one *idea* of another. . . . the whole doctrine of Propositions, together with the theory of Reasoning . . . was stated as if Ideas, or Conceptions, or whatever other term the writer preferred as a name for mental representations generally, constituted essentially the subject matter and substance of these operations. (*CW* VII:87)

Against Conceptualism Mill insists on the

difference between a doctrine or opinion, and the fact of entertaining the opinion; between assent, and what is assented to. . . . Logic, according to the conception here formed of it, has no concern with the nature of the act of judging or believing; the consideration of that act, as a phenomenon of the mind, belongs to another science. (*CW* VII:87)

Propositions (except sometimes when the mind itself is treated of) are not assertions respecting our ideas of things, but assertions respecting the things themselves. (*CW* VII:88)

What explains, then, the attribution of 'psychologism' to Mill? In the *Examination*, he writes: "Logic is not the theory of Thought as Thought, but of valid Thought; not of thinking, but of correct thinking." He then continues, in a passage quoted by Husserl and cited many times since:

It is not a Science distinct from, and coordinate with Psychology. So far as it is a science at all, it is a part, or branch, of Psychology; differing from it, on the one hand as the part differs from the whole, and on the other, as an Art differs from a Science. Its theoretic grounds are wholly borrowed from Psychology, and include as much of that science as is required to justify the rules of the art. (*CW* IX:359)

To give this a psychologistic reading is to take it out of context. Mill is not here repudiating his view that logic rests on completely universal empirical truths. But he thinks the logician's main task is not the scientific one of discovering such truths (since they are so obvious); the logician's task rather is to advance the art of thinking by formulating clear rules of reasoning. He must formulate these rules in a manner which will be as helpful as possible to inquirers, and must draw on the psychology of thought to do so. It is in that sense that the art of the logician borrows from the science of the psychologist. How best to promote the art of clear thinking is in part a psychological question. Nonetheless, "the laws, in the scientific sense of the term, of Thought as Thought – do not belong to Logic, but to Psychology: and it is only the *validity* of thought which Logic takes cognisance of" (*CW* IX:359).

So it is wrong to accuse Mill of psychologism about logic. When logic is considered as a set of truths, then his view of it, like his view of mathematics, is universalist and empiricist. Geometry formulates the laws of physical space, arithmetic the laws of aggregation, and logic (on the account given in section IV) the laws of truth itself. Indeed if one takes a universalist view of logic and combines it with rejection of Kant's Copernican revolution then Millian empiricism can appear inevitable. "Our thoughts are true when they are made to correspond with Phaenomena" (*CW* IX:384) – so how could we know that they are true other than by inductive evidence which shows that they correspond with phenomena? And that includes our logical thoughts, since they too are true when they are made to correspond with phenomena.

It is from this universalist and empiricist standpoint, and on its behalf, that Mill criticises what he sees as the three main attempts to vindicate the apriority of logic. 'Conceptualism', which we have already considered, is one of these. The other two he calls 'Nominalism' and 'Realism'.[9]

The Nominalists – Mill cites Hobbes as an example – hold that logic and mathematics are entirely verbal. Mill takes this position much more seriously than Conceptualism. Indeed he refutes it in extensive detail. He argues that Nominalists are only able to maintain their view because they fail to distinguish between the denotation and the connotation of names, "seeking for their meaning exclusively in what they denote" (*CW* VII:91). In contrast Mill shows how the import of propositions depends (with the exceptions mentioned in section II) on the connotations of their constituent names. He grounds his distinction between real and verbal propositions on his doctrine of denotation and connotation, and demonstrates on its basis that logic and mathematics contain real propositions.[10]

Nominalists and Conceptualists both hold that logic and maths can be known non-empirically, while yet retaining the view that no real proposition about the mind-independent world can be so known – but both are confused. What if one abandons the thesis that no real proposition about the mind-independent world can be known a priori? The Realists do that; they hold that logical and mathematical knowledge is knowledge of universals existing in an abstract Platonic domain; the terms that make up sentences being signs that stand for such universals. This is the view Mill takes least seriously – but versions of it were destined to stage a major revival in philosophy, and semantic analysis would be their main source.

It is relevant, however, to distinguish between a semantic and an epistemologically driven realism. The semantically driven view holds that we are justified in accepting the existence of abstract entities, particular or universal, if the best semantic account of the propositions we have reason to hold true is one which postulates the existence of such entities. The epistemologically driven view is an attempt to account for the aprioricity of certain propositions. It holds that such propositions are true because they correspond to facts about language-independent abstract entities. We have knowledge of these facts by virtue of some faculty of non-empirical intuition and that is why the knowledge is a priori. Proponents of the first view (Quine, for example) may argue that it can be defended without resorting to the epistemology propounded by the second and indeed without acknowledging the possibility of a priori knowledge at all.

Mill is a nominalist in the contemporary sense: he rejects abstract entities. Thus he treats aggregates as concrete objects, and attributes as natural properties rather than universals. By now the difficulties of giving a nominalist ontology of arithmetic or indeed general semantics are familiar. We cannot know how Mill would have responded to these difficulties had they been made evident to him, though there is a very decided nominalist flavour (in the current sense of 'nominalism') throughout his discussion. But what Mill is mainly concerned to reject is realism as an account of the possibility of a priori knowledge. It is the rejection of *that* possibility which is central to his philosophy.[11]

VI. EMPIRICISM AND THE NORMATIVITY

The aprioricity of logic and mathematics has been a central tenet of the analytic tradition – and descendants of 'Nominalism' and 'Realism' have played a leading role in its defence. Perhaps that made it easier to forget that Mill was not rejecting Nominalism and Realism in favour of some *other* account of the aprioricity of logic – 'psychologism'. He was rejecting the central tenet, that logic is a priori, itself. But the question remains, can epistemology dispense with the a priori altogether?

At this point the idea that Mill's *System of Logic* is psychologistic in some broader sense returns. The psychologism, in this broader sense, would not be about deductive logic, but about induction itself. For what epistemological account can Mill offer of that? How, at *this* point, does he respond to the Kantian claim that the very possibility of knowledge requires that there be a priori elements in our knowledge? Even if we accept his inductive account of logic and mathematics, must we not accept that the principle of induction itself is a priori?

Mill holds that the only fundamentally sound method of reasoning is enumerative induction, generalisation from experience. Other methods must in one way or another be based on it. This inductivism puts great strain on his empiricist epistemology of logic and mathematics – for example, when it leads him to suggest that the principle of exclusion is "one of our first and most familiar generalisations from experience" (see p. 41 above). One may well argue that if it is to be plausible, empiricism needs a more capacious cognitive armoury, one which allows for the conservative-holist and hypothetical elements in our knowledge. It is an interesting question how far an essentially Millian inductivism could be developed to take account of these elements.

But this is not the central issue at stake. Consider an optimal account of inductive logic, perhaps different from Mill's – let us refer to the set of its basic canons as {C}. The question then is, are the canons in {C} a priori, or if not, how are they established? Apparently we can apply to them Mill's own distinction betwen verbal and real propositions. They must emerge as real. Does he not therefore have to be a universalist about them? That is, does he not have to consider them as maximally general truths about the world?

And does that not provide a case against viewing them as a priori? Yet how else could we know them – and hence know anything? This is one central thrust of the Kantian critique of empiricism. It is not an issue about the acceptability or otherwise of inductivism but about the status of {C}.

Mill is not interested in inductive scepticism. He says that we learn "the laws of our rational faculty, like those of every other natural agency", by "seeing the agent at work" (see the Introduction, p. 8). We bring our most basic reasoning dispositions to self-consciousness by critical reflection on our practice. Having examined our dispositions, we reach a reflective equilibrium in which we endorse some – and perhaps reject others. We endorse them as sound norms of reasoning.

Consider then his favoured canon of inductive logic, enumerative induction. We can distinguish between that canon itself – which is a normative proposition – and a factual claim. The normative proposition is

(i) Enumerative inductions – given appropriate premises – defeasibly warrant belief in universal propositions about the world.

This proposition is topic-neutral and applies to all domains of inquiry. And of course the warrant for believing a universal proposition which an induction supplies is defeasible by further evidence. Given Mill's view of universal propositions as inference-rules, (i) says that enumerative induction is a valid source of real inference-rules.

The factual proposition is

(ii) Enumerative inductions – in some specified or in all domains of inquiry – frequently produce undefeated rules of inference (or produce them increasingly as time goes on, etc.).

(ii) is itself a general proposition, or a class of general propositions, about the world. Thus – granting (i) – we may acquire a warrant to believe it by a second-order enumerative induction, in some specified domain for which we have sufficient confirming instances. Equally, since induction is defeasible it is possible – granting (i) again – that a second-order induction will justify us in *disbelieving* (ii) in some or all domains. In the first case induction is internally self-vindicating in the domain. In the second case it is internally self-undermining. By induction we come to realise that induction is not be relied upon. The normative proposition, (i), remains correct but the warranting force of inductions is defeated.

Mill is quite rightly very interested in the fact that "the inductive process" has turned out to be largely self-vindicating. He is also struck by the fact that enumerative induction is differentially reliable in different domains. But he does not make the mistake of thinking that induction itself can produce an exhaustive justification of (i). That would indeed open him to Kantian critique. He accepts that an epistemology of induction must endorse (i) as primitively normative and not seek to derive it from (ii). On the other hand he does not claim that (i) is analytic, or in his term, 'verbal'. He refuses to treat (i) as a priori but he thinks we are entitled to accept it just because it is a primitive and stable feature of our practice of inquiry.

But this way of grounding (i) involves a transition from a psychological to a normative claim. This is the truth in the allegation that Mill's system of logic is 'psychologistic'. How can one defend such a transition from Mill's own criticism of the a priori school – unless one moves in a Kantian or transcendental idealist direction?

The answer perhaps is to take quite seriously the *normative* status of enumerative induction (or whatever primitive principles are found in (C)), along the lines suggested in the Introduction (pp. 13–16ff). The epistemology of fundamental norms must be distinguished from the epistemology of factual propositions. The appropriate epistemology for fundamental norms is the method of reflection and discussion. On the other hand factual propositions, just because they picture facts, are always open to refutation by empirical evidence. On this view we must formulate Mill's empiricism as follows: any *factual* proposition is refutable by evidence. In other words, Mill needs two distinctions, not just one: a distinction between the normative and the factual and a distinction between the verbal and the real. He must concede that fundamental normative propositions are real – but he could argue that they are not factual and so they do not need inductive support.

If we develop Millian empiricism in this way, a variety of further questions arises; in particular questions about its affinity to Reid and Kant. For example: what argument remains for Mill's minimalist, anti-Reidian view of the fundamental epistemic norms? Can we not apply a distinction analogous to that between (i) and (ii) to logic – or indeed arithmetic and geometry? Considered as sciences these are bodies of strictly universal propositions about the world. But may we not also hold that there are primitive logical or mathematical norms which stand to these strictly universal propositions as (i) stands to (ii)?

The thrust of Mill's empiricism could still survive, however, as the claim that any such primitive logical or mathematical norms are defeasible in just the way that (i) is. Empiricism becomes the thesis that all canons of rationality are empirically defeasible. That is, we may be led to reject universal factual propositions of logic, arithmetic or geometry as a result of empirical inquiry. The inquiry is itself of course guided by defeasible or default norms, some of which may have a logical or mathematical character. Inquiry cannot show any such norms to be incorrect; but it can defeat their warranting force.

If Mill has to endorse these two distinctions, between the real and the verbal and the normative and the factual, have we not pushed him into the Kantian camp? What difference is there between conceding that there are real normative propositions and conceding that there are synthetic a priori propositions? But to say that a fundamental normative proposition is a priori would add nothing to saying that it is normative. The distinction between the a priori and the a posteriori is a distinction *within* the factual. Because it is, Kant is led into transcendental idealism's constructive view of the knowing subject and its limitative doctrine that 'synthetic a priori' propositions cannot be asserted to hold of 'things in themselves'. In contrast, the distinction between the normative and the factual requires no such constructivism or limitative doctrine and no extra-scientific distinction between noumena and phenomena. In that sense it remains compatible with the only sort of naturalism that a Millian in ethics and epistemology need defend.

NOTES

1 It is contained in *System of Logic*, Book I, 'Of Names and Propositions'. His epistemology of logic is presented in Book II, 'Of Reasoning' (*CW* VII).

2 This comment requires qualification if we include inductive logic in logic, for in his account of scientific method Mill does develop a sub-

stantive inductive logic (the 'methods of experimental inquiry') as well as defending an empiricist conception of science.

3 See *System of Logic*, Book I, ch. 6, 'Of Propositions merely Verbal', and Book II, ch. 1, 'Of Inference, or Reasoning, in general' (*CW* VII). Mill writes of 'verbal' as against 'real' propositions but of 'merely apparent' as against 'real' inferences. I will use 'verbal inference' as a stylistic variant on 'merely apparent inference'.

4 There are evident similarities between Mill's 'verbal', Kant's 'analytic' and Wittgenstein's 'tautology'. The crucial difference, of course, is that Mill had no wish to show that logic as such was verbal.

5 He defines *A or B* as *If not A, then B, and if not B, then A.*

6 We could also stipulate that particular and singular propositions like 'Some fathers are parents' and 'My father is a parent' are verbal if they are directly deducible from an existential assumption ('There are fathers', 'I have a father') and a universal verbal proposition.

7 As will be clear from this discussion, much in Mill's *System* foreshadows the preoccupations of early analytic philosophy. I have already referred to the common spirit informing Mill's remarks about identity and Wittgenstein's treatment of identity in the *Tractatus*. Likewise Mill's two treatments of generality foreshadow Wittgenstein's in the *Tractatus* and the Vienna conversations. Crucially, of course, where Mill treats exclusion and bivalence as real, 'instructive' principles, Wittgenstein attempts to exhibit their formal or nonsensical character by his conception of the bipolarity of a proposition (the line it cuts through logical space). In many ways Mill's real heir in the analytic tradition was Frank Ramsey.

8 Mill discusses Hamilton's neo-Kantian view that the laws of thought are speculative truths applicable to things in themselves at *CW* IX:380–84.

9 He probably took Kantian views to be a form of Conceptualism.

10 The Nominalists, according to Mill, treat arithmetical equations as proper-name identities. As we have seen, Mill would agree that *proper-name* identities are in a certain sense verbal – but he holds that the names flanking the identity sign in an equation typically differ in connotation.

11 See his *Autobiography*:

The notion that truths external to the human mind may be known by intuition or consciousness, independently of observation and experience, is, I am persuaded, in these times, the great intellectual support of false doctrines and bad institutions. By the aid of this theory, every inveterate belief and every intense feeling, of which the origin is not remembered, is enabled to dispense with the obligation of justifying itself by reason, and is erected into its own all-sufficient voucher and justification. There never was such an instrument devised for consecrating all deep-seated prejudices. And the chief strength of this false philosophy in morals, politics, and religion, lies in the appeal which it is accustomed to make to the evidence of mathematics and of the cognate branches of physical science. To expel it from these, is to drive it from its stronghold. (*CW* I:233–35)

2 Mill, mathematics, and the naturalist tradition

I

John Stuart Mill's views about arithmetic and geometry have probably attracted more ridicule and disdain than the positions of any other thinker in the history of the philosophy of mathematics.[1] I believe that the unfavorable assessment of Mill is quite unwarranted, resting in part on misunderstandings of his position born of hasty misreading (sometimes, one suspects, of reading only the scornful remarks of his influential critics), in part on commitments to a view of philosophy quite different from that which moved Mill. In this chapter I shall try to set the record straight.

Because it is essential to any clear appreciation of Mill's ideas about mathematics to recognize the problems he attempted to address, we should begin by contrasting two large conceptions of philosophy in general and of the philosophy of mathematics in particular. One of these conceptions, which I shall call "transcendentalism", believes that a central task of philosophy is to identify fundamental conditions on human thought, representation, or experience, and that this enterprise is to be carried out by special philosophical methods that yield knowledge quite independently of experience or of the deliverances of the natural sciences. Prime examples of transcendentalist philosophy can be found in Kant, in Frege, and, in recent philosophy, in the writings of Michael Dummett. Opposed to transcendentalism is a quite different philosophical tradition, one that emphasizes the idea of human subjects

I am grateful to John Skorupski for his helpful comments, which have enabled me to improve the final version of this chapter.

as parts of nature, refuses to believe that there are special sources of philosophical knowledge whose deliverances are foundational to, or independent of, the methods and claims of the natural sciences, and conceives the philosopher as an "under-laborer", working cooperatively with scientists, artists, and makers of social policy on the problems that arise at particular moments in human history, endeavoring to shape more adequate visions of the world and our place in it. This conception of philosophy is appropriately called "naturalism".[2] It is found, I believe, in Aristotle, Locke, Hume, and Dewey, and its leading contemporary exponent is W. V. Quine. Mill is not only one of the most important naturalists in the history of philosophy, but also, perhaps, the most thoroughly consistent.[3]

Now it is quite apparent that my division is not exhaustive. Few philosophers would be happy counting themselves as either transcendentalists or naturalists – and some may question my assignment of labels to great figures of the past on the grounds that their writings suggest a more mixed picture. This is especially clear when we consider the views on mathematics expressed by philosophers in the empiricist tradition. Although empiricist philosophers like Locke and Hume display an apparent commitment to naturalism throughout much of their writing, their discussions of mathematics testify to the difficulty of avoiding transcendentalism in understanding mathematics and our mathematical knowledge. Faced with the two central questions in the philosophy of mathematics – What, if anything, are mathematical statements about? How do subjects achieve mathematical knowledge? – there is an inveterate tendency either to appeal to ethereal entities and special processes, or to reject such questions altogether in favor of inquiries into the conditions of the possibility of thought, language, and knowledge. Virtually all empiricists have succumbed to that tendency, and so deserted naturalism.[4]

But not Mill. At the heart of Mill's treatment of arithmetic and geometry is a serious attempt to understand these sciences as dealing with the physical properties of everyday things and our mathematical knowledge as grounded in our perceptual interactions with the physical world. This leads him to formulate views about mathematics that seem at a far remove from the contemporary practices of mathematicians, that dismiss the "special certainty" of mathematics and its "independence from experience". At first glance, his account appears crude, even childish.

So it appeared to Frege. In *The Foundations of Arithmetic*, a book that has been regarded, for almost half a century, as a model for the philosophy of mathematics, Frege engages in a review of the doctrines of his predecessors, reserving particular scorn for Mill. Frege's chief aim in criticizing Mill is to prepare the way for his own answer to the problem that occupies him, that of providing a characterization of the contents of arithmetical statements. What is not obvious from Frege's critique is the extent to which he has turned his back on one of the problems that Mill's account was supposed to address, the problem of explaining how human subjects acquire mathematical knowledge. In one sense, Frege's answer might appear implicit in the theses about the apriority of mathematical knowledge advanced in his book, and in the structure of the proofs that his subsequent work attempted to articulate. Mathematical knowledge is obtained by following proofs, and proofs ideally proceed by elementary logical steps (the steps identified in Frege's system of logic) from logical first principles (the basic laws of Frege's system of logic). But someone who is serious about the epistemological question is bound to feel that this only passes the buck. Ultimately we are owed an explanation of how the basic laws are known.

Frege addresses this question at only one point in his work, where he writes:

The question why and with what right we acknowledge a law of logic to be true, logic can answer only by reducing it to another law of logic. Where that is not possible, logic can give no answer. If we step away from logic, we may say: we are compelled to make judgments by our own nature and by external circumstances; and if we do so, we cannot reject this law – of Identity, for example; we must acknowledge it unless we wish to reduce our thought to confusion and finally renounce all judgment whatever. I shall neither dispute nor support this view; I shall merely remark that what we have here is not a logical consequence. What is given is not a reason for something's being true, but for our taking it to be true.[5]

To be sure, we would not expect from *logic* an answer to the question of how we recognize the truth of fundamental logical laws – but it appears that a complete philosophical account of logic and mathematics ought to provide *some* answer to this question. Frege's response is elusive, and allows for two modes of elucidation. One is to read him as admitting the validity of the question, and implicitly adopting a Kantian epistemological framework for answering it.[6] The other is to declare, in the spirit of Frege's repeated reminders to separate logical and psychological issues, that the epistemological task does not require us to describe some process through which human subjects can come to appreciate the truth of fundamental logical laws. It is enough simply to note that these laws are preconditions for the framing of any thought or for conducting any discussion.[7] In the passage I have quoted, Frege seems to distance himself from this type of transcendentalism – but perhaps it can be seen as according with his characterization of the laws of logic as "boundary stones set in an eternal foundation, which our thought can overflow, but never displace".[8] To a naturalistic sensibility, like Mill's, this kind of transcendentalist response will appear an even more outrageous error than invoking special knowledge-generating processes (as in Kant's brave attempt to say just how we gain fundamental knowledge in geometry[9]), for it simply ignores the fact that human beings come to know all the things they do, including laws of logic, by undergoing psychological processes, and we ought to be told just what these processes are and how they yield the knowledge in question.

Yet one or the other of these transcendentalist responses has been implicit in virtually all treatments of the philosophy of mathematics ever since Frege. Some philosophers have been happy with the old empiricist idea that elementary logical and mathematical knowledge can be gained by a process of conceptual analysis; others, like Kurt Gödel, have believed that we are able to know fundamental truths about a mathematical universe of abstract objects by engaging in processes of intuition that are akin to perception in important respects;[10] but, for the overwhelming majority of philosophers, the prevailing attitude seems to have been that the question of how we know the fundamental laws (whatever they are) from which proofs begin is one that either doesn't need answering or, perhaps, shouldn't even be asked.[11]

So Mill's attempt to grapple with the question is bound to look quaint. Moreover, the silence surrounding this question deprives Mill (and fellow-travelling naturalists) of their best defense, the pointed request to say just how mathematical truths are known if not by perceptual interactions with the physical world. From the naturalistic perspective, silence in response to a perfectly good question is a symptom of just how embarrassingly bad transcendentalist attempts to explain basic logic and mathematical knowledge turn out to be.

II

By the age of seven or eight, most children know some elementary facts of arithmetic, and, by their mid-teens, many know some truths of geometry. How has this knowledge been obtained? The obvious answers are somewhat different in the two cases, because of the special role that proof plays in geometrical instruction. Arithmetical knowledge is often founded upon rote learning, as children accept the practice of their teachers, but it is reinforced by manipulations of small groups of similar objects – beads, balls, fruit, vegetables, and so forth. Knowledge of geometry also involves acquiescing in prevailing practices. Students learn the axioms from a textbook, they are taught how to prove theorems from those axioms, and, as they gain confidence, they may emancipate themselves enough to come to accept a new theorem on the basis of a derivation they have constructed (although, even here, they may want to check the judgments of their peers, their teacher, or the text, before firmly committing themselves). As in the case of arithmetic, they may also gain empirical support from solving practical problems.

What does the child's knowledge have to do with that of the adult mathematician? Perhaps nothing. In the spirit of Descartes, Kant, Frege, and any number of later philosophers, we might think that, in epistemology, there comes a time to put away childish things, a time at which our knowledge becomes justified in a different, more adequate, way. For several centuries, epistemology has favored the myth of the synchronic reconstruction of the knowledge of a lone individual: true, each of us may have acquired all sorts of information from other people, but, it is possible, in principle, to reconstruct an individual's knowledge by tracing the chains of justification *within* that person's belief and experiences.[12] Applying the myth to the case of mathematics, we envisage rendering explicit the justification of mathematical beliefs in ways that make the early childhood training quite irrelevant. But if such synchronic reconstruction is possible, then we are owed an account of how the justification proceeds. Lacking any such account, it is worth exploring the straightforward suggestion that the simple story about the growth of mathematical knowledge in children is an indispensable part even of the knowledge of the sophisticated mathematician. Mill's account of mathematics is founded upon taking this possibility seriously.[13]

It is worth conceding, at this point, that the obvious account of how children learn mathematics may be wrong. Naturalists are committed to the doctrine that the mundane processes through which children learn are part of the justification for mathematical knowledge even for the sophisticates, but this doctrine is separable from any particular claims about the character of those processes. I have told a simple, "folk" story that might be superseded in the course of psychological and sociological inquiry. (Perhaps, as some writers have recently suggested, children have innate knowledge of some mathematical principles.[14]) However, Mill's explanation involves both theses: the "folk" account of children's knowledge acquisition as well as the commitment to understanding all mathematical knowledge as an outgrowth of the mundane processes.

Plainly, the rehearsal of the ways in which children are led into mathematical conformity is not completely satisfactory, for it takes for granted the ability of teachers to pass on items of knowledge. In giving a naturalistic account of any part of human knowledge (or of any complex human practice), it is quite correct to recognize the social and historical antecedents of the achievements of individuals, but we are then forced to wonder about the sources of the knowledge or skills transmitted. If children learn addition tables from their teachers, we need to ask how the teachers gained *their* knowledge. As we envisage a chain along which mathematical knowledge is transmitted and extended, it seems that we must stress the contribution of the interaction with the physical world that plays only a reinforcing role in the knowledge of contemporary children.[15] The manipulations of small groups of objects and the simple geometrical experiments that occupy only a subordinate position assume principal importance.

So we arrive at Mill's fundamental idea about arithmetical and geometrical knowledge: such knowledge is ultimately founded upon our interactions with the physical world. Seen in this light. Mill owes answers to three questions:

(1) What are the entities with which the statements of arithmetic and geometry are concerned?

(2) How do interactions with physical objects give us the knowledge of the properties of these entities recorded in the standard truths of arithmetic and geometry?

(3) How does the elementary knowledge obtainable by the simple physical interactions become extended into the complex knowledge of sophisticated contemporary mathematics?

I claim that Mill provides answers to the first two of these questions and outlines an answer to the third. Moreover, the answers seem to me to be correct (or correct as far as they go). I shall now attempt to explain and defend an assessment that will, no doubt, seem ludicrous to those whose primary acquaintance with Mill is through the traditional dismissal of his ideas.

III

In *A System of Logic*, Mill develops his account of arithmetic by inviting his readers to reflect on the fact that ordinary objects – like pebbles – can be rearranged so that they appear to us under different aspects. He writes:

Three pebbles in two separate parcels, and three pebbles in one parcel, do not make the same impression on our senses; and the assertion that the very same pebbles may by an alteration of place and arrangement be made to produce either the one set of sensations or the other, though a very familiar proposition, is not an identical one. It is a truth known to us by early and constant experience – an inductive truth; and such truths are the foundation of the science of Numbers. The fundamental truths of that science all rest on the evidence of sense; they are proved by showing to our eyes and our fingers that any number of objects, ten balls, for example, may by separation and rearrangement exhibit to our senses all the different sets of numbers the sum of which is equal to ten. All the improved methods of teaching arithmetic to children proceed on a knowledge of this fact. All who wish to carry the child's *mind* along with them in learning arithmetic; all who wish to teach numbers, and not mere ciphers – now teach it through the evidence of the senses, in the manner we have described. (*CW* VII:256–57)

This passage encapsulates the naturalistic approach to arithmetical knowledge I have outlined in the last section. For present purposes, its principal interest is in exposing the nature of the physical facts Mill takes arithmetic to be about.

We experience a world in which the same objects can present themselves differently to us, either because of our physical interactions or because of the ways in which we group them together in thought. To begin with, I shall proceed as Mill does (and as Mill's well-taught children do), focusing on the physical activities that give rise to different representations. The fact underlying the truth of "3 = 2 + 1" – or, as Mill sometimes puts it, underlying the definition of '3' as '2 + 1', a reformulation that will occupy us later – is human rearrangement of objects that collectively strike us as °°° so as to produce objects that affect us as °° °. Now although this is a plausible reinterpretation of what goes on in the experiments of Mill's progressive classrooms, it still leaves important points unspecified. Does the truth of "3 = 2 + 1" record the mere *possibility* of the kind of rearrangement of the world? Or does it describe the totality of human activities of a particular kind? To what, if anything, do the numerals refer?

Mill answers the last question much later in *A System of Logic*, where he provides two slightly different accounts. The first of these suggests that numerals are general terms picking out special sorts of entities.

What, then, is that which is connoted by a name of number? Of course, some property belonging to the agglomeration of things which we call by the name; and that property is the characteristic manner in which the agglomeration is made up of, and may be separated into, parts. (*CW* VII:611)

On a straightforward reading, this passage multiplies the number of entities in Mill's world. There are not only all the ordinary things, the pebbles, the balls, and so forth, but a vast number of "agglomerations", or "aggregates" as Mill goes on to call them. One interpretation of his terminology would be that numerical statements record properties of sets or classes, so that the account of arithmetic would turn out to be a species of Platonism. Mill's preferred rewriting of "3 = 2 + 1" would then be something like

$$(1) \qquad (x)\big(3x \supset (\exists y)(\exists z)(2y \,\&\, 1z \,\&\, y \cap z = \varnothing \,\&\, y \cup z = x)\big)$$

where the variables range over sets and the numerical terms '3', '2', '1', function as predicates. This reading would not only be in tension with Mill's nominalism, prominent throughout *A System of Logic*,[16] but it would also threaten to undercut the epistemological advantage of his account.[17] For while it is commonplace that people can perceive pebbles, it is far from clear that we can perceive *sets* of pebbles:[18] indeed, one of the most important problems of contemporary philosophy of mathematics has been that of understanding how any kind of knowledge of abstract objects is possible, given that these objects would be non-spatio-temporal and thus incapable of standing in causal relations to human subjects.[19]

However, if we give weight to "agglomeration" rather than to "aggregate", maybe we can avoid any commitment to abstract objects. Suppose we think of the agglomeration as something like a mereological union, for example by conceiving the agglomeration of pebbles as consisting of the space-time region occupied by those pebbles. Then the content of "$3 = 2 + 1$" can be represented by (1), provided that we now read the variables as ranging over space-time regions and interpret "$y \cap z = \varnothing$" as "y and z have no common part", and "$y \cup z = x$" as "x is the totality of space-time points in y and z". But the trouble with this proposal is that it opens the way to one of Frege's most effective criticisms. Because the *parts* of the agglomerations have now lost their identities, we cannot say that a particular agglomeration has any specific numerical property. Frege illustrates the point by asking us what number belongs to a pack of cards: is it 1 (for the pack), 4 (for the suits), or 52 (for the individual cards), or maybe something else entirely?[20] Mill is quite clear that attributions of number to agglomerations always carry with them some way in which the agglomeration is supposed to be divided up into parts – so the Fregean criticism is quite inept as an attack on Mill's own views. However, this does reveal that the reconstruction we have so far achieved fails to capture Mill's intentions.

If agglomerations are to be understood in terms of mereological sums, or chunks of space-time, the content of arithmetical statements must be represented in a more complex fashion. Agglomerations must either be seen as explicitly relational entities, or else we must see numerical identities as involving relations between agglomerations and properties that pick out a particular way of dividing the mereological sum into parts ("principles of division"). Thus we would rewrite "$3 = 2 + 1$" as

(2) $\left(x\right)\left(3\left[x,P\right] \supset \left(\exists y\right)\left(\exists z\right)\left(2\left[y,P\right] \& \text{ } 1\left[z,P\right] \& \text{ } y \cap z = \varnothing \& y \cup z = x\right)\right)$

where the lower-case variables range over space-time regions, where
P is a property variable, representing the parts into which the space-
time region is to be divided if the numerical predicate is to apply to
it. So, for example, in counting an agglomeration of pebbles as a
three, we would be saying that a particular space-time region counts
as a *three* with respect to division into pebbles. I think that a
consistent reconstruction of Mill's ideas can be elaborated along
these lines.[21]

However, this reconstruction of Mill has some disadvantages. It
is not clear that it can honor Mill's commitment to the universal
applicability of concepts of number: are there mereological sums
of concepts, ideas, angels, strokes of the bell, or figures of the
syllogism?[22] Further, as (2) makes plain, numerical identities would
now involve property variables, and this would seem to inflate
Mill's ontology. For, while Mill is content to talk of attributes,
his references are always particular – I do not think he would
countenance the idea of a well-defined totality of attributes.[23] The
worry about (2), especially if we read the free property variable as
tantamount to a universal quantification over properties, is that,
when the pertinent notion of property is explicated, our ontological
commitments will be equivalent to those of set theory, and our
epistemological access to general claims about properties will be
problematic.

The interpretations we have been considering so far take seriously
the idea of finding some special objects, about which we discover
facts by rearranging ordinary physical things. But do we need any
such objects to make sense of Mill's account? The remarks about
what properly instructed children do give no hint that they are
bringing new entities before them and exploring the properties of
these entities – rather, Mill seems to think, they are discovering,
through their activity of rearrangement, something about the ordinary physical things they manipulate. Perhaps we can manage without the new objects, alleged products of the activity, if we focus
directly on the activity itself.

Mill indicates as much in passages that develop his account of
number. He emphasizes the processes of joining and separating that
give rise to and decompose "aggregates".

What the name of number connotes is the manner in which single objects of the given kind must be put together, in order to produce that particular aggregate. (*CW* VII:611)

Every arithmetical proposition, every statement of the result of an arithmetical operation, is a statement of one of the modes of formation of a given number. It affirms that a certain aggregate might have been formed by putting together certain other aggregates, or by withdrawing certain portions of some aggregate; and that, by consequence, we might reproduce those aggregates from it by reversing the process. (*CW* VII:611)[24]

The talk of aggregates can either be read literally, as if our processes of manipulating the world brought a new object before us, or it can be understood as a convenient shorthand for discussing the processes by means of which we make salient previously unnoticed aspects of familiar entities. I think Mill's nominalistic scruples should incline him to the latter course. We can reconstruct his ideas about the content of arithmetical statements by viewing numbers as properties of human acts, acts of aggregating and disaggregating.[25]

Numerical identities are supposed to affirm that certain aggregates might have been formed, or decomposed, in particular ways. If we take a pebble and another pebble, placing them side by side, we perform a collective act, involving the representation of the pebbles together and as separated from other things, and we can call this act an act of "making 2". If we now perform a further collective act on a single pebble, different from those so far collected, separating it from other objects, we can call this an act of "making 1". If we now take the objects of our original "making 2" and the object of our act of "making 1", combining all the objects in a new act of collecting, we perform an act of "making 3". More concisely, a collection that unites the objects previously collected in acts of "making 2" and "making 1", where the objects collected in these previous acts are distinct, is an act of "making 3". So we can rewrite the numerical identity "2 + 1 = 3" as

$$(3) \qquad (x)(y)\big((2Cx \,\&\, 1Cy \,\&\, (z)\neg(Oxz \,\&\, Oyz))\supset (w)(Uxyw \supset 3Cw)\big)$$

where the variables range over human acts of collecting objects (rearranging them so as to achieve representations of them as together and separated from other things), the predicates '1C', '2C', and '3C' stand for acts of collecting a single object, two objects, and three objects, respectively, the relation O holds between a collecting and an object just in case the object is among those collected in that act (the collecting is "on" the object), and the relation U holds among three collectings if the third is an act of collecting the objects collected in the first two (the collecting analogue of set-theoretic union).

"Compositional" identities – those in which the left-hand side of the equation is arithmetically complex and the right-hand side simple – are thus not hard to understand. But Mill also explicitly considers "decompositional" identities, and these bring in new complications. The simplest way of rewriting "3 = 2 + 1" is

$$(4) \qquad (x)\big(3Cx \supset (\exists y)(\exists z)(2Cy \,\&\, 1Cz \,\&\, (w)\mathbin{\neg}(Oyw \,\&\, Ozw) \,\&\, Uyzx)\big)$$

This rewriting looks as though it commits the obvious error of replacing a true sentence with a false one. For "3 = 2 + 1" is true, but it is surely not the case that, for every act of "making 3" there are acts of "making 2" and "making 1" that are united in the original act. Nor does Mill claim that there are. As the passages I have quoted make plain, he emphasizes the *possibility* of various kinds of activity (or "aggregate formation"). So, perhaps, we should amend (4) to

$$(5) \qquad (x)\big(3Cx \supset \Diamond(\exists y)(\exists z)(2Cy \,\&\, 1Cz \,\&\, (w)\mathbin{\neg}(Oyw \,\&\, Ozw) \,\&\, Uyzx)\big)$$

where the '$\Diamond$' is a modal operator meaning "it is possible that".

But how exactly would Mill explain and justify this modal commitment? His worries about modal notions are evident throughout *A System of Logic*, and it is quite clear that he would find the contemporary semantics for modal logic epistemologically troublesome.[26] Insofar as he employs modal notions in his own explanations, his preference seems to be for the kind of linguistic reductionism beloved of empiricists, early and late. To say that we could perform various constructive acts is just to say that it is consistent to suppose that we do. The modal operator could thus be understood by supposing the '$\Diamond p$' just asserts that there is a consistent story that says that p. Indeed, we can improve the representation of arithmetical statements by making it plain, from the beginning, that these statements are part of a story.

Human collective activity is fragmentary, too sporadic to be neatly categorized and described. Instead of taking our task to be that of characterizing it exactly, we might proceed instead by imagining an *ideal collector*, one who performs all the acts of which we are capable. Indeed, for reasons that will become apparent later, we needn't suppose that this invocation of modality is anything more than a heuristic device, designed to get us started on understanding the story about the collector – our capabilities, far from being well-defined in advance, will, in fact, be pinned down through the way in which we develop the account of the ideal collector. Arithmetic, then, is seen as an idealizing theory, one that discloses facts about nature by reporting on the constructive activity of a fictitious character, whose performances contain actual human activities as an untidy part.

Developing Mill's ideas in this constructivist fashion may seem, in the end, to retreat from one of the most attractive features of his position, the linking of mathematical statements to facets of objective nature. Why should we think of the idealizing story as having anything to do with the structure of reality? I suggest that Mill's insight is that what we might call "the mathematical structure of reality" consists in the way that nature permits human rearrangement: we might think of this structure as a disposition for objects to be collected, manipulated, ordered, and arranged in some ways, but not in others, and that the manifestation of that disposition is simply the activity of an ideal collector. To adapt a Millian phrase, arithmetic concerns itself with permanent possibilities of rearrangement. The ideal collector is simply a device for showing those permanent possibilities.[27]

IV

The simplest kinds of collecting activity in which human beings actually engage involve manipulations of physical objects. The point of these manipulations is to help us achieve certain kinds of representations, to see some objects as "together" and "separated" from everything else, and Mill's diagrams remind us of what is essential. Although physical rearrangements serve as props in the early stages of collective activity, we quickly become able to manage without them and to collect objects in thought: indeed, it may be the case that the earliest stages of cognitive development already involve this ability and that the sole function of physical manipulation is to allow us to make arbitrary subdivisions in cases where we would naturally collect things whose salient characteristics are shared. In any event, the notion of collecting should be freed from any dependence on manipulation. Once this is understood, Frege's sarcastic comments that Mill's theory makes it appear fortunate that objects are not nailed down and that it cannot account for our ability to number strokes of the clock are obviously beside the point.[28]

Mill himself is eminently clear that arithmetical statements have wide application. He writes:

The properties of Number, alone among all known phenomena, are, in the most rigorous sense, properties of all things whatever. All things are not coloured, or ponderable, or even extended; but all things are numerable. (CW VII:221)

Propositions, therefore, concerning numbers have the remarkable peculiarity that they are propositions concerning all things whatever; all objects, all existences of every kind, known to our experience. (CW VII:255)

We should thus see Mill as introducing his account of collective activity with the idea of physical manipulation as a purely heuristic device. Our powers to collect things "in our mind" outstrip the crude shuffling of physical objects. By reading Mill in terms of "modes of formation" and not seeking some aggregate (or "agglomeration") that is to be the product of our collective activity, we can make sense of his ideas about the content of numerical statements and also do justice to his forthright acceptance of the universal applicability of arithmetic.

So far, we have been able to elaborate an account of arithmetical identities that answers the arithmetical part of the first question posed in section II: What are the entities with which the statements of arithmetic and geometry are concerned? Moreover, that account leads fairly directly to an answer to part of the second question, the question of how we could acquire arithmetical knowledge. As we engage in the collective activity with which arithmetic is concerned, we can notice regularities of the kind recorded in statements like (3). Our experience of instances serves as the basis for an induction to the generalization. So, as Mill says, the laws of arithmetic turn out to be inductive truths.[29]

Yet it is quite obvious that we would only achieve a fragmentary knowledge of arithmetic in this direct fashion. Perhaps we have a sufficient basis for asserting the identities that relate very small numbers – just as the children of the progressive classroom gain experience of the facts about collecting that underlie the addition and multiplication tables – but it seems ludicrous to think that we have any direct experience of the facts Mill connects with more ambitious arithmetical statements. Without venturing into the parts of arithmetic for which we standardly require calculators and computers, we can pose the problem by citing one of Mill's own examples.

Thus, when we say that the cube of 12 is 1782, what we affirm is this: that if, having a sufficient number of pebbles or of any other objects, we put them together into the particular sort of parcels or aggregates called twelves; and put together these themselves into similar collections; and, finally, make up twelve of these largest parcels: the aggregate thus formed will be such a one as we call 1728; namely, that which (to take the most familiar of its modes of formation) may be made by joining the parcel called a thousand pebbles, the parcel called seven hundred pebbles, the parcel called twenty pebbles, and the parcel called eight pebbles. (CW VII:611–12)

Now this is just what Mill's account of the content of "$12^3 = 1728$" ought to be, and it could be explicated (at some length!) along lines laid down in the previous section. However, surely there have been very few, if any, occasions, in the history of our species, on which someone actually performed the operations of collecting described here. So it is highly unclear that we have any basis for an induction to the general assertion that all of the complex collective operations that satisfy the conditions for "making 12^3" constitute a collective operation of "making 1728". Here it seems that we cannot simply read off the epistemology from an understanding of what the statement is about.

Once again, it is helpful to recall how children actually come to learn arithmetical identities of this kind. Mastery of the simple arithmetical identities provides them with rules that they can apply to arrive at more complicated truths. The addition and multiplication tables are used in working with numbers with several digits.

We can understand this as a matter of acquiring a notation and the rules for manipulating the symbols. The complex truths of arithmetic are justified through the exercise of conceptual abilities that are inculcated when children learn how to use the language of arithmetic.

But if Mill is to accept this view of our knowledge of non-elementary arithmetical truths, then it seems that he has reverted to a kind of epistemology favored by many other empiricists. From Locke and Hume to Ayer and Hempel, empiricists have insisted that mathematics can be accommodated in a view of knowledge that emphasizes the role of experience by reformulating the main empiricist slogan: instead of claiming that all knowledge is based upon experience, we are to say that all knowledge of matters of fact (all knowledge of synthetic truths) is based upon experience.[30] Now Mill seems to aspire to defend the slogan in its pure form. The whole point of alluding to experiments with pebbles appears to be to stress the role of everyday experience in mathematical knowledge, so that to acknowledge, in the end, that arithmetical knowledge rested upon notational conventions, or conceptual relations, or analytic first principles (to cite three popular versions of the dominant empiricist idea) would be to confess that the emphasis on physical manipulation was as irrelevant and misguided as Mill's critics have typically taken it to be.

To respond to this worry, we shall have to take up Mill's views about definition, and, in particular, his proposal that definitions carry with them an "associated matter of fact".[31] Mill believes that complex arithmetical knowledge is gained by applying definitions of the numerals (and of the symbols for arithmetical operations), but he does not think that the knowledge can be liberated from the recognition of the physical facts associated with the pertinent definitions. Unlike his fellow empiricists, he does not accede to the view that appeals to definitions, conceptual relations, or analytic principles constitute a mode of justification that is independent of experience. In twentieth-century terminology, Mill's empiricism rejects not only the synthetic a priori but the analytic a priori as well.

This apparently surprising doctrine rests on an appraisal of the ways in which definitions of important scientific terms respond to new discoveries. According to Mill, the main purpose of scientific definitions "is to serve as the landmarks of scientific classification. And since the classifications in any science are constantly modified as scientific knowledge advances, the definitions in the sciences are also constantly varying" (*CW* VII:139). The history of early nineteenth-century chemistry furnishes Mill with an obvious example. He notes that an older definition of 'acid' that required acids both to combine with alkalis to form salts and to contain oxygen had to be revised after the discovery of the composition of "muriatic acid" (hydrochloric acid, HCl).[32]

How does this bear on the issue of the analytic a priori? Mill is not explicit, but I think he envisages the following type of argument. Suppose, at a particular stage of inquiry, people accept a definition of some term so that, by appealing to that definition, they can defend a claim involving the term: for concreteness, imagine chemists working with the older definition of 'acid' maintaining that all acids contain oxygen and basing this judgment on the definition. Many empiricists seem to think that, in such cases, the subjects have a priori knowledge, knowledge that is independent of (and, perhaps, invulnerable to) experience.[33] If the knowledge were invulnerable to experience, then, after the discovery of the composition of muriatic acid, it would still be possible to retain the judgment. Perhaps the community of chemists would divide into traditionalists and innovators, speaking slightly different languages. For the traditionalists, "All acids contain oxygen" would still be true, and "Muriatic acid is an acid" would be false (perhaps what used to be called "muriatic acid" would be renamed). For the innovators, "All acids contain oxygen" would be false, and "Muriatic acid is an acid" would remain true. Mill believes that there is an important epistemic difference between traditionalists and innovators, that traditionalists have made an epistemic error by not revising their language. His point, I think, is that a language apt for the purposes of describing, explaining, and predicting natural phenomena ought to group together things over which we can make reliable inductive inferences, employ common patterns of explanation, and so forth. In other words, our language is subject to evaluation according to how well it serves the purposes of inquiry.

If this is correct, then the statement "All acids contain oxygen" is not invulnerable to experience, even though it is grounded in a definition. Moreover, although people could have justified that claim, prior to the discovery of the composition of HCl, by citing the definition, that would have been a purely *local* justification, one that failed to recognize the background conditions under which appeal to definition provides justification. If we are to elaborate the full justification, then we must bring out those features of the past practice of chemistry that made it justifiable to introduce the older definition – for example, the apparent concordance between the property of combining with an alkali to form a salt and containing oxygen. So it is only on a superficial view that the appeal to a definition can be regarded as yielding a priori knowledge in this case.

It is helpful to compare the arguments I have attributed to Mill with two lines of reasoning that Quine has elaborated with great lucidity.[34] At the end of "Two Dogmas of Empiricism", Quine articulates the point that, when a body of doctrine encounters a problematic ("recalcitrant") empirical finding, it may be reasonable sometimes to abandon quite high-level principles or to modify our definitions.[35] This is exactly the point that Mill makes concretely with the example of the definition of 'acid', but Quine extends it by asking after the precise epistemic difference between revising a definition and revising any other claim.[36] In an earlier essay, "Truth By Convention", a central argument consists in showing how any consistent body of doctrine we choose could be rendered "analytic" by framing the definitions of the constituent terms in the right way.[37] So if analyticity is the key to a priori knowledge, then a priori knowledge comes very cheap.[38] More to the point in elaborating Mill's theses about definitions, once we realize that virtually any thesis can be construed in a way that renders it a consequence of definitions, it becomes apparent that any attempt to justify our beliefs by citing definitions must be dependent on the justifiability of the linguistic conventions we employ. In other words, the citation of the definition cannot do justificatory work by itself. If we are sometimes justified in appealing to definitions, or to the conventions of our language, it is because we are justified in taking that language to be an apt vehicle for the purposes of inquiry.

Quine presents more completely a set of concerns about the apriority of our knowledge of conceptual truths (analytic truths, relations among ideas) that was overlooked by many empiricists, but was appreciated by both Kant and Mill. Kant's wide-ranging attempts to establish the legitimacy of certain concepts (and to formulate criteria for the employment of scientific concepts) can be seen as a valiant attempt to avoid the demolition of the a priori.[39] Mill goes in the opposite direction. Since he sees no possibility of any "transcendental" justification for our concepts, he draws the moral that all our knowledge is grounded in experience, and that the apparent independence from experience of our mathematical knowledge is an illusion, fostered by a myopic view of justification.

How, then, are particular linguistic practices justified? Like Kant before him, Mill has difficulty in saying precisely what the conditions for legitimacy of definitions are. His initial proposal (which he shares with Kant) offers the suggestion that adequate language must pick out objects in the world.

All definitions are of names only; but, in some definitions, it is clearly apparent that nothing is intended except to explain the meaning of the word. While in others, besides explaining the meaning of the word, it is intended to be implied that there exists a thing corresponding to the word. (CW VII:143)

Mill illustrates the contrast with a pair of examples. We define 'centaur' by saying that centaurs are animals with the upper parts of a man and the lower parts of a horse. Here (typically in the context of story-telling) there is no implication that any such object exists. On the other hand, when we define 'triangle' by declaring that triangles are rectilinear figures with three sides, we intend to assert the existence of triangles. So, Mill's first suggestion is that scientifically legitimate language should be referential, while language used for more playful purposes need not be.

This suggestion is far too simple, and, indeed, Mill's own example of the definition of a scientific term undermines the proposal.[40] For as he makes clear in the ensuing discussion, Mill does not think that geometrical figures correspond to any real objects. So it is no surprise to find him weakening his proposal to the thesis that the factual claim made in the definition "affirms the actual or possible existence of Things possessing the combination of attributes set forth in the definition; and this, if true, may be foundation sufficient on which to build a whole fabric of scientific truth" (CW VII:144). But this is hopeless. Not only does it bring in a modal notion that Mill is usually concerned to avoid, but it also weakens the original contrast (aren't centaurs possible on any conception of possibility that Mill can allow?).[41] Furthermore, as we reflect on the chemical example that started the entire chain of reasoning, we recognize that it is hard to fault traditionalists on grounds that they are failing to talk about possible objects – or even actual objects. (Since plenty of acids do contain oxygen, the traditionalist's term 'acid' has a nonempty extension.) The notion of legitimacy for scientific language must be explained differently.

As he proceeds, Mill does better, moving beyond simple existence criteria to recognize the need to fashion terms that conform to the resemblances in nature. In the concluding section of Book I of *A System of Logic*, he writes:

Although, according to the opinion here presented, Definitions are properly of names only, and not of things, it does not follow from this that definitions are arbitrary. How to define a name, may not only be a matter of considerable difficulty and intricacy, but may involve considerations going deep into the nature of the things which are denoted by the name. (*CW* VII:150)[42]

Later, in a passage commenting on the ills of language that grows haphazardly, he is more explicit about the ways in which a definition can go astray:

a name not unfrequently passes by successive links of resemblance from one object to another, until it becomes applied to things having nothing in common with the first things to which the name was given; which, however, do not, for that reason, drop the name; so that it at last denotes a confused huddle of objects, having nothing whatever in common; and connotes nothing, not even a vague and general resemblance. (*CW* VII:152)

Mill's final view, I believe, is that theses about the appropriateness of a language are to be judged by a complex set of desiderata. To point out that a term has, or lacks, reference is only the first step in appraising its legitimacy. If we discover that it is a predicate that applies to existing objects, then we have to inquire if those objects are sufficiently similar that we can expect to frame inductions about them.[43] If we find that the predicate applies to no existent objects, it may, nonetheless, be the case that we can still deploy it in generalizations that highlight regularities among entities that actually exist. These guidelines are rough, but they are no less precise (nor any less applicable) than the methodological standards we use in assessing inductive inferences.

We can now see that Mill's empiricist epistemology for arithmetic divides into two parts. The first part consists in recognizing the obvious ways of confirming judgments about regularities in collective activity, thus achieving an untidy corpus of simple arithmetical identities. So our predecessors gained knowledge of proto-arithmetic. The crucial step in moving beyond this situation was the subsumption of these simple regularities through the provision of a language, from whose definitions (or conventions, or semantical rules) they would emerge. Mill's own writings predate by decades the formulation of axioms for arithmetic by Peano and Dedekind, so he is unable to provide a systematic treatment of the entire science. He indicates briefly how he takes the definitions of the numerals to yield arithmetic identities.

We believe that five and two are equal to seven on the evidence of this inductive law [the law that the sums of equals are equal], combined with the definitions of those numbers. We arrive at that conclusion (as all remember how they first learned it) by adding a single unit at a time; $5 + 1 = 6$, therefore $5 + 1 + 1 = 6 + 1 = 7$: and again $2 = 1 + 1$, therefore $5 + 2 = 5 + 1 + 1 = 7$. (*CW* VII:613)

Frege correctly takes him to task for omitting, in this attempt at proof, the need for assuming the associativity of addition.[44] However, this does not touch the essentials of Mill's program: he can accept Frege's point as a friendly amendment to the twin claims that there is a definitional system that yields the truths of arithmetic and that this definitional system is justified through the recognition of basic properties of collective activity, which would justify us in believing the simple arithmetic identities.

After Peano, Dedekind, and Frege, we can add more detail. The standard Peano axioms can be reformulated as statements about collective activity. To do this, we need to be a little more careful than I have been so far, recognizing that Mill's version of arithmetic is concerned with types of operations, where two operations belong to a type just in case they can be *matched*, that is, if and only if the objects they segregate can be made to correspond to one another. Matchability plays a significant part of the role that identity plays in ordinary arithmetic.

Besides the notion of matchability, I shall take the notions of a *one-operation*, of one operation being a *successor* to another, and of an operation being an *addition* on other operations, as primitive.[45] These notions will be abbreviated as '*Mxy*', '*Ux*', '*Sxy*', and '*Axyz*', respectively. The basic axioms of Mill's version of arithmetic (or *Mill Arithmetic*) will recognize that matchability is an equivalence relation, that all one-operations are matchable, that anything matchable with a one-operation is a one-operation, that successors of matchable operations are matchable, and that an operation *a* matchable with an operation that is successor of some other operation *b* must itself be the successor of an operation matchable with *b*. More formally:

[M1] $(x)Mxx$

[M2] $(x)(y)(Mxy \supset Myx)$

[M3] $(x)(y)(z)(Mxy \supset (Myz \supset Mxz))$

[M4] $(x)(y)((Ux \& Mxy) \supset Uy)$

[M5] $(x)(y)((Ux \& Uy) \supset Mxy)$

[M6] $(x)(y)(z)(w)((Sxy \& Szw \& Myw) \supset Mxz)$

[M7] $(x)(y)(z)((Sxy \& Mxz) \supset (\exists w)(Myw \& Szw))$

These axioms only identify the fundamental features of collective acitivity. They need to be supplemented with analogues of the standard Peano postulates. In particular, we have to declare that if two operations are successor operations and are matchable, then the operations of which they are successors are matchable; that a one-operation is not the successor of any operation; and that whatever property is shared by all one-operations and is such that, if an operation has the property then all successor operations have the property, holds of all operations (i.e. universally). So we obtain two further axioms and an axiom schema.

[M8] $(x)(y)(z)(w)((Sxy \& Szw \& Mxz) \supset Myw)$

[M9] $(x)(y)\neg(Ux\&Sxy)$

[M10] $\left((x)(Ux \supset \Phi x)\&(x)(y)((\Phi y\&Sxy) \supset \Phi x)\right) \supset (x)\Phi x$

  for all open sentences 'Φx'

To capture the properties of addition, it suffices to mimic the recursive specification of addition in ordinary first-order arithmetic.

[M11] $(x)(y)(z)(w)((Axyz\&Uz\&Swy) \supset Mxw)$

[M12] $(x)(y)(z)(u)(v)(w)((Axyz\&Szu\&Svw\&Aywu) \supset Mxv)$

In precisely parallel fashion, we could introduce multiplication.

  Unfortunately, [M1]–[M12] are not adequate for the development of arithmetic. It is not hard to show that they have finite models. Moreover, when one tries to emulate the usual proofs of elementary arithmetic results, the source of the trouble is apparent: without some existence assumptions we cannot be sure that there will be the operations we need.[46] The trouble can be resolved quite straightforwardly by positing the necessary collective acts.

[M13] $(\exists x)Ux$

[M14] $(x)(\exists y)Syx$

[M15] $(x)(y)(\exists z)Azxy$

With these analogues of the ordinary ontological commitments of first-order arithmetic, it is a straightforward, if tedious, task to translate the usual proofs of arithmetical theorems.

  However, it may seem that the existential assumptions are unwarranted, given Mill's view of the entities with which arithmetic is concerned.[47] Can we really suppose that there is an infinite collection of collective acts? Plainly, actual human performance is finite. So, *interpreted as claims about actual human performance*, the axioms of Mill Arithmetic cannot all be true, for they jointly imply the existence of infinitely many entities – and these, we are assuming, are human acts of collecting. This is a large-scale version of the problem we encountered earlier in considering "decompositional" identities, and the same line of solution is in order. Mill Arithmetic is an idealized description of human collective activity, or, if you like, the exact description of the collective activity of an ideal agent.

The ideal agent is characterized through the principles [M1]–[M15], so that these may be taken to embody conventions of the language. The justification for introducing these conventions is that the resultant language provides a simple way of describing actual human collecting.

Could we manage with less? It is natural to think so. Perhaps we could set a boundary on the size of human collecting, and only introduce existential assumptions that commit us to collective acts below the boundary. However, when we think about what the relevant existential assumptions would be like, it is hard to regard them as anything but arbitrary. Notice that we can readily define the notions of "two-operation", "three-operation", and so forth in our primitive vocabulary: $(x)(2x \equiv (\exists y)(\exists z)(Uy \& Mxz \& Szy))$, $(x)(3x \equiv (\exists y)(\exists z)(2y \& Mxz \& Szy))$, etc. Now we can imagine replacing [M13]–[M15] with a finite number of axioms of the form

$$[\text{M}13^\star] \quad (x)\left(nx \supset (\exists y)Syx\right)$$

where 'nx' is replaced by one of the recursively defined number predicates. But why should we stop at any particular point? We obtain a simpler and more elegant theory by not making any arbitrary choice, by treating the ideal agent as one who can continue indefinitely. Hence, I claim that [M1]–[M15] represents the best idealization of our collective activity. If this is correct, then Mill's approach, developed as I have suggested here, solves the main problems of the ontology and epistemology of arithmetic.

V

Mill's account of elementary geometry is simpler and easier to defend. In part, this is because it is much easier to see how geometrical notions are to be linked to objects of our everyday experience, in part because Mill was already acquainted with a system of axioms for geometry (namely Euclid's, which although defective from the perspective of contemporary mathematics does not involve flaws that affect Mill's philosophical points). As with arithmetic, it is useful to start reconstructing Mill's account by looking at his conception of the entities with which geometry is concerned. Here he aims to repudiate an approach defended by Whewell (and stemming ultimately from Kant) that posits an ontology of ideal entities.

Ever since the ancient Egyptians, people have used geometry to deal with the edges of physical objects, to measure the areas of land and buildings, to evaluate the distances to inaccessible points, and so forth. However, it has been obvious to all who have reflected on Euclid's geometry, that the physical entities whose properties are established through geometrical reasoning do not, strictly speaking, conform to the definitions of the geometrical entities to which they are compared. Mill expresses the point in terms of his (crude) account of the legitimacy of language, according to which scientifically justifiable terms must correspond to actual or possible objects:

There exist no points without magnitude; no lines without breadth, nor perfectly straight; no circles with all their radii exactly equal, nor squares with all their angles perfectly right. It will perhaps be said that the assumption does not extend to the actual, but only to the possible existence of such things. I answer that, according to any test we have of possibility, they are not even possible. Their existence, so far as we can form any judgment, would seem to be inconsistent with the physical composition of our planet at least, if not of the universe. (*CW* VII:225)

The stringent requirement on possibility is beside Mill's main point. It is enough for him to claim that the truths of geometry do not precisely record the properties of physical objects, for his immediate concern is with what he takes to be an error that has infected a rival philosophical tradition.

Philosophers who want to defend the view that geometry is an exact science whose first principles are certain need to find objects that answer to the definitions of geometrical terms and that can be located in a place where it will be plausible to hold that we have a priori access to them. Once these demands are made explicit, there is a very tempting way to try to satisfy them, to wit by proposing that geometrical entities are "in the mind". But Mill responds that this does not solve the problem:

We can reason about a line as if it had no breadth; because we have a power, which is the foundation of all the control we can exercise over the operation of our minds; the power when a perception is present to our senses or a conception to our intellects, of *attending* to a part only of that perception or conception instead of the whole. But we cannot *conceive* a line without breadth; we can form no mental picture of such a line; all the lines which we have in our minds are lines possessing breadth. If any one doubts this, we may refer him to his own experience. I much question if any one who fancies that he can conceive what is called a mathematical line, thinks so from the evidence of his consciousness: I suspect it is rather because he supposes that unless such a conception were possible, mathematics could not exist as a science: a supposition which there will be no difficulty in showing to be entirely groundless. (CW VII:225)

In effect, Mill charges, the ontology and epistemology with which many philosophers have credited geometry is a fiction, at odds with subjective experience, and introduced solely to save a philosophical theory.

Hume had already pondered the idea that we can obtain certain knowledge of geometrical axioms by exhibiting to ourselves the relations among geometrical concepts. He envisaged this process as one of inspecting the properties of mental images. But, as he pointed out, these kinds of "inner perceptions" are no more accurate than "outer perceptions".

Now since these ideas are so loose and uncertain, I wou'd fain ask any mathematician what infallible assurance he has, not only of the more intricate and obscure propositions of his science, but of the most vulgar and obvious principles? How can he prove to me, for instance, that two right lines cannot have one common segment? Or that 'tis impossible to draw more than one right line betwixt any two points? Shou'd he tell me, that these opinions are obviously absurd, and repugnant to our clear ideas; I wou'd answer, that I do not deny, where two right lines incline upon each other with a sensible angle, but 'tis absurd to imagine them to have a common segment. But supposing these two lines to approach at the rate of an inch in twenty leagues, I perceive no absurdity in asserting, that upon their contact they become one.[48]

Between Hume and Mill, Kant had developed an influential philosophical account of geometry, according to which the process of constructing mental figures and inspecting their properties was supposed to provide a priori geometrical knowledge not by exposing the constituents of concepts but by revealing the structure of space, conceived as the form of outer intuition.[49] In responding to Whewell, Mill develops the Humean point that the mind's inspection of the properties of geometrical figures drawn in thought cannot work wonders that are unattainable by ordinary perception.[50]

Indeed, for Mill, the attempt to rescue geometry by ascribing a mental subject matter is a double failure, for the points and lines we imagine are no more able to satisfy the strict requirements of geometrical definitions than are external entities (the edges and corners of objects, for example), nor are their properties more epistemically accessible. Rather, as Mill suggests, we introduce a language that actually applies to nothing in the world at all, but which we treat as applying to external objects and images alike by abstracting from some of the features they actually present.

Mill states his position that geometry idealizes the properties of ordinary physical objects very clearly in the following passage:

> ...nothing remains but to consider geometry as conversant with such lines, angles, and figures as really exist; and the definitions, as they are called, must be regarded as some of our first and most obvious generalisations concerning those natural objects. The correctness of those generalisations, *as* generalisations, is without a flaw: the equality of all the radii of a circle is true of all circles, so far as it is true of any one: but it is not exactly true of any circle; it is only nearly true; so nearly that no error of any importance in practice will be incurred by feigning it to be exactly true. (*CW* VII:225–26)

Consider the Euclidean statement with which Mill is here concerned. We could formalize it in the following way:

(6) $\quad (x)\left(Cx \supset (y)(z)\left((Ryx \& Rzx) \supset Myz\right)\right)$

where 'Cx' means "x is a circle", 'Ryx' means "y is a radius of x", and 'Mxy' means "x and y are matchable" (I use the same notation and terminology as in the arithmetical case to signal a point that will occupy us later, to wit that a similar kind of constructive activity is involved in geometry).[51] Now, read in one way, (6) is exactly true – it flows from the conventions of the language (the conceptual relations, the semantical rules, etc.). Read in this way, it is vacuous. Nothing satisfies either of the predicates 'C', 'R'. There is an alternative way to read (6), for we can treat the predicates 'C', 'R' to apply to actual physical objects (for example, disks and chalk lines drawn upon them). Under this interpretation, (6) will not be exactly true, but approximately true. What this means is that a near relation of (6),

(6*) $\quad (x)\left(Cx \supset (y)(z)\left((Ryx \& Rzx) \supset M^*yz\right)\right)$

is exactly true. The difference between (6) and (6*) is that, in the one case, the radii can be operated on so that their ends become perfectly aligned, while, in the other, we get "near-alignment" – one of the segments protrudes by an amount, tiny in comparison with its length, beyond the other. 'M^{*}' stands for the relation of near-matchability.

Euclidean geometry not only contains universal principles that can be viewed as vacuously true and taken to be definitional in character, but also existential claims. Thus, corresponding to (6), there is the assertion that circles can be drawn with any center and radius.[52] Using the notation 'Lx' for "x is a line", this can be written as

(7) $$\left(x\right)\left(Lx \supset \left(\exists y\right)\left(\exists z\right)\left(Cy \& Rzy \& Mzx\right)\right)$$

So far, there is no difficulty, because (7) can be viewed as vacuously true (because of the nonexistence of entities satisfying 'L'). However, at some point, geometrical proofs will require unconditional existence assumptions, perhaps in the form of a declaration that there are points, and lines joining any two distinct points:

(8) $$\left(\exists x\right)\left(\exists y\right)\left(Px \& Py \& x \neq y\right)$$

(9) $$\left(x\right)\left(y\right)\left(\left(Px \& Py \& x \neq y\right) \supset \left(\exists! z\right)\left(Lz \& Oxz \& Oyz\right)\right)$$

Putting (7), (8), and (9) together, we shall find ourselves committed to the existence of points, lines, and circles. Although (8) is only a minimal existence assumption – one that only allows for a small fragment of Euclidean geometry – it cannot be strictly true. Thus we seem to face a choice between claiming that (6), (7), and (9) are strictly true and (8) is false; and claiming that (8) is true, and (6), (7), and (9) are approximately true.

In the end, I think that Mill's position is that the choice is unreal. The triumph of idealization in science, which he would trace to the first efforts in systematic geometry and in developing arithmetical notation, is that we can have it both ways. Because of the fact that, if we treat the existential assumptions as true, the other claims come out as approximately true, we are entitled to "feign" the joint truth of (6)–(9). Geometers have learned to liberate themselves from messy investigations of approximate equality, by introducing a language that, strictly speaking, applies to nothing at all, but works very effectively in studying the properties of actual things. The usage of that language rests upon the fund of experiences that acquaint us with its effectiveness.

Geometry, then, is an empirical science, whose ultimate justification rests on the regularities that physical objects approximate and that we build into our idealizing definitions. In a lucid passage, Mill records the role that experience plays in justifying the definitions:

We might suppose an imaginary animal, and work out by deduction, from the known laws of physiology, its natural history; or an imaginary commonwealth, and from the elements composing it might argue what would be its fate. And the conclusions which we might draw from purely arbitrary hypotheses might form a highly useful intellectual exercise: but as they could only teach us what *would* be the properties of objects which do not really exist, they would not constitute any addition to our knowledge of nature: while, on the contrary, if the hypothesis merely divests a real object of some portion of its properties without clothing it in false ones, the conclusions will always express, under known liability to correction, actual truth. (*CW* VII:229)

However, to complete his case about the epistemology of geometry, Mill must argue for two theses: first, that ordinary experience is able to justify us in thinking that ordinary physical objects approximate the properties attributed in the idealizing theory; and, second, that there are no procedures for gaining this justification independently of experience.[53]

Mill spends much more time on the second thesis than on the first. After noting that "Dr. Whewell" and his disciples maintain that we can perceive the truth of geometrical axioms a priori, Mill continues as follows:

They [the Whewellians] cannot, however, but allow that the truth of the axiom, Two straight lines cannot enclose a space, even if evident independently of experience, is also evident from experience. Whether the axiom needs confirmation or not, it receives confirmation in almost every instant of our lives, since we cannot look at any two straight lines which intersect one another without seeing that from that point they continue to diverge more and more. Experimental proof crowds in upon us in such endless profusion, and without one instance in which there can be even a suspicion of an exception to the rule, that we should soon have stronger ground for believing the axiom, even as an experimental truth, than we have for almost any of the general truths which we confessedly learn from the evidence of our senses. (*CW* VII:231–32)

These are strong words. But surely Mill is being too optimistic here, both in thinking that his apriorist opponents will concede the point, and in the confident assertion that there can be no "suspicion of an exception to the rule". Recall Hume's concern about the processes through which mathematicians are supposed to display to themselves the truth of related propositions. Hume agreed that, in the relatively gross instances in which the lines intersect at an appreciable angle, the mental image would display the property. Mill's swift treatment of the issue seems to indicate that he is thinking of such gross examples. But the trouble comes when we turn, as Hume reminds us we must, to the more subtle instances in which the separation of the lines is very slight. Moreover, as the Whewellian apriorists ought to point out, Mill's troubles are compounded by the fact that he must take the perceptions to be of physical objects, whose edges are not perfectly straight. If Mill has never encountered cases in which it appears that two (approximately) straight lines enclose a space, that surely testifies to the very sheltered life he has led.[54]

Of course, if Mill were to be confronted with an instance in which two physical edges appeared to be straight and also appeared to enclose a space, he would insist that the edges were not really straight after all. Would that disposition to treat the geometrical principles as legislative testify to the apriority of geometry? I do not think so. Even if Mill is too quick with this complex of issues, even if he does not provide an adequate defense of the possibility of experiential justification for geometrical definitions and axioms, a defense can be given. That defense would begin from the abundant successes, noted by Mill, in the gross instances. Confronting more problematic examples, it is quite legitimate to wonder whether the generalization has broken down or whether we should scrutinize assumptions about the straightness of the edges. The situation here is exactly parallel to that of a scientist whose hitherto successful theory has encountered a troublesome experiment. Just as the scientist would explore ways in which the apparatus might have been malfunctioning, so too, in this simpler predicament, Millian geometers could use their background knowledge about what objects best approximate straightness to test the linearity of the edges in question.[55] Presumably, they would appeal to the idea that certain kinds of materials are most rigid, and that deviations from perfect straightness can be assessed by aligning very long rods made from these materials with the edges. Finding that, where the generalization first appeared to break down, it was in fact supported by the further tests, they would ultimately come to treat the geometrical principle as legislative, not because they had a priori justification for it, but because of the ways in which it had survived even rigorous testing.

Mill's argument can thus be strengthened by articulating in somewhat more detail the methodology of empirical geometry – and it could be buttressed still further by exploring the ways in which experiments ultimately overthrew the doctrine that physical space is Euclidean. Let us turn now to the second part of his case. Mill concedes to his opponents the idea that we can indeed test geometrical propositions in imagination. Indeed, he goes further, suggesting that the scrutiny of mental pictures can play an important role in justifying some kinds of geometrical claims.

What says the axiom? That two straight lines *cannot* enclose a space; that after having once intersected, if they are prolonged to infinity they do not meet, but continue to diverge from one another. How can this, in any single case, be proved by actual observation? We may follow the lines to any distance we please; but we cannot follow them to infinity: for aught our senses can testify, they may, immediately beyond the farthest point to which we have traced them, begin to approach, and at last meet. Unless, therefore, we had some other proof of the impossibility than observation affords us, we should have no ground for believing the axiom at all. (*CW* VII:233)

Mill goes on to allow that the pictures we draw in the mind's eye serve the purposes of geometrical justification just as well as the pictures we draw on paper. His primary argument against the apriorist view is that our knowledge that the properties we discern in the mental images will also be found (or, at least, found approximately) in real objects has an empirical foundation, and thus that imagination is only useful as an ancillary to empirical justification because its reliability has been positively appraised in empirical terms.

Without denying, therefore, the possibility of satisfying ourselves that two straight lines cannot enclose a space, by merely thinking of straight lines without actually looking at them; I contend that we do not believe this truth on the ground of the imaginary intuition simply, but because we know that the imaginary lines exactly resemble real ones, and that we may conclude from them to real ones with quite as much certainty as we could conclude from one real line to another. (*CW* VII:234)

I think that Mill concedes too much here, and that, once again, his case can and should be strengthened.

To rest everything on the need for empirical justification of the transition from mental figures to objects of experience invites the Kantian rejoinder that, once the character of outer experience is properly understood, there is no need for any such justification.[56] Those firmly committed to transcendental idealism might simply have shrugged off Mill's challenge here. However, even the most ardent transcendental idealist would have to admit that mental picturing is actually inferior to our everyday observation, for reasons that stem ultimately from the Humean critique of geometrical imagination. Even if we waive the psychological difficulties of keeping mental images firmly in focus, there are things we can do to change and refine our perceptions of physical objects that are unavailable in the mental sphere. Faced with the challenging counterexample to the geometrical generalization, we can haul out the rigid rods. Of course, we can *imagine* doing the same with respect to a potentially misleading geometrical image, but we can *only* imagine what the result will be.[57] Nor, to take Mill's worry about lines' enclosing a space beyond the limits of our perception, can we settle that worry by appeal to imagination. Even in imagination we are limited – for only so much will fit on the mental "field" or "screen". Towards the end of his discussion, Mill seems to recognize this point, noting that our justification for believing the axiom rests on experiences that have shown us that "a line which, after diverging from another straight line, begins to approach to it, produces the impression on our senses which we describe by the expression 'a bent line' not by the expression 'a straight line'" (VII:235). If my earlier discussions were correct, then those experiences should include occasions on which we have revealed the crookedness of lines that initially struck us as straight, by using tests that are not applicable to mental images. The apriorists whom Mill opposed hoped to appeal to the geometrical imagination to account for the special exactness and certainty of geometrical knowledge. Ironically, ordinary experience turns out to have far greater probative power.

So it seems that Mill has answers to the main questions about the content of geometry and about our geometrical knowledge. However, the discussion so far has omitted – as Mill's own treatment omits – a truly difficult issue, one that will require us to develop further his picture of mathematics.

VI

In some parts of geometry – paradigmatically those concerned with the congruence or similarity of figures – it is easy to understand theorems as claims about the results of certain kinds of activity. If a particular figure were operated on in a particular fashion, by rotation, translation, or uniform stretching, for example, then it could be superimposed upon another figure. So these theorems can be regarded as being about the objects of the physical world and their fates under human rearrangement or, more exactly, under the activities of an ideal agent. Yet geometry also introduces the notion of measurement and of the assignment of real numbers to segments, areas, and volumes. This part of the subject, begun in antiquity, was a main stimulus to the seventeenth-century transformation of mathematics in which algebraic notation was deployed to allow for solution of problems previously deemed impossible (in the work of Descartes and Fermat)[58] and, subsequently, to develop the tools of the calculus (in the work of Newton and Leibniz). If Mill's account is to cover the entire subject, then he needs a way to discuss geometrical measurement.

Integral measurement is straightforward. Cases in which a particular line segment is some whole number of units of length, n units, allow us to decompose the object into segments that match the unit, and when we collect the segments we perform an n-collection. *Rational* measurement is almost as easy. To say that an object is m/n units long is to say that it can be split up into matchable parts such that (a) an assembly of an n-collecting on these parts matches the unit and (b) an assembly of an m-collecting on these parts matches the object. Intuitively, when we are dealing with commensurable magnitudes, we interpret measurement as a process in which we build up the object out of matchable parts and build up the unit out of (more or fewer) copies of those same parts.

Unfortunately, as the Greeks discovered, not all lengths are commensurable. They extended the language, using expressions of the form "*AB* measures *r* with respect to *CD*", even in cases where the conditions for rational measurement do not apply. Such expressions can no longer be interpreted literally in terms of whole-number collective operations. Instead, their meaning has to be assigned through connections that mathematical language makes possible: to say that the hypoteneuse of an isosceles right-angled triangle measures $\sqrt{2}$ with respect to the unit defined by either leg is to make an assertion about the areas of the *squares* constructed on legs and hypoteneuse; if we had an object matchable to a square constructed on the hypoteneuse, then, by judicious cutting and joining, we could divide it into two objects that matched squares constructed on the legs.[59] Understanding real numbers geometrically, through the constructions discussed in Euclid or through the methods of interpreting the calculus that flourished among those influenced by Newton (for example, the intricate geometrical proposals of Colin Maclaurin and other eighteenth-century British figures[60]), would allow Mill to extend his treatment of arithmetic and geometry in accordance with the fundamental claims of his philosophy of mathematics. He could continue to insist that mathematics requires no special entities other than physical objects and human operations upon them.

Mill does not make explicit how his treatment of elementary mathematics – simple arithmetic and the rudiments of geometry – is to be extended to the sophisticated work of his nineteenth-century contemporaries. Thus a major part of the third question I posed at the end of section II remains unanswered. Mill *has* explained how bits and pieces of rudimentary knowledge are systematized through the introduction of idealizing languages, but this only takes us as far as ordinary arithmetic and elementary Euclidean geometry, and we may be able to envisage how the story would go for the versions of analytic geometry and calculus developed in the Newtonian tradition.[61] He faces the *general* question of how mathematical knowledge grows, and what kinds of new entities, if any, are introduced in its growth. *In particular*, he has to come to terms with the articulation of real analysis by his Continental contemporaries.[62] How are we to justify the introduction of new principles, new language, and new definitions, of the kinds pioneered by Cauchy, Abel, Riemann, Dirichlet, and Weierstrass? Do the new forms of language take us beyond what can be represented in Mill's spare ontology of physical objects and human activity?

These are serious issues for obvious reasons. From a nineteenth- or twentieth-century perspective, the proper way to reconstruct Euclidean geometry is to recognize a commitment to the real-number continuum, and it is (to say the least) far from obvious that the continuum can be fitted within Mill's ontology.[63] Frege's perspective on Mill gains its force, I think, at least in part from the enormous distance between the mathematics Mill discusses and the power and sophistication of post-Weierstrassian analysis. Contemporary mathematicians, for whom set theory is a natural framework within which the whole of mathematics can be done, will identify real numbers in set-theoretic terms and wonder if Mill can replicate the set-theoretic constructions as simply as he reformulates the Dedekind-Peano axioms.

To provide a full-dress Millian reformulation of set theory would take more space than I have here, so I shall be content with an outline of an account I have given elsewhere.[64] As will become clear, this will expose both the potential of a Millian treatment and the chief philosophical problems that attend it.

Standard forms of set theory appear to involve references to abstract objects. I propose to generalize the trick for avoiding such references that I already attributed to Mill in the case of arithmetic. Instead of thinking about entities that are brought into being by our activities, or whose properties are disclosed by our activities, we focus on the activities themselves. So, just as the notions of "aggregate" and "agglomeration" earlier gave way to the idea of collective acts, we now drop the notion of a collec*tion*, the product of what we do, and think of collec*ting*. Generalizing the notion of matchability, we now think of collectings as being *equivalent* if there is an ideal operation of matching the entities they collect (intuitively, setting them in one-to-one correspondence). The idea of set-membership gives way to the concept of a collecting being *on* an entity. Thus, the unrestricted comprehension principle (the principle that for every property there is a set of just those things that have the property) would no longer be written as

(10) $\quad (\exists x)(y)(\varphi[y] \equiv y \in x) \quad$ for all open sentences $\varphi[y]$

but as

(11) $\left(\exists x\right)\left(y\right)\left(\varphi[y] \equiv Cxy\right)$ for all open sentences $\varphi[y]$.

(In [11] 'Cxy' can be read as "x is a collective act that is a collecting on y", where this does not preclude the possibility that the act collects other entities as well.)

How should we think of the activity of collecting? As in the case of arithmetic, it is natural to start with physical segregation – we move physical objects so that they are "together" and "apart from others". But most of our collecting is not like this. Typically, we don't require physical props. We can collect the monarchs of England or the presidents of the United States by thinking of them as "together", drawing a line around them in thought, or "lassoing" them (to use a suggestive phrase of Saul Kripke's). Less metaphorically, we can conceive of collecting as a process in which we achieve a new representation of entities, and it does not matter if this representation is won by moving the entities around, constructing pictures of all of them in the mind's eye and surrounding them with a mental line, or simply forming the temporary determination to consider anything satisfying a particular description as together with anything else that fits the description, whether or not we can depict the things individually.

However, if we are ultimately to obtain enough of the resources of set theory to allow the identification of the real numbers, then there has to be the possibility of iterated collecting. At first sight, this looks highly problematic. Collecting seems to require objects that are collected; we are trying to avoid the idea that acts of collecting have products; how then can we talk of collecting on prior collecting? The answer, I believe, is to recognize that what is fundamental to collecting is the attainment of a representation. We often represent collectings by drawing circles around symbols that stand for the objects collected. With this device in place, we can then take a group of circles as representing collectings, abstract from the objects of the collectings, and see the circles as "together" and "apart from everything else", initially, perhaps, by enclosing those circles in a larger circle.[65] Those accustomed to iterated collecting – set theorists and other well-trained mathematicians – quickly discard the crude scaffolding that is useful for the beginner. The idea of collecting on collecting becomes simply the commonplace notion of achieving a particular representation of prior acts of collecting.

Now, as I have suggested elsewhere, once we have given substance to the notion of iterated collecting, the way is open to reformulate the principles that underlie ZF set theory – indeed, we can provide a more natural interpretation of the stage theory that forms the principal motivation for ZF.[66] Once we have an analogue of ZF, then, of course, it is just a matter of translation to obtain the standard construction of the real numbers. So we reach a Millian reformulation of mathematics, *provided that we have a right to the existential assumptions required.*

In dealing with the natural numbers we were forced to go beyond the fragmentary collective activity in which human beings actually engage. At that stage, I proposed that we interpret the modalized existence principles in terms of the consistency of stories about an ideal agent whose collective activity was rich enough to cover number-aggregations of every size. The parallel move for set theory produces a conception of the ideal agent that is far more ambitious. Unless Millian mathematics is to "mutilate" classical mathematics by stopping short of the full ZF hierarchy, it will be necessary to assume that the stages of iterated collecting proceed far into the transfinite. The ideal agent first performs all collective acts on physical objects; at the second stage, the ideal agent performs all collectings on physical objects and first-stage collectings; at the third stage, the ideal agent performs all collectings on physical objects, first-stage collectings, and second-stage collectings; so it goes through all finite stages; after all the finite stages comes the first transfinite stage, the ωth stage, at which the ideal agent performs all collectings on physical objects and collectings performed at finite stages; at the next stage, the ideal agent performs all collectings on physical objects, on the collectings performed at finite stages, and on the collectings performed at the ωth stage; and so it goes on through all the transfinite stages. The total performance is staggering – and it is surely reasonable to wonder if the notion of collecting has been stretched beyond any bounds, so that, in effect, we are attempting to conceal a Platonistic metaphysics in constructivist dress.[67]

To this I can envisage three naturalistic replies, and, if Mill had developed his account of mathematics this far, I do not know which he would have chosen. The first, and most ambitious, would simply be to insist that the story about the ideal agent's collective activity is open-ended.[68] We begin with ourselves and the kinds of collecting that actual people do; we proceed from there to much more inclusive collectings, that range further but remain finite – the sorts of collecting that might be performed if human beings lived longer or worked faster; the next idealization conceives a being able to perform finite collectings of any size, the being whose prowess is recorded in Mill Arithmetic; now we can go further, imagining that the life and efficiency of the being are even further enhanced, that the representational abilities of the being are far greater than ours – the being engages in infinite as well as finite collectings; finally, just as we find no reason to stop the activity of collecting at any finite point, we see no reason to abridge it at any transfinite point either – the being's collecting generates the full resources of the ZF hierarchy. Stressing the continuity at each stage of this idealizing story, the first response insists that there is always a significant analogy to the notion of collecting previously introduced, so that there is no point at which the concept of collecting breaks down. Juxtaposing the final idealization with the starting point makes it hard to recognize that a common notion of collecting is involved, but the remedy for this sense of discontinuity is to insist on the intermediate steps.

The second and third responses reject this attempt to defend the semantic analogy among the various conceptions of the ideal agent, insisting that the notion of ideal collecting loses its sense once we go beyond some point, say, for the sake of definiteness, the point at which we assume the ability to collect any finite collectings (the ωth stage). They differ in their interpretation of the significance of this point. According to the second, "constructivist" view, the incoherence of a putative conception of the ideal agent provides reason to reject the language involved in that idealization.[69] Thus we should restrict ourselves to that part of mathematics that can be reconstructed in the theories of ideal collecting that do not stretch the concept of collecting to breaking point. The result would be a kind of naturalized intuitionism, shorn of the doctrines about the a priori evidence for mathematical principles and the distinctive ideas about logic.[70]

The third response is not so radical. For while disavowing the interpretation of the idealizing language that seeks to reformulate ZF set theory, and without proposing any other interpretation, pro-

ponents of the third response would insist on the usefulness of the
notation for systematizing the meaningful parts of mathematics,
those that can be construed as dealing with physical objects and
with (properly idealized) human operations on those objects. The
heart of the proposal is that mathematical language does not have to
be meaningful to be good, that we can retain a purely formal idiom
because of its utility.[71] This would be a naturalistic analogue of
formalism, without any commitment to the distinctive Hilbertian
ideas of the a priori status of "contentful" mathematics or to proving the consistency of the formal system in which "contentful"
mathematics is embedded.[72]

All three responses are Millian, in claiming that the ontology of
mathematics can be restricted to physical objects and (idealized)
human operations upon them. Where they disagree is in matters of
the scope of mathematical knowledge. For the first, "classical"
response, there is a chain of justification leading from the primitive
mathematical experiences of collecting and manipulating physical
objects, through the first systematizations that bring us the idealizing theories of arithmetic and Euclidean geometry, and on to the full
riches of contemporary mathematics. We learn, in this process, the
utility of new languages for solving problems that have been posed
in previously justified languages (as, for example, Descartes was able
to show how to resolve a host of locus problems, raised but not
answered by the ancient geometers). Moreover, as we go, it is possible always to provide a complete interpretation of the new vocabulary by articulating further the account of the collective powers of
the ideal agent (our story about the agent always remains consistent). The third response concurs in thinking that the utility of the
new languages warrants our employment of them: we are entitled to
count analytic geometry, calculus, real and complex analysis, topol-
ogy, and set theory as legitimate parts of mathematics, but some of
these disciplines ultimately outstrip our ability to provide a coherent interpretation in terms of acts of collecting (however idealized).
Finally, the second response takes our inability to extend the interpretation of earlier parts of mathematics to signal the illegitimacy of
the new languages – whatever their superficial charms. From this
perspective, the incoherence of the final task of the ideal agent
should lead us to mathematical reform.

Mill's own position cannot be identified because he did not

explicitly address the problem of how to account for the growth of mathematical knowledge. If we see him as a mathematical naturalist, for whom mathematical knowledge, like other parts of our knowledge (or other complex human practices), is extended by building on the earlier efforts of predecessors, then we must acknowledge a significant gap in his epistemology. Just as foundationalists in the philosophy of mathematics have typically spent much of their time in trying to show how to get from their first principles to all the theorems of the branches of mathematics they favor, so too, a naturalist must explain how mathematical knowledge is historically built.[73] I believe that Mill's story about elementary mathematics can be continued, but, given three possible lines of continuation, we can only speculate about which would have appealed most to Mill.

VII

Confronted with any putative item of human knowledge, we can generate two major philosophical questions: What, if anything, is the proposition we think we know about? How do we know (if we do know) that proposition? Answers to these questions have to fit together. If we specify a way of knowing that could not possibly yield information about the entities with which we take the proposition to be concerned, we are in philosophical trouble.

For some propositions, for example propositions about medium-sized physical objects, the answer seems to be relatively easy. We think of this knowledge as obtainable by individuals, through their own interactions with the objects around them. It is easy to overlook the role of the concepts they bring to their experience, the process of socialization through which they acquired those concepts, and the historical development out of which that kind of socialization emerged.[74] I believe, although I shall not argue the case here, that even in those instances that seem most to favor the idea of a synchronic reconstruction of human knowledge, we are forced to treat our present epistemic state as dependent on the epistemic performances of others.

In the case of mathematics, however, there is *no* obvious story about how we come to mathematical knowledge all by ourselves. If we suspend belief in philosophical theories and simply reflect on how we come to believe the mathematical propositions we do, the dependence on our predecessors is evident. However, generations of philosophers of mathematics have, either explicitly or tacitly, supposed that mathematics could be incorporated into a synchronic picture of human knowledge, one that allowed individuals to know some "first principles" and to derive the rest. A major problem for any such epistemology is to identify the way in which the first principles are known.

What are the possibilities? The popular empiricist idea that mathematical knowledge is obtainable (and obtainable a priori) by unfolding the definitions of mathematical terms has been decisively undermined by arguments present in rough form in Kant and Mill and refined in Quine's writings. Rationalist appeals to mathematical intuition either are specific (as in Kant's account of geometrical knowledge) and demonstrably inadequate, or retreat into vagueness, inspiring doubts about whether they have identified a process that could yield knowledge of anything. As I have already remarked, the most popular strategy is to ignore the question, perhaps by declaring that mathematics is a precondition for something important (experience of space, rational thought, or whatever). But this evasion is quite unsatisfactory. Even if a body of propositions would have to be true for us to perform a particular type of task, there is still a perfectly legitimate question about how we know it to be true – and the only way that the requirement that the propositions be true could bear on that question would be if it could plausibly be argued that we *know* that we can perform the task and *know* that the body of propositions has to be true for the performance to be achieved.

The chief motivations for these implausible exercises are, I believe, twofold: first is the obvious fact that mathematicians (typically) do not do experiments; second is the "felt necessity" of mathematics. From the first consideration arises a quick little argument: Mathematicians know some mathematics, and some of them know things that people have not known before. Their knowledge does not rest on experimentation, or on other interactions with the physical world. Hence, there must be some other mode of insight that yields mathematical knowledge. That argument depends crucially on accepting a synchronic picture of human knowledge, according to which individuals build knowledge in ways that are not dependent on the past. No naturalist should deny that, *as things now stand*, mathematicians proceed by sitting and thinking, scribbling on pieces of paper (or, occasionally, cutting equations into bridges[75]). They are not alone in this: theoretical physicists, biologists, political scientists, and economists sometimes do the same, as Mill already foresaw.[76] Yet mathematicians do it more dramatically, with more prestige and more success than any other group. For the naturalist, this practice has issued from a long history, one in which the language of mathematics has been enriched and extended, both by reflections on the state of mathematics that the present generation has inherited and, less frequently, by interactions with the physical world (sometimes direct, more often mediated by sciences that are clearly observational or experimental). Contemporary mathematical knowledge is dependent upon this history, and a *part* of articulating the justification for our mathematical beliefs is to understand how mathematics has grown, from the ancients to our own times.

We might inquire why the practice of "armchair science" has emerged, and why, in particular, it is dominated by the study of quantity. Mill sketches an answer to this question at *CW* VII:221–23. He believes, as we have seen, that it is possible to transform experimental sciences into deductive systems by introducing definitions that sum up the regularities that have been inductively confirmed. He takes mathematics to have an important role in this transformation because of the universality of the properties with which mathematics is concerned: "all things are numerable". In terms of the reconstruction I have given above, we might say that collective activity is always possible with respect to the objects of any inquiry, and recognizing the specific relations that obtain among our collectings in a particular domain provides us with a valuable way of systematizing our results. Why this is so, why "the Book of Nature is written in the language of Mathematics", Mill does not say. He envisages no transcendental argument that will derive the applicability of mathematics from something deeper. As a naturalist, he records the fact and sees it as the terminus of explanation.

The second main motivation for insisting that mathematical knowledge is thoroughly non-empirical is the sense that mathematical truths could not have been false. In his critique of

Whewell's account of mathematics, Mill is particularly concerned to rebut this claim. He states, quite forthrightly, that "this character of necessity ascribed to the truths of mathematics, and even (with some reservations to be hereafter made) the peculiar certainty attributed to them, is an illusion" (*CW* VII:224).[77] Mill has a ready explanation for why we have this illusory belief, since he thinks our everday experience is full of dramatic confirmation of mathematical truths. But his principal argument is that the invocation of the necessity of mathematics rests on confusing what we can imagine with what could be.

Mill launches his attack by asking what sense we can give to the notion of necessity. Recognizing that claims about metaphysical necessity, then as now, are backed by exercises in imagination, he interprets Whewell as supposing that a proposition is necessary if it is "not only false but inconceivable" (*CW* VII:238). Having framed the issue in this way, Mill gives brilliant expression to the naturalist worry that what we can and cannot conceive is due to the accidents of psychology and history:

Now I cannot but wonder that so much stress should be laid on the circumstances of inconceivableness, when there is such ample experience to show that our capacity or incapacity of conceiving a thing has very little to do with the possibility of the thing in itself, but is in truth very much an affair of accident, and depends on the past history and habits of our own minds. There is no more generally acknowledged fact in human nature than the extreme difficulty at first felt in conceiving anything as possible which is in contradiction to long-established and familiar experience, or even to old familiar habits of thought. (*CW* VII:238)

As Mill goes on to point out, the history of science abounds with examples in which people initially believed that a traditional doctrine had to be true because anything different was inconceivable – while their successors overthrew tradition, tamed the "inconceivable", and fashioned powerful theories.[78] Mill is even able to make the powerful rhetorical point that Whewell himself admits these phenomena from the history of the sciences, and stresses our ability to make sense of possibilities our ancestors deemed "inconceivable" (*CW* VII:242).

The obvious response to this critique is to divorce the notion of necessity from the inconceivability of the opposite. But this, Mill believes, leaves us without any way of justifying claims about necessity. How are we to decide if a proposition is necessary without employing the inconceivability test? In any event, the response is not pertinent to the main issue that Mill intends to address. For, in the case of mathematics, the sense of necessity results from our difficulties in imagining what a violation of mathematical truths would be like: we cannot say of an unarithmetical world how it would look. Given his thesis that we are bombarded with experiences that support mathematical laws, Mill can greet the phenomenon with equanimity. Further, his general account of why we find some things conceivable and others not, manifested in the critique of the inconceivability test, suggests that our failures of imagination should not be taken too seriously. Anticipating a Quinean point, he sees the inability to imagine breakdowns in arithmetic, the incapacity on which the "felt necessity" of mathematics rests, to be exactly analogous to the sense of pre-Copernicans that the earth could not move or the conviction of pre-Newtonians that there could be no action at a distance.

How, then, should we sum up Mill's overall achievement? I see him as laying out the general arguments against transcendentalist approaches to mathematics, and thus making the case for some kind of naturalism: his claims about the inability of appeals to definitions to ground a priori knowledge and the attack on the felt necessity of mathematics belong to this part of Mill's accomplishment. In our century, of course, the arguments have been articulated further, and with greater precision, particularly by Quine. Yet Mill was not content to leave the matter with a general brief for naturalism. He tried to say what kinds of entities mathematics is about, and how we can know about those entities. His focus was on the rudimentary parts of mathematics, the original disciplines from which contemporary mathematics has grown, and he neglected the problem of showing how mathematics is extended from its primitive origins, thereby leaving himself vulnerable to the charge that his story must be naive and crude.

Understanding the development of sophisticated mathematical knowledge was not a problem with which Mill was primarily concerned. As I have interpreted him, his is the complementary contribution of recognizing the empirical roots of mathematical knowledge. The starting point for contemporary knowledge of mathematics is the rudimentary activity of ordering physical objects around us – and Mill, the educationalist, believed that children should be reminded of this, that ontogeny should recapitulate phylogeny. In providing an account of the elementary parts of mathematics, Mill also responded to the difficult challenge of fitting the ontology and the epistemology together, giving an interpretation of the content of mathematical statements that could make it comprehensible how the kinds of knowledge-generating processes he assumed could yield knowledge about the right entities. In contrast to the rival transcendentalist proposals, this story is a smashing success.[79] To transform it into a complete philosophy of mathematics, it is necessary to turn away from the standard foundationalist programs and to think seriously about the rationale for the great transitions in the history of mathematics that have enriched the subject beyond anything that Mill's proto-mathematicians – even, perhaps, Mill himself – could have imagined. We need, in short, a complete change of perspective in philosophical thinking about mathematics. It is a measure of Mill's philosophical achievement that he pointed the way.

NOTES

1 The most influential attack was launched by Frege (1884/1950, 9–14, 22–24, 29–33). Another early indictment was that of W. S. Jevons (1877), in which Mill was described as a man "whose mind was essentially illogical". In an essay on the achievements of his godfather, Bertrand Russell singled out Mill's claims about mathematics as especially implausible: "I first read Mill's *Logic* at the age of eighteen, and at that time I had a very strong bias in his favour, but even then I could not believe that our acceptance of the proposition 'two and two are four' was a generalization from experience" (1951/1968, 3–4). Rudolf Carnap characterizes Mill's position on mathematics as one from which empiricists should try to escape (1963, 47, 65). A. J. Ayer's discussion of Mill's mathematical empiricism (1964, 291–93) is somewhat gentler but firm in its rejection. C. G. Hempel takes a similar tone (1964, 367–68).

Some recent writers have treated Mill's views on mathematics with more respect. Reginald Jackson 1941b is a thorough and lucid rebuttal of Jevons's complaints. David Bloor 1974 contains a thoughtful perspective on Mill's ideas about arithmetic. Glenn Kessler 1980 provides an important corrective to Fregean criticisms of Mill. John Skorupski 1989 is now the definitive work on Mill, and contains, among many other superb discussions, an excellent, sensitive treatment of Mill's ideas about mathematics. I have also attempted to rehabilitate Mill on mathematics in Kitcher 1980a and, less directly, in Kitcher 1983; I shall further develop the approach of these discussions in the present chapter.

2 I have developed my conception of philosophical naturalism – with respect to metaphysics and epistemology – in Kitcher 1992.

3 John Skorupski 1989 has provided a lucid account of Mill's naturalism. Mill's naturalism is evident in his choice of philosophical topics: his reflections on the methods of the natural sciences, his interest in freedom of thought, his concern with the status of women all represent the commitment of the naturalistic philosopher to take up the crucial questions of the age.

4 This is especially plain in the writings of twentieth-century logical empiricists who turned, with relief, to the logical investigations of Frege and Russell, thus avoiding what they saw as the unacceptable position defended by Mill. See the passages cited from Carnap, Ayer, and Hempel in note 1. As a number of recent writers, most notably Michael Friedman, have argued, the Vienna Circle can profitably be seen as pursuing a project that has affinities with Kant's transcendental program but that absorbs the advances in logic due to Frege and Russell.

5 From the Introduction to Frege 1893/1964; the passage quoted is from p. 15.

6 I elaborated this line of interpretation in Kitcher 1979. It now seems to me that it is *one* way of making sense of Frege's philosophical project with respect to mathematics, one that highlights his remark, in the passage quoted, that attempts to show why the laws of logic are true by way of transcendental arguments to the effect that we have to believe them do not really answer the question of justification. However, Frege's epistemological attitude now strikes me as more ambiguous than it did a decade or so ago, and I do not believe that there is a single coherent reconstruction that does justice to all his remarks. I remain convinced that prominent interpretations of Frege often overlook those aspects of his thought that Kitcher 1979 brings into the foreground.

7 The most fully articulated version of this position is given in the writings of Michael Dummett, especially Dummett 1991a and 1991b. An analogous approach to Kant's views about mathematics is given by Michael Friedman 1992. Dummett and Friedman highlight strands in the thought of Frege and Kant respectively that are complementary to those emphasized in Kitcher 1979 and 1975. I discuss the opposition between naturalism and transcendentalism in interpreting Kant's philosophy of mathematics in Kitcher 1996.

8 Frege 1884/1905, 13.

9 See Kitcher 1975.

10 Gödel 1964, 271–72.

11 Until recently this was the overwhelmingly dominant attitude in twen-tieth-century philosophy of mathematics. Questions about the episte-mology of fundamental mathematical principles were ignored in favor of concentrating on showing how to derive the mathematical corpus from a favorite set of axioms. Even today, it seems that the transcendentalist tradition of avoiding issues about how we know the axioms remains strong.

12 I have discussed this epistemological myth in a number of places: Kitcher 1993a, 1993b, 1994. Like many philosophical myths, this episte-mological story can sometimes be a benign idealization. However, as the works cited try to show, it sometimes introduces important distortions into our thinking about knowledge.

13 Mill writes: "Where then is the necessity for assuming that our recogni-tion of these truths [mathematical truths, and, in this context, specifi-cally laws of geometry] has a different origin from the rest of our knowledge, when its existence is perfectly accounted for by supposing its origin to be the same?" (A System of Logic, Book II, ch. 5, section 4). Citations will be to this text in its republishing as Volumes VII and VIII of CW. The passage just cited is from CW VII:232.

14 See Karen Wynn 1992a and 1992b. Even if Wynn's experimental results were taken to have the import she ascribes to them, it would still be possible to defend a fundamentally Millian view about arithmetical knowledge: the ultimate source for such knowledge would now be viewed as an interaction between early experiences and evolved neural structures. For an extremely helpful clarification of the philosophical issues, see Robert Schwartz 1995.

15 Here I envisage the kind of explanation of contemporary knowledge that I outline in Kitcher 1983, 1993a, and 1993b.

16 See, for example, CW VII:28, where Mill questions the idea of defining a general name as the name of a class by suggesting that this procedure would explain "the clearer of two things by the more obscure". It is worth pointing out that, throughout his discussions of mathematics, Mill attacks a position he calls "Nominalism", according to which mathematical propositions are "merely verbal" (see, for example, VII:277and Chapter 1 of this volume, section V). When I refer to Mill's nominalism, I have in mind his worries about classes and other abstract entities, and his skepticism about notions of necessity and possibility that cannot be given a linguistic gloss, not to the doctrine about the analyticity of mathematics that he opposes.

17 As John Skorupski has pointed out to me, there is a further problem with the suggested interpretation. Mill says that numerals *connote* properties of aggregates (agglomerations), but, on the account I have offered, the numerals seem to *denote* such properties. Perhaps then the numerals should be identified as denoting aggregates, and aggregates taken to be sets. That would reduce Mill's position to an orthodox brand of Platonism, with all the attendant epistemological difficulties.

18 However, the idea that we can perceive sets of objects has been defended in recent philosophy of mathematics. See Penelope Maddy 1990, ch. 2, and also Jaegwon Kim 1982.

19 This problem is posed with great force in a seminal article by Paul Benacerraf (1973).

20 See Frege 1884/1950, 28–29.

21 Kessler 1980 shows how the interpretation would go. Another possible approach would be to employ the theory of aggregates proposed by Tyler Burge (1977). As Kessler points out (p. 68), this would involve violating the Millian principle that "whatever is made up of parts is made up of the parts of those parts". The reconstruction of the present paragraph therefore follows Kessler rather than the possible development of Burge's ideas.

22 This signals another Fregean criticism of Mill. See Frege 1884/1950, 30–32. I shall consider it more extensively below. Kessler attempts to head off the criticism (1980, 76–77), but it is quite clear from his discussion that the interpretation of mereology I have employed in the text will not do, and I do not see that there is an alternative acceptable to Mill.

23 Kessler's reconstruction allows him to sketch a proof (1980, 77–78) of the exemplification of any finite number *n*, the principle corresponding to the existence of all finite numbers. Unfortunately that proof proceeds by invoking some very un-Millian attributes – the property of *being identical with 0 or 1*, for instance. This generates the suspicion that the wide-ranging invocation of properties that is involved in Kessler's interpretation is really set theory in disguise. If that is the case, then we will have made no epistemological or ontological progress in moving from (1) to (2).

24 Earlier passages in *A System of Logic* also look different in light of Mill's later discussions. See for example *CW* VII:256, where Mill takes the statement "1 + 2 = 3" to affirm "that if we put one pebble to two pebbles, those very pebbles are three".

25 Here I endorse the approach I advanced in Kitcher 1980a and in ch. 6 of Kitcher 1983.

26 Mill's concerns about modality surface in connection with mathematics in his critique of Whewell's claims about the necessity of geometrical

axioms (*CW* VII:236–51). I shall consider this discussion in the final section. Discussions in contemporary philosophy of mathematics have made it apparent that commitments to abstract entities can sometimes be avoided by introducing modalities; see, for example, Putnam 1983. However, this does not seem to make any progress in solving the epistemological problem posed by Benacerraf 1973. As Fabrizio Mondadori and Adam Morton point out (1976), given the standard interpretation of modalities, we can construct an analogue of Benacerraf's dilemma.

27 The view I am developing can be understood in either of two ways. First, we can treat the logical form of "3 = 2 + 1" as given by (5), and interpret the modal operator as claiming that *there is a consistent story that says that* so-and-so. Alternatively, we can take (4) to give the logical form, and claim that some parts of arithmetic are strictly false, although they would be true in any story that posited an ideal collector. As I understand Mill's position, he holds that these are both ways of making the same claim about the structure of the world, and that it is precisely the usefulness of the associated stories that reveals arithmetic as identifying that structure.

28 For Frege's objections, see Frege 1884/1950, 9.

29 Of course, the reference to "inductive truths" is shorthand. Mill means that arithmetical truths are established using the methods of the empirical sciences, and, since he lumps those methods under the umbrella term 'induction', he describes them as inductive truths. Despite his many insights, Mill's account of the methods of the natural sciences is somewhat impoverished, and we best read his discussions about mathematics by treating 'induction' as covering modes of inference that he does not officially allow.

30 For Locke, see *Essay Concerning Human Understanding*, Book IV, ch. 4, section 6; for Hume, see *Enquiry Concerning Human Understanding*, section IV, Part I; for Ayer and Hempel, see the references cited in note 1. It is quite clear that twentieth-century logical empiricists saw themselves as being able to use the logical advances of Frege and Russell to transform the imprecise theses of earlier empiricists.

31 See *CW* VII:142–48.

32 Mill provides an excellent account of this episode in chemistry at *CW* VII:139–40.

33 I gloss over some complex issues here. In offering an account of a priori knowledge (in Kitcher 1980b), I took the idea of knowledge "independent of experience" to entail that such knowledge should be invulnerable to future experience. Several critics have attempted to rehabilitate the notion of a priori knowledge by arguing that knowledge can be independent of experience (warranted by a process that is independent of experi-

ence) and also vulnerable to future experience. This objection was first raised by Charles Parsons (1986), and has been most fully articulated by Albert Casullo (1988). Although I think that my original approach to a priori knowledge is defensible, I shall not try to resist the notion of fallible a priori knowledge here. Instead, I adapt the Millian argument to show that the process of relying on linguistic conventions would not satisfy either the strong condition (requiring invulnerability to future experience) or the weaker condition (requiring that the justification be independent of past experience). Perhaps, in the end, the attempt to show that mathematical knowledge is not a priori (carried out in Kitcher 1983) does not need the strong commitments of the account of a priori knowledge invoked there.

34 Quine's critique of analyticity can be divided into two main parts: objections to the notion of meaning and arguments to the effect that appeals to meaning cannot ground a priori knowledge. As I read Mill, he would not be in sympathy with the first part, but the second part of Quine's attack can readily be viewed as developing Millian themes. In effect, both Mill and Quine are challenging the principle that analyticity secures apriority, by attempting to show that this principle is part of a bad theory of knowledge. Quine takes a further step, urging that the notion of meaning should be discarded, since truth by virtue of meaning cannot serve the epistemological purposes for which it was intended. For a similar analysis of some of Quine's seminal texts, see Harman 1967.

35 Quine 1963, 20–46. See section VII of this chapter.

36 Perhaps Mill even comes close to the Quinean formulation at VII:143, where, quoting an earlier review essay, he writes: "It is some confirmation of our opinion that none of those writers who have thought that there were definitions of things have ever succeeded in discovering any criterion by which the definition of a thing can be distinguished from any other proposition relating to the thing."

37 Quine 1966, 70–99.

38 Both Mill and Kant anticipated the point, and it *may* be implicit in Locke's concerns about "real" knowledge. I trace the insight to Kant in Kitcher 1981. For Mill's anticipations, see his assessment of the important role of reconceptualization in presenting inductive sciences in deductive form (VII:218).

39 See Kitcher 1981.

40 Mill also seems to go astray in these passages through overlooking a possible strategy for coping with existential assumptions in an area of science. He does not see that we can frame definitions in such a way as to make even the existential postulates of geometry come out automatically true. The trick is to suppose that the existential

postulates have to be satisfied in any Euclidean space, and to treat all geometrical propositions as involving a tacit relativization to a Euclidean space. Thus, "There are points" would become "In any Euclidean space, there are points". Of course, there would then be legitimate questions about whether any Euclidean spaces exist, but the truth of all the standard geometrical axioms would apparently have been guaranteed.

41 Skorupski 1989, 155–59, gives an excellent discussion of Mill's attitudes to modal notions.

42 Mill's reference here is plainly not to Aristotelian natures, but to linked properties covered by a system of inductive generalization. See *CW* VII:218–19 for a discussion of the ways in which some of the physical sciences have been reformulated by introducing definitions to cover systems of inductive generalizations, and for Mill's interesting assessment of the limitations of the strategy in systematizing the chemistry of his day.

43 In an intriguing passage, Mill seems to contrast the use of language for scientific purposes, taken to be subject to strict constraints, with the employment of everyday idioms. He notes that it may be a mistake to demand overall similarity among the instances of a general term, allowing that language may grow by noting local similarities. "Even when a name, by successive extensions, has come to be applied to things among which there does not exist this gross resemblance common to them all, still at every step of its progress we shall find such a resemblance. And these transitions of the meaning of words are often an index of real connexions between the things denoted by them, which might otherwise escape the notice of thinkers; of those at least who, from using a different language, or from any difference in their habitual associations, have fixed their attention in preference on some other aspect of the things" (*CW* VII:153). Perhaps there is an anticipation here of famous Wittgensteinian proposals about the character of ordinary language, and even the suggestion of the method of "ordinary language philosophy" practiced by Austin.

44 Frege 1884/1950, 10.

45 Here I again follow my earlier treatment in Kitcher 1980a and 1983.

46 See Kitcher 1980a, Appendix.

47 This contrasts with Kessler's reconstruction, on which we can prove that each finite number is exemplified. But, as observed in note 23, the price of being able to establish the existential claims is a commitment to properties that seems to reintroduce set theory in disguise. I think it would be open to Kessler to adopt a more restrained view of properties, and to allow that not every finite number is exemplified. He could then

mimic the approach offered in the text, according to which arithmetic is an idealizing theory.

48 David Hume, *A Treatise on Human Nature*, ed. L. A. Selby-Bigge (Oxford: Oxford University Press, 1967), p. 51.

49 For development of this interpretation of Kant's views, see Kitcher 1975.

50 See Parsons 1964; Hopkins 1973; Kitcher 1975; and Friedman 1992, ch. 1.

51 Mill plainly thinks of geometry in terms of the performance of various kinds of operations on geometrical figures (or on the objects that approximate such figures). See, for example, his discussion of the fifth proposition of the First Book of Euclid, where he states a principle of congruence: "Things which being applied to each other coincide are equals" (*CW* VII:215).

52 Mill seems to think of this as a paradigm of an existence assumption in geometry. See *CW* VII:145.

53 He also has to undermine the sense that arithmetic and geometry have a special necessity and certainty. This is a general task for his philosophy of mathematics, and, in the final section, I shall consider how he tries to discharge it.

54 As Skorupski (1989, 153) points out, virtually everyone who has studied geometry has had the experience of being misled by a superficially plausible – but inaccurate – diagram.

55 In an extended footnote to VII:232, Mill hints at something similar, although he is, I think, handicapped in expressing the point by his conception of scientific method.

56 As I interpret him, Michael Friedman emphasizes this aspect of Kant's thinking (most prominent in the "Axioms of Intuition" section of the *Critique*). See Friedman 1992, chs. 1 and 2.

57 Again, Mill comes close to the point. See his discussion of the difference between seeing a stone thrown into the water and merely imagining the stone (VII:233).

58 Mill recognizes the importance of this episode in the history of mathematics. See *CW* VII:222.

59 As is made evident by some proofs of the Pythagorean Theorem.

60 See Maclaurin 1742. I discuss the post-Newtonian tradition in mathematics in Kitcher 1983, 238–41.

61 Mill explicitly takes his theses about mathematics to apply to the calculus (VII:253). However, in his most elaborate discussion of the mathematics developed in the eighteenth century, he suggests that his view of algebra is restricted to the algebra of rational functions (polynomials, trigonometric and logarithmic functions, and compounds of them). See *CW* VII:613–15.

62 It is interesting to ask just how much mathematics Mill knew. His remarks indicate that he takes the limit of mathematics to be the calculus of variations (developed by Euler and Lagrange in the eighteenth century). See *CW* VII:221–22. I suspect that Mill, like most of his English contemporaries, however well-educated, was not abreast of Continental mathematics – that he knew nothing of the advances of Cauchy, Fourier, and Abel, let alone of their successors, who were revolutionizing analysis at the time he was writing. The backwardness of British mathematics may not only have made his task seem easier (since he did not have to argue for the empirical status of advanced algebraic analysis) but also have lent his presentation an air of ignorance that made his views easier to dismiss.

63 Thus it may seem that Mill's account only appears to work because he has failed to embed geometry within the proper framework.

64 Kitcher 1983, ch. 6.

65 Kitcher 1983, 128–29.

66 For a superbly lucid account of the stage theory, see George Boolos 1971. As I note (Kitcher 1983, 133), it seems to me that the Millian reconstruction avoids the tension between thinking of sets as eternally present and as brought into being in stages.

67 This concern is forcefully and lucidly expressed by Charles Chihara (1990, 242–43).

68 This is effectively the stance taken in Kitcher 1983.

69 Thus, on these approaches, there would be no *consistent* story about the collecting of an ideal agent that would suffice for the full resources of contemporary set theory.

70 This version of intuitionism would be closer to that of Brouwer and Heyting – especially Brouwer's theory of the creative subject – than to Dummett's account. For the ideas of the former writers, see Brouwer 1975, especially the essay "Consciousness, Philosophy, and Mathematics", and Heyting 1956. For Dummett's approach, see Dummett 1978.

71 More precisely, some mathematical statements would have the logical form either of existence statements that would not only be actually false but also false of the collecting of any consistently describable agent, or else of modalized existence statements in which the modality could not be interpreted in terms of the consistency of a story.

72 A position of this type is articulated in H. B. Curry 1964.

73 For my own attempt to do this, see Kitcher 1983, chs. 7–10.

74 I explore this dependence upon our society and its history in Kitcher 1993b.

75 On discovering quaternions, Mill's great contemporary, William Hamilton (not the philosopher whom Mill criticized but an Irish mathemati-

cian), carved the fundamental equations of the algebra of quaternions into the woodwork of a bridge.

76 See, for example, VII:616: "The advance of knowledge has, however, made it manifest that physical science, in its better understood branches, is quite as demonstrative as geometry. The task of deducing its details from a few comparatively simple principles is found to be anything but the impossibility it was once supposed to be; and the notion of the superior certainty of geometry is an illusion, arising from the ancient prejudice, which, in that science, mistakes the ideal data from which we reason for a peculiar class of realities, while the corresponding ideal data of any deductive physical science are recognised as what they really are, hypotheses". See also the passage from VII:229 about the possibility of deriving the features of an "ideal animal", quoted on p. 85 above.

77 Mill's "reservations" result from his belief that the experiences that confirm mathematical truths are omnipresent, and thus induce very firm convictions in us. So, in one sense, the claim that mathematics is especially certain is defensible, so long as we don't think of its certainty as having some peculiar source. I think Mill is inclined to overrate the role of experience and underplay the role of acculturation. By contrast, David Bloor (1974) overemphasizes the role of acculturation and minimizes the contribution of experience. I claim that the cultural practice is present because of the wealth of supporting experiences, that the cultural tradition plays a major role in the ontogeny of the sense of mathematical certainty, and that we cannot ignore the crucial phylogenetic role of experience (and should not ignore its more limited ontogenetic role).

78 It is also worth noting that something may be held to be conceivable – even in some detail – and yet turn out to be judged impossible by later inquirers. I see no reason to deny that Hilbert conceived of a finitary consistency proof for formal systems of arithmetic (in any ordinary sense of the term 'conceive'), even though we now hold that Gödel's theorems preclude any such possibility.

79 It is also superior to other ventures in naturalism. Quine's arguments develop Mill's fundamental point about the failure of analyticity to secure apriority, but Quine neither achieves a naturalistically adequate ontology nor offers a detailed story about how mathematical knowledge is obtained. These points are, I think, related. Quine's early nominalist scruples could be discarded because he did not perceive the necessity of showing how the knowledge developed by the individual could be knowledge about the kinds of entities posited in his ontology for mathematics. That oversight testifies, I think, to the continuing influence of

a kind of transcendentalism that dulls the urgency of questions about how people come to know what they do. Quine's ideas about mathematics are strikingly nonconstructive: they make a powerful case for the existence of an empiricist account of mathematics but do not actually exhibit one. This means that Quine's response to such fundamental questions as those posed by Benacerraf (1973) remain quite unclear. Mill, I think, does better.

3 Mill on induction and scientific method

I. INTRODUCTION

Books III and IV of *A System of Logic* lie at the heart of Mill's empiricist enterprise, ambitiously aiming to provide "a reduction of the inductive process to strict rules and to a scientific test, such as the syllogism is for ratiocination" (*Autobiography, CW* I:215–17).[1] Mill's lengthy examinations 'Of Induction' and 'Of the Operations Subsidiary to Induction' constituted, in his own estimate, the principal part of his theory of logic, because – by the arguments of Book II – inductive inference was the only form of 'real' inference capable of leading us to genuinely new knowledge. Since deductive processes enable us to do no more than 'interpret' inductions, identifying the particular cases which fall under general propositions, it is induction alone "in which the investigation of nature essentially consists." Consequently, "What Induction is . . . and what conditions render it legitimate, cannot but be deemed the main question of the science of logic – the question which includes all others" (*A System of Logic, CW* VII:283).

Mill defined induction as "the operation of discovering and proving general propositions" (*CW* VII:284). Inductive rules, as he conceived them, in their paradigmatic use simultaneously reveal and confirm general propositions that we have not considered before. But they also enable us to infer to new 'single facts' as readily as

I am very grateful to Barry Gower and to John Skorupski for very helpful comments on earlier drafts of this chapter. Section II is closely based on ch. 4, 'The Possibility of Inductive Reasoning,' in Scarre 1989.

general ones, since generals are 'but collections of particulars,' while the same evidence which entitles us to a draw a conclusion about a single unknown instance entitles us to draw a similar conclusion about a whole class of cases (*ibid.*). In scientific contexts our interest is usually in the derivation of fresh general principles, whereas in everyday life we are more often concerned with inferences to particular facts. In both kinds of circumstance, Mill thought, the same set of inductive principles could be applied, and thus "a complete logic of the sciences would be also a complete logic of practical business and common life" (*ibid.*). The soundness of an inductive argument is context-independent, and "must be tried by tests which are the same for all descriptions of inquiries, whether the result be to give A an estate, or to enrich science with a new general truth" (*CW* VII:285).

Mill's contentions that induction is the only form of real inference, and that a single set of inductive rules serves us outside as well as inside science, have, however, the implication that there is nothing fundamentally distinctive about the methodology of science. Mill's conception of the continuity of the modes of scientific enquiry with the knowledge-seeking processes of everyday life is clearly evident throughout the *Logic's* discussion of induction. While some sciences, particularly mathematics, are allowed to involve deductive interpretation, new knowledge about external reality is always held to be ultimately dependent on an *a posteriori* basis. Science differs from everyday concerns not in its methods but in its special subject-matter – its directedness on the uncovering and proof of laws of nature.

Mill's view of the purpose of science is signalled plainly by the epigraph from Dugald Stewart at the head of Book III:

According to the doctrine now stated, the highest, or rather the only proper object of physics, is to ascertain those established conjunctions of successive events, which constitute the order of the universe; to record the phenomena which it exhibits to our observations, or which it discloses to our experiments; and to refer these phenomena to their general laws. (*CW* VII:282).

Shorn of the restriction to physics, this expresses very well Mill's own understanding of the nature of the scientific project. It is a

quintessentially empiricist understanding, metaphysically abstemi-
ous in its construal of causes as constant conjunctions, devoid of
any hint of a priorism in the definition of scientific ideas, and
disposed to evaluate successful science in terms of its provision of
lawlike generalisations to explain phenomena. Mill's notion of a
satisfactory scientific explanation is that of a (possibly complex)
structure of general propositions expressive of relevant causal relationships. Thus if we ask why a given subject died after drinking
arsenious acid, we begin by noting that all men die if they drink
more than the smallest quantities of this acid. This leaves the
question of what makes arsenious acid a poison. Mill's completion
of the explanation is that when this substance comes into contact
with animal tissue, the acid leaves the water in which it is dissolved
and enters into chemical combination with the tissue, thus depriving it of its tendency to spontaneous decomposition which is part of
the continual process of composition and decomposition in which
all organic life consists (CW VII:407–08). Mill saw the role of an
inductive logic as the identification of rules for the production of
sound causal generalisations like these, and scientific knowledge as
the set of such generalisations, hierarchically arranged.

Despite his belief that the same inductive principles do duty in
everyday life as in scientific contexts, Mill approached the writing
of the Logic's chapters on induction with considerable hesitation.
Composition halted for several years in the 1830s because Mill felt
that he knew insufficient about the physical sciences to make a
success of this part of the work: "since I knew not of any book, or
other guide, which would spread out before me the generalities and
processes of the sciences, and I apprehended that I should have no
choice but to extract them for myself, as I best could, from the
details" (CW I:215). Exactly why Mill thought that his ignorance of
the physical sciences impeded the writing of a general study of
inductive logic is unclear. By his own admission, the only science of
which he had much first-hand knowledge was botany, which he had
studied with enthusiasm during his youthful trips to France. But
whether he thought that a closer knowledge of the core sciences of
physics and chemistry would assist him to isolate the rules of an
effective inductive logic, or that his theories would appear more
cogent if supported by examples drawn from the latest scientific
advances, the opportune publication in 1837 of William Whewell's

History of the Inductive Science provided him with 'a considerable approximation' to what he had been looking for. Whewell's massive work on the evolution of the sciences, in conjunction with Sir John Herschel's *Discourse on the Study of Natural Philosophy*, which he reread at this time, afforded a rich source of raw material for his own philosophising, and the stalled writing of the *Logic* resumed (*CW* I:215–17).

Mill's relationship with William Whewell (1794–1866), his senior by a dozen years and the greatest contemporary English historian and philosopher of science, was an ambivalent one. Whewell, who held the chair of moral philosophy at Cambridge from 1838 to 1855 and was master of Trinity College from 1841 until his death, knew vastly more than Mill did (as Mill candidly conceded) about the history and present state of the sciences. Possessed of a reputation as one of the most brilliant and learned men of the age (the Reverend Sydney Smith said of him that "Science is his forte; omniscience his foible"), Whewell seemed far better placed than Mill to construct a convincing account of scientific methodology. Yet Mill (never a man to be intellectually overawed) coolly drew for his own book on Whewell's encyclopaedic knowledge of the sciences, while rejecting almost entirely the older writer's philosophy. Mill's central objection to Whewell was that he represented the "German, or *a priori* view of human knowledge, and of the knowing faculties" inspired by Kant, and was therefore an enemy of the empiricist tradition to which he himself belonged, "which derives all knowledge from experience" (*CW* I:231–33). Whewell held that scientific, like all, knowledge was possible only because the mind supplied fundamental *ideas* to link together the data of sense – in scientific contexts, the ideas of time, space, number, force, mass, causality, and others. Mill objected to this doctrine of imposed mental conceptions on two counts: first, because it seemed to him to threaten the objectivity of human knowledge and to introduce an unappealing element of idealism into the account of reality; second, because there appeared to be no independent criterion for validating the conceptions so imposed:

By the aid of this theory, every inveterate belief and every intense feeling, of which the origin is not remembered, is enabled to dispense with the obligation of justifying itself by reason, and is erected into its own all-sufficient voucher and justification. There never was such an instrument devised for consecrating all deep-seated prejudices. (*CW* I:233)

Intending *A System of Logic* to supply a textbook of the 'school of experience' in opposition to apriorism or neo-Kantianism, Mill aimed to provoke a debate with Whewell by setting out the points of difference between them as starkly as possible. The hoped-for response was slow in coming, but in 1849, six years after the first edition of the *Logic*, Whewell published a powerful but tetchy critical essay[2] to which Mill in his turn replied in a series of elaborate footnotes to the third (1851) and later editions of the work. The exchanges between Whewell and Mill raise profound questions not merely about the methodology of science but about the nature of knowledge in general, and we shall return to them later in this chapter. But first we must examine some of the leading themes of Mill's treatment of inductive logic, beginning with his explanation of its possibility.

II. THE JUSTIFICATION OF INDUCTION

To the modern reader, the phrase 'the justification of induction' immediately brings to mind Hume's famous attack on the soundness of inductive reasoning. The importance of his treatment of induction is scarcely disputed even by those who are loath to believe his startling sceptical conclusion that there can be no such thing as a sound inductive argument; for it is normally accepted that that claim must be refuted and not merely ignored. Yet the refutation of Hume was not an objective of Mill, though he did regard himself in Book III as justifying inductive inference. Indeed, Mill seems not to have grasped what Hume's problem was, and his chief concern was to explain how inference from particulars to particulars – the standard pattern of valid reasoning – despite its appearance of slightness was really the only form of inference which science either needed to, or could, admit.

It is possible to distinguish three strands of thought in Book III which are suitably described as concerned with the justification of inductive inference. None is designed to rebut Hume.

(A) Not all inductive extrapolations from examined instances are justified; but how do we establish which ones are legitimate, and, in particular, how should we decide what kind of projections to make in an area of research of which we have had little or no direct previous experience?

(B) The uniformity of nature Mill called the "fundamental principle" of induction (*CW* VII:307). But does a person need to believe this sophisticated principle before his inductions can be considered rational?

(C) Mill maintained that "the uniformity of the course of nature . . . [is] the ultimate major premise of all inductions" (*CW* VII:308). But what sort of support does the uniformity of nature provide for inductive reasoning, given that by the theories of Book II universal propositions do not *deductively* warrant any conclusions?

A fourth very important strand in Book III is concerned less with justification than with psychological explanation. Mill was interested in the question of the origin of the notion of uniformity, and he urged that we should seek a source for it in experience rather than in some form of rational intuition. We would not form a belief in uniformity, he thought, unless we were confronted in daily life by patterns of regularity. Characteristically, he also held that it is experience which *justifies* the belief in uniformity, and thus unwittingly exposed himself to the objection that he was proposing an inductive justification of the very principle which he takes to warrant our inductive practice. Hume's question about induction (which was anticipated in antiquity by the Pyrrhonian sceptic Sextus Empiricus)[3] is: When we make inductive projections from a sample, what guarantee have we that further particulars will resemble those already examined (in other words, what guarantee that uniformities hitherto noted will be sustained)? In the view of Hume and of Sextus the answer is: None. But the fact is that there was nowhere a lively interest in this *sceptical* problem of induction before the Green and Grose edition of Hume's works in 1874 – and by that date Mill was dead.

At the beginning of Book III Mill addressed himself to the question of justification in sense (A). He complained that the detailed study of inductive methods had been hitherto neglected; some of the "generalities of the subject" had been discussed, but previous analyses of the "inductive operation" had "not been specific enough to be made the foundation of practical rules, which might be for induction itself what the rules of the syllogism are for the interpretation of inductions" (*CW* VII:283). Mill's interest here was in the practical task of locating sound methods of inductive enquiry – a search that culminated in the statement of his famous canons of induction. It is noteworthy that to some later philosophers, the task in which Mill was engaged here concerns the only worthwhile puzzle about induction. For instance, Keith Campbell has written that "The genuine problem of induction is that of finding criteria whereby acceptable procedures may be distinguished from unacceptable. There are instances of both types."[4] There is no doubt that Campbell and Mill are identifying an important research project into the justification of induction. Yet the success of the Mill/Campbell project presupposes that Hume's scepticism is in the last analysis baseless: for it is impossible to distinguish sound from unsound inductive methods if there cannot in principle be any sound ones.

Mill tended to speak almost interchangeably of the principle of uniformity and the law of causation, because he regarded patterns of uniformity in nature as depending on the causal relationships generalised by the law of causation: "There is, however, no other uniformity in the events of nature," he wrote, "than that which arises from the law of causation" (*CW* VII:577; cf. 323–27, 562, 567). When in Book III, ch. 21, he redeemed a promise made in ch. 3 to speak of the evidence for the principle of the uniformity of nature, 'the fundamental axiom of induction,' it was the evidence for the law of *universal causation*, as the presupposition of all inductive methods, which he discussed. Mill explained the principle of uniformity as an "assumption with regard to the course of nature and the order of the universe; namely, that there are such things in nature as parallel cases; that what happens once, will, under a sufficient degree of similarity of circumstances, happen again; and not only again, but as often as the same circumstances recur" (*CW* VII:306). A few pages later, he remarked that it is the law of causation on which "depends the possibility of reducing the inductive process to rules," and characterised the law as follows:

To certain facts, certain facts succeed. The invariable antecedent is termed the cause; the invariable consequent, the effect. And the universality of the law of causation consists in this, that every consequent is connected in this manner with some particular antecedent, or set of antecedents. Let the fact be what it may, if it has begun to exist, it was preceded by some fact or facts, with which it is invariably connected. (*CW* VII:327)

This close association of the two principles is natural and reasonable for an empiricist like Mill who disbelieved in the existence of causal necessity (CW VII:326–27); causal relationships will consist, for such a philosopher, in some variety of constant conjunctions of phenomena, while the uniformity of nature as a whole is simply the sum of those uniformities.

Book III, ch. 3, 'Of the Ground of Induction,' is at the heart of Mill's attempt to answer the question, How is inductive reasoning possible? After referring to the assumption of uniformity involved in every induction, he revealingly continues:

And, if we consult the actual course of nature, *we find that the assumption is warranted*. The universe, so far as is known to us, is so constituted, that whatever is true in any one case, is true in all cases of a certain description; the only difficulty is, to find what description. (CW VII:306; my emphases)

The words I have emphasised here make plain that Mill saw no reason for scepticism about the truth of the uniformity principle/ law of causation. He spoke of uniformity as a "universal fact" (*ibid.*), and of "the uniformity *which we know* to exist in nature " (CW VII:310; my emphases). Later in the *Logic* he talked of the law of causation as standing "at the head of all observed uniformities, in point of universality, and therefore . . . in point of certainty":

we shall find ourselves warranted in considering this fundamental law, though itself obtained by induction from particular laws of causation, as not less certain, but on the contrary, more so, than any of those from which it was drawn. (CW VII:570)

Mill was, admittedly, willing to allow that we can conceive of the universe's dissolving into chaos (CW VII:565–66), but this remained for him a bare conceptual possibility, and not what it is if Hume's argument is correct, a prospect which we have no good reason for believing to be less probable than the alternative prospect of continuing order. On Mill's thinking, we can confidently deny that there is any likelihood of a collapse into chaos, the "progress of experience" having "dissipated the doubt" that might have hung over the universality of the law of causation in those days "before there were sufficient grounds for receiving it as a certainty" (CW VII:574).

In a note added to the 1872 edition of the *Logic*, Mill also set out to refute the anti-empiricist claim he attributed to Reid, Stewart and W. G. Ward that "whatever knowledge experience gives us of the past and present, it gives us none of the future," declaring that "I see no force whatever in this argument" (*CW* VII:577).[5] Mill found nothing questionable in the notion that the past offers a wholly reliable guide to the future. Joseph Priestley, he argued, had settled the issue by pointing out that "though we have had no experience of what *is* future, we have had abundant experience of what *was* future" (*ibid.*); and our predictions about the future have invariably been verified by experience. Mill's treatment of the issue shows clearly his insensitivity to Hume's problem. Grant to Priestley and Mill that 'present futures' are constantly becoming 'past futures,' and that inductive predictions made about what was presently future have, when those futures arrived, frequently turned out to be correct. Yet it is open to question whether this past experience of the correctness of predictions is an adequate basis for confidence that our predictions about what is future to us *now* will turn out to be equally reliable; for there can be a sound inductive argument from the past correctness of predictions to the future reliability of predictions only if the patterns of uniformity that have hitherto held continue to hold; but it is precisely the assumption that they will hold which Hume claimed that we cannot rationally defend. But Priestley, Mill and their opponents simply assumed that knowledge of the future is possible, warranted by the uniformity of nature – a uniformity which they agreed could be known with certainty, though they disagreed about the *source* of that certainty.

While Mill never betrayed any doubt that nature is, in a degree to make possible the practice of induction, a regular affair, he conceded that "the proposition, that the course of nature is uniform, possesses rather the brevity suitable to popular, than the precision requisite in philosophical language" (*CW* VII:311). We do not, for example, expect the succession of rain and fine weather to be the same every year, or to have the same dreams every night. "The course of nature," said Mill, "is not only uniform, it is also infinitely various" (*ibid.*); and he observed with a touch of hyperbole that "The order of nature, as perceived at first glance, presents at every instant a chaos followed by another chaos" (*CW* VII:379). Yet we are sometimes prepared to accept generalisations on the basis of relatively slight

experience, as when a chemist draws conclusions about the properties of a newly discovered substance from experiments on a single
sample (*CW* VII:313–14). Mill rightly noted that he who would
construct a 'scientific theory of induction' should ponder cases like
these, and seek to establish the conditions under which sound
generalisations can be inferred. The "problem of induction," he
concluded, which even the wisest of the ancients could not solve,
was to answer the question: "Why is a single instance, in some
cases, sufficient for a complete induction, while in others, myriads
of concurring instances, without a single exception known or presumed, go such a very little way towards establishing an universal
proposition?" (*CW* VII:314). But this problem can only be set up on
the assumption that nature at root possesses a large measure of
uniformity – that it has, so to speak, a 'deep structure' of uniformity
beneath its often confusingly complex 'surface structure.'

The name of "empirical laws" can be given, Mill proposed, to
"those uniformities which observation or experiment has shown to
exist," but which cannot wholly be relied on "in cases varying
much from those which have been actually observed, for want of
seeing any reason *why* such a law should exist" (*CW* VII:516). Such
laws we can reasonably attempt to explain in terms of more
ultimate laws concerning universal causal relations, but before
we have achieved this kind of explanation of an empirical regularity
we should maintain a healthy scepticism about whether it will
hold in cases spatially or temporally distant from those we have
witnessed. We cannot be sure that observed regularities concerning
tides, weather conditions, the expansion of bodies by heating, the
poisonousness of substances containing a high proportion of nitro-
gen, and many others, will be preserved in distant parts of the
universe or at remote periods of time (for instance, changes in
the movements of the bodies in the solar system may one day
cause the pattern of tides on Earth to alter). But there is no such
problem about inductions regarding 'ultimate laws,' which can
be expected to hold always and everywhere, or those concerning
the continuance of empirical regularities in 'adjacent' cases: thus
"We have . . . the warrant of a rigid induction for considering it
probable, in a degree indistinguishable from certainty, that the
known conditions for the sun's rising will exist to-morrow" (*CW*
VII:516, 551).

Most ultimate of all laws is, of course, the law of causation itself – the 'axiom of induction.' Mill devoted Book III, ch. 21, to defending the view that our knowledge of it is empirically grounded. This chapter was directed against philosophers who sought to explain our deepest conceptions about the nature of the world, logic, mathematics and morality by means of rationalist theories of non-empirical, *a priori* apprehensions. Mill consistently opposed "the school of metaphysicians who have long predominated in this country" who affirmed that

the universality of causation is a truth which we cannot help believing; that the belief in it is an instinct, one of the laws of our believing faculty. As the proof of this, they say, and they have nothing else to say, that everybody does believe it; and they number it among the propositions, rather numerous in their catalogue, which may be logically argued against, and perhaps cannot be logically proved, but which are of higher authority than logic, and so essentially inherent in the mind. . . . (CW VII:563)

Mill stressed as firmly as Wittgenstein was to do a century later that rational beliefs must measure up to an external criterion, something independent of their merely seeming to be right: for "to say [as the apriorists do] that belief suffices for its own justification is making opinion the test of opinion; it is denying the existence of any outward standard" (CW VII:564).[6] Asserting, like Stewart, that belief in the universality of causation was a 'principle of our constitution' seemed to Mill at once psychologically implausible and epistemologically indefensible.[7]

Yet at the beginning of the same chapter occurs a passage which can easily mislead readers into thinking that Mill's primary concern was with the Humean problem:

But is this assumption [of the law of causation] warranted? Doubtless (it may be said) *most* phenomena are connected as effects with some antecedent or cause, that is, are never produced unless some assignable fact has preceded them; but the very circumstance that complicated processes of induction are sometimes necessary, shows that cases exist in which this regular order of succession is not apparent to our unaided apprehension. If, then, the processes which bring these cases within the same category with the rest, require that we should assume the universality of the very law which they do not at first sight appear to exemplify, is not this a *petitio principii*? (CW VII:563)

Mill here claims that a fallacy of *begging the question* threatens if we assume all phenomena to be subject to a law of uniform causation that we have no right to take to be a law unless we can be sure that it has no exceptions. This certainly sounds close to the Humean claim that we should not affirm uniform causation outside the narrow realm of phenomena we have experienced. But the subsequent discussion makes plain that Mill was not casting doubt on the thesis that our experience provides massive and conclusive evidence for the general prevalence of uniform causal relations. The problem he was raising in this passage is the much more limited one of how we come to be justified in carrying our belief in underlying uniformity into realms where we are at first hard put to detect any regularity. Can we, without making unjustified assumptions, Mill was asking, deny that there are in nature any random events? His answer was that even in the difficult cases, we may rationally, and without *petitio*, assert that the law of causation holds, on the *inductive* basis that the course of scientific research has so far provided no grounds for doubting that all phenomena are governed by causal laws. "When every phenomenon," he wrote,

that we ever knew sufficiently well to be able to answer the question, had a cause on which it was invariably consequent, it was more rational to suppose that our inability to assign the causes of other phenomena arose from our ignorance, than that there were phenomena which were uncaused. . . . (*CW* VII:574)

Discoveries in physics since Mill's death have proved wrong his expectation that science would never uncover indeterminacy in nature, yet that expectation was not an unreasonable one in the light of the rapid advances of the science of his day; assuming the soundness of inductive argument, it was rational enough to infer that human ignorance rather than any intrinsic randomness in things was the best explanation of the fact that for some classes of phenomena deterministic laws could not (yet) be stated.

"Whatever be the most proper mode of expressing it," Mill declared, "the proposition that the course of nature is uniform, is the fundamental principle, or general axiom, of Induction." Yet the inference to the law is itself "an instance of induction, and induction by no means of the most obvious kind," being a sophisticated generalisation about generalisations (*CW* VII:307). But how then, he wondered, could a person rationally make his earliest inductions, if the uniformity principle was not known to him *a priori*, as Reid and Stewart had held, but was only proved 'along with' particular inductions? Mill's preference for an empiricist explanation of the belief in uniformity produced a need for a justification of induction of type (B): a justification of a person's early inductions, made before he could be aware (via induction) of the general causal uniformity holding in the world. As Mill plausibly remarked, a conviction of the existence of general uniformity is secondary, in the order of evidence, to the discovery of uniformities in particular contexts. The task was to explain how justified inductions could be made without an explicit consciousness of the principle which justified them.

For Mill, this problem was no more than a special aspect of the broader problem of justification which I have labelled (C): that of explaining how the uniformity principle warrants inductions. His rather complicated response to this draws heavily on the theory of reasoning and the syllogism developed in Book II: the uniformity principle is "the ultimate major premise of all inductions," a generalisation to the effect that all events are subject to regularity, and like all syllogistic major premises can play a role in a justificatory schema without being known in advance of that schema's conclusion.

A major premise, on Mill's theory, is not essential to the proof of a syllogistic conclusion, but serves only as a kind of useful signpost (his technical term is 'memorandum') to the conclusion which the minor premise entitles us to draw; if it were false, that conclusion would not be a satisfactory induction from the premise. This is not the place to enter into the details of Mill's peculiar views on deductive inference,[8] and we may merely note that the thesis that all 'real inference' is inductive inference from particulars to particulars sits uneasily with the claim that the uniformity principle is the 'fundamental principle' of induction. Despite Mill's description of it as the *ultimate* major premise of all inductions, there seems nothing very fundamental about the uniformity principle if it plays no more powerful role than major premises, on his view, ever do play. To be sure, he contended that the uniformity principle, while not contributing to the proof of inductive conclusions, is yet 'necessary' to their being proved, since "no conclusion is proven, for which there cannot be found a true major premise" (*CW* VII:308; cf. 310). But as a major premise, for Mill, is a premise only in name and not in real function, talk of the uniformity principle as a necessary condition of proofs is hardly justified: for it cannot consistently be held that a major promise is superfluous to the true movement of proof from particulars to particulars yet is necessary for that proof to go through.

III. THE ELIMINATIVE METHODS

Mill firmly dismissed the idea that causal relations involve necessity, and insisted that experience supports only a constant-conjunction analysis of causation. The cause of a phenomenon is the sum total of contingent conditions "which being realized, the consequent invariably follows" (*CW* VII:332). The main aim of science, in Mill's opinion, is to trace causal relationships, and a major role of inductive logic is to help it to do so. Despite his claim that effects normally depend not on a single factor but on a complex of factors acting together, Mill's famous methods of experimental enquiry are designed specifically to locate, by means of eliminative reasoning, a salient condition preceding or accompanying a phenomenon "with which it is really connected by an invariable law" (*CW* VII:388). It has been fairly objected to this conception of science that the most interesting research is concerned much more with the discovery of novel entities and processes than with the identification of causes. But if causal explanation is not the whole of science, as Mill supposed, it is still a legitimate part of it; and the eliminative methods have also a useful role to play in everyday causal enquiry.

The most important of the experimental methods are those of Agreement and of Difference:

Method of Agreement [MA]: If two or more instances of the phenomenon under investigation have only one circumstance in common, the circumstance in which alone all the instances agree, is the cause (or effect) of the given phenomenon. (*CW* VII:390)

Method of Difference [MD]: If an instance in which the phenomenon under investigation occurs, and an instance in which it does not occur, have every circumstance in common save one, that one occurring only in the former; the circumstance in which alone the two instances differ, is the effect, or the cause, or an indispensable part of the cause, of the phenomenon. (*CW* VII:391)

The thought behind MA is that no feature *not* common to the circumstances in which the phenomenon occurs can be its cause, since the phenomenon is capable of occurring in its absence; so if there is a sole feature common to the different cases, this is the only remaining candidate to play the causal role. But this is problematic for two reasons: there is frequently great difficulty in obtaining different instances of a phenomenon coinciding in only one aspect, and there are often – as Mill himself reluctantly conceded – different causal routes to the same effect (as a man can be killed by shooting, stabbing or poisoning). Strictly, MA establishes only that a condition not invariably present among the antecedents of a given phenomenon cannot be *necessary* for its occurrence. MD corresponds to a familiar intuitive pattern of causal reasoning, but the difficulty of determining with certainty that all relevant differences between the instances in which a phenomenon occurs and those in which it does not have been taken into account leaves it unable to fulfil Mill's purpose for it of conclusively demonstrating nomological causal relationships. At most, MD can prove that a particular factor is not a *sufficient* condition of some phenomenon, where the factor occurs and the phenomenon does not. Nevertheless, as J. L. Mackie has pointed out, both MA and MD are suggestive and useful modes of causal investigation where we already have a good idea of the range of possible causes of the phenomenon at issue; though this implies that the methods will only be of much service in relatively well-understood areas of enquiry, and will do little to advance more path-finding research.[9]

What Mill calls the Joint Method of Agreement and Difference identifies as the cause of a phenomenon the only factor always present when the phenomenon occurs and always absent when it fails to occur. This is a particularly hard method to employ, involving the need to secure one pair of cases with a single similarity and another pair with a single difference; it will also only locate a cause in the uncommon cases where there is a *unique* cause to be found (where, that is, plurality of causes does not apply).

The remaining methods of inductive enquiry are those of Residues and of Concomitant Variation:

Method of Residues [MR]: Subduct from any phenomenon such part as is known by previous inductions to be the effect of certain antecedents, and the residue of the phenomenon is the effect of the remaining antecedents. (*CW* VII:398)

Method of Concomitant Variations [MCV]: Whatever phenomenon varies in any manner whenever another phenomenon varies in some particular manner, is either a cause or an effect of that phenomenon, or is connected with it through some fact of causation. (*CW* VII:401)

Like the preceding methods, MR can be useful in signalling causal possibilities, but as a mode of proof it fails because it falsely assumes that separate parts of a compound phenomenon always have separate causes. Finally, MCV properly, if vaguely, draws attention to the probability of some causal linkage between phenomena which vary in tandem.

IV. INDUCTION VERSUS HYPOTHESIS

Mill saw his inductive methods as the guiding principles of the first of three stages into which sound scientific reasoning could be divided: induction, ratiocination and verification. On this picture, the initial inductive stage ascertains the laws of causes; the second, ratiocination, computes deductively from those laws "how the causes will operate in the particular combination known to exist in the case in hand"; while the third, verificatory, step compares "this calculated effect with the actual phenomenon" (*CW* VII:491–92). Such inducto-deductive methodology represents, in Mill's view, the ideal format for discovery and justification in science. Appropriate inductive processes yield general statements of causal law from which, with suitable premises about particular circumstances, empirically verifiable conclusions about individual instances can be inferred; these verified instances then corroborate the original statements of law. But Mill recognised that undirected and random inductive processes are scarcely likely to lead to the discovery of significant causal laws: hence the scientist must begin with a *hypothesis*, a plausible conjecture suggestive of fruitful observations and experiments (*CW* VII:496).

Without such assumptions, science could never have attained its present state: they are necessary steps in the progress towards something more certain; and nearly everything which is now theory was once hypothesis. (*ibid.*)

The fact is, however, that Mill never entirely made up his mind about the proper role of hypotheses in science. The idea of a hypothesis as a shrewd and imaginative guess to the causal relationships worth testing for sometimes gives way, in the pages of the *Logic*, to a different, and from Mill's perspective altogether more problematic, conception, whereby a hypothesis is not merely a valuable preliminary to the use of the inductive methods, but an *alternative* first stage in the three-stage proof process. What Mill termed the 'Hypothetical Method'

suppresses the first of the three steps, the induction to ascertain the law; and contents itself with the other two operations, ratiocination and verification; the law which is reasoned from, being assumed, instead of proved. (*CW* VII:492)

But if "nearly everything which is now theory" began from (or could in principle have begun from) an act of hypothesising of this second sort, the inductive methods to which Mill devoted so much careful attention seem in danger of becoming redundant: for science can, as a matter of logic, get along without them and, as a matter of history, often has. But at this point Mill laid down an extra, and very exacting, condition on the Hypothetical Method. For the conclusion reached by the method to be acceptable, he suggested, it must be capable of verification by the Method of Difference (*CW* VII:492–93). Mill's proposal was that a double 'deduction' should be performed (each component step is in fact really a more complex inference, with inductive elements included) of the observational implications of the hypothesis's truth and the observational implications of its falsity, all other features of the world being held constant; then only if the former set of implications matches the world and the latter fails to do so is the hypothesis confirmed, difference reasoning thereby demonstrating the hypothesised cause to be alone capable of producing the observed results. But the problem, as Mill fully recognised, with this rigorous mode of verification is that from any hypothesis in any slight degree *recherché* or dissimilar to already familiar principles, it is very difficult to infer with certainty what the results of its holding, and of its not holding, will be. Consequently he concluded that acceptable hypotheses must always be simple hypotheses which bear a strong degree of analogy to already well-established principles.

To clarify the notion of desirable analogy with known principles, Mill distinguished between hypotheses about casual agents and hypotheses about the laws of operation of causes:

[e]ither the phenomenon assigned as the cause is real, but the law according to which it acts, merely supposed; or the cause is fictitious, but is supposed to produce its effects according to laws similar to those of some known class of phenomena. (CW VII:490)

Mill offered as examples of the first kind of hypothesis "different suppositions made respecting the laws of the planetary central force, anterior to the discovery of the true law" (i.e. Newton's law of universal gravitation – itself originally a hypothesis of the same kind). Examples of the second sort were the vortices of Descartes and the luminiferous ether, both of which, though 'fictitious' (by which misleading term Mill meant not yet known to exist) were taken to operate according to established laws (ibid.). Hypotheses of both kinds were, in Mill's view, theoretically capable of confirmation or disconfirmation; but the line had to be drawn at hypotheses which posited both a novel cause and a novel law of operation. Of the two varieties of tolerable hypothesis, however, he strongly preferred those which ascribed a 'fictitious' law to a known cause to those which posited a known law for a 'fictitious' cause. It was simpler, he thought, to observe or experiment on causes which were known to us than to 'deduce' the effects, on the basis of familiar laws, of Cartesian vortices or the luminiferous ether. Since hypotheses like these could not, that is, be effectively verified or falsified by difference reasoning, they were best avoided.

Mill's attitude to any but the mildest and most unexciting hypotheses was one of suspicion. Confronted by the historical evidence recounted in Whewell's History, he was forced to concede that many major advances in science had depended on the "large temporary assistance" rendered by the hypothetical method (CW VII:496). Yet his abhorrence of anything that smacked remotely of apriorism made him unwilling to countenance the admission to a process of reasoning of any proposition which could not be rigorously confirmed by observation or the use of the inductive methods (a condition which a large number of historically important hypotheses actually failed to satisfy). In Mill's view, doubtless influenced by Bacon and Newton, a hypothesis is always guilty until proved innocent. This caution may seem unjustified to the modern reader. Yet in defending it, Mill hit upon one powerful argument against the multiplication of hypotheses which parallels a popular present-day argument for an instrumentalist interpretation of theories. Mill noted the simple but vital logical fact that a hypothesis which fits the observed data is not thereby proved to be true, because there may be an indefinite number of alternative but incompatible hypotheses (most of which we will not have thought of) which fit those data equally well. Hypotheses are underdetermined by evidence except (according to Mill) in the limited range of cases where they are amenable to inductive verification by difference reasoning. This was a truth, he patronisingly remarked, which Whewell, despite his many "abilities and attainments," had failed to grasp:

he recognises absolutely no mode of induction except that of trying hypothesis after hypothesis until one is found which fits the phenomena; which one, when found, is to be assumed as true. . . . And this without the slightest distinction between the cases in which it may be known beforehand that two different hypotheses cannot lead to the same result, and those in which, for aught we can ever know, the range of suppositions, all equally consistent with the phenomena, may be infinite. (CW VII:503)

Yet Mill did not consider the underdetermination argument to support a non-realist conception of scientific theories, in the manner of modern instrumentalism. The idea that a hypothesis which has wide explanatory scope, unifies the data, suggests novel experimental tests and aids the successful prediction of phenomena, can be an eligible one *whether or not its referring terms are taken to refer to anything*, was not a Millian one. Admittedly Mill allowed that hypotheses not yet known to be true were worth further investigation if they seemed to explain known facts and successfully predicted previously unknown ones: for "any suspicion, however slight, that sets an ingenious person at work to contrive an experiment, or affords a reason for trying one experiment rather than another may be of the greatest benefit to science" (CW VII:560). But theories, in Mill's view, were more than merely conceptual devices for instilling order in the observational data and for facilitating predictions of phenomena: they were attempts at a literal description of the world.[10]

Here, at least, he was in superficial agreement with Whewell, who likewise required of a satisfactory scientific theory that it provide a *true* account of reality. This surface agreement masks, though, a more basic difference of view concerning the nature of the phenomenal world encountered in experience. Whewell, profoundly influenced by Kant, considered reality-as-we-know-it to be in some part a construction of the human mind. On this conception, the data of sense, including observations made under experimental conditions, need to be shaped and organised by 'fundamental' and 'appropriate' ideas, or conceptual categories, before they can represent to us a comprehensible external world; and it is precisely *this* function of shaping and organising the sensory data which scientists perform when they frame hypotheses. "Facts are the materials of science," Whewell wrote; and "all Facts involve Ideas."[11] Whewell's Kantianism incorporates, as Gerd Buchdahl has remarked, a strong version of the doctrine that all observation is 'theory-laden'; for Whewell, no realm of facts exists independently of our intellectual activity.[12] Whewell's enthusiasm for hypothetico-deductive methodology was the product, therefore, not of any instrumentalist stance on theoretical structures as convenient mental tools for unifying and attaining a power of prediction over phenomena, but of a dynamic, neo-Kantian view of reality as moulded by the conceptualising power of the mind. Scientific hypothesising was not for Whewell, as it was for Mill, merely a form of sophisticated guessing about the nature of reality, but instead the crucial operation *by which we impose form and order on the formless, disordered data of scientific enquiry.*

Whewell's major original contribution to the Kantian tradition was to emphasise the *continuity* of the process whereby, over time, science develops and refines the ideas which serve us in the constructive interpretation of nature. His historical studies trace the intellectual unfolding not only of the most general fundamental ideas, such as space and time, force and causality, but also of the more particular 'appropriate Conceptions' in the special sciences of astronomy, mechanics, chemistry, biology and physiology.[13] But while Whewell took the categorical ideas expressed in hypotheses to be man's contribution to the construction of nature, he did not suppose that all imposed ideas were of equal worth. He was enough of an empiricist to admit that scientists can make unfortunate choices in the detailed application of a fundamental idea within an area of research, and that many initially promising hypotheses turn out to be ineffective at making good sense of the data, or incompatible with other simpler, more capacious or better-integrated organising principles. Yet he strongly disbelieved that the production of satisfactory theory could be reduced to rules:

> Scientific discovery must ever depend upon some happy thought, of which we cannot trace the origin; – some fortunate cast of intellect, rising above all rules. No maxims can be given which inevitably lead to discovery. No precepts will elevate a man of ordinary endowments to the level of a man of genius: nor will an inquirer of truly inventive mind need to come to the teacher of inductive philosophy to learn how to exercise the faculties which nature has given him.[14]

Whewell's opinion that innovation in science required a quality of judgement, even genius, rather than a set of principles devised by "the teacher of inductive philosophy," was paralleled by a conviction that the evaluation of hypotheses could not be turned into a rule-governed process of the sort envisaged by Mill. Their disagreement on this issue produced one of their sharpest exchanges, in which each writer marred his position by overstatement.

Mill began by playing his best card, that of the underdetermination of theories by data. That one hypothesis accounts for all the known phenomena is no guarantee of its truth, for some other hypothesis might account for the evidence equally well; indeed "there are probably many others which are equally possible, but which, for want of anything analogous in our experience, our minds are unfitted to conceive" (CW VII:500). But his next contention is more doubtful. If its accounting for presently known facts offers no proof of the truth of a hypothesis, its leading to "the anticipation and prediction of others which experience afterwards verified" fails to provide much more, such "coincidences between its prophecies and what comes to pass" deserving to impress only the "uninformed" who lack scientific attainments (CW VII:500–01). While Mill is not alone in questioning the evidential value of predictive success (Keynes, for instance, affirmed that "The peculiar virtue of prediction or predesignation is altogether illusory"),[15] there is force in Whewell's claim that predictive success is a sign that a hypothesis is tracking the truth, because otherwise "concidences between its prophecies and what comes to pass" are improbable. False theories do sometimes enjoy a measure of explanatory and predictive success, and it would have been candid for Whewell to have admitted this; yet the prediction by a hypothesis of novel, and especially of surprising, facts is some real evidence (not proof) that a genuine principle of nature has been located.[16] In any case, Mill's reluctance to grant much confirmatory force to a hypothesis's predictive success is dubiously compatible with his claims on behalf of the third, or verificatory, stage of his own inducto-deductive methodology, where the truth of the inferred prediction about a particular case is held to corroborate the lawlike premise or premises. His acute distaste for Whewellian hypotheses, with their background of Kantian apriorism, led him to something of a double standard, whereby predictive success serves to confirm inductively attained lawlike premises but not hypothesised ones, which require a further step of difference reasoning to demonstrate that predicted cases would not have occurred had alternative hypotheses been true.

But Whewell was on weaker ground in denying the justness of Mill's claim about the underdetermination of hypotheses by data.

[W]hen he says that the condition of a hypothesis accounting for all the known phenomena is "often fulfilled equally well by two conflicting hypotheses," I can only say that I know of no such case in the history of Science, where the phenomena are at all numerous or complicated; and that if such a case were to occur, one of the hypotheses might always be resolved into the other.[17]

Steven Lukes has written: "Many philosophers of science have supposed that theories determine, in the sense of entail, data, but who has supposed that a given set of data, however large, entails one and only one theory?"[18] The answer is: Whewell did so. Philosophical and historical considerations alike cast doubt on his belief that the level of confirmation of a hypothesis can be raised so high as to render superfluous any attention to alternatives. A hypothesis may exclude all rivals for a long time, but few scientific hypotheses have enjoyed the gift of eternal life. Recalcitrant experimental data, or lack of coherence with other theories in related areas, can seal the fate of even the most favoured and long-lived hypotheses. Moreover, at a time of revolutionary change in a problem area, there may be no consensus in the scientific community as to which of a number of incompatible hypotheses best accounts for the available data.[19] Such uncertainties and controversies do not mean, of course, that scientists should not hypothesise; but they do indicate that Whewell was wrong to dismiss so lightly Mill's worries about verification. Whewell's contentions that 'complete evidence'[20] may be obtained for a hypothesis, and that conflicts between hypotheses are normally more apparent than real, could only be well supported on a more thoroughgoing version of transcendental idealism, whereby hypotheses constitute facts so entirely as not to be answerable to an objective reality at all.

The depth of the rift between Mill and Whewell on the nature of scientific progress is illustrated by their dispute over the correct description of one of the milestones of Western science, Kepler's theory of the elliptical orbits of the planets. Mill contended that Kepler's advance was not even a proper instance of inductive reasoning: Kepler had merely plotted the carefully observed positions of planets at certain temporal intervals, then 'colligated' the observations by drawing ellipses to connect them (CW VII:292–94). Whewell retorted that Kepler had done much more than that; he had tried out numerous geometrical constructions before lighting on the idea of an ellipse, his discovery therefore being a clear (and brilliant) instance of hypothetical method.[21] The question central to this debate was the origin of Kepler's idea of an elliptical orbit. Was this, as Mill maintained, simply *discovered* by him in the data? Or was it, as Whewell insisted, a notion Kepler *imposed* on the data in an act of constructive interpretation?

A conception [Mill proposed] implies, and corresponds, to, something conceived: and though the conception itself is not in the facts, but in our mind, yet if it is to convey any knowledge relating to them, it must be a conception *of* something which really is in the facts, some property which they actually possess, and which they would manifest to our senses, if our senses were able to take cognizance of it. (CW VII:295)

Whewell, by contrast, argued that Kepler could never have formulated his theory without performing 'a special mental operation,' to bind together the successive positions of the planets by the idea of an ellipse:

Before this, the facts are seen as detached, separate, lawless; afterwards, they are seen as connected, simple, regular; as part of one general fact, and thereby possessing innumerable new relations before unseen.[22]

Despite the stridency with which Mill and Whewell condemned each other's views, it is possible to see them as grasping *different but complementary* elements of a more complex story about scientific discovery. Mill's special merit was to stress the answerability of theory to fact, reminding the reader of the plausible realist requirement that sound science should represent the world as it actually is. Kepler was correct (on this view) to claim that planetary orbits are elliptical *only if* the planets really do travel in elliptical orbits. Whewell, however, was right to emphasise, as Mill did not, the intellectual sophistication of Kepler's interpretation of a highly confusing and incomplete set of data – a task demanding an act of constructive imagination to make those data intelligible. On this eirenic proposal, the ellipse is genuinely 'in the facts' of planetary motions, yet the *idea* of an ellipse needs to be formulated by the scientific mind before the character of the facts can be elicited. To be sure, this line of thought cannot wholly reconcile the historical Whewell and Mill, who disagreed fundamentally over whether a fully determinate external world exists prior to the application of concepts. But the non-partisan reader of the present day may prefer to think that while neither Mill nor Whewell told the whole of the truth about scientific method, each told a part of it.

V. CONCLUSION: MILL'S STATUS AS A PHILOSOPHER OF SCIENCE

Great philosophers intrigue and stimulate, even when they fail to convince us. Mill's philosophy of natural science is not always clear or cogent, and it is sometimes (as in its treatment of hypotheses) blinkered or inconsistent. But it is notable too for its single-minded devotion to a thoroughgoing empiricism, its subtle analysis of the notions of cause and of law, its attempt to probe the murky subject of the conditions of reliable inductive inference, and its defence of the idea of science as a progressive programme of ever more general and unified explanations of phenomena.[23]

Nevertheless, it is hard to avoid the impression that Mill lacked the sophisticated grasp of the dynamic of the modern scientific enterprise which first-hand experience of research would have given him. He aimed to reduce scientific methodology to a small number of very specific rules for the determination of causes, seemingly unaware that much of the most interesting research is concerned not with causal analysis but with the discovery of novel entities and processes. Mill's rules could not have produced the theories of relativity or quantum mechanics, or revealed the nature of DNA, the electromagnetic spectrum, lasers or superconductors. The weakness at the heart of his methodology is a profound theoretical timidity, a reluctance to offer hostages to fortune in the shape of hypothetical entities or forces whose explanatory fruitfulness can compensate for their lack of straightforward verifiability. That many of the most successful modern theories make crucial reference to unobservable (or only indirectly observable) entities and qualities (electrons, quarks and other subatomic particles, antimatter, 'charm,' 'strangeness,' black holes, the big bang, etc.) indicates the limitations of Mill's understandable, but over-cautious, predilection for explanation by the homely and familiar. It is an unfortunate accident of history that his distrust of the hypothetical method was fuelled by his strong and understandable dislike of the apriorism of Kantian philosophers like Whewell. Had Mill not regarded his conflict with Whewell over hypotheses as a battle in his wider war against the 'school of intuition,' he might have seen more merit in adventurous styles of scientific speculation. It is ironic that Mill's naturalistic-empiricist style of mind produced a deeply conservative philosophy of science. How different his views would have been had he written in the age of Einstein, we can only speculate.

Mill was the spokesman for what might be dubbed a 'museum conception' of natural science. By that I mean that he understood scientists to be primarily concerned with the following tasks: (1) the explanation and classification of observable phenomena, distinguished by their observable properties; (2) the production of inductive generalisations descriptive of causal principles of observable phenomena; (3) the arrangement of these causal principles into hierarchically structured systems of higher-level and lower-level laws; (4) the reduction of the more surprising or *recherché* features of nature to more familiar ones; (5) the attainment of theoretical closure in areas of research where careful application of the inductive methods leaves nothing further to explain. In addition, we may note that Mill paid little attention to the role of quantitative methods in science, and none at all to the provision of mathematical models in the development of theory. Statistical reasoning receives a short chapter of the *Logic*; but statistical judgements are held to be "of little use . . . except as a stage on the road to something better" – namely, universal generalisations (*CW* VII:592). Mill saw science as yielding, for the most part, a glass-cabinet sort of knowledge, in which the vertical and horizontal relationships among phenomena are meticulously displayed, classified by reference to relevant causal principles. On the Millian picture, science progressively uncovers the complex of causal interconnections among often *prima facie* very disparate kinds of things, and reveals new and unexpected elements of a pyramidal system of laws.

If the deficiencies of this 'museum view' of science are obvious, its merits too should not be overlooked. Mill's advocacy of inductive reasoning according to strict and precise rules, his Ockhamite dislike of unnecessary theoretical entities, and his constant tendency to demystify science and stress its continuity with the knowledge-gathering activities of everyday life, remind us that discipline and restraint are among the scientific virtues. Admittedly, he vastly underrated the importance of those other virtues of theoretical imagination and courage in conceptual innovation. Yet there is some justice in his remark that whilst a few persons, "by extraordinary genius, or by the accidental acquisition of a good set of intellectual habits," may profitably work without pre-set principles, "the bulk of mankind require either to understand the theory of what they are doing, or to have rules laid down for them by those who have understood the theory" (*CW* VII:11). That science, for those lacking the genius of a Kepler or an Einstein, should be, at least in part, a rule-governed activity, is a perfectly defensible view. Whether Mill himself 'understood the theory' well enough to propose the rules is, of course, another question.

NOTES

1 Mill is quoting from Dugald Stewart 1814, II:321.
2 Whewell 1849, reprinted under the title 'Mr Mill's Logic' in Butts 1968.

3 Sextus Empiricus 1933, 148.

4 Campbell 1974, 148.

5 To be more precise, Reid and Stewart did not deny that *if* uniformity can permissibly be presupposed, experience will then be a guide to the future; but they disagreed with the claim that knowledge of *uniformity* itself is a product of experience. They thought it more probable that our knowledge of uniformity was either instinctive, or the result of rational intuition, or a gift of divine providence.

6 Cf. Wittgenstein 1953, Pt. I, sect 258 and *passim*.

7 Dugald Stewart 1854–58, 5:101f.

8 See Chapter 1 of this book, and Scarre 1989, chs. 2 and 3.

9 Mackie 1974. For an extensive treatment of the eliminative methods, see also Skorupski 1989, ch. 6.

10 It will be clear from these remarks that I do not share John Skorupski's belief (1989, 202) that the passage at VII:560 indicates Mill's sympathy for an instrumentalist position.

11 William Whewell, *Novum Organon Renovatum being the Second part of the Philosophy of the Inductive Sciences* (London: Parket), ch. III, aphorism IV.

12 Buchdahl 1971, 350.

13 See, e.g., Butts 1968, 116.

14 Butts 1968, 117.

15 Keynes 1963, 305.

16 Mill comes closest to admitting Whewell's claim in the passage cited above (*CW* VII:560) on the promising nature of hypotheses which predict phenomena successfully. For further discussion of the Mill-Whewell debate on prediction, see Laudan 1981, ch. 10.

17 Butts 1968, 292.

18 Lukes 1978, 96.

19 Cf. Kuhn 1962.

20 Butts 1968, 292.

21 'Mr Mill's Logic,' sections II, III.

22 Butts 1968, 278.

23 "[T]he whole problem of the investigation of nature, viz. What are the fewest assumptions, which being granted, the order of nature as it exists would be the result? What are the fewest general propositions from which all the uniformities existing in nature could be deduced?" (*CW* VII:472).

4 Mill, phenomenalism, and the self

I. THE ORIGINS OF MILL'S PHENOMENALISM: BERKELEY, HAMILTON AND THE RELATIVITY OF KNOWLEDGE

"Matter, then, may be defined as the Permanent Possibility of Sensation". With this famous phrase, Mill put phenomenalism firmly on the philosophical map. The origins of phenomenalism – the standpoint which regards sensations as the basic constituents of reality, and attempts to construct the external world from sensations and the possibilities of sensation – can be traced back to Berkeley. But the analysis of matter as the "permanent possibility of sensation" and the attempted application of that analysis to mind in the best-known chapters of Mill's *Examination of Sir William Hamilton's Philosophy* constitute the first developed presentation of the doctrine.[1] After Mill, a commitment to phenomenalism became standard among scientific philosophers, until superseded by physicalism in the 1930s. Figures associated with the doctrine included Mach, Russell, Carnap, C. I. Lewis and A. J. Ayer, and with these it took an increasingly "linguistic" or "semantic" form.[2]

Mill's phenomenalism is a direct descendent of Berkeley's idealist immaterialism. Mill indeed characterised himself as an "idealist", a follower of Berkeley who rejected the reality of matter. In his review of "Berkeley's Life and Writings", Mill expresses his boundless admiration for the earlier writer: "of all who, from the earliest times, have applied the powers of their minds to metaphysical enquiries," Mill writes, giving a list that includes Plato, Descartes

I am grateful for comments from C. V. Borst, Chris Hookway, E. J. Lowe, Alan Millar, Alan Richardson, Geoffrey Scarre and John Skorupski.

and Kant, "he is the one of greatest philosophic genius". Mill explains how his own position nonetheless improves on Berkeley's. The "common notion of matter" says that material objects are "not mental, or such as can only exist in a mind. . . . It was competent to Berkeley to maintain that this part of the common notion is an illusion; and he did maintain this, in our opinion successfully".[3] Where he was less successful, Mill claims, was in *explaining* how this illusion is produced; here Berkeley should have employed the psychological methods of his own *Theory of Vision*, subsequently exploited by the associationist psychology of Hartley's *Observations on Man*.[4]

This was the method Mill himself employed; so in brief, Berkeley + Hartley = Mill. For Mill, the process of association of ideas generates our belief in the "permanent possibilities of sensation", and these possibilities are really what we refer to when we talk of an external world. The introduction of the possibilities of sensation marks the crucial difference between Mill and Berkeley, and indeed defines the phenomenalist as opposed to idealist variety of immaterialism. For Berkeley, objects are essentially groups of *actual* ideas, whether had by human subjects or, in some sense, by a divine subject. As Mill correctly notes, Berkeley "had not thoroughly realised the fact, that the permanent element in our perceptions is only a potentiality of sensations not actually felt". He had, however, seen that "*to us* the external object is nothing but such a potentiality", and Mill quotes one of the passages where Berkeley came close to phenomenalism:

The table I write on, I say, exists, that is, I see and feel it; and if I were out of my study I should say it existed – meaning thereby that if I was in my study I might perceive it, or that some other spirit actually does perceive it.[5]

But "in itself the object was, in his theory, not merely a present potentiality, but a present actual existence . . . in the Divine Mind" (p. 461).

This, for Mill, is the "illogical side of Berkeley's theory" (p. 465). The possibilities of sensation are intended as an insubstantial replacement for Berkeley's God. They "are not a positive entity . . . they did not exist as sensations, but as a guaranteed belief; implying constancy in the phenomena, but not a spiritual substance for the phenomena to dwell in when not present to my own mind" (p. 464). (It is notable that in the review, Mill says nothing of any difference between himself and Berkeley concerning minds or selves.) Phenomenalism, then, seems to assume an ontology purely of sensations, but unlike Berkeleian idealism, it maintains that what we mean by an external world involves appeal not just to actual, but also to possible, sensations. But spelling out just what this definition involves will be a major concern of the present chapter.

If Berkeley is central, the *absence* of Hume as an influence on Mill's phenomenalism is striking, since he is sometimes regarded as a phenomenalist.[6] But Hume did not assume his current eminence in the philosophical canon until T. H. Green's edition of his works appeared after Mill's death. Moreover, the Philosophic Radicals – Bentham, the Mills and their circle – distrusted the philosopher whose scepticism seemed to be a pretext for his Toryism. Mill refers to Hume as "the most extreme of Phenomenists" (p. 165n), but he was by no means a phenomenalist in the modern sense. His view is that belief in an external world has no rational basis, but is nonetheless compelled by "natural instinct": "We may well ask, *What causes induce us to believe in the existence of body?*, but it is in vain to ask, *Whether there be body or not?* That is a point which we must take for granted in all our reasonings".[7] Hume and Mill both wanted to explain this belief as acquired through experience by the association of ideas, but Humean scepticism does not imply that external objects do not exist; consequently, it has no use for "possible perceptions". For Hume, matter could not be defined as the permanent possibility of sensation.[8]

Mill's discussion of Berkeley shows that there are both ontological and psychological strands to phenomenalism – concerning what the belief in an external world amounts to and how it arises. In the *Examination* these are intertwined. But Mill's explicit target is the psychological theory of the "school of intuition" – principally Thomas Reid and his successor Sir William Hamilton. Reid (1710–96), critic of Hume and founder of the Scottish "common sense" school, is, after Hamilton, the writer most extensively referred to in the *Examination*.

In important respects, Reid's work sets the agenda for Mill's discussion. Reid maintained that belief in an external world is – as Mill puts it – "intuitive" (we feel compelled to believe it) and "original" (innate); it is therefore legitimate. Thus, "that those things do really exist which we distinctly perceive by our senses, and are what we perceive them to be", is taken by Reid as one of the self-evident principles of "common sense".[9] Mill denies that there is any such body of self-evident principles. He follows Hume in using association to analyse apparently "intuitive" beliefs – in an external world, or cause and effect, or the self – as an acquired product of sensations. But he opposes Hume in apparently accepting Reid's argument from "intuitive" and "original" to "legitimate" (on Mill's affinity with Reid see the Introduction to this volume, section II).

Although Mill's "school of experience" is certainly empiricist, the "original beliefs" of the "school of intuition" are not rationalist. For the "intuitionists", such beliefs are "principles of common sense" and not products of the "inward light" of reason. (Though it is not clear Mill recognised this; as when he denies that there is "knowledge a priori; [i.e.] truths cognisable by the mind's inward light, and grounded on intuitive evidence".) Reid, Hume and Mill are all committed to naturalism; Hamilton, as we will see, seems to be simply confused.[10]

Mill had long felt there ought to be a "hand to hand fight" between the "two schools of philosophy, that of Intuition, and that of Experience and Association". In 1854 he expressed the intention of developing a philosophy which would succeed in "placing metaphysics and moral science on a basis of analysed experience, in opposition to the theory of innate principles".[11] Mill saw such innate principles as a bastion of conservative social thought, as his Autobiography makes clear. His alternative philosophy received its fullest expression in An Examination of Sir William Hamilton's Philosophy, which appeared in 1865.

Sir William Hamilton (1788–1856) was eminent, in Mill's eyes, as "the great fortress of the intuitional philosophy in this country". Given the subsequent sharp decline in his reputation, it is important to recognise that in the first half of the nineteenth century, Hamilton and Mill were the two most celebrated philosophical thinkers in Britain. It was the Examination, as its author correctly noted, that "reduced [Hamilton's] too great philosophical reputation within more moderate bounds".[12] In fact, as an early reviewer declared:

The whole fabric of the Hamiltonian philosophy is not only demolished, but its very stones are ground to powder. Where once stood Sebastopol bidding proud defiance to rival systems is now "a coast barren and blue/ Sandheaps behind and sandhills before."[13]

Though the "great fortress" of intuitionism turns out to be a rambling edifice, cobbled together in a patchwork of earlier styles, its most obvious structural defect lies in the treatment of the "relativity of human knowledge". Hamilton's philosophy may have been, as Mill says, "the latest form of the Reidian theory" (p. 110 – in fact it was the last). But Scottish common sense left Hamilton when he hit upon the quixotic enterprise of combining Reid's direct realism with Kant's critical philosophy. Hamilton's "Philosophy of the Conditioned" declared the "great axiom that all human knowledge . . . is only of the relative or phaenomenal", and that "we know nothing absolutely" – that our knowledge of mind and of matter is properly of phenomena, not substances.[14] As Mill recognised, this principle could hardly be reconciled with direct realism, and thus Hamilton's "synthesis" of Reid and Kant is quite unstable. It was the burden of Mill's criticism in the *Examination* that, despite his protestations, Hamilton never properly supported the "great axiom" at all.[15]

Mill himself holds to the relativity of knowledge unequivocally. He is totally antipathetic to direct realism. This position clearly goes together with his rejection of the view that belief in the external world is "intuitive". The relativity of knowledge rules out the possibility that we could be directly, non-inferentially aware of external objects:

We know no more of what they are, than the senses tell us, nor does nature afford us any means of knowing more. . . . our knowledge of objects . . . consist [s] of nothing but the sensations which they excite, or which we imagine them exciting, in ourselves. (pp. 5–6)

The relativity of knowledge is an *epistemological* doctrine. But it comes in two forms, Mill writes; and here he attaches distinct *ontological* claims to the epistemological doctrine. According to the first, preferred by philosophers of an "Idealist" persuasion – among whom it becomes apparent Mill numbers himself – an object is "but a complex conception made up by the laws of association. . . . There is nothing real . . . but these sensations". Sensations occur in fixed groups, but we have no evidence of any "substratum or hidden cause of sensations". This view virtually amounts to phenomenalism. According to the second, Kantian version of the doctrine, "there is a real universe of 'Things in Themselves' . . . but all we know [them] to be is merely relative to us, consisting in the power of affecting us in certain ways" (pp. 6–7). The term "phenomenalism" was not used by Mill or his contemporaries, but when it first appeared in the philosophical literature, it was, confusingly, to this latter view that it referred.[16]

Mill criticised Hamilton for conflating the weak sense of the doctrine, with which both "Idealists" and Kantians could agree, with the idealist interpretation Mill himself preferred. As regards its weak sense, Hamilton was indeed correct in regarding the "great axiom" as one that almost all philosophers accepted, at least "in modern times".[17] The philosophical situation as Mill found it was largely hostile not only to direct realism but also to what is now termed "scientific realism": the view that science can provide a route to the absolute nature of things. However, Mill was distinctive among his contemporaries in making the further commitment to phenomenalism.

The relativity of knowledge lies behind Mill's commitment to an ontology purely of sensations. His view is that since we can know nothing beyond our sensations, our knowledge of the external world cannot be knowledge of something "intrinsically distinct" from sensation. But although epistemological and ontological assumptions motivate Mill's attack on Hamilton's "intuitionism", Mill's ontology and epistemology were always kept largely implicit, and the connection is a veiled one. With the principle of the relativity of knowledge held in the background, we return to the foreground, Mill's detailed critique of Hamilton's intuitive "introspective method", where the debate is at least overtly on a psychological level, concerning how our beliefs in an external world arise. It is in the course of this critique that full-fledged phenomenalism makes its undramatic first appearance.

II. THE "PSYCHOLOGICAL" VERSUS THE "INTROSPECTIVE" THEORY CONCERNING BELIEF IN AN EXTERNAL WORLD

The terms of the Mill–Hamilton debate may seem arcane, but they have important echoes in current discussion of the *a priori*, for instance by Christopher Peacocke.[18] Hamilton's "introspective" theory scrutinised our beliefs to arrive at the ones which are "irresistible", hence "innate", and therefore "intuitive" or legitimate. Belief in matter or in an external world is one such belief. Mill rejects the move from irresistible to innate, as we will see. But he seems not to question the subsequent move from irresistible and innate to legitimate – this was Reid's line of argument as given above. Certainly some of what he says indicates that he accepts this argument:

Could we try the experiment of the first consciousness in any infant – its first reception of the impressions which we call external; whatever was present in that first consciousness would be the genuine testimony of consciousness, and . . . there would be as little possibility of discrediting it, as our sensations themselves. (p. 140)

Furthermore, Mill does argue from the unavoidability and inexplicability of certain basic principles directly to their legitimacy, notably in the case of memory, as we will see. Against this, however, are passages where Mill insists that "a conviction might be really innate . . . and yet not be true".[19] Nor does Mill ever explain *why* the "testimony of consciousness" concerning our original convictions should bestow legitimacy on them – a question that will surely strike the modern reader. (Compare Peacocke: "Even though a transition is primitively compelling, we can still raise the philosophical question of whether what we find primitively compelling can also be justified".[20])

Mill wants to argue that, though apparently "irresistible", belief in an external world is not "intuitive" or legitimate. His use of the term "intuitive" will not be clear to modern readers either, and is in itself rather obscure (as becomes evident when Mill moves on to the self). "Intuitive knowledge" for Mill is immediate knowledge – what seems "unavoidable" or "necessary" – and he regards immediate knowledge derived from sensory experience, or from memory, as "intuitive". But "we certainly do not know by intuition" – "by mere introspection of ourselves" – "what knowledge is intuitive" (pp. 136, 138). We must first exclude the possibility that the belief in question is an "acquired product".[21] For this reason, Mill may conflate "original" or innate with "intuitive"; though the two kinds of expression may be co-extensional, the first is meant to be a psychological notion and the second an epistemic one. "Intuitive" for Mill should properly be paraphrased "compelling and not explicable as an acquired belief" – in Peacocke's terminology, "primitively compelling". (For more on Mill's epistemology, see the Introduction to this volume, section II.)

So although epistemology is "the interpretation of Consciousness" (p. 110), Mill's objection to Hamilton's "school of intuition" is that it takes a too simple view of this interpretation. The kernel of the dispute is that, according to Mill, beliefs that *appear* intuitive – i.e. that are "irresistible" – are mistakenly regarded *as* intuitive, because the possibility that they are an "acquired product" is not considered. Mill's own "psychological" theory, in contrast, shows how a belief, though possessing "the character of necessity", *could* have been acquired through experience. Thus in ch. IX of the *Examination* Mill outlines the view that "the laws of association . . . are capable of creating, out of those data of consciousness which are uncontested [viz. sensations], purely mental conceptions, which become so identified in thought with all our states of consciousness, that we seem, and cannot but seem, to receive them by direct intuition". The belief in matter may be one such "mental conception":

Idealists, and Sceptics, contend that the belief in Matter is not an original fact of consciousness, as our sensations are, and is therefore wanting in the requisite which, in . . . Sir W. Hamilton's opinion, gives to our subjective convictions objective authority. (p. 140)

If the belief in matter is not innate, then by Hamilton's lights it cannot be "objective", i.e. imply an external world over and above sensations. This is precisely what Mill the idealist goes on to argue.

Mill focuses on matter and mind in ch. X of the *Examination*, which, in line with the generally negative tone of the work, is an attack on "Sir William Hamilton's View of the Different Theories Respecting the Belief in an External World". Mill painstakingly surveys these archaically named theories, from Reid's "natural realism" to "absolute idealism" via "cosmothetic idealism". (The latter is really indirect or representative realism, so maybe Mill should have termed it "cosmetic idealism".) It is hard not to become impatient when Mill criticises Hamilton's criticism of Brown's interpretation of Reid; the "stones" of the Hamiltonian philosophy are certainly being "ground to powder" here.[22]

The upshot of the famous chapter that follows, ch. XI, "The Psychological Theory of the Belief in an External World", is that, contrary to Hamilton, the belief is "not intuitive, but an acquired product" (p. 177). The formation of our perceptual judgments is explicable, Mill argues, *without* assuming that we perceive anything but sensations; this is what leads him to phenomenalism. His "psychological theory" will show how, "supposing no intuition of an external world to have existed in consciousness", the belief in one would inevitably be generated, and would mistakenly be regarded as "intuitive" (p. 178).

But what do we mean when we say "the objects we perceive are external to us, and not a part of our own thoughts?"

We mean, that there is concerned in our perceptions something which exists when we are not thinking of it; which existed before we had ever thought of it, and would exist if we were annihilated; and further, that there exist things which we never saw, touched, or otherwise perceived, and things which never have been perceived by man. This idea of something which is . . . fixed and the same, while our impressions vary . . . and which is always square (or of some other given figure) whether it appears to us square or round – constitutes altogether our idea of external substance. (pp. 178–79)

Mill then turns to the question of acquisition, and develops his "Psychological Theory". It is based on the premises of "Expectation" – that "after having had actual sensations, we are capable of forming the conception of Possible sensations" – and "Association of Ideas" (pp. 177–78). Mill's story is that processes of association operate on the notion of contingent or possible sensations, to generate the "complex conception" of external objects or substance just outlined. The essence of association, as Mill understands it, is this:

"When two phaenomena have been very often experienced in conjunction . . . it is impossible to think the one thing disjoined from
the other"; as a result, "the facts . . . answering to those ideas come
at last to seem inseparable in existence", and "the belief we have
in their coexistence, though really a product of experience, seems
intuitive" (pp. 177–78).

Possible sensations are sensations which are not and individually
never were in our consciousness, "but which . . . we know that we
should have felt under given supposable circumstances, and under
these same circumstances, might still feel" (p. 179). It is features of
the concept of possible sensations which, Mill argues, lead by association to the generation of the concept of permanent, external
objects. First, the possibilities are "conditional certainties", not
"vague possibilities" (p. 180). Mill has in mind the following: I
confidently expect, on the basis of past experience, that if I were to
experience certain sequences of sensation associated with approach-
ing a strong flame, I would then experience a sensation of burning
pain. While the conditional could never be a certainty, Mill's
point is that it is more than a mere epistemic possibility. "Guaranteed or certified" is a better description than "permanent", since
there is change in the possibilities whenever there is change in the
external world. (Mill seems to think there is no circularity in this
formulation.)

Furthermore, these "certified or guaranteed possibilities" refer to
groups of actual and possible sensations, between which there is a
fixed "Order of succession" which gives rise to the ideas of cause
and effect. Therefore it is the possible sensations which become
most important to me: "My present sensations are generally of little
importance, and are moreover fugitive: the possibilities, on the
contrary, are permanent, which is the character that mainly distinguishes our idea of Substance or Matter from our notion of sensation" (p. 180).

The possibilities are therefore regarded by us as grounding a common, public world – they "present the character of objectivity" (p.
184). Mill evidently believes his account avoids the multiple private
worlds implicit in Berkeley's idealism:

The permanent possibilities are common to us and to our fellow-creatures;
the actual sensations are not. . . . The world of Possible Sensations succeed-

ing one another according to laws, is as much in other beings as it is in me; it has therefore an existence outside me; it is an External World. (pp. 181–82)

What is important for our everyday beliefs is the converse of what is ontologically basic: "The sensations, though the original foundation of the whole, come to be looked upon as a sort of accident depending on us, and the possibilities as much more real than the actual sensations. . . ." (p. 181). Thus it is that any sensation experienced is regarded as belonging to a group of actual and possible sensations, which is itself mistaken for, or regarded as, a permanent, external object.

Mill believes he has now refuted Hamilton's introspective account, since on the latter's principle of "Parcimony", "Where there is a known cause adequate to account for a phenomenon, there is not justification for ascribing it to an unknown one" (p. 183). (Mill's theory is extended in ch. XIII, "The Psychological Theory of the Primary Qualities of Matter".) The psychological theory accounts for our belief in an external world, so there is no reason to regard that belief as innate. Thus the idea of permanent possibilities of sensation starts out, for Mill, as part of an explanation of our belief in an external world; it is part of the *cause* of our belief. To reiterate, Mill is explaining how possibilities of sensations come to be mistaken for or, more neutrally, regarded as, permanently existing external objects.

The more neutral formulation seems advisable because of the rather different use to which Mill subsequently puts the concept of possibilities of sensation. This concept comes to figure in the *definition* of the belief in external objects: "Matter, then, may be defined as the Permanent Possibility of Sensation" (p. 183). Only at this point does Mill's account become genuinely phenomenalist, offering a *semantic* rather than a *psychological* analysis. Mill's subjunctive conditionals now come to constitute what may be regarded as the first developed statement of the modern phenomenalist analysis of "material object statements". According to this analysis, statements such as "There is a table in the next room" are equivalent in meaning to "If X were in such-and-such circumstances (in the next room), then he or she would have so-and-so (table-like) perceptual experiences". (Further analysis, including elimination of the subject, is required. As Ayer notes, phenomenalists tend not to be very specific here, preferring "more or less vague descriptions of how such translations might run".[23]) This analysis is a semantic implementation of the defining ontology of phenomenalism – that all that exists are sensations and the possibilities thereof.

III. COMPETING STRANDS IN MILL'S ACCOUNT: "ERROR THEORY", PHENOMENALISM AND ONTOLOGICAL NEUTRALITY

Before exploring further this semantic turn in Mill's treatment, it will be useful to explore the options open to him. Skorupski's succinct analysis points up the alternatives that Mill should have recognised:

The inference required from pure sensings to mind-independent physical objects cannot possibly be recognised in Mill's inductivist logic of truth. So Mill must either accept that we have no grounds at all for any beliefs about external objects, or must reject the assumption that physical objects are mind-independent.[24]

(Direct realists, in contrast, will question the starting point in "pure sensings", perhaps denying that there is any such category.) Certainly Mill rejects the initial inference from "pure sensings" to "mind-independent physical objects". He is clear that his psychological theory does not constitute a *legitimation* of our belief in an external world – construed as a belief in the supposed hidden causes of sensations. Concerning that belief he writes, "I am only accounting for it; and to do so I assume only the tendency, but not the legitimacy of the tendency, to extend all the laws of our own experience to a sphere beyond our experience" (p. 187n). Such a legitimation would run counter to Mill's account of inductive inference.

But which of the ensuing alternatives indicated by Skorupski does he espouse? I will argue that, depending on the sense in which "external object" is taken, Mill may be seen as pursuing both alternatives – though I will also argue that this is not an explicit strategy on his part. In one sense – that in which "external object" denotes a "hidden cause of our sensations" – he holds that we have no grounds for our beliefs. To that extent he advocates what is nowadays termed an "error theory" – a theory explaining how our mistaken beliefs arise. This is the account suggested by Mill's psychological theory as just outlined. But in another sense, in which "external objects" are *not* in "a sphere beyond our experience", he holds that talk of them is not erroneous. It simply amounts to, i.e. is perhaps to be reduced to, talk of mind-dependent entities, viz. possibilities of sensation – though as we will see in the next section, Mill is ambivalent on how "mind-dependent" the possibilities actually are.

But what *do* we believe? In claiming that all that exists are sensations and, perhaps, possibilities of sensation, phenomenalism, like idealism, seems to conflict with common sense. Berkeley, however, saw himself as a friend to common sense, outraged by the allegedly sceptical consequences that can be drawn from Locke's realist philosophy (and were, by Hume). Mill, though less explicit on this question, took the same position. It is a sentiment common among phenomenalists that there is a conflict with common sense only insofar as ordinary people are seduced by the views of realist philosophers. Mill's view seems to be that there is an error in what people say they think, rather than in what they actually do think; but he is far from clear on the matter.

This equivocation reinforces the feeling that there are two competing tendencies in Mill's account, those of eighteenth-century psychological analysis, and what would become twentieth-century semantic analysis. The latter tendency – what is sometimes called "linguistic" phenomenalism – treats Mill's subjunctive conditionals as "meaning-equivalences", and may therefore be viewed as an attempted "vindication", or perhaps a reduction, of ordinary discourse. Russell, for instance, taking "sense-data" as certain, tried to justify common-sense beliefs in material objects by showing that they involve "logical constructions" from such data.[25] Thus modern phenomenalists, assuming the falsity of direct realism, try to bridge the logical gap between a subjective "given" and an external world. On their view, the question of whether external objects exist does not arise. In contrast, psychological analyses have a tendency towards "error theory", explaining *away* the ordinary conception of external objects as "imaginary" or mistaken. (Whether the semantic analysis of "linguistic" phenomenalism involves a "reduction" depends on one's understanding of that dubious concept, of which there are as many varieties as Heinz tinned foods; if "reduction" implies elimination there may be a tendency towards an error theory.)

Returning now to Mill's discussion, we see how it exhibits tendencies both of "error theory" and semantic analysis. As outlined so far, his account has largely invited an "error theory". Mill has argued that belief in an external world is acquired and so has no "objective authority". The permanent possibilities of sensation are "what leads us to say" that there are external objects; a psychological, not a semantic analysis. However, Mill has also claimed that the possibilities of sensation *constitute* "an External World", and what he now says suggests that he *does* believe that the Possibilities are "what we mean" when we talk of external objects. Mill seems to think he is stating a conclusion when he gives his famous definition:

Matter, then, may be defined as the Permanent Possibility of Sensation. If I am asked, whether I believe in matter, I ask whether the questioner accepts this definition of it. If he does, I believe in matter; and so do all Berkeleians. In any other sense than this, I do not. But I affirm with confidence, that this conception of Matter includes the *whole meaning attached to it by the common world*, apart from philosophical, and sometimes from theological, theories. The reliance of mankind on the real existence of visible and tangible objects, means reliance on the reality and permanence of Possibilities of visual and tactual sensations, when no such sensations are actually experienced. (p. 183, my emphasis)

But the conclusion doesn't follow. The psychological theory doesn't show that matter may be *defined* as the permanent possibility of sensation. It may, however, granting Mill's further inductivist assumptions, show that matter does not *exist*. When he writes, "If I am asked, whether I believe in matter . . .", Mill clearly assumes such ontological implications will be drawn. He makes the same assumption in a further defence of his new, phenomenalist definition of "matter":

I believe that Calcutta exists, though I do not perceive it, and that it would still exist if every percipient inhabitant were suddenly to leave the place, or be struck dead. But when I analyse the belief, all I find in it is, that were these events to take place, the Permanent Possibility of Sensation which I call Calcutta would still remain; that if I were suddenly transported to the banks of the Hoogly, I should still have the sensations which, if now present, would lead me to affirm that Calcutta exists here and now. We may infer, therefore, that both philosophers and the world at large, when they think of matter, conceive it really as a Permanent Possibility of Sensation. (p. 184)

However, "the majority of philosophers fancy it is something more; and the world at large, though they have really, as I conceive, nothing in their minds but a Permanent Possibility of Sensation, would, if asked the question, undoubtedly agree with the philosophers". So Mill now makes explicit his "error theory", whereby the association of ideas explains *away* the belief in a strictly fictional matter:

There is . . . no psychological obstacle to our forming the notion of a something which is neither a sensation nor a possibility of sensation [i.e. the notion of substance], even if our consciousness does not testify to it; and nothing is more likely than that the Permanent Possibilities of sensation, to which our consciousness does testify, should be confounded in our minds with this imaginary conception. (p. 185)

So there is an error in what people say, and also in some sense in what they think, Mill maintains. This stance is echoed elsewhere. In the essay on Berkeley discussed above, Mill agrees with his hero that "the common notion of matter" is an "illusion". And in a letter to Herbert Spencer, he writes that "sensations, memories of sensations, and expectations of sensation . . . I maintain . . . are the only substratum I need to postulate; and that when anything else seems postulated, it is only because of the erroneous theory on which all our language is constructed". Instead, Mill suggests, "the concrete words used [should be] interpreted as meaning our expectations of sensations".[26]

The "psychological theory", to reiterate, seems to specify three processes: (i) expectation generates the idea of possibilities of sensation; (ii) through the association of ideas, the possibilities of sensation come to be regarded as "permanent"; (iii) the pernicious idea of a "hidden cause" or "mysterious substratum" is developed. The last of these surely implies an "error theory". However, in the Appendix that Mill added in the third and fourth editions (1867 and 1872), even this becomes unclear:

[My opponents] forget that to go into a room, to be asleep or awake, are expressions which have a meaning in the Psychological Theory as well as in theirs; that every assertion that can be made about the external world, which means anything on the Realistic theory, has a parallel meaning on the Psychological. [The latter] forms as vast and variegated a picture of the universe as can be had on the other theory; indeed, as I maintain, the very same picture. . . . (p. 197; this claim is reiterated on p. 198)

Note how the "Psychological Theory" is now being contrasted with the "Realist" rather than the "introspective" theory, indicating a new direction of interest. The realist theory – that which postulates substance "as a support for phaenomena, or as a bond of connexion to hold a group . . . of otherwise unconnected phaenomena together" – is not declared erroneous, but is held to offer "the same picture" as the psychological theory. These comments introduce a novel and sophisticated form of reduction, if it is reduction at all – the ontological neutrality later advocated by Mach, Carnap and Schlick.

On the most developed statement of this view, the conflict between phenomenalism and other metaphysical positions, and that between these and common sense, are empty of content. As Carnap wrote: "the realistic and the [phenomenalist or physicalist] constructional languages have actually the same meaning. . . . [Once they are] recognized as nothing but two different languages which express the same state of affairs, several, perhaps even most, epistemological disputes become pointless". Schlick, in the course of defining the "problem of the external world" as a pseudo-problem, argued that Mill, like Berkeley, "was not wanting to deny the reality of physical objects, but rather to explain it, when he declared them to be 'permanent possibilities of sensation'" – though he did think Mill's mode of expression to be "unsuitably chosen".[27] Mill, like Carnap in this respect, was an irenic philosopher, seeking to harmonise apparently rival metaphysical positions, drawing the line at the objectionable "school of intuition"; hence his tendency to write like a "self-appointed Royal Commission".[28] The irenic attitude is one of the roots of ontological neutralism; it also generates many of the ambiguities we are trying to elucidate.

Ontological neutrality is only adumbrated in Mill, and required verificationism to bring it into sharper focus. It is apparent not only in the remarks on the "two pictures", but also in Mill's claim that the "practical consequences" of his and the realist accounts are the same (see e.g. p. 183). This claim has led Skorupski to argue, in his portrayal of what appears to be a "Thoroughly Modern Mill", that the ambivalences in Mill's account result from a coherent distinction between the "literal meaning" of statements about the external world and their "practical content".[29] Skorupski maintains that Mill *does*, contrary to my earlier claim, explicitly implement a two-pronged strategy – the possibilities of sensation capture the "practical content" of the idea of substance, while the psychological account explains *away* the strictly literal but pernicious notion of the "external cause" or "propertyless substratum". Hence Mill intends *both* meaning-equivalence *and* an error theory.

The "two pictures" account would not, on this view, imply meaning-equivalence between the ostensibly rival "theories". Rather, it would imply that the idea of an external cause of sensation is "functionally redundant" in our thinking.[30] That is, when Mill asserts that the concepts of the possibilities and of external objects are equivalent, he is thinking of their "practical content" – as when he says that Hamilton "knew that the belief on which all the practical consequences depend, is the belief in the Permanent Possibilities of Sensation" (p. 183). In the *System of Logic*, in contrast, so this story goes, Mill is concerned with literal meaning, and claims that the names which make up propositions about the external world denote the external causes of our sensations, and connote the attributes of those causes. Hence: "A body, according to the received doctrine of modern metaphysicians, may be defined, the external cause to which we ascribe our sensations".[31] Mill is concerned in the *Logic* to demarcate logic from metaphysics, and claims that "every essential doctrine [there] could stand equally well" with rival metaphysical positions (p. 62n) (though the *Logic* would have to be made consistent with the relativity of knowledge).

No doubt there is some such distinction between "practical" and "literal" content in Mill's mind in ch. XI. But it cannot be maintained that Mill has a clear grip on the two-pronged strategy. (What one makes of Mill's alleged use of the distinction partly depends on whether one believes there *is* one, of course – denied by Wittgenstein in the *Philosophical Investigations*.) Mill refers to a variety of objects of belief without clearly separating them into pernicious and anodyne: "non-ego", "matter", "body", "external substance", "a kind of permanent substratum", "that the objects we perceive are external to us, and not part of our thoughts", "an existence transcending all possibilities of sensation" (p. 185), "the supposed hidden causes of our sensations", "a mysterious substratum" (p. 192). (Similarly with Mach; see below.) There is one crucial conflation, to be pursued below, between "external substance" – which includes other minds – and "matter". For instance, Mill writes in the review of Berkeley quoted above that Berkeley saw how "*to us* the external object is nothing but such a potentiality" – when he should have said "material object".

So it remains preferable to talk of competing tendencies in Mill's account, rather than an explicit strategy of combining them. Mill's position is transitional between eighteenth-century psychological explanation and twentieth-century semantic analysis. His avowed intention in the *Examination* is psychological: the rejection of "intuition". But it is possible that he had developed his views in the period between the *Logic* and the *Examination*, so that the second, reductive strategy increasingly comes to the fore.[32] Though he seems very pleased with his "psychological theory", Mill's account of the process of acquisition of belief is in fact very sketchy. Perhaps, at this late stage in his career, he was losing interest in his eighteenth-century associationist heritage; if the "possibilities of sensation" themselves constitute an objective world, there is less need for an associationist theory.[33]

The ambiguous status of the possibilities is another reason for denying that Mill clearly implements Skorupski's two-pronged strategy. "Mind-dependent" possibilities are not the clear practical import of our beliefs about the external world; for Mill wants the possibilities *both* to be "mind-dependent" *and* (somehow) to constitute an "objective world". His attempts to vindicate this requirement are the topic of the next section.

IV. MILL'S ONTOLOGY AND THE POSSIBILITIES OF SENSATION

Mill does have an "ontology of sensations" – he could hardly be a phenomenalist if he didn't. But in contrast to Berkeley's ontology of ideas and spirits, it is surprisingly uninfluential in his philosophy. A central justification for his ontology, the relativity of knowledge, is not mentioned in chs. XI and XII. His irenic attitude in any case leads him to circumspection in stating it, most notably in the *System of Logic*. Mill writes that "it was soon acknowledged by all who reflected on the subject, that the existence of matter cannot be proved by extrinsic evidence. The answer, therefore, now usually made to Berkeley and his followers, is that the belief is intuitive" (this is Hamilton's answer).

> But although the extreme doctrine of the Idealist metaphysicians, that objects are nothing but our sensations and the laws which connect them, has not been generally adopted . . . the point of most real importance is one on which those metaphysicians are now very generally considered to have made out their case: viz. that *all we know* of objects is the sensations they give us, and the order of the occurrence of those sensations.[34]

Here, the relativity of knowledge – "*all we know* of objects is the sensations they give us" – is regarded as more important than claims about what objects *are*. In contrast to this reticence, the ontological implications of the psychological theory are most clearly spelled out in the Appendix to chs. XI and XII of the *Examination*, where Mill writes that he has "shown that in order to account for the belief in Matter, or, in other words, in a non-ego supposed to be presented in or along with sensation, it is not necessary to suppose anything but sensations and possibilities of sensation connected in groups" (p. 204).

But what *is* it to "suppose . . . possibilities of sensation connected in groups"? Surely it is only *actual*, not *possible*, sensations that can be said to exist. There is in Mill's discussion a pervasive ambiguity on this question. It may be that the only coherent account of the possibilities of sensation will regard them as objects of belief had by minds (themselves analysable as groups of actual and possible sensations). But many commentators have recognised an obscure pull in Mill's account towards "reifying" the possibilities. This tendency perhaps goes with Mill's declining interest in associationism and hence in an error theory. It is expressed in his claim that the possibilities are objective and "independent of our will, our presence, and everything which belongs to us":

> the Permanent Possibilities are external to us in the only sense we need care about; they are not constructed by the mind itself, but merely recognised by it; in Kantian language, they are *given* to us, and to other beings in common with us. (p. 187n)

It may be that on close inspection, some passages which suggest a "reifying" interpretation turn out to be part of Mill's psychological story of how we acquire belief in an external world. But at least one early critic, Hugh O'Hanlon, was led to pose a dilemma for Mill between "Pure Idealism" and mind-independence of the possibilities; Mill patronises his "young antagonist", but his response is obscure and inadequate (p. 203n).

Among proponents of the reifying interpretation was H. H. Price, who felt Mill must maintain that the possibilities are "real *in some sense*", that they "subsist". In this he agreed with one of the most eminent nineteenth-century critics of Mill's phenomenalism, Josiah Royce. But as Royce asked, in common with many after him, "What kind of unreal reality is this potential actuality?" (Royce's Absolute Idealist response was that "all the conceived 'possible experiences' are actual in a Consciousness of which we suppose nothing but that it knows these experiences. . . .") In response to such doubts, McCloskey very sensibly comments: "One cannot have possibilities of mental sensations existing in the absence of all else; the apparent sense of the statement rests on the unspoken assumption that the possibilities are some sort of dispositional property of the mind".[35]

Hence the second interpretation, assumed by Skorupski and others: the possibilities are "certified beliefs" had by minds, and it is *we* who "reify" them, as the "psychological theory" shows. This interpretation is supported by Mill's assertion, in his review of Berkeley, that the possibilities "are not a positive entity . . . they did not exist as sensations, but as a guaranteed belief".[36] But what is the status of minds, and the implication for the ontological commitment of phenomenalism? There are two possible positions to take here. On the first, minds are a category distinct from, and perhaps more fundamental than, sensations; on the second, minds are constructions from sensations.

The first view implies that there is a question: "in virtue of what are the conditional statements which express the possibilities true?" And the answer suggested is: in virtue of the categorical properties of minds. It is notable, however, that the question "In virtue of what . . . ?" is not one that Mill shows any signs of addressing. Should he have addressed it? I think not, since the question suggests an appeal to a category more ontologically basic than sensations. The true phenomenalist ought to reject any grounding for the subjunctive conditionals.

This is not an interpretation that is universally accepted. Winkler, for instance, writes of Berkeley's "phenomenalism":

> if Berkeley is a phenomenalist he is a theocentric one, who grounds the existence of perceptions, actual and possible, in the will of God. . . . The difference between the perception and phenomenalist interpretations of Berkeley's views on unperceived objects . . . is not that the former assigns a role to God while the latter does not, but that the former emphasizes God's role as perceiver, and the latter his role as agent.[37]

But talk of "grounding" the existence of possibilities of perception has the effect of collapsing phenomenalism into idealism. If Mill is serious about his ontology, the subjunctive conditionals should be ontologically ungrounded, and "barely" true. This is not to say that *particular* subjunctive conditionals have no inductively based evidential support, though formulating this support is problematic in itself. (Compare the claim that statements about mental states are true in virtue of statements about brain-states – mind-brain identity – and the distinct claim that the evidence for the former is behavioural. But the issue is far from straightforward.)

The phenomenalist viewpoint is strange but distinctive. It expresses a curiously insubstantial, indeed "magical" solution to the problem of the external world which arises on an assumption of the relativity of knowledge. Since phenomenalists must regard regularities in sensations simply as "brute" facts, the most fundamental laws of nature will concern mental entities (sensations). Intractable problems of generating an objective world and understanding our scientific knowledge of it result from this picture. For instance, if the conditionals are ungrounded and barely true, it seems inexplicable how one conditional may be inferred from another – that if it is true that "If I go into the next room, I will have an experience as of a table" then it seems to follow, other things beings equal, that it is also true that "If you go into the next room, you will have an experience as of a table". More fundamentally, the phenomenalist understanding of a world in which there happen to be no minds appears sophistical.[38] Given such difficulties, it is no surprise that many have sought to find a basis for the subjunctive conditionals – at the cost, I claim, of the disappearance of phenomenalism.

Hence the phenomenalist is compelled to adopt the position that minds are constructions from sensations, and thus has to attempt a dual construction of both matter *and* mind. Only if there is this dual construction can the phenomenalist avoid sliding into a non-phenomenalist idealism. Mill's extension of the psychological theory from matter to mind in ch. XII constitutes such an attempt, as is suggested when he says that he is entitled to imply an Ego in the notion of Expectation, since "up to this stage it is not Self, but Body, that I have been endeavouring to trace to its origin as an acquired notion" (p. 203). This aim, however, and with it the ontology of sensations, is impeded, and in the end fatally undermined, by understandable Berkeleian tendencies, as I will now argue.

V. THE "PSYCHOLOGICAL THEORY" AS APPLIED TO MIND

The points of comparison in Mill's account of mind or the self are Berkeley and Hume. Mill's tendency to conflate mind and self results from his precursors' neglect of the subject's embodiment, though he himself is less guilty here. If embodiment is not recognised as an essential feature of the subject's situation, the analysis of self and mind seems to converge. At first sight Mill's account echoes Hume's – the rejection of minds as substances, an explanation of how we mistake a bundle (or in Mill's case, series) of perceptions for a substantial self, and a final perplexity about the status of the rejection.

But on further inspection, there are affinities with Berkeley's view of the mind as substantial. These are implicit from the outset in Mill's postulation of other minds, for reasons that will become apparent. He denies that "the real externality to us of anything, *except other minds*, is capable of proof" (p. 187n; my emphasis), and goes on to offer a proof, lacking in Berkeley, of the existence of other minds. Indeed, Mill was probably the first philosopher properly to recognise the problem of other minds that arises from a "relativity of knowledge" or Cartesian starting point. His "argument from analogy" is rightly regarded as the classic statement of a "Cartesian solution" – one which addresses the problem on its own Cartesian terms rather than attempting to "dissolve" it, as Ryle and Wittgenstein were to do. Together with the definition of matter as "the permanent possibility of sensation", it is the best-known passage in the *Examination*.

Mill seems to see no inconsistency between the series account and the postulation of other minds; why they are inconsistent will be explored below. These conflicting aspects will be apparent as his account is outlined. It certainly *begins* like Hume's. Mill asks whether "we already have in our consciousness the conception of Self as a permanent existence; or whether it is formed subsequently" (not quite Hume's question, admittedly, but the answer is Humean):

our knowledge of mind, like that of matter, is entirely relative. . . . We have no conception of Mind itself, as distinguished from its conscious manifestations. We neither know nor can imagine it, except as represented by the succession of manifold feelings which metaphysicians call by the name of States or Modifications of Mind. (pp. 188–89)

(Note that it is "metaphysicians", not Mill himself, who view sensations as "States of Mind" rather than as ontologically basic.) However, our *notion* of mind, like that of matter, is that of

a permanent something, contrasted with the perpetual flux of the sensations and other feelings or mental states which we refer to it. . . . The belief I entertain that my mind exists when it is not feeling, nor thinking, nor conscious of its own existence, resolves itself into the belief of a Permanent Possibility of these states. (p. 189)

Mind itself, however, is

nothing but the series of our sensations . . . as they actually occur, with the addition of infinite possibilities of feeling requiring for their actual realization conditions which may or may not take place, but which as possibilities are always in existence, and many of them present. (p. 189)

The terms of this account, and its unclarities, are familiar from Mill's treatment of matter. He goes on to note disanalogies between the notions of self and the notion of matter. In contrast to matter, interestingly, "My notion of Myself . . . includes all possibilities of sensation . . . certified by experience or not, which I may imagine inserted in the series of my actual and conscious states"; and most importantly, this series is "confined to myself", and is not shared with others (p. 189). This last claim leads into the most significant difference between the two accounts, in that Mill holds that inferences to other minds *are* justified, while those to matter are not. This is brought out in his response to Reid's objection that if Hume's theory were correct, I would have no evidence "of the existence of my fellow-creatures". Mill responds that "All that I am compelled to admit . . . is that other people's Selves also are but series of feelings, like my own" (p. 190).

So how do I know that there are other minds? Even "the most strenuous Intuitionist" must recognise that it is not by "direct intuition". (Reid would dispute this claim.) Mill now states his famous argument from analogy to the existence of other minds. It marks an important advance on Hume's discussion in its recognition of the different grounds of first- and third-person judgments, and of the importance of embodiment:

I conclude that other human beings have feelings like me, because, first, they have bodies like me, which I know, in my own case, to be the antecedent condition of feelings; and because, secondly, they exhibit the acts, and other outward signs, which in my own case I know by experience to be caused by feelings. I am conscious in myself of a series of facts connected by an uniform sequence, of which the beginning is modifications of my body, the middle is feelings, the end is outward demeanour. In the case of other human beings I have the evidence of my senses for the first and last links of the series, but not for the intermediate link. I find, however, that the sequence between the first and last is as regular and constant in these other cases as it is in mine. (p. 191)

(In his Appendix, Mill gives a better account of this process, properly relativised to his conditional analysis [p. 204n].) So Mill believes that in the case of mind, unlike that of matter, an account of *how* we infer to other minds, *does* legitimate that "inference". By Mill's own canons of inductivist logic, however, this is no more a "good . . . inductive process" than is the inference to matter. He overlooks this problem because, for reasons that will become apparent, it is essential for him to legitimate the belief in other minds.

To reiterate, Mill seems to think that the postulation of other minds is quite consistent with a series account. But from this point on, for reasons that are obscure, he backtracks over the psychological theory of mind. He now sees "intrinsic difficulties" which seem "beyond the power of metaphysical analysis to resolve":

The thread of consciousness which composes the mind's phaenomenal life, consists not only of present sensations, but likewise, in part, of memories and expectations. . . . In themselves, [these] are present feelings. . . . But they are attended with the peculiarity, that each of them involves a belief in more than its own present existence . . . [a belief] that I myself formerly had, or that I myself, and no other, shall hereafter have, the sensations remembered or expected. (pp. 193–94)

Hence if the mind is a series of feelings, it is one which "is aware of itself as past and future". This involves the "paradox" that "something which . . . is but a series of feelings, can be aware of itself as a series".

The result, Mill believes, is fatal for his theory:

we are here face to face with that final inexplicability, at which, as Sir W. Hamilton observes, we inevitably arrive when we reach ultimate facts. . . . The real stumbling block is perhaps not in any theory of the fact, but in the fact itself. The true incomprehensibility perhaps is, that something which has ceased, or is not yet in existence, can still be, in a manner, present: that a series of feelings, the infinitely greater part of which is past or future, can be gathered up, as it were, into a single present conception, accompanied by a belief of reality. I think, by far the wisest thing we can do, is to accept the inexplicable fact, without any theory of how it takes place. . . . (p. 194)

This was not wise enough for many commentators. F. H. Bradley sneered that when Mill had "the same fact before him, which gave the lie to his whole psychological theory, he could not ignore it, he could not recognize it, he would not call it a fiction; so he put it aside as a 'final inexplicability', and thought, I suppose, that by covering it with a phrase he got rid of its existence". William James referred to "the *definitive bankruptcy of the associationist description of the consciousness of self*", commenting that "Mr. Mill's habitual method of philosophizing was to affirm boldly some general doctrine derived from his father, and then make so many concessions of detail to its enemies as practically to abandon it altogether".[39]

Contemporary protests, no doubt less eloquently expressed, led Mill to expand on his apparent non-conclusion in the Appendix added to the third and fourth editions. Here he argues that, despite his retractions, he is still not compelled to accept the ego as "an original presentation of consciousness" (p. 207). He may be correct to say that he has not accepted "the common theory of Mind, as a so-called Substance" (p. 206), but he is certainly close to doing so, and clearly advocates a *non-reductive* account. That is, the self is not merely a series of sensations tied together by processes of association; there is a "real tie" between the present memory-impression and the original sensation of which it is a "copy or representation":

the inexplicable tie . . . which connects the present consciousness with the past one, of which it reminds me, is as near as I think we can get to a positive conception of Self. That there is something real in this tie, real as the sensations themselves, and not a mere product of the laws of thought without any fact corresponding to it, I hold to be indubitable. (p. 207)

I ascribe a reality to the Ego – to my own Mind – different from that real existence as a Permanent Possibility, which is the only reality I acknowledge in Matter: and by fair experiential inference from that one Ego, I ascribe the same reality to other Egoes, or Minds.

This wonderfully equivocating passage illustrates Mill's ambivalent treatment of the possibilities. Matter has a "real existence" as permanent possibility; but as this is the "only reality" Mill acknowledges in matter, it is clearly an inferior kind of "real existence" to that which he now postulates for mind! Nonetheless, Mill is confident he has "more clearly defined my position in regard to the Ego, considered as a question of Ontology", though he insists, very dubiously given his concessions, that "the Mind is only known to itself phaenomenally, as the series of its feelings of consciousness" (p. 208).

Mill is agnostic over what form a non-reductive account should take – whether we are "directly conscious of [a self] in the act of remembrance", or whether "according to the opinion of Kant, we . . . are [merely] compelled to assume it as a necessary condition of Memory" (p. 207). But although he cannot countenance "Transcendentalism", his final view does have affinities with Kant's "unity of consciousness" account, as will become apparent. (The nature of the "real tie" will also be further explored below.) Whatever form it takes, a non-reductive account cannot admit sensations as ontologically basic, and so is incompatible with phenomenalism as I have defined it – indeed there is a question whether it can admit sensations as objects at all, rather than as "states of mind". (The problem of the relation of mind and sensations has been much discussed in connection with Berkeley, and will not be pursued here.[40])

Mill's "final inexplicability" echoes Hume's confession of failure in his own Appendix to the *Treatise*, even if the tone appears unduly complacent rather than troubled. Hume was forced to concede that either a "real connexion" between perceptions or an ego in which they inhere is required; but "plead[s] the privilege of a sceptic", confessing "this difficulty is too hard for my understanding".[41] His reasons for abandoning the bundle theory are notoriously obscure; Mill's recantation is almost as compressed and obscure as Hume's. Both writers, perhaps, suspect that a yawning chasm is opening up around their philosophical viewpoint, and would prefer not to peer into it.

But the parallels should not be overstated. Although the series account may resemble Hume's as commonly understood, it is a "reinvention" of it, for reasons noted above. (Maybe it is association of ideas that causes us to confuse the two associationist theories, and regard them as one object with a "feign'd" permanence.) Moreover, Hume is probably no more a "phenomenalist" with regard to mind than he is with regard to matter. As in the case of body, Hume's view may simply be that we have no *conception* of a permanent self. As Edward Craig argues, "If there is no conception, no idea, then there is no rational argument, one way or the other", and Hume's stance on the self is that of an "ontological agnostic".[42] This is not Mill's view; again there is the contrast between his circumspection in making ontological claims and Hume's scepticism. Mill's philosophy is not driven by a theory of ideas; what motivates the series account is the relativity of knowledge.

Despite his retraction, the series account *is* an inevitable consequence of Mill's ontology and probably also his epistemology. The psychological theory of mind is no more a misapplication of the relativity of knowledge than is the theory of matter, contrary to Skorupski's claims. The appeal of a series account for idealists is shown by the fact that Berkeley considered eliminating the self, though his "official view" was that it is a substance.[43] But though Mill had to attempt a series account, his retraction has revealed internal pressures in the contrary direction. I will now explore these pressures further, hoping to clarify the reasons Mill gives for that retraction.

VI. WHY MILL RETRACTED THE "PSYCHOLOGICAL THEORY" AS APPLIED TO MIND: MEMORY AND OTHER MINDS

The reasons for Mill's retraction are not at all clear. Much of what he says in fact appears quite consistent with a series account. His concern over how "a series of feelings, can be aware of itself as a series", or "as past and future" (p. 194), has rightly been considered a bad reason for rejecting such an account. Though I have to *believe* that "I myself" had the sensations remembered, why can't such beliefs be explained in Humean terms as involving a "feign'd" permanence? (The fact that a series refers to itself as "I" does not of itself mean that Hume's account is question-begging.)

The immediate reason why Mill has to abandon a series account arises from his admission that memory constitutes "intuitive knowledge". This admission is the first of two sources of a nonreductive account in the *Examination*; the second, to which I will return in due course, is the postulation of other minds. Concerning the distinction between memory and other kinds of knowledge which he does not admit as intuitive, Mill writes:

The distinction is, that as all the explanations of mental phenomena presuppose Memory, Memory itself cannot admit of being explained. Whenever this is shown to be true of any other part of our knowledge, I shall admit that part to be intuitive. (p. 165n)

Mill believes that the formation of our perceptual judgments can be explained without assuming we perceive external objects; what he cannot then do, is explain our perceptual judgments, or our memory judgments, without assuming we really do remember things. Associative processes require the remembering of past conscious states; otherwise, there would be no mechanism whereby habits of mind are generated. This, for associationism, has to be a primitive and unexplained tendency. Mill thus regards memory as a second source of "intuitive knowledge", in addition to "present consciousness" (p. 165n). Memory judgments must be regarded as reliable.

However, the claim that memory is intuitive proves ambiguous, and deeply problematic for Mill's psychological theory; indeed, it seems that if the reality of past conscious states can be justified, so should the reality of external objects.[44] The intuitive status of memory is implicit in Mill's claim that "the fact which alone necessitates the belief in an Ego, the one fact which the Psychological theory cannot explain, is the fact of Memory" (p. 206). But how *does* "the fact of Memory . . . [necessitate] the belief in an Ego"? Is it the "intuitive status" of memory as just outlined that forces Mill's recantation?

If memory is intuitive knowledge, then it seems the self must be more than just a "feign'd" permanence. Memory beliefs are reliable; so much of what I seem to remember must have happened, so I must be a genuinely persisting self. But is this the whole story? First, one may ask why it is *memory* that requires the postulation of a self, and not simply sensation as such. After all, it has often been argued against Hume that "unowned perceptions" are inconceivable. But this would imply that "the Ego is an original presentation of consciousness", which Mill tries to resist (p. 207). More importantly, there is a further connection between memory and the self which he seems to recognise, and which does not simply involve its intuitive status.

Returning to the passages in which Mill retracts the series account, we find an ambiguity in his claims. He first says that "a remembrance of sensation . . . involves the suggestion and belief that a sensation, of which it is a copy or representation, actually existed in the past". This seems to be the point arising from the intuitive status of memory. However, he goes on to say that the phenomenon of memory "[cannot be] adequately expressed, without saying that the belief [it includes] is, that *I myself* formerly had . . . the sensations remembered" (p. 194, my emphasis). This is a different point – that the past sensation, assumed to have existed, belongs to myself.

It is the latter point, I think, that Mill insists on in the Appendix, though the same ambiguity is implicit. He claims that the self involves a "real tie . . . which connects the present consciousness with the past one, of which it reminds me . . . and not a mere product of the laws of thought without any fact corresponding to it". But what is the "fact" which this "real tie" guarantees? That there really *was* a past sensation, whose copy I am now having? Or that given there was such a sensation, it belonged to *me*? I would argue the latter. The series account itself, in postulating a series of sensations – that is, sensations extended in time – already assumes that the individual sensations actually exist or existed. The intuitive status of memory is not required to guarantee *that*. Moreover, it is the tie that Mill holds to be real, not just the past sensation. So the question Mill is addressing is not whether the past sensations existed, but rather, whose sensations are they? What is lacking, without a "real tie", is that the sensations do not necessarily belong to the same subject.

Mill is therefore looking for some principle of unity of consciousness. There is such a principle, but it is, I think, a product less of the general trustworthiness of memory judgments, than of a certain *kind* of immunity to error which they exhibit. If I seem to remember going on a childhood holiday to Bournemouth, then I cannot be mistaken about *who* went on holiday; if anyone went, it was myself. Though it may turn out that the apparent memory is a delusion, I cannot coherently begin to wonder, "Maybe someone went to Bournemouth, but was it myself?" This feature may be expressed, though I think misleadingly, by the claim that "I" is part of the content of memory judgments; better, that "I" involves an identification which spans past and present, which in memory judgments guarantees an immunity to error through misidentification. In making a memory claim, I do not identify two distinct subjects – the remembering subject and the subject who experienced or witnessed the remembered events – who are conceivably not identical, though they normally are. There is, rather, a *guaranteed* identity here. It is the resulting specific immunity to error which Mill is groping for in his postulation of a "real tie".

This line of thought connects with an interesting discussion in Mill's only other treatment of these questions, his Notes, written in 1867–68, to James Mill's *The Analysis of the Human Mind*. There he writes that "the notion of Self is . . . a consequence of Memory"; "a being, gifted with sensation but devoid of memory", would not have it. More important, the notion is more than just a *consequence* of memory:

The phenomenon of Self and that of Memory are merely two sides of the same fact. . . . We may, as psychologists, set out from either of them, and refer the other to it. . . . But it is hardly allowable to do both. At least it must be said, that by doing so we explain neither.[45]

There is here an implicit rejection of the complaint Butler and Reid made against Locke's account – a complaint of which Mill would have been aware – viz. that memory presupposes personal identity and so cannot be the criterion for it.[46] Unfortunately, Mill's discussion is clouded by an unresolved tension between first- and third-person criteria for personal identity. He criticises Locke and the "psychologists" for ignoring third-person (bodily) criteria, but endorses Locke's analysis of first-person (psychological) criteria: "My personal identity consists in my being the same Ego who did, or who felt, some specific fact recalled to me by memory". Mill doesn't really explain why the different sets of criteria should come up with the same answer to questions of personal identity – or maybe he doesn't really believe it is the same question that they address. Nonetheless, what he says suggests a novel response to Butler and Reid's "circularity objection". It marks the beginnings of a neglected and, I believe, correct account, which specifies a benign circularity between the concepts of memory (and expectation) and personal identity. Despite deficiencies in his formulation, Mill is correct in pointing to a circularity whilst, unusually, not finding it vicious.

The benign circularity of the memory criterion is, I would argue, demonstrated by the status of memory judgments as immune to error through misidentification. Self-conscious ways of knowing such as memory *constitute*, and do not – as Reid and Butler assumed – merely furnish evidence for, personal identity. These claims suggest a Kantian "unity of consciousness" account of personal identity: the self is not an object definable independently of one's self-conception, notably through memory. Thus there is an interesting connection between a Kantian account and Mill's claim that "The phenomenon of Self and that of Memory are merely two sides of the same fact". It is less the general reliability of memory judgments that is implicated in generating the self, than their immunity to error through misidentification.[47]

As noted above, Mill tries to salvage something of the "psychological theory" by arguing that although the notion of an ego is not acquired *simply* in accord with the laws of association, but requires memory as a mode of intuitive knowledge, it *is* nonetheless acquired and not innate. He "[sees] no reason to think that there is any cognizance of an Ego until Memory commences" (p. 207). Now the whole point of showing that an idea is acquired is to cast doubt on its legitimacy. Mill's demonstration that we can acquire the idea of matter without acquaintance with anything genuinely permanent constituted an *undermining* of the latter notion. The case is quite different with the self, where Mill has conceded that there *is* something genuinely permanent. On Mills' "interpretation of consciousness", there ought to be no philosophical point in arguing that an idea is acquired, if one has already conceded its legitimacy. Indeed, the fact that it is acquired ought to undermine its legitimacy. That he goes on to insist that the idea of the self may nonetheless be acquired, reveals some confusion in his epistemology.

Leaving direct consideration of memory, the second source of a non-reductive account of the self lies in Mill's treatment of other minds. Mill's phenomenalism aims to be "pluralistic", not solipsistic; on his view there are, irreducibly, experiences other than my experiences. But he cannot simply assume the existence of other minds, he has to prove it. This is because of his starting point in the relativity of knowledge. Without such a proof the putative sensations of others would remain unacceptable "hidden causes of sensations" – causes of the sensations I experience when I observe others. It remains the case that other minds are, or are made up from, objects external to me which are not *mere* "possible sensations" (to me), but which have a real existence independent of any possibility of being perceived (by me). So in a pluralistic phenomenalism the permanent possibilities could only constitute *matter*, not "external substance". (This is to assume, as Mill seems to, a subjective starting point. But the issue is a clouded one.)

The "proof" is inadequate, as has been noted above. But the problem is more fundamental. Mill asks how I *know* there are other minds. But does his account have the resources to make the *distinction* between self and others in the first place – can it yield criteria of personal identity and individuation? In contrast to Hume, Mill is at least aware of the problem of other minds, yet he makes no attempt to "tie" the perceptions with the "string" of causality or resemblance. Such an attempt would have failed nonetheless, since to admit that there are, irreducibly, other minds, is to admit a "real tie" between sensations – and so the demise of the psychological theory as applied to mind follows. *"Pluralistic* phenomenalism" implies a non-reductive account of the self, and is therefore not phenomenalism on the strict definition I have been defending. Phenomenalism is necessarily solipsistic. It follows that Mill was wrong to distinguish between the allegedly baseless "extrinsic objections" of Reid – which provoked his argument from analogy – and the insoluble "intrinsic difficulties" of memory (p. 193). They are intimately connected, and Reid's objection, rejected by Mill, was correct: on the series account, "the proposition . . . that there are any Selves except mine, is but words without a meaning" (p. 190). (Even "mine" would be a word without a meaning, of course.)

Mill's positivist and logical positivist successors – from Mach and Carnap to Ayer – tried to avoid the dilemma of pluralistic idealism versus solipsistic phenomenalism. They sought to transcend a "subjectivist" starting point, and to make their doctrine in some elusive sense ontologically "neutral". (We have seen how Mill's discussion of the "two pictures" of the realist and psychological theories anticipates their position.) In Mach's "neutral monism", unlike Mill's phenomenalism, sensations are in themselves neither mental nor physical, neither subjective nor objective. Though Mach talks of a "functional dependence" between sensations, there is no analysis of matter in terms of "possibilities of sensation". This position is echoed in later positivist viewpoints, and for Mach and Russell, though not for Ayer, a lack of interest in possibilities of sensation means that their "neutral monism" is, strictly, not phenomenalism. Despite Mach's neutralist aspirations, however, Schlick argued convincingly that "a real world common to all individuals is out of the question" on his account.[48]

In this crucial respect Mach's actualism and Mill's possibilism are equally unsatisfactory. The general failure of empiricist standpoints to allow "a real world common to all individuals" was diagnosed by Mill's acute critic Henry Sidgwick, in his sustained attack on the empiricist notion of "experience". In the article "Incoherence of Empirical Philosophy", a lively defence of (implicitly Scottish) "common sense" that was anachronistic in the late nineteenth century, Sidgwick asks "who are the 'we' who have this knowledge" that is necessarily relative or immediate?

Each one of us can only have experience of a very small portion of this world; and if we abstract what is known through memory, and therefore mediately, the portion becomes very small indeed. In order to get to what "we" conceive "ourselves" to know as "matter of fact" respecting the world, as extended in space and time – to such merely historical knowledge as we commonly regard not as "resting" on experience, but as constituting the experience on which science rests – we must assume the general trustworthiness of memory, and the general trustworthiness of testimony under proper limitations and conditions. . . . I do not see how we can prove that we have such a right, from what we immediately know.[49]

Though he was forced to accept memory as "intuitive knowledge", with a resulting incoherence, Mill could never have included testimony.

More plausible, non-phenomenalist varieties of anti-realism would have satisfied the doctrine of the relativity of knowledge. But there was never a chance in a Millian of that doctrine itself being questioned; and it is in Mill's starting point of "pure sensation" that his fundamental errors originate. An even longer chapter would have had more to say about this question. But I hope that Hamilton's examination of Mill's examination of Hamilton has at least shown what an intriguing, elusive and puzzling doctrine phenomenalism is.

NOTES

1 First edition, 1865. All unqualified page references are to the *Examination* in *CW* IX. The phrase "possibilities of sensation" first appears in Mill's *System of Logic* from 1843, in *CW* VII:58.

2 On Mill's relative lack of influence on scientific philosophers, see Mandelbaum 1971, 13–14.

3 1871 review of "Berkeley's Life and Writings", ed. A. Fraser. *CW* XI:459–60.

4 See *Autobiography*, *CW* I:71. On associationism, see section II of this chapter.

5 Berkeley 1962, Part 1, section 3, p. 66. There are other passages where Berkeley inclines to phenomenalism. See Bennett 1971, sections 29, 31–32; Winkler 1989, chs. 6, 7.

6 See, for instance, Fogelin 1985, 68. Pears (1990, ch. 10) argues against this interpretation.

7 Hume 1973, 1.4.2, p. 187.

8 The interpretation of Hume is a fraught business, but it is not even clear that he subscribes to the doctrine of the relativity of knowledge; see below. Fogelin writes: "The central difference between Hume's position and twentieth-century phenomenalism is that Hume is attempting to explain the origin of the plain man's belief in the continued existence of what he sees, whereas twentieth-century phenomenalists are attempting to vindicate it" (Fogelin 1985, 68n3). Mill, as I will explain, is attempting to do *both*; but the latter project, involving a definition of the plain person's belief in terms of permanent possibilities of sensation, is essential to what I am calling phenomenalism.

9 Reid 1872, 445.

10 Mill quotation: *CW* X:125. On the status of Reid's "principles", and the surprising extent of agreement between Hume and Reid, see Skorupski 1993a, 11–14. That Reid borrowed from Descartes as well as the "British empiricists" points up the deficiencies of the modern classification of philosophers as empiricist or rationalist.

11 *Autobiography*, *CW* I:270; letter to Gomperz, *CW* XIV:239.

12 Mill quotations: *CW* I:270 and 271.

13 Pattison 1865, 562. On the other hand, one recent commentator has found Hamilton a superior philosopher to Mill; see Mounce 1994.

14 W. Hamilton 1865, 136–37.

15 On Hamilton's philosophy and these criticisms, see A. Ryan's Introduction in *CW* IX, especially pp. xxiff.

16 See, for instance, Schlick 1974 (first published 1918), 235–44. As we have seen, Mill referred to Hume as a "Phenomenist", a term which Royce and W. G. Ward both applied to Mill (as he noted on p. 165n; comments on his critics were added to later editions of the *Examination*). Royce seems to be referring simply to Mill's allegiance to the relativity of knowledge; Royce 1882, 50; and see section IV of this chapter. The different interpretations of the relativity of knowledge are characterised as two forms of phenomenalism, "strong" and "weak", in Skorupski 1993a, 56. But I am reserving the term "Phenomenalism" for Mill's own "Idealist" interpretation.

17 W. Hamilton 1866, 639–40.

18 See the discussion of a "primitively compelling transition" in Peacocke 1992.

19 *CW* VII, 276. See Skorupski 1989, 226–29 and 158–59; and below.

20 Peacocke 1992, 134.

21 Henry Sidgwick, in his important critique "Incoherence of Empirical Philosophy" (1882), explores these assumptions. Taking empiricism to be based on the trustworthiness of "immediate [i.e. non-inferred] cognitions", he argues that it is "practically of no avail to say that

immediate cognition is infallible, unless we have a no less infallible criterion for ascertaining what cognitions are immediate" – and that this is deeply problematic (p. 539). Sidgwick's article – further discussed below – is useful as a clear account of the context and assumptions of Mill's discussion by a writer of the following generation.

22 On this chapter, see Skorupski 1989, 223–25.

23 Ayer 1954, 134.

24 Skorupski 1989, 225. See also Skorupski 1989, 233 and, on Mill's inductivism, 206ff.

25 See Russell 1972 and 1963. Examples of "linguistic phenomenalism" are found in Carnap 1967 and Ayer 1940.

26 *CW* XVI:1090, discussed in Skorupski 1989, 234.

27 Carnap 1967, 87; Schlick 1981, "Positivism and Realism" (first published 1932–33), 99. On ontological neutrality, see A. Hamilton 1992.

28 Skorupski 1989, xii.

29 See Skorupski 1989, 232–35.

30 See Skorupski 1989, 235; it becomes "meaning-equivalence" only with verificationism.

31 *CW* VII:56.

32 Packe claims that in the latter Mill was forced to abandon his earlier "professional" neutrality, though he must be wrong to see the *Logic* as "following faithfully from Hume"; see Packe 1954, 440–41.

33 I owe this suggestion to Geoffrey Scarre. Scarre 1989, 172–76, teases out many of the obscurities and confusions in Mill's account.

34 *CW* VII:58–59.

35 Royce 1882, 53; Price 1926–27; McCloskey 1971, p. 158. Price holds that Mill is an "idealist" but not a "phenomenalist", on the grounds that the latter view denies any reality to the possibilities; a curious inversion of present nomenclature.

36 *CW* XI:464.

37 Winkler 1989, 206.

38 On the fundamental problems facing phenomenalism and the conflicts with naturalism that result, see Skorupski 1989, 240–47.

39 Bradley 1962, 39n and 40n; James 1950, 359 and 357.

40 See Winkler 1989, 290–300.

41 Hume 1973, 635–36.

42 Craig 1987, 114.

43 Skorupski 1989, 237. On Berkeley, see Pitcher 1977, ch. X; Winkler 1989, ch. 9. In the *Philosophical Commentaries* Berkeley entertained the view of the mind as "a congeries of Perceptions" (entry 580). But Berkeley's "official view" is expounded by Philonous when he rejects Hylas's claim that "in consequence of your own principles, it should

follow that you are only a system of floating ideas, without any substance to support them" (*Three Dialogues Between Hylas and Philonous* in Berkeley 1962, 223–24). In the *Principles* Berkeley writes, "That which I denote by the term 'I' is the same with what is meant by *soul* or *spiritual substance*" (Berkeley 1962, entry 139).

44 See Skorupski 1989, 228–29.

45 *CW* XXXI:138, 212–13.

46 On their "circularity" objection, see Noonan 1989, ch. 3.

47 These rather compressed claims about immunity to error through misidentification are developed in A. Hamilton 1995, which criticises Parfit's denial, through "q-memory", of the guaranteed identity of remembering and remembered subject, and further argues that the dichotomy between Lockean "psychological" criteria and "bodily" criteria is a false one.

48 Mach 1959; Schlick 1974, 225–27. On these questions see A. Hamilton 1990 and 1992.

49 Sidgwick 1882, 542–43.

5   Mill on religion

In his *Autobiography* Mill declares himself to be "one of the very few examples, in this country, of one who has, not thrown off religious belief, but never had it" (*CW* I:45). Yet Mill could hardly avoid engaging with religion in pursuit of his main concerns. It is no surprise that he does so in setting out the utilitarian morality,[1] in defending liberal principles in the face of restrictions on free speech and discussion,[2] and in assessing the quality of current University education.[3] But only in the posthumously published *Three Essays on Religion* (1874)[4] was religion itself the focal point of his analysis. In these essays Mill attacks orthodox theology on both epistemological and moral grounds. He argues, however, that there is some evidence that the universe was created by an intelligent being and he takes seriously the possibility that something important might be missing from a life in which religion had no place.

The *Three Essays*, 'Nature', 'Utility of Religion' and 'Theism', are the main focus of the present discussion. According to Helen Taylor,[5] the first two were written between 1850 and 1858 and the third between 1868 and 1870. Though it was the last to be written there is good reason to discuss 'Theism' first since the general position it defends underpins the thinking behind the other two essays. Accordingly, in sections I and II I discuss some of Mill's central epistemological objections to orthodox theology relying mainly on 'Theism' but drawing also on the impassioned discussion of H. L. Mansel in Mill's book on Hamilton.[6] In the ensuing sections I explore themes mainly from the other two essays.[7]

I

The orthodoxy which Mill attacks assumes a division of theology into natural, which deals with what can be established about God by the exercise of our cognitive capacities without recourse to divine aid, and revealed, which deals with those truths which are supposed to have been made accessible as a result of divine revelation. At the core of natural theology are arguments for the existence of a God who is conceived to be omnipotent, omniscient and omnibenevolent, but natural theology may also incorporate claims about human nature and destiny in so far as they are thought to be supported by evidence or otherwise argued. Revealed theology in Christian tradition includes received Christological doctrines, such as that of the incarnation. An important strand in orthodox Christian theology took it that revealed doctrines were communicated by supernatural means to prophets and the like, who then related them to others. Locke, developing a line of thought already found in Aquinas,[8] had argued that we have reason to believe in revealed truths since we have reason to trust 'proposers' of supposedly revealed truth whose divine commission is accredited by external signs, notably miracles. This view is the target of Hume's essay 'Of Miracles'.[9]

By far the largest portion of 'Theism' is devoted to natural theology. Mill deals in turn with traditional arguments for the existence of God, the attributes of God, and considerations pertaining to immortality. Like Hume, Mill thinks that the best argument for the existence of God does not suffice to make it probable that there is a God as conceived by orthodox natural theology. Unlike Hume, he thinks that the marks of design constitute some, though not particularly strong, evidence that the universe in its present form is the work of an intelligent Creator.[10] But this evidence, he argues, does not support the hypothesis that the Creator is either omnipotent or omniscient, nor does it provide grounds for thinking that it is all-good or principally concerned with the good of humankind. The hypothesis of immortality fares no better, though Mill does not think that it is ruled out a priori. So far as revealed theology is concerned, Mill tightens up the Humean view on miracles, arguing that "miracles have no claim whatever to the character of historical facts and are wholly invalid as evidences of any revelation" (*CW*

X:481). In this section I focus on Mill's treatment of the argument from marks of design; in section II I examine his discussion of the divine attributes.

Mill thought that the only argument for the existence of God which is truly scientific in character is that from (apparent) marks of design in nature. What makes this argument scientific is the fact that it is "wholly grounded on experience" (CW X:446) and does not draw on a priori assumptions. Stated in its simplest terms the argument has two stages, as follows:

> (1) There are artifacts (e.g. machines) and things in nature (e.g. animals and their organs) which are analogous in that they have parts which conspire to some end. The analogy and the fact that the artifacts are produced by intelligent design provide adequate evidence (i.e. evidence strong enough to warrant acceptance) that the relevant things in nature have an analogous cause and thus are also produced by intelligent design. We may thus infer that these things are indeed the products of intelligent design.
>
> (2) The relevant things in nature are so far beyond the power of man that they must have been produced by God.

In assessing the argument Mill makes an important distinction between a mere argument from analogy and a truly inductive argument. Both, he says, "argue that a thing known to resemble another in certain circumstances . . . will resemble it in another circumstance" (CW X:447). The point is that if X and Y resemble one another in respect of properties $P_1 \ldots P_n$ and X has a further property P_{n+1} then these facts constitute evidence for the proposition that Y resembles X in respect of the further property P_{n+1}. In a truly inductive argument, Mill suggests, evidence is adduced for what I shall call a connectivity thesis to the effect that P_{n+1} depends on, or is in some other way connected with, $P_1 \ldots P_n$. In a *mere* argument from analogy the evidence does not support such a thesis. Such arguments may be very weak. In any case their strength depends on whether the points of resemblance between X and Y are many and the points of difference few.[11] Now, as set out above, the argument from marks of design is a mere argument from analogy, since nothing is assumed about the connection between the property of being the product of intelligent design and the property in respect of which human artifacts and things in nature resemble one another. But, Mill thinks, there is a stronger version of the argument which is truly inductive, for it relies on evidence that the property in question, having parts conspiring to a particular end, has "a real connection with an intelligent origin" (CW X:447).[12] Mill does not explicitly spell out what the connection is, but he surely has in mind a causal connection. Artifacts like machines have the property of having parts which conspire to an end because they have been designed so that the parts conspire to the end in question. To take Paley's favourite example: A watch has parts which conspire to the end of showing the time and it has such parts because it has been designed to show the time.

The upshot is that the evidence that natural things like animals and their organs are produced by intelligent design is provided not just by the fact that such things are analogous to artifacts which have parts conspiring to an end and which have been produced by intelligent design, but, in addition, by the fact that the respect in which the natural things resemble the artifacts is a property, having parts conspiring to an end, which the artifacts have because they have been designed to conspire to the end in question.

Mill proceeds to illustrate the case for design with reference to the eye, another example which had been used by Paley. The considerations which he adduces are meant to support the claim that the eye has parts which conspire to an end because it was designed so that the parts would conspire to that end. The first consideration is that the only relevant respect in which the elements of the eye and the arrangement of these elements resemble one another is their enabling the animal to see. The second is that the vast number of instances of eyes is evidence that the particular arrangement of their parts could not have come about by chance but had a common cause. The third is that since "the elements [of eyes] agree in the single circumstance of conspiring to produce sight" (CW X:448), the cause in question must be appropriately connected to sight. This last point, Mill suggests, is as far as induction can take us. "The natural sequel of the argument", he writes, is this:

Sight, being a fact not precedent but subsequent to the putting together of the organic structure of the eye, can only be connected with the production of that structure in the character of a final, not an efficient cause; that is, it is not Sight itself but an antecedent Idea of it, that must be the efficient cause. But this at once marks the origin as proceeding from an intelligent will. (CW X:448)

Given Mill's previous remarks about what constitutes a truly inductive argument, one would expect the considerations about the eye to take the following form: Granted (i) that the eye has parts which conspire to an end, (ii) that in this respect the eye resembles a machine, and (iii) that machines have parts conspiring to an end because made by intelligent design (the relevant connectivity thesis), we may infer that the eye has parts conspiring to an end because made by intelligent design. Mill's actual procedure is to argue that the parts of the eye must have come together through a common cause which is suitably connected to sight and then infer as a 'natural sequel' that intelligent design is the only plausible cause. There is no mention of the analogy between eyes and machines or of the connection, in the case of machines, between having parts conducive to an end and being made by intelligent design. The resemblances which Mill actually talks about are those between "[t]he parts of which the eye is composed, and the collocations which constitute the arrangement of those parts" (CW X:448).

A feature of Mill's discussion which is initially puzzling is that he takes the considerations about the eye to conform to the Method of Agreement (CW X:448), whereby, according to A *System of Logic*, "if two or more instances of the phenomenon under investigation have only one circumstance in common, the circumstance in which alone all the instances agree is the cause (or effect) of the given phenomenon" (CW VII:390). The method is meant to identify a cause from candidate causal factors which are known to be present. If one thinks of the inductive argument under consideration as yielding the conclusion that the eye is the product of intelligent design, one might be inclined to object that since in the case of the eye intelligent design is not known to be present, the argument cannot be an example of the Method of Agreement. However, what Mill has in mind is that the known factor in which the relevant phenomena agree is that they all conspire to produce sight. That, he thinks, is the cause, albeit the final cause, of the coming together of the parts of the eye. Even so, it is strange that Mill should, without comment, assume that the Method of Agreement applies to final causes. The very notion of a final cause, as indeed of an efficient cause, is foreign to the thinking about causation in *A System of Logic*, where the methods for discovery are introduced as pertaining to antecedent 'conditions' of phenomena and their consequences.[13] Note, however, that the sort of connection for which Mill is looking, between conspiring to produce sight and the cause or causes of there being eye structures as we now know them, can be expressed without recourse to the notion of final causes. Mill is seeking an explanation for the fact that there are many species of animal with complex eyes; organs which are extremely well suited to enabling their possessors to see. The considerations he adduces about the eye suggest that any explanation should satisfy a certain constraint: the fact that the structures have parts conspiring so well to produce sight should figure in the explanation of there being animals which possess such structures. Once this is granted the hypothesis that eyes are the products of intelligent design comes in as a plausible explanation which satisfies the constraint.

We know now that there is an alternative explanation which also satisfies the constraint. According to the Darwinian theory of evolution, eyes as we have them now have evolved by natural selection from much more primitive structures, perhaps arrays of light-sensitive cells on the surface of the body. Such structures would have appeared in some individuals of a population as chance variations distinguishing these individuals from others in the population. They would have conferred an advantage on the creatures having them in that it raised their chances of surviving to reproduce. Since they were heritable, the advantage would have been passed on to offspring; thus the proportion of creatures in the population having the variant structures would have increased. Complex eyes such as we find now evolved over a vast period of time through the accumulation of small but advantageous variations on these original variations. The theory satisfies the explanatory constraint mentioned above since the property of having parts which conspire to produce sight figures in the explanation of there being species of animals with eyes. It is a property of structures which conferred selective advantage on the creatures which had them and thus accounts for there being species with such structures.

Mill recognized that the theory of natural selection was a possible alternative to the hypothesis of intelligent design and that its availability weakened the evidence in favour of that hypothesis. On balance he thought that the design hypothesis was still the more probable but only because the theory of natural selection was at that time speculative. The evidence accumulated since fatally weakens the argument from design in the form in which Mill considers it.

II

The discussion of the attributes in 'Theism' focuses on omnipotence, but Mill has interesting things to say about the 'moral attributes' of the Creator both there and in other writings.

Mill argues not just that the hypothesis of omnipotence is not well supported by evidence. He thinks it is actually inconsistent with known facts. The very marks of design which provide evidence of a Creator testify against the possibility that the Creator is omnipotent. Design is contrivance, the adaptation of means to an end, but, according to Mill, "the necessity for contrivance – the need of employing means – is a consequence of the limitation of power" (CW X:451). In support of this Mill argues "[t]hat the very idea of means implies that the means have an efficacy which the direct action of the being who employs them has not". The upshot is that an omnipotent being would have no need to employ means to ends and, by implication, would have no need to construct things which are adapted to certain ends. There is, however, a rather obvious objection to this line of thought. We need to distinguish between the claim that there are things in nature structured in a manner which conspires to some end and the claim that the Creator had to employ means to achieve ends which it was not capable of bringing about by fiat. Granted that the Creator formed the eye so that it would enable its possessor to see, it does not follow that the eye was not created by fiat. Mill seems to confuse the notion of means whereby the eye has the capacity for sight with the notion of means by which the eye was made. He might have more effectively pursued a somewhat different, though related, line of argument. Theists sometimes argue not just that particular animals and organs provide evidence of design but that the larger order of things in nature and in human life testifies to the Creator's purposes. It is claimed, for example, that God arranges that human beings suffer so that they will grow spiritually. This would be a clear case of the Creator's employing means to an end which it wills to achieve. Mill's point would then be that since an omnipotent creator could have brought it about immediately that his creatures had the desired level of spirituality, it follows that if the Creator had to adopt the means described, or any other means to the chosen end, then it is limited in power. It is open to theists to argue that it is logically impossible to bring about spirituality in individuals without the provision of the means to grow towards it. It is not easy to see what could justify such a claim. In any case, Mill is right to insist that such evidence as there is in favour of an intelligent Creator does not establish the Creator's omnipotence. The most that the marks of design show is that the Creator was responsible for functional structures in nature. They do not show, and no other available argument establishes, that the materials out of which these structures are made, or even the forces to which the materials are subject, were brought about by the Creator.

As to the precise limitations on the power of the Creator, Mill points out that "they are wholly unknown to us" (CW X:456), though he thinks it likely that they are due to the nature of the substances and forces available rather than to any devilish intelligence. On omniscience Mill has little to say beyond claiming, plausibly, that the hypothesis of an omniscient Creator, though not contradicted by known facts, is nonetheless not supported by them. While the Creator's knowledge of the powers and properties of things must vastly exceed the human, there is no ground on which it can be inferred to be perfect.

Turning to consider what can be inferred about the Creator's purposes, Mill asks, "To what purpose, then, do the expedients in the construction of animals and vegetables, which excite the admiration of naturalists, appear to tend?" (CW X:456). For those who seek inspiration from the contemplation of a divine purpose, his initial answer is bleak.

There is no blinking the fact that they tend principally to no more exalted object than to make the structure remain in life and in working order for a certain time: the individual for a few years, the species or race for a longer but still a limited period. And the similar though less conspicuous marks of creation which are recognized in inorganic Nature, are generally of the same character.

The marks of design, for the most part, suggest only that the Creator wills "not the good of any sentient creature" but "the qualified permanence, for a limited period, of the work itself, whether animate or inanimate" (CW X:457). In view of this it is puzzling that Mill is prepared to concede that "there is a preponderance of evidence that the Creator desired the pleasure of his creatures". He cites, in particular, the availability of sources of pleasure, and the fact that pain usually arises from external interference rather than from the ends to which the contrivances of nature tend. Such considerations, he rightly points out, do not show that the Creator's "sole or chief purposes are those of benevolence". On the contrary, "if God had no purpose but our happiness and that of other living creatures it is not credible that he would have called them into existence with the prospect of being so completely baffled" (CW X:458). What is puzzling is that essentially the same considerations would seem to count against the view that the Creator so much as cares about the pleasure of his creatures. Granted that the basic design of living creatures does not work towards their experiencing a balance of pain over pleasure, this fact hardly supports Mill's concessionary view that the Creator positively desires the pleasure of his creatures when account is taken of the circumstances in which so many are placed and the susceptibility to disease to which so many are subject.

Defenders of orthodoxy argue that the pain of living creatures does not impugn the goodness of the Creator. Mill has no truck with such arguments when deployed in defence of belief in God as traditionally conceived. He refers to "the impossible problem of reconciling infinite benevolence and justice with infinite power in the Creator of such a world as this". To try to effect such a reconciliation, he says, "not only involves absolute contradiction in an intellectual point of view but exhibits to excess the revolting spectacle of a jesuitical defence of moral enormities" (CW X:456). The defensive strategy would indeed involve contradiction, as many have pointed out,[14] given some auxiliary assumption about goodness which has the effect of not permitting a completely good being to tolerate the sufferings to which living creatures are subject. Orthodox theodicies, however, challenge such assumptions and thus raise the question whether Mill can press home his claim that they are actually contradictory. It is at this point that the discussion of Mansel becomes relevant.

Mill quotes the following passage from Mansel.

It is a fact which experience forces upon us, and which it is useless, were it possible, to disguise, that the representation of God after the model of the highest human morality which we are capable of conceiving, is not sufficient to account for all the phenomena exhibited by the course of his natural Providence. The infliction of physical suffering, the permission of moral evil, the adversity of the good, . . . these are facts which no doubt are reconcilable, we know not how, with the Infinite Goodness of God, but which certainly are not to be explained on the supposition that its sole and sufficient type is to be found in the finite goodness of man. (CW IX:101)

Any orthodox theological view must acknowledge that God's goodness is vastly different from that of humankind. But, as Mill goes on to note, Mansel holds that God's goodness differs from that of humans not just in degree but in kind. If the difference were only in degree it could rightly be argued that God must, for example, care for his creatures in something like the way in which we acknowledge that we should care for others. The difference would be that God cares so much more than we ever could, but what counts as caring for God would be akin to what counts as caring for us. So it would mean having regard for the well-being of those cared for, and, in God's case, the caring would be informed by perfect knowledge of what makes for well-being. On Mansel's view, by contrast, God's goodness is so different from that recognised by us that we have no adequate conception of what it is like. The intended upshot is that we are in no position to infer that the pain and suffering in the world is incompatible with God's having the traditional divine attributes.

It is by no means unusual these days to hear what is essentially Mansel's view advanced in discussions of the theological problem of evil, yet Mill's assault upon it is hard to resist once understood. Mansel's view amounts to the claim that we have no conception at all of what is meant by declaring God to be good. Mill points out that if this is so then no one has any ground for venerating God. Anything which is a proper object of veneration must be conceived to be good and thus worthy of veneration. If we have no idea of what it is for God to be good we are in no position to regard him as worthy of veneration and so can have no reason for venerating him. It is important to appreciate this line of thought in assessing what is perhaps one of the most outspoken passages in all of Mill's writings:

If, instead of the 'glad tidings' that there exists a Being in whom all the excellences which the highest human mind can conceive, exist in a degree inconceivable to us, I am informed that the world is ruled by a being whose attributes are infinite, but what they are we cannot learn . . . I will bear my fate as I may. But when I am told that I must believe this, and at the same time call this being by the names which express and affirm the highest human morality, I say in plain terms that I will not. . . . I will call no being good who is not what I mean when I apply that epithet to my fellow creatures; and if such a being can sentence me to hell for not so calling him, to hell I will go. (CW IX:103)

Some religions may dismiss this as an impious outburst which arrogantly sets Mill's or some accepted human standard of goodness above God's. That would miss the central point, which does not have to do with setting up a standard of goodness in opposition to God's (higher) standard. The point is that in regarding any being as worthy of veneration one is committed to regarding that being as good in a sense of that term which is intelligible and intelligibly linked to worthiness of veneration.

The case against Mansel is strong but does it suffice to block *any* attempt to show that pain and suffering are compatible with the traditional divine attributes? Attempts at theodicy do not in general rely on Mansel's position. Rather, they try to show at the very least that even a being who is good in some commonly accepted sense of that term *could* have morally adequate reasons to permit the pain and suffering in the world. They may, for example, suggest that people may allow loved ones to suffer for the sake of a worthy end and be no less good for that. Whether this sort of point can be made effective given that God is not subject to human limitations seems to me to be doubtful in the extreme. Nonetheless, Mill is too quick in claiming that orthodox theodicies involve 'absolute contradiction'. Whether they involve moral enormities is a further matter.

III

The aim of the essay 'Nature' is "to inquire into the truth of the doctrines which make Nature a test of right and wrong, good and evil, or which in any mode or degree attach merit or approval to following, imitating, or obeying Nature" (*CW* X:377–78). From this alone it is not immediately evident what the essay has to do specifically with religion. Mill makes the connection explicit in the following passage:

[T]here still exists a vague notion that . . . the general scheme of nature is a model for us to imitate: that with more or less liberty in details, we should on the whole be guided by the spirit and general conception of nature's own ways: that they are God's work and as such perfect . . . and that if not the whole, yet some particular parts of the spontaneous order of nature, selected according to the speaker's predilections, are in a peculiar sense, manifestations of the Creator's will; a sort of finger posts pointing out the direction which things in general, and therefore our voluntary actions, are intended to take. (*CW* X:382)

Mill's attack on these ideas is preceded by some useful conceptual analysis. He notes that the nature of a thing may mean the aggregate of its powers or properties. So when we talk of nature in the large we may mean the totality of the powers and properties of all things. In this sense nature is all things actual and physically possible. But there is another sense of 'nature' in which nature is contrasted with art or contrivance. In this sense nature is "only what takes place without the agency, or without the voluntary and intentional agency, of man" (*CW* X:375). Mill's basic argument is just this: The injunction to follow or imitate nature is intended, as all injunctions are, to urge us to do something which we might or might not do. If then 'nature' is taken in the first sense the injunction is meaningless. Following nature in this sense is not something which we might or might not do since everything we do, being "the exertion of some natural power" (*CW* X:379), is in conformity with nature. On the other hand, taking 'nature' in the second sense the injunction is irrational and immoral:

Irrational, because all human action whatever, consists in altering, and all useful action in improving, the spontaneous course of nature:

Immoral, because the course of natural phenomena being replete with everything which when committed by human beings is most worthy of abhorrence, any one who endeavoured in his actions to imitate the natural course of things would be universally seen and acknowledged to be the wickedest of men. (CW X:402)

The case against the injunction to follow nature on the first interpretation of 'nature' needs little comment. In the course of his discussion Mill exhibits his commitment to a naturalistic view of human beings. He thinks that human beings in their entirety are parts of nature like any other organisms and as such are as much subject to nature's laws as anything else. Such naturalism is open to dispute. But even if human actions involve the effects in the natural order of the operation of a soul or spirit which is not natural in the requisite sense, the basic thrust of Mill's case against the injunction to follow nature, on the first interpretation, is unaffected. All Mill needs is the conditional: if by 'nature' is meant everything actual and physically possible and if all human actions are the exertions of natural powers, then the injunction to follow nature is meaningless. This is clearly true and the anti-naturalist can without inconsistency accept it.

The attack on the injunction to follow nature on the second interpretation of 'nature' is more controversial. The aim is to show that on this interpretation the injunction is irrational and immoral. To show that it is irrational Mill relies on an assumption about human action. At one point this is expressed as the claim that "the very aim and object of action is to alter and improve Nature" (CW X:380). In a passage already quoted from the conclusion of the essay (CW X:402) the point is more prudently expressed as the claim that "all human action whatever, consists in altering, and all useful action in improving, the spontaneous course of nature". One could pick away at either of these formulations. Clearly not everything we do is aimed at the improvement of nature. Perhaps in an attenuated sense everything we do is aimed at altering nature in that it makes something happen which would not have happened otherwise. Be that as it may, what Mill needs is surely just the assumption that we all have an interest in there being activities which aim to alter the spontaneous course of nature. Since, for example, we rely on manufactured shelter and clothing it would be irrational to submit to a principle which implies that manufacturing should not take place. The problem for Mill's argument is simply that defenders of the injunction to follow nature would hardly wish to deny such points. Their claim must presumably be that there is general order in nature with which human beings may or may not align themselves, and that to aim so to align oneself is not irrational on the grounds that Mill supposes, since it need not involve holding back from or subverting rational attempts to alter the spontaneous course of nature.[15] Mill may be right to suggest as he does that the religious have too often obstructed progress out of a concern not to tamper with the creation. But if they may on this account be justifiably convicted of irrationality, the irrationality would spring not from a failure to appreciate the very general point about action on which Mill relies, but rather from lack of evidence for the world view which provides the rationale for resisting particular attempts at improving on nature.

In support of the charge of immorality Mill graphically and rhetorically illustrates the death and destruction wrought by the natural elements and the diseases which debilitate or kill the good and the bad alike. There is no point in rehearsing the details. Those with the good fortune to live in an environment which is rarely life-threatening and in social circumstances which, relative to the range of such circumstances throughout the world, provide for a high degree of comfort and health, may find Mill's review of the horrors of nature over-pessimistic or at least one-sided. But that the horrors occur is not in doubt. The question is how far they tell against the defender of the injunction to follow nature. Mill has two main points. The first, which figures in the concluding summary of his position (CW X:402) already quoted, is that to imitate nature, given what nature does, would be wicked. If imitating nature includes wreaking death and destruction, then the point is not in dispute. Again though, the defender of the injunction to follow nature is hardly likely to find it compelling because the injunction is not meant to direct people to imitate nature's horrors, but rather to align themselves with an order which is conceived to be benign. Mill's second and more telling point is then that the horrors he has been illustrating constitute evidence against the view that there is such a benign order. The traditional problem of evil is at the root of the problem he discerns in the injunction to follow nature. He is saying in effect, 'If you follow nature as it really is, then you will act immorally *and* you have no good reason to think that nature is otherwise'.

It is arguable that Mill does not fairly represent the range of positions open to those who defend the injunction to follow nature. It is fundamental to the thought of, for example, St. Augustine of Hippo that the nature of everything is good. Rational agents may violate their nature, but their nature, for all that, remains something which is good. It is clear that by the nature of a thing Augustine cannot mean the aggregate of its powers or properties, for under that interpretation the nature of a human being would incorporate any tendencies toward evil which that being has, and Augustine would conceive of such tendencies as violations of the being's nature. In speaking of the nature of X, Augustine must have in mind something such that, if it functioned properly, X would be as God had intended and would thus be good. In *On Free Choice of the Will*, one of his most Platonic works, he provides an account of the soul as having various components including reason, whose function it is to govern the rest and thus preserve order in the parts. Though Augustine does not talk explicitly of following one's nature, he clearly conceives of virtue as a matter of sustaining an order in the soul and conceives of sustaining such order as a matter of actualising one's nature. This basic idea is taken up by Joseph Butler in the eighteenth century. In his *Fifteen Sermons* Butler speaks of our nature as a system or constitution adapted to virtue and makes that notion central to his explanation of how it can be that we may either conform to or deviate from our nature. As with Augustine the key idea is that we violate our nature when we wilfully act in ways which do not respect the proper order of the components of our nature, as when, for example, we act from passion contrary to the deliberations of our reflective faculty, conscience. Against this background Butler develops his central thesis that virtue consists in following one's nature.[16]

A defender of the Platonic-Christian tradition as exemplified by Augustine and Butler could claim with some justification that Mill does not explicitly address the particular conception of nature required to make the most plausible sense of the injunction to follow nature. That conception focuses on human nature rather than nature in the large and conceives of that nature in terms of an orderly arrangement of components. Mill does discuss specifically human nature (*CW* X:392ff). As one would expect he applies the distinction he has already made between two senses of 'nature'. If by our nature is meant the aggregate of our powers and properties, then we cannot but follow our nature, and we do so as much when we do evil as when we do good. The analogue of the second sense of 'nature' is to think of our nature as comprising those of our tendencies to act which are not formed or molded by reason. Mill comments:

> The result is a vein of sentiment so common in the modern world (though unknown to the philosophic ancients) which exalts instinct at the expense of reason; an aberration rendered still more mischievous by the opinion commonly held in conjunction with it, that every, or almost every, feeling or impulse which acts promptly without waiting to ask questions, is an instinct. Thus almost every variety of unreflecting and uncalculating impulse receives a kind of consecration, except those which, though unreflecting at the moment, owe their origin to previous habits of reflection. . . . (CW X:392)

While such remarks have some point against Rousseau and others of the Romantic movement they have little bearing on the Platonic-Christian tradition whose representatives could not be further from consecrating 'unreflecting and uncalculating impulse'. The discipline of impulse is crucial to what they conceive to be natural to humankind, since it accords with the order with which the human soul was designed to conform. Given the influence of Butler in the nineteenth century[17] it is perhaps a little surprising[18] that Mill does not devote some attention to Butler's analysis. Butler was very much aware of the need to deal with the conceptual problems in the notions of following and deviating from one's nature, and developed his conception of our nature as a system adapted to virtue with the express aim of making sense of these notions. It may be that Mill would have included Butler amongst those thinkers whose talk of nature concerns not what is but what ought to be.[19] Any such interpretation of Butler would be inaccurate. For Butler, following our nature does not mean just living as we ought but rather living in accord with the ways for which our constitution is adapted, and it is for him a matter of fact that we are so adapted through being designed by God. Nevertheless, though Mill, in this context, does not explicitly address the thought of Butler or others in the Platonic-Christian tradition it is clear what stance he would take towards their ideas. The claim that we are adapted to virtue, because literally made for virtue, turns on the optimistic teleological theology against which Mill takes considerations about evil to be decisive. It is thus for him no more plausible than the more general claim that there is a benign providential order in nature with which we should align ourselves, but from which in practice we may depart. Once again the problem of evil is the heart of the matter.

IV

Sceptical as to the truth of religious claims, Mill turns in 'Utility of Religion' to consider whether religion in general has been beneficial to humankind and whether any benefits it may have produced could have been achieved without it. Such an enquiry was very much to the point, since it could not simply be assumed "that if religion be false, nothing but good can be the consequence of rejecting it". On the contrary, it is "perfectly conceivable that religion may be morally useful without being intellectually sustainable" (CW X:405). Utilitarian considerations would dictate that if the benefits of religion could not be obtained by other means, then, provided that religion does not result in more harm than good, it would be wrong to undermine it.

To believers the restrictions on Mill's discussion will seem to miss out the most important matters. Mill is concerned to estimate the benefits of religion on the supposition that religious beliefs are false or at least not 'intellectually sustainable'. He must therefore leave out of account any supposed benefits which would accrue only if religious beliefs were true. Being strengthened or guided by God and receiving everlasting life are thus not germane to the discussion.

Mill could have made more than he does of the evils brought about by religious institutions and practices.[20] In what is, from any reasonable point of view, a remarkably fair and balanced analysis, he chooses instead to focus on respects in which religion could fairly be argued to have been an instrument of both social good or individual good. As to social good he concedes that religious teaching has had a substantial role in inculcating a regard for principles of justice, veracity and beneficence, and that humankind would be in a sorry state had such principles not been inculcated. He argues, however, that it was not because the teaching was religious that it had such benefits, but rather because it presented a "generally accepted system of rules for the guidance and government of human life" (CW

X:407). This prompts an instructive analysis of the factors which contribute to the widespread acceptance of such a system. Mill distinguishes three influences. There is, first, the influence of what he calls simple authority, by which he means the influence exerted by the mere fact that fellow human beings share a certain belief or attitude. Then there is the power of education conceived as the deliberate inculcation of beliefs and attitudes in the young whether by parents or formal schooling. Both of these influences, Mill points out, "operate through men's involuntary beliefs, feelings and desires" (CW X:410). A third influence, public opinion, he suggests, "operates directly on their actions, whether their involuntary sentiments are carried with it or not". By 'public opinion' he does not mean just widely held beliefs and attitudes, but rather the tendency of the public to attach praise and favour to sharing certain beliefs and attitudes, and blame and disfavour to failing to share them.

In a society in which religion has absorbed "the best human morality which reason and goodness can work out" (CW X:406) and for which the time is long past when "the divine agency was supposed habitually to employ temporal rewards and punishments" (CW X:412), these are, Mill thinks, the main influences responsible for the continued acceptance of religious beliefs and attitudes and, through them, the continued acceptance of associated practical principles. To the influence often attributed to the anticipation of divine retribution or reward Mill gives little weight. He will have no truck with those who fear the collapse of civilized life, for want of supernatural threats and inducements, were religion not widely accepted.[21]

Religion is not necessary as an enforcer of social morality, nor, Mill goes on to argue, is it necessary as a teacher.

[B]ecause, when men were still savages, they would not have received either moral or scientific truths unless they had supposed them to be supernaturally imparted, does it follow that they would now give up moral truths any more than scientific, because they believed them to have no higher origin than wise and noble human hearts? Are not moral truths strong enough in their own evidence, at all events to retain the belief of mankind when once they have acquired it? (CW X:416)

Besides, Mill suggests, the attribution of a supernatural origin to received moral principles has a positively harmful effect in that it renders them immune from discussion and criticism and so works against the possibility of rational revisions in the light of increased scientific knowledge and changing sensibilities.

The upshot, then, is that although religion has indeed been socially beneficial there is no reason to suppose that it is necessary as either an enforcer or a teacher of morals. But what about the influence of religion on the good of individuals? Here is a key passage:

Religion and poetry address themselves, at least in one of their aspects, to the same part of the human constitution: they both supply the same want, that of ideal conceptions grander and more beautiful than we see realized in the prose of human life. Religion, as distinguished from poetry, is the product of the craving to know whether these imaginative conceptions have realities answering to them in some other world than ours. The mind, in this state, eagerly catches at any rumours respecting other worlds, especially when delivered by persons whom it deems wiser than itself. To the poetry of the supernatural, comes to be thus added a positive belief and expectation, which unpoetical minds can share with the poetical. Belief in a God or Gods, and in a life after death, becomes the canvas which every mind, according to its capacity, covers with such ideal pictures as it can either invent or copy. In that other life each hopes to find the good which he has failed to find on earth, or the better which is suggested to him by the good which on earth he has partially seen and known. (CW X:419)

Religion thus conceived is unquestionably "a source of personal satisfaction and of elevated feelings" (CW X:420) and to that extent a factor for good in the lives of individuals. Again, though, the crucial question is whether comparable benefits could be achieved without religion or, at any rate, without supernatural religion. How without such religion can we be moved by something "grander and more beautiful than we see realized in the prose of human life"? The importance of being so moved was, by his own account, borne in upon Mill by the mental crisis which he endured in 1826. The key feature of this crisis was the sense that the realization of the goals towards which he was working would not bring with it any great joy or happiness. That the goals were worth pursuing he did not doubt, but it disturbed and depressed him to feel that he would not delight in their achievement.[22] The crisis passed, but it led to a reappraisal of his attitudes towards life and towards the analytical style of his intellectual pursuits, as the following passage from the *Autobiography* indicates.

I had now learnt by experience that the passive susceptibilities needed to be cultivated as well as the active capacities, and required to be nourished and enriched as well as guided. I did not, for an instant, lose sight of, or undervalue, that part of the truth which I had seen before; I never turned recreant to intellectual culture, or ceased to consider the power and practice of analysis as an essential condition both of individual and of social improvement. But I thought that it had consequences which required to be corrected, by joining other kinds of cultivation with it. The maintenance of a due balance among the faculties, now seemed to me to be of primary importance. The cultivation of the feelings became one of the cardinal points in my ethical and philosophical creed. And my thoughts and inclinations turned in an increasing degree towards whatever seemed capable of being instrumental to that object. (*CW* I:147)

If Mill takes seriously the notion that supernatural religion makes for the good of its adherents, it is because he appreciates its role in the cultivation of feelings and, in particular, the range of feelings associated with taking delight in the pursuit of worthwhile ends. But, he argues, this is a good which can flow from "the idealization of our earthly life, the cultivation of a high conception of what *it* may be made" (*CW* X:420). Though individual human lives are transient, "the life of the human species is not short; its indefinite duration is practically equivalent to endlessness; and being combined with indefinite capability of improvement, it offers to the imagination and sympathies a large enough object to satisfy any reasonable demand for grandeur of aspiration" (*CW* X:420). The cultivation of such sentiments is the Religion of Humanity,[23] deservedly so-called, Mill suggests, since "[t]he essence of religion is the strong and earnest direction of the emotions and desires towards an ideal object, recognized as of the highest excellence, and rightfully paramount over all selfish objects of desire" (*CW* X:422). But not only does the Religion of Humanity make possible 'grandeur of aspiration', it also avoids the moral defects of supernatural religion in so far as it is free of doctrines which encourage undue concern for personal salvation and does not require a dubious ethic of belief.

In 'Utility of Religion' Mill is primarily concerned with the Religion of Humanity in so far as it is productive of the sort of individual good which he took to flow from supernatural religion at its best. But Mill was clearly also concerned with the question whether morality, conceived as grounded in utilitarian considerations, would take hold of people's minds, as the discussion of the ultimate sanction of the principle of utility in *Utilitarianism* indicates:

[M]oral associations which are wholly of artificial creation, when intellectual culture goes on, yield by degrees to the dissolving force of analysis: and if the feeling of duty, when associated with utility, would appear equally arbitrary; if there were no leading department of our nature, no powerful class of sentiments, with which that association would harmonize, which would make us feel it congenial, and incline us not only to foster it in others (for which we have abundant interested motives), but also to cherish it in ourselves; if there were not, in short a natural basis of sentiment for utilitarian morality, it might well happen that this association also, even after it had been implanted by education, might be analysed away. (*CW* X:230–31)

The worry about 'the dissolving force of analysis' echoes that which sprang from the mental crisis and, here too, the response is to recognize the importance of feeling.

[T]here *is* this basis of powerful natural sentiment; and this it is which, when once the general happiness is recognized as the ethical standard, will constitute the strength of the utilitarian morality. This firm foundation is that of the social feelings of mankind; the desire to be in unity with our fellow creatures, which is already a powerful principle in human nature, and happily one of those which tend to become stronger, even without express inculcation, from the influences of advancing civilization. (*CW* X:231)

The emphasis is on the naturalness of social feeling, but Mill goes further.

If we now suppose this feeling of unity to be taught as a religion, and the whole force of education, of institutions, and of opinion, directed, as it once was in the case of religion, to make every person grow up from infancy surrounded on all sides by the profession and by the practice of it, I think that no one, who can realize this conception, will feel any misgiving about the sufficiency of the ultimate sanction for the Happiness morality. (*CW* X:232)

These passages from *Utilitarianism* make it plain that Mill is not interested in the Religion of Humanity purely as a means to bringing about the benefits to individuals which hitherto they had derived from supernatural religion. Rather, the Religion of Humanity is to be seen as the deliberate nurturing of sentiments which are the natural basis of utilitarian morality, but which might easily become faint through the want of a culture which would encourage them.

The modern reader may feel that it takes a highly developed sense of moral superiority to suppose that one's favoured morality should be propagated as a religion.[24] Such a reaction may spring from a general antipathy to commending *any* moral point of view. But it may also spring from a more reasonable worry as to whether the attitudes nurtured by the Religion of Humanity really have anything to commend them or whether anyone has the right to inculcate them through the formal educational system. Might not the high-minded secular priests of this religion simply be out to impose their views on the masses? Mill has the resources for a response to this line of thought. To cultivate social feeling, and encourage therefore the pursuit of the good of humanity, is not to impose on the masses an ideal dreamt up by an intellectual elite bent on reform. As we have seen, Mill thinks that social feeling is natural and a part of an individual's good. Such a claim is no mere dogma, for it is not immune to criticism. It may only be plausibly held so long as the generality of humankind on reflection find that they actually do care about the good of humanity and find satisfaction in promoting that good.

Mill's fairly brisk and highly general remarks about the Religion of Humanity hardly suffice to impart a vivid sense of its inspirational powers. We may find it hard to be inspired by humanity as such and may reflect that a professed concern for the good of humanity can all too readily co-exist with blindness to the needs of those closer to home.[25] But though Mill's high and earnest tone may grate we should not lose sight of the fact that he sought to foster a genuine regard for the good of others and, with some justification, feared that the passing away of supernatural religion might drain away the emotional resources required for the pursuit of the worthwhile ends[26] and deprive individuals of that cultivation of feeling which he took to be a crucial ingredient of a satisfying life.

The seriousness with which Mill took the cultivation of feeling is further evidenced by his reflections on imagination in the final part of 'Theism'. The "rational principle of regulating our feelings as well as opinions strictly by evidence" (*CW* X:483) is not incompatible, Mill argues, with "the indulgence of hope, in a region of imagination merely, in which there is no prospect that any probable grounds of expectation will ever be obtained". He goes so far as to suggest that "the indulgence of hope with regard to the government of the universe and the destiny of man after death, while we recognize as a clear truth that we have no ground for more than a hope, is legitimate and philosophically defensible" (CW X:485). So too is the hope "that Christ actually was what he supposed himself to be . . . a man charged with a special, express and unique commission from God to lead mankind to truth and virtue" (CW X:488). Such hopes, Mill thinks, meet our need for 'grandeur of aspiration' and thus "aid and fortify that real, though purely human religion" which is the Religion of Humanity.

It is important to see that there is no suggestion in all this of turning a blind eye to evidence which renders hope futile. Changes in our state of information and understanding may make hope no longer 'legitimate and philosophically defensible'. Many would hold that this is now the status of all supernatural hopes, and there is nothing in what Mill says which rules out such an attitude if it is properly related to the evidence. Still, I think Mill goes too far. It is one thing to be hopeful about what for all we know might be the case when we think there is at least some chance that it may be so. It is another to indulge hope where we have no reason to think there is such a chance. This latter speculative hope is what Mill enjoins, yet there is an obvious danger. The hopes which he seeks to encourage are those which release vital resources and energies in the pursuit of worthwhile ends. But directing such resources and energies behind hopes which are entirely speculative diverts them from more realistic hopes and may get in the way of reconciling oneself to a situation which in reality may be less pleasing than that hoped for. Clearly this can happen. Imagine parents who in the absence of any evidence continue to hope that their long lost child is alive. Such a hope might be sustaining, but it might equally detract from coming to terms with the loss. Nonetheless, Mill's exploration into the territory of imagination and feeling is suggestive. Imaginative visions of how things might become and, indeed, of how, for all we know, things might actually be, are, if Mill is right, no mere embellishment of life, but a condition for both happiness and the energetic pursuit of the good.

It has been suggested that in *Three Essays on Religion* Mill appears "to be a man who had sought to salvage as much as he could from traditional faith".[27] The concluding section of 'Theism' on 'supernatural hopes' lends substance to this remark, though it gives a misleading impression of the tenor of the essays taken as a whole. There are no concessions to religious beliefs and attitudes in 'Nature' and the whole thrust of 'Utility of Religion' is towards replacing supernatural religion with the Religion of Humanity. So far as 'Theism' is concerned there is no hint until its concluding section that Mill would wish to indulge supernatural hopes. The limited theism defended in his discussion of the marks of design is treated, in that discussion, as an explanatory hypothesis, not as a source of either consolation or inspiration. Against this background the remarks on hope come as a surprise. They do not follow from what has come before. Imaginative vision does not require, and need not pave the way for, speculative hope.

V

Morality and virtue are usually conceived in such a way that the morally commendable or virtuous life is one which is suited to meeting the demands of social existence and thus requires the restraint of self-interested or aggressive inclinations and the encouragement of regard for the good of society. Since the time of Plato there have been many philosophers who have suspected, perhaps feared, that the way human beings are constituted as a matter of fact works against their satisfying the demands of morality and virtue thus conceived. Plato can be seen as addressing this suspicion, and attempting to banish it, by meeting the challenge to Socrates in Book II of the *Republic*. An important element of the challenge was to show that justice is good in itself. In meeting the challenge Plato argued that if the elements of our psychological make-up function properly then we shall be virtuous. Contrary to appearances, our nature actually conduces to, rather than works against, our being virtuous. This theme is carried over into Christian tradition. Christians turned their suspicion that we are not up to virtue into a doctrine of sin which served to demonstrate our need, not just for guidance, but for redemption. For all that Christianity had to acknowledge that we were not created evil and so was under strong pressure to think of evil as a violation of a nature which is good. As indicated earlier this theme may be found in the work of St. Augustine, and also that of Joseph Butler in the eighteenth century. But while for Augustine our original nature is ravaged and rendered impotent by original sin, Butler is quite explicitly concerned to encourage us to virtue by showing that virtue is a matter of following our nature. His worry is not posed by the doctrine of original sin, but by a view of human motivation which would suggest that we were made for private good and not for public.

Mill and other Victorian thinkers took up the traditional concern with whether we are up to virtue – with whether we have the resources required for the pursuit of noble ends. In Mill's case the problem is acute. The considerations advanced in 'Nature' and in 'Theism' show him to be far removed from the optimistic Platonic-Christian vision of a natural order in harmony with the moral order – a vision underpinning Butler's thought and which the Kant of the *Critique of Practical Reason* was still trying to preserve. Unable to rely upon that vision, Mill cannot draw strength from a conception of the proper functioning of the elements of our nature. It is not nature, under such a vision, but art, in the form of education, which fashions us for virtue. It can do so, Mill suggests, only if it feeds our imaginations in ways which cultivate those feelings which are the natural basis of the utilitarian morality. Seen in the light of these considerations the *Three Essays on Religion* are more than an attack on orthodox religious thought, and more too than an expression of nostalgia for religion by a reluctant sceptic. They show Mill exercised by the traditional suspicion about our aptitude for virtue, in the light of his scepticism about religious belief, and actively seeking ways of bridging the gap between the way we are and the way we ought to be.

NOTES

1 See *Utilitarianism*, CW X:209–33.
2 See *On Liberty*, CW XVIII:228–59, and also Mill's early contributions to newspapers gathered together in *CW* XXII. Mill's preoccupation with prevailing restrictions on the expression of unbelieving opinions is well documented in Hamburger 1991.
3 As in *Civilization*, CW XVIII:117–47.

4 *CW* X:369–489.

5 See her introductory notice, *CW* X:371–72.

6 *An Examination of Sir William Hamilton's Philosophy*, *CW* IX.

7 For a useful general survey of Mill's thought on and attitudes to religion, see Carr 1962.

8 Thomas Aquinas, *Summa Contra Gentiles*, Bk. 1. Locke's discussion may be found in *An Essay Concerning Human Understanding*, Bk. IV, especially chs. 18 and 19.

9 *Enquiry Concerning Human Understanding*, sec. X.

10 One might have expected Mill to refer in these essays to Hume's *Dialogues Concerning Natural Religion*. In fact, there is no such reference and the Indexes to Mill's *Collected Works* cite just one reference to the *Dialogues*, in *CW* XXIV:1083. Mill's treatment of the argument from marks of design is similar to Hume's, but seems to be explicitly geared to the discussion in Paley's *Natural Theology*, which is cited.

11 A somewhat similar line of thought occurs in *A System of Logic*, *CW* VII:555–58.

12 It is on this point that Mill may have regarded his own formulation of the argument as advancing beyond Paley's.

13 See, in particular, *CW* VII:326ff.

14 See, for example, Mackie 1955.

15 Mill recognizes (*CW* X:482) that the crucial issue has to do with the idea that there is a benign providential order rather than with the idea that no one should ever try to improve on nature, but does not qualify the charge of irrationality as he should.

16 For discussions of Butler which focus on the idea of our having a constitution adapted to virtue, see Millar 1988 and 1992.

17 On this see Garnett 1992.

18 But not so surprising. Mill's attitude to Butler was no doubt coloured by the not altogether inaccurate thought that Butler was an intuitionist in ethical matters. See the passing remarks in 'Sedgwick's Discourse', *CW* X:64.

19 Compare Mill's remarks on the Stoics and the natural law tradition, *CW* X:376ff.

20 In this respect his essay contrasts strikingly with those of Russell 1975.

21 Freud was not so sanguine. See Freud 1985.

22 For an illuminating discussion of such 'arrests of life' touching on, among others, Mill and Tolstoy, see Hepburn 1965.

23 The expression 'Religion of Humanity' had been used by Comte, for whom Mill had a qualified admiration. See *August Comte and Positivism*, *CW* X: especially 332ff. Note, however, that Mill found Comte's advocacy of a kind of liturgy for the Religion of Humanity simply

ridiculous. See *CW* X:341ff. The history of the idea of a Religion of Humanity in Victorian Britain is traced in Wright 1986.

24 Somewhat similar sentiments underlie Cowling 1963. Cowling writes: "Mill was one of the most censorious of nineteenth-century moralists. At every turn, denigration of existing society was offered with inquisitorial certainty" (p. 143). He also claims that the Religion of Humanity has no more claim to acceptance than the religions Mill criticizes.

25 A failing cruelly but effectively satirized in Dickens's *Bleak House* in the character of Mrs Pardiggle.

26 The concern of Victorian moralists with motivation is interestingly explored in Collini 1991. See especially ch. 2.

27 Semmel 1984, 173.

6 Mill on psychology and the moral sciences

> They [Coleridge and Bentham] agreed in recognising that sound theory is the only foundation for sound practice, and that whoever despises theory, let him give himself what airs of wisdom he may, is self-convicted of being a quack. If a book were to be compiled containing all the best things ever said on the rule-of-thumb school of political craftsmanship, and on the insufficiency for practical purposes of what the mere practical man calls experience, it is difficult to say whether the collection would be more indebted to the writings of Bentham or of Coleridge. ("Coleridge," CW X:121)

John Stuart Mill held, with his father, James Mill, and with all utilitarians, that the end of morality and of practice in general is to maximize the general welfare of humankind. However, to achieve any end, including this ultimate end, requires a knowledge of the means to that end, a knowledge of causes and effects that may be used to realize the end. Practice can only be as solid as the theoretical knowledge of fact upon which it is based. But the younger Mill disagreed with his father and the older generation of utilitarians on the nature of that knowledge and on the methods to be used to justify claims to have acquired such knowledge. To be sure, both the older and the younger Mills must be counted within the empiricist camp, with regard to the nature of human knowledge.[1] On this view, human knowledge begins and ends in sense experience, and knowledge of causes is, as Hume argued, knowledge of matter-of-fact regularities (cf. James Mill 1869, I:350, 402ff). Mill understands causation in terms of necessary, sufficient, and necessary and sufficient conditions.[2] Understood strictly, a statement of causation is simply a statement of necessary and sufficient conditions: "whenever something is A then, and only then, it is B."[3] It is through the use of such generalizations that we *explain* events. An explanation of why an A is a B is provided by subsuming these events under the relevant law:

> Whenever something is A then, and only then, it is B.[4]
> This is A.
>
> ───────────────
>
> Hence, this is B.

As Mill puts it, "An individual fact is said to be explained, by pointing out its cause, that is, by stating the law or laws of causation, of which its production is an instance" (*CW* VII:464). Mill thus adopts what has subsequently come to be called the "covering law model" of explanation.[5] Now, these generalizations used in explanations and for practical reasoning are always statements regarding a complete population. Our empirical data, in contrast, are always limited to a sample. The generalizations that we use in explanation and in practical reasoning therefore always make a claim that goes beyond the available evidence. For this reason knowledge of such generalizations can never be certain. However, some generalizations (those that we count as laws) – unlike others (those that we count as accidental generalizations) – can be used for purposes of prediction ("what will happen") and contrary-to-fact reasoning ("what would happen if"), both of which are essential to rational action. Those generalizations that we use for prediction and contrary-to-fact reasoning, that is, those generalizations that we use in practical inferences, are those that are more solidly based evidentially; these, according to the Mills, are those for which the data have been gathered in conformity to the methodological rules of the empirical science (James Mill 1869, I:437–38). The knowledge required for action may be of the biological realm, in the case of agricultural production, or of mechanics, physics and chemistry, in the case of the production of material goods. But the Mills both take as solidly established the factual generalization that *for every property there is a generalization that gives its necessary and sufficient conditions in terms of other properties.*[6] This is the principle of universal causation. It is a law about laws – as Mill puts it, it states that "it is a law that there is a law for everything"; and it is justified, Mill argues, by the fact that we have been successful in discovering causes.[7] The law entails that for any property there is a law that can be discovered and which explains the presence and absence of that property.[8] It applies to the biological and physical realms, as we just noted, but also applies in particular, according to the Mills, to human beings. In that context it is the thesis that there are laws of the human mind and of human behaviour – the Mills are convinced determinists;[9] and if we are to deal in practice in an effective way with social processes then we also need to know these laws of human nature.[10] It is with respect to the latter, the laws that one needs to know to achieve one's social ends, that the Mills, elder and younger, disagreed. Where the elder Mill began with psychology, the younger Mill argues that the basic form of knowledge that is required for social action is sociological.[11] And where the elder Mill used what came to be called the "geometrical" method for justifying the theoretical conclusions to be used for social action, the younger Mill proposed instead what he referred to as the "deductive" method. Both the geometrical and deductive methods can rightly be called "inductive," and they both conform to the general patterns of the canons of scientific inference, yet they imply very different ways of marshalling evidence. In this respect John Stuart Mill differs from his father and the older utilitarians on the proper method for the social sciences.

One can see the older utilitarian patterns of thought in the work of James Mill on government and in the work of David Ricardo on economics.

James Mill wrote his "Essay on Government" (1820) as a plea for political reform during the period of a narrow franchise and rotten boroughs.[12] It presented in an effective polemical form arguments that Bentham presented in a less pellucid way in his essay *Plan of Parliamentary Reform, in the form of a Catechism* (1817).[13] Mill, following Bentham, argued that the effects of widening the franchise and eliminating the rotten boroughs would be a government more responsive to the interests of all, and would therefore serve the general utilitarian end. The thesis that these actions would have those effects was justified by deducing it from the assumption that each person seeks to maximize his or her own pleasure, where "pleasure" is understood in a fairly narrow sense, to mean material well-being. Mill proposed to "lay a foundation for the science of Government" by reference to the principle that "every human being is determined by his pains and pleasures; and that his happiness corresponds with the degree in which pleasures are great, and his pains are small" (James Mill 1978, 55–56). According to Mill, the greatest happiness is to be achieved when each receives the full return from his or her labour.

if you give more to one man than the produce of his labour, you can do so only by taking it away from the produce of some other man's labour. The greatest possible happiness of society is, therefore, attained by insuring to every man the greatest possible quantity of the produce of his labour. (James Mill 1978, 57)

But given the premise about human nature, people will be inclined to take from others in order to satisfy their own desires: "it is obvious that every man, who has not all the objects of his desire, has inducement to take them from any other man who is weaker than himself" (ibid.). How is this to be prevented? How are we to ensure that every person receives the greatest possible quantity of the produce of his or her labour? The answer Mill gives is that people combine together to "delegate to a small number the power necessary for protecting them all" (ibid.). The government is the group to whom this power is delegated.

[T]he end to be obtained, through government as the means, is, to make that distribution of the scanty materials of happiness, which would insure the greatest sum of it in the members of the community, taken altogether, preventing any individual, or combination of individuals, from interfering with that distribution, or making any man to have less than his share. (James Mill 1978, 56)

But government is one thing, good government another. One still needs various means to secure good government, to secure the identity of interests between the community as a whole and those to whom power is delegated. Mill deduces from his premise about human nature that the means to good governing is a representative form of government: "in the representative system alone the securities for good government are to be found" (James Mill 1978, 72). If the representatives are chosen by a small number of the community, the latter will elect those who will further the interest of the minority that chooses them. To ensure therefore that the representatives act in the interest of the community as a whole, the electors should consist of the community at large:[14] "It is very evident, that if the community itself were the choosing body, the interest of the community and that of the choosing body would be the same" (James Mill 1978, 79). Mill thus defends a broad franchise with few qualifications.

Ricardo[15] began his economics from the same premise about human nature. He assumes that persons are out to maximize their pleasure, and that exchanges are made on this basis. For most objects, labour is required for their production, and it is this pain that must be compensated in an exchange. Labour therefore determines the exchange value of an object.[16] Ricardo quotes Adam Smith approvingly:[17] "What every thing is really worth to the man who has acquired it, and who wants to dispose of it, or exchange it for something else, is the toil and trouble which it can save to himself, and which it can impose on other people."[18]

From this premise concerning human psychology that he shared with Bentham and James Mill, and from the appropriate Malthusian assumptions about the growth of population, it could be deduced that population would grow in such a way that competition in a free market for work would eventually drive wages down so that the latter tend to hover about the subsistence level. This was the so-called "iron law of wages." On the basis of this "law," Ricardo and the other utilitarians argued that any attempt to ameliorate the conditions of the working class through legislation, e.g., by means of the Poor Laws, would in fact make conditions worse. Any long-run gains could be made only through knowledge and the use of entrepreneurial skills, and if these were not adequately rewarded they would not be exercised. But to ameliorate conditions of the working class would require transfers of goods from those who had them to those who did not, thereby depriving the innovators and the entrepreneurs of their fair reward. So, in spite of the short-term gain, in the long run all would be made worse off by taxing the well-off to favour the poor. As Ricardo put it, speaking about the Poor Laws, "instead of making the poor rich, they are calculated to make the rich poor."[19] One cannot, it was concluded, without impunity, interfere with the "laws" of economics.

The principle of gravitation is not more certain than the tendency of such laws to change wealth and power into misery and weakness; to call away the exertions of labour from every object, except as providing mere subsistence; to confound all intellectual distinction; to busy the mind continually in supplying the body's wants; until at last all classes should be infected with the plague of universal poverty.[20]

The principle of utility therefore argued against any attempt to remedy the lot of the poor through legislation.

In each case, that concerning government and that concerning economic organization, the central premise was a thesis about human nature. This premise states that human beings are moved primarily by self-regarding desires for material pleasures. This premise had the form of a statement of law about human beings, and in particular about human motivation. This thesis was part of the general theory of associationist psychology, and was taken to be well established by the methods of science. Since the thesis was taken as an axiom by James Mill and Ricardo and their results were deduced from it, the method they used can reasonably be called "geometrical," as it was both by their opponents and by the younger Mill.

James Mill's essay on government was strongly criticized by the Whig polemicist and historian T. B. Macaulay in his discussion of "Mill's Essay on Government: Utilitarian Logic and Politics" (Macaulay 1978).[21] He attacked the conclusions, but more importantly also attacked the method: no conclusions could be expected to be sound if the geometrical method was used in the social sciences. Macaulay emphasized in effect that political science and the science of government in particular was a *social* science, dealing with large groups of people. In order to discuss the issue of the best form of government, we need to have a good understanding of human motives. To assume material self-interest alone is simply false of a single individual.

But when the question is propounded generally about the whole species, the impossibility of answering is still more evident. Man differs from man; generation from generation; nation from nation. Education, station, sex, age, accidental associations, produce infinite shades of variety. (Macaulay 1978, 126–27)

Given the fact that these many individuals were interacting, it was simply not possible to deduce from psychological laws about individuals the laws for the group phenomena. That is, Macaulay argued, given the facts of interaction, the geometrical method was inappropriate for the social sciences. We need instead to proceed inductively, "by observing the present state of the world" and "by studying the history of past ages," "generalizing with judgment and diffidence," "perpetually bringing the theory which we have constructed to the test of new facts" (Macaulay 1978, 128). Macaulay argued that instead of the geometrical method one needed to proceed historically and through the study of different societies, using the simple inductive methods of Bacon. In the absence of such an adequate method, and given the reliance upon one that cannot work, it is no wonder then that James Mill had arrived at mistaken conclusions, and potentially disastrous policy recommendations.

Proceeding thus, – patiently, – dilligently, – candidly, – we may hope to form a system as far inferior in pretension to that which we have been examining, and as far superior to it in real utility, as the prescriptions of a great physician, varying with every stage of every malady, and with the constitution of every patient, to the pill of the advertising quack, which is to cure all human beings, in all climates, of all disease. (Macaulay 1978, 128)

This point was related to the economic points of Ricardo. If indeed people acted only for their own profit, then if they were given the vote they would immediately act to expropriate the rich. That would perhaps lead in the long run to disaster for succeeding generations. But the lot of those latecomers would be irrelevant since the voters would be acting to maximize their own profit, and not to secure additional gain for future generations; they would act in their own interests and not those of succeeding generations.

The point was made explicitly by Samuel Taylor Coleridge in his *Treatise on Method* (1818).[22] Coleridge criticizes the case for universal suffrage that had been made by the reform agitator Major John Cartwright in the pamphlet *A Bill of Rights and Liberties; or, An Act for a Constitutional Reform of Parliament*. Cartwright based his argument for Parliamentary reform on a premise that Coleridge puts this way: "all without exception are capable of feeling happiness or misery, accordingly as they are well or ill governed."[23] As Cartwright puts it,

according to the just theory of government, every male commoner . . . who directly, or indirectly, contributes to the public taxes, or whose property, character, liberty, and life are affected by legislation, is entitled to his suffrage in the election of those Representatives of the Commons, by whom taxes and laws are imposed.[24]

His proposed bill therefore contains the clause that "every male commoner . . . shall be entitled to, and enjoy the right of suffrage in the election of a representative to serve his electoral district in Parliament" (Cartwright 1817, 3). Cartwright's argument here takes up that of Bentham,[25] who began his claim for the universality of suffrage with the rhetorical question, "Who is there, that is not susceptible of discomfort and comfort – of pain and pleasure?" To this argument of Cartwright, Bentham, James Mill, and the other utilitarian reformers, Coleridge replied with rhetorical questions paralleling those of Bentham:

But are they not then capable of feeling happiness or misery accordingly as they do or do not possess the means of a comfortable subsistence? And who is the judge, what is a comfortable subsistence, but the man himself? Might not then, on the same or equivalent principles, a leveller construct a right to equal property? The inhabitants of this country without property form, doubtless, a great majority; each of these has a right to a suffrage, and the richest man to no more; and the object of this suffrage is a legal power of abolishing or equalizing property: and . . . a power which ought never to be used ought not to exist.

Therefore, unless he carries his system to the whole length of common labour and common possession, a right to universal suffrage cannot exist; but if not to universal suffrage, there can exist no natural right to suffrage at all.[26]

Macaulay emphasized the same argument. James Mill had asserted, as we saw, on the one hand that "the greatest possible happiness of society is . . . attained by insuring to every man the greatest possible quantity of the produce of his labour," and, on the other hand, that "it is obvious that every man, who has not all the objects of his desire, has inducement to take them from any other man who is weaker than himself. . . ." It follows, Macaulay argued, that levelling would result: rather than maintain security of property, ensuring that all maintained the fruits of their labour, the majority would plunder the rich.

It may perhaps be said that, in the long run, it is for the interest of the people that property should be secure, and that therefore they will respect it. We answer thus: – It cannot be pretended that it is not for the immediate interest of the people to plunder the rich. Therefore, even if it were quite certain that, in the long run, the people would, as a body, lose by doing so, it would not necessarily follow that the fear of remote ill consequences would overcome the desire of immediate acquisitions. Every individual might flatter himself that the punishment would not fall on him. (Macaulay 1978, 119)

The utilitarian premises concerning human nature lead directly to the conclusion that any broadening of the franchise will lead inevitably to a disastrous levelling of society. On the elder Mill's own grounds, extending the franchise could lead only to disaster.

Macaulay, like Coleridge, in fact *can* provide an account of why the poor do not plunder the rich: most persons have sentiments that restrain them from harming others.

If all men desired wealth so intensely as to be willing to brave the hatred of their fellow creatures for sixpence, Mr Mill's argument . . . would be true to the full extent. But the fact is, that all men have some desires which impel them to injure their neighbours, and some desires which impel them to benefit their neighbours. (Macaulay 1978, 107)

People are in fact moved by moral sentiments, and these are, often enough, sufficiently strong to restrain inclinations to violate the norms of property. People on the whole do not plunder the rich because they *feel* that it is wrong to do so. Mill is not only methodologically inadequate but he begins from a false premise about human nature: people are in fact not moved solely by material self-interest. Mill proceeds in his "reasoning as if no human being had ever sympathized with the feelings, been gratified by the thanks, or been galled by the execrations, of another" (Macaulay 1978, 127). Mill's premises create a problem – how to prevent the poor from plundering the rich – which on Mill's own terms is insoluble, but which in fact is easily solved once a more adequate view of human nature is adopted – once we recognize that there are human motives, moral sentiments, in particular, as well as such things as aesthetic feelings, and so on, that are not simply matters of self-interest, not merely matters of material pleasure and pain.

The political economist Richard Jones[27] and the Cambridge scientist, moralist, and philosopher of science William Whewell[28] criticized Ricardo's economics on grounds similar to those used by

Macaulay against James Mill's political views.[29] They pointed out that in fact the distribution of wages, like the ownership of land and the distribution of rent, depended upon social institutions; it was a matter of human law, not an "iron law" of nature.[30] Economics therefore required one to take into account the social institutions of a society, and that in turn required an historical orientation. Again the claim was that the geometrical method was inappropriate in economics, and that one should approach the group phenomena of economics employing Baconian inductive methods after a thorough examination of historically based data.

For Whewell and Jones, social institutions, such as the rules of property that determined the nature of distribution in economics, were rooted in our moral sentiments. It was these sentiments that moved people to interact in their relationships in such a way that they conformed to the rules governing these institutions. Now, if it were indeed true, as both James Mill and Ricardo held, that people act to maximize their own profit, then, since the poor are in the vast majority, it would seem that they should be expected to act to expropriate the rich. But they do not. In fact, in general they respect the rules of property. That shows that there is something deep and fundamental about the moral sentiments that protect property, something that cannot be accounted for by the simple assumption that people act only to maximize their own profit. James Mill and the utilitarians could offer a long-run argument why the poor *ought not* to expropriate the rich, but, given their premise concerning human motivation, it seemed as if they could offer no explanation why they *do not* do so in the short run.

This shows, Jones and more especially Whewell concluded, as had Macaulay, that the utilitarian description of human beings is simply inadequate: it does not take into account the basic moral sentiments. These latter have to be taken to be irreducible. Moral rules are not merely prudential norms adopted by people whose motives are primarily self-regarding, as James Mill and Ricardo claimed. Conformity to moral norms is rather a matter of moral sentiments that are irreducible to self-regarding motives. So much the worse for the account of human nature upon which the utilitarians based their social policy recommendations.

The younger Mill agreed substantially with these criticisms. Thus, as early as 1833 he wrote critically of his father's emphasis upon a "common universal nature":

We seldom learn from Mr. Mill [*Analysis of the Phenomena of the Human Mind*] to understand any of the varieties of human nature; and, in truth, they enter very little into his own calculations, except where he takes cognizance of them as aberrations from the standard to which, in his opinion, all should conform. . . . I believe the natural and necessary differences among mankind to be so great, that any practical view of human life which does not take them into account, must, unless it stop short in generalities, contain at least as much error as truth; and that any system of mental culture, recommended by such imperfect theory in proportion as it is fitted to natures of one class, will be entirely unfitted for all others.[31]

The younger Mill also attempted, however, to show that these objections could be met through a more soundly based empiricist methodology of science. As the comments here hint, the younger Mill became aware of the real problems during the well-known mental crisis that he went through as a young man. But if that crisis made him aware of the problems as he had not before been, it also pointed the way towards the solutions.

On his father's view of human psychology, people sought to maximize their own pleasure. It was claimed that the method of *psychological analysis* revealed this fact.[32] To be sure, we do have moral sentiments, and feelings are aroused by reading poetry, but these can be *analyzed*. Such analysis reveals that these sentiments and feelings have arisen through processes of association. It turns out that feelings of pleasure are consequent upon moral behaviour and upon reading poetry. These feelings come to be associated with those actions. What originally was sought as a means to pleasure now comes to be sought as part of pleasure. Analysis reveals that moral sentiments and aesthetic responses are mental complexes which have as their parts on the one hand ideas of the ends sought or of the aesthetic object and, on the other hand, feelings of pleasure with which these ideas have come to be associated. This account of human motivation made it seem that poetry was nothing more than prose for which certain decorations had been provided to add to the pleasure of reading, while, with regard to moral action, those patterns of action which were apparently required by our moral sentiments and deeply felt social ties were in fact nothing other than patterns of behaviour adopted prudentially as means for maximizing our own material pleasures. But if, for example, the rules of property are nothing but prudential norms, we cannot explain why the poor do not expropriate the rich. Whewell and Jones concluded that these moral sentiments are therefore not learned by association but are, rather, innate, native to the human disposition.

John Stuart Mill was to criticize the moral and political thought of Whewell in detail, criticizing both the nativism and the moral intuitionism with which it was connected (see his 'Sedgwick's Discourse" and "Whewell on Moral Philosophy," CW X). But his discovery of how to meet the criticisms began during his mental crisis. This crisis, as he describes it in his Autobiography,[33] arose from a sense that nothing was really worthwhile. He attributed it to the role that analysis had played in his education: he had come to believe that there was no intrinsic value to anything. The problem was due to the method of analysis used by Bentham and his father. The use of this method was Bentham's originality. As the younger Mill was to express it after his crisis, "It is the introduction into the philosophy of human conduct, of this method of detail – of this practice of never reasoning about wholes until they have been resolved into their parts, nor about abstractions until they have been translated into realities – that constitutes the originality of Bentham in philosophy, and makes him the great reformer of the moral and political branch of it" ("Bentham," CW X:86). But the consequence of applying this method without care was to dismiss too much: Bentham, Mill tell us,

had a phrase, expressive of the view he took of all moral speculations to which his method had not been applied, or (which he considered as the same thing) not founded on a recognition of utility as the moral standard; this phrase was "vague generalities." Whatever presented itself to him in such a shape, he dismissed as unworthy of notice, or dwelt upon only to denounce as absurd. He did not heed, or rather the nature of his mind prevented it from occurring to him, that these generalities contained the whole unanalysed experience of the human race. (CW X:90)

Mill's reading of Wordsworth led him to recognize that to the contrary there were aesthetic responses in which the object and the feeling were inseparable.[34] He concluded that the same was true of our moral sentiments. Whewell and Jones were indeed correct in holding that our moral sentiments are not merely an external connection of end and pleasure; they are to the contrary unified wholes that are not reducible to their parts.[35] Bentham simply ignored pleasures of any order other than the material: "Nor is it only the moral part of man's nature, in the strict sense of the term – the desire of perfection, or the feeling of an approving or of an accusing conscience – that he overlooks; he but faintly recognises, as a fact in human nature, the pursuit of any other ideal end for its own sake" (CW X:95). As Mill came later to emphasize, moral and aesthetic sentiments are pleasures of a qualitatively superior order than the material pleasures that Bentham emphasized, those material pleasures the search for which was assumed axiomatically by Bentham and by the elder Mill in his essay on governmental reform.

Yet from the fact that our moral and aesthetic pleasures are different from and irreducible to the lower pleasures, it does not follow that they must be taken to be innate or native. It was precisely this inference, from irreducibility to innateness, that intuitionists such as Whewell and, earlier, Thomas Reid, had made, and that the younger Mill was willing to dispute. So to dispute this inference was to agree with his father, against the nativists and intuitionists, that our moral sentiments and aesthetic feelings are acquired through learning. In order for the younger Mill to defend this position, he had to modify his father's account of associationism, and more specifically the account of psychological analysis, in order to allow that the products of association can have properties that are not present in their genetic antecedents. He had to find a way in which it was possible to allow that in learning processes, in association, the effect is "heterogeneous" with its causes; or, what is the same, that it is "dissimilar" to the latter. His father's doctrine of association had to be rethought so as to allow that, in these processes, "it is proper to say that the simple ideas generate, rather than that they compose, the complex ones" (CW XII:854).

In this context, that of psychological analysis, it is necessary to distinguish two senses of 'part', that of logical or integrant or real part, and that of what Mill came to call a "metaphysical" part. Real or integrant parts *compose* the whole of which they are parts; metaphysical parts, in contrast, *generate*, but do *not* compose, the whole of which they are said to be parts (CW IX:259).

Bentham and the elder Mill held that mental phenomena were simply the additive sums of real parts. Their model for psychological analysis was logical analysis. Thus, for example, the idea 'human' is analyzed into the conjunction or logical sum of the simpler parts 'rational' and 'animal'. This model is applied to all ideas – e.g., the idea of a *house* consists of the sum of the ideas of the various parts of a house, walls, floors, etc., and then more basically the ideas of bricks, etc., while the idea of *everything* includes the idea of every thing.[36] The parts of these complex ideas are not only logically more basic but also, according to this older generation of utilitarian radicals, genetically basic. The complex idea gradually arises through a process of association which unites the causally precedent and logically simpler parts into the complex whole. For these thinkers, psychological analysis and logical analysis amount to the same: a complex idea is the logical sum of its parts, these parts are the literal parts of the idea and are together as a result of association, and analysis reveals these parts of mental phenomena. Psychological analysis therefore reveals the genetic antecedents of the mental phenomena, or, in other words, how it was that they came to be acquired through a process of associative learning. On this account of psychological analysis, learned mental phenomena are groups of separable parts, and analysis of them consists of locating those parts much as the analysis of a concept consists of locating the parts that define the concept. Psychological analysis of a mental phenomenon thus appears to be more *a priori* than empirical, on the model of analyzing the concept of 'human' into the concepts of 'rational' and 'animal'.[37]

John Stuart Mill never rejected the associationist claim of his father and the other utilitarians that our moral and aesthetic feelings are for the most part learned responses acquired through processes of association. Moreover, he never abandoned the notion that analysis reveals the genetic origins of these phenomena. However, he did come to realize during his mental crisis that such mental phenomena as our aesthetic responses to poetry or our moral sentiments are more than the sums of whatever parts analysis reveals; they are unified wholes with qualities that are not present in any of the parts. As Skorupski has put it, for Mill "states of consciousness . . . causally combine to produce emergent states of consciousness with a wholly new intrinsic or qualitative character."[38] In association a sort of mental chemistry occurs in which the product of the process has properties not present in its genetic antecedents, as water has properties not present in either hydrogen or oxygen. This notion of mental chemistry "gives him [Mill] a clear distinction between philosophical analysis of the content of a concept, and psychological analysis of its aetiology."[39] Hence, if psychological analysis is to reveal genetic origins, it could not be a matter of breaking a phenomenon into its constituent parts. Moreover, to speak of genetic antecedents is to speak of *causes*, and causes cannot be discovered *a priori*. This means that we must recognize that no psychological analysis could proceed *a priori*, breaking a mental event into real parts of which it is supposed to be the logical sum.

What, then, is psychological analysis? As John Stuart Mill (re-)conceived it, it involves first attending to a mental phenomenon as a whole, phenomenologically, and then attending to it analytically so as to bring to one's attention parts not previously present to consciousness. If *A* and *B* become associated to produce *C*, then equally there will be an association between *C* on the one hand and its genetic antecedents *A* and *B* on the other: each is necessary and sufficient for the other. Psychological analysis is a process that uses this association to bring to consciousness the genetic antecedents of the mental phenomenon ("idea") with which one is concerned. Psychological analysis, as the younger Mill conceived it, is thus itself a process of association which recovers, not real or integrant parts really present, but what Mill later called metaphysical parts, genetic antecedents which are present only dispositionally (*CW* IX:259). The product of analysis is knowledge of an association. Since an association is a regularity, analysis proceeds empirically, according to the methods of empirical science, and not *a priori*.[40] The metaphysical parts that analysis reveals are not there as real parts, though they can, through association (under the appropriate set), be recovered: that is precisely what analysis does. In general, there will be no reason to assume that the analytical parts, that is, the parts that are recovered during analysis, the genetic antecedents, are the logical parts. Analysis thus still reveals the processes of learning by which the later mental phenomena arose, but as now understood it does not require us to think of the latter as literally reducible to those parts. Rather, as we have said, in associative processes of learning the elements interact as it were chemically, rather than mechanically, to produce new phenomena that are qualitatively different from those elements[41] (*CW* VII; James Mill 1869, II:321).

In this way our aesthetic responses and our moral sentiments can, on the one hand, be taken to be, as Jones and Whewell insisted that they be taken to be, things that are greater than mere external or conjunctive connections of ideas with feelings of pleasure. They are indeed pleasures but pleasures that are qualitatively distinct from, and in that sense irreducible to, the more physical pleasures which they have as their associative antecedents; as well as, often at least, having greater motivating power than the latter. This yields a conception of human nature that is richer than that of the older utilitarians, and enables the younger Mill to provide a fully adequate response to the objection that the poor, if permitted, would act to plunder the rich.

On the other hand, this reformed account of the appropriate method for scientific psychology, and the more plausible account of human nature that it yields, also permits John Stuart Mill to argue, contrary to Jones and Whewell, and in conformity to the earlier utilitarian tradition of Bentham and James Mill, that our moral sentiments and aesthetic responses are for the most part learned rather than innate.[42] Though they are simple and unique, that is compatible with the claim that psychological analysis (not logical analysis) reveals them to have been learned. Moreover, since our moral sentiments are the basis for our conforming to the rules that govern our interactions with others, this permits Mill to acknowledge, with Macaulay and against his father, that social ties must be acknowledged as playing a role in social processes. Still further, the younger Mill agrees with Jones and Whewell that, since economic distribution is based on rules of property and contract, these are a matter of human laws rather than some sort of "iron law" of nature. John Stuart Mill thus agrees with Macaulay and with Jones and Whewell that the geometrical method is inappropriate in the social sciences, and that policy recommendations should not be based on propositions whose justification is based on that method. If the younger Mill is to take up the reformist programme of the older utilitarians, he must base it upon a social theory that is more sociological than psychological, and one, moreover, that is based upon a sounder method than that used by his father or by the classical economists such as Ricardo.

Mill discovered what became the roots of his sociological thought in two ways. One was his practice as Examiner in the East India

Company.[43] In this role he had as one of his major tasks that of drafting policy concerning the Indian states that were under the control of local princes within the general framework established for the British by the East India Company. Mill, during and subsequent to his mental crisis,[44] came to understand that engrained habits and norms of social interaction were involved in land tenure and that the latter could therefore not easily be transformed. One can locate a steadily increasing willingness, during and after Mill's mental crisis, to work within the limits set by existing institutions and customs, in the interest of reform, and even to respect those institutions. People with those habits were not so readily to be transformed as a more mechanical view of human nature would imply. Commenting on an attempt by the English at land reform in India, Mill notes how

the measure proved a total failure, as to the main effects which its well-meaning promoters expected from it. Unaccustomed to estimate the mode in which the operation of any given institution is modified even by such variety of circumstances as exists within a single kingdom, they [the English governors] flattered themselves that they had created, throughout the Bengal provinces, English landlords, and it proved that they had only created Irish ones. The new landed aristocracy disappointed every expectation built upon them. They did nothing for the improvement of their estates, but everything for their own ruin. (CW III:321–22)

One must work within the established patterns, and accept them as established, if one is to begin to have any effect that could be counted as improvement. Perhaps under the impact of the realism that comes from administrative duties, and certainly under the influence of the ideas of British Indian administrators, such as Munro, Elphinstone, and Malcolm, all of whom favoured a sympathetic and positive use of indigenous Indian social structures, groups, and customs, Mill came to move away from his father's more narrow and more mechanical Benthamism to recognize that utilitarian-inspired reform could be successful only if it was combined with a dose of organic conservativism.[45] He came even to see how existing institutions and customs could provide value for those participating in those institutions. This sense of how reformers should approach existing institutions appears in an illuminating way in a passage written much later in his life:

To determine the form of government most suited to any particular people we must be able, among the defects and shortcomings which belong to that people, to distinguish those that are the immediate impediment to progress; to discover what it is which (as it were) stops the way. The best government for them is the one which tends most to give them that for want of which they cannot advance, or advance only in a lame and lopsided manner. We must not, however, forget the reservation necessary in all things which have for their object improvement, or Progress; namely, that in seeking the good which is needed, no damage, or as little as possible, be done to that already possessed. (*Considerations on Representative Government, CW* XIX:396)

Thus, he opposed, for example, "all interference with any of the religious practices of the people of India, except such as are abhorrent to humanity" – by which he means such customs as those of *Sati* and *Thagi*; and when the British government was in the process of abolishing the Company in favour of more direct rule, he expressed concern with regard to the inhabitants of India, that "their strongest and most deeply-rooted feelings will henceforth be treated with much less regard than heretofore" ("The Petition of the East India Company," *CW* XXX:81).

This is one way in which the younger Mill arrived at the "complexity of [his] understanding of the relationship between abstract utility and the given fabric of ethical life."[46] The other source of his thought was more theoretical, located in two groups of thinkers, both of whom were part of the Romantic reaction to the Enlightenment. There was on the one hand the speculations of the English idealist Samuel Taylor Coleridge, who provided a more speculative basis for the measure of organic conservativism that Mill came to embrace. In contrast to Bentham, Coleridge thought that "the long duration of a belief . . . is at least proof of an adaptation in it to some portion or other of the human mind; and if, on digging down to the root, we do not find, as is generally the case, some truth, we shall find some natural want or requirement of human nature which the doctrine in question is fitted to satisfy: among which wants the instincts of selfishness and of credulity have a place, but by no means an exclusive one" ("Coleridge," *CW* X:120). The younger Mill accepted the general point, and also some of the more detailed suggestions about the role in society of those sentiments that Bentham and his method ignored.[47] Thus, the systems of education in a society are seen by Coleridge, with the younger Mill agreeing, as inculcating moral sentiments that function to restrain one's "personal impulses and aims, to what were considered the ends of society; of adhering, against all temptation, to the course of conduct which those ends prescribed" (CW X:133). Among those feelings are those of allegiance, which constitute the institution of government, that is, those feelings that lead people to accept the rule of their government as that of a legitimate authority, even where they disagree with some of the details of what the government has done (CW X:133–34). Finally in any society there are the shared feelings of sympathy and union, contrasted to feelings of hostility and separation, which constitute "a feeling of common interest among those who live under the same government" (CW X:135).

But Coleridge was not the only theorist who pointed to the moral sentiments that provided the glue that as it were cemented people together into societies and into social institutions. There was also the perhaps more carefully grounded social thought of the French thinkers Saint-Simon and Comte (see Mill's "August Comte and Positivism," CW X).[48] Comte, like Coleridge, held that "as society proceeds in its development, its phænomena are determined, more and more, not by the simple tendencies of universal human nature, but by the accumulated influence of past generations over the present. The human beings themselves, on the laws of whose nature the facts of history depend, are not abstract or universal but historical human beings, already shaped, and made what they are, by human society" ("Auguste Comte and Positivism," CW X:307). Comte taught Mill, as Coleridge, immersed in the contagious idealism of German thought, could not, that these habits and sentiments that his father ignored could be understood using the methods of empirical science. But there was a common message that he learned from Coleridge and from Comte, namely, that there are patterns of thought and action that coordinated the behaviour of whole societies and indeed whole ages; it was these that one tried to sketch when one attempted to characterize the "spirit of the age," to use the name of a series of essays in which Mill explored this topic. From Coleridge and Comte he also learned that these patterns of thought could involve deference to authority and that this authority could operate through such social institutions as the church. Finally, again from these two, as well as Saint-Simon, he came to understand how social and economic activities are bound up with the institutionalization of these activities.

Now, although Mill does not speak this way, he views social institutions as constituted by interrelated roles, with people acting in ways characteristic of the institution. He speaks, rather, of a "consensus" in social groups and society in general, "similar to that existing among the various organs of man and the more perfect animals, and constituting one of the many analogies which have rendered universal such expressions as the 'body politic' and 'body natural'" (CW VIII:899), but the point is the same: an institution is not a heap of individuals any more than an animal is a heap of organs; an institution is, rather, constituted by *relations among the parts*, social relations, that is, patterns of coordinated action and behaviour. These ways of acting and behaving are determined by the norms that define the roles, with people moved to conform to these norms by their moral sentiments: they have learned to value those characteristic ways of behaving. One of the simplest, yet most fundamental of social institutions, and one to which Mill gave considerable thought, is that of promising. There are two roles, that of promisor and that of promisee. Two persons, ego and alter, enter into the roles of promisor and promisee when ego says to alter that "I promise you that I shall do x." Humans early acquire the moral sentiment that people ought to keep their promises. That is, there is a general pattern of behaviour.

(G_1) Every promisor does for the promisee what was promised.

which has attached to it moral sentiments such that people feel that

(R_1) It ought to be that every promisor does for the promisee what was promised.

These moral sentiments shared by all people are, of course, learned, acquired through association, rather than innate as thinkers such as Jones and Whewell had claimed; but they are very deeply embedded in our human nature. The point is that the sentiment that people ought to conform to the norm (R_1) moves people to conform their own behaviour to it. Thus, when the promisor and promisee enter into their roles by ego promising alter to do x, ego comes to feel the moral obligation to do x, what was promised, and also to feel that alter has the moral right to expect that x be done; similarly, alter comes to feel that ego is morally obliged to do x and to feel that he or she has a moral right to expect that x be done by ego. Since we feel that it is obligatory that all conform to this norm, we take care to raise children so that they conform to the rule (R_1); we put them in situations where they come to internalize this standard,[49] that is, in situations where pleasure comes to be associated with behaviour conforming to this rule, both their own behaviour and also others'. Moreover, since we feel that it is obligatory that all conform to (R_1), when a promise is not kept we are liable to take steps to punish the violation, or at least we feel that it is morally appropriate to punish the violator.

There are of course other rules besides (R_1) that are involved. There is, for example, the pragmatic rule of language that makes 'I promise . . .' a performative utterance that moves ego and alter into the roles of promisor and promisee. Moreover, it is clear that most institutions have many more roles than two and that the norms governing those roles are much more complex. Mill did not subject these institutions to detailed analysis, and, although sociologists since have gone into greater detail on occasion, it is still true that most institutions have not been carefully mapped. What, for example, were the differences in the norms defining the roles of Chief Examiner as opposed to clerk in the East India Company? Often enough, no doubt, there would be very little to be gained by providing an abstract description of the rules, formal and informal, that define social roles. The point here is that if one is to think clearly about social relations then one must have at least a basic outline for how one proposes to think about them, and Mill has provided himself with this in his account of promising.

This basic account – "model" if you wish – can be extended to other social relationships, e.g., kinship relations:

(R_2) It ought to be that every person in the bear clan marries a person who is not in the bear clan.

What is important about norms like (R_1) and (R_2) is that, provided the moral sentiments are in fact efficacious in motivating people, then these sentiments will bring it about that the pattern deemed obligatory will in fact hold in the group. Thus, if the sentiments attaching to (R_1) are efficacious, then the generalization (G_1) will *as a matter of fact* truly describe the people in the group. Similarly, if the sentiments attaching to (R_2) are efficacious, then it will be a true generalization about the group that

(G_2) Every person in the bear clan marries a person who is not in the bear clan.

Rules such as (R_1) and (R_2) provide models that people have of their social relations. If these normative models are efficacious, then they will in fact be true models.

Note that (R_1) and (R_2) are models in the minds of those *in* the social group. They are normative for these people. And in so far as they make descriptive claims (G_1) and (G_2), these generalities are explanatory of the observed behaviour of members of the society.[50] But these prescriptive norms, which provide an explanatory model for those in the group, can also constitute an explanatory model for the scientist who is studying the group; the patterns they prescribe are explanatory not only for those in the group but for those studying the group. However, those studying the group must also take these patterns as the object of study; the social scientist thus not only uses the model but also studies it.[51] Often he or she studies it in order to understand how change might be effected in the institution being studied. One's cognitive interest in the institutional structure might be the disinterested concern of the research social scientist or the pragmatic interests of the reformer or administrator, but in any case does not require one to have internalized the norms governing the institution. Thus, it has been suggested that, with regard to the social institutions of India, John Stuart Mill lacked "any special regard for existing institutions or traditions, except that they formed the given, the datum line in any particular case."[52] But for those who are participating in the institution, the structure is not, or at least not merely, an object of study but a set of norms to which their moral sentiments move them to conform.

In recognizing this, we also recognize a further explanatory element. The moral sentiment expressed by the normative statement

It is obligatory that *p*

brings it about that

p

That is, there is a causal relationship to the effect that

(C) The sentiment that it is obligatory that p brings it about that p.

In this sense, (R_1) and (R_2) *explain*, respectively, the patterns (G_1) and (G_2). In other words, we can explain the observed patterns by appeal to the causal efficacy of the moral sentiments that make such behaviour felt to be obligatory. The model in the minds of the members of the group thus not only explains in so far as it is descriptive, it also explains in so far as it is prescriptive. In fact, the latter explanation, since it is based on a more comprehensive causal principle (C), which takes into account more relevant factors, provides a fuller explanation of the observed behaviour.

Yet more comprehensive explanations are possible. (C) holds only because of certain learning situations. What we in fact have is something like the following:

(L) Whenever a person is in a learning situation of such and such a sort, then that person comes to be such that he or she feels the sentiment that it is obligatory that p.

In order to explain why persons feel the sentiment, we turn to their past history, the learning experiences they have had. These experiences, together with the law (L), provide a (covering law) explanation of why they feel the sentiment. This, when conjoined with (C), explains (via the covering law model) why they act as they do. The law (L) yields a yet more comprehensive explanation than (C). Of course, (L) as stated is just a sketch of a law or theory, specifically a sketch of a psychological theory of learning. For John Stuart Mill, of course, the relevant theory of learning is associationism, or, behaviouristically restated, classical conditioning – with more than a touch of reinforcement theory.[53] As Mill puts it, "The laws of mind . . . compose the unversal or abstract portion of the philosophy of human nature; and all the truths of common experience, constituting a practical knowledge of mankind, must to the extent to which they are truths, be results or consequences of these" (*CW* VIII:861). But the point that needs here to be emphasized is that Mill's account of social theory and of the methods for justifying its acceptance for purposes of explanation and of practice do not presuppose the commitment to any specific theory of learning. Associationism, that is, classical conditioning, is one possible theory. But there are others, such as that of Piaget, which one could hold – we need not go into the details. Mill, of course, was prepared to defend associationism, and the movement of his own thought, before, during, and after his mental crisis, remained within this context. But the account of social theory, of its justification, and of its relation to psychological theory does not depend upon the details of Mill's own theory of learning: for these things all that is required is that there be some learning theory or other, some account of how the norms for social roles become internalized, how our moral sentiments become attached to these patterns of behaviour and not others.

If the structural patterns (R_1) and (R_2), or what, for purposes of explanation, is much the same, the patterns (G_1) and (G_2), are explanatory, then at the same time it is essential to recognize that the events that these patterns describe are the evidential basis for any claim or thought that those patterns in fact describe correctly the social reality. The observed social relations provide the data for the scientist attempting to ascertain the social structure.[54] At the same time those relations are a consequence of that structure. Lévi-Strauss seems to put the relationships in pretty well the correct order: observed social relations are the raw material in which social structural relations "inhere"[55] and out of which non-statistical models are "constructed." Lévi-Strauss distinguishes "mechanical" from "statistical" models; he characterizes this distinction as one of level, but it is clear that with a "mechanical" model on the level of structure, there is associated a "statistical" model which describes, with some degree of precision, the actual distributions of behaviours that conform and do not conform with the non-statistical or mechanical model.[56] Such structural models explain structural features exemplified in concrete social relations, and are "translatable" into statistical models.[57] The structural models serve to explain the social relations that can be observed, with the approximation to reality of those models measured by the probabilities in the statistical model. It is to be sure an approximation, but if the approximation is close enough then a degree of social control is possible. As Mill makes clear, the empirical generalizations which are the starting point of any social science are only "approximate generalizations"; but these laws which cannot be used to give firm predictions are nonetheless useful: "whenever it is sufficient to know how the great majority of the human race, or of some nation or class of persons, will think, feel, and act, these propositions are equivalent to universal ones" (*CW* VIII:847).

But why is there only an approximation? Why do the structural models not fit precisely the realities of social behaviour?

It remains true, as we have insisted with Mill, that the norms that define social roles do, in their own way, provide explanations of human action and behaviour. But we must also recognize that these norms are not always efficacious. It is for this reason that the models are not always quite true. Most of the time most people keep their promises; to this extent (R_1) is efficacious and to this extent (G_1) is true. But not all promises are kept. A promise might be broken for good reasons; it could not be kept, for example, because one was delayed in saving a drowning child. Or they may be broken for bad reasons; some people are knaves, and some even just forgetful. As Lévi-Strauss once put it, models that are prescriptive in the minds of the members of the group may be preferential in practice.[58] This means that (G_1) is only approximately true. What we have instead is

$(G_{1'})$ $q\%$ of the time promisors do for the promisee what was promised.

where 'q' is some fairly large percentage representing the probability that a promisor will keep his or her promises. The statistical generalization $(G_{1'})$ holds because there are in fact variables that are not mentioned in (G_1) but which are relevant – those variables in individual psychology that in the real world of everyday life transform prescription into preference! What holds in fact is not the generalization (G_1), which has, as one says, "exceptions," but rather

$(G_{1''})$ There are certain factors of a motivational sort such that, for every promisor, if they are absent, then and only then that promisor does for the promisee what was promised.

The law (G_1) attempts to leave no factors unmentioned; the law $(G_{1''})$ in contrast asserts the existence of certain factors but does not mention them. Laws like (G_1) can be said to be deterministic, while laws like $(G_{1''})$ have been called "gappy."[59] John Stuart Mill recognizes the existence of laws that are gappy in just the way that $(G_{1''})$ is gappy. They exist in many areas of science, but particularly in the social sciences. What they mark is the existence of certain variables that we do not know, but which we would like to know.[60] For, clearly, laws like (G_1), if we have them, are better than gappy laws like $(G_{1'})$ for purposes of prediction and contrary-to-fact reasoning. For the gaps represent unknown interfering factors which, when they do, unknown to us, interfere, bring it about that our predictions using the gappy law are false. By that fact, of course, we infer the presence of the interfering factors, and thereby account for the inaccuracy of our prediction.[61] The falsity of the prediction does not falsify the gappy law.[62] But it does mean that the law is not as useful for purposes of prediction as one would be in which those gaps were filled. The ultimate aim of empirical science is a set of laws which have as few gaps as possible.[63] Gappy laws therefore pose a research problem; the task of the research is to discover the factors that the gappy law asserts to be there but which we do not yet know, or do not know in all detail.[64] Yet, until that task is complete we must make do with gappy knowledge. Or rather, we can at least approach the matter statistically, as in $(G_{1'})$, to enable us to estimate the extent to which we may reasonably bet upon the relationship holding in a given case.[65] But Mill's thought was formed too early for him to take seriously into account the developments in statistics that were happening with increasing frequency as the century passed.

Mill did see, however, the relevance of such procedures for the social sciences. The starting point of such sciences was "approximate generalizations," but such a generalization is, "in social inquiries, for most practical purposes equivalent to an exact one; that which is only probable when asserted of individual human beings indiscriminately selected, being certain when affirmed of the character and collective conduct of the masses" (CW VIII:847). Mill is as clear as we could reasonably expect on the statistical nature of much of social science. He is equally clear on the imperfect or gappy nature of such knowledge, and of the desirability of removing, to the extent that they can be removed, those gaps:

the science of Human Nature may be said to exist in proportion as the approximate truths which compose a practical knowledge of mankind, can be exhibited as corollaries from the universal laws of human nature of which they rest; whereby the proper limits of those approximate truths would be shown, and we should be enabled to deduce others for any new state of circumstances, in anticipation of specific experience. (CW VIII:848)

As the case of kinship relations (R_2) makes clear, the norms defining social relationships can form a complex set. This set of norms defining the institution may itself exhibit a more abstract structure that it shares with a quite different set of norms defining a different set of social relationships. Lévi-Strauss discovered that this is indeed the case with respect to certain kinship structures; marriage systems that were specifically different could nonetheless share a certain generic logical form.[66] Mill was aware of the same sort of thing, though he did not put it in those terms, nor did he try to make a nice neat system out of it, as Lévi-Strauss found he could do when an algebraic structure was created to describe the different marriage systems with which he was concerned. It is this general sort of generic structure shared by different patterns of thought and behaviour that Mill had in mind when he spoke of such things as the "spirit of the age."

The social structures, then, do indeed move one, as the structuralists claim. The point is that Mill would not disagree. But these structures that move the individual are not at the same time somehow independent of the individual or of human psychology. There have been philosophers of the social sciences and sociologists who have argued that social factors should be construed as basic entities, irreducible to the individual persons who participate in those institutions. Such views have been held by idealists such as Coleridge and those in the Hegelian tradition, and by certain Marxists;[67] and they have been attributed to Durkheim and Lévi-Strauss. However, Mill's empiricism will permit him to introduce a concept into science only if it refers to things presented in experience or is defined in terms of such concepts. We do not see the Law in its majesty condemning the thief, we see Judge Iacobucci pass sentence; we do not see the Inquisition torture poor Juan, we see Torquemada persecuting. Empiricism must claim that there is nothing to social institutions over and above the individuals who participate in them – *and the social relations among these individuals.* The latter is of course important, because it is simply wrong to say that social institutions are *nothing more than* the individuals in them; for social institutions *do* involve something more: the social relations among those individuals. Social institutions are *constituted* by the *coordinated* behaviour of several individuals; if the coordination does not exist, we have mere individuals, no institution. Mill is clear on the importance of social relations; as we noted, he here agrees with Coleridge, Jones, and Whewell. Hence, while Mill does insist that social factors do not exist somehow over and above individual persons, he cannot be reckoned as some sort of social atomist who holds that there is nothing to society besides those individuals.

Of course, to say that social phenomena may in this way be reduced to psychological phenomena does not imply that social processes must be traced back to some intention or passion that set the process in motion. It is simply not true that every social process has an intended target or end. For, as Mill realizes, social phenomena often have unintended consequences. He was clearly aware of this in, for example, his discussion of the market where people act on the preference of a greater gain to a smaller and in so doing effect an equilibrium between supply and demand. No one intends the latter, it is the unintended consequence of actions that have other motives. Popper has suggested that Mill is somehow forced by his methodological individualism to deny that there are social processes that involve unintended consequences.[68] The reason Popper gives for so supposing is that reduction of the sociological to the psychological requires that the relevant psychology be somehow pre-social, that it presupposes "the idea of a human nature and a human psychology as they existed prior to society."[69] But it does nothing of the kind. What it presupposes is the idea that social factors can be understood in terms of individuals standing in certain sorts of social relations, where these are understood in terms of coordinated action and behaviour. It does not require that the social be reduced to the non-social.

Of course, Mill also holds that we can explain the acquisition of the capacity to participate in groups and to conform to the norms of social roles by reference to psychological learning theory, and, more specifically, to associationism – though, as we have said, the last detail is not really necessary: Mill's point stands, no matter what specific learning theory one defends. What happens is that persons are put in certain contexts in which they learn. The contexts for learning social roles are clearly social. They involve, for example, the family: being a parent is a social role that requires one to socialize one's infant in certain ways; that is, to do that is among the norms defining that role. They also involve other institutions, e.g., schools, churches, prisons, training programmes, etc. The infant is certainly non-social when he or she enters the world; but the learning itself is a social process. No doubt, of course, in the mists of time past, the social arose out of the non-social – though even our primate ancestors were certainly social in important ways! But how the social first arose, and how primate sociality became specifically human, are things we simply do not know, and perhaps never shall. But in any case, contrary to what Popper apparently thinks, there is no need to suppose that the reduction of the social to the psychological is the same thing as the elimination of the social in favour of behaviour which is somehow pre-social.

Social structure, then, does shape human behaviour. It can do so because, through learning, moral sentiments become attached to these ideas. It is precisely because they are embedded in our individual psychologies that such structures do not always move us. As in the case of promising, there can be factors that move us to act contrary to the way the structures incline us to act. Such structures do describe and explain human action, but to see the full significance of such action it must be placed in the context of the whole, and developing, characters of the individual actors. Mill is perfectly clear on this important point, one which is often missed by those who insist that the sociological is somehow independent of the psychological.[70]

At the same time Mill also recognized there is no reason to suppose that one cannot discover laws that describe changes and developments in the social realm, laws that describe the interactions of social factors without (explicitly) mentioning the individuals who, *qua* standing in certain social relations, constitute those factors. Thus, he learned from Saint-Simon and Comte that one could begin to discern patterns of change within the patterns or structures of thought and sentiment that describe the "spirit of an age." There were, he came to hold after his mental crisis, when he had come to recognize the importance of sociological variables, patterns of social development which one could discover. That is, the patterns describing the coordination of persons in groups serve to define a certain sort of social whole, and wholes of this sort are followed in due course by wholes of a different sort. More abstractly put, the patterns that define social wholes define group variables, and changes in these group variables occur according to some more general pattern to the effect that

(G$_3$) Whenever patterns A hold then there is a later time at which patterns B hold and there is a still later time at which patterns C hold.

The most famous example of a suggested law of this sort, and one in which Mill saw great significance and was even inclined at one time to accept, is Comte's law of the three stages: human societies have been characterized by a development in which theological or animistic patterns of thought are dominant, succeeded by a stage in which metaphysical patterns of thought are dominant, succeeded in turn by a stage in which empiricist or positivist patterns of thought are dominant. Laws of this sort – developmental laws[71] – are clearly gappy since they do not mention precisely how long it takes for each subsequent stage to arrive, nor do they describe changes that occur in the transitional periods. In this respect, even if such hypotheses could be confirmed, they would not come up to the ideal of scientific knowledge that Mill proposed, that of gapless laws. That would not of course detract from their usefulness as far as they go; a gappy law is still a law, and can still play a role in helping us to understand social change.

But we should also recognize that it is unlikely that we would ever discover gapless laws that relate only social variables, as certain Marxists have sometimes implied.[72] For, after all, as Mill clearly understands, individuals do have a role to play in history; some do, at times, make a difference to what happens among the social variables. And in so far as individuals do make a difference, there can be no purely social laws.

There is continuity in history and across a society or group. Structure, in other words, reproduces itself in individuals. Mill came to understand from Coleridge the importance of "a system of *education*, beginning with infancy and continued through life, of which, whatever else it might include, one main and incessant ingredient was *restraining discipline*" (*CW* X:133). Thus, given that we ourselves are moved by the norm (R$_1$), the norm that approves *general* conformity to the standard it expresses, we are moved by it to subject our children to learning processes that will ensure that this norm will come to be internalized in their consciousnesses as it is in ours. And if we see others violating this norm we will take steps, from punishment to help in relearning, that will ensure that they too, in the future at least, will conform. It is the institution of the family that is most important in the process of learning. This institution is itself a structure, of course, and reproduces itself along with such norms as (R_1) and (R_2). And there are other institutions, e.g., schools, which provide the context in which other structures come to be internalized. But the learning situations are never quite the same, and all the various norms, standards, and motives acceptable and unacceptable, are acquired in slightly different ways. Within our individual psychologies such things as strength of motives and meaningfulness can differ in ways that vary from the subtle to the gross. Structural norms thus come to be violated, and violated in many different ways. It is this, our individuality, that accounts for deviations from social norms, and, more deeply, one must recognize, accounts for social change, that is, the change over time in our social norms.

It is individuality that accounts, in the end, according to Mill, for whatever social and economic progress that we have achieved.[73] Social progress has depended upon moral leaders such as Jesus and Socrates who have, through example and argument, reshaped the moral sentiments of humankind. Economic progress depends upon improved methods of production, that is, upon new knowledge and inventions and upon entrepreneurial skills. The principle of utility thus demands that we encourage human beings to develop their individuality. This means that we should, as we raise our children, attempt to bring them to value their own individuality, so that they will come to cultivate themselves, and to value the individuality of others, encouraging those others also to develop themselves as individuals.

Here there is a major contrast to Comte, who argued that social progress required that each member of society be singly motivated by a concern for maximizing the general welfare. Mill disagreed. As he put it in his study of Comte,

Why is it necessary that all human life should point but to one object, and be cultivated into a system of means to a single end? May it not be that the fact that mankind, who after all are made up of single human beings, obtain a greater sum of happiness when each pursues his own, under the rules and conditions required by the good of the rest, than when each makes the good of the rest his only object, and allows himself no personal pleasures not indispensable to his faculties? The regimen of a blockaded town should be cheerfully submitted to when high purposes require it, but is it the ideal perfection of human existence? ("Auguste Comte and Positivism," *CW* X:337)

Skorupski has expressed it this way: "One central point which [Mill] sees with complete clarity is that the utilitarian need not and cannot require that 'the test of conduct should also be the exclusive motive of it'. Confusing those two things was, he thought, the error of Auguste Comte. He most decidedly does not share Comte's vision of a society permanently mobilised for the general good."[74] To be sure, some people, some of the time, are moved by the general welfare as an end. But the general welfare, while the ultimate moral standard, is in fact not best served by all the people, all the time, being moved by this end.

The very possibility that Comte envisages presupposes that men can come to seek the general welfare as a moral end. This in turn presupposes, contrary to the main thrust of the older utilitarian tradition concerning human motivation, that people are not intrinsically selfish and that morality can come to be sought for its own sake. Mill's message, that other things, too, can – and ought to be – sought for their own sakes, also presupposes that same psychological point. In this way Mill's social thought presupposes his rethinking of the nature of our ideas and of psychological analysis as the proper method of psychology.

At the same time, his urging the development of individuality presupposes that values are not innate but acquired, learned in the relevant contexts, primarily social, but also in contexts into which one can deliberately and voluntarily place oneself so that one's psychological development is a sort of *self*-development.[75] Mill's defence of individuality thus presupposes that on this matter his psychology agrees with that of his father rather than with the nativism of Whewell and the other intuitionists.

The major social means for encouraging individuality are, according to Mill, the institutions of a free society. We need to develop systems of education which encourage people not only to understand but also to question authority and received wisdom and custom so that these might be improved. These are the sorts of values that the institutions should inculcate, relying upon a knowledge of the laws of learning on how best to do this. We need to encourage and develop social institutions, such as freedom of speech, that both permit people to exercise their individuality, and, through that exercise, encourage and, with the appropriate associations, reinforce that individuality.

It is in this context that we must place Mill's views on economics.[76] In one respect his views are very much of a piece with those of the classical economists such as Ricardo who preceded him. In his economic thought Mill was the culmination of a tradition rather than a revolutionary or radical innovator.[77] But his justication of the economic institution of the free market was different from that of the earlier generation of philosophic radicals, the generation of his father and of Ricardo, and was moreover significantly qualified.

Mill referred to the science that we call economics as "political economy." It deals with those social phenomena that result from the pursuit of wealth, abstracting from all other human motives; it takes as its starting point, the psychological law that a greater gain is preferred to a smaller. Political economy therefore treats of the laws of the production and distribution of material goods. Clearly, the laws of political economy will have to be gappy, since they abstract from all human motives save that of gain. That does not mean that they are useless for shaping policy decisions, but it does mean that they have their limitations and that when one applies them one must take account of other collateral causes that might modify the usual effects. Mill, unlike many more recent economists such as Milton Friedman, recognizes that the science of economics is only relatively autonomous and that in the end its claims must be embedded in the laws of a broader, more inclusive social science and, ultimately, in the laws of psychology.

Within the science of political economy, the laws of production are, Mill held, natural laws, but the laws of distribution are not, in that sense, natural laws. Rather, distribution depends upon social structure; "the Distribution of Wealth . . . is a matter of human institution solely" (*CW* II:199). It depends, for example, on the rules for land tenure and rent – Mill takes over much of Jones's discussion of various forms of land tenure and rent;[78] and it depends, for another example, upon the property rules for the ownership of capital. Patterns of distribution depend upon the existence of such social structures. Among the patterns of distribution are those which occur in a free market. In such a market people buy and sell goods, including land, capital, and their own labour, in conformity with the rule of maximizing one's profit: buy low and sell high. Such free markets presuppose certain social structures, e.g., the rules of property, the rules of exchange or contract (promising), and the rules that restrict the legitimate use of governmental authority to policing and enforcing contracts. Many would now attempt to justify the use of free markets for distribution because they do so with maximal efficiency. That is not Mill's justification.

Material well-being is not the end-all of life, but it is the begin-all. If we are to develop our full potentials as human beings, then we must satisfy our material needs. Indeed, we must come to more adequately satisfy those needs; nothing stifles individuality more than poverty. Some social structures perpetuate poverty by discouraging economic development. Land tenure systems in parts of India and in Ireland were of this sort; by transferring the profits resulting from any improvement from the renter to the landlord, they removed any incentive for the worker to improve his holdings: "in such a condition, what can a tenant gain by any amount of industry or prudence, and what lose by any recklessness?" (CW II:318). In contrast, the system of distribution in a free market does reward those who, through their knowledge or entrepreneurial skills, improve production.

Communistic management would . . . be, in all probability, less favourable than private management to that striking out of new paths and making immediate sacrifices for distant and uncertain advantages, which, though seldom unattended with risk, is generally indispensable to great improvements in the economic condition of mankind, and even to keeping up the existing state in the face of a continual increase of the number of mouths to feed.

As for labourers, "these, under Communism, would have no interest, except their share of the general interest, in doing their work honestly and energetically" ("Chapters on Socialism," CW V:742). Such incentives are important for motivating people to make improvements, and therefore social structures such as the free market which provide such incentives are to be preferred on utilitarian grounds, and those such as the Irish land tenure system are to be discouraged. To be sure, such social change cannot be achieved overnight, as the earlier utilitarians seemed to think; they neglected the role of social structure, where the younger Mill had come to recognize its significance. In any case, Mill's approach to economics did not involve simply exploring the mechanisms of the market. To be sure, that he did. But this was placed within the broader context of what we would now refer to as developmental economics.[79] Mill's concern in the end was not simply for *distribution* of the product but in *economic development* that would increase production and make the human lot a materially better one.

The justification that Mill offers for a system of free markets is not that of the older utilitarians, that this is simply a matter of "natural law." Mill is clear: if it were a matter of law, the so-called laws of economics could not be violated; but they often are – even, or especially, the "iron law of wages" – and so they could not be laws. Rather, the workings of the market presuppose, as we have said, certain social institutions. It is with this in mind that Mill offers a two-fold utilitarian justification of a system of free markets. On the one hand, in general it works more efficiently for the individual: "as a general rule, the business of life is better performed when those who have an immediate interest in it are left to take their own course, uncontrolled either by the mandate of the law or by the meddling of any public functionary" (*CW* III:946). Further, for the most part competition eliminates monopoly and therefore the sort of tax that the latter can impose to make goods more expensive than they need be; socialists tend to "forget . . . that with the exception of competition among labourers, all other competition is for the benefit of the labourers, by cheapening the articles they consume" (*CW* III:794). *Laissez faire* is thus the general rule, although there are a number of important exceptions. Moreover, as we noted, it provides incentives for improvement, and this contributes to the utilitarian end: "competition may not be the best conceivable stimulus, but it is at present a necessary one, and no one can foresee the time when it will not be indispensable to progress' (*CW* III:795). On the other hand, the system of free markets enables people to exercise their individuality in their free choices in the market, again contributing to the utilitarian end. But the market has negative consequences also. In certain circumstances, in particular that of growing population, it tends to drive wages for labour to the subsistence level. This was the "iron law of wages" of the earlier generation. It was hardly an "iron law," however, for it depended upon social structures, and there is no inevitability about those structures: they can be changed. As Mill saw it, the central social problem was the poverty of the working class: "first among existing social evils may be mentioned the evil of Poverty" (*CW* V:712). This stifles the individuality of the labourers, preventing them from developing their full potentialities, thus running contrary to the utilitarian end. Mill argued, in fact, that if the system of free markets could not solve the problem of the poverty of the working class, then, on utilitarian principles, it would have to be changed to a system, a social structure of distribution, that would do a better job.

If, therefore, the choice were to be made between Communism with all its chances, and present state of society with all its suffering and injustices; if the institution of private property necessarily carried with it as a consequence, that the produce of labour should be apportioned as we now see it, almost in an inverse ratio to the labour – the largest portions to those who have never worked at all, the next largest to those whose work is almost nominal, and so in a descending scale, the remuneration dwindling as the work grows harder and more disagreeable, until the most fatiguing and exhausting bodily labour cannot count with certainty on being able to earn even the necessaries of life; if this or Communism were the alternative, all the difficulties, great or small, of Communism would be but as dust in the balance. (*CW* II:207).

If socialism were necessary, then socialism it would have to be. Mill's acceptance of the system of free markets is thus seriously qualified.

The point is, of course, that John Stuart Mill recognized, as the earlier generation of thinkers had not, that social institutions do exist. To be sure, these institutions are a matter of learned conventions and can, therefore, be changed. On this idea, that the world can be changed through learning, or relearning, Mill agrees with his predecessors. What such change requires is the discovery of the relevant social and psychological theories that will provide us with insight into the means by which we can most efficiently achieve those ends. Mill disagrees with his predecessors on what the relevant social theories are. And more deeply, he disagrees with them on method: they adopted the wrong theories, the younger Mill argues, because they inadequately conceived the method of investigation proper to social science.

In order to discover the laws explaining social change and development, one needs a method adapted to that (cognitive) end. Mill's father, and the older generation of utilitarians, had used the geometric method to justify the theories upon which they based their policy recommendations. The younger Mill recognized the correctness of the criticisms of this method by Macaulay, Jones, and Whewell. But he rejected the inductive methods of Bacon that these critics proposed as an alternative. These methods of Baconian induction – what we have come to call Mill's Methods in recognition of John Stuart Mill's superb formulation of them – are the methods of eliminative induction. They aim to discover which among a series of competing hypotheses is the true one. They do this by successively eliminating hypotheses with falsifying instances. The one which, at the end, remains uneliminated is the one that is true. Clearly, these methods will work only if it is taken for granted that one among the several hypotheses is true; that is, one must assume that *there is* a cause there to be discovered. But as we have noted, John Stuart Mill does in fact assume this; this is the principle of universal causation. Moreover, it is not a mere assumption: Mill argues that he in fact has good inductive evidence to justify its assertion. But it is also clear that if the method of elimination is to lead to the truth, then one must also have a complete enumeration of the alternative hypotheses. This is the principle of limited variety.[80] This is required, for, if one alternative had not been enumerated, it could turn out that it is the true one and not the hypothesis so far unelimated. What the younger Mill pointed out to the critics of the earlier generation of utilitarians is that in the area of social theory, which deals with large groups of people, there are simply too many variables for them all to be enumerated; the principle of limited variety simply cannot be achieved. If we look at social institutions, we can discover relevant "differences without any assignable limit, . . . in more ways than can be enumerated or imagined," from which Mill concludes that "there is thus a demonstrated impossibility of obtaining, in the investigations of the social science, the conditions required for . . . inquiry by specific experience" (*CW* VIII:882). The methodology for political economy and sociology that was proposed by Macaulay, Jones, and Whewell is therefore as defective as the geometrical method that they criticized – and on the same grounds, the complexity of social phenomena.

The best that one can achieve by looking at the relations among social or group phenomena in history is a set of merely empirical laws. These are matter-of-fact patterns that we discern in the actual course of history. The evidence for them is nothing more than the instances whose occurrences they cover; in effect, the evidence for them is gathered by the rule of induction by simple enumeration. But where the phenomena are complex, such a method does not rule out the possibility that there are other causal factors at work that we have overlooked. Ideally we should use the methods of eliminative induction to eliminate the possibility that such relevant causal factors exist. But social phenomena are too complex for these methods, as we know Mill also argued. So the empirical laws discerned in history are only weakly grounded, and as such can hardly be called scientific, and cannot form the secure basis of policy recommendations. If, therefore, these laws are to become scientific, they must be placed on a more secure basis than the data from which they are abstracted. Mill proposed that empirical laws could be so transformed by embedding them in a more comprehensive theory that could be used to distinguish which of the empirical laws were genuinely causal, which merely accidental generalities.

In the case of history and social phenomena, Mill argued that such a theory does exist. It is the science of psychology. This science deals with human motives and agency, the basic causes of social phenomena. And he argued that social science could proceed deductively from this more basic science; specifically, he proposed that social science could use what he called the "deductive" method to deduce whether or not the observed empirical laws really flowed from human action and motives, that is, whether they were genuinely causal or not.[81]

According to Mill "the effect produced, in social phenomena, by any complex set of circumstances, amounts precisely to the sum of the effects of the circumstances taken singly" (CW VIII:895). This is not true of every science; in chemistry, for example, or in psychology itself, effects often have properties which are not reducible to the properties of the causes. The laws in these cases are said to be "chemical." But in the case of social phenomena, there is nothing in the resultant whole that is not already in the parts; the resultant whole is simply, as Mill says, the "sum" of the parts. We may therefore consider each cause that is operating and use the science of psychology to infer what effect it would have. We can then deduce the social laws. For the social cause is the sum of the individual causes taken as parts, and the social effect is the sum of the individual effects taken as parts. The problem with the geometrical method is that it simply assumes one cause, instead of taking into account "all the causes which conjunctly influence the effect" (CW VIII:895). But once *all* the causes are taken into account, then one can indeed proceed deductively, in principle at least, as the elder Mill and Ricardo proposed.

Where the many causes acting are all of a single kind, it is possible to discover the laws for the group phenomena simply by deducing them from the assumed conjunction of the many single causes. This is what Mill calls the "physical" or "concrete deductive" method. It can be used in political economy, where one assumes everyone is acting on the motive of preferring the greater gain to the smaller. However, where one is interested in development over time, as one more generally is in sociology and history, it is necessary to trace out over time the detailed effects of all the many causes. But this detailed set of inferences is beyond the powers of human computation. The best that we can do is begin with the empirical laws of social phenomena and show by deduction that this was *likely* to result from what we know of the nature of humankind and the circumstances in which the many individuals then existed. This is the "inverse deductive" method.

In either case, however, we can never safely take for granted that we have located all the operative causes. That means, in effect, that we must always take for granted that the laws of social phenomena that we have located are in fact gappy. Social science can therefore never be anything more than a science of *tendencies* rather than one in which positive predictions are possible. This is in fact the best that we can do, given the complexity of the phenomena; but even so, such knowledge can be useful in proposing policy. After all, weather forecasting, too, is useful, even though it too is only a science of tendencies.

It is evident that this proposed method for social science can work only if the deductions that Mill describes are really valid. Mill, naturally, argues that they are. In fact he holds that they occur elsewhere in science, in physics in particular. In mechanics it is possible to deduce the laws for a complex system from the laws for simple systems. If we have a three-body system, we can conceptually divide it into three two-body systems, and knowing the forces that would operate in the two-body systems were they isolated, we can deduce what the forces are that are operating in the three-body system. Mill holds that this deduction proceeds *a priori*; in these cases, as opposed to those such as chemistry and psychology where the effect is "heterogeneous" with its causes, "the joint effect of causes is the *sum* of their separate effects" (*CW* VII:373, italics added), and, while we know the law of the separate causes by induction, the inference to their joint effects involves no further induction but only "ratiocination." In fact, he is wrong on this point.[82] In order for the deduction to go through one must take into account *the relations by which the simpler systems are constituted into the more complex system*, and *there is no* a priori *reason for assuming that a given relational structure will yield one sort of law for the complex system rather than another.*[83] This means that the deduction of the law for the complex system depends not only upon the laws for the simpler system but also upon *another factual assumption* that relates the laws of the complex system to *both* the laws for the simpler system *and* the relational structure that constitutes the complex system out of the simpler systems. This factual assumption relating the laws for the complex system to both the laws for the simpler system and the relational structure is itself a *law*, not a specific causal law but rather *a law about such laws*. Since it is a law, the step from the causal laws for the simpler systems is not one of pure ratiocination or pure deduction but one that also involves an inductive feature. This law, this inductive step the existence of which Mill denies, has been referred to as a "composition law."[84] When Mill asserts that the inference is a deduction that proceeds wholly *a priori* without any inductive step beyond those that provided the laws for the simple systems, he is neglecting to take into account this additional factual premise. In effect *this amounts to neglecting the causal role of the relations which constitute the whole out of the parts.* Mill, then, is wrong in his claim that in mechanics the deduction of a law for the complex system can be deduced *a priori* from the laws for simpler systems; what he calls the "deductive" method does not in fact have any place in mechanics.

Mill makes a similar mistake in the case of the social sciences.[85] When he claims that the deduction of the laws for the complex social wholes can be deduced *a priori* from the laws for the parts, that is, from the laws for persons taken individually, he is claiming in effect that there is no need for a composition law, or, what amounts to the same, no need to take into account the *social relations* which, by virtue of holding among individuals, constitute the social whole out of those individuals. Mill suggests that in the social sciences, the individual cases act "conjunctively," in just the way that they act in mechanics:

The Social Science . . . is a deductive science; not, indeed, after the model of geometry, but after that of the more complex physical sciences. It infers the law of each effect from the laws of causation on which that effect depends; not, however, from the law merely of one cause, as in the geometrical method; but by considering all the causes which conjunctly influence the effect, and compounding their laws with one another. (*CW* VIII:895)

But a conjunction is merely that and not a relational whole. He indicates the same neglect of relations when he speaks of "computing the *aggregate* result of many co-existent causes" (*ibid.*, italics added). Mill also indicates that the inference from the laws of the co-existent causes to the "aggregate" effect is something that we can "calculate *a priori*" (*ibid.*); the inference will, of course, be *a priori* if it proceeds on the basis of a *conjunction* of premises, but not if it requires additional factual premises concerning the relational structure and a composition law. He also suggests, as we have noted, that the total social effect is merely the "sum" of the individual effects. He makes the same point when he explicitly compares social phenomena to those of mechanics. For, he tells us, "in social phenomena the Composition of Causes is the universal law" (*CW* VIII:879), where the Composition of Causes is "the principle which is exemplified in all cases in which the joint effect of several causes is identical with the *sum* of their several effects" (*CW* VII:371, italics added). But again, on the one hand, a mere sum is not a relational whole, while on the other hand, if the connection is merely that of a sum, then the deduction does proceed *a priori*, like any other inference based on the mathematical notion of addition.[86] In short, *when Mill proposes the "deductive" method for the social sciences he is neglecting to take into account social relations as relevant factors.* It is much as if Newton failed to take into account the relative positions of the planets when he inferred the forces acting in the solar system from the assumption that gravity would act among the planets and the sun taking them pairwise; but then, Mill's account of mechanics implies that Newton did just that![87]

We may therefore conclude that Mill did not provide an adequate account of the scientific method appropriate for the social sciences. He did suggest, however, an alternative means by which empirical laws could be transformed into scientific laws. This was the use of probability theory to try to separate out those cases where all the relevant factors might not be known but where it is *likely* that the generalization one is considering is genuinely causal. The use of probability and statistics was only beginning when Mill was trying to think through the problem of method in the social sciences;[88] we cannot reasonably expect him to have done more than he did in giving its role in the social sciences. But, as we know, it has in fact become the basic method in the social sciences for the discovery of causes.

What is ironic is that Mill's own proposals for a method in the social sciences made much the same error as the geometrical method of his father, and were open to much the same criticism: he neglected to take into account the social relations among individuals which unite the latter into social wholes. Mill distinguished the geometrical method of his father from his own proposal for an inverse deductive method by arguing that the former failed to acknowledge what the latter insisted upon, namely, the complexity of the relevant causes. But to recognize complexity is not yet to recognize the relevance of the relations that hold amongst the many individuals in the complex phenomena. It is these relations that Mill ignores when he proposes his own methodology of social science, ignoring them just as much as his father had ignored them. The younger Mill justified this dismissal of the relevance of the relations that structure the social whole with the following argument:

The laws of the phenomena of society are, and can be, nothing but the laws of the actions and passions of human beings united together in the social state. Men, however, in a state of society, are still men; their actions and passions are obedient to the laws of individual human nature. Men are not, when brought together, converted into another kind of substance, with different properties. . . . Human beings in society have no properties but those which are derived from, and may be resolved into, the laws of the nature of individual men. (*CW* VIII:879)

Mill is here conflating two different things.[89] On the one hand he is asserting the empiricist thesis that concepts either refer to what is presented to us in ordinary sense experience or inner awareness or are defined in terms of such concepts, and using this to conclude that there is nothing to social institutions and groups over and above the individuals that form those institutions and groups. On the other hand he is asserting that the laws for the complex systems, the social institutions and groups, can be deduced from the laws for individuals taken alone. What he neglects to note is that, while groups do not have properties that cannot be resolved into the properties of individuals, individuals in groups do have properties that they do not have *qua* individuals, that is, taken in isolation. For, individuals in groups do exhibit behaviour that they do not exhibit when they are taken alone. This behaviour that appears only in groups, these properties that people have only in groups, is precisely the behaviour that defines those groups, that is, *the reciprocal and coordinated behaviour that constitutes social relations*. Mill of course does not neglect social relations. Even when he applies what he calls the deductive method, and gives us to understand that there are no relations that are relevant to the deduction, he does in fact implicitly introduce them. When he infers the laws of the market in political economy from the assumption that the individuals in the market prefer a greater gain to a smaller, he has to assume that they stand in a variety of social relations, those for example of buyer and seller, and those of capitalist, labourer, and renter. What the one hand giveth the other taketh away. And so, in the passage quoted just above, we see Mill totally missing the significance of social relations. This is ironic, of course, because, as we suggested, it takes him back to the philosophy of his father and the earlier generation of utilitarians. It is even more ironic because, as we have also seen, he is at the same time fully aware of the importance of social relations! Mill came out of his mental crisis recognizing the limitations of the social thought of his father, but as we now see he could never quite escape those limitations.

NOTES

1 For a general discussion of Mill's philosophy of science, see F. Wilson, 1990, ch. II.
2 If we have (1) $C \to E$, then C is sufficient for E. If we have (2) $E \to N$, then N is necessary for E. If we have (3) $C \leftrightarrow E$, then C is necessary and sufficient for E. If we have (4) $(C \,\&\, D) \to E$, then $(C \,\&\, D)$ is a complex sufficient condition, with two parts, each of which is itself insufficient. If, besides (4), there is a second sufficient condition, say (5) $(F \,\&\, G) \to E$, then we have what Mill calls a plurality of causes. Each of these conditions is sufficient, but neither is necessary. If (4) and (5) are both true, then so is (6) $[(C \,\&\, D) \vee (F \,\&\, G)] \to E$, where 'v' represents "or". In other words, where there are several sufficient conditions, the logical sum of the sufficient conditions is itself a sufficient condition.

Where there are several conditions each of which is sufficient, the effect E will be caused sometimes by the one and sometimes by another, depending upon the conditions. But clearly, wherever one sufficient condition is present, so is the logical sum of all sufficient conditions. The latter therefore occurs unconditionally: it is the unconditional sufficient condition.
3 What Mill says explicitly is that science aims to discover causal laws and that a cause is an unconditional sufficient condition. However, in general each sufficient condition will be a conjunction (logical product) of several conditions, each of which is in itself insufficient. Moreover, in general there will be several sets of such complex conditions each of which is itself sufficient though to be sure none is by itself necessary. That is, in general there will be a plurality of causes. Where there is a plurality of causes, the disjunction (logical sum) of those sufficient conditions is the unconditional sufficient condition, or cause.

Mill argues that "it is a law that there is a law for everything" (CW VII:325). To thus hold that every event has a cause, i.e., that if an event occurs then there is a cause for that event, is to hold that it is a necessary condition for any event that there is a cause for it, that is, that there is an unconditional sufficient condition for that event. The logical sum of the sufficient conditions will be this condition, and its occurrence will therefore be not only sufficient for the event but also necessary.

For Mill, then, what science aims at ideally is set of laws giving necessary and sufficient conditions for all events.

But in practice we are often concerned not with the whole unconditional cause, but only with individual sufficient conditions, or even with the insufficient parts of the sufficient conditions – what J. L. Mackie was later to call INUS conditions: "Insufficient Necessary Parts of Unnecessary Sufficient" conditions. (See Mackie 1975.)

Mill develops methods ("Mill's Methods") for the discovery of necessary conditions (method of agreement), sufficient conditions (method of difference), and necessary and sufficient conditions (joint method of agreement and difference). Mill does not develop the methods to apply to conjunctive or disjunctive conditions, though this is easily done; see Mackie 1974. But Mill clearly allows for complex causal conditions when he allows for a plurality of causes, and therefore points the way for others, such as W. E. Johnson and C. D. Broad, culminating in Mackie, to extend his ideas from simple cases to the more complex.

Although Mill allows for the indicated wide variety of cases, in the present chapter we shall, for the sake of simplicity, assume that the laws with which we are concerned are all statements of necessary and sufficient conditions, and that these conditions are all incomplex.

4 This is the form of a statement of necessary and sufficient conditions. The laws could also be those that state a sufficient condition, or those that state a necessary condition. Or they could even involve complex conditions, formed conjunctively and disjunctively out of simpler conditions. (See note 2 above.) Furthermore, some of the conditions might be described only generically rather than specifically. (See the discussion of "gappy" laws, below; cf. note 60.) All these complications we can safely ignore; all we need for our present purposes is the basic idea that explanation proceeds by deduction from laws.

5 Karl Popper has suggested (1950, 2:367 n. 7) that it was he who discovered this model. Popper is clearly wrong in this claim: it was first explicitly stated by Mill. And Mill was clearly anticipated by Hume and Bacon.

6 Note that this law is not only universal, containing the universal quantifier "all," but also makes an existence claim, since it also contains an existential quantifier asserting "there is." Now, a statement like "all A are B" containing a universal quantifier is falsifiable by a single instance of an A which is not B. But an existentially quantified statement cannot be falsified by a single instance – though it can be verified by a single instance. And, of course, universally quantified statements, while they can be falsified by a single instance, can never be conclusively verified. But the causal principle contains both sorts of quantifier. Thus, it can neither be conclusively falsified nor conclusively verified. This shows clearly that Mill, like other empiricists, rejects the suggestion of Karl Popper, in his *Logic of Scientific Discovery* and elsewhere, that a statement, if it is to be reckoned as scientific, must be conclusively falsifiable.

(Of course, an observation falsifies a hypothesis conclusively only if the further *epistemic* condition is met, that the observation is itself certain. The latter seldom holds, and so no hypothesis can be said to be falsified with certainty. In this sense, all falsification remains tentative. But there cannot even be *tentative falsification* of this sort unless the [non-epistemic] *logical* condition is met, that the falsity of the observation statement *entails* that the hypothesis is false. And that *logical* condition will hold only if the hypothesis contains no existential quantifiers.)

7 Mill's argument here is often spoken of with derision. For a sympathetic examination of Mill's case, see Wilson 1985, sec. 1.3.

8 As is well known, each of Mill's Methods works by using observational or experimental data to eliminate all but one from a range of hypotheses, and concludes that the remaining unelimited hypothesis is true. If this inference is to be conclusive, then one must assume that there is at least one condition that is a cause (determinism) and that it is among those in the delimited range (limited variety). Each of the eliminative methods requires, in other words, for its logical working the assumption of certain matter-of-fact premises known as the principle of determinism and the principle of limited variety (Skorupski 1989, 179, refers to these as the causation assumption and the exhaustiveness assumption). See G. H. von Wright 1957. In effect, whether he knew it exactly or not, Mill recognized the need for these principles when he assumed that the principle of universal causation is logically both necessary and sufficient for the working of his methods of eliminative induction. It is this principle that we have just stated.

9 Here too they disagree with Popper. See note 41 of this chapter.

10 We should not fall into the dogma of Popper (1954, II:ch. 14) that the "task" of the social sciences is to explain the "indirect, the unintended and often the unwanted by products of" intentional human action. The "task" of the social sciences, according to Mill, in so far as it is possible to define such a "task," is a cognitive one: it is to discover cause-and-effect relations in the area of the social, just as it is the task of mechanics to discover the causes that operate in the physical realm. Because we know some causal relations in the realm of the social, we can, sometimes at least, bring about among our friends, and, where necessary, our foes, what we desire.

11 This has been established in detail by John Robson in his important study, *The Improvement of Mankind* (Robson 1968).

12 James Mill, "An Essay on Government" (James Mill 1978). James Mill wrote this article, along with a number of others, for the *Supplement* to the fifth edition of the *Encyclopædia Britannica*. The *Supplement* was

planned in 1814, and was issued in half volumes from December 1815 onwards. It was issued as a whole in six volumes in 1824. Mill's "Essay on Government" first appeared in the second part of Volume IV, which was published in September 1820.

13 *Plan of Parliamentary Reform, in the form of a Catechism, with Reasons for Each Article: with an Introduction, showing the Necessity of Radical, and the Inadequacy of Moderate, Reform*, in Bentham 1962, 3:459. The *Plan* was first published in 1817.

14 Excluding "all those individuals whose interests are indisputably included in those of other individuals," who "may be struck off without inconvenience" (James Mill 1978, 79) – where among those who are thus excluded are children and women.

15 See Ricardo 1951. For a comparison of Ricardo and Mill, see Wilson 1990, ch. VI, especially sec. 1.

16 Ricardo 1951, 12f.

17 Ricardo 1951, 13.

18 Smith 1904, Bk. I, ch. 5, p. 32.

19 Ricardo 1951, 106.

20 Ricardo 1951, 108.

21 This essay first appeared in the *Edinburgh Review*, no. xcvii (March 1829), Article vii.

22 Coleridge 1934. The *Treatise* was written in 1818, when it was published in a quarto edition. Alice D. Cooper's text is that of the edition of the *Encyclopædia Metropolitana* of 1849.

23 Coleridge 1934, I:277.

24 Cartwright 1817, 2. Cartwright excluded "infants, the insane, and such as have, for criminality, legally forfeited their franchise" (p. 2). He does not even bother to mention women.

25 Cartwright (1817, xvi, 28) refers to Bentham's arguments.

26 Coleridge 1934, I:277.

27 Jones taught first at Cambridge, then briefly at King's College, London; he then succeeded Malthus in the chair of political economy and history at the East India Company college at Haileybury. For his criticisms of Ricardo, see R. Jones 1831. He contrasts the methods of Ricardo with his own inductive method in the Preface, p. xxi.

28 At Cambridge, Whewell was successively a tutor, Knightbridge Professor of Moral Philosophy, and Master of Trinity College. For his work on Ricardo, see Whewell 1829 and also Whewell 1831 and 1859. Whewell (1831, 52ff; 1859, xi) praises Jones's use of the inductive method. As Whewell's own essays on Ricardo indicate, he was prepared to take the game of deduction even further than Ricardo, by introducing a higher degree of mathematical sophistication, but at the same time he insisted

that such an approach if taken alone could only lead to "perversions of facts," and had to be preceded by the sort of inductive inquiry that Jones had undertaken (see Whewell 1831, 43f).

Whewell was also a critic of both Mill's moral philosophy (see Whewell 1845) and Mill's philosophy of science (see Whewell 1847). Mill replied to both; see his "Whewell on Moral Philosophy" (CW X) and his *System of Logic* (CW VII–VIII).

Needless to say, Whewell was also a Tory and a defender of unreformed universities. Mill wrote of Whewell, commenting on both the moral philosophy and the philosophy of science, that

> We do not say the intention, but certainly the tendency, of his efforts, is to shape the whole of philosophy, physical as well as moral, into a form adapted to serve as a support and a justification to any opinions which happen to be established. A writer who has gone beyond all his predecessors in the manufacture of necessary truths, that is, of propositions which, according to him, may be known to be true independently of proof; who ascribes this self-evidence to the larger generalities of all sciences (however little obvious at first) as soon as they have become familiar – was still more certain to regard all moral propositions familiar to him from his early years as self-evident truths. His *Elements of Morality* could be nothing better than a classification and systematizing of those opinions which he found prevailing among those who had been educated according to the approved methods of his own country; or, let us say, an apparatus for converting those prevailing opinions, on matters of morality, into reasons for themselves. (CW X:168–69).

It has been said that if Whewell had not existed as an opponent, Mill would have had to invent him.

29 Samuel Hollander (1985, I:149ff) discusses these Cambridge critics of Ricardo and James Mill.

30 The main thrust of Jones's book on rent is to show how rents vary with the conventions defining the social structure of land ownership. Whewell, in his review of Jones's book (1831, 49) and again in Whewell 1859, xi, emphasizes how this view of rent differs from that of Ricardo. It is a point he takes up, quoting Jones extensively, in Whewell 1862, 76ff.

Whewell, referring to Jones, makes the same point in the second of his essays on Ricardo (Whewell 1829, 4), and then immediately turns, in order to reject it, to the claim that it is a *natural law* that wages for labour always tend to the subsistence level (p. 5ff), and indicates (p. 7) that social convention plays a role in determining the equilibrium level of wages. Jones (1831, xxvff) makes a similar point, that wages depend upon social institutions.

31 John Stuart Mill [unsigned], Appendix to Bulwer's *England and the English*, *CW* I:591.
32 For a detailed discussion of this method, see Wilson 1990, ch. III.
33 See also William Thomas 1979.
34 Wordsworth's place in Mill's thought has been discussed in Wilson 1989. See also Woods 1961.
35 For a discussion of the notion of psychological analysis in the context of his mental crisis, see Wilson 1990, ch. I, sec. 3.
36 For the idea of a house, as described by James Mill, see James Mill 1829, I:115–16; he describes the idea of *everything* in the same passage. But the notion that the idea of *everything* contains as integrant or real parts the ideas of every (other) thing shows that something has gone wrong. As E. G. Boring (1957, 226) has commented, "in this *reductio ad absurdum* we see the persistent danger of philosophical psychology, unchecked by scientific control. A rational principle is captured by the empirical method and may then be turned loose to carry us even to the brink of absurdity. There is no logical reason to suppose that the idea of *everything* might not be an association of every idea of a thing, but there is not the slightest observational ground for maintaining, even with the maximal telescoping, that a consciousness can contain a literally unlimited number of ideas at once. What meaning can one give to the conception that ideas [that is, sensory images] coexist when indistinguishable? . . . Mill has admitted to systematic psychology a rational principle capable of devouring observational effects."
37 See Boring 1957, 226; Wilson 1990, ch. IV; and Wilson 1991b.
38 Skorupski 1989, 263.
39 *Ibid.*
40 "The aetiology is established by eliminative methods of induction, not by an analysis of the conceptual content of the feeling." *Ibid.*
41 Popper (1961) argues that the human being escapes from the web of causation because there is novelty, in human knowledge in particular, as such novelty cannot be predicted or reduced to law. We see here that Mill rejects this claim; novelty *can* be explained by deterministic laws. For a discussion of Popper's argument on this point, see Addis 1975.
42 See Wilson 1990, ch. VII.
43 For the relations between the utilitarians and India, see Moir 1990; Forbes 1951; Stokes 1959; Moore 1983; Lloyd 1991; and Zastoupil 1981.
44 The connections between Mill's work in the East India Company and his mental crisis are discussed in an illuminating way in Zastoupil 1981.
45 Zastoupil 1981, 54.

46 Skorupski 1989, 17.

47 Skorupski (1989) describes the "complexity of Mill's understanding of the relationship between abstract utility and the given fabric of ethical life" as "one aspect of his general project, that of opening up philosophic radicalism to the insights of the 'Germano-Coleridgean' school, which stood in all apparent opposition to it."

48 For Mill's relations with these French thinkers, see Filipiuk 1991.

49 I am not suggesting that "internalization" is an *explanation* of this event; it merely describes it. The explanation is to be found in the learning theory that provides a law or generalization that relates learning experiences to the fact of internalization.

50 Lévi-Strauss 1967, 273–74.

51 Lévi-Strauss 1967, 121; also Lévi-Strauss 1969, Preface.

52 Moore 1983, 518.

53 For a discussion of the connections between John Stuart Mill's theories of psychology and more recent theories, now stated in the language of behaviourism, see Wilson 1990, ch. VIII.

54 ". . . social relations consist of the raw material out of which the models are built, while social structure can, by no means, be reduced to the ensemble of social relations to be described in a given society." Lévi-Strauss 1967, 271.

55 Cf. Lévi-Strauss 1969, 483.

56 Lévi-Strauss 1967, 275–76.

57 Lévi-Strauss 1967, 292.

58 "Rather let us own that the notions of prescriptive and preferential are relative: a preferential system is prescriptive when envisaged at the model level; a prescriptive system must be preferential when envisaged at the level of reality." Lévi-Strauss 1969, xxxiii.

59 The term is due to J. L. Mackie (1975).

60 The role of gappy laws in the covering law model of explanation is discussed in Bergmann 1957, ch. II; M. Brodbeck 1968a; and in considerable detail in Wilson 1985.

61 For details on the logic of inferences of this sort using gappy laws, see Wilson 1985.

62 The point is that the imperfect or gappy law contains an existential quantifier – "there are factors f of such and such a generic sort F and which are such that, whenever an x is G then x is H if and only if x is f." The presence of the existential quantifier prevents falsification by counterexamples. The presence of the universal quantifier is what marks it as a law, of course.

63 Cf. Bergmann 1957, ch. II.

64 Cf. Wilson 1986, ch. I. The point is that gappy laws with the form suggested in note 62 have the form exemplified by principles of determinism and limited variety. That is why gappy laws guide research.

65 On the role that statistics thus plays in science, see Wilson 1986, ch. I, sec. i; and Wilson 1991a, ch. VII and VIII.

66 Cf. Lévi-Strauss 1967, 271–73. See also the algebra of kinship constructed by André Weil, which Lévi-Strauss included as ch. XIV of Lévi-Strauss 1969.

67 Cf. Addis 1968.

68 Popper 1950, II: ch. 14.

69 *Ibid.*

70 This point has recently been stated in a particularly persuasive and illuminating form in Carrithers 1992.

71 For a detailed discussion of such laws, and their relations to the causal ideal of scientific explanation, see Addis 1975.

72 Cf. Addis 1975.

73 For the details of Mill's commitment to individuality, see Donner 1991.

74 Skorupski 1989, 17.

75 Donner 1991 emphasizes Mill's stress on self-development.

76 For a remarkable survey of Mill's views on political economy, see Hollander 1985.

77 Cf. Bladen 1965.

78 This point is noted by Whewell (1859, xvii).

79 Cf. Bladen 1965.

80 On the principles of determinism and limited variety, see note 8 of this chapter.

81 For a detailed discussion of Mill's account of the deductive method and its relation to other features of his philosophy, see Wilson 1983.

82 Cf. Russell 1956, 484.

83 See Bergmann 1957, ch. III; Madden 1962; Wilson 1991a, ch. III; and Wilson 1990, ch. II, sec. 2.

84 Cf. Bergmann 1957, ch. III.

85 For the importance of the notion of a composition law in the philosophy of the social sciences, see Brodbeck 1968b and Addis 1975.

86 It is worth noting a further confusion on Mill's part, between the *logical* notion of "conjunction" and the *arithmetical* notion of "addition." The inferences of logic and mathematics both proceed *a priori*, but they are for all that very different sorts of inference. This was finally made clear to empiricists by Mill's intellectual heir, Bertrand Russell.

87 Hollander (1985) fails to note this central defect of Mill's proposed methodology of social science. To be sure, he does (1985, I:91) mention

the "Composition of Forces," but he does not notice how Mill lacks an adequate understanding of this principle.

88 Cf. Goldman 1983.

89 For an important discussion of this sort of confusion, see Brodbeck 1968b.

7   Mill's utilitarianism

INTRODUCTION

Mill's *Utilitarianism* was not written as a scholarly treatise but as a series of essays for a popular audience. It was first published in three instalments in *Fraser's Magazine* in 1861 and appeared in book form in 1863. *Fraser's Magazine* was a magazine with a general audience and the essay was written with this readership in view. Although many commentators have examined the arguments Mill puts forward in this work in isolation from his other writings, in fact it cannot be properly appreciated unless it is placed in the context of the larger body of his work. In particular, this work needs to be read against the background of his more scholarly writing in *A System of Logic* and in his editorial footnotes to James Mill's *Analysis of the Phenomena of the Human Mind* (*Logic*, *CW* VII and VIII; James Mill 1869).

John Stuart Mill is rightly considered to be a major figure in the history of utilitarianism; his theory is a touchstone to which contemporary ethical theorists regularly return for insights. Yet at the same time, Mill's utilitarianism is boldly revisionist, breaking free of many of the constraints and confines of the narrower and simpler utilitarianism of his predecessors Jeremy Bentham and his father James Mill. Although John Stuart Mill was carefully educated and prepared by his father to be the transmitter and torch bearer of Benthamite utilitarianism, he instead radically transformed it. The result is a theory which is both inspiring and frustrating in its

Some of the ideas in this chapter were worked out in an earlier form in Donner 1983, 1987, 1989, 1991, and 1993. I would like to thank Roger Crisp and John Skorupski for comments on earlier drafts.

sophistication, richness and complexity. While I argue that Mill's theory is consistent and unified, there is no doubt that it expands and enlarges the familiar boundaries of his predecessors' utilitarianism at times almost to the breaking point. But his theory also shares with theirs some familiar foundations.

Although utilitarianism as a moral theory has many faces, a core idea informs all of them. Utilitarianism makes utility or intrinsic value the foundation of morality. Utilitarianism "evaluates actions in terms of their utility" (Sumner 1979, 100) rather than in terms of any intrinsic properties of the actions. Utilitarianism is distinguished from moral theories which hold that certain kinds of acts are right or wrong in themselves, and we are obliged to perform them or refrain from doing them for that very reason. According to utilitarianism, on the other hand, concepts of the good are more basic than or prior to concepts of right and obligation, and obligations are determined by reference to intrinsic value. This core idea leaves much room for differing interpretations of the nature of the good to be produced as well as the method of determining obligations on the basis of this good. This latter issue is often formulated as the dispute which divides act utilitarianism and rule utilitarianism. Bentham, James Mill and John Stuart Mill all hold to mental state accounts of utility, that is, accounts which maintain that the good we seek to promote consists in mental states such as pleasure, happiness, enjoyment or satisfaction. The attractive intuitive idea of utilitarianism is the importance of the promotion of well-being in its many forms. But this still leaves open the questions: what is the best account of utility or welfare? and what is the best method for maximizing or promoting (utilitarians can differ over this) utility or welfare, however construed?

THE NATURE OF THE GOOD

Classical utilitarians have usually agreed that human good consists in the experience of pleasure or happiness or that pleasure or happiness is the one thing desirable in itself. But utilitarians disagree about the nature of utility. John Stuart Mill holds that the principle of utility is the supreme or foundational principle of morality, which plays the role of justifying all obligations and secondary principles or standards. He says that

The creed which accepts as the foundation of morals, Utility, or the Greatest Happiness Principle, holds that actions are right in proportion as they tend to promote happiness, wrong as they tend to produce the reverse of happiness. (*Utilitarianism*, *CW* X:210)

In this formulation Mill's theory puts forward a single standard for morality. However, the principle of utility is most directly a principle of the good which is the foundation for all practical reasoning, including moral reasoning, and so provides the grounding for the moral evaluation of action. In another formulation, the principle of utility is more clearly advanced as a principle of good: "The utilitarian doctrine is, that happiness is desirable, and the only thing desirable, as an end; all other things being only desirable as means to that end" (*CW* X:234). He expands: "By happiness is intended pleasure, and the absence of pain; by unhappiness, pain, and the privation of pleasure" (*CW* X:210). This "theory of morality" is grounded on "the theory of life" that

pleasure, and freedom from pain, are the only things desirable as ends; and that all desirable things (which are as numerous in the utilitarian as in any other scheme) are desirable either for the pleasure inherent in themselves, or as means to the promotion of pleasure and the prevention of pain. (*CW* X:210)

These quotes signal some important breaks from the Benthamite utilitarian tradition. Good resides in internal mental states of pleasure or happiness. But while for Bentham these mental states are sensations of pleasure, for Mill they are far more complex states of experience. Mill thought that Bentham's conception of the good, his quantitative hedonism, was narrow and misconceived and made him vulnerable to the criticism that utilitarianism is "a doctrine worthy only of swine" (*CW* X:210). Mill expands the conception of the good in two separate but related respects. He takes value to reside in complex mental experiences rather than sensations and he takes the quality of happiness as well as the quantity to be productive of its value. Mill's qualitative hedonism is a complex mental state account of utility which takes into account the quality as well as the quantity of pleasurable experiences in measuring their value and stands as a sophisticated alternative to Bentham's quantitative hedonism. I first explore the views on complex mental states before turning to the question of what makes these experiences valuable.

Mill's qualitative hedonism is intended to fend off criticisms that utilitarianism is a narrow theory appropriate for swine; nevertheless it has drawn more than its share of criticism. Mill stands accused of a list of inconsistencies because he defends a complex mental state account which expands the good-making properties of pleasures to encompass quality as well as quantity of states of experience. Mill concurs with Bentham that pleasurable mental states are what have value or are the things that are valuable. However, Mill dissents from Bentham over the issues both of the nature of these valuable states and of which properties produce their value. Many mistaken or misguided objections to Mill's position arise from the failure of critics to keep separate the quite distinct issues of what things are valuable – pleasurable mental states – and what properties of these states are their good-making properties. A position on the issue of what things have value still does not settle the question of what properties of those things produce or create their value.

John Stuart Mill, James Mill and Bentham all share an associationist psychology.[1] When Mill says that "by happiness is intended pleasure, and the absence of pain", he indicates that happiness consists of a composite in which pleasures outbalance pains over time (*Utilitarianism, CW* X:210).[2] Mill's empiricism and psychological associationism provide the impetus for his claim that our mental life is created out of the basic data of sense experience. Sensations are the basic original mental entities and are defined as "the feelings which we have by the five senses – Smell, Taste, Hearing, Touch, and Sight" (James Mill 1869 I:3). Sensations and ideas, which are the subsequent mental copies of sensations, become linked through association and in the normal course of psychological development what were originally simple mental states are turned into much more complex states of experience. Moreover, Mill thinks that association often operates as a quasi-chemical process to create chemical unions of elements in which the original parts or elements merge into a new and complex whole (*Logic, CW* VIII:852–56). He says,

When many impressions or ideas are operating in the mind together, there sometimes takes place a process of a similar kind to chemical combination. When impressions have been so often experienced in conjunction, that each of them calls up readily and instantaneously the ideas of the whole group, those ideas sometimes melt and coalesce into one another, and appear not several ideas, but one. (*CW* VIII:853)

The complexes that result occupy an important place in Mill's moral psychology, for they are bearers of value, rather than the simple ideas which generate them.

While Mill's theory can be classified as a sophisticated kind of hedonism because of the role that pleasures and pains play in generating complex pleasurable experiences, it would be a mistake to view his theory as primarily focussed on the evaluation of pleasures. Out of the building blocks of pleasures are built human happiness and satisfaction, and on this base is erected the edifice of human beings of firm and distinctive character freely choosing the projects and activities of meaningful life. Mill's fundamental purpose is to promote human self-development and so he is centrally occupied with exploring the forms of character that allow humans to pursue meaningful lives.

Mill is sometimes misconstrued as maintaining the related thesis of *psychological* hedonism, understood as the thesis that all actions are motivated by the anticipation of pleasure or pain. But Fred Berger, among others, has argued convincingly that Mill is not a psychological hedonist and thus does not hold that all actions are motivated by the anticipation of pleasure or pain (Berger 1984, 12–17). For example, we are not so motivated when we act from habit and especially when we have a confirmed character. Mill explains,

When the will is said to be determined by motives, a motive does not mean always, or solely, the anticipation of a pleasure or of a pain. I shall not here inquire whether it be true that, in the commencement, all our voluntary actions are mere means consciously employed to obtain some pleasure, or avoid some pain. It is at least certain that we gradually, through the influence of association, come to desire the means without thinking of the end: the action itself becomes an object of desire, and is performed without reference to any motive beyond itself. Thus far, it may still be objected, that, the action having through association become pleasurable, we are, as much as before, moved to act by the anticipation of a pleasure, namely, the pleasure of the action itself. But granting this, the matter does not end here. As we proceed in the formation of habits, and become accustomed to will a particular act or a particular course of conduct because it is pleasurable, we at last continue to will it without any reference to its being pleasurable. . . .

. . . A habit of willing is commonly called a purpose; and among the causes of our volitions, and of the actions which flow from them, must be reckoned not only likings and aversions, but also purposes. It is only when our purposes have become independent of the feelings of pain or pleasure from which they originally took their rise, that we are said to have a confirmed character. (*Logic, CW* VIII:842–43)

Acting from habit does not contradict the claim that "happiness is desirable, and the only thing desirable, as an end" (*Utilitarianism, CW* X:234). As well, the textual evidence indicates that pleasures not only play a causal role but must also be phenomenally present in the product of association, albeit not as uniform and distinct components, if the complex as a whole can rightly be said to be valuable. Mill's exploration of the role of habit supports the claim that pleasure must be phenomenally present in valuable experiences.

How can the will to be virtuous, where it does not exist in sufficient force, be implanted or awakened? Only by making the person *desire* virtue – by making him think of it in a pleasurable light, or of its absence in a painful one. It is by associating the doing right with pleasure, or the doing wrong with pain, or by eliciting and impressing and bringing home to the person's experience the pleasure naturally involved in the one or the pain in the other, that it is possible to call forth that will to be virtuous, which, when confirmed, acts without any thought of either pleasure or pain. Will is the child of desire, and passes out of the dominion of its parent only to come under that of habit. *That which is the result of habit affords no presumption of being intrinsically good;* and there would be no reason for wishing that the purpose of virtue should become independent of pleasure and pain, were it not that the influence of the pleasurable and painful associations which prompt to virtue is not sufficiently to be depended on for unerring constancy of action until it has acquired the support of habit. Both in feeling and in conduct, habit is the only thing which imparts certainty; and it is because of the importance to others of being able to rely absolutely on one's feeling and conduct, and to oneself of being able to rely on one's own, that the will to do right ought to be cultivated into this habitual independence. *In other words, this state of the will is a means to good, not intrinsically a good; and does not contradict the doctrine that nothing is a good to human beings but in so far as it is either itself pleasurable, or a means of attaining pleasure or averting pain.* (*Utilitarianism, CW* X:238–39, emphasis added)

Mill's comments quoted above lend credence to the interpretation that pleasure must be present phenomenally in a mental state as a condition of its claim to value. But because of the process of "mental chemistry" described above, this pleasure may be mixed with other elements of the mental state so that it cannot be "picked out" as a distinct aspect of the experience. Hence it is the mental complex as a whole which must have value rather than the sensations of pleasure "in" the experience.

I have claimed that it is important to keep separate the issues of what things have value and of what properties of these things make them valuable or increase or decrease their value. The things that have value are complex mental states with pleasure as a component. Now I take up the notorious and contentious question of Mill's qualitative hedonism.

QUALITATIVE HEDONISM

In propounding qualitative hedonism, Mill moves beyond Benthamite quantitative hedonism in a decisive and notable way. His insistence that the quality of states of happiness is crucial to their value justly earns for him the reputation of revisionary utilitarian. This break with orthodox Benthamism provides an opening for his radical expansion of the conception of the good at the heart of his moral philosophy. It allows him a means to counter decisively the objections of opponents that hedonistic utilitarianism is worthy only of swine; it also enables him to set out an attractive and plausible alternative.

Mill has been subjected to a good deal of less than sympathetic treatment because of his inclusion of quality as a good-making characteristic. The recent excellent revisionary scholarship which has countered many earlier distorted interpretations of aspects of Mill's thought has still tended to accept what I claim are mistaken interpretations of Mill's qualitative hedonism. Many of the harshest criticisms of Mill take him to task for including quality in the assessment of value. Mill's views on quality are taken to be inconsistent with hedonism, and he is accused of abandoning both utilitarianism and hedonism.

Before I delve into the question of the alleged inconsistency of Mill's recognition of quality with hedonism, I will look at what Mill means by the quality of pleasurable states. Many commentators treat quality and value as synonymous, but this is seriously mistaken. Confusion over just what Mill means by quality has led to misconstruals; it is instructive to clarify this question first. In *Utilitarianism* Mill is insistent that pleasures differ in quality as well as quantity:

> It is quite compatible with the principle of utility to recognize the fact, that some *kinds* of pleasure are more desirable and more valuable than others. It would be absurd that while, in estimating all other things, quality is considered as well as quantity, the estimation of pleasures should be supposed to depend on quantity alone. (*CW* X:211)

> What is there to decide whether a particular pleasure is worth purchasing at the cost of a particular pain, except the feelings and judgment of the experienced? When, therefore, those feelings and judgment declare the pleasures derived from the higher faculties to be preferable *in kind*, apart from the question of intensity, to those of which the animal nature, disjoined from the higher faculties, is susceptible, they are entitled on this subject to the same regard. (*CW* X:213)

> According to the Greatest Happiness Principle . . . the ultimate end . . . is an existence exempt as far as possible from pain, and as rich as possible in enjoyments, both in point of quantity and quality. (*CW* X:214)

> If I am asked, what I mean by difference in quality of pleasures, or what makes one pleasure more valuable than another, merely as a pleasure, except its being greater in amount, there is but one possible answer. Of two pleasures, if there be one to which all or almost all who have experience of both give a decided preference, irrespective of any feeling of moral obligation to prefer it, that is the more desirable pleasure. If one of the two is, by those who are competently acquainted with both, placed so far above the other that they prefer it, even though knowing it to be attended with a greater amount of discontent, and would not resign it for any quantity of the other pleasure which their nature is capable of, we are justified in ascribing to the preferred enjoyment a superiority in quality, so far outweighing quantity as to render it, in comparison, of small account. (*CW* X:211)

> From this verdict of the only competent judges, I apprehend there can be no appeal. On a question which is the best worth having of two pleasures, or which of two modes of existence is the most grateful to the feelings, apart from its moral attributes and from its consequences, the judgment of those who are qualified by knowledge of both, or, if they differ, that of the majority among them, must be admitted as final. (*CW* X:213)

> . . . the test of quality, and the rule for measuring it against quantity, being the preference felt by those who, in their opportunities of experience, to

which must be added their habits of self-consciousness and self-observation, are best furnished with the means of comparison. (*CW* X:214)

Quality as well as quantity of happiness is to be considered; less of a higher kind is preferable to more of a lower. (*Journals and Debating Speeches, CW* XVII:663)

The obstacle to a correct interpretation of what Mill means by quality is that he uses the term ambiguously to mean either a kind or a normative property. This vacillation has made him vulnerable to criticisms and misinterpretations. By choosing a consistent sense of quality we can demystify this dimension and put Mill's view of value in clearer perspective. Many interpretations of Mill place quantity (intensity and duration) on one side as a straightforward empirical property and quality on the other side as a mysterious, obscure, normative property (Edwards 1979). This interpretation misses the point of what both Mill and Bentham are doing. Bentham regards the quantities of pleasures as empirical, but he also regards them as normative, that is, productive of good, or that in virtue of which the pleasures that have them are good. Mill does not regard only the quality as normative; he regards both quantity and quality of pleasures and satisfactions as normative or productive of good. He also regards both as empirical. He simply adds one further property, quality, as a normative property. It is often assumed that by including quality as productive of good Mill introduces a radically new and mysterious kind of dimension. This is not the case. In Mill's view, quality is just another ordinary property, and so in all of my discussions of quality of pleasurable experiences I use quality to mean that additional good-making characteristic of pleasures. Quality is thus assigned a consistent meaning, and notions that quality is the only normative aspect of pleasurable experiences should be dispelled. Quality is clearly not synonymous with overall value. Overall value or goodness is produced by quantity and quality, the two basic good-making characteristics. When competent agents express preferences for different pleasurable experiences, they are ranking these experiences on a scale of value. What is being measured is value of experience. The properties that contribute to value are quantity and quality.

In *Utilitarianism* Mill equates the quality of pleasure with its kind. He says, for example, that "the pleasures derived from the higher faculties [are] preferable *in kind* (*CW* X:213). Thus intellectual pleasures can be a kind. But kinds of pleasure are not categorized solely by the faculty affected; they are also classified by cause and by phenomenal differences in the pleasurable experiences themselves. Thus causal and intentional properties enter the picture. Mill's notion that quality of pleasurable experiences is roughly equivalent to kind and his particular view of kind give his view a flexibility that Bentham's lacks.

Many critics have not accepted Mill's bold revisionism. Mill's inclusion of quality raises special problems because of its very complexity, and it calls for a more complicated method for measuring value. But many of the common criticisms of Mill's qualitative hedonism are misdirected and insubstantial and confuse the issues at stake. Some of the worst offenders in this regard are historical critics such as G. E. Moore and F. H. Bradley. An examination of some of the weaker objections they advance will clear away some of the thicket and allow for an exploration of the more substantial questions at stake.

An example of a weak objection is the claim, baldly stated without explanation or argument, that Mill abandons hedonism by introducing quality into the measurement of value of pleasurable experience. F. H. Bradley says,

If you are to prefer a higher pleasure to a lower without reference to quantity – then there is an end altogether of the principle which puts the measure in the surplus of pleasure to the whole sentient creation. (Bradley 1962, 119)

But this view simply misinterprets the claims of hedonism. All that hedonism holds is that pleasure is good and is the only thing that is good, but hedonists differ over the question of which dimensions or properties of pleasure should be used to measure its overall value. Bradley's criticism defines hedonism very narrowly as maintaining that only quantity of pleasure can be counted in the measurement of value, but this definition straightforwardly begs the question. Mill maintains that quality is to be included in the measurement of the overall value of pleasurable experience, and this standard criticism offers no argument for excluding this dimension out of hand.

A second shallow criticism claims that the "something" that an object of more value has to a greater degree can only be quantity (intensity and duration). This argument regards degree and degree of quantity as identical – it is meaningless to talk about "higher" and "lower" unless we are referring to degrees of quantity. As Bradley puts his version, "so that apart from quantity, apart from degree, there is no comparison, no estimation, no higher and lower at all" (Bradley 1962, 118).

This claim that "higher quality" must be referable to more degrees of something can be understood in a strong or a weak sense. In the weak sense, the claim is that pleasures that are more valuable qualitatively have more degrees of something, namely, whatever quality is. In the strong sense, the claim is that pleasures that are more valuable qualitatively have more degrees of quantity, that is, of intensity and duration. The objection trades on the ambiguity between these two senses. The strong sense is needed to draw the conclusion (if quality is not referable to degrees of quantity, then no measurement of value can be obtained), but the assumption of the strong sense begs the question. On the other hand, the conclusion does not follow from the weak sense (pleasures that are more valuable qualitatively must have more degrees of whatever quality is). And this weak sense is not one that Mill would resist. In fact, this objection again construes the question in a narrow and limiting way. As the work on utility theory and social-choice theory of the past few decades has shown, there is a wide range of possibility about the kinds of scale on which utility is to be measured as well as on what the utility to be measured is. The objection in question assumes that measurement must be on strong scales, measuring only quantity (intensity and duration) of pleasure. This assumption also begs the question. Scales of utility can be of many different strengths and can measure utility construed in many different ways (Griffin 1986, 75–124).

There is another problem with this second superficial objection. If we take the objection seriously, we accept that all comparative qualitative judgments are meaningless; not only qualitative differences among pleasures, but also qualitative differences among beautiful objects, or noble characters, for example, must be referable to such quantitative degrees. Acceptance of the objection eliminates the possibility of any comparative purely qualitative judgments. To say the least, this is a very strong position to take, yet its proponents adopt it with regard to quality of pleasurable experience without even an attempt at providing an argument.

Most more recent commentators have also reacted warily to Mill's inclusion of quality. Some false friends, who are concerned that his use of quality makes him vulnerable to objections, have attempted to develop reductionist or correlationist interpretations of his views to save him from his supposed inconsistencies. Reductionists claim that quality of pleasure is reducible to quantity, and so there is no inconsistency. For example, Ernest Sosa claims that, according to Mill, "qualitative pleasure-differences [are] basically differences in degree" (Sosa 1969, 162). However, Sosa's attempt to save Mill from himself does not succeed, and his interpretation clashes, with Mill's clear statements on quality. His interpretation is not in harmony with the spirit of Mill, for it is apparent from even a superficial examination of Mill that quality is quite significant for him. He would have no reason for arguing so forcefully for the need for quality if indeed he intended to reduce it to quantity. Correlationists hold that differences of degree of quantity are correlated in some precise way with differences of degree of quality. They maintain that quantity is thus an absolutely reliable indicator of quality. Richard Bronaugh has made one of the best attempts at providing a correlationist account (Bronaugh 1974). However, this attempt fails for the same reason that Sosa's theory does not succeed. The textual evidence that Mill treats quality as an independent variable is just too strong to ignore.

David Brink argues that Mill rejects hedonism and "instead, he defends (consistently) a conception of human happiness whose dominant component consists in the exercise of one's rational capacities" (Brink 1992, 68). But Brink's argument gets off on the wrong foot and as a result many of his points are misapplied. Brink's misstep occurs early in his argument when he says that "hedonism claims that pleasure is the good (that pleasantness is the one and only good-making property) and that pain is the bad (that painfulness is the one and only bad-making property)" (Brink 1992, 71). Brink clearly conflates here the two issues which need to be kept separate, namely, what things have value and what are the good-making properties of these things which produce their value. Thus he prematurely and incorrectly concludes that Mill's doctrine of the "higher pleasures" is inconsistent with hedonism as well as with a subjective conception of happiness.

Brink's alternative interpretation of Mill as maintaining a non-hedonistic "deliberative conception of happiness" is thoughtful; nevertheless many of his insights are weakened because of his failure to integrate Mill's views on the value of the development and exercise of certain human capacities with the internal mental state account Mill actually holds.

Roderick Long has recently proposed an indirect reductive reading. He says,

The superiority of higher pleasures is indeed quantitative, but only *indirectly* so; in choosing a higher pleasure over a lower one, we are *ipso facto* choosing a nobler character over a baser one, and it is the pleasantness of the noble character, not of the higher pleasure itself, that provides the needed quantitative superiority. (Long 1992, 279)

This reading brings forward the too-much-neglected (until quite recently) elements of Mill's theory which tie it in with the philosophies of Plato and Aristotle which were so influential in Mill's character and intellectual development (*Autobiography*, *CW* I:9–63). Virtue ethics is currently undergoing a revival of interest, and the elements of Mill's thought which resonate with these theories, namely, the emphasis upon character development and nobility, are nicely brought out by Long's discussion. But Long's interpretation also suffers from its reductionist elements, for there is ample evidence that Mill views quantity and quality as completely independent factors.[3]

The important questions that remain after these objections and alternative interpretations are cleared away are: How are the scales of value to be constructed (conceived of) and what measurement procedure is to be substituted for Bentham's felicific calculus? Mill must also explain how degrees and scales of quantity and quality are put together on the central scale of value. In all of this it must be remembered that the scale we are working with is the scale of value. This scale measures the value of pleasures. A look back at Bentham's felicific calculus, which is a quantitative approach, is instructive as background and in comparison with Mill's measurement procedure.

Both Mill and Bentham require methods of measuring the value of different mental states, but they come up with very different procedures. Bentham's felicific calculus is a method designed to measure the total quantity of pleasure and pain caused by an action. The method calls for a calculation of the quantity of each pleasure and pain of every person whose interests are affected. Then the balance of quantity of all the pleasures and pains is worked out to determine which action will produce the greatest balance of pleasure over pain. The method quantifies intensity and duration and integrates them into the scale of value. Since value is a function of quantity, the higher on the scale of quantity each pleasure is placed, the greater is its value. Since Benthamite scales are cardinal, units that can be added and multiplied and so aggregated are required for each of the dimensions.

Mill's measurement procedure for value of pleasurable experience thus does not break with Bentham in taking the key step from unidimensional to multidimensional measure, since Bentham has already done this with the dimensions of intensity and duration, combined into quantity. But Mill's theory does have more dimensions of value to contend with and is more complicated. Applying Mill's procedure, after intensity and duration have been synthesized, the resulting scale of quantity must in turn be integrated with that of quality to form an overall judgment of value. Some kinds or qualities of pleasurable experience are judged to be more valuable and thus placed higher on the scale of quality by competent agents. Competent agents rank pleasurable experiences on scales that measure their value. Their preferences represent a judgment of the value of the experiences resting on the good-making properties of quantity and quality (Wilson 1990, 257–93).

Mill's method of value measurement, as I interpret it, is a general and inclusive procedure for assessing the worth of all enjoyments. Significantly, it allows in principle for the inclusion and comparability of all good-making properties of enjoyments, and does not restrict the domain of the sorts of enjoyments that may be scrutinized and compared for value or disvalue. While there is little doubt that Mill himself regards the enjoyments of intellectual activity and pursuits of justice as the prime examples of highly valuable kinds of pleasures, it is a mistake, I contend, to read his comments on the value of these kinds of enjoyments as doing any more than providing enduring examples of valuable satisfactions. I claim that it is mistaken to restrict the good-making features that may be assessed and compared and to interpret Mill as holding that some kinds of enjoyments are lexically preferable to other kinds, in the sense that a quantity of the lexically preferable kind of enjoyment will always outweigh any quantity of the other.

Jonathan Riley's recent interpretation illustrates the dangers of this move (Riley 1988). I note in passing, without exploring in detail, Riley's restrictive interpretation of Mill's view of kinds of enjoyments. Riley's interpretation allows for only four kinds: "'utilities of justice' . . . 'private utilities' (including 'aesthetic utilities') . . . 'utilities of charity', and . . . 'merely expedient utilities'" (Riley 1988, 87). These fixed categories of kind do not do justice to the complexity and sophistication of Mill's actual position on the myriad kinds of satisfactions which may, in the course of life, be experienced and enjoyed.

The error which concerns me here is related. Riley's interpretation is also restrictive in arguing for lexical "dominance" of certain kinds of utilities, as well as the view that different kinds of utilities cannot be compared (Riley 1988, 210). He says that "each kind of utility is non-comparable with other kinds in terms of quantity or intensity" (Riley 1988, 166). This interpretation is rather difficult to uphold as a general approach to value measurement and lacks intuitive plausibility. In the course of daily life agents are constantly called upon to make such comparisons, and they do so successfully, albeit in a rough and ready way. Since Mill does intend his method to be used in constructing actual agents' plans of life and guiding actual value assessments and moral decisions, the plausibility of Riley's approach is called into question.

In addition, one of Riley's central claims is flatly contradicted by Mill's own words. Riley claims that "utilities of justice" – these refer to principles of justice which I discuss in the latter part of this essay – are lexically preferable to the other kinds of utility in Riley's schema. But Mill specifically repudiates this:

Justice is a name for certain moral requirements, which, regarded collectively, stand higher in the scale of social utility, and are therefore of more paramount obligation, than any others: *though particular cases may occur in which some other social duty is so important, as to overrule any one of the general maxims of justice.* (*Utilitarianism*, CW X:259, emphasis added)

While self-developed agents will concur in most cases concerning the value of certain sorts of enjoyments, any absolutist approach which determines in advance that certain pleasures are always and without exception superior, is doomed to fall prey to the inevitable exceptions.

The problems with this general lexical priority are pointed out by James Griffin's discussion of trumping in cases of the ranking of values. Trumping occurs when we encounter an example of "one value outranking the others as strongly as possible. It takes the form: *any* amount of A, no matter how small, is more valuable than *any* amount of B, no matter how large. In short, A trumps B; A is lexically prior to B" (Griffin 1986, 83). Strictly speaking, according to Griffin, trumping in the case of general categories of value is

far too strong. How do we rank, say, autonomy or liberty, on the one hand, and prosperity or freedom from pain on the other? Nearly all of us would sacrifice some liberty to avert a catastrophe, or surrender some autonomy to avoid great pain. So people who would call certain values "trumps" or give them "lexical priority" probably do not mean these terms entirely seriously. (Griffin 1986, 83)

Griffin zeroes in on why this is the case. Part of the reason is that the categories used are too abstract or general, and fail to allow for particularity of circumstance or specific contexts.

The mistake here seems to be to think that certain values – liberty, for instance – as *types* outrank other values – prosperity, for instance – as types. Since values, as types can vary greatly in weight from token to token, it would be surprising to find this kind of discontinuity at the type – or at least at a fairly abstract type – level. (Griffin 1986, 85–86)

The strongest claim, I believe, that can be maintained on a Millian account is that there may be *particular occasions* when, as Griffin puts it, "when informed, I want, say, a *certain* amount of one thing more than *any* amount of another. . . . it may be that I think that no increase in *that* kind of value, even if constant and positive, can overtake a certain amount of this kind of value" (Griffin 1986,

76). Mill's approach to measurement of value is too open and flexible, and puts too much weight upon the considered judgments (which may turn out to be mistaken) of self-developed agents to uphold any claim stronger than the one that it is possible that a judgment such as that described by Griffin may be made on particular occasions in specific contexts. Abstract categories or types of value cannot be evaluated in advance, apart from concrete circumstances, to have the great weight that lexical priority or trumping demands.[4]

There are, as well, more general reasons for being wary of approaches such as Riley's in which certain general kinds of enjoyments are deemed to be lexically weightier than others. These approaches have a built-in elitist character and violate the spirit of Mill's theory, which, I contend, is radically egalitarian (Donner 1991, 159ff). And, while the value of certain kinds of satisfactions can confidently be judged to be enduring, Mill himself is acutely aware of the fallibility of human judgment, including judgment about value, and builds into his theory an expectation of progress and improvement in human affairs, which will of necessity involve the recognition that earlier judgments were mistaken (*On Liberty*, *CW* XVIII:229ff).

Those who argue that Mill elevates the pleasures of justice and intellect above others overlook that, in Mill's view, mental development always needs to be accompanied and balanced by what he calls moral development. I take up these ideas in more detail in the next section. But here I note that the pleasures of intellectual pursuits must be balanced by the pleasures of sociality, caring and connectedness to others. An interpretation of Mill which argues for the lexical priority of utilities of justice opens itself up to, and, in my view, succumbs to, contemporary objections from feminist moral philosophers. Mill's utilitarianism, correctly interpreted, is in harmony with feminist ethics in its acknowledgment of the importance of development of feelings and relationships with others as well as intellect and justice. In his exploration of the capacities that require development for human well-being, he is careful always to include feelings. Yet in his actual examples of highly valuable pleasures, he tends to use those of intellectual activities and to overlook pleasures of activities which involve the exercise of human capacities of caring and relationship. This is a misapplication of his theoretical commitment to affective development, and it opens him up to criticism for placing too much emphasis on the value of intellectual pursuits and consequently undervaluing pleasures of activities of nurturing and relationship. Mill's general method of value measurement, as well as his fundamental commitment to moral and affective development, allow room to correct the imbalance in his choice of examples of more valuable kinds of enjoyments and to correct the mistakes of the past which undervalued the pleasures of the activities historically associated with women. An adequate interpretation of Mill's qualitative hedonism must value the pleasures of caring and relationship, such as friendship and childrearing, equally with the pleasures of intellectual pursuits.

This is but one example, albeit an important one, of the dangers of interpreting Mill's measurement procedure as consisting of a lexicographical ranking system. But my central point is that any kind of enjoyment which is deemed to be lexically preferable to others will fall prey to similar problems. If Mill's method of value measurement is seen to be general and unrestricted, this allows room for exceptions as well as for improvement and progress over time and recognition of the mistakes of earlier ages. This places great weight upon the education and character of moral agents, issues which I take up shortly.

In summary, Mill's qualitative hedonism is an appealing and plausible alternative to the Benthamite utilitarian aggregative approach. I have argued that Mill differs from Bentham in regarding valuable things as being complex pleasurable states of experience and in claiming that both quantity and quality or kind are good-making properties which produce value. Mill quite clearly maintains that these two properties are separate, independent good-making features. It is consistent with hedonism to maintain that the kind of pleasure is relevant to its overall value and it begs the question simply to assume without argument that the only relevant good-making property is quantity. Mill's own words apply here aptly: "It would be absurd that while, in estimating all other things, quality is considered as well as quantity, the estimation of pleasures should be supposed to depend on quantity alone" *Utilitarianism*, *CW* X:211). And yet, many commentators have done just this, pointing out in somber tones the "problems" in Mill's argument. As Fred Wilson says,

Can the fact that one prefers some qualitatively different pleasures to others seriously compromise any claim to be a hedonist? . . . the answer is . . . clearly negative. It is hard to understand how these things can really be questioned. In fact, the points would seem to be sheer common sense. (Wilson 1990, 271)

Mill's theory opens a path for hedonism in which the sorts of pleasures, activities, characters and lifestyles people enjoy and choose are very much in the picture. I now turn to these issues.

DEVELOPMENT AND SELF-DEVELOPMENT

Mill's reliance upon the preference rankings of competent agents to assess value signals some other profound differences with Benthamite utilitarianism. Many twentieth-century commentators focus on the treatment of action and of moral rules and obligations in Mill's utilitarianism. But Mill himself seems to be as concerned about issues of good character and good lives as he is about right action. Instead of focussing primarily on calculations of consequences of actions, he also turns his attention to the proper education and socialization of moral agents, believing that agents who are self-developed are much more likely to promote good in the world as well as lead satisfying lives. More good will come about if self-developed agents act in character or out of habit, and questions of character take on a much weightier role in Mill's theory than in Bentham's. So it is important to give due place to his discussion of the ways in which people are appropriately socialized.

Mill jettisons the Benthamite felicific calculus; he offers in its place a method employing the preferences of self-developed agents. In the relevant passage in *Utilitarianism*, he refers to agents who "have experience of" or "are competently acquainted with" those pleasurable experiences which are being evaluated and ranked (*CW* X:211). But in making this remark, as in the case of many other points of his argument in *Utilitarianism*, Mill draws upon a wealth of background detail and argumentation worked out in other writings. Mill's point is that if such agents prefer or judge more valuable certain enjoyments, then these enjoyments should be taken to be more valuable. The test is the preferences of agents who are in the best position to know.

The first stage of the education and socialization of competent agents is the process of development. During this part of the process, generic human intellectual, affective and moral capacities are nurtured, usually as part of childhood socialization. Mill's doctrine of development, formulated and explained in many writings, sets out the educative process by which these capacities are fostered. Mill's doctrine of development is multifaceted; it plays more than one role in his theory. This doctrine describes a form of education which is foundational in the sense that someone who has undergone it is the kind of person who is in a position to be maximally happy, and in addition has achieved a perspective appropriate to evaluate the experiences, pursuits, character and ways of life which are worth pursuing.

Thus developed and self-developed agents are the pivot of Mill's theory, because their preferences provide the best indicators of value of different kinds of happiness. They are at the same time both the best judges of value and the source and locus of value. The most valuable forms of happiness are those which involve the development and active use of generic human capacities which are the focus of development. The sort of educative process which concerns Mill is one of character formation. Using his psychological theory of association, Mill argues that if our educational goal is to create certain features of character, or to nurture certain human capacities, we must take care to use the laws of association to further these educational goals, creating the right associations to encourage certain forms of character. Our education should encourage the character traits that would produce the most utility if manifested by members of a community (*Logic*, *CW* VIII:869–70).

Mill regards affective development, or the development of feelings, as the foundation of all types of development. This puts his theory in the lineage of Hume and historical utilitarians who regard morality as the domain of feeling as well as of reason. In the *Autobiography* Mill says that he felt that his own education had focussed too narrowly on intellectual training, and when, in early adulthood, he suffered his well-known "mental crisis", a bout of severe depression, he later traced his problems to deficiencies in his education, including the deprecation of internal culture and the lack of nurturing of feeling. He was determined to rectify this imbalance in his own philosophy and to find an appropriate place for "internal culture" (*Autobiography*, *CW* I:147). In his personal experience, encounters with writings of romantic poets such as Wordsworth and Shelley helped to pull him out of his depression and revitalize his feelings (Michele Green 1989). But many other activities and pursuits can be relied upon to train and enlarge the feelings (*CW* I:143ff).[5]

Intellectual development is more standardly associated with Mill, and his love of intellectual pursuits is well known. He says that "it is . . . better to be Socrates dissatisfied than a fool satisfied" (*Utilitarianism*, *CW* X:212). Intellectual powers can be trained in various ways, and Mill offers various suggestions which revolve around a rejection of methods using rote learning and an endorsement of those which develop critical thinking and reflection. For example, Mill's impassioned defence in *On Liberty* of the value of free and open debate for mental development is well known and justly celebrated (*CW* XVIII:243).

The process of moral development teaches children to feel sympathetic connection with others and to take pleasure in their happiness. Cultivation of sympathy with others is the foundation of moral development. Many of Mill's concerns are echoed in contemporary claims about the need for the capacity of empathy for moral agency.

> But there *is* this basis of powerful natural sentiment. . . . This firm foundation is that of the social feelings of mankind; the desire to be in unity with our fellow creatures, which is already a powerful principle in human nature, and happily one of those which tend to become stronger, even without express inculcation, from the influences of advancing civilization. The social state is at once so natural, so necessary, and so habitual to man, that, except in some unusual circumstances or by an effort of voluntary abstraction, he never conceives himself otherwise than as a member of a body. (*Utilitarianism*, *CW* X:231)

Mill harshly criticizes Bentham for holding to a belief in the "predominance of the selfish principle in human nature" ("Remarks on Bentham's Philosophy," *CW* X:14). The original basis of moral feelings is explained:

> The idea of the pain of another is naturally painful; the idea of the pleasure of another is naturally pleasurable. From this fact in our natural constitution, all our affections both of love and aversion towards human

beings . . . originate. In this, the unselfish part of our nature, lies a foundation, even independently of inculcation from without, for the generation of moral feelings. ("Sedgwick's Discourse," *CW* X:60)

Our moral/social side is an element of our nature that needs development along with our intellectual/individualist side, and Mill's refusal to create a hierarchy among these capacities and his insistence upon a balance among them has important consequences for his conception of self-development, as well as for his liberal political theory. On Mill's account, moral development is the appropriate accompaniment to mental development, and one without the other is a caricature of development.

When people who are tolerably fortunate in their outward lot do not find in life sufficient enjoyment to make it valuable to them, the cause generally is, caring for nobody but themselves. . . . Next to selfishness, the principal cause which makes life unsatisfactory, is want of mental cultivation.
. . . As little is there an inherent necessity that any human being should be a selfish egotist, devoid of every feeling or care but those which centre in his own miserable individuality. (*Utilitarianism, CW* X:215–16)

This picture of the process of development prepares the way for the next stage of self-development. In the usual course of events, when children mature and reach adulthood they assume control of the development process and continue it as one of self-development. In the continuation, the higher-order capacities of individuality, autonomy and sociality and cooperativeness are constructed on the groundwork of the generic human capacities. These capacities of sociality/cooperativeness and autonomy/individuality must all be balanced against each other; none must be allowed to take over a dominant role. Individuality is the capacity to discover our own unique mix of the generic human capacities. Autonomy is the capacity to reflect critically upon, choose and endorse the character, projects and pursuits in harmony with our nature. While we do not have one fixed and unchangeable essence, we do have a range of potential and a range of characters, lifestyles and pursuits in harmony with this. The greatest happiness results from seeking out and discovering this range and then choosing and creating traits of character, lifestyles and commitments on this foundation. There are a range of options within our potential, and thus the process is partly one of discovery and partly one of creation (Gray 1983, 80).

Mill's individualism assumes social beings and not isolated individuals lacking deep social bonds.

In the comparatively early state of human advancement in which we now live, a person cannot indeed feel that entireness of sympathy with all others, which would make any real discordance in the general direction of their conduct in life impossible; but already a person in whom the social feeling is at all developed, cannot bring himself to think of the rest of his fellow creatures as struggling rivals with him for the means of happiness, whom he must desire to see defeated in their object in order that he may succeed in his. The deeply-rooted conception which every individual even now has of himself as a social being, tends to make him feel it one of his natural wants that there should be harmony between his feelings and aims and those of his fellow creatures. . . . few but those whose mind is a moral blank, could bear to lay out their course of life on the plan of paying no regard to others except so far as their own private interest compels. (*Utilitarianism*, CW X:233)

Mill's concept of individualism is centered around the value he places on the individual as the generator, focus and evaluator of value. Value is located in each and every individual, and whatever value groups or communities have flows only from the value of its members. Such individuality requires that persons are in control of their own lives, that they are accustomed to making and carrying through on their own choices and that their own ideas, activities and projects are an expression of their own particularity.

From this brief overview of the different elements which must be balanced intricately against each other, I hope some of the flavour of Mill's conception of self-development has emerged. Mill's theoretical commitment to self-development is fundamental; as Alan Ryan says, "Mill's concern with self-development and moral progress is a strand in his philosophy to which almost everything else is subordinate" (Ryan 1988, 255). Judgments of value are the evaluative basis of all human practical reasoning about ends or goals not only of morality but also of self-interest, beauty, nobility and all other practical arts. But humans cannot fully make such judgments of value unless they have reached a certain threshold level of self-development. To deny someone the opportunity of development and self-development is thus to deny that person the status of full moral agency. Although much goes into the socialization and educational experience of self-development, almost everybody, in Mill's view, has the potential to attain such status, and it is usually their social circumstances that determine whether their potential unfolds. Thus Mill's ideals and commitments require that all adult members of society have the opportunity and social resources effectively to gain the status of self-developed agent. I claim then that Mill's utilitarianism, with its fundamental commitment to and dependence upon self-developed competent moral agents, inclines his moral theory towards a form of radical egalitarianism. According to the fundamental tenets of Mill's utilitarianism, people have a right to liberty of self-development and their rights are violated if their social circumstances bar them or do not provide adequate resources for them to attain and exercise self-development. To elaborate in great detail upon these matters would be to stray beyond the confines of this chapter and into the territory of other essays on Mill's political philosophy. However, to conclude the subject of Mill's utilitarianism, it is necessary to survey some issues regarding his views on moral rules and in particular on rules of justice and rights.

THE PRINCIPLE OF UTILITY AND MORAL RULES

My discussion thus far has been preoccupied with questions regarding Mill's conception of value or the good. Since in a utilitarian moral theory the notion of good is prior to that of right, and since Mill's views on the good are distinctive, this is appropriate. However, some issues regarding Mill's views on right or obligation also need to be pursued.

Utilitarians can differ over their conceptions of utility or the good which is to be promoted or maximized. They can also differ over their views about how moral rules setting out duties, obligations or rights are to be constructed and justified. The principle of utility is the one ultimate principle in a utilitarian system. But this principle can play different roles vis-à-vis decisions of right and wrong. In the twentieth century these questions have tended to congeal around what is called the dispute between act and rule utilitarianism.[6] The literature regarding the appropriate place of rules in a utilitarian moral theory is already vast. However, I contend that the amount of light shed upon the underlying substantive issues is not at all commensurate with the magnitude of this literature. In fact, I claim that

this literature rapidly becomes so caught up in abstract technical-
ities that it gets bogged down and as a result these underlying issues
tend to be obscured.

Fred Berger sets out a standard position on what is taken to be at
issue in this debate. He says,

> Act-utilitarians hold that an act is right if, and only if, it would produce the
> best consequences among all the acts the agent can perform. . . . Rule-
> utilitarians hold that acts are right if, and only if, they are prescribed by
> rules which are in turn justified by the consequences of their being adopted
> or conformed to. (Berger 1984, 64)[7]

According to act utilitarianism, then, we decide what is right by
looking at the consequences or the utility of performing a particular
act on a particular occasion. This approach makes moral decisions
on a case-by-case basis. According to rule utilitarianism, we do our
duty by following general moral rules such as the rule forbidding
killing. These general moral rules are those which will promote the
greatest balance of happiness if everyone were to follow them.
Agents ought to follow justified moral rules, and these justified
rules are the ones that would produce the greatest balance of happiness if they were adhered to by moral agents. According to rule
utilitarianism, then, if on a particular occasion following the rule
would not lead to the best consequences, we should still follow the
rule. This means that if a rule is generally useful we should follow
it, because others need to have assurance that moral rules will be
followed. We undermine this general confidence when we break
justified rules on particular occasions. But the point that needs to be
kept in view is that these rules must be justified by utility. The
general practice of these rules produces the greatest balance of
happiness.

Berger claims, as I do, that Mill's theory is "neither an act- nor a
rule-utilitarian theory as those terms are strictly defined" (Berger
1984, 65).[8] I would go further and claim that few utilitarian theories
are, as these two options offer a false dichotomy to which few can
strongly adhere in practice. In Mill's view, as I shall set it out, there
is a strong and central role for secondary moral principles; but there
are also instances where a direct appeal is made to the principle of
utility in particular cases, a procedure which is ruled out by at least
some versions of rule utilitarianism. Mill himself does not appear to

see the issue in these either/or terms, and it is uncharitable to insist that his reflections be fitted into categories developed in the twentieth century and uncritically read back onto his discussion in ways with which he probably would not agree.

The underlying substantive issue, which is sometimes lost in the discussion, arises from reflection upon a common type of criticism directed at utilitarian theories, namely, that they allow or justify cases of injustice which conflict with our usual moral intuitions. One classic form of this objection holds that ideals of justice and utility can conflict, that is, that on particular occasions we are morally obliged to protect an innocent person even though "the common good" might be promoted on this occasion if this person's rights were violated. For example, we send an innocent person to jail or to be executed because we maintain that this is the only way to quell the public's demand for a "law and order" response to a grisly killing for which the police have no apparent suspects.

The underlying question in dispute is whether Mill's utilitarianism can formulate rules of justice or obligation which are strong enough to withstand being easily overturned, for minor or moderate gains in utility to others, yet flexible enough to be outweighed in rare cases of catastrophe. That is, we want to strike a balance between a too-rigid adherence to moral rules, or what J. J. C. Smart calls "rule worship", and a too-easy tendency to overturn or make exceptions to generally useful rules (Smart 1982, 10). After all, such secondary moral principles are those which are generally useful in promoting utility, and have been found to be so through the long history of human experience.

Berger proposes to interpret Mill as holding a "strategy conception of rules" (Berger 1984, 67). He explains:

the view that I claim to have been Mill's holds that in *practical* deliberations, we should follow useful rules in determining our moral duties, except in extreme or special circumstances where a great deal is at stake, or the rules conflict, in which case we determine what morality requires by appeal to the consequences of the act. (Berger 1984, 66–67)

Well-accepted general rules of obligation, which are built upon a long history of experience about what is beneficial to humans, should be followed on most occasions. When agents are considering whether to follow or make an exception to a justified rule, they must be careful to take into consideration the effects of following or violating the rule.

One sees the rule-related utilities of the particular act better by asking what it would be like if this sort of act were not generally done, and by considering that doing it is the rule. (Berger 1984, 70)

However, no set of rules ultimately will suffice.

Knowledge of the consequences of acts in the innumerable circumstances in which they occur can never be complete; and accepted rules must not be too complex to be useful in practical situations. Morever, while the accepted rules of a society embody its wisdom, they also embody its foolishness and stupidity. People are wont to blindly follow what is generally done, so the mere survival of a rule is no guarantee of its having been found useful through careful examination. There is, then, always room for moral reform, and where time and knowledge permit calculation, it is in order to look at the consequences of the act at hand, and apply the Principle of Utility itself, rather than some subordinate moral rule, to the act. (Berger 1984, 71)

It must also be kept in mind that direct appeal to the principle of utility may be required not just on particular occasions but also when we are considering moral reform. Mill's own words here are instructive:

The corollaries from the principle of utility, like the precepts of every practical art, admit of indefinite improvement, and, in a progressive state of the human mind, their improvement is perpetually going on. But to consider the rules of morality as improvable, is one thing; to pass over the intermediate generalizations entirely, and endeavour to test each individual action directly by the first principle, is another. It is a strange notion that the acknowledgment of a first principle is inconsistent with the admission of secondary ones. To inform a traveller respecting the place of his ultimate destination, is not to forbid the use of landmarks and direction-posts on the way. . . . Whatever we adopt as the fundamental principle of morality, we require subordinate principles to apply it by: the impossibility of doing without them, being common to all systems, can afford no argument against any one in particular: but gravely to argue as if no such secondary principles could be had, and as if mankind had remained till now, and always must remain, without drawing any general conclusions from the experience of human life, is as high a pitch, I think, as absurdity has ever reached in philosophical controversy. (*Utilitarianism*, *CW* X:224–25)

This then, I take it, sets out the rough contours of Mill's position on moral rules. Once again, his views rely upon a model of balance, in this case balancing whether to follow generally useful rules or to engage in further reflection on the case by directly appealing to the principle of utility. These views can be extended and applied to his perspective on rules of justice which concern rights.

JUSTICE, RIGHTS AND UTILITY

Recent revisionist work on Mill's moral philosophy has clarified its complex structure, which includes a theory of justice which sets out the place of principles of justice or rights.[9] Until the recent wave of revisionary scholarship, the chapter of *Utilitarianism* entitled "On the Connexion between Justice and Utility" tended to be ignored. (Indeed, all but a few pages of this work shared this fate.) In this chapter Mill responds to the sorts of objections I have raised in the previous section, namely, those objections which claim that justice and utility are opposed or can conflict. In the course of this he offers an account of the origin of the sentiment of justice, an issue which I sidestep here, as well as an analysis of the concept of a right and a utilitarian defence of rights. In this final section I concentrate on these latter two issues. While Mill's utilitarian justification of rights does not provide as secure a grounding for rights as some might wish, because utilitarian rights are not foundational and so are not "trumps", it is nonetheless a robust defence.[10] The issue, once again, concerns the strength and foundation of rights. Mill's moral theory is not rights-based, because, as his rights are utilitarian rights, they are grounded in well-being. But Mill argues effectively that utilitarianism can strongly support rights and retain a central place for them in the theory. Thus, while rights are not foundational, nonetheless they are weighty and not easily overturned.

I begin by sketching out the architecture of Mill's utilitarianism, and then turn to some possible lines of response to those critics who argue that utility and rights conflict and that utility cannot support strong rights.

In *Utilitarianism*, the *Logic*, and other writings, Mill claims that the principle of utility is a general principle of the good which governs all of the practical arts, including those of the art of life: morality, prudence and nobility. In the *Logic* he speaks of the need for "an ultimate standard, or first principle of Teleology" and claims that "the promotion of happiness is the ultimate principle of Teleology" (*CW* VIII:951). This is the backdrop for the discussion in *Utilitarianism* in which the structure of his moral philosophy is presented. Mill first sets off the category of morality from the broader class of expediency, or general promotion of utility, of which morality constitutes a sub-class.

We do not call anything wrong, unless we mean to imply that a person ought to be punished in some way or other for doing it; if not by law, by the opinion of his fellow creatures; if not by opinion, by the reproaches of his own conscience. This seems the real turning point of the distinction between morality and simple expediency. It is part of the notion of Duty in every one of its forms, that a person may rightfully be compelled to fulfill it. Duty is a thing which may be exacted from a person, as one exacts a debt. . . . I think there is no doubt that this distinction lies at the bottom of the notions of right and wrong; that we call any conduct wrong, or employ, instead, some other term of dislike or disparagement, according as we think that the person ought, or ought not, to be punished for it; and we say that it would be right to do so and so, or merely that it would be desirable or laudable, according as we would wish to see the person whom it concerns, compelled, or only persuaded and exhorted, to act in that manner. (*Utilitarianism, CW* X:246)

This passage gives rise to some puzzles and ambiguities in Mill's theory which have been the subject of recent commentaries and debates among revisionary scholars. The most widely known formulation of the principle of utility, which is presented early, in chapter 2 of *Utilitarianism*, and which has been called the "proportionality criterion of rightness and wrongness", states that "actions are right in proportion as they tend to promote happiness, wrong as they tend to promote the reverse of happiness" (Berger 1984, 105; *Utilitarianism, CW* X:210). Most discussion of the principle of utility in the literature has focussed on this formulation of the principle. But in the chapter on justice and utility, Mill relies on what Berger and others call the "punishability" criterion (Berger 1984, 66).[11] The primary concept in this formulation is of the wrongness of action, as Mill begins by saying in the quote above that "we do not call anything wrong..." David Lyons's article "Mill's Theory of Morality" illuminates the puzzles that arise (Lyons, 1994). Lyons interprets and reconstructs Mill as maintaining that not every action which does not maximize utility is wrong. To be wrong, an act must deserve or be liable to punishment. According to Lyons, Mill's theory uses "a model based on coercive social rules" (Lyons 1994, 54). Lyons conceptually links moral obligation and punishment or sanctions. The sanctions include not only legal sanctions, but also social disapproval and internal guilt or pangs of conscience. Lyons claims that

These considerations suggest that Mill had the following view. To call an act wrong is to imply that guilt feelings, and perhaps other sanctions, would be warranted against it. But sanctions assume coercive rules. *To show an act wrong, therefore, is to show that a coercive rule against it would be justified.* The justification of a coercive social rule establishes a moral obligation, breach of which is wrong. (Lyons 1994, 55, emphasis in original)

L. W. Sumner has summarized Lyons's point here as follows:

We begin with an analysis of concepts on which asserting that a particular act *a* is wrong is identical with asserting that the existence of a coercive social rule against doing acts of kind A would be justified. Coercive rules are rules backed by sanctions. . . . The wrongness of an action is thus connected with the justifiability of imposing sanctions against the doing of that sort of action. (Sumner 1979, 104)

In Mill's utilitarian defence of moral rules, the costs of setting up, maintaining and enforcing a coercive moral rule, which include restrictions on freedom as well as the listed sanctions, must all be taken into account in deciding whether a particular moral rule is justified. As Sumner explains,

if we employ the notion of a positive balance of utility to mean an excess of benefits over costs then the existence of a coercive rule against doing some kind of act would be justified if and only if it would yield a positive balance of utility. (Sumner 1979, 104–05)

Mill's moral theory thus separates moral rules of obligation from the broader class of rules of expediency or general promotion of the good. But Mill also differentiates rules of justice from moral rules of obligation; the former also constitute a sub-class within the class of moral rules. Mill claims that rules of justice "involve the idea of a personal right – a claim on the part of one or more individuals"

(*Utilitarianism, CW* X:247). Injustice "implies two things – a wrong done, and some assignable person who is wronged" (*CW* X:247). This leads to the definition of a right:

When we call anything a person's right, we mean that he has a valid claim on society to protect him in the possession of it, either by the force of law, or by that of education and opinion. If he has what we consider a sufficient claim, on whatever account, to have something guaranteed to him by society, we say that he has a right to it. (*CW* X:250)

Elaborating on this, he continues, "To have a right, then, is, I conceive, to have something which society ought to defend me in the possession of" (*CW* X:250).

Recent commentators have pointed out that in this first part of the passage Mill analyzes the concept of a right in general, and that this analysis is distinct from his utilitarian defence of rights and could be accepted by thinkers even if they are not committed to utilitarianism (Lyons 1994, 51). Now Mill sets out his utilitarian justification of rights. He says that "if the objector goes on to ask why it ought, I can give him no other reason than general utility". The moral justification is based on "the extraordinarily important and impressive kind of utility which is concerned" (*Utilitarianism, CW* X:250–51). Mill's substantive theory of justice goes beyond both the analysis of the concept of a right and the utilitarian justification to discuss particular rights. The two most basic rights, according to Mill, are the right to security and the right to liberty (including the right to liberty of self-development).[12] But Mill reiterates his claim that justice and utility are not in conflict, but on the contrary rules of justice must be based on well-being:

While I dispute the pretensions of any theory which sets up an imaginary standard of justice not grounded on utility, I account the justice which is grounded on utility to be the chief part, and incomparably the most sacred and binding part, of all morality. Justice is a name for certain classes of moral rules, which concern the essentials of human well-being more nearly, and are therefore of more absolute obligation, than any other rules for the guidance of life. (*Utilitarianism, CW* X:255)

Finally, he emphasizes this central claim again:

Justice is a name for certain moral requirements, which, regarded collectively, stand higher in the scale of social utility, and are therefore of more paramount obligation, than any others; although particular cases may occur in which some other social duty is so important, as to overrule any one of the general maxims of justice. (*CW* X:259)

Rights protect the most vital human interests. Since they are specifically designed to protect and guarantee such interests, rights claims ward off casual trade-offs which would permit some people's important interests being overridden to promote unimportant or moderately important interests of others, even large groups of others. Mill analyzes rights as involving claims which are socially guaranteed by institutions collectively set up and maintained to carry out these guarantees effectively (*Utilitarianism*, *CW* X:251). Thus, it would be inconsistent to maintain on the one hand that rights ought to be effectively protected and guaranteed, and on the other hand that they can easily be traded off for unimportant or moderately important gains to others. Mill obviously does not intend to endorse such inconsistencies, but instead intends to propound a robust view of rights which can give this protection.

Sumner has advanced a recent defence of the claim that consequentialism, including utilitarianism, can indeed "protect the integrity of rights" (Sumner 1987, viii). He presents the apparent problem as follows:

What distinguishes consequentialist theories from their rivals is that they are goal-based – that is, at bottom they counsel the pursuit of some global synoptic goal. By contrast, rights appear to function normatively as constraints on the pursuit of such goals. (Sumner 1987, vii)

But Sumner maintains that, contrary to appearances, "the supposed incompatibility between commitment to a basic goal and acceptance of constraints on the pursuit of that goal is an illusion" (Sumner 1987, vii). Once again, the complexity of the theory provides the solution, for the misleading appearance "has been fostered chiefly by an oversimplified view of the structure of consequentialism" (Sumner 1987, viii). Sumner elaborates on the apparent puzzle involved in a consequentialist foundation for a right, for, as he puts it,

if a right is to be grounded in a goal then the goal must justify constraints on its own pursuit. But surely if we once adopt a goal then we are committed to doing on every occasion whatever will best achieve it, in which case we are committed to ignoring or overriding any such constraints. (Sumner 1987, 177)

However, the mere statement of the assumption illuminates its weakness. The assumption is that, for consequentialists, there is a "very simple linear relationship between their moral theory and their moral practice". The assumption illicitly conflates a "theory of justification" and a "theory of decision-making" (Sumner 1987, 177, 179). The best strategy is the one which is the most successful in promoting the goal, but "whereas a theory of moral justification takes the perspective of an omniscient observer, a theory of moral decision-making takes the perspective of a real-life moral agent" (Sumner 1987, 180). The question of whether a direct or an indirect strategy is the most successful in attaining the goal is empirical, not philosophical. Viewed in this light, the assumption of a direct strategy is another example of objectors begging the question. In matters of practical decision-making across a wide range of human activities, there is a great deal of evidence that indirect strategies are as successful as or more successful than direct ones. Thus the constrained indirect strategy of entrenching rights within consequentialism, which "rests heavily on the imperfections of our own nature and of our decision-making environment", has much plausibility (Sumner 1987, 197).

So utilitarianism has strong resources to counter this common complaint. But other issues remain. The painful dilemmas occur in cases which involve conflicts among the rights or vital interests of a number of persons, in which choices concerning whose rights are to be protected and whose overridden are unavoidable. Although such dilemmas are sometimes presented as objections to utilitarianism, I claim that such cases on the contrary reveal the strength of utilitarianism in allowing a method to attempt to resolve such painful dilemmas. One example of this is the by now classic case put forward by Bernard Williams as an allegedly powerful objection to utilitarianism. Williams describes a scenario in which an American botanist, Jim, stumbles across a scene of horror in a South American village. Twenty of the village's inhabitants are tied up and facing execution by a group of soldiers. The captain informs Jim that the people are "a random group of the inhabitants who, after recent acts of protest against the government, are just about to be killed to

remind other possible protestors of the advantages of not protest-
ing" (B. Williams 1982, 98). The captain offers Jim the opportunity
to save nineteen of the inhabitants. However, in order to bring about
this outcome, Jim must kill one of the inhabitants himself. If Jim
refuses to kill one innocent villager himself, all of the twenty inhabitants will be executed by the soldiers. "The men against the wall,
and the other villagers, understand the situation, and are obviously
begging him to accept. What should he do?" (B. Williams 1982, 99).
According to Williams, what Jim should do (or in this case, not do)
is clear. Jim would undermine his integrity if he were to enter into
the moral situation and kill one innocent person in order to save
many others. Williams goes much further. Jim should not even
contemplate the various alternatives open to him on this occasion,
for even to do this would be to undermine his integrity.

One might have the idea that the *unthinkable* was itself a moral
category. . . . It could be a feature of a man's moral outlook that he regarded
certain courses of action as unthinkable, in the sense that he would not
entertain the idea of doing them. . . . Entertaining certain alternatives, regarding them indeed as *alternatives*, is itself something that he regards as
dishonourable or morally absurd. . . . For him, there are certain situations
so monstrous that the idea that the processes of moral rationality could
yield an answer in them is insane: they are situations which so transcend in
enormity the human business of moral deliberation that from a moral point
of view it cannot matter any more what happens. Equally, for him, to spend
time thinking about what one would decide if one were in such a situation
is also insane. (B. Williams 1982, 92)

Williams puts forward this example as though it obviously reveals
a fatal flaw in utilitarian thinking, and as though the mere contemplation of the alternatives would violate deeply felt moral intuitions
in his readers. Thus, according to Williams, utilitarianism violates
our deepest moral understandings. But on the contrary, I claim that
it is Williams's own musings on this example which are deeply at
odds with many people's reflective moral sensibilities. The sort of
moral narcissism involved in the line of thinking which maintains
that we are entitled, or obliged, to turn our backs on such scenarios
is out of touch with many agents' reflective approach to such examples. The world is filled with situations of moral horror as bad as or
much worse than that described by Williams. From privileged sanc-

tuaries it may appear as if agents are entitled to remove themselves from even thinking about such circumstances, but from the perspective of the village inhabitants in his example, or the countless other people who must live days, months or years of their lives with monstrosity as their daily reality, it may well appear that Williams's approach to moral reflection is both bankrupt and baneful.

Utilitarianism, and in particular Mill's utilitarian rights theory, is not, I claim, undermined by such cases where agents are required to make painful choices among conflicting rights where it is impossible to avoid overriding some person's vital interests. It is, I maintain, a strength rather than a weakness that this approach provides agents with a procedure for attempting to bring about the best possible, or least horrific, outcome in such terrible circumstances.

Mill's moral theory, with its central and strong place for rights grounded on well-being, does not permit trade-offs of persons' vital interests, those very interests protected by rights and backed by social institutions designed to secure and guarantee their effective protection, for small increases in the good of even large numbers of others. When the vital interests enshrined in rights of a number of persons conflict, and when it is impossible to protect all of these rights, then Mill's utilitarianism provides a method for trying to minimize the harm to interests. John Skorupski, whose nuanced discussion of Mill's views of justice and rights takes full note of the complexities and difficulties involved, puts the point this way:

There *are* situations – call them cases of 'abnormal peril' in which we are willing to accept sacrifices of individuals' primary utilities to safeguard the primary utilities of others, sacrifices which would in the normal case, the case in which ordinary life is going on, be considered unacceptable. (Skorupski 1989, 330)

This is not to say that there is a blueprint set out to resolve such dilemmas. Reflective Millian utilitarians will disagree about how to approach particular cases. But what they will agree on is the obligation to decide in ways which protect fundamental interests from being traded off. This leads into a final point about *Mill's* utilitarianism which needs to be highlighted. Many of the usual cases brought forward as objections to utilitarianism are based upon a conception of moral agents which is firmly rejected by Mill. The sorts of cases which are commonly discussed, in which agents are quite content to sacrifice the vital interests or rights of minorities in order to advance the trivial or moderately important interests of others, depend upon a view of moral agents as rational self-interested agents, concerned primarily to promote their own interests and unconcerned or uncaring about the serious harm inflicted upon others by their pursuit of their own interests. Although this conception of moral agents is commonly and uncritically accepted in twentieth-century discussions, it is a view of agents from which Mill would recoil in horror. It is not sufficiently appreciated, I believe, in contemporary discussions which blithely talk about how easy it is to sacrifice minority interests, that the objectors are accepting without question that this is how moral agents normally go about their deliberations. Moral agents must be *constrained* from sacrificing or ignoring the interests of others by recognizing through reason the *force* of their rights claims. But in Mill's conception of moral agents as self-developed, agents are appropriately socialized spontaneously to take account of the good and interests of others and to care about their well-being without being *forced* to do so. It would be degrading for such a self-developed agent to come to the sorts of decisions that these counterexamples assume is the appropriate utilitarian response.

One other respect in which twentieth-century perspectives on moral philosophy have been uncritically and uncharitably read back into Mill's approach is the excessive concern with abstract consequentialist debates, or with debates focussed primarily on action and obligation. Mill was much more concerned with questions of good character and good lives. His primary commitment, which ties in with the formative influence of classical Greek philosophy on his views, is to ways of life and character development. This is why his conception of human self-development is so much more carefully worked out and occupies so much more space in his writings than his views on action and rights. *Mill's* utilitarianism is organized around a core concept of human happiness which cannot be separated out from socialization practices which nurture agents to be self-developed, that is, to be morally, intellectually and affectively developed so that they could not, in their deliberations, ignore the happiness of others in the way these cases demand.

This links Mill's approach to certain aspects of contemporary virtue, communitarian, and feminist approaches to ethics which also reject the concept of moral agency underlying these cases. This is not at all to say that Mill would accept these new theories uncritically either; many elements of communitarian and virtue ethics in particular would not meet with his approval. But the insight they all share which he would welcome is the view of moral agents as connected to others, caring for others, regarding themselves as social beings as well as individuals. Recall his eloquent words:

The social state is at once so natural, so necessary, and so habitual to man, that, except in some unusual circumstances or by an effort of voluntary abstraction, he never conceives himself otherwise than as a member of a body. . . . In this way people grow up unable to conceive as possible to them a state of total disregard of other people's interests. . . . They are also familiar with the fact of co-operating with others, and proposing to themselves a collective, not an individual, interest, as the aim (at least for the time being) of their actions. . . . He comes, as though instinctively, to be conscious of himself as a being who *of course* pays regard to others. The good of others becomes to him a thing naturally and necessarily to be attended to, like any of the physical conditions of our existence. (*Utilitarianism, CW* X:231–32)

If "self-developed" agents make decisions to sacrifice the primary interests of others, they reveal their lack of concern for and connection to those others, and they by these very actions and deliberations undermine their claim to this self-developed status. Thus these sorts of scenarios are not only disallowed on Mill's view of moral agents, but these sorts of deliberations are self-defeating, for by the very engaging in such actions agents would undermine their own claim to be self-developed moral agents.

Mill's utilitarianism continues to fascinate and frustrate because of its richness, its complexity and its refusal to back away from and remain uninvolved with the messiness of social and political reality. Mill was as much a social activist as a philosopher, and his views were tested and refined in the light of their actual results in his own life. Mill's work tests us in another way. In all of his work Mill defies easy analysis or categorization, instead enriching and expanding the theories he elaborates until they threaten to burst the familiar boundaries into which those who want neat categories would like to contain him. But if ethical and political life are as complex as they seem, we need a theory as complex as Mill's to encompass them.

NOTES

1 James Mill's *An Analysis of the Phenomena of the Human Mind* sets out this associationist psychology. John Stuart Mill's editorial notes to the 1869 edition set down the few points of dispute with his father's discussions.

2 See also Sumner 1992.

3 For other noteworthy additions to the recent debate, see Edwards 1979; Wilson 1990, 224–93; Sumner 1992; Riley 1988, 133–234; Riley 1993; Skorupski 1989, 283–336; Berger 1984, 30–63; Gray 1983, 70–89; Hoag 1992; West 1976.

4 For a much fuller treatment than I can give here of the nature of utility and well-being, as well as the difficult and complex issues of measurement of utility and well-being, see Griffin 1986, especially 7–124.

5 See also J. M. Robson 1968 and Sharpless 1967.

6 The standard account of the various forms of utilitarianism is Lyons 1965. See also Lyons 1994; Urmson 1953; Rawls 1955; Schneewind 1968; Cooper, Nielsen and Patten, 1979.

7 There are actually several different versions of rule utilitarianism, but Berger sets out the core theme.

8 See also Brink 1992, 69.

9 For examples of this recent scholarship on moral rules and justice, see Lyons 1994; Brown 1982; Berger 1984; Gray 1983; Skorupski 1989.

10 See Dworkin 1977, xi, 184–205.

11 See also Brown, 1973 and 1974; Lyons 1994.

12 For a careful and comprehensive treatment of Mill's theory of justice, see Berger 1984, 123–225.

8 Mill's political economy: Ricardian science and liberal utilitarian art

I. A GRAND PROJECT

John Stuart Mill undertook to rehabilitate the utilitarian radicalism of Bentham and his followers, "to show that there was a Radical philosophy, better and more complete than Bentham's, while recognizing and incorporating all of Bentham's which is permanently valuable".[1] To carry out his grand project, he studied the insights into will, imagination, and character offered by German Idealists (including Goethe, Kant, and Schiller) and their British disciples (notably Coleridge, Frederick Maurice, John Sterling, and Carlyle). He was also far more open than his utilitarian predecessors to egalitarian social utopias of the sort proposed by French 'socialists' (including Saint-Simon, Fourier, Comte, and Louis Blanc). Moreover, at his death in 1873, he was lampooned as a 'feminine philosopher' for his insistence that justice demanded equal rights for women as well as men independently of race or colour. In his view, as they gained equality with men, women would tend to demand more prudent family practices (including birth control measures) than had hitherto been observed or could otherwise be expected under the prevailing system of male domination.

Such psychological insights and improved ideas of society, Mill believed, could somehow be integrated with the basic tenets of the Benthamite approach. Bentham, James Mill, and Ricardo, whatever their other differences, analyzed political and economic affairs by assuming that any agent is motivated by his own particular interests as he conceives them. In addition to universal education, therefore, they generally advocated social institutions (including majoritarian democracy and competitive capitalism) designed to give predominantly self-interested individuals adequate incentives to act so as to promote the general happiness (understood as the sum or perhaps average of the enlightened self-interests). Such reforms retained appeal for the younger Mill as far as they went. But he also looked beyond them by imagining that certain aesthetic and moral feelings might eventually come to trump self-interest (enlightened or otherwise) in political and economic matters. This opened his eyes to possibilities not entertained (or insufficiently considered) by Benthamite radicals. He emphasized that if certain moral feelings of mutual cooperation trumped self-interest in the political arena, for example, democratic majorities could accept various 'counter-majoritarian' constitutional checks designed to prevent majority domination over minority interests.[2] If similar moral feelings emerged in the economic sphere, he also claimed, existing competitive capitalism might eventually be transformed into a more cooperative type of private property economy, involving much less inequality in the distribution of wealth than hitherto observed. Indeed, cooperative capitalism might evolve even further, he speculated, by a kind of 'spontaneous process', into an ideal decentralized socialism in which competition among small-scale worker cooperatives is constrained by some higher morality of distributive justice.

Mill's novel brand of utilitarian radicalism (henceforth, 'liberal utilitarianism') is more cognizant than its Benthamite ancestor of human capacities of imagination (including sympathy for others) and mutual cooperation, more open to the possibility that individuals might form noble characters that reflect repeated acts of imagination and cooperation, and consequently less committed to social institutions that presuppose the predominantly selfish type of characters observed hitherto. Yet Ricardo's science of political economy, an essential tool of the older radicalism, remains essential. In this chapter, I propose to outline Mill's Ricardian scientific principles and relate his applications of them to his liberal utilitarian values. For my purposes, it is important to keep in mind his distinction between the *science* and *art* of political economy. His Ricardian view of the science must not be conflated with his liberal utilitarian view of the art which he indicates owes little to Ricardo. The science consists of abstract 'laws' or theorems which presuppose that any person is motivated primarily by a desire for wealth, although that motive is limited by certain relevant auxiliary desires, including the desire for leisure and the desire for enjoyment of the things which wealth can buy. Persons are also assumed to be capable of reasoning about the effective means of attaining their desires, and to be situated in a competitive market environment. The art takes the 'laws' of the corresponding science, converts and rearranges them into a system of practical rules, and then applies the rules in concrete circumstances to promote the general welfare. That ultimate end is apparently conceived in terms of certain subordinate social goals or "permanent interests of man as a progressive being",[3] including a permanent interest in 'abundance' which may be interpreted as the efficient production, allocation, and growth of national wealth. More generally, the art of political economy is a component of the liberal utilitarian 'Art of Life' that attempts to apply the entire stock of scientific knowledge to promote the general happiness conceived thus.[4]

Despite his reliance on Ricardo's scientific principles, Mill looked to Smith rather than Ricardo when it came to practical use of economic science in service of a liberal utilitarian 'Art of Life':

For practical purposes, political economy is inseparably intertwined with many other branches of social philosophy. . . . Smith never loses sight of this truth. . . . [A] work similar in its object and general conception to that of Adam Smith, but adapted to the more extended knowledge and improved ideas of the present age, is the kind of contribution which political economy at present requires.[5]

By implication, Ricardo does not always make clear the links between political economy and the other components of social philosophy. Indeed, by failing to elaborate the values (Benthamite or otherwise) which he thought should guide and constrain applications of his principles, he at times gave the impression that his science could stand alone as a body of universal truths. His focus on competitive capitalist institutions and on the predominantly selfish type of character moulded under such institutions threatened to become the only possible focus, unqualified by other considerations.

Mill seeks to rework Smith's practical art by applying Ricardo's advanced scientific principles in light of a suitably 'enlarged' utilitarian philosophy that goes beyond Benthamism to accommodate a more complex psychology (involving higher moral and aesthetic kinds of motivations that may trump narrow self-interest) as well as improved ideas of social cooperation and equal justice. In particular, he emphasizes that contemporary ideas and institutions of private property, and the highly inegalitarian distribution of wealth associated with them, are a matter of social choice and therefore need not be accepted as 'natural' or inevitable. By the time he published the third edition of his great treatise in 1852, he and Harriet Taylor (whom he married in 1851) had firmly concluded that socialists were right to hold out the possibility of a radically egalitarian social ideal, even if any progress toward it must be gradual and difficult.[6]

Mill's liberal utilitarian 'Art of Life' (including the art of political economy) owes much to its Benthamite progenitor, or so I will argue.[7] His grand project is properly seen as an 'enlargement' and 'reorientation' of Benthamism rather than an outright rejection of it. As is well known, Bentham conceived the general welfare in terms of "four subordinate objects", namely, "subsistence, abundance, equality, and security".[8] In his view: "The more perfect the enjoyment of all these particulars, the greater the sum of social happiness".[9] He seems to have believed that an optimal mixture of the four particulars could be achieved under a legal code that distributes equal rights and correlative duties of a certain content and order of precedence. More specifically, by distributing private property rights that secure to each producer the fruits of his own labour and saving (net of fair taxation), an ideal system of rules would promote economic abundance and foster equality in the distribution of wealth. At the same time, each person must also be assigned basic rights to subsistence, safety, and freedom from undue coercion. The system of equal rights and duties permits each person to enjoy security of expectations with respect to certain vital elements or 'primary goods' in his plan of life.

Mill's view as I interpret it shares much in common with this picture of Benthamite utilitarianism but also 'enlarges' upon it in significant ways. For example, Mill goes beyond Bentham to allow for the possibility that an ideal code might abandon private property altogether in favour of equal rights for members of self-managed socialist enterprises to participate in internal collective decisions, including decisions as to fair distribution of market returns. In short, general welfare maximization might involve a decentralized form of socialism rather than a more cooperative and egalitarian form of capitalism.

Moreover, Mill prescribes a so-called 'stationary state' rather than continued economic growth beyond a reasonable threshold of national wealth and population. By implication, economic rights associated with the interest in abundance – whether private property rights or rights to participate in socialist enterprises – come into conflict with superior types of rights beyond that threshold. Those superior rights might include rights to breathe clean air and drink clean water, for example, as well as rights to contemplate unspoiled natural beauty in solitude, rights to engage freely and exclusively with other consensual adults in intimate activities of no legitimate concern to anyone else, and so on. At some point, if growth of wealth and population continues unchecked and natural beauty is increasingly sacrificed to mankind's economic purposes, such rights will be endangered for many of us. Liberal utilitarianism at that point prescribes a halt to further economic growth.

Mill's liberal utilitarian scheme of equal rights is also distinctive because of the absolute protection afforded to the individual's liberty to choose as he likes with respect to certain 'purely self-regarding actions' said to directly cause no 'perceptible damage' to other persons against their wishes. Bentham does not seem to have conceived of an equal right to liberty of similar scope or weight.[10] Rather, he seems to have identified a person's liberty with his set of rights distributed under the rules, in which case "the spheres of liberty and security are extensionally equivalent" even in the absence of any right to liberty of a Millian sort.[11] In effect, Mill's conception of general welfare recognizes a distinctive 'permanent interest' in 'individuality' which is not captured by the 'subordinate objects' comprising the Benthamite conception.

If my view is accepted, Mill reconceives the general welfare by adding to Bentham's list of permanent interests, by imagining the possibility of a distinctive optimal mix of those permanent ingredients, and by identifying novel codes of rights and duties associated with that ideal blend of security, subsistence, abundance, equality, and individuality. Given that his idea of general welfare ultimately motivates his art of political economy, his practical applications of the Ricardian principles will illustrate that ultimate end and help clarify the structure of his general philosophy. Before such clarification can be expected, however, an understanding of at least the main Ricardian principles themselves is required.

II. RICARDIAN SCIENCE

Mill described Ricardo as Britain's "greatest political economist" and referred to his *Principles of Political Economy and Taxation* (1817) as "the book which formed so great an epoch in political economy."[12] Ricardo's theories admittedly required some clarification and even modification in view of subsequent contributions by various economists, including Mill himself. But Mill's understanding of the science remained essentially Ricardian: "I doubt if there will be a single opinion (on pure political economy) in [my own *Principles of Political Economy*]", he remarked in a letter dated February 22, 1848, to John Austin, "which may not be exhibited as a corollary from [Ricardo's] doctrines".[13]

In contrast, Mill claimed that Smith's pioneering treatise exhibits the science 'almost' in its 'infancy': "The 'Wealth of Nations' [1776] is in many parts obsolete, and in all, imperfect".[14] Smith's various theoretical shortcomings are said to include: (1) his inadequate appreciation of the advantages and disadvantages associated with the division of labour; (2) his inattention to key considerations (including general excess supply of labour and certain natural and artificial monopolies) that largely explain the highly unequal wages hitherto observed across different occcupations; (3) his botch of the distinction between exchange value and use (or utility) value; (4) his mistaken notion that labour may serve as a measure of value (whether Smith meant exchange value or utility value or both in this context remains ambiguous); (5) his failure to grasp the theory (developed by Ricardo and Torrens) that comparative cost advantage (rather than foreign demand for surplus domestic production) determines international trade flows in a world of imperfect factor mobility; and (6) his apparent acceptance of the unsound doctrine that "competition of capital lowers profits by lowering prices".[15] Moreover, Mill is generally quick to rebut anti-Ricardian critics, including Malthus, Chalmers, and Sismondi, who he thinks are still labouring under the influence of Smith's errors.[16]

Samuel Hollander argues forcefully, in his magisterial study of

Mill's political economy, that Mill "was perfectly objective" in depicting "his scientific work as Ricardian".[17] He claims further that Mill's science displays substantial continuity not only with Ricardo's theory but also with modern neoclassical theory: "the economics of Ricardo and J. S. Mill in fact comprises in its essentials an exchange system consistent with the neo-classical elaborations". This scientific continuity thesis liberates Mill from a received interpretation of him as a muddled transitional figure attempting in vain to bridge incompatible theoretical frameworks: "[T]hat we find both neo-classical and Ricardian features in Mill's *Principles* implies neither inconsistency . . . nor a process of attempted escape from his Ricardian heritage".[18] Rather, Mill emerges as a key contributor to an ongoing scientific enterprise, as I will attempt to illustrate by summarizing his Ricardian views of exchange value, production, distribution, growth, and the stationary state. At the same time, he does not always place emphasis where modern analysts do, nor does he always confine himself to their behavioural and institutional premises. I also note some of those peculiar elements of his theory.

Exchange value

Mill affirms that competitive exchange values are determined by demand and supply. Against Smith, he argues that a commodity's exchange value depends on both its 'effective' utility value (or use value) and its scarcity, where by 'effective' utility value is meant pleasure or preference-satisfaction of individuals with purchasing power, and by scarcity is meant 'difficulty of attainment' or costliness of supply. Exchange value is nil, he indicates, if there is no effective demand for the commodity *or* if nature supplies it in such abundance that any demand for it can be satisfied without incurring any costs of production.

Mill discusses three different cases of what he and Ricardo call 'natural values' (or what Marshall calls 'normal values'). In one case, admittedly 'peculiar', where a desired commodity is scarce and its supply cannot be increased at any cost (that is, its supply is fixed in the long run), natural value is limited only by the wants of individuals with the means to purchase. No limits are placed on natural value by costs in this case, given the assumption that costs of reproducing the commodity are infinite. Such exchange values are termed 'scarcity values' or 'monopoly values' because individuals or firms in possession of the fixed supply face no threat of competition from other producers entering the industry. Existing producers (however numerous) have power and incentive to exploit purchasers by colluding to suitably restrict sales of the commodity. By restricting supply, those firms can set prices at any level which maximizes industry revenues given demand. Purchasers have no alternative sources of supply and thus are forced to make their demand conform to the available supply.[19]

This case exhibits the *unrestrained* law of supply and demand, Mill says, anterior to considerations of cost of production. Although of limited scope for purposes of long-run analysis, he insists, that law is nevertheless of fundamental importance for short-run analysis where supply is temporarily fixed as a result of input constraints:

In the case of most commodities, it requires a certain time to increase their quantity; and if the demand increases, then until a corresponding supply can be brought forward, that is, until the supply can accommodate itself to the demand, the value will so rise as to accommodate the demand to the supply.[20]

More on this in a moment.

In a second case, where the desired commodity is scarce yet its supply can be increased indefinitely at constant unit costs (including ordinary profits), natural value is equal to the constant cost of production. Evidently, the law of supply and demand is not set aside in this instance. Rather, it is now *restrained* by the law of cost of production which comes into play precisely because purchasers now do have alternative sources of supply at constant costs. As Mill puts it:

[T]he law of demand and supply . . . is acknowledged to be applicable to all commodities. . . . [In the present case, this fundamental law] is controlled, but not set aside, by the law of cost of production, since cost of production would have no effect on value if it could have none on supply. . . . [P]otential alteration [of supply] is [generally] sufficient; and if there even be an actual alteration, it is but a temporary one, except in so far as the altered value may make a difference in the demand, and so require an increase or diminution of supply, as a consequence, not a cause, of the alteration in value.[21]

Given that the commodity can be reproduced at constant (marginal and average) cost to satisfy whatever level of effective demand appears at this cost, producers have no credible threat to force purchasers to pay more than the constant cost of production in the long run unless government creates artificial barriers to competitive entry. Even if few producers are observed, the threat of entry forces those producers to set prices no higher than this long-run cost. At the same time, the natural value must at least cover that cost because otherwise firms will shut down.

In a third case, which Mill suggests is intermediate between the first two, where the commodity is scarce and its supply can be increased only at increasing unit costs, natural value is still equal to long-run marginal cost of production, yet producers of so-called intramarginal units (involving superior types of inputs) will also receive rents from purchasers. Purchasers have alternative sources of supply but now only at the increasing marginal cost. Producers still have no credible threat to set prices above marginal costs in the absence of political barriers to competitive entry. But they do have power to set prices at a level which covers the cost of that unit of the commodity which is produced with the least productive inputs. Otherwise, that unit cannot be supplied and demand will not be satisfied in the long run. As fewer and fewer productive combinations of inputs are called into production with increases of scale, producers can raise prices to cover the increasing marginal cost. Competitive entrants could do no better.

Mill largely ignores a fourth case where the desired commodity is scarce but its supply can be increased indefinitely at decreasing unit costs. The case is problematic for the existence of what neoclassical economists call 'perfectly' competitive equilibrium. Given that marginal costs are falling everywhere over the relevant range of production, perfectly competitive firms (which are powerless to drive a wedge between prices and marginal costs) are unable to recover their average costs and thus cannot survive in the long run.[22] Government intervention might be advocated to preserve the appearance of a perfectly competitive market structure in this case. More specifically, many small producers might be permitted by government to set prices to recover their average costs. But that policy would sacrifice the efficiencies of large-scale production for the semblance of an ideal of competition.[23]

Given that decreasing costs are observed over a 'large' range of production, the production technology seems to dictate the emergence of few large-scale producers. But that may not be inconsistent with the invisible hand, despite the absence of many small-scale producers. Indeed, the threat of potential entrants may force even a 'natural' monopolist to set prices no higher than long-run average costs. It seems unreasonable to expect competitive forces to do more than minimize the industry's total costs of production subject to the industry remaining viable in the long run. If this seems acceptable, then natural values in the problematic case are equal to long-run average costs rather than marginal costs. Moreover, reasonable competition may obtain even in the absence of perfectly competitive markets.

Mill goes on to emphasize that natural exchange values are 'permanent' or 'average' values towards which actual market values are constantly gravitating even though at any time market values may deviate from natural values. As a result of short-run constraints on input supplies, market values generally oscillate above and below natural values so that possessors of the fixed inputs temporarily receive (positive or negative) excess profits (Marshallian 'quasi-rents'). The unrestrained law of demand and supply governs those market oscillations. But for any commodity whose natural value is a cost value as opposed to a scarcity or monopoly value, the deviation between market and natural values tends to be corrected through anticipated alterations of supply. As Mill explains:

There is a demand for a certain quantity of the commodity at its natural or cost value, and to that the supply in the long run endeavours to conform. . . . [I]f a value different from the natural value be necessary to make the demand equal to the supply, the market value will deviate from the natural value; but only for a time; for the permanent tendency of supply is to conform itself to the demand which is found by experience to exist for the commodity when selling at its natural value. If the supply is either more or less than this, it is so accidentally, and affords either more or less than the ordinary rate of profit; which, under free and active competition, cannot long continue to be the case.[24]

To recapitulate: the pure law of demand and supply governs, on the one hand, the natural values ('monopoly values') of commodities whose supply is fixed or cannot be increased sufficiently to satisfy the whole of the demand for them in the long run, and, on the other hand, the temporary market values of *all* commodities, including those whose supply can be increased to satisfy any demand for them in the long run. The natural values of the latter commodities, however, are governed by the law of cost of production, 'a superior force' which constrains the law of demand and supply by making market value gravitate towards long-run cost and "which would settle it and keep it there, if fresh disturbing influences were not continually arising to make it again deviate".[25]

Among other things, Mill extends his value analysis to include money and defends a duly qualified version of the quantity theory of money.[26] He also offers an intriguing discussion of the business cycle.[27] He explains some 'peculiar cases' (for example, the case of joint production) where the law of demand and supply is not constrained in the usual way by the law of production cost.[28] And he provides what is considered even by modern practitioners as one of the finest discussions ever written on the theory of international trade, highlighted by his celebrated chapter XVIII ('Of International Values').[29]

Although he admits that the theory of exchange value and price is of fundamental interest in the context of a competitive market economy 'entirely founded on purchase and sale', Mill also indicates that political economy has other concerns perhaps even more fundamental.

Production constraints

"The laws and conditions of the production of wealth partake of the character of physical truths", Mill asserts. "There is nothing optional or arbitrary in them. . . . [They] would be the same as they are, if the arrangements of society did not depend on exchange, or did not admit of it".[30] The science of political economy is ultimately concerned with the *production* of wealth, he insists, where wealth refers to "all useful or agreeable things except those which can be obtained, in the quantity desired, without labour or sacrifice".[31] Production is a process whereby natural materials are transformed by labour and abstinence into scarce objects that embody utility value, in other words, objects that are not naturally abundant and are desired by persons with the means to reimburse those (perhaps themselves) who by their exertions and savings create the objects.[32] That transformation process is governed by constraints that are independent of what people may wish or think in the matter: "Whatever mankind produce, must be produced in the modes, and under the conditions, imposed by the constitution of external things, and by the inherent properties of their own bodily and mental structure".[33]

With few exceptions, for example, labour is required to transform natural resources into any sort of wealth.[34] To carry on all but the most simple transformations, moreover, capital goods and permanent improvements to natural resources are also required. But these latter requisites are themselves products of labour. For labour to be devoted to the production of such inputs as machinery or more fertile land, however, some individuals must abstain from their own present consumption to support that of the workers during the production period. Thus, whether mankind like it or not, wealth cannot be produced without the required labour and abstinence. But the labour will not be forthcoming in the long run unless workers are paid a commodity wage sufficient to keep them at their customary subsistence level, with the caveat that customary expectations cannot fall below what is required for bare survival. If workers do not receive their customary 'necessaries', then population (labour supply) tends to decline (whether from a fall in the birth rate or a rise in the death rate) below the quantity wanted for production. Nor will capital goods or resource improvements be forthcoming in the long run unless abstainers expect additional output from the future use of those inputs sufficient to repay, with some customary minimum rate of profit, the commodity wages which must be advanced to the workers. Customary profit rate expectations are also bounded from below by the requirement that output must be sufficient to permit all participants in the production process (including workers and abstainers) to survive over the long run.

There are still other production constraints that are not a matter of choice. For any given state of technical knowledge, for example, certain combinations of inputs are more technically efficient than others:

Whether [mankind] like it or not, their production will be limited by the amount of their previous [capital] accumulation, and, that being given, it will be proportional to their energy, their skill, the perfection of their machinery, and their judicious use of the advantages of combined labour.

Like it or not, "the unproductive expenditure of individuals will *pro tanto* tend to impoverish the community, and only their productive expenditure will enrich it".[35] Like it or not, 'the niggardliness of nature' will cause decreasing returns beyond some scale of agricultural production because (despite the apparently unlimited increases of labour and capital which mankind are capable of producing) there are physically limited supplies of the most fertile types of land in the long run. Technological advance may obscure these limits by revealing far more productive ways of combining labour with natural materials and agents.

But howsoever we may succeed in making for ourselves more space within the limits set by the constitution of things, we know that there must be limits. We cannot alter the ultimate properties either of matter or mind, but can only employ those properties more or less successfully, to bring about the events in which we are interested.[36]

The upshot is that non-optional laws and conditions of production, not the machinery of exchange and price, underlie the natural cost values of those commodities which are reproducible by labour and abstinence with a given stock of technical knowledge. For production to satisfy any given market demand in the long run, any commodity's exchange value must tend to award at least a customary subsistence wage and a customary minimum profit to the workers and savers who employ the least productive types of natural resources in its production. Technological advance may continually lower those cost values. But it can hardly be expected to reduce them to zero. That would mean that the commodities could be produced indefinitely without labour of abstinence; in effect, nature would freely supply the goods. In such a utopia, the science of political economy would cease to be of any practical concern.

Distribution constraints

Whereas the organization of production is constrained by certain laws and conditions in which "there is nothing optional or arbitrary", Mill says, institutions for distributing wealth are entirely matters of social choice: "The rules by which [distribution] is determined, are what the opinions and feelings of the ruling portion of the community make them, and are very different in different ages and countries; and might be still more different, if mankind so chose".[37] Thus, in an advanced moral culture, society may choose to establish far more egalitarian institutions than hitherto observed anywhere. Such institutions may be implemented because most persons have learned to pursue higher moral purposes that suitably constrain their respective material self-interests. Most might eventually come to be motivated by a moral conviction to share wealth equally or on the basis of need, for example, conjoined with a desire to contribute whatever labour and saving one is capable of.

But the science of political economy, Mill makes clear, abstracts from moral motivations altogether and does not attempt to explain why some rules of distribution rather than others are established in any given social context. Rather, the science "is concerned with [man] solely as a being who desires to possess wealth and who is capable of judging of the comparative efficacy of means for obtaining that end". It

makes entire abstraction of every other human passion or motive; except those which may be regarded as perpetually antagonizing principles to the desire of wealth, namely, aversion to labour, and desire of the present enjoyment of costly indulgences [luxuries and fleeting pleasures].[38]

Moreover, given the assumption that man is motivated thus, the science is concerned with the economic *consequences* of society's chosen rules of distribution, whatever the rules may be:

Those [consequences] . . . are as little arbitrary, and have as much the character of physical laws, as the laws of production. . . . Society can subject the distribution of wealth to whatever rules it thinks best: but what practical results will flow from the operation of those rules, must be discovered, like any other physical or mental truths, by observation and reasoning.[39]

In particular, the science considers the incentives which personal wealth-maximizers have under the given rules so as to ascertain what actual distributions of wealth may be expected in the long run.[40]

Up to now, Mill emphasizes, societies have generally relied on rules of private property for distributive purposes: "Unless in some exceptional and very limited cases, the economical arrangements of society have always rested [on the institution of individual property], though in its secondary features it has varied, and is liable to vary".[41] Moreover, societies will probably continue to do so for the foreseeable future: "[T]he political economist, for a considerable time to come, will be chiefly concerned with the conditions of existence and progress belonging to a society founded on private property and individual competition".[42] As a result of such rules of private property, society's wealth is distributed among the *individual* owners of the factors of production in the form of wages, profits, and rents. But private property per se does not imply the existence of three distinct classes of, respectively, workers, capitalists, and resource owners: "though these three sometimes exist as separate classes, dividing the produce among them, they do not necessarily or always so exist". Indeed, 'the ordinary case' is that the same person owns two or even all three factors.[43]

Nevertheless, the special case of three distinct classes is of particular scientific interest. In this regard, to the extent that the same persons own two or more factors, *competition* among distinct classes of owners cannot account for the division of the output. Such competition is, however, the mechanism supposed by the science to deduce the distributive consequences of rules of private property: "[O]nly through the principle of competition has political economy any pretension to the character of a science". Mill admits that "it would be a great misconception of the actual course of human affairs to suppose that competition exercises in fact this unlimited sway".[44] Rather, 'custom or usage' generally hinders or even replaces individual competition in determining the distribution of wealth in any observed private property economy. For example, in a slave economy where the master class owns all three inputs, the masters own the whole product and share it with their slaves according to customary opinion (if greed does not lead them to work their slaves to death). Even in a modern industrial economy where three distinct classes of persons do compete to determine the distribution, custom may still interfere with the competition insofar as unequal retail prices are charged to different consumers of the same good, for example, or unequal wages are paid to similarly skilled workers of different sexes or races. Indeed, custom will also generally frame the competition in the sense that division of the output is ultimately tied to certain customary expectations of workers and capitalists as to, respectively, a subsistence wage and minimum profit rate.

Assuming for analytic convenience that inputs are matched to mutually exclusive classes of workers, capitalists, and resource owners, Mill indicates that the consequences of unlimited competition in product and factor markets may be summarized in terms of laws of distribution that (like the laws of production) "partake of the character of physical truths". He insists that the "mechanism of exchange and price . . . is quite powerless to alter" those distributive consequences. At the risk of oversimplification, the competitive process works like this. Given that profits are only made possible by the power of labour to produce *more* than the commodity wages necessary to keep workers at their customary subsistence, what goes to the worker from production at the margin *must* come at the expense of his competitor, the owner of capital: "whatever of the ultimate product, is not profit, is repayment of wages".[45] Rent goes to those who possess superior types of resources to that used at the margin. But, extraordinary scarcity values aside, such rent emerges *as a result* of the competition between capitalists and workers. It is equivalent to the additional product (profits and wages) made possible for capitalists and workers who use the superior resources:

> The superiority of the instrument is in exact proportion to the rent paid for it. . . .Whoever does pay rent gets back its full value in extra advantages, and the rent which he pays does not place him in a worse position than, but only in the same position as, his fellow producer [at the margin] who pays no rent, but whose instrument is one of inferior efficiency.[46]

So, independently of the machinery of exchange and price, competition underlies the basic Ricardian distribution principle that "the rate of profit and the cost of labour vary inversely as one another".[47] If the separate owners of the different inputs each bring their essential ingredient to the production process and then compete over the division of the product, then, whether or not they actually buy and sell anything at a price, an inverse relation exists between the ordinary rate of profit and the cost of labour to the capitalist.[48]

Competition between owners of the same factor also works its effect. Consider workers. They seek wealth for themselves. But once

their commodity wage exceeds the level required to support a customary subsistence, their aversion to labour and their desire for
present enjoyment encourage them to pursue wealth for themselves
through the efforts of others. Once above the habitual minimum, in
other words, they tend to have children on the expectation that
these offspring will soon be capable of earning the same above-
standard commodity wage as themselves. Given a sufficient number
of children, each bringing in a surplus beyond what is necessary to
her own subsistence, the entire family (including the parents) might
eventually be supported by the work and savings of the children
alone. But if all workers pursue similar wealth-seeking strategies,
then increased population (labour supply) tends in the long run to
outpace the demand for labour (roughly equivalent to the stock of
circulating capital). With due caveats relating to wage differentials
across industries, the general level of commodity wages is directly
proportional to the ratio of (circulating) capital to population; and,
therefore, in the absence of legal or customary checks on population, this wage level tends to be driven down to the customary
minimum. In short, if workers are motivated as political economists
suppose, then competition within the working classes tends to
make the customary minimum into a maximum commodity wage
in the long run.[49]

Competition among owners of capital also tends to make some
customary minimum rate of profit into the maximum that capitalists may reasonably expect in the long run. With due allowances for
inequalities of risk and of required degrees of managerial skill across
different investments, the minimum profit rate is a uniform rate of
return "which is barely adequate, at the given place and time, to
afford an equivalent for the abstinence, risk, and exertion implied in
the employment of capital".[50] Capitalists will generally not invest
the wealth required to employ productive labour in the given society unless they expect to earn at least a minimum profit rate. Now,
actual profits are simply that portion of output which is produced by
workers in excess of what is required for their own customary
support. Given that the commodity wages advanced by capitalists
are roughly equivalent to the stock of circulating capital, profits
must be equal to output net of that capital stock. The uniform profit
rate thus cannot *exceed* the ratio of net output to capital. If capitalists are convinced that labour is sufficiently productive to generate

the net output required to yield some customary minimum profit rate, however, capital will be forthcoming. But then competition among the owners of capital will tend to ensure that this minimum is also the maximum rate in the long run. Given that the effective desire to save has been triggered by net output expectations among most investors (including those with no unusual risk-taking proclivities or managerial skills), capital will tend to be invested until the ratio of expected net output to capital stock approaches the minimum rate.

Finally, competition among resource owners will tend to ensure that the rents which flow as a result of the competition between capitalists and workers are also the maximum rents. But, in extraordinary cases where even the worst types of resources receive rents in the long term, competition is at best only partially operative. Resource owners in these cases have monopoly power to extract scarcity values from capitalists and workers for the use of resources, such values being a function of long-run demand and supply (taking for granted that resource owners may credibly threaten to further limit access).

The competitive capitalist economy tends on this Ricardian view to gravitate toward a stationary long-run equilibrium (or 'stationary state') in which market values converge on natural cost values, population is stationary with the working classes receiving a customary subsistence wage, capital stock is stationary with capitalists receiving a customary minimum profit rate, and different qualities of natural resources are employed in production with owners of (at least) the superior qualities receiving rents from their mere possession. At such a stationary state, market demand has settled at a maximum sustainable level, that is, a level which owners of inputs are just willing (given customary expectations of subsistence wages and minimum profits) and able (given the state of technological knowledge) to sustain indefinitely. Natural cost values are thereby tied to a given state of technology and customs governing the long-run supplies of labour and capital. More specifically, the competitive process of adjustment to the stationary state (which might involve either growth or decline of population and capital) ensures that cost values are not only the minima required to sustain production but also the maxima that wealth-seekers may reasonably expect in the long run.

Growth and the stationary state

Mill claimed that any 'opulent' economy such as Britain, with a large output and virtually no idle supplies of fertile land, is habitually "on the very verge of the stationary state" at all times.[51] Nevertheless, actual convergence is continually postponed for various reasons, for example, technological innovations that prevent profits from falling to their customary minimum rate.[52] Might it not be possible that technological advance and other sources of sustained economic growth would fundamentally alter the Ricardian analysis?

As a practical matter, Mill reaffirms Ricardo's conclusion that, in the absence of voluntary birth control not to be expected from selfish economic agents of the sort assumed by the science, economic growth tends to enrich the owners of resources without improving the lot of workers or capitalists:

The economical progress of a society constituted of landlords, capitalists, and labourers, tends to the progressive enrichment of the landlord class; while the cost of the labourer's subsistence tends on the whole to increase, and profits to fall [to their customary minimum level].[53]

Technological advance may counteract the last two effects for an indefinite period, he admits, but it ultimately must exacerbate the first – the benefits of the improvements will eventually flow to the resource owners in the form of higher rents. According to the Ricardian view, population tends to adjust to capital stock in such a way that market wages and profits are driven toward their respective customary minimum levels. Moreover, this adjustment process is not fundamentally altered by technological improvements per se, even though its operation may be hidden for a considerable period. If a relatively sudden improvement occurs in the means of producing the commodities making up the customary subsistence wage, for example, with little or no change in the existing population or capital stock (and perhaps even withdrawal from production of the least productive natural resources), money wages (the cost of labour) and rents tend to fall, whereas the profit rate tends to rise above the customary minimum rate.[54] These initial effects on distribution would be permanent rather than merely temporary if population and capital could somehow be held constant. By raising the market profit rate, however, the improvement stimulates net investment and increased demand for labour. If self-interested motivations and customary expectations remain unchanged, growth of population and capital will eventually upset the initial distributional effects; indeed, the effects will tend to be reversed. Moreover, if, as Mill admits has generally been the case up to his time, improvement occurs not suddenly but gradually so that population and capital are enabled to grow sufficiently rapidly all along (the least productive natural resources never being withdrawn from production) even worse resources are continuously called into production to help supply the increasing demand. The same distributional effects as those ultimately associated with the other case are implied: rents and the cost of labour tend to rise whereas the profit rate tends to fall to its minimum rate.[55]

The Ricardian analysis suggests that technological advance alone might postpone but cannot significantly alter the rather gloomy stationary state that awaits a ruthlessly competitive economy of self-interested economic agents. If we assume for analytic convenience that continuous technological progress can somehow take place without any improvement in the characters and customary expectations of market participants, the stationary state is associated with ever larger populations and capital stocks at the same customary subsistence wage and customary minimum profit rate. Technological advance, says Mill, makes the stationary state "fly before us" by raising the productivity of inputs. As a result, market profits tend to be prevented from falling to their customary minimum rate, perhaps for a considerable period of time, until growth of population forces up the cost of labour (due to the higher cost of producing the commodities comprising the customary subsistence wage) and thereby causes profits to fall. In the meantime, population and capital stock are enabled to grow. Eventually, however, further technological progress must cease. At that point (however distant), the sustained growth of wealth and population made possible by technological advance must come to an end. Moreover, despite the sustained economic growth, individual workers and capitalists are no better off. As Mill puts it:

There is a greater aggregate production, a greater produce divided among the labourers, and a larger gross profit; but the wages being shared among a larger population, and the profits spread over a larger capital, no labourer is better off, nor does any capitalist derive from the same amount of capital a larger income.[56]

Only owners of resources have benefited through larger and larger rents.

Scientific continuity?

Despite substantial continuity between Mill's Ricardian science and the modern theoretical mainstream, some important shifts of emphasis have occurred which some may even be inclined to view as discontinuities. One important shift, for example, relates to the conception of competitive markets. Whereas neoclassicists tend to focus on the ideal of perfectly competitive equilibrium, classicists apparently preferred to view the competitive mechanism in less rarified terms. More specifically, whereas perfectly competitive markets feature many small producers without significant power to affect equilibrium prices fixed as if by an invisible hand at marginal costs of production, Mill seems to equate competition with the freedom of potential entrants to replicate the production technology of existing producers given the same market demand. In the latter case, even a natural monopolist may be constrained by competitive forces in the sense that freedom of entry forces prices to be set at long-run average cost. More generally, the law of production cost regulates classical competitive exchange value to the extent that existing firms recognize that entrants can credibly threaten to satisfy the given demand at similar costs.[57] At the same time, the pure law of demand and supply (unconstrained by costs) is associated with imperfections (including temporary constraints on supplies of inputs) in the competitive environment which give some agents 'monopoly' power to exploit buyers of their commodities.

A second important shift of emphasis relates to the general interdependence between factor and product markets and potentially complex implications for exchange values and distribution of factor rewards. Neoclassicists tend to focus attention on general equilibrium analysis and to view the classicists as at best dimly aware of even the idea (let alone the technical details) of that analysis. Hollander has argued persuasively, however, that Ricardian theory incorporates general equilibrium insights.[58] Even so, Mill and Ricardo seem inclined to treat the details of the interactions between factor and product markets as being of less interest than the role of certain customary expectations (concerning, respectively, a subsistence wage and a minimum profit rate) in determining the character of the stationary state toward which the competitive economy gravitates, including the size of the population (labour supply) and capital stock as well as the per capita rewards of the classes of workers, capitalists, and resource owners in the long run.

A final important shift of emphasis worth noting here relates to the possibility of continuous growth of wealth and population. Moderns have tended to stress the feasibility of continuous balanced growth (i.e., growth at a constant ratio of capital to labour), whereas classicists were more inclined to stress that technological improvement alone cannot prevent (however long it might defer) the ultimate arrival of a stationary state.[59] Indeed, moderns have even argued recently that indefinitely sustained growth of per capita wealth is made possible by continuous technological innovation.[60]

Despite their disagreement over its feasibility, however, classicals and moderns generally agree that indefinite growth is *desirable*. No significant normative shift of emphasis seems to have occurred. Indeed, Ricardo and the Benthamite radicals apparently equated economic growth with the advance of civilization. Civilization would thus cease to advance at the stationary state. Mill's philosophical novelty lies in part in his view that a stationary state is compatible with, even essential to, the advance of civilization (including moral and political development). In his view, once a certain threshold of population and material prosperity is reached, increased technological knowledge should be used for ends other than further growth. Unlike most classicals and moderns, he advocates a stationary state in which a stable population maintains itself at some reasonable average level of material comfort, yet most persons also attach more importance to certain 'higher pursuits' than to further labour, investment, and exploitation of natural resources. Those 'higher pursuits' require leisure time and might include academic studies, contemplation of natural beauty, intimate activities between consenting adults, helping others with their projects, and political efforts to promote fair distribution of wealth. Progress in these higher pursuits conflicts with, and, according to his liberal utilitarian scale of value, takes priority over, continued growth of wealth and population beyond the relevant threshold.[61]

III. LIBERAL UTILITARIAN ART

Mill's liberal utilitarian art of economics requires clarification at many points, only a few of which can be broached here. An initial step is to recognize the priority of security, subsistence, and individuality over other 'permanent interests' in his conception of welfare. The next steps are to outline the ideal stationary state at which he thinks general welfare would become supreme, clarify some features of the gradual process of transition to that ideal, and indicate the sorts of economic reforms which he recommends. Finally, although a utilitarian 'continuity thesis' analogous to Hollander's scientific one may be plausible, I suggest that Mill's utilitarianism is so distinctive that his view of the economic art is outside the mainstream of classics and moderns alike.

Priorities

The importance of security, subsistence, and individuality in Mill's utilitarianism is commonly recognized in the literature, although the meanings of those permanent interests and how they function in the structure of his doctrine continue to be disputed. Hollander, for example, interprets Mill as giving great weight to "the supreme social utility of security (on a par, it will be recalled, with that of subsistence)".[62] In his view, not only security and subsistence but also "human character formation itself, and ultimately social progress" are included as vital components of Mill's conception of the general welfare.[63] Once the non-standard idea of general utility is properly understood, he argues, other pieces of Mill's philosophy, including the ideas of liberty and individuality regarded as means to the end, fall into place.[64] He also suggests that Mill's recognition of a hierarchy of different interests within his idea of general utility represents "a return to Bentham".[65]

Hollander's interpretation is one of many which cannot be adequately discussed here.[66] My own interpretation, elaborated elsewhere,[67] is perhaps closer to Hollander's than to competing interpretations. Moreover, it shares much in common with some of the recent interpretations of Bentham's philosophy noted earlier, especially those of Kelly and Rosen.[68] In my view, general security is an ingredient of general welfare, which, in social contexts beyond some minimum threshold of material and moral development at which a basic right to subsistence becomes feasible,[69] takes lexical priority over other ingredients in cases of conflict.[70] Security is a product of social rules (laws, customs, and/or shared dictates of conscience) that distribute and sanction (possibly unequal) personal rights and correlative duties. The rules give rise to a pattern of legitimate expectations the complete fulfilment of which is equivalent to the meaning of general security under those rules. Security is maximized, however, only in the context of ideal rules that distribute equal rights and also promote substantial economic equality for all.[71] This claim that general security is perfected under certain rules of equal justice may be contestable. But if it is accepted, then all persons ought to develop preferences for such ideal rules because those rules alone afford supreme protection for each and every person's vital concerns or primary goods. More on this in due course.

Security understood thus is a kind of utility associated with the satisfaction of certain legitimate expectations formed around a given system of rules of justice.[72] It may be associated with many rights beyond rights to personal safety and freedom from coercion by others. In large part, it can be interpreted to subsume the other 'permanent interests' which help to shape the content and order of precedence among rights. Subsistence, abundance, individuality, and equality are then seen as elements of the general welfare which complement security by indicating the nature of a utilitarian moral code. Thus, subsistence and equality apparently implied for Mill a weighty basic right to some minimal level of material benefits and services, for example.[73] Such positive rights seem essential to maximization of general security, since without means of subsistence no person can even survive. Yet rights of this sort are feasible only if a state of abundance has been achieved sufficient to enable producers to provide not only their own means of subsistence but also the means of the disabled. Moreover, subsistence rights must not unduly discourage self-interested individuals from the work and saving of which they are capable.[74] What rights are required to promote abundance, and how they relate to equality, will be the focus of discussion in the next couple of subsections.

Individuality and equality apparently implied for Mill an equal absolute right to liberty – in the sense of choosing to do whatever one likes – with respect to 'purely self-regarding' actions.[75] His famous liberty principle, according to which the individual's liberty ought to take precedence over competing considerations in the context of purely self-regarding matters (and only in that context), is distinct from his general policy of laissez-faire in economic matters. As he stresses:

[T]rade is a social act. Whoever undertakes to sell any description of goods to the public, does what affects the interests of other persons, and of society in general; and thus his conduct, in principle, comes within the jurisdiction of society. . . . [T]he so-called doctrine of free trade [or laissez-faire] . . . rests on grounds different from . . .the principle of individual liberty.[76]

His rather complicated laissez-faire policy, marked by various 'large exceptions', is driven by considerations of mere economic efficiency: the line it prescribes between free competition and government intervention in any social context is defended as expedient for achieving 'abundance'.[77] Moreover, the location of the expedient line may vary across different civil societies. But the 'one very simple principle' of liberty is grounded on considerations of security and justice: its assignment of equal rights to choose as one likes is defended as essential not only to the individual's self-development but also to the maintenance of whatever intellectual and moral capacities she has developed.[78] Moreover, the just line it prescribes between individual liberty and social authority is invariant across civil societies.

A proper distinction between these respective doctrines of laissez-faire and of liberty is crucial for understanding Mill's art of political economy. He expresses no doubts about the feasibility of implementing a general policy of laissez-faire under socialism, for example. A decentralized socialist economy, in which many producer cooperatives compete with each other in product and factor markets, is evidently the only form of socialism he takes seriously. What he fears, however, is that equal rights to liberty of purely self-regarding actions will never be adequately protected under any form of socialism. Given the present state of moral and intellectual imperfection, socialism is likely to make worse what is 'already one of the glaring evils' of existing society. Even if a decentralized socialism could be somehow established, intolerant majorities *within* producer associations would likely suppress unconventional ideas and impose a uniform private life-style on all of the members. Moreover, laissez-faire might actually exacerbate this injustice: competition *between* the associations might tend to eliminate remaining inter-group differences with respect to ideas, opinions, and life-style. Indeed, this sort of commercial competition already encourages undue social conformity under capitalism.[79] Still, it remains an open question, he insists, whether competitive capitalism will always afford relatively more protection for individual liberty and spontaneity than would decentralized socialism. Perhaps moral and intellectual improvement will one day make socialism hospitable to the greatest amount of individuality.

A liberal utopia

Mill suggests that general welfare (and thus the mix of its permanent ingredients) would become supreme at an ideal stationary state. That stationary state cannot be attained, he makes clear, unless workers learn to voluntarily restrict their numbers and thereby appropriate for themselves much of the net output that would otherwise be distributed to resource owners as rent. For any given stock of technological knowledge, society might take steps in the direction of such a stationary state by encouraging the working classes to develop tastes for material comforts beyond their customary subsistence, a point already recognized by Ricardo. A complementary strategy emphasized by Mill would be for society to encourage the workers to develop the capacities and desires for moral and aesthetic rewards distinct from material wealth. Workers could be educated to assign more value to things other than the indefinite increase of population and capital, including fair distribution, philanthropy, solitude and privacy, an unspoiled natural environment, and a diversity of life-forms in addition to human beings. Once accustomed to such tastes and desires, workers would tend to practice birth control to maintain a customary standard of living which includes not only material luxuries but also substantial leisure and non-material forms of wealth.

Evidently, a Millian stationary state is not a traditional Ricardian equilibrium where a 'superabundant' population of predominantly self-interested workers maintains itself at a spartan subsistence wage. Rather, highly educated workers voluntarily limit their numbers to support a highly civilized standard of living. Moreover, technological advance and moral and political improvement remain feasible, allowing the Millian stationary state to become even more civilized and happy:

It is scarcely necessary to remark that a stationary condition of capital and population implies no stationary state of human improvement. There would be as much scope as ever for all kinds of mental culture, and moral and social progress. . . . Even the industrial arts might be as earnestly and successfully cultivated, with this sole difference, that instead of serving no purpose but the increase of wealth, industrial improvements would produce their legitimate effect, that of abridging labour.[80]

In this context, social goals other than economic abundance are elevated to prominence. In particular, "what is economically needed is a better distribution" of wealth for the given population.[81]

Although he leaves open the possibility that society might eventually progress to a decentralized form of socialism involving perfect economic equality or even higher criteria of distributive justice, Mill concentrates attention on the gradual development of a more cooperative and egalitarian form of capitalism. More specifically, he calls for reform of existing laws and customs of private property in light of a desert principle upon which he thinks the justification of private property rests, namely, the principle (also apparently endorsed by Bentham) that individuals deserve to own the competitive market fruits of their own labour and saving.[82] Existing rules of property deviate from that 'equitable principle' in important respects and, to that extent, are illegitimate from the perspective of capitalism itself. Capitalism reformed in conformity with the principle would not recognize individual rights to own natural resources per se, for example, so that any rents associated with mere possession of resources could in principle be taken by the community through the tax system.[83] Nor would capitalism thus understood recognize a right to acquire unlimited wealth by gift or inheritance. Instead, any surplus which a person acquired above some limited "amount sufficient to constitute a moderate independence" would properly be confiscated, in which case givers would have a strong incentive to spread the wealth among various recipients.[84] These and other reforms of the existing idea of property would tend to promote a far more egalitarian distribution of wealth without subverting capitalism itself.[85]

As moral, political, and technological improvements brought society near a type of perfection that is only dimly recognizable from our imperfect vantage point, the Millian stationary state would begin to resemble a liberal social utopia. At that utopia, general security would be perfected under a system of universal equal rights accompanied by substantial economic equality. Whether associated with a more egalitarian capitalism or a decentralized socialism, such an ideal liberal society would be composed of highly educated and productive workers with strong dispositions to cooperate mutually by pooling their capital, to practice suitable birth control, and, generally, to respect each other's equal rights (including the right to liberty in purely self-regarding concerns). All able-bodied persons would exert themselves, none would be idle rich living off vast inheritances or resource rents. Technological advances would facilitate more and more leisure for all.

A gradual process of egalitarian reform

It emerges that Mill, like Bentham, associates the increase of general welfare (and its chief ingredient, security) with extension of basic rights and reduction of economic inequality:

We hold with Bentham, that equality, although not the sole end, is one of the ends of good social arrangements; and that a system of institutions which does not make the scale turn in favour of equality, whenever this can be done without impairing the security of the property which is the product and reward of personal exertion [labour and saving], is essentially a bad government – a government for the few, to the injury of the many.[86]

In particular, egalitarian reform of private property in accord with the desert principle is essential to general security maximization. Equal property rights of that sort are necessary for predominantly self-interested producers to feel as secure as possible in providing for their own subsistence (and that of their dependents) through their own exertions. Such rights guarantee the producer the fruits of his own labour and saving, where society takes steps to minimize (without pretending to remove altogether) inequalities of opportunity by, for example, limiting inheritance and ensuring reasonable access to natural resources. Private property reformed thus would be associated with a far more egalitarian distribution of wealth than hitherto observed under capitalism.[87] Moreover, while private property might eventually become dispensable if producers develop moral sentiments that suitably constrain their material self-interest, it is "at present [the] sole reliance for subsistence and security" and is likely to remain so for an indefinite period.[88] By implication, to increase the level of general security and advance toward liberal utopia, egalitarian reform of capitalism must preoccupy reformers for the foreseeable future.

Given that general security would be perfected under a system of equal rights accompanied by substantial economic equality, progress toward that ideal must nevertheless be gradual rather than immediate. A time-consuming process of mass education is needed, for example, to inculcate moral and aesthetic dispositions requisite to the ideal stationary state, including habits of mutual cooperation and respect together with a love of 'the graces of life' beyond material wealth and human reproduction. At an even more fundamental level, however, security itself is a value that can only be increased in a gradual manner.

Starting from any non-ideal position, where rights and wealth may be distributed in a highly unequal way, Bentham and Mill both insist that legitimate expectations formed around the existing rules of property must not be disappointed by any egalitarian reform of those rules if security is to increase.[89] It is not sufficient to justify reform that security takes on its supreme value at an egalitarian utopia. Society is not at utopia. Also required is that reform not destroy even the imperfect degree of security achieved under the existing rules. That imperfect security, associated with the existing system of unequal rights and holdings, has priority such that a reduction of security cannot be balanced or offset by increases in other values. Thus, if existing rules of property are reformed to abolish slavery, for example, or to terminate any other sort of property right, then persons whose expectations were formed prior to the reform ought to receive fair market compensation for the taking of their property to avoid arbitrary disappointment of their plans of life. Such compensation tends to perpetuate existing economic inequalities for a certain period of time, until the relevant generations of persons pass away and are replaced by new generations whose expectations have been formed after the reform.[90] Similarly, although sharply progressive taxation of estates and resource rents would foster diffusion of wealth, protection of existing expectations requires that those special taxes must not be applied retroactively. The present market values of inheritances and resources should thus be exempt from new special taxes.[91]

In effect, supreme general security can only be approached by a gradualist strategy of egalitarian reform. Any reform must protect the existing pattern of expectations associated with individual rights in place prior to the change, while simultaneously introducing a new pattern associated with a more egalitarian system of rules. That new pattern of expectations is inculcated in generations whose expectations are formed after the change. Moreover, the original right-holders have no reason to oppose the reform because they are not taxed retroactively and are fairly compensated for any taking of their property: the old pattern of expectations associated with their rights has not been upset *for them*. A gradualist strategy of this sort is essential because there is no other feasible way to increase general security. Any attempt at egalitarian reform through retroactive special taxation or through non-payment of fair compensation would tend to reduce security, by disappointing the legitimate expectations of existing right-holders. Violation of even a single person's existing rights is sufficient to reduce security and thereby render the reform self-defeating in utilitarian terms, since other considerations of value cannot make up for that reduction of security. In short, raising the present level of general security requires egalitarian reform of the existing rules together with protection for any individual's legitimate expectations formed under the existing system. In the absence of such protection, general security tends to fall and opposition to the reform is more likely.

Given that any progress toward a liberal utopia must be gradual, not only because of the need for mass education but also because of the need to protect the expectations of existing right-holders as egalitarian reforms proceed, it follows that Mill does not give precedence to equal rights to autonomy in economic and political (as opposed to purely self-regarding) matters during the process of transition. Otherwise, he would advocate a socialist revolution and immediate imposition of some form of radical participatory democracy, rather than gradual egalitarian reform of existing arrangements. He certainly highlighted the possibility that equal rights to participate in economic and political decisions might be characteristic of an ideal liberal society. But, in the meantime and for the foreseeable future, he defended in principle greater voices for the more industrious (e.g., profit-sharing in proportion to private capital contribution) and the more educated (e.g., plural voting).

Rising security and falling profits

Mill also indicates that general security is inversely related to the customary minimum rate of ordinary profit. That minimum profit rate, we may recall, is the minimum uniform rate of return that rewards the ordinary investor in any given social context for the "abstinence, risk, and exertion implied in the employment of capital".[92] It varies across social contexts, however, depending on the degree to which property put to *any productive use* is generally protected by law and custom from wanton damage or theft. Its level depends on the strength of the average investor's disposition to accumulate capital (that is, save and invest wealth for productive purposes) in the given social context. But the strength of the disposition in question is in turn ultimately determined by the degree of general security of persons and property in that social context. It is worth spelling this out in a bit more detail.

The customary minimum profit rate is "exceedingly variable" across different societies, Mill says, because of "the great variableness of two out of its three elements", to wit, the rate of return required for abstinence and the rate of compensation required for ordinary risk-taking.[93] Now, the reward for abstinence in any society depends on the intensity of the general desire to accumulate capital. In turn, the strength of that desire to save and invest for productive purposes varies directly, he insists, not only with expected profits but also with moral and intellectual development:

The effective desire of accumulation is of unequal strength, not only according to the varieties of individual character, but to the general state of society and civilization. . . . Deficient strength of the desire of accumulation may arise from improvidence, or from want of interest in others. Improvidence may be connected with intellectual as well as moral causes. Individuals and communities of a very low state of intelligence are always improvident. A certain measure of intellectual development seems necessary to enable absent things, and especially things future, to act with any force on the imagination and will. The effect of the want of interest in others in diminishing accumulation will be admitted, if we considered how much saving at present takes place, which has for its object the interest of others rather than of ourselves; the education of children, their advancement in life, the future interests of other personal connexions, the power of promoting, by the bestowal of money or time, objects of public or private usefulness.[94]

Higher intelligence implies a better capacity to discern the prudence of saving for future needs not presently felt; and stronger moral sentiments imply a stronger desire to save for the interests of others (including one's fellow workers in a cooperative association). Thus, as 'the general state of society' improves in the sense that the moral and intellectual capacities of most people improve, the general desire to accumulate capital strengthens. As a result, a lower interest reward is customarily expected for abstinence, *ceteris paribus*.

The second variable component of the customary minimum profit rate across social contexts is the required reward for risk-taking, not for taking unusual risks in some particular investment but for taking the ordinary risks associated with any investment in the given society. Mill suggests that this required insurance reward in any society depends on the degree of general security of property. But (and this is the key point) the degree of general security also determines the strength of the general desire to accumulate capital: "The more perfect the security, the greater will be the effective strength of the desire to accumulate".[95] Even if it does not alter the general disposition to hoard, Mill insists, a greater degree of security does strengthen the desire to save of all wealth-seeking individuals, including "those who live on the mere interest of their capital, in common with those who personally engage in production".[96] Moreover, the risk of using wealth as capital (that is, for productive purposes) rather than letting it sit idle "is great in proportion as the general state of society is insecure . . . and for this, the expectation of profit must be sufficient to compensate".[97]

It follows that variations in the degree of general security of property are ultimately the source of 'the great variableness' of the customary minimum profit rate across social contexts. Variations in both the reward conventionally expected for *ordinary* abstinence and the reward expected for *ordinary* risk-taking can be traced to differences in the degree of general security.[98] As general security rises, the customary minimum profit rate falls. By implication, an ideal stationary state at which general security is perfected must also feature a lowest feasible (or *infimum*) rate of profit.[99] Moreover, that infimum profit rate must be associated with the highest general state of moral and intellectual improvement. Violation of civil and property rights would be rare in such an ideal setting. From the imperfect vantage point of our own society, Mill makes clear, we cannot be sure whether general security will be perfected under an egalitarian form of capitalism or some decentralized form of socialism. All that can be inferred for the present is that the minimum profit rate will continue to fall as individuals become more disposed to mutually cooperate and to respect each other's person and property under rules that favour a broad dispersion of wealth. Note that on the implausible assumption that the profit rate falls to zero, Mill's ideal stationary state can be made to resemble the familiar Marxist utopia where labour receives the whole product.

To the extent that capital is insecure in *every* productive use in a given society, the customary minimum profit rate is higher in that society because investors require higher rewards for ordinary abstinence and risk-taking than would be received under ideal conditions of supreme security. In part, insecurity may arise in non-ideal social contexts because persons do not comply fully with the given system of rules. Thus, the ordinary profit rate might remain above the customary minimum in those contexts because property is arbitrarily damaged or stolen, often by government officials, in almost every productive use.[100] Even if it could be supposed that rules of property are perfectly enforced in every social context so that non-compliance is never a source of insecurity, however, the minimum profit rate itself would vary with the nature of the social rules. Mill and Bentham both imply that inegalitarian rules as such – rules that distribute unequal property rights and/or yield great and persistent inequality of wealth unconnected to personal desert – are a source of insecurity. If rights unequal to the fruits of one's own labour and saving are distributed by law and custom among predominantly self-interested wealth-seekers, for example, then the privileged are permitted by society to ignore any moral claims pressed by others to the means of subsistence, thereby rendering them insecure. The unprivileged, lacking an equal claim to the fruits of their own savings, would thus have inadequate incentives to invest, with the implication that available capital is not allocated efficiently among alternative uses. Given that the extent of the capital market is thereby limited artificially by the unequal rules, the customary minimum profit rate is higher than needs be in comparison with the ideal case.[101]

Normative continuity?

An argument might be made for the essential continuity of normative economics, analogous to Hollander's scientific 'continuity thesis'. In this regard, it is important to recognize that the 'marginalist revolution' involved a normative reaffirmation of the 'old' Benthamite utilitarianism. Jevons, Edgeworth, and even Marshall paid short shrift to the modifications of utilitarianism proposed by Mill. Rather, those neoclassical pioneers proposed more or less to operationalize a Benthamite art of economics by precisely measuring and comparing units of happiness across persons.[102] That normative program was later refined (if not rendered vacuous) by the 'ordinalist revolution' of the 1930s and beyond, associated with Lord Robbins, Hicks, Samuelson, and Arrow. The upshot is that interpersonally comparable cardinal utility information has been abandoned in favor of noncomparable preference orderings, and Pareto efficiency has become the main (perhaps sole) surviving criterion of the economic art.[103]

Even from a Benthamite perspective, modern 'ordinalist utilitarianism' represents a significant shift of emphasis in the utilitarian tradition. In effect, Bentham's faith in a utilitarian harmony of abundance, security, subsistence, and equality has been replaced by a virtually exclusive focus on efficiency and growth, with little concern for conflicts between these values and others (including basic rights and distributive justice).

Mill's novel brand of liberal utilitarianism breaks with both Benthamites and moderns over the appeal of indefinitely sustained economic growth. Indeed, given its vision of an ideal stationary state at which general security is perfected under a liberal system of basic rights and substantial economic equality, liberal utilitarianism may seem closer in spirit to influential non-utilitarian liberalisms which give similar prominence to certain equal rights, fair distribution of wealth, encouragement of diverse life-styles, and so on.[104] Nevertheless, Harsanyi, Brandt, Hare, and others have variously argued that utilitarianism might be reworked to take rights and other liberal concerns seriously.[105] It remains an open question whether any of these modern 'rule utilitarianisms' and 'institutional utilitarianisms' improves upon Mill's peculiar doctrine or captures its liberal spirit.[106]

NOTES

1 In this chapter Mill's *Principles of Political Economy* (1848) will be denoted as *POPE*; *Chapters on Socialism* (1879) as *COS*; *On Liberty* (1859) as *OL*; *Utilitarianism* (1861) as *UTIL*; *Considerations on Representative Government* (1861) as *REPGOV*; *The Subjection of Women* (1869) as *SUBJ*; and the *Autobiography* (1873) as *AUTO*. The present reference is to *AUTO, CW* I:221.

2 For Mill's defence of liberal democracy (involving checks against majority power) as opposed to majoritarian democracy (involving no such checks), see *REPGOV, CW* XIX: esp. 422–533. His distinction between "the desire to exercise power over others" and the "disinclination to have power exercised over themselves" is crucial in this context (*CW* XIX:420).

3 *OL, CW* XVIII:224.

4 See *System of Logic, CW* VIII:943–52.

5 *POPE, CW* II:xci–xcii.

6 *AUTO, CW* I:239–41.

7 For insights into Bentham's doctrine, see Harrison 1983; Rosen 1983 and 1987, 121–38; Postema 1986; and Kelly 1990.

8 For clarification of Bentham's conception of the general welfare in terms of these four components, see, e.g., Harrison 1983, 244–62; and Kelly 1990, 73–94, 104–31.

9 Bentham, "Principles of the Civil Code," in John Bowring, ed., *The Works of Jeremy Bentham*, 11 vols. (Edinburgh, 1838–43), I:302 as quoted in Kelly 1990, 73.

10 Kelly (1990, 150–54) suggests, however, that Bentham may have anticipated Mill's famous principle of liberty.

11 Kelly 1990, 103.

12 *POPE, CW* II:392; *AUTO, CW* I:31.

13 *CW* XIII:731. Mill also claimed, in a letter to William Tait dated September 24, 1833, that his earlier work, eventually published as

Essays on Some Unsettled Questions of Political Economy (1844), contained views "in continuation and completion of Ricardo's doctrines" (*CW* XII:178).

14 *POPE, CW* II:xcii. When describing with admiration the 'thorough' mode in which Ricardian political economy was taught to him by his father, Mill emphasizes that "it was one of my father's main objects to make me apply to Smith's more superficial view of political economy, the superior lights of Ricardo, and detect what was fallacious in Smith's arguments, or erroneous in any of his conclusions" (*AUTO, CW* I:31).

15 See, respectively, *POPE, CW* II:116–30; *CW* II:380–99; *CW* II:456–57; *CW* II:577–81; *CW* II:587–617; and *CW* III:733–35. Smith may not really have subscribed to the last 'unsound doctrine', Mill admits, because he occasionally writes as if he believed that the competition of capital lowers profits by raising money wages, and, at other times, even "seems on the very verge of grasping" the basic Ricardian distribution theorem according to which the rate of profits is inversely related to the cost of labour. Telling against Smith's grasp of the basic Ricardian theorem, however, is his view that a general wage tax would raise general prices rather than lower the rate of profits (*CW* III:829–30).

16 See, e.g., *CW* II:570–76.

17 Hollander 1985, II:917.

18 Hollander 1985, 931.

19 In this case, for any given market demand schedule, firms have joint power to shift the perfectly price-inelastic supply schedule toward the origin. Given that demand is not perfectly price-elastic, they have a strong incentive to withhold supply and thereby force purchasers to move upward along their downward-sloping demand curve until natural value or price reaches a level at which industry revenues are as high as possible (even though some goods may remain unsold). Indeed, by even *threatening* to withhold goods from sale, firms might be able to induce *shifts* in the demand schedule away from the origin such that the entire fixed supply can be sold at higher and higher prices.

20 *POPE, CW* II:469.

21 *CW* II:521–22. Mill makes these statements in the context of his discussion of the value of convertible money. As a defender of a version of the quantity theory of money, he makes clear that money is an exceptional commodity in the sense that actual (not merely anticipated) alteration of supply is necessary before the value of money conforms to its cost of production.

22 Neoclassical theorists have pointed out that the problem essentially vanishes if decreasing costs are confined to a range or sector of production that is 'small' relative to the size of the economy. If so-called 'non-convex production' is bounded thus, then an approximation to competitive equilibrium is known to exist. See, for example, Arrow and Hahn 1971, 169–82. An analogous strategy is employed with respect to non-convex consumer preferences.

23 Mill clearly recognizes the phenomenon of increasing returns to scale (*POPE, CW* II:131–52). Moreover, he underscores the fact that efficient production in this case is in tension with the preservation of a perfectly competitive regime of many small-scale producers. He is notably ambivalent about the emergence of large-scale producers as a result of decreasing costs: the economic efficiency gains must be weighed against the social drawbacks associated with the disappearance of "the regime of independent small producers" (*CW* II:141).

24 *POPE, CW* II:475.

25 *CW* II:476. Mill goes on to say in this context that "demand and supply always rush to an equilibrium, but the condition of *stable* equilibrium is when things exchange for each other according to their cost of production, or, in the expression we have used, when things are at their natural value". See also *CW* II:570.

26 See also Baumol and Becker 1952; Hollander 1985, II:483–601.

27 See Forget 1990.

28 For relevant discussion, see Negishi 1989, 155–90.

29 See Chipman 1965 and 1979.

30 *POPE, CW* II:199, 455.

31 *CW* II:10. Note that among the things classed as wealth are scarce objects which *cannot be produced* at all by labour and abstinence. Mill would prefer to include human beings as wealth but he thinks that popular usage precludes this. As he uses the term, therefore, wealth does not include persons or fleeting utilities not embodied in any object (*CW* II:45–50). See also his "important distinction in the meaning of the word wealth, as applied to the provisions of an individual, and to those of a nation, or of mankind" (*CW* II:8).

32 The relevant things have exchange value if the machinery of exchange and price is in place. But exchange need not actually take place or even be possible.

33 *CW* II:199.

34 'Productive labour' means labour that creates wealth. 'Unproductive labour' is not a term of deprecation and means labour that creates other persons or fleeting utilities not embodied in objects.

35 *CW* II:199. 'Productive expenditure' means all forms of capital invest-
    ment, including consumption by workers and their families of the
    'necessaries' required for their habitual standard of living during the
    production process. Expenditure on 'luxuries' and fleeting pleasures is
    'unproductive expenditure'. Productive expenditure tends to enrich the
    community by maintaining or increasing its capacity to produce
    wealth, that is, its stock of capital, including human capital. Unproduc-
    tive expenditure is certainly not to be regretted in an opulent com-
    munity, however. Such expenditure is a sign of the community's
    enjoyment of things other than wealth, and may be directed to 'higher
    purposes' than mere material well-being (*CW* II:53–54).
36 *CW* II:199.
37 *CW* II:200.
38 Mill, 'On the Definition of Political Economy and the Method of
    Investigation Proper to It' (1836), *CW* IV:321. For further discussion, see
    also Hollander 1985 I:66–187.
39 *POPE, CW* II:200.
40 See also V. R. Smith 1985.
41 *POPE, CW* II:200–01.
42 *CW* II:214.
43 *CW* II:235–36.
44 *CW* II:239.
45 *CW* II:412.
46 *CW* II:429.
47 *CW* III:700. See also Hollander 1985, I:335–62.
48 'The cost of labour' is distinct from the commodity wage. What labour
    costs to the capitalist is "a function of three variables: the efficiency of
    labour; the wages of labour (meaning thereby the real reward [or com-
    modity wage] of the labourer); and the greater or less cost [in terms of
    labour and saving] at which the articles comprising that real reward can
    be produced or procured" (*POPE, CW* II:414). If money may be assumed
    an invariable standard of value, then the "the cost of labour . . . is
    correctly represented by the money wages of the labourer" (*CW* III:698).
    The money wage level rises and the rate of profit falls if the commodity
    wage level rises and/or the natural cost values of the 'chief articles'
    comprising the commodity wage basket rise. "But the opposition of
    pecuniary interest thus indicated between the class of capitalists and
    that of labourers, is to a great extent only apparent" (*CW* III:700). This
    is because the commodity wage may be high when the cost of labour is
    relatively low, the articles making up the commodity wage basket
    being produced so efficiently that an ample supply can be provided to
    the workers at comparatively low cost. Thus, a high real wage may
    coexist with a high rate of profit.

49 If customary opinion denies an equal opportunity to acquire job skills
   and thereby impedes the free flow of workers between different
   employments, however, then different habitual standards may exist
   and the commodity wage in each employment tends in the long run to
   be regulated by population increase among the class of workers customarily admitted into that employment (CW III:385–88).

50 CW III:402. The minimum profit is composed of three components: an
   interest payment for providing capital to workers during some period of
   time 'on the best security', that is, on the best guarantee of getting back
   the principal; an insurance payment for bearing the ordinary risk of loss
   across investments; and a salary payment for performing the ordinary
   managerial tasks across investment projects. No insurance reward is
   included for what in this social context is considered extraordinary
   risk-taking in particular investments. Nor are any wages included for
   unusual managerial skills on the part of the investor. As Mill points
   out, the different components of profit might be paid to different
   (classes of) individuals.

51 CW III:738. America is not an 'opulent' country because it has "a large
   reserve of fertile land still unused" for production.

52 CW III:752. Mill says that the ordinary rate of profits may not fall to the
   customary minimum for any of several reasons. In any given social
   context, for example, ordinary profits may be prevented from falling to
   the minimum rate by unproductive waste of capital as a result of rash
   speculation, by technological improvements, by cheap capital imports,
   by capital exports, and so on (CW III:741–46). Moreover, the minimum
   profit rate itself varies across social contexts depending on the degree of
   general security of property. As security improves, therefore, the minimum rate may fall below its level in the earlier context, leaving ordinary profits to adjust accordingly. Finally, when different countries are
   at very different stages of progress, profit rates in the more opulent
   countries cannot fall to their respective minima because, below 'some
   practical minimum', their circulating capital would fly to the less
   opulent countries (CW III:746).

53 CW III:731–32.

54 CW III:723–29. As a result, Mill and Ricardo both claimed (against
   Adam Smith, among others) "that the interest of the landlord is decidedly hostile to the sudden and general introduction of agricultural
   improvements" (CW III:726–27).

55 CW III:729–32.

56 CW III:731.

57 This Ricardian idea of competition is similar to the notion of 'contestable markets' developed recently by William Baumol and his colleagues. See, for example, Baumol 1982; Baumol, Panzar, and Willig

1982; Baumol, Panzar, and Willig 1986, 339–65. Indeed, it may be fair to say that the contestable markets approach represents a rediscovery and elaboration of the Ricardian view.

58 "In particular", Hollander emphasizes, the Ricardian

> cost-price analysis is pre-eminently an analysis of the allocation of scarce resources, proceeding in terms of general equilibrium, with allowance for final demand, and the interdependence of factor and commodity markets. There was a simultaneous (and consistent) attachment to cost theories of value and to the general-equilibrium conception of economic organization as formulated by J. B. Say and much admired by Walras. The demand side, the functional relation betweem cost and output, the supply and demand determination of wages and profits, far from being "radical departures" from Ricardianism, are central to that doctrine. . . . Serious and long-lived misconceptions regarding classicism flow from a failure to recognize that its notions of wages and interest as compensation for effort and abstinence were pertinent only at the macro-economic level where the determinants of aggregate factor supplies are under investigation. . . . (Hollander 1985, II:931–32)

59 See, for example, Solow 1956 and Cass 1965. Unlike the classical approach, these standard neoclassical models view population growth as an exogenous process. In effect, balanced growth involves a stationary ratio of capital to labour, i.e., capital and population are growing at the same rate.

60 For recent models of sustained growth, see, for example, Romer 1986; Jones and Manuelli 1990 and 1992; and Fisher 1992.

61 In his early essay on 'Civilization' (1836), Mill distinguishes a narrow sense of civilization from a larger sense (CW XVIII:117–47). Civilization in the restricted sense (with which the essay is concerned) is "that kind of improvement only, which distinguishes a wealthy and powerful nation from savages or barbarians" (CW XVIII:119). As he makes clear, it involves increasing population, wealth, cooperation, and security. Civilization in the larger sense means "more eminent in the best characteristics of Man and Society; farther advanced in the road to perfection; happier, nobler, wiser" (CW XVIII:119) The abandonment of further economic growth as a means of promoting 'utility in the larger sense' seems to involve a switch from civilization in the narrow sense to civilization in the larger sense.

62 Hollander 1985, II:650.

63 Hollander 1985, II:663.

64 Hollander 1985, II:663–68.

65 Hollander 1985, II:605, 638–68.

66 See, e.g., Berger 1985; Gray 1989, 120–39, 217–38; Lyons 1994; and Skorupski 1989, 283–388.

67 See Riley 1988 and forthcoming.

68 See note 7 of this chapter.

69 In social contexts below the relevant threshold, subsistence cannot be secured or guaranteed by society for any person, even the strong. Something like a Hobbesian state of nature prevails. In effect, general security, made possible by a system of social rules of justice, is impossible, as is the sort of civil liberty which is extensionally equivalent to security. In such a context, subsistence becomes the most valuable ingredient of personal and general welfare: any person must take whatever 'physical nutriment' and other resources are needed for his own survival at the expense of that of others. This may explain Mill's otherwise puzzling admissions that subsistence is more valuable than security and liberty. He refers to "security" as the "most indispensable of all necessaries, after physical nutriment" (*UTIL, CW* X:251), for example, and also says that "liberty" becomes most valuable to any person "after the means of subsistence are assured" (*POPE, CW* II:208–09). Beyond the relevant threshold of development, where a basic right to subsistence can be assured by society, general welfare can and should be promoted by giving priority to general security and subsuming subsistence within security.

70 Even with the caveat expressed in the previous note, Mill may not mean to give security lexical priority over other values. See, e.g., *POPE, CW* III:880–86. But in my view the weight he generally assigns to it is such that lexical priority provides a reasonable interpretation of his approach. See, e.g., *UTIL, CW* X:250–51, 255–56, 259. Keeping in mind that security is equivalent to liberty in the sense of a system of rights and correlative duties, Rawls also reads Mill in this way. See Rawls 1971, pp. 42–43 (n. 23), 122–26, 315–25, 501–02.

71 For ease of exposition, I ignore the idea that general security may vary across different levels of enforcement of the given system of rules. Rather, general security is defined such that no person deviates from the given rules. Given that nobody's legitimate expectations are disappointed, security is in a sense 'maximized' in the context of any given code. But my focus is on the different degrees of general security associated with *distinct* systems of rules and their respective distributions of rights and duties. If security is a function both of the nature of the rules and of their enforcement, and if enforcement is invariably perfect (so that this source of security is always maximized), then my claim may be restated as being that general security is maximized at its highest feasible (or *supremum*) value only in the context of the relevant ideal code.

72 P. J. Kelly (1990, 84) refers to such "expectation utilities" as being of "supreme importance within [Bentham's] legislative project". He tends to argue that Bentham's utilitarian account of justice in terms of general security is superior to Mill's similar account (P. J. Kelly 1990, 7, 109 [n. 17], 205–06, 218).

73 *POPE, CW* III:960–62.

74 Mill leaves to 'private charity' the provision of assistance beyond a bare minimum, and recommends exceptional legal penalties (including denial of the franchise and of permission to procreate) to encourage welfare recipients to support themselves if they are able. See *REPGOV, CW* XIX:467–74, 488–90; *POPE, CW* II:357–60; and *OL, CW* XVIII:304–05.

75 See Riley 1991a.

76 *OL, CW* XVIII:293.

77 *POPE, CW* III:936–71.

78 *OL, CW* XVIII:260–75.

79 In *On Liberty*, Mill discusses this problem of mass conformity at length and proposes to remedy it through a package of various measures. These include: legal enforcement of the individual's right to choose as he likes with respect to purely private matters such as his ideas on all subjects, his intimate life-style, and so on; a program of national education designed to promote tolerance of what others choose in such private matters; and active government support for social pluralism. The last policy might include special subsidies for intellectual and agricultural classes within a predominantly commercial society, for example, as well as suitable immigration measures.

80 *POPE, CW* III:756.

81 *CW* III:755.

82 *CW* II:208, 215. Bentham, in passages quoted by P. J. Kelly (1990, 112–13), mentions a guarantee only for the fruits of labour. Kelly seems to interpret this to imply that, for Bentham, there was no right to a return on capital: "[I]n the long term all unearned benefits [might be redistributed], *even those which are a return on capital*" (p. 127). But Bentham may not have meant to exclude a legitimate reward for capital, given that capital goods are themselves the fruit of labour. Indeed, in his *Defence of Usury* (1816), he agrees in effect with Mill that a return on capital is legitimately earned for abstinence, risk, and/or managerial efforts on the part of investors.

83 *POPE, CW* II–III:227–32, 819–22, 868.

84 *CW* III:755. See also *CW* II–III:218–26, 887–95.

85 For further discussion of the desert principle of distributive justice

associated with capitalism in its best form, see Riley 1989, 122–62, and references cited therein.

86 Mill, 'Vindication of the French Revolution of February 1848', *CW* XX:354. See also his discussion of an ideal 'society between equals' in *UTIL, CW* X:231–33, 243–44, 257–59; and *SUBJ, CW* XXI:293–95, 324–40.

87 Kelly also suggests that, for Bentham, great economic inequality constituted a threat to general security

for two reasons: firstly, the concentration of wealth and power in too few hands is likely to result in both not being used for the benefit of all; and, secondly, this could result in the threat of the economically disenfranchised attempting to restructure the social order [violently] for their own [exclusive class] benefit. (P. J. Kelly 1990, 125)

88 *COS, CW* V:750. See also Mill's letter to Charles Elliot Norton dated June 26, 1870, reprinted in *CW* XVII:1739–40.

89 For Bentham's view, see Kelly's (1990, 168–206) discussion of what he calls Bentham's 'disappointment-preventing principle'. Kelly emphasizes that the

"disappointment-preventing principle" . . . is largely concerned with extending access to property, . . . while protecting those expectations which are derived from the existing distribution of property rights. . . . [It] enables the Benthamite legislator to pursue a policy of the substantial equalization of property holdings while also respecting the pattern of expectations embodied in the existing distribution of property. (pp. 8–9)

Mill clearly recognizes a similar principle. See, e.g., *UTIL, CW* X:242–43, 247–48, 256; *POPE, CW* II:230–33; *COS, CW* V:753; and Riley forthcoming. He apparently intended to offer a full discussion of the principle in his 'Chapters on Socialism' but did not live to complete the task.

90 Fair compensation is due to an owner for any taking of her property by the state but, as Mill makes clear, every legal reform does not amount to a taking. Individuals do not hold title to 'confessedly variable' general taxes or tariffs, for example, and thus cannot claim compensation for changes in those institutions (with the caveat that such changes cannot apply retroactively). The line between a taking of property and a reform with incidental effects on the distribution of property is not always easy to draw, however. If the state has never exercised its power to tax estates or resource rents, for example, or has left taxes fixed for generations, then existing property owners may have some moral claim for compensation if taxes are reformed. See *POPE, CW* II:217–18, 230–33; III:819–22.

91 See, e.g., *CW* III:819–22, 868. More generally, for Mill's principles of fair taxation, see *CW* III:805–72. With the caveat that all persons should be legally guaranteed a basic income exempt from taxation, he generally argues for proportional taxation of any surplus income earned from one's own labour and saving under competitive conditions, and for sharply progressive taxation of all unearned surplus income including gifts, inheritances, resource rents, and the like.

92 *CW* II:402.

93 *CW* II:402–03. Mill does not seem to think that much variation in ordinary management skills exists across social contexts.

94 *CW* II:162–64.

95 *CW* II:163.

96 *CW* II:403.

97 *CW* II:736–37.

98 Recall that the minimum profit rate in any given social context does not include any rewards for what is considered in that context to be *extraordinary* abstinence, risk-taking, or management skills.

99 Given existing customs governing the minimum profit rate in any society, we might say that general security *in that social context* is maximized when the ordinary profit rate falls to the customary minimum rate. But customs undergo improvement under the process of transition ('civilization') to liberal utopia. As development proceeds, the minimum profit rate falls to its lowest possible (or *infimum*) rate and the maximum level of general security rises to its highest possible (or *supremum*) level.

100 *CW* II:162–63, 736–37.

101 Similarly, if rules of property give rise to great and persistent inequality unconnected to personal exertions, that inequality could lead producers to rebel against the regime. Such a risk of revolution endangers every capital investment, and thereby raises the customary minimum profit rate relative to the ideal case.

102 Not only did Mill want to go beyond the old radicalism, he also made clear his aversion to what he considered the false precision of the marginalist gloss on it. In a letter to John Elliot Cairnes dated December 5, 1871, for example, he complains that Jevons has "a mania for encumbering questions with useless complications, and with a notation implying the existence of greater precision in the data than the questions admit of". In his view, this "vice . . . is one preeminently at variance with the wants of the time, which demand that scientific deductions should be made as simple and as easily intelligible as they can be without ceasing to be scientific" (*CW* XVII:1862–63). He seems to be alluding in this passage to the contemporary need to make

political economy as accessible as possible to the working classes, to forestall their acceptance of revolutionary socialistic doctrines which he argued involved serious errors of political economy.

103 According to the (weak) Pareto principle, one outcome (market allocation or growth path) is judged better than another if everyone prefers the one to the other. In the absence of unanimity, no judgement is prescribed.

104 See, e.g., Rawls 1971 and 1993a; Dworkin 1981, 1987a, 1987b, and 1991.

105 See, e.g., Harsanyi 1977a, 1977b, and 1992; Brandt 1979 and 1992; and Hare 1981.

106 For further discussion, see Riley forthcoming.

9 Civilization and culture as moral concepts

Much has been written, admiring and dismissive, on Mill the preeminent champion of individuality. And appropriately so; *On Liberty* is likely to remain the most widely known of his social and political writings, one that seems never to lose its power to stimulate both thought and emotion. Analysis of *Utilitarianism* and his other writings on ethical questions properly centres on what he says about individual motivation and behaviour. And as one of the greatest of Classical economists, Mill was in the tradition whose analysis and values were based on the individual's self-interest. This insistent concern for individuality should not, however, preclude attention to his portrayal and evaluation of humans as social animals.

It is significant – to touch only on the most contentious area, economics – that the full title of Mill's major treatise is *Principles of Political Economy with some of their applications to social philosophy*. And that after finishing his other great treatise, *A System of Logic*, he told Alexander Bain that his next project was a work on ethology (Bain 1901, 159; Bain 1882, 78–79), one that L. S. Feuer thought would have been a "masterpiece of sociology" (Feuer 1976, 87). What he had in mind was an analysis and exposition of "the science which corresponds to the art of education; in the widest sense of the term, including the formation of national or collective character as well as individual" (*System of Logic, CW* VIII:869). Though he never wrote this work, it is not fanciful to look for his views of civilization and culture in this context.

There are here at least four related implications. First, the study is of "improvement"; second, a science and an art are needed; third, "character" implies that human nature in general and in particular is the basic focus; fourth, normative as well as descriptive and analytic evidence is essential. The first of these, being fundamental to everything in the discussion below, needs no special comment here, except that, as I have written in another context, "If one believes in and strives for the 'improvement of mankind' . . . one must believe that mankind needs improvement and also that mankind can be improved" (J. M. Robson 1976, 143).[1] Brief discussions of the other implications will serve as introduction to more specific discussions of Mill's views.

Mill's formulation of the relation between science and art is as instructive as it is unusual, connecting as it does apparently abstract analysis of large subjects or even particular issues with practical precepts and moral goals.

The art proposes to itself an end to be attained, defines the end, and hands it over to the science. The science receives it, considers it as a phenomenon or effect to be studied, and having investigated its causes and conditions, sends it back to art with a theorem of the combination of circumstances by which it could be produced. Art then examines these combinations of circumstances, and according as any of them are or are not in human power, pronounces the end attainable or not. The only one of the premises, therefore, which Art supplies, is the original major premise, which asserts that the attainment of the given end is desirable. Science then lends to Art the proposition . . . that the performance of certain actions will attain the end. From these premises Art concludes that the performance of these actions is desirable, and finding it also practicable, converts the theorem into a rule or precept. (*System of Logic, CW* VIII:944–45)[2]

Applying this formulation to Mill's outline of ethology, one sees that if he follows his own precepts, his own accounts of national as well as individual character will be guided by educational goals, though its findings will not be determined by them. And this, though he never developed a science of ethology, will be seen to be the case in his accounts of civilization.

Of even more importance is Mill's understanding of human nature. When assessing it, one must remember that since his time relevant evidence as well as attitudes developed in anthropology, sociology, evolutionary biology, and especially in genetics, create a necessary gap between our concepts and his. Seeing what those concepts are, however, is important not only in establishing his position but also – because his programme is essentially practical – in appreciating the arguments and policies of the period.

Just how important the questions are is seen in his account of the changes that marked his revision of his teachers' precepts, though he is able to place the blame for dangerous beliefs on an enemy as much his as theirs, intuitional metaphysics. By the 1850s, when he drafted his *Autobiography*, he had "long felt" that a disposition "so agreeable to human indolence," that it must be "attacked at the very root," was the prevailing tendency

to regard all the marked distinctions of human character as innate, and in the main indelible, and to ignore the irresistible proofs that by far the greater part of those differences, whether between individuals, races, or sexes, are such as not only might but naturally would be produced by differences in circumstances. . . .

This tendency "is one of the chief hindrances to the rational treatment of great social questions and one of the greatest stumbling blocks to human improvement" (*CW* I:270).

In Mill's account, human beings by nature display certain characteristics and behaviours beyond what the "human" narrowly denotes logically.[3] Not being an adherent of natural law, he does not see these as valuable either by definition or necessity; that is, the "natural" may not, and if and when uncontrolled and undeveloped by man's "art," probably will not, conduce to individual and social utility.

For convenient discussion, his comments on human nature can be placed in three categories: *needs*, *constituents*, and *capacities*. The *needs* are both individual (physical) and social. Of the former, Mill ranks liberty as coming second only to the means of subsistence ("food and raiment") (*Principles of Political Economy*, *CW* II:208; *Subjection of Women*, *CW* XXI:336.) With liberty must be placed the desire to choose one's own mode of life, expressed in a passage that merits quotation as an example of how deeply based in personal experience were the supposedly icy Mill's precepts:

Let any man call to mind what he himself felt on emerging from boyhood – from the tutelage and control of even loved and affectionate elders – and entering upon the responsibilities of manhood. Was it not like the physical effect of taking off a heavy weight, or releasing him from obstructive, even if not otherwise painful, bonds? Did he not feel twice as much alive, twice as much a human being, as before? (*Subjection of Women*, *CW* XXI:337)

The freedom he seeks escapes inhuman "moulds," "patterns," "compression," "stunting and dwarfing," "restrictions," "restraint" (*On Liberty*, *CW* XVIII:esp. 265–72; *Autobiography*, *CW* I:260; *Subjection of Women*, *CW* XXI:340). The solitude that enables self-development, he says, has both social and individual utility (*Principles of Political Economy*, *CW* III:756). The universal need for internal culture, cultivation of feelings and of both active and passive capacities (*Autobiography*, *CW* I:147), shows that growth and change are naturally desired; diversity and the development resulting from free choice of one's mode of life are "co-ordinate" with "civilization, instruction, education, culture," and are, indeed, "a necessary part and condition" of them (*On Liberty*, *CW* XVIII:261).

That what he says about the social needs of humans can be summarized quickly does not hide their importance, as will be seen when other aspects of human nature are considered. Specifically he observes that humans require sympathizing support and objects of admiration and reverence ("Bentham," *CW* X:96), and need to pay (not just should pay) attention of others' opinions (*Principles of Political Economy*, *CW* II:206, 370ff).

Turning to what Mill offers as *constituent* characteristics defining human nature, which are closely related to needs, one finds very little that is strictly physical: humans are feeling creatures who are capable of reason. Another constituent, essential to practical reason and hence to improvement, is expectation based on foresight.[4]

Two lists of the non-physical constitutes of human nature, one from his "Bentham," the other from *Utilitarianism*, are comprehensive, if not analytically admirable. In the former one finds love of justice; a sense of honour and personal dignity; love of beauty, order, congruity, consistency, and conformity to end; love of power, of action and of ease; and love of loving (*CW* X:95–96). In the latter list, as part of the argument for higher pleasures, which they define, appear pride; love of liberty and of personal independence; love of power, excitement, and tranquillity; and a sense of dignity (varying in proportion to higher faculties) (*CW* X:212ff).

It will be noted that improvement is more than casually connected with most of the needs and characteristics Mill mentions, and the relation is brought out even more obviously when one looks to the *capacities* of human nature: "there is hardly anything valuable in the natural man except capacities – a whole world of possibilities, all of them dependent upon eminently artifical discipline for being realized" ("Nature," *CW* X:393). The most important capacity, unquestionably, is for good behaviour in the most exalted sense, which cannot be expected to occur automatically among the passive. Though, Mill avers,

> the moral feelings are not innate, but acquired, they are not for that reason the less natural. It is natural to man to speak, to reason, to build cities, to cultivate the ground, though these are acquired faculties. The moral feelings are not indeed a part of our nature, in the sense of being in any perceptible degree present in all of us. . . . Like the other acquired capacities above referred to, the moral faculty, if not part of our nature, is a natural outgrowth from it; capable, like them, in a certain small degree, of springing up spontaneously; and susceptible of being brought by cultivation to a high degree of development. (*Utilitarianism*, *CW* X:230)

The *capacities* Mill dwells on, unlike the *tendencies* of human nature,[5] are all laudable, but no one could assert that he held an extreme Romantic view that humankind has no capacity for evil, particularly when one considers that the categorizing words most commonly associated with "capacities" in his accounts are "powers" and "susceptibilities." A more useful judgment is that he employs the term in hortatory passages where the improvement of mankind is at issue. (Mill shared with his father, though in a less grim sense, the Manichean view that human history revealed a constant battle between the forces of good and evil, and that morality entails a recognition of evil so that it can be combatted.)

In two places in his "Bentham," "desire" and "wish" are significantly brought very close to "capacity" and "power." In the first of these he says that Bentham never recognized man as "a being capable of pursuing spiritual perfection as an end; of desiring, for its own sake, the conformity of his own character to his standard of excellence"; in the second, that Bentham's system of ethics recognized "no such wish as that of self-culture, we may even say no such power, as existing in human nature" (*CW* X:95, 98). And in *Utilitarianism* the *capacities* mentioned are for the cultivation of sensibilities, sacrifice for others, disinterested devotion to one's fellow man and to God, labouring and combining for generous, public, and social purposes, and, perhaps now annoyingly to some, as an explicit distinction between man and brute, "acquiring a love of cleanliness" (*CW* X:230).[6]

It seems clear that there are in human nature, whether physical or moral, elements necessary to but not sufficient for improvement. Judgments and decisions about priorities and entailments are needed to promote the best available results. One must consequently recognize the importance to Mill of qualitative differences among moral motives and outcomes, a recognition that has resulted in much controversy over the appropriateness of such tests in the utilitarian ethical system initiated by Bentham's insistence on quantitative measures. That matter is treated elsewhere in this volume; here attention need be paid only to its implications for interpretation of Mill's views on civilized societies.

His accounts are marked by sets of paired correlative terms. "Quick," "strong," "active," energetic," and "open," are frequently attributed to nature, as well as "slow," "weak," "passive," "susceptible," and "close": the contrast is markedly in favour of the former set, even when "impulsiveness" is seen as a concomitant, and even when the necessity of "prudence" and "reserve" is admitted.[7] The clear qualitative judgment is even more evident when one realizes that these are on a scale from little to much (zero is impossible, as the attributes are evidently universal, and infinity is not realizable or even desirable for separate attributes). That is, quantity curiously becomes a test in kinds of judgment where quality normally reigns. (It is as though a person of many judgments were equivalent to – or better than – one of much judgment.) Negative assessments appear in two well-known passages: in *On Liberty* Mill refers to the "general average of mankind" as being "moderate in intellect" and in "inclinations"; in the *Autobiography* the "great majority of mankind" are presented as having "but a moderate degree of sensibility and of capacity for enjoyment" (*CW* XVIII:271; *CW* I:147). The clearest statements of all come in the third chapter of *On Liberty*, where, for example, we find this: "To say that one person's desires and feelings are stronger and more various than those of another, is merely to say that he has more of the raw material of human nature, and is therefore capable, perhaps of more evil, but certainly of more good." "Strong," "vivid," "powerful": these are the proper modifiers of "the stuff of which heroes are made" (*CW* XVIII:263–64).

For Mill, then, energy, activity, and growth are essential and available; this cluster of words implies that humankind *must*, physiologically and psychologically, move and change, and *should* move and change in particular ways. Another cluster of terms points to the engines for that movement: enthusiasm, high aspirations, and the pursuit of spiritual perfection; the desire for conformity to a standard of excellence, the love of congruity and of consistency in all things. He chose as epigraph to *On Liberty* Von Humboldt's desideratum: "a harmonious development of human powers to a complete and consistent whole."

This analysis serves cynical practice if one believes that *plus ça change, plus c'est la même chose. Universal* human nature, by pre-evolutionary definition, is fixed, ahistorical, given, and history will continue to be one damn thing after another. Knowing the facts about human nature can contribute to reform only if *individual* human nature can alter and be altered. And that is Mill's position. Particular variable manifestations of human nature should not be taken as fixed characteristics of universal human nature. From the study of history, he says, one comes to appreciate "the astonishing pliability of our nature, and the vast effects which may under good guidance be produced upon it by honest endeavour" ("Civilization," *CW* XVIII:145).[8]

In sum, when he alludes to, comments on, describes, or analyzes "human nature," normally, and especially when the passages are extensive, he is referring (a) to individual character or type, or (b) to group or class or nation. His interest lying in modification of behaviour, he looks not at abstract human nature, but at individuals and groups from and in which action emerges. Evidence is seen in what may have been unconsciously presented pairs of terms such as "human nature and [human] life,"[9] "man's nature and circumstances," "man and . . . man's position in the world" ("Bentham," *CW* X:90, 89), "humanity and human affairs" (*System of Logic, CW* VIII:925), "human nature and human history" (Notes to James Mill's *Analysis, CW* XXXI:162), "human nature and . . . fact" (*Subjection of Women, CW* XXI:295), "human nature and conduct" (*Inaugural Address Delivered to the University of St. Andrews, CW* XXI:229), "human nature and human society" (*ibid., CW* XXI:256; *System of Logic, CW* VIII:943, 950), and "human and social life" (*Autobiography, CW* I:245). There is evident a mental habit, reflected I believe in his recommendations for action, of distinguishing between, while connecting, individual and society, general and particular, logical and pragmatic.

If Mill is seen as a renegade from philosophic radicalism (his own label and one he did not think he betrayed), the charge may be based on his mature views about the means – and the possibility – of improving mankind, which resulted from his adopting a radically different philosophy of history.[10] He thought, following the lead of Thomas Carlyle and the Saint-Simonians, that he could identify in the early 1830s a "Spirit of the Age," different from but also inheriting from the "spirits" of past ages, and containing the seeds of the coming one. The term is consonant with other contemporary ones, all indicating that change was occurring, whether for good or ill,[11] but the dominant attitude, in which Mill shared and to which he contributed, was that there was improvement. Indeed, belief in process almost insists on belief in at least the possibility of progress.

In essence what Mill adopted was a cyclical pattern explaining human history as a succession of "critical" and "organic" periods; "transitional periods" – such as the one he lived in – grow out of the former and into the latter. In organic periods people are united by shared positive beliefs that bond them in sympathy and hence in mutual action; when shared belief collapses, a critical period begins, marked by negativism, scepticism, and selfishness. The exact details of this scheme, particularly as elaborated into positivism by Auguste Comte (originally a Saint-Simonian), did not attract Mill, but its outlines can be seen in his later thought. Though he continued to hold that the order characteristic of an organic period is needed to preserve the social union, he mandated the diversity essential for advance; the best social arrangements are those that nourish the beneficial aspects of critical periods within the framework of an organic state – though one radically unlike the pedantocracy insisted on by Comte.

Even more significant for Mill's views on civilization is his extracting from these and other sources, including his experience in the Examiner's Office of the East India Company, an acceptance of the relativity of social and institutional norms. He came to argue that each element of social organization should be seen in its historical context. Old and prevailing forms should be neither despised nor revered, but examined for their significance historically and consequently practically. As early as the later 1820s, he says:

> ... I ceased to consider representative democracy as an absolute principle, and regarded it as a question of time, place, and circumstance; though I now looked upon the choice of political institutions as a moral and educational question more than one of material interests, thinking that it ought to be decided mainly by the consideration, what great improvement in life and culture stands next in order for the people concerned, as the condition of their further progress, and what institutions are most likely to promote that; nevertheless this change in the premises of my political philosophy did not alter my practical political creed as to the requirements of my own time and country. (*Autobiography*, CW I:177)

Now, as one approaches a more precise account of Mill's positions on culture and civilization, the importance of the fourth consideration can be seen. In his allusions to human nature, as in many other places, one can see a blend of description, analysis, and judgment. That is, one cannot always discern whether comments apply specifically and restrictively to human nature as it is seen to be, or as it essentially must be, or as it should be; and, furthermore, one cannot always discern whether such comments are intended to apply to individuals, to classes, or to humankind in the abstract.

What is certain is that determining the purely abstract is of less interest to him than using description to support inductions leading to proper judgment. While he refers to universal human nature, individual human nature, and the human nature of groups (class or nation), the majority of his references are to the latter two, and individuals and groups are shown to have "better" and "higher" characteristics, as well as "worse" and "lower" ones.

What direction the constituents of human nature should be given can be seen through a study of varied individuals and groups to determine what their "natures" are, and then to apply criteria determining which are "higher" and which "lower." Mill did not make an initial induction according to his canons of proof (*System of Logic*, CW VII:388–404), but he does present evidence of different kinds, some of it derived from personal experience.[12] And in his essay specifically on civilization, he adopts the praiseworthy practice of providing a defining distinction that can guide analysis and comment. "Civilization," he says, "like other terms of the philosophy of human nature," has two significations; it "sometimes stands for human improvement in general, and sometimes for certain kinds of improvement in particular" ("Civilization," *CW* XVIII:119). Significant parameters of his thought are here indicated: terms of this kind come within the purview of "the philosophy of human nature," and this one centres on human improvement in general and in particular circumstances.

Human nature, it may be said, is both the efficient cause and final end of improvement; therefore the desired movement from actual to ideal states depends on assessment of motivation and agreement on values. For Mill, as for almost all his contemporaries, one certain characteristic of a "high" civilization is that it displays a "high" culture, the judgment being a moral more than a material one. This understanding is most evident in the polemics of Matthew Arnold, whose *Culture and Anarchy* brought the implications of the term into public dispute. Though he and Mill are usually seen to hold incompatible views on individual liberty, on culture there is sufficient consonance to make Arnold's criteria useful in looking at Mill's desiderata. Essential to Arnold are disinterestedness, curiosity, a blending of "Hellenism" ("spontaneity of consciousness") and "Hebraism" ("strictness of conscience"), a harmonious and general expansion of individual and social powers, the triumph of reason and the will of God, the playing of a fresh current of thought upon our stock notions and habits, the supremacy of the best self in individual and nation, and, perhaps most characteristically, a union of "sweetness" and "light." Extracting from this list the will of God and the implication that the best self of the nation might cramp that of the individual, and allowing for some dissonance in terminology, one can make of Arnold's views a fairly good summary of Mill's. Important aspects of their programmes overlap: both see that improving individual culture is essential in improving society (though for Arnold the danger is anarchy rather than stagnation); both hold to the notions of organic and critical periods in history; and both insist on the vital cultural importance of education.

The similarities with Arnold are more evidence of Mill's concern to broaden the utilitarian account of values. Among the less welcome similarities in this context is a shared use of scatter-gun definitions that inhibit confident summary. In Mill's analyses of human action and character most commonly one finds a three-fold distinction that is initially inviting to the tidy mind.

That in "Bentham" is clear enough. Bentham, in judging only the moral aspect of behaviour and character – Mill might here have omitted character – ignored other elements by which "our sentiments towards the human being may be, ought to be, and without entirely crushing our own nature cannot but be, materially influenced." (Not to be overlooked here are the three-fold requirements, "may," "ought," and "can.")

Every human action has three aspects: its moral aspect, or that of its right and wrong; its aesthetic aspect, or that of its beauty; its sympathetic aspect, or that of its loveableness. The first addresses itself to our reason and conscience; the second to our imagination; the third to our human fellow-feeling. According to the first, we approve or disapprove; according to the second, we admire or despise; according to the third, we love, pity, or dislike. The morality of an action depends on its foreseeable consequences; its beauty, and its loveableness, or the reverse, depend on the qualities which it is evidence of. . . . It is not possible for any sophistry to confound these three modes of viewing an action; but it is very possible to adhere to one of them exclusively, and lose sight of the rest. (CW X:112–13)

Similarly, in *Utilitarianism* Mill asserts that judging goodness only by a moral standard blinds one to "the other beauties of character which go towards making a human being loveable or admirable," that is, "their sympathies" and "their artistic perceptions" (CW X:221). One can infer that without a fuller vision the engine of improvement cannot be started nor its goals properly conceived.

These accounts indicate that Mill wants all human actions judged according to their *moral, aesthetic*, and *sympathetic* aspects, and holds that consideration of them all is necessary for good policy. Elsewhere he gives accounts somewhat different from, if not inconsistent with, these. In another section of *Utilitarianism*, for instance, three distinct categories again appear, when he asserts that one element, punishability, marks off "morality in general" from expediency and worthiness (CW X:247). More extensively in the *System of Logic*, when setting forth the basis of sound policy, he argues that justifying one's judgment to others depends on establishing premises. These, with their principal conclusions, would provide an "Art of Life," with "three departments, Morality, Prudence, or Policy, and Aesthetics; the Right, the Expedient, and the Beautiful or Noble, in human conduct and works" (*CW* VIII:949). In the opening page of the chapter that argues that case, Mill claims that ethics or morality "is properly a portion of the art corresponding to the sciences of human nature and society." Until the third edition (1851) that sentence continued, "the remainder consisting of prudence or policy, and the art of education" (*CW* VIII:943). And in the manuscript an earlier, cancelled version of this clause was: "Morality together with Prudence or Policy comprising the whole of the Art."

Another three-fold distinction appears when, in his *Inaugural Address at St. Andrews*, Mill designs an ideal university education perhaps suited only to those of his capacity. At the moment, the "two kinds of education" that schools and universities are "intended to promote" (he would not say "do promote") are

intellectual education, and moral education: knowledge and the training of the knowing faculty, conscience and that of the moral faculty. These are the two main ingredients of human culture; but they do not exhaust the whole of it. There is a third division, which, if subordinate, and owing allegiance to the two others, is barely inferior to them, and not less needful to the completeness of the human being; I mean the aesthetic branch; the culture that comes through poetry and art, and may be described as the education of the feelings, and the cultivation of the beautiful. (*CW* XXI:251)

This classification is comparable to that in *On Liberty* where reference is made to the "mental, moral, and aesthetic stature" of which human nature is capable (*CW* XVIII:270).[13] The place that utility has in these schemes is most concisely indicated in "Centralisation," when Mill asserts that the "greatest" of collective interests, which are not usually classed "under the head of interest," i.e., "*l'utile*," are "*le vrai, le beau, et le bien*." Pursuit of these leads to "inward, not outward" rewards, and "external fruits only in a distant future" (*CW* XIX:595–96).

In "Civilization" Mill provides a definition sufficient to introduce his prescriptions for the best life for social animals. In the wider sense, Mill says, a "country" (perhaps "nation" would be closer in modern usage) is called "more civilized if we think it[14] more improved; more eminent in the best characteristics of Man and Society; farther advanced in the road to perfection; happier, nobler, wiser" (*CW* XVIII:119). The repetition of the comparative "more" indicates not just temporal but cultural placing on the "road to perfection" – a path with a terminus defined as "happier, nobler, wiser." (That they are comparatives rather than superlatives is indicative of Mill's insistence on active process.)

In this sense, use of the term "civilization" implies a moral judgment, but Mill is aware of the apparent neutrality of its narrower sense, in which it stands for "that kind of improvement only, which distinguishes a wealthy and powerful[15] nation from savages or barbarians." In that acceptation, one properly can refer to "the vices or the miseries of civilization," and seriously ask if "civilization is on the whole a good or an evil." Though, he says, using what is probably the editorial "we" characteristic of journalism, "we entertain no doubt on this point" and hold "that civilization is a good, that it is the cause of much good, and not incompatible with any," there is "other good, much even of the highest good, which civilization in this sense does not provide for, and some which it has a tendency (though that tendency may be counteracted) to impede" (*CW* XVIII:119).

Comparison blends with definition of the term: the "civilized" excels the "savage" through size and density of population and fixity of location, and in commerce, manufacture, and agriculture, in cooperation,[16] in acceptance of guidance and discipline, and in taking pleasure in society.[17] Also, "in an early stage of civilization," both of the "two elements of importance and influence among mankind," property and "powers and acquirements of mind . . . are confined to a few persons" (*CW* XVIII:121). Another fundamental distinction is that in savage life

there is little or no law, or administration of justice; no systematic employment of the collective strength of society, to protect individuals against injury from one another; every one trusts to his own strength or cunning, and where that fails, he is generally without resource.

The prerequisites for communities to become and continue "progressive" in these desirable "elements" are seen in similar terms as "sufficient knowledge of the arts of life, and sufficient security of property and person." Mill judges (not surprisingly) that considering both past achievements and present "rapid advances," the term "civilization" in this sense is most properly applied to modern Europe and preeminently to Great Britain (*CW* XVIII:120–21).

This last observation should be signal enough that description does not imply approval or forestall criticism. In fact, "the age" is not "equally advanced or equally progressive" in all kinds of "improvement"; indeed in some it seems "stationary, in some even retrograde."[18] In various contexts Mill is scathing about the mores and manners of the dominant middle class: celebrating the ability to make money does not entail celebration of blind dedication to money-making. Modern civilization is marked by "a relaxation of individual character: or rather, the concentration of it within the narrow sphere of the individual's money-getting pursuits"; the "energies of the middle classes are almost confined to money-getting, and those of the higher classes are nearly extinct" (*CW* XVIII:129, 130).

Another observation indicating the need for judgment will be familiar to readers of *On Liberty*;[19] one remarkable effect of civilizing tendencies is "that power passes more and more from individuals, and small knots of individuals, to masses: that the importance of masses becomes constantly greater, that of individuals less" (*CW* XVIII:121). Among the "moral effects" of civilization is "the insignificance into which the individual falls in comparison with the masses"; everyone "becomes dependent, for more and more of what most nearly concerns him, not upon his own exertions, but upon the general arrangements of society." The "growing insignificance of the individual in the mass ... corrupts the very fountain of the improvement of public opinion itself; it corrupts public teaching; it weakens the influence of the more cultivated few over the many" (*CW* XVIII:129, 133–34).

Similarly, he asks rhetorically in "Civilization" whether, given the "wonderful development of physical and mental power on the part of the masses," there has been any increase in the "corresponding quantity of intellectual power or moral energy" in those who have "enjoyed superior advantages?" His answer is "No." "There is a great increase of humanity, a decline of bigotry, as well as of arrogance and the conceit of class[20] among our conspicuous classes," but "no increase of shining ability, and a very marked decrease of vigour and energy" (CW XVIII:125–26).

Because the "spectacle, and even the very idea, of pain, is kept more and more out of the sight of those classes who enjoy in the fulness the benefits of civilization," the cruelty evident in Classical cultures – and he should have added, but did not, in contemporary less civilized cultures – is judged differently by moderns. The "pain which they inflicted, they were in the habit of voluntarily undergo-ing from slight causes; it did not appear to them as great an evil, as it appears, and as it really is, to us, nor did it in any way degrade their minds" (CW XVIII:130–31). (He seems not to make the same allowance for contemporary cruelty in other "uncivilized" lands.) Negatively, then, "the more opulent classes of modern civilized communities" are much more "amiable and humane," but much less "heroic," that is, much less 'ready, for a worthy object, to do and to suffer, but especially to do, what is painful or disagreeable." They lack what is essential for "a great character": "Heroism is an active, not a passive quality" (CW XVIII:131–32).

Mill's ideas developed and were expressed, it should be recalled, in a period when ethnography was an amateur pursuit, and distinc-tions among and judgments about various "races," "cultures," and even "nations" were based more on traditional and geographic con-siderations than on inductive analysis of causes and effects.[21] It is well also to consider that, after more than a century of both dispas-sionate and passionate discussion, very different responses are likely to such questions as, Can different civilizations be equally called civilized? and Are all cultures cultured?

What can one say, in terms appropriate to Mill's own time of his own role in the consideration of such questions? While he was not himself a collector of social scientific data, he read widely in the literature, and interpreted the evidence from the position of a leading student of method with an intense interest in results. What he wished to ally himself with was the encouraging European tendency towards "the philosophic study of past and of foreign civilizations," a tendency "not wholly imperceptible even in this country, the most insular of all the provinces of the republic of letters" ("State of Society in America" [1836], CW XVIII:94). In this context his aspirations are well expressed in a letter to Auguste Comte:

Malgré la brièveté de la vie humaine, nous pouvons l'un et l'autre espérer de voir la position sociale et le caractère national de chaque portion importante du genre humain rattachés aux lois de la nature humaine et aux propriétés du milieu organique général ou particulier par une filiation aussi certaine sinon aussi complète que celle qui existe aujourd'hui dans les sciences les plus avancées. Je serais bien heureux si je me croyais capable de prendre une part vraiment importante, bien que secondaire, à ce grand travail. (*Earlier Letters*, CW XIII:510 [22 Mar. 1842])

It is in this light that one may attempt to assess his disparate comments on different cultures and national characteristics. Specifically on "race" he had little to say; in a biological sense, he considered it, like sex, an "accident of birth," not a measure of worth. But like others of his time, he tended to apply it to groups that were indeed genetically loosely interrelated, but distinguished from one another by behaviour and belief. His position is best seen in a letter to Charles Dupont-White, where he asserts that, as his article on Michelet shows, he did not deny, but in fact admits "pleinement," "l'influence des races." What he objects to is the current tendency – the result especially of the reaction of the nineteenth century to eighteenth-century ideas – to attribute all varieties among peoples and individuals to "des différences indélébiles de nature," without considering whether the influences "de l'éducation et du milieu social et politique" do not supply sufficient explanation. With reference to observed "différences de caractère entre les peuples celtiques et les peuples anglo-saxons," Mill agrees that "la race y entre pour beaucoup," but asks – rhetorically – if "la diversité dans le développement historique de la France et de l'Angleterre . . . ne suffisait pas à elle seule comme explication?" (*Later Letters*, CW XV:691 [6 Apr. 1860]).

The term that better expresses Mill's attitude in that passage and elsewhere, and avoids the danger of introducing anachronistic biological explanations, is "national character," which takes a prominent place in Mill's criticism of Bentham's universalism.

That which alone causes any material interests to exist, which alone enables any body of human beings to exist as a society, is national character: *that* it is, which causes one nation to succeed in what it attempts, another to fail; one nation to understand and aspire to elevated things, another to grovel in mean ones; which makes the greatness of one nation lasting, and dooms another to early and rapid decay. . . . A philosophy of laws and institutions, not founded on a philosophy of national character, is an absurdity. ("Bentham," *CW* X:99)

Because he took little account of "national character and the causes which form and maintain it," Bentham

was precluded from considering, except to a very limited extent, the laws of a country as an instrument of national culture: one of their most important aspects, and in which they must of course vary according to the degree and kind of culture already attained; as a tutor gives his pupil different lessons according to the progress already made in his education. (*CW* X:105)

Laws, then, as well as education and the social and political milieu, as he remarked to Dupont-White, are essential considerations. And the same insistence is found in a letter to Charles Wentworth Dilke, where he comes down on Dilke for apparently assuming in his *Greater Britain* that there are "no sources of national character but race and climate." But since in some places Dilke displays "a strong sense of the good and bad influences of education, legislation, and social circumstances," Mill infers only that Dilke does not go so far as he "in believing these last causes to be of prodigiously greater efficacy than either race or climate or the two combined" (*CW* XVII:1563 [9 Feb. 1869]).

The passage quoted above, in which Bentham is criticized for failing to consider the state of development of the national character when prescribing laws, continues with a strong argument for comparative studies in deciding on policy.

The same laws would not have suited our wild ancestors, accustomed to rude independence, and a people of Asiatics bowed down by military despotism: the slave needs to be trained to govern himself, the savage to submit to the government of others. The same laws will not suit the English, who distrust everything which emanates from general principles, and the French, who distrust whatever does not so emanate. Very different institutions are needed to train to the perfection of their nature, or to constitute into a united nation and social polity, an essentially *subjective* people like the Germans, and an essentially *objective* people like those of Northern and Central Italy; the one affectionate and dreamy, the other passionate and worldly; the one trustful and loyal, the other calculating and suspicious; the one not practical enough, the other overmuch; the one wanting individuality, the other fellow-feeling; the one failing for want of exacting enough for itself, the other for want of conceding enough to others.[22]

What should supersede Bentham's universalism is indicated in Mill's "State of Society in America":

Each nation, and the same nation in every different age, exhibits a portion of mankind, under a set of influences, different from what have been in operation anywhere else: each, consequently, exemplifies a distinct phasis of humanity; in which the elements which meet and temper one another in a perfect human character are combined in a proportion more or less peculiar.

Were all alike, "improvement" could occur only within national limits, but fortunately each can see "in some other a model of the excellencies corresponding to its own deficiences," and so no longer "go on confirming themselves in their defects by the consciousness of their excellencies, but betake themself, however tardily, to profiting by each other's example." Abandoning universalism obviously does not mean accepting amoral cultural relativism.

Looking only at the present age, Mill asserts that each of the "four great nations," England, France, Germany, and the United States of America, shows, "either in its social condition, in its national character, or in both, some points of indisputable and pre-eminent superiority over all the others," as well as "some deep-seated and grievous defects" peculiar to itself. As a result, the "state of society in each, and the type of human nature which it exhibits, are subjects of most instructive study to the others" (CW XVIII:94 [1836]).

Specific characteristics of the European nations mentioned in "Bentham" (omitting the Italian) are somewhat differently referred to in an earlier discussion, where Mill asserts that "the German nation is eminently *speculative*, the English essentially *practical*, and the French endeavour to unite both qualities, having an equal turn for framing general theories and for reducing them into practice," and implies what may usefully be learned from this comparison: "it might be shown that every one of the three nations possesses some intellectual and some moral qualities in a higher state of developement than either of the other two nations; and that each excels in some department, even of industry" ("Comparison of the Tendencies of French and English Intellect" [1833], CW XXIII:444–45).

The fullest discussion of this question, with comments on English, German, Italian, Spanish, and French cultures, comes in an article, "Guizot's Lectures on European Civilization," that Mill (as editor of the *London and Westminster Review*) wrote jointly with Joseph Blanco White.[23] First, as to England, its civilization has worked mainly for "the improvement of the social arrangements, and of everything relating to external life." As a result, society "has developed itself more nobly and more brilliantly than *man*: immediate and narrow applications have been more thought of than principles: the *nation* makes a greater figure in history, than the individuals who compose it" (*CW* XVIII:374–75 [1836]).

Germany provides a contrast: there "social or external progress has . . . been difficult and slow: the coarseness of German manners has been proverbial till our own days. But compare "the mental powers displayed by the German [religious] reformers . . . with the semi-barbarous manners which they themselves betray, and which . . . may be taken as samples of those which prevailed in the nation." Further, German literature, showing a disdain for the "social structure," has "created a world for itself, into which the possessors of power have generally had the good sense not to intrude" (*CW* XVIII:375–76).

Italian civilization is unlike both, being "not essentially practical like the English, nor almost exclusively speculative like the German." In the past "Man and society have . . . displayed themselves with considerable lustre: the Italians have excelled . . . in science, art, philosophy and in the practical concerns of government and life." But for a long time Italy has "stood still," advancing on "neither of the two paths of civilization." But this failure is the result of "a foreign yoke." What she has ever lacked is

faith in truth. It is not enough to have intellect for speculation and talent for conduct; there must be a link to connect the two; there must be a deep conviction that they who know, can and ought to act according to what they know: That the truths which are known do not exist solely for speculation, but have the power and the right to prevail in the government of the outward world. (*CW* XVIII:376, 377)

Spain is dismissed quickly, the central comment being that the "chief character of civilization – general, continuous progress, has been denied in Spain both to intellect and society" (*CW* XVIII:377). France is the most civilized country for Guizot, though Mill is quick to point out that the judgment is made not out of "national vanity."

France demonstrates, in Mill's approving paraphrase of Guizot, the "parallel and harmonious" advance of "the two elements of civilization – the internal and the external development." "Side by side with every great event, every revolution, every public improvement," one can note "some general doctrine, corresponding to them" (*CW* XVIII:378).

While Mill's comments on various national cultures contribute to our understanding of what "civilization" meant for him, his more detailed discussions of two very different countries, Ireland and India, touch specifically on the major issues.

Throughout the century, "The Irish Question" was a distressing preoccupation for the English; since the question, which involved strongly held political, religious, economic, and even military views, could never be precisely stated, conclusive answers never were given. For Mill, the question took at least a slightly more amenable form, "What Is to be Done with Ireland?"[24] And he focussed it by starting his recommendations from and energizing them with practical economic facts, as in his most concentrated discussion of Irish conditions, a long series of articles in the *Morning Chronicle* immediately responding to the terrible famine of the late 1840s. But just here his own comment shows that the driving force behind his recommendations was moral: "the stern necessities of the time seemed to afford a chance of gaining attention for what appeared to me the only mode of combining relief to immediate destitution with permanent improvement of the social and economic condition of the Irish people" (*Autobiography*, *CW* I:243).

Essential to achieving and maintaining civilization is property. In the most direct words: "Ireland's politicians and legislators" must "recognise the duty of civilizing her people," and learn "from the experience of nations how high a rank among civilizing agents belongs to the wide diffusion of property in land" ("Condition of Ireland [32]," *CW* XXIV:997 [15 Dec. 1846]). The scheme for reclamation of waste lands offers the best hope "for the permanent advantage of the rural Irish"; it is "as well suited to educate them into better habits and higher civilization, as our past conduct was calculated to barbarise and anarchise, if the expression may be permitted, even a civilised people" ("Condition of Ireland [7]," *CW* XXIV:903 [17 Oct. 1846]).

Most of Mill's cultural evidence was agricultural. His most detailed descriptions are of Irish, Indian, and Western European agricultural societies and economies.[25] Mill takes his text from Arthur Young: "The magic of property turns sand into gold. . . . Give a man the secure possession of a bleak rock, and he will turn it into a garden; give him a nine-year's lease of a garden, and he will convert it into a desert" (*Principles of Political Economy, CW* II:274, 278). This, quoted from Young's *Travels in France*, is part of the massive amount of European evidence Mill gives in his *Principles* to show that the best economic results arrive when cultivation and husbandry are in the hands of those who can reap the rewards of their own labour, foresight, and ingenuity through secure tenure or actual ownership.

It is more than an innocent mistake to look for the causes of observed uncivilized group conduct in fixed human nature:

Is it not . . . a bitter satire on the mode in which opinions are formed on the most important problems of human nature and life, to find public instructors of the greatest pretension, imputing the backwardness of Irish industry, and the want of energy of the Irish people in improving their condition, to a peculiar indolence and *insouciance* in the Celtic race? Of all vulgar modes of escaping from the consideration of the effect of social and moral influences on the human mind, the most vulgar is that of attributing the diversities of conduct and character to inherent natural differences. What race would not be indolent and insouciant when things are so arranged, that they derive no advantage from forethought or exertion?

What Mill is repudiating is not the existence of "inherent natural differences" (it will be observed that the Irish and French share a "Celtic" nature), but their being sufficient cause of the observed differences in behaviour.

It is very natural that a pleasure-loving and sensitively organized people like the Irish, should be less addicted to steady routine labour than the English, because life has more excitements for them independent of it; but they are not less fitted for it than their Celtic brethren the French, nor less so than the Tuscans, or the ancient Greeks. An excitable organization is precisely that in which, by adequate inducements, it is easiest to kindle a spirit of animated exertion. . . . No labourers work harder, in England or America, than the Irish; but not under a cottier system. (*CW* II:319)

And elsewhere, again with the Celtic argument, he asserts that emigration is not the proper solution for Irish woes; giving the Irish peasant landed property in Ireland "would precisely supply what is wanting to the formation of his character."

The possession of property would make him an orderly citizen. It would make him a supporter of the law, instead of a rebel against all law but that of his confederacy. It would make him industrious and active, self-helping and self-relying, like his Celtic brother of France. And it would (if anything would) make him, like the same Celtic kinsman, frugal, self-restraining, and provident, both in other things, and in the main article of all, population. ("Condition of Ireland [25]," *CW* XXIV:973–74 [2 Dec. 1846])

And so, in large measure, civilized. It may seem that this emphasis on land ownership distorts the definition of civilization, but it may be that even a few more words are appropriate, because here one can see the entailment of those essentials, justice and the rule of law.

What the abundant evidence proved to Mill's theoretical and practical satisfaction was that two beneficial systems are available in different conditions, small-scale farming and peasant proprietorship – both with security of tenure. Mill's description and analysis take into account historical, legal, national, and geographic variations, and cooperative experiments, but the overall conclusion is single: "unwearied assiduity" and "affectionate interest in the land" bring forth the treasure. "The magic of property turns sand into gold." Mill uses this argument as economic justification for reform of the land laws, but he knew that strong moral arguments were needed to induce belief in the reforms sufficient for social and legislative change.

Once again the key concept is "improvement" in a broad utilitarian sense. Property "rights" are to be understood in those terms. "Though no man made the land," he says, "men, by their industry, made the valuable qualities of it; they reclaimed it from the waste, they brought it under cultivation, they made it useful to man, and so acquired a title to it as men have to what they have themselves made" ("Chichester Fortescue's Land Bill," *CW* XXVIII:80 [17 May 1866]). Like Bentham, he dismisses the "natural rights" argument – used in his day as later – that because no man made the land private property is simply robbery. For him, improvement justifies the right to landed property – and that right is not automatically inherited. The virtue must be renewed in heirs: "no exclusive right [in land] should be permitted to any individual, which cannot be shown to be productive of positive good" (*Principles of Political Economy*, *CW* II:231–32).

Improvement alone engages a moral principle (Mill uses the terms "moral claim" and "moral basis" in this context); in the lack of it, the landlord's right is only that of "the dog in the manger" ("Chichester Fortescue's Land Bill," *CW* XXVIII:81, 80). As in that passage, Mill used the moral argument often and vigorously against the landed aristocracy, and so might be seen seeking simply to remove injustice. But the positive results of reform were much more important to him. In his judgment, as more than implied above, security of tenure makes not just better *farmers* but better *people*. Better in what ways? In being civilized citizens, their behaviour characterized by greater foresight, self-respect, self-control, prudence, moderation, etc.

Even more important in the development and strengthening of Mill's views was his professional involvement in the civil affairs of India, not least with reference to land ownership and use. During the quarter century (1823–58) he spent in the Examiner's Office of the East India Company, which he headed in his final years of office, his daily concern was the development of appropriate and practicable policies for the governance of the subcontinent. For him – as for his father, who had also been Chief Examiner, and who was one of the major European authorities on Indian affairs – effective policies could be founded only on an understanding of the history and present state of Indian civilization. It may well be said, in fact, that this belief was one of his father's most effective teachings. Reporting in his *Autobiography* on his proofreading of the *History of India* (when he was eleven years old), he says:

The number of new ideas which I received from this remarkable book, and the impulse and stimulus as well as guidance given to my thoughts by its criticisms and disquisitions on society and civilization in the Hindoo part, on institutions and the acts of governments in the English part, made my early familiarity with it eminently useful to my subsequent progress. (*CW* I:27–29)

Europeans, while finding aspects of Indian, especially Hindu, culture intriguing and attractive, found little to admire in its social, political, and civil manifestations. Basically, there was a clash of civilizations,[26] and a general belief that the Indian needed improvement, though not necessarily by accepting everything in the European model. The curious expansion of an eighteenth-century trading company into the superior governing body of a vast territory allowed for a gradual development of policies in this direction, especially as control more and more moved from the Company to the British government. The primary motives for change, often dictated by military considerations, shifted with the control from economic to political.

As to what policies would bring about improvement, there were two schools, one advocating an empire of reform, the other an empire of opinion: the first arguing, in Benthamite style, that only sweeping institutional reforms *would* produce a civilized state; the other, in Coleridgean style, that only reforms taking into account existing beliefs and practices *could* produce such a state.[27] Neither held that true civilization in India could be achieved by preserving the present "national" Indian governments; all, including Mill and the Court of Directors, believed that extending direct British rule was necessary.

Success of the "engraftment" policy that Mill adopted from the empire of opinion school required recognition of the three conditions he laid down in *Considerations on Representative Government* for effective reform:

The people for whom the form of government is intended must be willing to accept it; or at least not so unwilling, as to oppose an insurmountable obstacle to its establishment. They must be willing and able to do what is necessary to keep it standing. And they must be willing and able to do what it requires of them to enable it to fulfil its purposes.... The failure of any of these conditions renders a form of government, whatever favourable promise it may otherwise hold out, unsuitable to the particular case. (*CW* XIX:376)

Full understanding of national cultures is therefore needed for reform – but it should be obvious that understanding does not entail unqualified approval, for otherwise reform would be unnecessary.

Understand both what is good and what is bad; discourage the bad, adopt the good, and improve slowly through educating by precept but mainly by practice.

People are more easily induced to do, and do more easily, what they are already used to; but people also learn to do things new to them. ... The amount of capacity which a people possess for doing new things, and adapting themselves to new circumstances, is itself one of the elements of the question. It is a quality in which different nations, and different stages of civilization, differ much from one another. The capability of any given people for fulfilling the conditions of a given form of government, cannot be pronounced on by any sweeping rule. Knowledge of the particular people and general practical judgment and sagacity, must be the guides. ... To recommend and advocate a particular institution or form of government, and set its advantages in the strongest light, is one of the modes, often the only mode within reach, of educating the mind of the nation not only for accepting and claiming, but also for working, the institution. (CW XIX:379)

The grand project for the civilization of humankind comes down finally to education, to teachers and taught, to those who know and those who need to know, and to the means of getting the knowledge from one to the others.[28] It is only a slight injustice to see James Mill's views on these issues as deriving from Bentham's definition of the goal of punishment, "to grind rogues honest." But John Mill came to a different conclusion: there is a legitimate goal (civilization), and there are rogues (savages and children), but grinding will not make them civilized citizens. Civilization involves the moralizing of individuals in society, an active process that is fueled by a practiced will and has predictable consequences.

There is a conundrum in the process, like the classical Quis custodiet ipsos custodes? Who will teach the teachers? The answer for Mill is, of course, experience, general and external, and personal and internal. The required general experience – neither necessarily nor desirably abstract – is of human nature and behaviour. Limiting the range only for occasional reasons, Mill says: "The true teacher of the fitting social arrangements for England, France, or America, is the one who can point out how the English, French, or American character can be improved, and how it has been made what it is" ("Bentham," CW X:99). And without geographic limitation:

No one who attempts to lay down propositions for the guidance of mankind, however perfect his scientific acquirements, can dispense with a practical knowledge of the actual modes in which the affairs of the world are carried on, and an extensive personal experience of the actual ideas, feelings, and intellectual and moral tendencies of his own country and of his own age. ("On the Definition of Political Economy," *CW* IV:333)

The study of civilizations is itself civilizing, and, by becoming the subject of instruction, transfers its benefits from teacher to student.[29] To be civilized is a process in which one becomes civilized, and so in the broadest sense the civilized society is itself the best teacher.[30] This connection is most evident in a part of the definition Mill stresses, cooperation, which is an instance of civilization feeding on itself: the cooperation that it practices develops cooperators.

It is probably not unfair to say that for Mill, the subject being civilization, the teachers had something to learn from the students, but the students did not have much to teach the teachers. Only the civilized can create and maintain civilization, though the comparatively uncivilized contribute some goods to it, and are not merely its passive consumers.[31]

For Mill the connection between learning and teaching is even closer when one turns from general to personal experience. He dwells in his *Autobiography* on the ways in which his self-culture, aesthetic as well as intellectual, contributed to his mature views, and indeed its effects can be seen in all his central writings, including the one devoted specifically to the content and purpose of education, his *Inaugural Address*.[32] And, as has been apparent throughout this discussion, learning and teaching are for him crucial in the civilizing process.

That conclusion is not surprising, of course, when one recalls that Mill's overall plan for improvement depends on the cooperation of artist and scientist in his understanding of the terms. As a social scientist – the first and only ethologist? – he looked to various kinds of evidence showing what human nature was in the abstract and in the concrete – in individual and general behaviour. And his education, both early and continuing, can be seen as a gathering of evidence towards an ethology.

An attempt to be specific about influences would produce a massive tome, and just mentioning them all would be no more instructive than an invitation list or the citation of procedures in medical reports.[33] It is important, however, even if apparently otiose, to say that as scientist Mill was depending not just on his personal and professional experience, important as that was, but on close study of a host containing such as Aristotle, Hume, Locke, Bentham, James Mill, Comte, Tocqueville, Guizot . . . but I must not do what I have eschewed. In sum, one can say that his "science" was based on observation, analysis of history and literature, and imaginative projection and introspection.

The initial role of the artist, it will be recalled, is to set ends. In the same sense, and with not much less importance for his project of human improvement – the fashioning of "a second nature, far better and more unselfish" than that humans were "created with" ("Theism," *CW* X:459) – Mill presents civilization as like utility, both end and means, and as an ideal both for individuals and nations. Individuals and societies must, and can, make choices. As he was aware, sound policy depends on analysis based on accurate observation and description, and on comparison. And evaluative comparison implies a standard, in this case of civilization and culture. While defending the emphasis of political economy on the study of wealth, he comments:

All know that it is one thing to be rich, another thing to be enlightened, brave, or humane; that the questions how a nation is made wealthy, and how it is made free, or virtuous, or eminent in literature, in the fine arts, in arms, or in polity, are totally distinct enquiries. Those things, indeed, are all indirectly connected, and react upon one another. A people has sometimes become free, because it had first grown wealthy; or wealthy, because it had first become free. The creed and laws of a people act powerfully upon their economic condition; and this again, by its influence on their mental development and social relations, reacts upon their creed and laws. (*Principles of Political Economy, CW* II:3)

Emphatically, the ideal end is not merely abstract, and one becomes aware of the artist's final role in devising and applying wise policy, judged by utility in the widest sense, both moral and practical. So what does he finally recommend?

Given that improvement – defined by him in moral terms – should and can occur, policy makers and movers should attempt to encourage the best aspects of civilization in all individuals and nations.[34] That formulation is bland enough, but it seems less vapid and neutral if interpreted in language inoffensive in Mill's time and apt to his concerns, as Lynn Zastoupil does: it was Mill's "mature conviction, expressed in several works, that primitive nations must follow the path to modern civilization laid out by the Western world."[35] That of course sounds now more like a battle cry than a mature policy document. Its correct interpretation needs the context given by attention to time, place, and circumstances that I here can only appeal to, not supply.

Another less obvious context, however, may be briefly elucidated as assisting understanding. Believing that he lived in an age of transition, being an empiricist and inductivist, a liberal, and a close student of persuasion, Mill seldom gave way to apodictic assertions. His arguments often seem allied to his notions about the dialectic blending of opposites, seen in his descriptions of "half-men" as "completing counterparts." Shaping his argument to occasion and audience, he was dedicated to rhetorical strategies that are offensive to dogmatists who like switches that have only *on* and *off* positions, preferably fixed at *on*. Mill held that "circumstances alter cases," and some see that position as not permitting firm beliefs – though that the phrase is Edmund Burke's might suggest a compatibility. What he employed may be described as a rhetoric of tendencies and a rhetoric of qualification; it is not shilly-shally, because the end is action when means can be made to produce the desired ends. And it does not freeze: democratic "improvement" can come, but can come only from the success of what Mill perfected if he did not invent, the rhetoric of the moving average. It is the major instrument of his ethology as an applied science.

NOTES

1 The importance I attach to the notion is evident in the title of my book *The Improvement of Mankind: The Social and Political Thought of John Stuart Mill* (J. M. Robson 1968).

2 For discussion of this model, see J. M. Robson 1968, 64–67; and J. M. Robson 1966, 167–86.

3 In examining the notion of "Natural Kinds" in his *Logic*, Mill identifies "mankind" as a basic *infima species*, having the attributes of "corporiety, animal life, rational, and a certain external form" (elsewhere,

"corporiety, organization, life, rationality, and certain peculiaries of external form"). He expressly rules out as "logical kinds" classes produced by artificial distinctions, such as the "various races and temperaments, the two sexes, and even the various ages," which are no more natural kinds than are "Christian, Jew, Mussulman, and Pagan" (*CW* VIII:31–32, 124–25).

4 J. S. Mill's note to James Mill's *Analysis of the Phenomena of the Human Mind*, CW XXX:178–79.

5 The following list of natural human *tendencies* (or *propensities*) is too heterogeneous for strict classification; the separate terms, however, suggest much necessary to any programme for "civilizing." Humans – seemingly all humans, though in different degrees – have a tendency to theorize ("Bentham" [perhaps the subject of the essay affected Mill's judgment], *CW* X:102); to abstract and generalize ("Notes on The Phaedrus," *CW* XI:75n); to interpret the complicated as mysterious (*Utilitarianism, CW* X:228–29); to anarchy (*System of Logic, CW* VIII:922, from Coleridge); to extend the bounds of moral police (*On Liberty, CW* XVIII:284); to disparage feelings and mental states not their own ("Bentham," *CW* X:93); to intolerance in whatever one really cares about (*On Liberty, CW* XVIII:222); to believe that subjective feelings not otherwise accounted for are revelations of objective reality (*Utilitarianism, CW* X:230 – called a *predisposition*); and – a sad list – "to pugnacity, irascibility, enthusiasm, destructiveness, domination, and cruelty" ("Nature," *CW* X:393).

In specific contexts he also refers to various natural human *feelings*: of the infinite (*Auguste Comte and Positivism, CW* X:334); of fear ("Nature," *CW* X:393); of the rightness of the *lex talionis* and its reverse (*Utilitarianism, CW* X:253–56); and of gratitude to protectors (*Principles of Political Economy, CW* III:760) and to those who, having power, do not use it to crush the weak (*Subjection of Women, CW* XXI:286–87). He also refers to social and selfish feelings and conscientious feelings (e.g., *Utilitarianism, CW* X:231, 229).

In most of these, given Mill's general view of *tendencies*, one can detect a sense in which momental as well as initial inertia is a human characteristic.

6 It is clear that for Mill, though men are animals, their animality is lower than their humanity, and their animality can and should be suppressed. For example, he compares human "prudence," "foresight," and "social affections," on the one hand, with animal "blind instinct" on the other, when talking of population control (*Principles of Political Economy, CW* II:156–58). The contrast is most apparent when Mill alludes to – "discusses" is too specific – sexual desire.

7 See, e.g., *Autobiography*, *CW* I:33, 155–57; *Principles of Political Economy*, *CW* II:206, 210, 213, 222; "Thoughts on Poetry," *CW* I:363–64.

8 In his *Autobiography* he says he picked up from John Austin the phrase "the extraordinary pliability of human nature" (*CW* I:187).

9 "Bentham," *CW* X:89, 89–90, 97 (in the second of these "this subject" was revised to "these subjects"); *On Liberty*, *CW* XVIII:271n; *Autobiography*, *CW* I:15.

10 The best discussion of this matter is in Burns 1976.

11 As I have said elsewhere: "*The Spirit of the Age, Characteristics, Signs of the Times, Tracts for the Times, Hard Times*, even *The Nineteenth Century* – such titles imply an awareness of identifying marks that distinguish the nineteenth century from other ages, and may be taken to imply also, behind the awareness of change and history, an uneasiness about at least some of the marks" (J. M. Robson 1976b, 78).

12 I am content to use such evidence while watching from a distance the battles of those, mostly literary critics, who reject it as resulting from the "biographical fallacy," and those theorists, mostly social scientists, who discount it as corrupted by class, race, gender, or other bias.

13 It would be disingenuous (or worse) not to call attention to other passages where comparable divisions appear in different contexts. In *Representative Government*, the three varieties of mental excellence are described as "intellectual, practical, and moral" (*CW* XIX:407, cf. 400), and the human "faculties" are identified as "moral, intellectual, and active" (*CW* XIX:404).

14 "We think it" is probably here not just a form of words; it reflects the human judgment that goes beyond mere observation of natural phenomena.

15 In article form (1836), "populous."

16 That this important element of Mill's political and economic thought has been little commented on justifies quotation:

There is not a more accurate test of the progress of civilization than the progress of the power of co-operation. . . . Co-operation, like other difficult things, can be learnt only by practice: and to be capable of it in great things, a people must be gradually trained to it in small. . . . The division of employments – the accomplishment by the combined labour of several, of tasks which could not be achieved by any number of persons singly – is the great school of co-operation.

He cites as examples navigation, military operations, commerce, and manufacture (*CW* XVIII:122, 123).

17 In describing savage life in this essay, Mill offers no empirical evidence, just assuming agreement in shared general knowledge, saying for instance, "Consider the savage" (*CW* XVIII:122). But there are some examples. When referring to cooperation in warlike activity, he cites positive and negative examples – the Spanish in the Peninsular War, the native states of India, Turkey and Russia during the French invasion, the inept opponents of Rome – and then illustrates at greater length the elements in recent European history (*CW* XVIII:123ff).

18 For Mill's important analysis of the "stationary state" economically, see his *Principles of Political Economy, CW* III:752–57. See also Chapter 8 of this volume.

19 Much material relevant to my argument here will be found in other chapters in this volume, especially those dealing more specifically with *Considerations on Representative Government* as well as *On Liberty* and *Utilitarianism* (Chapters 7, 10, and 14).

20 In the original version, "and of many of the repulsive qualities of aristocracy."

21 That is not to say that late twentieth-century judgments are uniformly and pragmatically based on the better scientific evidence available.

22 "Bentham," *CW* X:105. These comments of 1838 were closely anticipated in Mill's "Remarks on Bentham's Philosophy" (1833), where he equally finds fault in Bentham's assuming that "mankind are alike in all times and all places, . . . and that if the same institutions do not suit them, it is only because in the more backward stages of improvement they have not wisdom to see what institutions are most for their good." Had he seen that political institutions are "the principal means of the social education of a people," he would have understood "the same institutions will no more suit two nations in different stages of civilization, than the same lessons will suit children of different ages." And the instances of difference follow:

> For a tribe of North American Indians, improvement means, taming down their proud and solitary self-dependence: for a body of emancipated negroes, it means accustoming them to be self-dependent, instead of being merely obedient to orders: for our semi-barbarous ancestors it would have meant, softening them; for a race of enervated Asiatics it would mean hardening them." (*CW* X:16)

23 While all the opinions cannot be uniquely assigned to Mill, and there is much quotation from Guizot, he chose what was to go into the article, and there is nothing inconsistent with views he expressed elsewhere.

24 Though that is the title of an unpublished paper (*CW* VI:497–503), it would have served as well for all his comments on Ireland.

25 That is not to say that he is an agrarian determinist, or even an economic one.

26 The simplification involved in pretending that the widely varying religious, political, tribal, and legal beliefs and practices made up one "Indian" civilization is for convenience. In practice the East India Company, and *a fortiori* J. S. Mill, took account of these differences in designing practical policies. But, though this awareness made for different judgments about specific aspects of the various cultures, in effect there was no opposition to the view that they should change in the direction of the essential aspects of European civilization (also in this context seen as unitary).

27 My discussion here draws heavily on Zastoupil 1994, esp. 53, 84, 124–25. His careful argument is the first based on a full examination of Mill's official "despatches." (The 1713 despatches are listed in *CW* XXX, with a list of published extracts from them.) Because it is unlikely that those despatches will be published in full, Zastoupil's argument will remain valuable not just in itself, but as a useful research document.

28 Because Mill places so much emphasis on self-development, it is perhaps wise to point out that he would not have been in the company of those angry romantics of the later twentieth century who pressed their battle against authority to the point where teaching in its traditional senses was seen as an evil, and not even a necessary one.

29 In one of his early denunciations of education at Oxford and Cambridge, Mill avows that, because those universities have neglected their essential functions, almost no one has "any curiosity respecting the nature and principles of human society, the history or the philosophy of civilization; nor any belief that, from such inquiries, a single important practical consequence can follow" ("Professor Sedgwick's Discourse," *CW* I:34).

30 Mill's exposition of Coleridge's conditions for a stable, "permanent political society" are illustrative of such teaching. The conditions are, first, "a system of *education*, beginning with infancy and continued through life, of which, whatever else it might include, one main and incessant ingredient was *restraining discipline*"; second, "the existence, in some form or other, of the feeling of allegiance, or loyalty"; and third, "a strong and active principle of cohesion among the members of the same community or state. . . . [a] principle of sympathy, not of hostility; of union, not of separation" ("Coleridge," *CW* X:133–35).

31 Though the point is not germane to my argument, the uncivilized are also civilization's opponents and potentially its destroyers.

32 Much of "Civilization" bears directly on this point, and some passages call for quotation as giving substance to Mill's definition of civilized and

civilizing studies. The weakness of the traditional educational institutions would not "be cured by bringing their studies into a closer connexion with what it is the fashion to term 'the business of the world,'" by removing the classics and logic and adding modern languages and science. Better to have "classics and logic taught far more really and deeply than at present, and . . . add to them other studies more alien than any which yet exist to the 'business of the world,' but more germane to the great business of every rational being – the strengthening and enlarging of his own intellect and character." What they do not seek is precisely what is wanted; their object is

not that the individual should go forth determined and qualified to seek truth ardently, vigorously, and disinterestedly; *not* that he be furnished at setting out with the needful aids and facilities, the needful materials and instruments for that search, and then left to the unshackled use of them; *not* that, by a free communion with the thoughts and deeds of the great minds which preceded him, he be inspired at once with the courage to dare all which truth and conscience require, and the modesty to weigh well the grounds of what others think, before adopting contrary opinions of his own. . . .

On the positive side, classical literature should be retained "because it brings before us the thoughts and actions of many great minds, minds of various orders of greatness, and these related and exhibited in a manner tenfold more impressive, tenfold more calculated to call forth high aspirations, than in any modern literature." History is valuable

because it is the record of all great things which have been achieved by mankind, and because when philosophically studied it gives a certain largeness of conception to the student, and familiarizes him with the action of great causes. In no other way can he so completely realize in his own mind . . . the great principles by which the progress of man and the condition of society are governed. Nowhere else will the infinite varieties of human nature be so vividly brought home to him, and anything cramped or one-sided in his own standard of it so effectually corrected; and nowhere else will he behold so strongly exemplified the astonishing pliability of our nature, and the vast effect which may under good guidance be produced upon it by honest endeavour.

Literature should be presented along with history or as part of it; and logic and the philosophy of mind emphasized, "the one, the instrument for the cultivation of all sciences; the other, the root from which they all grow." And more: "all those sciences, in which great and certain results are arrived at by mental processes of some length or nicety: . . . sciences of pure ratiocination, as mathematics; and sciences partly of ratiocination, and partly of what is far more difficult, comprehensive observation and analysis." "The philosophy of morals, of government, of law, of political economy, of poetry and art, should form subjects of systematic instruction. ..." (CW XVIII:139–46).

33 Such lists can be found in CW XXXIII, which contains various kinds of index that will simplify influence studies.

34 And discourage the worst. In "Civilization," having listed the bad effects of civilization in its descriptive sense, Mill asks if they can

be avoided by checking the diffusion of knowledge, discouraging the spirit of combination, prohibiting improvements in the arts of life, and repressing the further increase of wealth and of production? Assuredly not. Those advances which civilization cannot give – which in its uncorrected influence it has even a tendency to destroy – may yet coexist with civilization; and it is only when joined to civilization that they can produce their fairest fruits. (CW XVIII:135–36)

So the battle will never end – not a bad quality in a battle for Mill, who saw contention as vital to the health of true beliefs and practices.

35 Zastoupil 1994, 168. This judgment is based on his earlier analysis of the way that Mill, initially attracted to Herder's doctrine of cultural pluralism, based on the observation – similar to Coleridge's – that "every national group has its own culture and system of national education for keeping that culture alive in its members," later repudiated the related belief that "all cultures are good in themselves and should not be measured against one standard of civilization." Zastoupil argues (p. 129) that Mill did not, of course, consequently repudiate his strong advocacy of individual diversity.

10 Democracy, socialism, and the working classes

I

When Mill was addressing a public meeting in his campaign to be elected as a member of Parliament, he was handed a placard with a quotation taken from one of his works that "the lower classes, though mostly habitual liars, are ashamed of lying", and he was asked whether he had written those words. When he answered "I did", the meeting, consisting largely of the working classes, applauded loudly. This incident epitomizes some of Mill's characteristic attitudes towards the working classes. He did not think much of their present intellectual and moral qualities.[1] But he was prepared to speak frankly about them.[2] His obvious pleasure at their favourable response to his openness confirmed his view that they had the capacity and willingness to improve themselves. He wanted to provide them with the opportunities for such improvement.[3] He saw himself as their friend, or "a person whom they could trust" (*CW* I:274). But his idea of improvement was not to impose paternalistically his own conception of their interests on them, but instead to increase the scope for them to voice their interests, while at the same time subjecting them to various influences, including the influences, though not the direction, of abler persons, in order to advance their mental cultivation and thereby to broaden their interests. His hopes for their future well-being were tempered by his fears about letting them dominate social and political life in their present unenlightened state. So another part of his case for social and political reform focussed on finding a counterpoise to the prevailing views and on ensuring greater diversity. In the end, it was his overriding concern for the fate of individual freedom and development which guided all his social and political proposals.

372

II

Mill was elected a Liberal member of Parliament for Westminster in 1865 and served for one term until 1868. He devoted much of his energies to trying to extend the franchise. He himself regarded his unsuccessful, but encouraging, attempt to give women the suffrage as "perhaps the only really important service I performed in the capacity of a Member of Parliament" (*CW* I:285). His motion, which would have given the vote to all women who had the qualifications required of male electors, won more votes than expected, and he was justifiably proud of the impetus it gave to the movement to extend the suffrage to women.

Mill also supported Gladstone's unsuccessful Reform Bill of 1866, which, if passed, would have extended the franchise to the extent of making working-class voters constitute about a quarter of the total electorate of England and Wales.[4] When the bill was defeated, the government, with Lord John Russell as Prime Minister and Gladstone as Chancellor of the Exchequer and Leader of the House, resigned and was succeeded by a Tory government led by Lord Derby and Disraeli. Soon thereafter the Reform League, dedicated to extending the franchise, tried to hold a meeting in Hyde Park. The huge gathering was denied entry to the park. Some of the men tore down the park railings and people were injured in the ensuing scuffle. Mill blamed the police for maltreatment of "many innocent persons" and for causing extreme exasperation to working men.[5] The League again planned to hold a meeting in Hyde Park about a week later. There was a danger of serious violence breaking out as the government made military preparations to foil the meeting. Mill met with the leaders of the League to persuade them to cancel the meeting. There was resistance from the working-class leaders in the group, but Mill's view eventually prevailed. He also agreed to address a meeting of the Reform League held in the Agricultural Hall a day before the now-abandoned Hyde Park meeting.

Mill's detailed account of these events showed how he consistently sided with the aspirations of the working class. He believed that he had an almost unique rapport with the working class and that at the time he was the only one who could avert the disaster of a clash between the demonstrators and the troops. "No other person, I believe, had at that moment the necessary influence for restraining the working classes, except Mr Gladstone and Mr Bright, neither of whom was available" (*CW* I:279).

Mill believed that it would be to the benefit of the workers themselves and to the nation as a whole if the working class could be brought into the mainstream of politics and given a significant voice in Parliament. But he did not want them, or any other single group, to dominate social and political life. We can now examine how his theory of representative government was in line with his activities as a member of Parliament.

III

The development of Mill's views on democracy has been well traced by J. H. Burns in his paper "J. S. Mill and Democracy, 1829–61".[6] Mill originally supported the secret ballot, which was a crucial element of the platform of the philosophic radicals. It was a means of protecting the voter from the pressure of sinister interests. But when Mill changed his mind about the desirability of the ballot, it was precisely its secrecy to which he objected. If voters had to account publicly for their vote, they would act more responsibly. But although Mill's views on specific devices such as the ballot changed, there was a fierce consistency in the way he held to his fundamental principles of good government. Burns acknowledges this, but maintains that Mill was not in the strict sense a democrat: "A consistent viewpoint unites Mill's political thought from start to finish; but it is not, in the strict sense he would himself have adopted, the viewpoint of a democrat".[7] On the other hand John M. Robson believes that Mill was a consistent democrat: "So when the question is asked, by whom should the government be selected? There is no doubt about Mill's answer. He is a democrat. From the time of his earliest sympathy with the Roman populace to his last writings the theme of popular control runs through his thought."[8] Of course whether Mill is a democrat depends on how the term is used. He is certainly not a democrat if a democrat is someone who believes that each person's vote should have exactly the same value as everyone else's. Mill quoted with approval the remark "Some are wise, and some are otherwise" (*CW* XXIII:497), and he wanted to give greater weight to the views of the wise. But I have also indicated how Mill thought of himself as a friend of the working class.

The interesting question is how he combined his different concerns and perspectives into a coherent account of the fundamental principles of good government. *Representative Government* presents his mature and most developed views on these issues.

IV

Mill believes that a form of government will not operate effectively unless certain conditions are satisfied. There must be a willingness on the part of the people to accept it. They must be prepared to do what is necessary to preserve the form of government, such as defending it when it is under attack. And they must be willing and able to perform the duties required of them under the form of government. Thus a people who are unwilling or unable to actively co-operate with the law and to restrain themselves from exacting private revenge will only be fit for despotic forms of government. But within the limits set by these condition, the appropriate form of government in a particular society is a matter of choice.

But what principles should determine the choice? What are the criteria of a good form of government? The most important criterion for Mill is that the form of government should promote the capacities of the people, their "virtue and intelligence". The political institutions of a society are for Mill "an agency of national education". If the people are not yet ready to govern themselves, and they require a despot to rule over them, then the despot's function is to prepare them for the next stage of social progress. A self-perpetuating despotism is never justified. A form of government must be geared to the prevailing capacities of people, but it must also prepare them to move forward by developing their capacities to a higher level. Political institutions should also put the existing capacities of the people to the best use in the conduct of public affairs.

Applying these criteria for good government, Mill concludes that democracy is ideally the best form of government. By that he means that if the social conditions which make it feasible are present, then a democratic form of government will satisfy the criteria of a good government to a greater degree than all the alternatives. Despotism concentrates the exercise of mental activity in one person, leaving the people at large mentally passive. The intellectual and moral capacities can best be developed by active participation in practical affairs.

Wherever the sphere of action of human beings is artifically circumscribed, their sentiments are narrowed and dwarfed in the same proportion. The food of feeling is action: even domestic affection lives upon voluntary good offices. Let a person have nothing to do for his country, and he will not care for it. It has been said of old, that in a despotism there is at most but one patriot, the despot himself; and the saying rests on a just appreciation of the effects of absolute subjection, even to a good and wise master. (CW XIX:400–01)

Mill believes in the superiority of the active to the passive character, and democracy best promotes the active character. "The maximum of the invigorating effect of freedom upon the character is only obtained, when the person acted on either is, or is looking forward to becoming, a citizen as fully privileged as any other" (CW XIX:411). He emphasizes the educative effects of participation in public affairs. People develop interests other than their self-interests, and their perspectives are enlarged. He cites the public education which Athenian citizens obtained from her democratic institutions. A similar, though lesser, benefit is conferred on the lower middle-class English by their service on juries and parish offices.

Still more salutary is the moral part of the instruction afforded by the participation of the private citizen, if even rarely, in public functions. He is called upon, while so engaged, to weigh interests not his own; to be guided, in case of conflicting claims, by another rule than his private partialities; to apply, at every turn, principles and maxims which have for their reason of existence the common good: and he usually finds associated with him in the same work minds more familiarised than his own with these ideas and operations, whose study it will be to supply reasons to his understanding, and stimulation to his feeling for the general interest. He is made to feel himself one of the public, and whatever is for their benefit to be for his benefit. (CW XIX:412)

Given these educational benefits of participation, the community gains most when participation is spread out as widely as possible. But since it is impossible in any community beyond a certain size for all to participate directly and extensively in the affairs of the state, representative government is the best system. Ultimate sovereignty will be exercised by all the citizens, each one of whom will also occasionally have the opportunity to participate personally in public affairs either at the local or the national level.

Apart from promoting "the virtue and intelligence" of the people at large through political participation, a democratic system of government also harnesses the existing capacities of the people to the highest degree. People's rights and interests are only secure to the extent that they themselves have the power to protect them. It is not just that those who are excluded from the political process will have their interests overlooked. It is also that, even when others are motivated by good will towards them, their interests will be viewed and interpreted from a different and misleading perspective. It is for these reasons that Mill sees the importance of extending the franchise to the working classes. He has a high opinion of the attitude of the other classes towards the working classes: they are prepared to make financial sacrifices for the benefit of the working classes. But even so, the interests of working people are not properly catered for because issues are never viewed from their point of view. Mill gives the example of strikes to illustrate how the issue would get a more balanced treatment if only there were workers' representatives in Parliament to argue their side of the case.

It is an inherent condition of human affairs, that no intention, however sincere, of protecting the interests of others, can make it safe or salutary to tie up their own hands. Still more obviously true is it, that by their own hands only can any positive and durable improvement of their circumstances in life be worked out. (*CW* XIX:405–06)

The political participation of the working classes ensures not only their self-protection but it also makes them self-dependent, and it will maximize the general prosperity of the community. On the other hand, their exclusion from the political process will result not in their interests and rights being deliberately ignored, but in their being simply overlooked even by sincere and well-meaning members of the other classes. The community as a whole will be the poorer for such neglect.

Having explained why it is important that no section of the population should be excluded from political participation, Mill goes on to delineate the essential features of representative government. It is a system in which the ultimate controlling power resides in the representatives periodically elected by all the people. But although the representative body should have the ultimate control, it does not follow that the same body should exercise all the functions that governments are expected to perform. The business of legislation and of administration is to be left in professional hands. There should be a small commission of legislation. The elected Parliament may instruct the commission to draft laws for particular purposes, but once legislation has been drafted, Parliament may not itself amend the legislation. It may pass or reject it, or send it back to the commission for amendment. In this way Mill wishes to combine the idea, crucial to his conception of democracy, that Parliament should be the ultimate authority in the enactment of all laws, with the idea that there should be a proper place for expertise in legislation and administration. The main function of Parliament is to be "the nation's Committee of Grievances, and its Congress of Opinions" (CW XIX:432). It is a place in which a whole range of different opinions will be voiced and discussed.

However, the idea of Parliament as a place in which ideas are discussed in order to ascertain the truth would be hollow if it turns out that the various opinions voiced merely reflect sectional interests, with the interests of the majority always prevailing in the end. Many of Mill's proposals may best be seen not as ends in themselves, but as attempts to give strength to his conception of the role of Parliament in the social and political life of the community. He mentions the dangers of "sinister interests" and of class legislation which would undermine the general welfare. The main division of interests in a modern community is between labourers and employers of labour, both broadly conceived. Included in the latter group are highly paid members of the professions whose education and ambitions place them in the same category as the rich employers of labour and the inheritors of wealth. On the other hand, Mill groups together the small employers of labour with the manual labourers. Most of the members of each group would seek to promote their sectional interests. But if the composition of Parliament could be so structured that these conflicting sectional interests are roughly equally divided, then neither side would prevail in promoting its self-interest because there would be a minority on each side who are motivated by higher, non-sectional interests, and the two minority groups would combine with the majority of each group to defeat the class interests promoted by the majority of the other group.

> The representative system ought to be so constituted as to maintain this state of things: it ought not to allow any of the various sectional interests to be so powerful as to be capable of prevailing against truth and justice and the other sectional interests combined. There ought always to be such a balance preserved among personal interests as may render any one of them dependent for its successes, on carrying with it at least a large proportion of those who act on higher motives, and more comprehensive and distant views. (*CW* XIX:447)

The danger of class legislation by the numerical majority is one danger to the pursuit of truth and justice. Another danger is that Parliament will be dominated by "a low grade of intelligence" (*CW* XIX:448). Of course it is possible to raise the intellectual level of the parliamentary representatives by restricting the franchise. But Mill's belief that each group in society is the only safe guardian of its own rights and interests precluded such a solution. In any case his belief in the educative effects of political participation also means that people with a low grade of intelligence need not be stuck with that level of development if they have the opportunity to actively engage with others in the common affairs of the community.

In order to improve the intellectual and moral standards of parliamentary representatives, Mill proposes a system of proportional representation based on suggestions published a few years earlier by Thomas Hare. The basic idea is to have units of representation or quotas, with each quota consisting of the number of voters divided by the number of seats in Parliament. Each voter expresses several preferences, but his vote will only count for one candidate. If the candidate of his first choice fails to obtain the quota, his vote will go to the candidate who is his second preference, and so on. When a candidate has obtained the quota, the remainder of those who voted for him will transfer their vote to their next preferences. Voters need not therefore vote for local candidates but may instead choose from the whole range of candidates. Again, candidates whose supporters are not confined to one locality but are scattered throughout the country can have the benefit of the pooling of the votes of all their supporters. Talented candidates will be encouraged to stand for elections and the national competition for votes will ensure that more able candidates are pitted against one another.

Every member of the House would be the representative of a unanimous constituency. He would represent a thousand electors, or two thousand, or five thousand, or ten thousand, as the quota might be, every one of whom would have not only voted for him, but selected him from the whole country; not merely from the assortment of two or three perhaps rotten oranges, which may be the only choice offered to him in his local market. (CW XIX:455)

Although proportional representation will check the tendency of representative democracy towards "collective mediocrity", it will not change the fact that "superior intellects and characters" will still be outnumbered in Parliament. However, Hare's proposals will at least ensure that the voices of the "instructed minority" will be heard, and Mill was optimistic about the salutary effects of their presence in Parliament. Unpopular views, which would normally only be presented in books and periodicals, will now have a wider audience. The less instructed will have their views subjected to cogent criticisms. They can no longer simply assume that their opinions are correct, and may occasionally be persuaded that they are wrong. Contact with the minds of the instructed will lift the mental level of the average person.

Two more general features of Mill's thought also support his belief in the beneficial effects of increasing the influence of superior minds. The first is his view that social progress depends on a clash between different centres of power. If any single power succeeds in suppressing all the others, then social stagnation will result.

Human improvement is a product of many factors, and no power ever yet constituted among mankind includes them all: even the most beneficent power only contains in itself some of the requisites of good, and the remainder, if progress is to continue, must be derived from some other source. No community has ever long continued progressive, but while a conflict was going on between the strongest power in the community and some rival power; between the spiritual and temporal authorities; the military or territorial and the industrial classes; the king and the people; the orthodox and religious reformers. (CW XIX:459)

So in a democracy there must be some rallying point against the ascendant public opinion.

The second relevant aspect of Mill's thought is his faith in the power of ideas to bring about social changes. "One person with a belief, is a social power equal to ninety-nine who have only interests" (*CW* XIX:381). Mere physical and economic power are not the whole of social power, but "speculative power is one of the chief elements of social power". He points to the ending of slavery through "the spread of moral convictions" and the emancipation of the serfs in Russia through "the growth of a more enlightened opinion respecting the true interest of the State" (*CW* XIX:382).

It is what men think, that determines how they act; and though the persuasions and convictions of average men are in a much greater degree determined by their personal position than by reason, no little power is exercised over them by the persuasions and convictions of those whose personal position is different, and by the united authority of the instructed. (*CW* XIX:382)

It is therefore possible for the representatives of majority interests, who come into contact with the ideas and arguments of the instructed, to rise above their material or class interests, and consider issues from the perspective of rational considerations. The stronger arguments of the instructed will have an influence greater than their numerical strength.

But Mill also wants to increase further the influence of the instructed by increasing their numerical strength, although not to the point where they could on their own form the majority in Parliament. He argues that the votes of the mentally superior should be given greater weight. He believes that this is not incompatible with the democratic principle that everyone should have a voice in political affairs. So he suggests a system of plural voting which gives certain people two or more votes while others receive only one each. Since it is mental superiority and not wealth which is relevant, and since there is no reliable national system of examination that will identify intellectual ability, Mill argues that plural votes should be given on the basis of a person's occupation.

An employer of labour is on the average more intelligent than a labourer; for he must labour with his head, and not solely with his hands. A foreman is generally more intelligent than an ordinary labourer, and a labourer in the skilled trades than in the unskilled. A banker, merchant, or manufacturer is likely to be more intelligent than a tradesman, because he has larger and more complicated interests to manage. (CW XIX:475)

But since it is the successful performance of the relevant occupations and not just the holding of certain jobs which is relevant, Mill requires that people should have performed superior functions for some length of time before they qualify for plural votes. Mill also believes that those who have passed major examinations, such as members of the liberal professions and university graduates, may also be given extra votes. It should also be possible for individuals who do not belong to the favoured professions, or who do not perform the superior functions, to prove that they have the requisite intelligence to be entitled to plural votes. But although Mill holds the general principle that superior minds should have greater influence in Parliament, which is a place for discussion, he is not wedded to the specific proposals he makes about plural voting. There is, however, another general principle to which he adheres, namely that the total voting strength of those with plural votes should not outweigh that of the rest of the community who have only single votes. Those privileged with additional votes should not be in a position to enact their own class legislation.

Mill also suggests that the value of having superior intellects in Parliament would be diminished if they were required to pledge that they would vote in accordance with the wishes of their supporters, rather than use their own judgement to decide on the issues as they arise. Those of superior mental capacities should accept a duty to use these capacities for the benefit of the community. The ordinary voters are entitled to know the views of their parliamentary representatives on issues relevant to the performance of their public duties. The voters need not be expected to elect a representative who will act against their fundamental interests, but they may be persuaded to defer to his superior judgement on other issues. The absence of pledges by parliamentary candidates is for Mill another device to ensure that minorities are represented and unpopular views are heard in Parliament. In any case Mill's conception of Parliament as a forum of public discussion rules out the idea that members of Parliament are merely delegates of their constituents, bound to passively reflect their views. A parliamentary delegate would not be able to change his views in the light of discussion, and a Parliament, consisting of members whose views are already determined before the debate begins, would not be a place in which ideas live or die with the strength of the arguments in their favour.

Mill's opposition to secret ballots is also largely motivated by his desire to minimize the chances of class legislation. The vote has a function of protecting voters from unjust treatment, but it is not to be used solely for private benefit, but in order to promote the public good. Voting, being a public duty, requires accountability. Secret ballots will enable voters to get away more easily with the acts which serve their personal or class interests at the expense of the general interest. Publicity will make voters pay more attention to the grounds for their actions. It may of course also subject them to external vested pressure. But Mill is of the opinion that such pressure was, at the time he wrote, less of a danger than the use of a secret vote to promote the sinister class or personal interest of the voter.

Mill's conception of democracy is therefore one in which government is ultimately accountable to the people, and in which each group is able, through the franchise, to protect its interests. But for him democracy is also a system of government in which no single group has absolute power over all others. Minority opinions can assert an influence on the process by which decisions are made. In particular, the instructed have a crucial role to play, being given an influence greater than their numerical strength. Political participation is seen not just as a means of protecting one's legitimate interests, but also as an educative process in which one enlarges one's sympathies and interests. The functions of legislation and administration are to be in the hands of experts, while the main function of Parliament is to be a place for the discussion of ideas. It is his hope, backed up by various devices, that disagreements will be based on different opinions, and not on different sectional interests.

Given his conviction that no group can have its interests securely defended by another group, it is somewhat surprising that Mill excludes certain groups from the franchise. Relying on the view that "universal teaching must precede universal enfranchisement", Mill argues that the suffrage should not be given to those who are unable to read, write, or do simple arithmetic. Mill also excludes from the vote those who do not pay taxes on the ground that giving them the vote "amounts to allowing them to put their hands into other people's pockets, for any purpose which they think fit to call a public one" (*CW* XIX:471). The third group of people excluded consists of those who receive parish relief. This is for the same reason that such people should not be in a position to help themselves to the money of others. But if these are groups of people with distinct interests which can only be adequately protected or fully understood by others if they have the vote, then Mill's reasons for exclusion seem rather feeble. The same kinds of consideration which led Mill to plead for the extension of the suffrage to the working class generally and to women should also be sufficient to outweigh his arguments for the exclusion of the three groups mentioned. If political participation has an educative effect, then those excluded from the franchise are denied one valuable avenue for their improvement. Again, Mill's concern that minorities should be adequately represented counts against their exclusion. There are sufficient safeguards in Mill's various proposals to prevent any single group from getting its way without the support of others, and to combat any damage to the general interest which the uneducated, the non-taxpayers, and the recipients of parish relief may be expected to inflict. Mill seems to have too much faith in the impartiality of the educated, and too little in that of the uneducated and the poor, almost as if he believes that to be well educated is both necessary and sufficient to secure the moral virtues.

V

Two fundamental principles shaped Mill's attitudes towards the working classes. The first is that they themselves are ultimately the best defenders of their own interests. The second is that they need to be educated to a higher moral and intellectual level, and when they have so developed, they will have a better conception of their interests and integrate them with the general interest. These principles sustained Mill's belief that the franchise should be extended to them in order that they may both protect their interests and develop their capacities through the educative effects of political participation. The representatives of the working classes are also to be educated by being subjected to the influences of the instructed in Parliament.

These principles guided not just Mill's proposals about democracy but also his account of economic organization. Thus Mill points out that there are two conflicting theories about the desirable social position for manual labours. The theory which he accepts is that they should be independent. The other theory is that they should be dependent on the higher classes who have the responsibility of protecting them. Mill points out that the privileged and powerful classes have always used their power to advance their own interest. People need to be protected from their so-called protectors. Husbands who are supposed to protect their wives, and parents their children, have been guilty of brutality and tyranny, as many a police report has shown.

The working classes will not accept the state of dependence on their employers whose interests are perceived to be opposed to their own. As workers become better educated through schools, newspapers, public discussions, and trade union activities, they are confirmed in their opposition to the employment of others as their protectors. One valuable effect of the improvement in education and intelligence of the workers is the reduction in overpopulation. Women will achieve a degree of social independence as they move into industrial occupation. They will no longer regard the bearing and nurturing of children as their exclusive function, filling their entire lives.

Workers are not prepared to treat the employer–employee relationship as permanent, for it is a relationship of dependence. Workers and capitalists will not do justice to one another in such a relationship. Workers will generally try to get as high wages for as little work as possible, and it is in the interests of the capitalists themselves to have the operations of industry conducted on a different basis that brings together their interests and those of the workers. Mill suggests a co-operative partnership between workers and capitalists in which the partners each have a share of the total profits. He believes that such a partnership is both economically efficient and morally beneficial in elevating the characters of the parties involved. Each will give of its best in making the partnership a success.

But Mill regards co-operatives of capitalists and workers as but a step to the ultimately desirable association of workers among themselves. Workers will then collectively own the capital, and work under managers they have elected. In such associations workers do not have to pay capitalists a "tax" for the use of the capital. They would accumulate the capital themselves. Mill gives examples of the successful operation of such workers' associations in Paris, built up from humble beginnings by disciplined and demanding savings from meagre incomes.

> The same admirable qualities by which the associations were carried through their early struggles, maintained them in their increasing prosperity. Their rules of discipline, instead of being more lax, are stricter than those of ordinary workshops; but being rules self-imposed, for the manifest good of the community, and not for the convenience of an employer regarded as having an opposite interest, they are far more scrupulously obeyed, and the voluntary obedience carries with it a sense of personal worth and dignity. (CW III:780–81)

Mill pays some attention to the detailed operations of these associations, noting with satisfaction that they abandoned the idea with which they started out that all should get equal wages, irrespective of the type of work done. "Almost all have abandoned this system, and after allowing to every one a fixed minimum, sufficient for subsistence, they apportion all further renumeration according to the work done: most of them even dividing the profits at the end of the year, in the same proportion as the earnings" (CW III:782–83). New members do not have to bring capital to the associations. They enter as partners but they receive for a few years a smaller share of the profits. Members are free to leave the associations although they cannot take away any of the capital. The capital is never to be divided.

Mill also details the successful operations of workers' associations in England. His reason for going into such details is apparently to show that the idea of workers' co-operatives is not a pie-in-the-sky, but a fully feasible idea.

> It is hardly possible to take any but a hopeful view of the prospects of mankind, when in two leading countries of the world, the obscure depths of society contain simple working men whose integrity, good sense, self-command, and honourable confidence in one another, have enabled them to carry these noble experiments to the triumphant issue which the facts recorded in the preceding pages attest. (CW III:791)

Mill explains that one of the sources of efficiency in a co-operative association of workers is the limitation in the number of distributors, thereby freeing more people to engage in productive activities. The other source of efficiency is the incentive given to workers to do their best to increase productivity. In the early stages, workers' co-operative associations will compete with co-operative associations of capitalists and workers. Mill sees this competition as healthy. But eventually no worker would want to work outside co-operative associations of workers. Society will then be transformed: "the best aspirations of the democratic spirit" would be realized "by putting an end to the division of society into the industrious and the idle, and effacing all social distinctions but those fairly earned by personal services and exertions" (CW III:793). Mill regards it as "the great social evil" that there should be a non-labouring class. When industrial organization is entirely based on associations of workers' co-operatives, this social evil is eradicted and there will be a kind of classless society in which nobody is "exempt from bearing their share of the necessary labours of human life, except those unable to labour, or who have fairly earned rest by previous toil" (CW III:758).

Mill writes in glowing terms about the social and moral changes that will be generated by this change in industrial organization. The non-material benefits to all, and especially to the working classes, far outweigh the material benefits, which are themselves quite great.

It is scarcely possible to rate too highly this material benefit, which yet is as nothing compared with the moral revolution in society that would accompany it: the healing of the standing feud between capital and labour; the transformation of human life, from a conflict of classes struggling for opposite interests to a friendly rivalry in the pursuit of a common good to all, the elevation of the dignity of labour; a new sense of security and independence in the labouring class; and the conversion of each human being's daily occupation into a school of the social sympathies and the practical intelligence. (CW III:792)

However, until this ideal state is reached, there will continue to be conflicts between the working classes and the capitalists who are their employers. Workers were entitled to join together in trade unions for the purpose of trying to raise their wages. Mill does not believe that they will often succeed, but it is wrong to legislate against trade unions, or against strikes. Trade unions are not a hindrance to the free market for labour but "the necessary instrumentality of that free market" (*CW* III:932). Mill supports trade unions and the right to strike only to the extent that no compulsion is imposed. He recognizes that the voluntary activities of trade unions can sometimes work against the public good, as, for example, when they refuse to allow any differentials in pay between skilled and unskilled workers. But here, as elsewhere, Mill's commitment to individual liberty prevails.

> It does not, however, follow as a consequence that the law would be warranted in making the formation of such associations illegal and punishable. Independently of all considerations of constitutional liberty, the best interests of the human race imperatively require that all economical experiments, voluntarily undertaken, should have the fullest licence, and that force and fraud should be the only means of attempting to benefit themselves, which are interdicted to the less fortunate classes of the community. (*CW* III:934)

Mill was also aware of the fact that some workers might hope to gain the benefit to workers generally of the activities of trade unions, without at the same time making the sacrifice of being a member of a union that goes on strike. Such non-members gain from the higher wages which result from trade union activities, but they do not pay the membership fee or submit to restrictions which are needed to gain the higher wages. Mill disapproves of such free-riding, and believes it proper for members of trade unions to show their public disapproval of non-members, and to put some social pressure on non-members to join. However, members should be prevented by law from going further and infringing, or threatening to infringe, "any of the rights which the law guarantees to all – security of person and property against violation, and of reputation against calumny" (*CW* V:660).

VI

Mill's concern for the welfare of the working classes led him to seriously consider fundamental changes to social organization and to challenge the established system of private property. Admission to the franchise and the acquisition of "purely political rights" by the working classes do not in themselves remove all the social injustices from which they suffer. In particular there is still the great evil of their being "debarred by the accident of birth both from the enjoyments, and from the mental and moral advantages, which others inherit without exertion and independently of desert" (CW V:710).

In the *Autobiography* he described one of the important changes in his views as his acceptance of "a qualified Socialism" (CW I:199). He went on to describe some of the details of the changes, which involved a willingness to consider fundamental alterations in social institutions, including changes in the institution of private property which he had previously regarded as sacrosanct (CW I:239). He had thought that there were only limited possibilities of improving the lot of the vast majority who were poor. The numbers of the poor were to be reduced by their voluntary restraint on population brought about by universal education. But now he acknowledges the possibility of a more equitable division of goods, and a major social transformation in the character of both the labouring classes and their employers to the extent that they will both develop an interest in the common good, and will no longer be motivated by self-interest.

Mill's greatest sympathy with socialism lies with its account of the evils of existing society. There is a passionate intensity in the way he describes these evils both in the *Autobiography* and in the posthumously published *Chapters on Socialism*. There is a vast contrast between the few who are rich and the many who are poor. The great majority of people are still forced by poverty to be "chained to a place, to an occupation, and to conformity with the will of an employer" (CW V:710). The existence of great poverty has little to do with desert. A very large proportion of the "industrious classes" are dependent on charity, while there are many idle rich. "Some are born without work, others are born to a position in which they can become rich *by* work, the great majority are born to hard work and poverty throughout life, numbers to indigence" (CW V:714).

The evil of misconduct, including crime, in existing society can be traced to poverty, idleness, and bad education or lack of education, which are themselves the results of defective social arrangements. So far Mill is in agreement with what he takes to be the socialist analysis of our present discontents. But he emphatically rejects the socialist case against competition. Socialists raise both moral and economic objections to competition. Competition is morally bad because it sets people against one another and places them in a zero-sum situation in which a person can only gain at the expense of others. It is also economically bad because it is the cause of low wages to labourers and of ruin and bankruptcy to producers. But Mill argues that if competition can lower wages, it can also raise them. The working classes benefit from the competition among producers which leads to a lowering of the prices of commodities. Competition among producers seldom leads to a monopoly, although in some areas producers with larger capital to invest in better machinery will have advantages over smaller producers. But the concentration of businesses in larger competitors produces efficiency and a lowering of the prices of commodities. Mill acknowledges that the intensity of modern competition may lead to the adoption of fraudulent practices in order to increase profits. But the cure for this evil need not depend on the adoption of socialism.

Mill also disagrees with the socialists about whether the profits to capitalists are disproportionately large compared with the wages of labourers. He believes that the return to capitalists for the investment of their capital, for the risks they take of losing, for the exercise of their skill, and for the work they put in, is quite fair. Workers would not gain much if some of the profits of capitalists were divided among them. Greater gains would be made by the invention of machinery and by cutting back on the cost of having unnecessary distributors of goods. Mill also argues that contrary to the claims made by socialists, the evils of existing social arrangements are not increasing, but in fact the conditions of the working classes are gradually improving.

While Mill is in substantial agreement with socialists about the evils of the current operation of the system of private property, he is less sympathetic to their proposed solutions. He distinguishes between the revolutionary socialists and the socialism of people such as Owen and Fourier. He has little time for the former, centralized version of socialism, in which the working classes or their agents take over and manage all the property of the country. Revolutionary socialists attempt to change society "at a single stroke", heedless of the "frightful bloodshed and misery that would ensue if the attempt was resisted" (*CW* V:737). They will forcibly and unjustly take over property currently held in private hands. They will plunge society into chaos and drag everybody down to the present low level of the worst off. Why should we give up the "large possibilities of improvement" available in the present system for a completely untried system? Revolutionary socialism will prove to be a "disastrous failure".

However, Mill takes much more seriously the socialism of Owen and Fourier and "the more thoughtful and philosophic Socialists generally". In this case socialism is decentralized, being applied to smaller units such as villages or townships, and being extended to the whole country only by a multiplication of such self-contained units. So the movement away from private property can be made on an experimental basis. Socialism, brought about in this way, will only be implemented on an increasingly broad scale when it has been shown to be successful on a smaller scale.

Mill defines socialism as follows:

What is characteristic of Socialism is the joint ownership by all the members of the community of the instruments and means of production; which carries with it the consequence that the division of the produce among the body of owners must be a public act, performed according to rules laid down by the community. Socialism by no means excludes private ownership of articles of consumption; the exclusive right of each to his or her share of the produce when received, either to enjoy, to give, or to exchange it. . . . The distinctive feature of Socialism is not that all things are in common, but that production is only carried on upon the common account, and the instruments of production are held as common property. (*CW* V:738)

Whereas he thinks that revolutionary socialism is impractical in seeking to manage the whole production of the nation through one central organization, he does not doubt the practicability of the decentralized socialism of Owen and Fourier. But one crucial consideration is the relative efficiency of socialist management when compared with the system of management under capitalism. Under capitalism the owners of capital will reap all the profit accruing from good management, and will therefore have a great incentive to maximize efficiency. But in a socialist system, this incentive is missing. This would be the case under the form of socialism which Mill calls Communism, in which everyone gets an equal share of the produce. With people as they now are, the greatest inducement to maximum exertion is some prospect of their own economic betterment or that of their families. Duty and honour are more likely to prevent wrongdoing than lead to the fullest application of energies to overcome "the ever-present influence of indolence and of ease" (CW V:740). Under a Communist system those with the greatest managerial skills will not be drawn into the job because they will not receive greater remuneration than others for the performance of more onerous work.

As far as the welfare of ordinary workers is concerned, Mill believes that Communism may be more efficient than the existing system in which hired labourers are paid fixed wages. Trade unions often discourage their members from being too efficient as this would reduce the number of jobs available. They also oppose the introduction of machinery which economizes on the use of labour. On the other hand, in a Communist system it is in the general interest of the workers that everyone reach the highest level of efficiency. However, Mill argues that the inefficiency of the present system can be remedied by switching to a system of industrial partnership in which all the labourers obtain a share of the profits. So the advantage of Communism in this area is only against the present system of private property, and not against better arrangements for the remuneration of workers which can be made within a system of private property.

Mill believes that a Communist society will often "fail to exhibit the attractive picture of mutual love and unity of will and feeling which we are often told by Communists to expect" (CW V:745). There are many sources of discord. People's material interests are placed outside the area of dispute by equality of treatment. But there will still be rivalry for reputation and for personal power and influence, which will be more intense as energies are diverted to these areas from the area of material interests. A Communist society will make collective decisions about the education of children, and there will be strong disagreement about the appropriate forms of education. Major differences of opinion will also arise about the use of common productive resources and about the conditions of social life generally. Mill harbours great fears for individual freedom, as the intrusions into private life will be very great in a Communist society.

Already in all societies the compression of individuality by the majority is a great and growing evil; it would probably be much greater under Communism, except so far as it might be in the power of individuals to set bounds to it by selecting to belong to a community of persons like-minded with themselves. (*CW* V:746)

Apart from Communism, the other form of socialism that Mill considers is Fourierism, in which inequalities in rewards are permitted. Mill also adds that Fourierism allows "individual ownership of capital, but not the arbitrary disposal of it" (*CW* V:747). This seems to go against his earlier characterization of all forms of socialism in terms of the common ownership of all the means of production. But by capital he means the savings made from the remunerations received. Workers are to be divided into groups, with each group performing a different kind of work. Workers choose which group to join, and they may belong to more than one group. Each group is paid in proportion to its contribution of labour, capital, and talent. If there are too many in one group and too few in another, then the remuneration of the groups will change in order to get a better balance of members. This arrangement allows for a greater degree of freedom of choice than alternative socialist schemes, and Mill believes that "the picture of a Fourierist community is both attractive in itself and requires less from common humanity than any other known system of Socialism" (*CW* V:748). He is prepared to see it tested in social life.

He keeps an open mind about the eventual superiority of some form of socialism over a system of private property. But he is convinced that socialist schemes are "at present workable only by the *elite* of mankind, and have yet to prove their power of training mankind at large to the state of improvement which they presuppose" (*CW* V:748). Given that at present people do not have the moral and intellectual qualities to make socialism successful, and that there is no quick way of inculcating those qualities in them, we would have to live with a system of private property, for a considerable period of time. But we do not have to live with that system as it now stands with all its injustices. The few who currently benefit from the present system should be prepared to make those changes which will help the majority. This is a requirement both of justice and of prudence, because otherwise there will be attempts made to move prematurely into a socialist society. Just as Mill is impatient with the revolutionary socialists who wish to transform society radically and immediately, so too is he impatient with the defenders of the existing social order who are complacent about its virtue and who misrepresent the socialist alternative to it.[9]

VII

Speaking of the working classes, Mill notes, "The prospect of the future depends on the degree in which they can be made rational beings" (CW III:763). He was optimistic about the future towards which we should move by non-violent, piecemeal, political, social, and economic reforms. As the working classes participate more fully in the life of the community, they will improve themselves materially, intellectually, and morally, and they will contribute to the improvement of everybody else. But for Mill the desirable future is not one in which wealth and production keep on increasing endlessly. Increased production is important for backward countries, but in the most advanced countries better distribution is crucial. He envisages a stationary state in which there is no increase in capital and production, and in which population is kept in check so that the condition of the lower classes will not deterioriate. There will be no poverty, and better distribution will produce a society with the following features:

... a well-paid and affluent body of labourers; no enormous fortunes, except what were earned and accumulated during a single lifetime; but a much larger body of persons than at present, not only exempt from the coarser toils, but with sufficient leisure, both physical and mental, from mechanical details, to cultivate freely the graces of life, and afford examples of them to the classes less favourably circumstanced for their growth. (CW III:755)

Among "the graces of life" made possible by the stationary state is the enjoyment of solitude. A society which is not dedicated to ever-increasing production, and in which there is no excessive population, will be one where people can have the solitude to appreciate "natural beauty and grandeur". It will not destroy all "the spontaneous activity of nature",

> [w]ith every rood of land brought into cultivation, which is capable of growing food for human beings; every flowery waste or natural pasture ploughed up, all quadrupeds or birds which are not domesticated for man's use exterminated as his rivals for food, every hedgerow or superflous tree rooted out, and scarcely a place left where a wild shrub or flower would grow without being eradicated as a weed in the name of improved agriculture. (CW III:756)

Material prosperity will not increase in the stationary society, but there will be improvement in other areas – in our cultural, moral, and social life generally. But a high level of material comfort will be enjoyed by all, and no one will any longer be subjected to a "life of drudgery and imprisonment": "no one is poor, no one desires to be richer, nor has any reason to fear being thrust back, by efforts of others to push themselves forward" (CW III:754). There will certainly be no industrious poor, nor any idle rich. All will be "labourers", earning an income on the basis of their labour, and rewarded in proportion to their industry. And all labourers will be able to cultivate the graces of life.

NOTES

1 *Autobiography*, CW I:274.
2 *CW* I:239.
3 *CW* I:272.
4 Kinzer, Robson, and Robson 1992, 90. This book gives an excellent account of Mill's parliamentary career.
5 *Autobiography*, CW I:278. See also Kinzer, Robson, and Robson 1992, 94–99; and Packe 1954, 457–62.
6 See Schneewind 1968.
7 Schneewind 1968, 328.
8 J. M. Robson 1968, 224.
9 See his essay "Newman's Political Economy", CW V:441–57.

11 The subjection of women

When John Stuart Mill married Harriet Taylor in 1851, he wrote out a formal protest against the laws that would govern their marriage. He objected to

the whole character of the marriage relation as constituted by law ... for this amongst other reasons, that it confers upon one of the parties to the contract, legal power & control over the person, property, and freedom of action of the other party, independent of her own wishes and will. ... [H]aving no means of legally divesting myself of these odious powers ... [I] feel it my duty to put on record a formal protest against the existing law of marriage, in so far as conferring such powers; and a solemn promise never in any case or under any circumstances to use them. (Hayek 1951, 168)

This critique of the injustices of English marriage law formed the core of Mill's later work, *The Subjection of Women*. Although *The Subjection of Women* was enthusiastically welcomed and widely circulated among the small circles of women's rights advocates on both sides of the Atlantic in the latter nineteenth century, beyond these groups when the book was not ignored it was frequently ridiculed or excoriated by philosophers and politicians alike. James Fitzjames Stephen, one of the foremost jurists of the century, wrote that he disagreed with *The Subjection of Women* "from the first sentence to the last" (Stephen 1873/1967, 188). Thirty years later, Frederic Harrison said it smacked of "rank moral and social anar-

This chapter revises and expands material that originally appeared in my "Marital Slavery and Friendship: John Stuart Mill's *The Subjection of Women*," *Political Theory* 9 (May 1981) 229–47.

chy" (quoted in Packe 1954, 495). This chilly reception was due in large part to the book's subject matter, the relationship between the sexes and the organization of both domestic and political power in English society.

As Mill's denunciation of English marriage law at the time of his wedding demonstrates, he saw a clear relationship between his ideas about women's subordination and contemporary legal structures. On several occasions he worked to influence legislation and public policy concerning issues affecting women. His best-known effort was his sponsorship while a member of Parliament of a women's suffrage amendment to the Reform Act of 1867, but he also cosponsored a Married Women's Property bill the next year, testified before the Royal Commission on the Contagious Diseases Acts in 1871, and was in regular correspondence with women's rights activists. Not surprisingly, these activities also subjected him to ridicule from conservative forces.

In recent years Mill's ideas about women's subordination and how it is to be remedied have generated a different sort of controversy. Where nineteenth-century women's rights activists by and large embraced Mill's contention that women and men deserved equality before the law, some contemporary feminists have asserted that Mill's vision of "equality" did not adequately challenge the existing sexual division of labor and that it subtly reinscribes gender roles (Annas 1977, Okin 1979, Goldstein 1980, Eisenstein 1981, Elshtain 1981, Krouse 1982). Christine di Stefano argues that Mill was only prepared to grant women equality with men if they manifested traditionally male characteristics like working in the public sphere, and that he did not attend sufficiently to women's differences both from men and among various class, racial, and other categories of women (di Stefano 1991, 144–86). Yet others see in Mill's discussions of the working class a tendency to see in the poor the same chaos and disorder that much of his society found in women (Zerilli 1994; see also Ring 1985, 37).

This chapter pays heed to these criticisms but argues that Mill's denunciation of "marital slavery" in *The Subjection of Women* and his insistence that it be replaced by "marital friendship" reconstituted the understanding in much previous liberal political theory and English and American law concerning what kinds of relationships were legitimate in the private or domestic realm. In Mill's eyes the relationship between husband and wife had to be grounded in legal equality. Nearly two hundred years earlier John Locke had, like Mill, concluded that the legal subordination of wife to husband violated the principle that all rational beings had a right to equal freedom, but Locke nonetheless had accepted legal rules giving domestic authority of the male head-of-household as "the abler and the stronger" (Locke 1988, 321). For Mill, however, legally created and enforced inequality in the domestic realm made what should have been a private and intimate relationship into one infused with state-sanctioned power. Legal reforms such as giving married women the right to hold property, equal custodial rights for mothers and fathers, and equal grounds for legal separation were necessary to eliminate the spousal domination that corrupted the relationship between husband and wife. That corruption affected their relationship both as intimate companions and as fellow citizens.

Mill's reflections on the relationship between the public and domestic world also emphasized the extent to which the rights-bearing individual of much liberal political thought is constituted in important ways by intimate as well as public relationships. In Mill's eyes, no "individual" can properly be viewed as an isolated or atomistic entity.[1] His view of the individual as fundamentally constituted in and by interpersonal relationships was an important contribution to the liberal understanding of individual autonomy.[2] Mill's insights concerning both the inextricable relationship between the public and private worlds and the nature of the individual and individual autonomy make *The Subjection of Women* an important text not only in the history of feminist theory but for contemporary liberal political theory, public policy, and law as well.[3]

The Subjection of Women is divided into four untitled chapters which contain overlapping and complimentary themes. The first chapter sets forth Mill's depiction and critique of the social and legal status of women in his society. The oppressive nature of Victorian marriage law and Mill's proposals for marriage law reform are the subjects of the second. The third discusses both the injustice of shutting women out of most remunerative occupations and the vote, and the social disutility or cost to society of those exclusions. In the fourth, Mill sets forth his vision of the ways in which the acceptance of the principle of equality between the sexes would transform marriage and family relationships, civil society, and even the individual capacity for happiness and fulfillment. *The Subjection of Women* both argued that justice demands that women be admitted to the rights held by men, and expressed Mill's belief that legal equality would help usher in a radically different and better future for women and men alike.[4]

I. "AN EMINENTLY ARTIFICIAL THING": WOMEN'S PRESENT NATURE AND ITS CAUSES

Mill sets forth the fundamental argument of *The Subjection of Women* in the first paragraph: it is that "the principle which regulates the existing social relations between the two sexes – the legal subordination of one sex to the other – is wrong in itself and now one of the chief hindrances to human improvement; and that it ought to be replaced by a principle of perfect equality, admitting no power or privilege on the one side, nor disability on the other" (*CW* XXI:261). His concern was to show that women's lack of equality has deprived them of their freedom: legal inequality has created not simply different resources and realms of action for men and women, but a relationship of active domination in which women had to conform themselves to men's wills. In an image that permeates the book and that captures his belief in the inseparability of inequality and active domination, Mill compared women's subordination to slavery. The dependence of women on men "is the primitive state of slavery lasting on" (*CW* XXI:264), a striking example of "a social relation grounded on force" that has survived despite "generations of institutions grounded on equal justice" (*CW* XXI:265). Moreover, the slave-like relationship between women and men made it impossible, in Mill's eyes, to know the "nature" or capacities of either sex, or whether these differ in any way, for such power relationships inevitably distort both the actions and perceptions of those involved in them. Men and women alike were harmed by such distortion.

The subordination of women was not only an unjust violation of the principle of equal liberty, but an anachronism. Mill referred to the abolition of legal chattel slavery in "all the countries of Christian Europe" (*CW* XXI:264) as proof that women's unequal status is a "relic of the past [that] is discordant with the future and must necessarily disappear" (*CW* XXI:272). The individual's place in the world used to be based on status, but now each person is free from ascribed roles and responsibilities:

> For, what is the peculiar character of the modern world – the difference which chiefly distinguishes modern institutions, modern social ideas, modern life itself, from those of times long past? It is, that human beings are no longer born to their place in life, and chained down by an inexorable bond to the place they are born to, but are free to employ their faculties, and such favourable chances as offer, to achieve the lot which may appear to them most desirable. (CW XXI:272–73)

Freedom of choice was not only conducive to individual happiness, but also provided the best hope for human progress. Not only would things go best for the individual when they "are left to his own discretion," but "freedom of individual choice is now known to be the only thing which procures the adoption of the best processes" to lead to social betterment (CW XXI:273). This interweaving of the principle of justice that dictates women's right to equality before the law and of the principle of utility that anticipates social benefits to follow from overturning relationships of domination and subordination recurs repeatedly in *The Subjection of Women*.

II. THE INJUSTICE OF MARITAL SLAVERY

Having set forth in chapter I the basic argument that the inequality of women and men before the law was both unjust and harmful to individuals and society, Mill devoted chapter II to a discussion specifically of marriage law and its role in creating and perpetuating the conditions of domination and subordination that marked relationships between the sexes. Reformation of marriage law was essential, in Mill's eyes, if marriage were to become, as he very much desired, a "school of genuine moral sentiment" (CW XXI:284). Marital relations based on equality would transform not only the domestic but also the civic characters of men and women, and provide a model of mutual respect and reciprocity that children would imitate in their own adult relationships.

Mill asserted that despite the supposed advances of Christian civilization, the "wife is the actual bond-servant of her husband: no less so, as far as legal obligation goes, than slaves commonly so called" (CW XXI:284). Mill's analysis of women's servitude was not confined to *The Subjection of Women*. In his speech on the Reform Bill of 1867, Mill talked of that "obscure feeling" that is "ashamed to confess itself openly" that women had no right to care about anything except "how they may be the most useful and devoted servants of some man" (*CW* XXVIII:154). To Auguste Comte he wrote comparing women to "domestic slaves" and noted that women's capacities are spent "seeking happiness not in their own life, but exclusively in the favor and affection of the other sex, which is only given to them on the condition of their dependence" (*CW* XIII:609, my translation).

Mill frequently made an analogy between the situation of married women and that of chattel slaves. He thought that the position of married women resembled that of slaves in several ways: the social and economic system gave women little alternative except to marry; once married, the legal personality of the woman was subsumed in that of her husband; and the abuses of human dignity permitted by custom and law within marriage were egregious.

In Mill's eyes, women were in a double bind: they were not free within marriage, and they were not truly free not to marry.[5] What could an unmarried woman do? Even if she were of the middle or upper classes, she could not attend any of the English universities, and thus she was barred from a systematic higher education. If somehow she acquired a professional education, the professional associations usually refused to allow her to practice her trade. "No sooner do women show themselves capable of competing with men in any career, than that career, if it be lucrative or honorable, is closed to them" (*CW* XXI).[6]

Working-class women were even worse off. In the *Principles of Political Economy*, Mill argued that their low wages were due to the "prejudice" of society which, "making almost every woman, socially speaking, an appendage of some man, enables men to take systematically the lion's share of whatever belongs to both." A second cause of low wages for women was the surplus of female labor for unskilled jobs. Law and custom ordained that a woman has "scarcely any means open to her of gaining a livelihood, except as a wife and mother" (*CW* II:394; III:765–66). Marriage was, as Mill put it, a "Hobson's choice" for women, "that or none" (*CW* XXI:281).[7]

Worse than the social and economic pressure to marry, however, was women's status within marriage. Mill thoroughly understood the stipulations of the English common law which deprived a married woman of a legal personality independent of that of her husband. The doctrine of coverture or spousal unity, as it was called, was based on the Biblical notion that "a man [shall] leave his father and his mother, and shall cleave to his wife, and they shall be one flesh" (Genesis 2:22–23). If "one flesh," then, as Blackstone put it, "by marriage, the husband and wife are one person in law." And that "person" was represented by the husband. Again Blackstone (1765–69, I:430) was most succinct: "The very being or legal existence of the woman is suspended during the marriage, or at least is incorporated and consolidated into that of the husband."[8] One of the most commonly felt injustices of the doctrine of spousal unity was the married woman's lack of ownership of her own earnings. As the matrimonial couple was "one person," the wife's earnings during marriage were owned and controlled by her husband.[9] During his term as a member of Parliament, in June 1868, Mill supported a Married Women's Property Bill, saying that its opponents were men who thought it impossible for "society to exist on a harmonious footing between two persons unless one of them has absolute power over the other," and insisting that England had moved beyond such a "savage state" (CW XXVIII:285).[10] In *The Subjection of Women* Mill argued that the "wife's position under the common law of England [with respect to property] is worse than that of slaves in the laws of many countries: by the Roman law, for example, a slave might have his peculium, which to a certain extent the law guaranteed to him for his exclusive use" (CW XXI:284). Similarly, Mill regarded the husband's exclusive guardianship over the married couple's children as a sign of the woman's dependence on her husband's will (CW XXI:285). She was denied any role in life except that of being "the personal body-servant of a despot" (CW XXI:285).

Both common and statute law also sanctioned domestic violence. The two legal stipulations that to Mill most demonstrated "the assimilation of the wife to the slave" were her inability to refuse her master "the last familiarity" and her inability to obtain a legal separation from her husband unless he were guilty of desertion or extreme cruelty in addition to his adultery (CW XXI:285–86). While middle-class Victorian wives were clearly not subject to the conditions of chattel slavery (most importantly, neither they nor their children could be sold), Mill chose the slave image to impress upon his readers that by marriage a husband assumed control of his wife's property and her body.[11] Mill was appalled by the notion that no matter how brutal a tyrant a husband might be, and no matter how a woman might loathe him, "he can claim from her and enforce the lowest degradation of a human being," which was to be made the instrument of "an animal function contrary to her inclination" (CW XXI:285). A man and wife being one body, rape was by definition a crime which a married man could not commit against his own wife. By law a wife could not leave her husband on account of this offense without being guilty of desertion, nor could she prosecute him. Rape within marriage was particularly vicious because it was legal.

Wife-beating was so rarely prosecuted and so lightly punished that society appeared to condone such physical violence against women. During the parliamentary debates on the Representation of the People Bill in 1867, Mill argued that women needed suffrage to enable them to lobby for legislation which would punish domestic assault:

I should like to have a return laid before this House of the number of women who are annually beaten to death, kicked to death or trampled to death by their male protectors: and, in an opposite column, the amount of sentences passed. . . . I should also like to have, in a third column, the amount of property, the wrongful taking of which was . . . thought worthy of the same punishment. We should then have an arithmetical value set by a male legislature and male tribunals on the murder of a woman. (CW XXVIII:158–59)

Knowledge that courts put a low value on a woman's life and rarely provided women protection from brutal husbands made *all* women vulnerable and contributed to their submissiveness in marriage.[12] For Mill, domestic slavery was not an aberration found in a few unhappy marriages, but a legally sanctioned system of male domination that rendered some women's lives nearly unbearable, and that affected the character of even the happiest marriages in his day.

Despite these strong denunciations of women's position under marriage law, Mill by and large accepted the notion that once they marry, women should be solely responsible for the care of the household and children, men for providing the family income: "When the support of the family depends . . . on earnings, the common arrangement, by which the man earns the income and the wife superintends the domestic expenditure, seems to me in general the most suitable division of labour between the two persons" (CW XXI:297). He did not regard it as "a desirable custom, that the wife should contribute by her labour to the income of the family" (CW XXI:298). Mill indicated that women alone would care for any children of the marriage; repeatedly he called it the "care which ... nobody else takes," the one vocation in which there is "nobody to compete with them," and the occupation which "cannot be fulfilled by others" (CW XXI:297–98, 300, 340). For all his insight into the dynamics of domestic domination and subordination, Mill did not suggest altering domestic arrangements, but seemed to think that providing equal opportunity to women in areas outside the family would solve the power imbalances within. In *On Liberty* he wrote that "nothing more is needed for the complete removal of [the despotic power of husbands over wives] than that wives should have the same rights and receive the same protection of the law in the same manner, as all other persons" (CW XVIII:30).

Despite his inability to see that women's exclusive responsibility for domestic chores was itself an impediment to their entry into public life, by the end of chapter II Mill had posed a radical challenge to one of the most preciously held assumptions about marriage in the modern era, which is that it is a relationship grounded on the consent of the partners to join their lives. Mill argued to the contrary that the presumed consent of women to marry was not in any real sense a free promise, but one socially coerced by the lack of meaningful options. Further, the laws of marriage deprived a woman of many of the normal powers of autonomous adults, from controlling her earnings, to entering contracts, to defending her bodily autonomy by resisting unwanted sexual relations. Indeed, the whole notion of a woman "consenting" to the marriage "offer" of a man implied from the outset a hierarchical relationship. Such a one-way offer did not reflect the relationship that should exist between those who were truly equal, among beings who should be able to create together by free discussion and mutual agreement an association to govern their lives together.

To create conditions conducive to a marriage of equals rather than one of master and slave, marriage law itself would have to be altered, women would have to be provided equal educational and employment opportunity, and both men and women would have to become capable of sustaining genuinely equal and reciprocal relationships within marriage.

III. THE DISUTILITY OF EXCLUDING WOMEN FROM PUBLIC LIFE

One of the most interesting aspects of Mill's writings on women was his assertion that domestic and political life were inextricably connected. This challenged the traditional distinction in liberal political theory between that which is public and that which is private. The public discrimination against women, Mill contended, was a manifestation of a desire for dominance rooted as much in familial and intimate relationships as in public considerations: "[women's] disabilities [in law] are only clung to in order to maintain their subordination in domestic life: because the generality of the male sex cannot yet tolerate the idea of living with an equal" (CW XXI:299). Indeed, men's fear of equality in the household was the driving force behind their resistance to granting women political rights. Ending the subjection of women would therefore require both marriage law reform and changes in women's participation in public and political work. This dual agenda was reflected in the fact that Mill's denunciation of the injustice and corrupting influence of marriage law in chapter II was followed in chapter III by a long argument – or series of arguments – meant to refute a panoply of prejudices against women entering the professions and other remunerative work, higher education, and politics, and to show that women should be admitted "to all the functions and occupations hitherto retained as the monopoly of the stronger sex" (CW XXI:299).

While Mill's discussion of women's opportunities for education, employment, and public service seems to be the thematic complement to his analysis of marriage, the *form* of Mill's argumentation in chapter III is at odds with that of the rest of The Subjection of Women. Where Mill argued in chapters I and II that one could not know women's true nature because the character of women as well as men had been distorted by the relationships of domination and subordination between the sexes, in chapter III he frequently invoked women's nature (that is, their present nature) as a reason for dropping barriers to their wider social and political participation.[13]

The degree to which Mill referred to women's present characteristics in support of his brief for eliminating barriers to their participation in public life seemed not only to contradict his earlier
assertions that these characteristics were themselves the product of
women's subordination, but also to argue that women be admitted
to the franchise and public life not because their humanity entitled
them to the same rights as men, but because of various sex-based
traits. The depictions of supposedly female traits also tended to
obscure relevant distinctions among women of different classes and
social groups.

Throughout chapter III Mill made a two-pronged argument about
women's exclusions from public life: these were "a tyranny to them,
and a detriment to society" (*CW* XXI:300). The first such disability
Mill addressed was women's exclusion from both the "parliamentary and municipal franchise" (*CW* XXI:301); when Mill served as a
member of Parliament he attempted to put theory into practice by
proposing a women's suffrage amendment to the Reform Act of
1867. In *The Subjection of Women* he argued first that the vote is an
aspect of the right to self-protection, and then moved on to argue
that "high considerations of practical utility" suggest that whatever
public offices are open to men should be open to women too (*CW*
XXI:302). He reviewed the manifest political talent of Queens Elizabeth and Victoria of England, Blanche of Castile, Margaret of Aus-
tria, and other female rulers. He went on to suggest that women's
aptitude for politics was rooted in their "more rapid insight into
character," their tendency to abjure "abstraction" and "imaginary
entit[ies]" in favor of attention to "individuals," and "the general
bent of their talents towards the practical." All these qualities made
women fit for "practice" and a life of public action (*CW* XXI:304–
06).

The danger in Mill's appeal to the "practical utility" of giving
women the vote on the basis of their "bent . . . towards the practical" was that it might suggest that women were not well suited to
systematic thought, which required the "absorption of the whole
mind in one set of ideas and occupations" (*CW* XXI:310). Anticipating this challenge, Mill replied that it was impossible to know
whether it was women's fundamental nature that made them concentrate on "the management of small and multitudinous details,"
or whether this trait resulted from the circumstances of their daily

lives which required them to take care of "things in general" (*CW* XXI:310). Either way, Mill argued, the public would benefit from public servants with the capacity for attention to detail, and for that reason if no other women should be admitted to public office.

Before directly addressing the related question of whether women did have the capacity for speculative thought, philosophy, and high art, Mill engaged in discussion about the relative brain size of men and women. In the context of his discussions about the limitations of so-called scientific observation to link innate sexual or racial characteristics to social behavior, this discussion seems bizarre and even, in Julia Annas's eyes, "pathetic" (Annas 1977, 186). At first, Mill decisively dismissed the alleged fact that men had larger brains than women: the supposed discrepancy was unproved, and moreover brain size alone did not correlate with intelligence, as was shown by the fact that whales (mammals with larger brains) were not smarter than humans. But then Mill backtracked and said that men probably did have larger brains than women, but slower cerebral circulation, and this would explain why men's thinking was slower but could be sustained longer, while women's thinking was rapid and quicker to rebound when fatigued. And, indeed, Mill concluded this interlude by remarking that it was highly uncertain whether "there was any natural difference at all in the average strength or direction of the mental capacities of the two sexes, much less what that difference is" (*CW* XXI:312). Moreover, psychology and the mental sciences sought answers to questions concerning sexual difference in the wrong places, in individual characteristics rather than in "the different relations of human beings to society and life" (*CW* XXI:312).

Mill also insisted that social context was central to any consideration of the frequent charge that "No production in philosophy, science, or art, entitled to the first rank, has been the work of a woman" (*CW* XXI:314). The reasons for this lack of achievement at the highest level of the creative arts and sciences did not have to do with women's capacities but with their social situation: women hadn't had education until recently, and women of both the upper and lower classes were distracted by tending to their pressing and time-consuming, albeit very distinct, household duties. "The superintendence of a household, even when not in other respects laborious, is extremely onerous to the thoughts; it requires incessant vigilance . . . at every hour of the day, from which the person responsible for them can hardly ever shake herself free" (*CW* XXI:318). Until these burdens were lessened, it made no sense to speculate on what women's intelligence and artistic capacity might be, for women were warped creatures.

The severe role division in society distorted women's capacity in another way by making them appear more moral than men. Women's supposed greater moral character was as artificial as their absence from the first ranks of science. Women's morality was, rather, "an admission by men, of the corrupting influence of power" (*CW* XXI:320–21). Women, like "negro slaves," seldom broke that law: "Those who are under the control of others cannot often commit crimes" (*CW* XXI:321). What Mill saw in women and men alike was not natural sexual difference, but "the influences of social circumstances" (*CW* XXI:321).

These reflections brought Mill back to his fundamental premise that nothing certain about supposed differences between men and women could be known by observing contemporary women and men, because the characters of men and women were shaped by relationships of domination and subordination. But this situation itself suggested the grounds to hope for a better future: if social circumstances had created these differences, then social circumstances could again alter both men's and women's dominant traits or characteristics. The desired transformation in male and female characteristics could not be achieved by intellectual conviction alone, however, but only if women began to participate in public life. Mill's resort to arguments based on what he took to be society's general view of women's present characteristics and capabilities reflected his "anxiety to add as many arguments as possible based upon women's actual (and supposedly actual) qualities, in spite of having pointed out clearly all the pitfalls of this approach in Chapter I" (Annas 1977, 186).

Mill thought that it would be extremely difficult for women by themselves to bring about the necessary legal changes: "A woman who joins in any movement which her husband disapproves, makes herself a martyr, without even being able to be an apostle, for the husband can legally put a stop to her apostleship." It was therefore crucial for women's emancipation, Mill believed, for men "in considerable number . . . to join with them in the undertaking" (*CW*

XXI:332). But only men willing to accept their loss of domestic as well as political dominance would enter the lists on women's behalf. Domestic subordination fueled the injustices of law and social custom concerning both family and political life. Reforming women's legal status would not be sufficient for the social and political transformations that Mill sought. Resolution of "the woman question" would only come through changes in the lived relationships between women and men. It was the hope for and belief in the possibility of that transformation that animated all of *The Subjection of Women*, and particularly its final chapter.

IV. MARITAL FRIENDSHIP

A necessary first step in reconstituting marriage as "a union of thoughts and inclinations" which created a "foundation of solid friendship" between husband and wife (*CW* XXI:333–34) was to gain women access to education, remunerative work, and political representation, and to abolish the inequalities of coverture. All of these reforms would require, said Mill, that men sacrifice those political, legal, and economic advantages they enjoyed "by the mere fact of being born a male" (*CW* XXI:324). In line with these views Mill supported such concrete measures as women's suffrage, the Married Women's Property Bills, the Divorce Act of 1857, the repeal of the Contagious Diseases Acts, and the opening of higher education and the professions to women. Suffrage, Mill contended, would both develop women's faculties through participation in civic decisions and enable married women to protect themselves from male-imposed injustices such as lack of control of their own income and equal rights to custody of their children. Access to education and jobs would give women alternatives to marriage. It would also provide a woman whose marriage turned out badly some means of self-support if separated or divorced. The Divorce Act of 1857, which established England's first civil divorce courts, would enable women and men to escape from intolerable circumstances (although Mill protested the sexual double standard ensconced in the act). And for those few women with an income of their own, a Married Women's Property Act would recognize their independent personalities and enable them to meet their husbands more nearly as equals.[14]

Mill further insisted that the subjection of women could not be ended by law alone, but only by law and the reformation of education, of opinion, of social inculcation, of habits, and finally of the conduct of family life itself. This was so because the root of much of men's resistance to women's emancipation was not simply their reluctance to give up their position of material advantage, but many men's fear of living with an equal. It was to retain marriage as "a law of despotism" that men shut all other occupations to women, Mill contended (CW XXI:156). Men who "have a real antipathy to the equal freedom of women" were at bottom afraid "lest [women] should insist that marriage be on equal conditions" (CW XXI:156). The public discrimination against women was a manifestation of a disorder rooted in family relationships. The progression of humankind could not take place until the dynamics of the master–slave relationship were eliminated from marriages, and until the family was instead founded on spousal equality.

Mill intended *The Subjection of Women* not only to convince men that their treatment of women in law was unjust, but also that their treatment of women in the home was self-defeating, even self-destructive. Women were those most obviously affected by the denial of association with men on equal footing. Women's confinement to domestic concerns was a wrongful "forced repression" (CW XXI:148). Mill shared Aristotle's view that participation in civic life was an enriching and ennobling activity. In *Considerations on Representative Government* Mill lambasted benevolent despotism because it encouraged "passivity" and "abdication of [one's] own energies," and he praised the Athenian dicastry and ecclesia because they required the participation of the citizenry (CW XIX:399–400, 411). But no similar public-spirited dimension to life was possible for women in his own day. During his speech on the Reform Bill of 1867 Mill argued that giving women the vote would provide "that stimulus to their faculties ... which the suffrage seldom fails to produce on those who are admitted to it" (CW XXVIII:157). Without such a reform, there was no impetus for women to consider with others the principles which were to govern their common life, no incentive to conform to principles which defined their mutual activity for the common good, no possibility for the self-development which comes from citizen activity. The cost to women was obvious; they were dull, or petty, or unprincipled (CW XXI:290–338). The cost to men was less apparent but no less real; in seeking a reflection of themselves in the consciousness of these stunted women, men deceived, deluded, and limited themselves.

Mill was convinced that men were corrupted by their dominance over women. The most corrupting element of male domination of women was that men learned to "worship their own will as such a grand thing that it is actually the law for another rational being" (CW XXI:293). Such self-worship arose at a very tender age, and blotted out a boy's natural understanding of himself and his relationship to others. A boy may be "the most frivolous and empty or the most ignorant and stolid of mankind," but "by the mere fact of being born a male" he is encouraged to think that "he is by right the superior of all and every one of an entire half of the human race: including probably some whose real superiority he had daily or hourly occasion to feel" (CW XXI:324). By contrast, women were taught "to live for others" and "to have no life but in their affections," and then further to confine their affections to "the men with whom they are connected, or the children who constitute an additional indefeasible tie between them and a man" (CW XXI:272). The result of this upbringing was that what women would tell men was not, could not be, wholly true; women's sensibilities were systematically warped, and both they and men suffered the consequences of the inevitable distortions of reality that women conveyed to men.

This depiction was strikingly similar to that which Hegel described in his passages on the relationship between master and slave in *The Phenomenology of Mind*.[15] The lord who sees himself solely as master, wrote Hegel, cannot obtain an independent self-consciousness. The master thinks he is autonomous, but in fact he relies totally upon his slaves, not only to fulfill his needs and desires, but also for his identity: "Without slaves, he is no master." The master could not acquire the fullest self-consciousness when the "other" in whom he viewed himself was in the reduced human condition of slavery: to be *merely* a master was to fall short of full self-consciousness, and to define himself in terms of the "thing" he owns. So for Mill, men who have propagated the belief that all men are superior to all women have fatally affected the dialectic involved in knowing oneself through the consciousness others have of one. He made a similar point in *Considerations on Representative Gov-*

ernment, where he lamented the effects "fostered by the possession of power" by "a man, or a class of men" who "finding themselves worshipped by others ... become worshipers of themselves" (*CW* XIX:455). The present relationship between the sexes produced in men that "self-worship" which "all privileged persons, and all privileged classes" have had. That distortion deceives men and other privileged groups as to both their character and their self-worth.

Philosophers prior to Mill who had considered the social relations between men and women had argued either that the authority of men over women was natural (Aristotle, Grotius); or that while there was no natural dominance of men over women prior to the establishment of families, in any civil society such preeminence was necessary to settle the dispute over who should govern the household (Locke); or that men's dominance was the result of women's consent in return for protection (Hobbes) or the consequence of the development of the sentiments of nurturance and love (Rousseau). None had suggested that domestic arrangements might diminish a man's ability to contribute to public debates or to the governing of a democratic republic. Mill wished to show that the development of the species was held in check by a domestic slavery that produced the fear of equality, spousal hierarchy, and a lack of reciprocity and the mutuality of true friendship.

Mill's remedy for the evils generated by the fear of equality was what he called marital friendship. His praise of marital friendship was almost lyrical, and struck resonances with Aristotle's, Cicero's, and Montaigne's similar exaltations of the pleasures as well as the moral enrichment of this form of human intimacy.[16] Mill wrote:

> When each of two persons, instead of being a nothing, is a something; when they are attached to one another, and are not too much unlike to begin with; the constant partaking of the same things, assisted by their sympathy, draws out the latent capacities of each for being interested in the things ... by a real enriching of the two natures, each acquiring the tastes and capacities of the other in addition to its own. (*CW* XXI:334)

This expansion of human capacities did not, however, exhaust the benefits of friendship. Most importantly, friendship developed what Montaigne praised as the abolition of selfishness, the capacity to regard another human being as fully as worthy as oneself. Therefore friendship of the highest order could only exist between those equal in excellence (Montaigne 1976, 135–44). And for precisely this reason, philosophers from Aristotle to Hegel had consistently argued that women could not be men's friends, for women lacked the moral capacity for the highest forms of friendship. Indeed, it was common to distinguish the marital bond from friendship not solely on the basis of sexual and procreative activity, but also because women could not be part of the school of moral virtue which was found in friendship at its best.

Mill therefore made a most significant break with the past in adopting the language of friendship in his discussion of marriage. For Mill, no less than for any of his predecessors, "the true virtue of human beings is the fitness to live together as equals." Such equality required that individuals "[claim] nothing for themselves but what they as freely concede to every one else," that they regard command of any kind as "an exceptional necessity," and that they prefer whenever possible "the society of those with whom leading and following can be alternate and reciprocal" (CW XXI:294). This picture of reciprocity, of the shifting of leadership according to need, was a remarkable characteristic of family life. Virtually all of Mill's liberal contemporaries accepted the notion of the natural and inevitable complimentariness of male and female personalities and roles. Mill, however, as early as 1833 had expressed his belief that "the highest masculine and the highest feminine" characters were without any real distinction (Letter to Thomas Carlyle, 5 October 1833, CW XII:184). That view of the androgynous personality lent support to Mill's brief for equality within the family (Urbinati 1991).

Mill repeatedly insisted that his society had no general experience of "the marriage relationship as it would exist between equals," and that such marriages would be impossible until men rid themselves of the fear of equality and the will to domination (Letter to John Nichol, August 1869, CW XVII:1634). The liberation of women, in other words, required not just legal reform but a reeducation of the passions. Women were to be regarded as equals not only to fulfill the demand for individual rights and in order that they could survive in the public world of work, but also in order that women and men could form ethical relations of the highest order. Men and women alike had to "learn to cultivate their strongest sympathy with an equal in rights and in cultivation" (CW XXI:336). Mill struggled, not always with total success, to talk about the quality of such associations. For example, his views on divorce fluctuated. In a letter of 1855, written as Parliament was considering the measure that became the Matrimonial Causes (Divorce) Act of 1857, he wrote, "My opinion on Divorce is that . . . nothing ought to be rested in, short of entire freedom on both sides to dissolve this like any other partnership" (Letter to unidentified correspondent, November 1855, *CW* XIV:500). Writing to Henry Rusden in 1870, however, Mill denied that he advocated that marriage should be dissoluble "at the will of either party," and stated that he could put forward no well-grounded opinion until women achieved equality under the laws and in married life (*CW* XVII:1750–51). In *On Liberty*, Mill argued that von Humboldt's characterization of marriage as a contractual relationship which could be ended by "the declared will of either party to dissolve it" was misguided. That kind of dissolution was appropriate when the benefits of partnership could be reduced to monetary terms. But marriage involved a person's expectations for the fulfillment of a "plan of life," and created "a new series of moral obligations . . . toward that person, which may possibly be overruled, but cannot be ignored" (*CW* XVIII:300). Mill was convinced that difficult though it might be to shape the law to recognize the moral imperatives of a relationship such as marriage, there were ethical communities that transcended and were not reducible to their individual components.

In the course of discussing what he hoped would be the new relationship between spouses, Mill did not attack the traditional assumption about men's and women's different responsibilities in an ongoing household, although he was usually careful to say that women "chose" their role or that it was the most "expedient" arrangement, not that it was theirs by "nature." As noted in section II, he by and large accepted the notion that once they marry, women should be solely responsible for the care of the household and children, men for providing the family income. He seemed to shut the door on combining household duties and a public life: "like a man when he chooses a profession, so, when a woman marries, it may be in general understood that she makes a choice of the management of a household, and the bringing up of a family, as the first call upon her exertions . . . and that she renounces . . . all [other occupations] which are not consistent with the requirements of this" (*CW* XXI:298).

In this discussion of family life, Mill seemed to forget his own warning that women could be imprisoned not only "by actual law," but also "by custom equivalent to law" (CW XXI:340). He did not consider that men might take any role in the family other than providing the economic means of support, and overlooked his own cautionary observation that in any household "there will naturally be more potential voice on the side, whichever it is, that brings the means of support" (CW XXI:291). Nor did he entertain the possibilities that nurturing and caring for children might provide men with useful knowledge and experience, and that sharing the experience of raising children might contribute to the friendship between spouses that he so ardently desired. Mill also let pass the opportunity to supplement his condemnation of undesired sexual relations as the execution of "an animal function" with an appreciation of the possible enhancement a physical expression of delight in one's companion might add to marital friendship.[17] Especially puzzling, given his concerns with representative government, was the fact that although Mill had brilliantly depicted the narrowness and petty concerns of contemporary women who were totally excluded from political participation, he implied that the mistresses of most households might content themselves simply with exercising the suffrage (were it to be granted), a view hardly consistent with his arguments in other works for maximizing the level of political discussion and participation whenever possible.

Mill's acceptance of the traditional gender-based division of labor in the family has led some critics to fault him for supposing that legal equality of opportunity would solve the problem of women's subjection, even while leaving the sexual division of labor in the household intact. For example, Julia Annas, after praising Mill's theoretical arguments in support of equality, complains that his suggestions for actual changes in sex roles are "timid and reformist at best. He assumes that most women will in fact want only to be wives and mothers" (Annas 1977, 189). Leslie Goldstein agrees that "[t]he restraints which Mill believed should be imposed on married women constitute a major exception to his argument for equality of individual liberty between the sexes – an exception so enormous that it threatens to swallow up the entire argument" (Goldstein 1980, 328). Susan Okin contends that "Mill never questioned or objected to the maintenance of traditional sex roles within the family, but expressly considered them to be suitable and desirable" (Okin 1979, 237).

Mill often wrote as if all that was necessary to break the dynamics of domestic domination and subordination was providing equal legal rights and equal opportunity to women. In *On Liberty* he wrote that "nothing more is needed for the complete removal of [the almost despotic power of husbands over wives] than that wives should have the same rights and should receive the same protection of law in the same manner, as all other persons" (*CW* XVIII:301). In the same vein, Mill seemed to suggest that nothing more was needed for women to achieve equality than that "the present bounties and protective duties in favour of men should be recalled" (*CW* XXI:280). This focus on legal equality has led Christine di Stefano to argue that in order to accommodate women in public life, Mill had to conceptualize women as if they were men: "In Mill's hands, women are dealt with in the terms of exceptional and masculine individualism. . . . Women must be disembodied, desexed, degendered, and made over into the image of middle-class and upper-class men if they are to benefit from the promises of rational liberalism" (di Stefano 1991, 176). While di Stefano's analysis identifies the false gender-neutrality of much of liberal discourse about "the individual" that obscures sex, or class, or race, or other distinguishing features, *The Subjection of Women* contained its own critique of the liberal subject in suggesting the importance of relationship to creating any individual. While correctly identifying the limitations of antidiscrimination statutes as instruments for social change, di Stefano fails to recognize that Mill's final prescription to end the subjection of women was not equal opportunity but spousal friendship; equal opportunity was a means whereby such friendship could be encouraged.

Mill's commitment to equality in marriage was stronger, and of a different theoretical order, than his acceptance of a continued sexual division of labor. On the one hand, Mill's belief in the necessity of equality as a precondition to marital friendship was a profound theoretical tenet. It rested on the normative assumption that human relationships between equals were of a higher, more enriching order than those between unequals. Mill's belief that equality was more suitable to friendship than inequality was as unalterable as his conviction that democracy was a better system of government than despotism; the human spirit could not develop its fullest potential when living in absolute subordination to another human being or to government (*Considerations on Representative Government, CW* XIX:399–403). On the other hand, his belief that friendship could be attained and sustained while women bore nearly exclusive responsibility for the home was a statement that might be modified or even abandoned if experience proved it to be wrong. In this sense it was like his view that the question of whether socialism was preferable to capitalism could not be settled by theoretical argument alone, but must "work itself out on an experimental scale, by actual trial."[18] Mill believed that marital equality was a moral imperative; his view that such equality might exist where married men and women moved in different spheres of activity was a proposition subject to demonstration. Had Mill discovered that managing the household to the exclusion of most other activity created an impediment to the friendship of married women and men, *The Subjection of Women* suggests that he would have altered his view of practicable domestic arrangements, but not his commitment to the desirability of male–female friendship in marriage.

CONCLUSION

Despite Mill's overly sanguine belief in the efficacy of equal opportunity, his adoption of a male subject as the supposedly universal citizen, and his blindness to what conditions might promote a vital friendship between spouses, the contribution of *The Subjection of Women* to both liberal and feminist theory transcended the book's prescriptions for actual reform. As he did in *On Liberty*, Mill argued forcefully that the development of human civilization was dependent on the continual expansion of possibilities for self-expression and action by all members of society. The cultural and ethical well-being of the whole depended upon the equal right of each person to undertake freely whatever projects and life activities he or she regarded as desirable.[19] There was, therefore, no disjuncture between Mill's commitment to the principle of advancing "the permanent interests of man as a progressive being" (*On Liberty, CW* XVIII:224) and his support of equal social, economic, and political rights for women.

The Subjection of Women also contributed to liberal feminism's assault on patriarchal understandings of the domain of personal authority.[20] Mill insisted that the relationship between husband and wife, traditionally thought of as "private" and hence not appropriately subject to public or legal scrutiny, was in fact infused with power that was sustained by state action.[21] The state enforced male dominance in marriage not only directly by the laws of coverture, but also indirectly by denying women higher education, employment, and professional training and licensing, thus closing off alternatives to marriage. In this context of laws and social practices, for the state to refuse to intervene in family matters out of respect for family "privacy" reflected a failure to understand how deeply civil society was already implicated in domestic as well as public structures of power and authority.[22] In both *The Subjection of Women* and his work in Parliament, Mill insisted that there was a reciprocal influence between men's and women's resources and authority in the home and the public realm. If women were to be self-determining, they needed not only the vote and the ability to support themselves, but also the abolition of coverture and of social customs of male dominance in the home. Neither public life nor domestic life could be understood or properly ordered without consideration of the other; the boundaries between the two were permeable, and configurations of power in one influenced relationships in the other.

Mill's discussion of marital friendship was also important to liberal and feminist theory in its insistence upon the ineluctably social character of every human life.[23] Marital friendship was important because people did not become who they were in isolation from others, but through social interactions. Mill insisted that the individuals whose rights the liberal state was meant to defend had to be considered as beings-in-relationship. This was important not only for adults, but also for the children in their care. Children would most readily learn that all human beings were of equal moral worth and deserving of equal political rights in households where father and mother regarded one another and were treated in law as equals (Okin 1989, 20–23).

The Subjection of Women not only contained one of liberalism's most incisive arguments for equal rights for men and women, but embodied as well a belief in the importance of friendship – of human affection, mutuality, reciprocity, and interdependency – for human development and progress. Mill's plea for an end to the subjection of women was not made, as critics such as Gertrude Himmelfarb assert, in the name of "the absolute nature of the principle of liberty, the exaltation of individuality whatever its particular form," but in the name of the need of both men and women for community (Himmelfarb 1974, 181). *The Subjection of Women* was an eloquent brief for equal rights for men and women and a devastating critique of the corruption of marital inequality. Beyond that it also expressed Mill's profoundly held belief that any "liberal" regime must promote the conditions under which friendship, not only in marriage but in other associations as well, will take root and flourish.

NOTES

1 This is not to say that Mill has not been misread as an exponent of atomistic individualism, particularly with respect to his views on the centrality of negative liberty to any account of government's role in protecting human freedom. See the interesting account of the nineteenth-century idealist critics of Mill, particularly T. H. Green and Bernard Bosanquet, in Nicholson, Chapter 13 of this volume.

2 On the concept of autonomy in liberal political theory see Held 1993, especially "Noncontractual Society: The Postpatriarchal Family as Model," pp. 192–214; and Nedelsky 1989 and 1990.

3 Excellent introductions to Mill's work are Skorupski 1989 and Ryan 1974 (which, however, pays scant attention to *The Subjection of Women*). Also useful with respect to the relationship between Mill's theory and policy issues of his day is Duncan 1973.

4 There is much dispute over whether the controlling principle of Mill's critique in *The Subjection of Women* is equality or utility. Julia Annas 1977, 179–94, discusses this conflict.

5 Mill's analysis of women's choice of marriage as a state of life reminds one of Hobbes's discussion of some defeated soldier giving his consent to the rule of a conquering sovereign. Women, it is true, could decide which among several men to marry, while Hobbes's defeated soldier had no choice of master. But what could either do but join the only protective association available?

6 Mill described the plight of Eleanor Garrett, sister of Millicent Garrett Fawcett, the suffrage leader, in his speech introducing the women's suffrage amendment:

A young lady, Miss Garrett, ... studied the medical profession. Having duly qualified herself, she ... knocked successively at all the doors through which, by law, access is obtained into the medical profession. Having found all other doors fast shut, she fortunately discovered one which had accidentally been left ajar. The Society of Apothecaries, it seems, had forgotten to shut out those who they never thought would attempt to come in, and through this narrow entrance this young lady found her way into the profession. But so objectionable did it appear to this learned body that women should be the medical attendants even of women, that the narrow wicket through which Miss Garrett entered has been closed after her. (*CW* XXVIII:159)

7 Tobias Hobson, a Cambridge liveryman, would only hire out the horse nearest the door of his stable, even if a client wanted another. *Oxford English Dictionary*, II:369.

8 The consequences of the doctrine of spousal unity were various: a man could not make a contract with his wife since "to covenant with her would be to covenant with himself"; a wife could not sue without her husband's concurrence; a husband was bound to "provide his wife with necessaries . . . as much as himself"; a husband was responsible for certain criminal acts of his wife committed in his presence; and, as a husband was responsible for his wife's acts, he "might give his wife moderate correction . . . in the same moderation that [he is] allowed to correct his apprentices or children." Blackstone 1765–69, I:430.

9 The rich found ways around the common law's insistence that the management and use of any income belonged to a woman's husband by setting up trusts which were governed by the laws and courts of equity. A succinct explanation of the law of property as it affected married women in the nineteenth century is contained in Reiss 1934, 20–34.

10 Several Married Women's Property Bills which would have given married women possession of their earnings were presented in Parliament beginning in 1857, but none was successful until 1870.

11 On women's lives under chattel slavery see J. Jones 1985. A first-person narrative of a slave woman's life during Mill's lifetime is H. Jacobs 1987.

12 Mill's depiction of marriage departed radically from the majority of Victorian portrayals of home and hearth. John Ruskin's praise of the home in *Sesame and Lilies* reflected the feelings and aspirations of many: "This is the true nature of home – it is the place of Peace; the shelter, not only from all injury, but from all terror, doubt, and division. . . . It is a sacred place, a vestal temple, a temple of the hearth watched over by Household Gods." Ruskin 1902–12, XVIII:122.

13 Jennifer Ring 1985 and 1991 are very critical of Mill's empirical method in *The Subjection of Women*.

14 For an account of the legal reforms mentioned here and Mill's relationship to them, see Shanley 1989. The Matrimonial Causes Act of 1857

allowed men to divorce their wives for adultery, but women had to establish that their husbands were guilty of either cruelty or desertion in addition to adultery in order to obtain a separation. Mill was reluctant to say what he thought the terms of divorce should be in a rightly ordered society, but he never wavered in his condemnation of the sexual double standard.

15 Hegel 1931, 228–40. Mill's analysis also calls to mind Simone de Beauvoir's discussion of "the Other" in *The Second Sex* (Beauvoir 1974).

16 Badhwar 1993 collects a number of essays on various philosophers' discussions of friendship.

17 One of the striking features of Montaigne's lyrical praise of friendship was that it was devoid of sensuality, for Montaigne abhorred "the Grecian license," and he was adamant that women were incapable of the highest forms of friendship. Mill's notion of spousal friendship suggested the possibility of a friendship that partook of both a true union of minds and sexual pleasure, although (undoubtedly to the relief of such contemporaries as James Fitzjames Stephen) Mill himself was not disposed to make such an argument.

Throughout his writings Mill displayed a tendency to dismiss or deprecate the erotic dimension of life. In his *Autobiography* he wrote approvingly that his father looked forward to an increase in freedom in relations between the sexes, freedom which would be devoid of any sensuality "either of a theoretical or of a practical kind." His own twenty-year relationship with Harriet Taylor before their marriage was one of "confidential friendship" only. *Autobiography, CW* I:109, 251. In *The Principles of Political Economy* Mill remarked that in his own day "the animal instinct" occupied a "disproportionate preponderance in human life" (*CW* III:766).

18 *Chapters on Socialism, CW* V:736. On Mill's socialism see Sarvasy 1985.

19 Donner 1991 analyzes Mill's moral psychology and his views on the interdependent and reciprocal nature of the moral development of the individual and communities.

20 On patriarchalism in political thought see Schochet 1975; on liberal feminism's assault on patriarchalism see Eisenstein 1981.

21 On the public/private distinction see Elshtain 1981; and Ackelsberg and Shanley, 1996.

22 For contemporary discussions of the impossibility of state neutrality toward the family see Okin 1989 and Olsen 1985.

23 Excellent discussions of the ways in which classical liberal theory pays insufficient attention to the ways in which individuals are constituted in and by their relationships to others are found in Held 1993, Nedelsky

1989 and 1990, and Tronto 1993. Regon 1993 explores ways in which recognition of the degree to which the "self" is constituted by relationships might affect family law and public policy dealing with the family in our own day.

12 Mill and the Classical world

I. MILL'S CLASSICAL INTERESTS

Mill began learning Greek at the age of three and Latin at eight. From about the age of twelve his Greek and Latin reading focussed on works "such as were worth studying, not for the language merely, but also for the thoughts". He mentions especially Demosthenes, Tacitus, Juvenal, and Quintillian. His father laid special emphasis on Plato.[1] Throughout his literary career, from his discussion of Sedgwick on education in Cambridge to his own rectorial address on education in St Andrews, Mill retained a keen interest in Classical studies and their place in education.[2] Moreover, he took an active part in encouraging the study of Classical antiquity among readers who were beyond the years of formal education. In 1834–35 he published 'Notes on some of the More Popular Dialogues of Plato'[3] – really an abbreviated translation-cum-paraphrase. In 1840 he reviewed two publications on Plato.[4] In 1846 and 1853 he reviewed two sections of the multi-volume history of Greece by his friend and (with some qualifications) ally, George Grote, and in 1866 and 1873 he reviewed Grote's works on Plato and Aristotle.[5]

Though Mill's intellectual life was certainly not dominated by his Classical (especially Greek) interests, his publications in this area were not thoughtless pot-boilers. He had compiled the versions of Plato several years before they were actually published.[6] In preparation for the first review of Grote's *History*, he says he "had to read

I am grateful to the editor of this volume for helpful criticisms of an earlier draft of this chapter.

and think a good deal for it first";[7] among other things, he re-read Homer. In preparation for his review of Grote's book on Plato, he re-read Plato in Greek. Though the reviews of Grote are not discussions of one scholar by another, they are the work of a critic who could test Grote's assertions by reference to his own knowledge of the main primary sources.

To estimate the significance and value of Mill's engagement with Classical antiquity, we may consider two questions: (1) What is the nature and value of his contribution to the understanding of Classical antiquity? (2) What are the effects of his Classical interests on his philosophy, and are these effects good or bad?

II. MILL AND GROTE

To understand and evaluate Mill as a student of Classics, we must begin from some account of Grote. Mill's main Classical publications are reviews of Grote. They are highly – and quite justifiably – enthusiastic; they have the appearance of a mere summary of Grote; and casual readers (especially those who have not recently read the sixteen or so volumes of Grote being reviewed)[8] may suppose that Mill is simply recommending Grote without assessing him from any independent point of view. This would be a mistaken view of Mill's attitude to Grote. Some of his discussion highlights some areas of disagreement between Mill and Grote, and in doing so highlights some areas of difficulty in Mill's own philosophical position.

Grote's work constitutes a contribution of the first rank both to the study of Greek history and to the study of Greek philosophy. None of his English contemporaries equalled his contribution to either area of study; and no one at all has equalled his contribution to both areas. Both his *History* and his book on Plato still deserve to be read by anyone who is interested in Greek history or in Plato, not simply by those who are interested in the history of scholarship.[9]

Both of Grote's major works are thoroughly penetrated by his philosophical outlook. He formed this outlook primarily under the influence of James Mill, and in many ways he was a more orthodox follower of the elder Mill than the younger Mill was. Mill notices this difference between himself and Grote long before the publication of Grote's major works:

You ask me about Grote; I happen to be able to tell you more about him than almost any one, having been intimate with him almost from my boyhood, though less so than formerly in proportion as I have diverged from his opinions: he is a Utilitarian; in one sense I am so too, but *he* is so in rather a narrow sense; has therefore a belief, a firm one, in *him* most deep and conscientious, for which chiefly he lives, and for which he would die. He is a highly instructed man; an excellent scholar; has made great progress in writing a History of Greece, some of the manuscript of which I have seen; it will be a work of great, though not of consummate merit. . . . He is a man of good, but not first-rate intellect: hard and mechanical; not at all quick; with less *subtlety* than any able and instructed man I ever knew; with much logical and but little aesthetic culture; *narrow* therefore; even narrower than most other Utilitarians of reading and education; more a disciple of my father than of any one else. . . . After all I have said of him you will be surprised to learn that he reads German.[10]

In a later letter Mill compares Grote more directly with himself:

I believe if I have done any good a large share of it lies in the example of a professed logician and political economist who believes there are other things besides logic and political economy. . . . [O]ne that will never be made to believe it at all, at least in the sense that I do, is one of the best of men and a highly instructed man too, Mr Grote.[11]

Mill's prediction about the merits of Grote's history is rather an underestimate, but the general picture of Grote's strengths, weaknesses, and general outlook is largely vindicated both by Grote's work and by the later conflicts resulting from Mill's deviations from the position of James Mill.

Is Grote's hard-line utilitarianism a weakness in his historical and philosophical writing? In many ways, as we will see, it is an advantage; for it makes him more vividly aware of aspects of Greek history and of Plato that his predecessors overlook or neglect. James Mill's philosophy is a powerful instrument for use in Grote's inquiries, and Grote uses it effectively. Still, it fails to reveal the whole truth; some questions that reveal the limitations of Grote's outlook emerge, clearly though unobtrusively, from Mill's discussion of him.

III. INTERPRETATIONS OF ATHENIAN DEMOCRACY

Both Grote and Mill noticed that Greek history, thought, and culture were used as a weapon by the people whom Mill calls "the Tory perverters of Grecian history".[12] Mill had learnt this lesson in his childhood from his father:

History continued to be my strongest predilection, and most of all ancient history. Mitford's Greece I read continually; my father had put me on my guard against the Tory prejudices of this writer, and his perversion of facts for the whitewashing of despots, and blackening of popular institutions. These points he discoursed on, exemplifying them from the Greek orators and historians, with such effect that in reading Mitford my sympathies were always on the contrary side to those of the author, and I could, to some extent, have argued the point against him; yet this did not diminish the ever new pleasure with which I read the book.[13]

The fact that the careful and well-informed James Mill could find nothing more suitable than Mitford for his son to read on Greek history shows why a history free of Tory prejudice would find some eager readers.

The first person to rescue Greek history from the Tories (as we may call them loosely, following Mill) was Connop Thirlwall, whose work was warmly praised by both Mill and Grote.[14] One major dispute between Grote and Thirlwall and the Tories was about Athenian democracy, and especially about whether Athenian history in the fifth century B.C. illustrated the folly of extreme democracy and the wisdom of aristocracy.

It is easy to say, in a rather positivist vein, that Grote showed that the Tories interpreted the facts of Athenian history in the light of their political outlook, and that he presented the bare facts free of this interpretation. If this positivist judgment seems unsophisticated, we might prefer the anti-positivist view that Grote wrote a history from a radical democratic point of view as a rival to histories written from a Tory point of view. Instead of saying that he liberates the facts from ideology, we might say that he substitutes one ideology for another. Neither the positivist nor the anti-positivist judgment expresses the most important aspect of Grote's achievement.

The Tories could make a good case for their view of Athenian history, and it is not entirely fair to accuse them of perverting it, as though they were intent simply on forcing their own political judgments into the understanding of the Greek political experience. They could point to a great deal of support for their view in the

Greek sources themselves. Plato's opinion of democracy is evidently hostile, and Aristotle's opinion, though more complex, is evidently not entirely friendly. From the fifth century, the modern historian could quote the hostile attitude that Thucydides displays towards the democracy, and the abusive remarks of Aristophanes about individual democratic politicians. Thucydides describes specific incidents (the Athenians' treatment of Pericles, the Sicilian expedition)[15] in terms that seem to vindicate his own view of the incompetence of democratic government.

It would have been easy to refute the Tories if it could have been shown that the ancient sources did not support them, and that their attitude to Athens was simply the product of anachronistic modern preoccupations. In fact, however, the reverse seemed to be true. The sources for this period of Athenian history are not plentiful, and they are largely literary – the works of intelligent, reflective students of history and politics with their own political judgments; these political judgments seemed to confirm the Tory point of view. If we do not acknowledge the ancient support for modern anti-democratic critics of democratic Athens, we cannot understand Grote's achievement in answering these critics.

Mill himself does not adequately prepare us to appreciate Grote. He remarks that "Mr Grote had already shown grounds for believing that Cleon,[16] and men of his stamp, had been far too severely dealt with by historians" (CW XI:331). He does not remark that one of the offending historians is Thucydides himself. He mentions Thucydides' report of Pericles' Funeral Speech (CW XI:319), but he does not mention Thucydides' generally hostile attitude to the post-Periclean democracy. In another general remark about Athenian democracy Mill comes closer to acknowledging the facts:

the Athenian democracy had been so outrageously, and without measure, misrepresented, that whoever had read, as so few have done, Thucydides and the orators with decent intelligence and candour, could easily perceive that the vulgar misrepresentation was very wide of the truth. (CW XI:329)

The crucial phrases here are "as so few have done" and "with decent intelligence and candour". Mill implicitly acknowledges that other people have read the texts that Grote read, and drawn different conclusions from them. He explains the different conclusions by a difference in intelligence and candour, as though the Tories were so blinded by partisan prejudice that they could not see what was plainly to be seen in the evidence. But Mill might himself be accused of some lack of candour in failing to admit that Thucydides himself might sometimes be taken to present a Tory picture of the democracy.[17]

Grote's desire to rescue Greek history from the Tories forced him to re-examine the ancient evidence, in order to show that the Tories had understood it wrongly. While he was certainly abreast of contemporary German scholarship, his main achievement does not consist in his use of ancient sources or modern discoveries that his opponents had neglected; it consists in the more careful examination of familiar texts that the Tories thought they knew well but had never properly understood. This feature of Grote's history makes it the pre-eminent modern history of Greece in English; its main historical and political argument has not been superseded (despite the evidence available to us and not to Grote), because it is based on careful and close argument from the main literary sources.[18]

A few examples will illustrate the character of Grote's argument. Cleon is often cited as one of the demagogues whose evil influence led the Athenians into disastrous error, once they began to listen to these vulgar, lower-class, self-seeking manipulators of popular opinion who mismanaged the war against Sparta. Grote and Mill believe that this judgment is the reverse of the truth:

The demagogues were, as he [Grote] observes, essentially opposition speakers. The conduct of affairs was habitually in the hands of the rich and great, who had by far the largest share of personal influence, and on whose mismanagement there would have been hardly any check, but for the demagogues and their hostile criticism. These opinions receive ample confirmation from the course of affairs, when, there being no longer any lowborn Cleon or Hyperbolus to balance their influence, Nicias and Alcibiades had full scope to ruin the commonwealth.[19]

This assessment receives no support from Thucydides' explicit comments; while he attributes the basest motives to Cleon, he says never a word in condemnation of Nicias and Alcibiades. Nor can we hope to correct Thucydides from any other source. Nonetheless, Grote's and Mill's judgment is quite justified, and can be amply supported from Thucydides himself. The reason is simple.

Thucydides not only offers political judgments of his own, but also presents a detailed narrative that allows us to correct his own judgment about the comparative merits and defects of Cleon, Alcibiades, and Nicias. Grote examines the evidence on which Thucydides bases his judgments, and finds that the evidence does not support the judgments.

Mill's failure to point this out clearly is not surprising, however, once we notice that Grote himself does not point it out clearly. It is a surprising fact about Grote's voluminous history that it contains no full appraisal of the value of Thucydides as a historical source. On one occasion Grote speaks of "the impartial voice of Thucydides".[20] He seems to rely on this impartiality when he appeals to Thucydides' estimate of Pericles to rebut Tory criticisms of Pericles' behaviour as a popular leader.[21] And yet he criticizes Thucydides sharply and fairly for the partisan judgments passed on Cleon and Nicias; these passages are splendid examples of Grote's careful and independent estimate of the evidence that Thucydides adduces in support of his judgments, but Grote never goes beyond them to a general estimate of Thucydides himself.[22]

A further count against democratic Athens was its acquisition and maintenance of its empire. As Mill says, "modern historians seem to have succeeded to the jealous animosity of the Corinthians, and other members of the Spartan alliance, at the opening of the Peloponnesian war" (CW XI:321). Once again, an unfavourable view of the Athenian empire can be supported from Thucydides himself. He suggests that at the beginning of the war the Spartans were generally expected to be the liberators of Greece from Athenian domination. He represents Pericles as telling the Athenians that they hold the empire 'as a tyranny', and several Athenian speakers insist that Athenian policy towards the empire should be guided by considerations of power, security, and expediency, not by any standards of justice.[23] It would be quite unfair to suggest that only blind anti-democratic prejudice could lead a modern reader to take an unfavourable view of the Athenian empire.

The best reply to this view rests on a more careful study of Thucydides and of the historical situation he describes. Mill rightly calls attention to the striking remark that Thucydides attributes to the oligarchical conspirator Phrynicus, whom he represents "as reminding his fellow-conspirators that they could expect neither assistance nor good-will from the allies, since these well knew that it was from the oligarchical Athenians they were liable to injury, and looked upon the Demos as their protector" (CW XI:322–23, citing Thucydides VIII.48).[24] Closer study of Athenian intervention in the government of cities in the empire, and of judicial relations with the allies, confirms the view of Grote and Mill. While, as Mill acknowledges, "the Athenians certainly were not exempt from the passion, universal in the ancient world, for conquest and dominion" (CW XI:321), the empire was neither especially oppressive nor especially exploitative, and for the subject cities it was immensely preferable to the other two available options of domination by the Spartans or by the Persians.[25]

The same need for critical study of the literary sources is shown in one of Grote's major achievements in the study of intellectual history – his treatment of the Greek sophists. Mill thoroughly endorses Grote's attack on the Tory view that the sophists were corruptors of conventional morality, and that their general outlook is represented by the immoral positions maintained by Callicles in the *Gorgias* and by Thrasymachus in the *Republic*. The Tories were right to suppose that Plato criticizes the sophists. Grote, however, shows that they were wrong to suppose that Plato accuses the sophists of being corruptors of conventional morality, or that Plato regards the views of Callicles and Thrasymachus as characteristically sophistical views. Grote is certainly biased in favour of the sophists; he presents them as respectable intellectuals and teachers of practical morality and politics. But this is not what makes his study of the sophists valuable and convincing; its value lies in his argument to show that a careful study of Plato does not support the Tory view of them.[26]

We miss the main value of Grote's history, then, if we treat it simply as the work of a liberal and utilitarian determined to rebut the Tory interpretation of Greek history. Its value consists in the careful and critical study of the sources from which any interpretation has to begin. The effect of Grote's philosophical and political biases is salutary; they encourage him to look for flaws in the arguments supporting the Tory view, and to look for evidence supporting a contrary argument. In finding the relevant flaws and arguments, he is not simply expressing his own philosophical and political biases; he is pointing to some genuine features of the evidence that his opponents have missed.

Mill recognizes Grote's critical handling of the evidence, and praises it in general terms:

This conscientious scrupulousness in maintaining the demarcation between conjecture and proof, is more indispensable than any other excellence in the historian, and above all in one who sets aside the common notion of many of the facts which he relates, and replaces it by a version of his own. Without this quality, such an innovator on existing beliefs inspires no reliance, and can only, at most, unsettle historical opinion, without helping to restore it. Anybody can scrawl over the canvas with the commonplaces of rhetoric or the catchwords of party politics. . . . But Mr Grote commands the confidence of the reader by his sobriety in hypothesis . . . and . . . explaining his reasons with the precision and minuteness of one who neither desires nor expects that anything will be taken upon trust.[27]

This judgment has been endorsed by later historians,[28] and it clearly picks out an important feature of Grote's work. It is not clear, however, that Mill recognizes its full significance. If he had acknowledged the extent to which Tory views could claim support from the primary sources for Greek history, Mill might have seen that something more than 'candour' or freedom from political prejudice was needed to dislodge the Tory account of Athenian democracy; if he had seen that, he could have argued more convincingly for his general evaluation of Grote.

IV. MILL AND GROTE ON DEMOCRACY AND LIBERTY

Does Mill add anything to Grote? It is not surprising that he emphasizes some themes in Grote that are particularly close to his own philosophical and political preoccupations. He does not usually advertise the fact that on some points he goes beyond Grote and on some points sometimes actually goes against him; but some of these points are nonetheless clear and important.

It is useful to begin with one point of clear disagreement; though it may seem remote from philosophical and political issues, it will turn out to be connected with them. Mill shows himself Grote's superior in literary criticism when he defends the substantial integrity of the *Iliad* against Grote's attempt (in harmony with contemporary German scholarship) to excise several books as later additions. In arguing against the excision of Books 2–7 Mill reveals some of his own response to the poem as a whole:

> but, above all, it is in those books that we become acquainted with, and interested in, most of the leading characters of the subsequent epos. . . . Without the books which Mr Grote strikes from the original plan, there would be, if we except the amiable characters of Patroclus and Sarpedon, scarcely anything in the poem that excites a really personal interest.[29]

A comparison between Mill's treatment and Grote's illustrates what Mill had in mind in describing Grote as a man of "much logical and but little aesthetic culture". In Mill's record of his mental development, the appreciation of poetry as a means of cultivating 'personal interest' and sympathy is closely connected with the growth of his favourable attitude to Coleridge and his more critical attitude towards the utilitarianism of Grote and James Mill.[30]

This division between Grote and Mill emerges more sharply from their different treatments of questions about liberty that preoccupied both of them. On many points, not surprisingly, they agree. Mill quotes at length from Grote's appreciative account of the liberty of thought and action in democratic Athens. Grote remarks:

> Within the limits of the law, assuredly as faithfully observed at Athens as anywhere in Greece, individual impulse, taste, and even eccentricity, were accepted with indulgence; instead of being a mark, as elsewhere, for the intolerance of neighbours or of the public.[31]

Mill endorses Grote's praise of Athenian tolerance, and argues that such tolerance is necessary for the encouragement of genius. A society that does not positively encourage individuality and originality "may have persons of talent . . . but genius, in such a soil, is either fatally stunted in its growth, or if its native strength forbids this, it usually retires into itself, and dies without a sign".[32]

Why does Mill suppose that the Athenian democracy provided a friendly environment for individuality and originality? His own remarks on democracy in *On Liberty* do not suggest that he regards the sovereignty of majority opinion as an automatic safeguard of tolerance. How, in his view, did Athens avoid the tendency towards a tyranny of the majority? Unfortunately, neither Grote himself nor Mill's discussion of Grote gives a definite answer to this question. Mill, however, offers a suggestion. He remarks that Athens not only allowed freedom of speech and debate, but accustomed citizens to listen to debate and to make up their minds as a result of it:

the daily working of Athenian institutions (by means of which every citizen was accustomed to hear every sort of question, public and private, discussed by the ablest men of the time, with the earnestness of purpose and fulness of preparation belonging to actual business, deliberative or judicial) formed a course of political education, the equivalent of which modern nations have not known how to give even to those whom they educate for states-men. To their multitudinous judicial tribunals the Athenians were also indebted for that habitual love of fair play, and of hearing both sides of a case, which was more or less a quality of the Greeks generally, but had so firm a hold on the Athenians that it did not desert them under the most passionate excitement.[33]

Mill's references to 'the ablest men of the time' and to 'a course of political education' suggest the crucial difference he sees between Athenian democracy and just any old democracy. The Athenian constitution was designed by "a succession of eminent men", begin-ning with Solon, and "calculated to secure as much caution and deliberation as were compatible with ultimate decision by a sover-eign Ecclesia" (*CW* XI:326). In Mill's view, decisions by ordinary citizens were not necessarily decisions by the ignorant or unin-formed or the irrationally prejudiced. Since citizens had experience in public offices (including service in the Council, on juries, and in the various other positions filled by sortition), they had the sort of experience in making political decisions that made them better able to make intelligent decisions in the Assembly. And since they listened to 'the ablest men of their time', they learned how to distinguish good advice from bad.

Mill's praise of Athenian democracy is perfectly consistent, there-fore, with his praise of Plato for insisting on the role of education and expertise in government. He praises Plato for seeing the part of the truth that Plato found 'neglected and left in the background by the institutions and customs of his country'. Mill agrees with the truth that he thinks Plato over-emphasizes:

His doctrine was an exaggerated protest against the notion that any man is fit for any duty; a phrase which is the extreme formula of that indifference to special qualifications, and to the superiority of one mind over another, to which there is more or less tendency in all popular governments, and doubtless at Athens, as well as in the United States and Great Britain, though it would be a mistake to regard it in any of them as either universal or incurable.[34]

In saying that indifference to 'the superiority of one mind over another' is neither universal nor incurable in a democracy, Mill suggests the benefit that was secured, though incompletely, by the Athenian method of political education. On this point he implicitly contrasts Athens with modern societies:

the mass do not now take their opinions from dignitaries in Church or State, from ostensible leaders, or from books. Their thinking is done for them by men much like themselves, addressing them or speaking in their name, on the spur of the moment, through the newspapers.[35]

Mill does not intend his views about the role of expertise and of intellectual superiority to imply a restriction of democratic participation. Indeed, he seems to draw the contrary conclusion, that ordinary people will be more likely to listen to good advice the more experience they have had in deciding for themselves about the sorts of questions on which advice is given to them. Political participation and responsibility, in his view, are aspects of moral and political education.

Institutions alone could hardly be expected to have this educating influence. Mill notices that Greek democracy also required concern for the public good:

In the greatest Greek commonwealth, as described by its most distinguished citizen, the public interest was held of paramount obligation in all things which concerned it; but, with that part of the conduct of individuals which concerned only themselves, public opinion did not interfere; while in the ethical practice of the moderns, this is exactly reversed, and no one is required by opinion to pay any regard to the public, except by conducting his own private concerns in conformity to its expectations.[36]

To illustrate this point Mill quotes a long passage from Grote, which, however, describes only Athenian tolerance for individuality. We may well wonder how the strong ties of solidarity and sense of common interest that were developed in democratic Athens could be consistent with the limited functions that Mill and Grote want to allow the state in regulating private opinions. But Mill claims that in Athenian democracy the proper balance was achieved. In chapter 3 of *Utilitarianism* he advocates the development of the social feelings. In *On Liberty* he advocates the liberty of thought and discussion and the tolerance of individuality. He points to Athens to show that these demands do not conflict, but actually support each other.

Mill does not pretend that civic sentiment came naturally to Greeks or to Athenians. He points out that the Athenian democracy was sometimes threatened by oligarchic dissenters who "ought always to be present to the mind, not merely as a dark background to the picture of the Athenian republic, but as an active power in it".[37] These people evidently challenged the moral and political assumptions underlying democracy; a good example of such a challenge is presented by Callicles in Plato's *Gorgias*. What, in Mill's view, ought Athens to have done about the opinion that principles of justice are simply matters of convention, the result of a conspiracy by the weak against the strong? If people are permitted to express such views, or to form associations for propagating them, and especially if they are to be protected from the non-legal sanctions of general disapproval and condemnation, it is reasonable to suppose that civic sentiment will be weakened.

In Plato's view, the maintenance of civic sentiment requires repression both by law and by non-legal sanctions. This is one of Plato's reasons for believing that Athenian tolerance undermines the civic spirit that is necessary for the maintenance of the tolerant society itself; the decline of democracy into tyranny shows the basic conflict between two aspects of the Athenian outlook. This is why the *Laws* prohibits not only the Calliclean and Thrasymachean outlook, but any religious, metaphysical, and scientific views that (in Plato's view) encourage people to hold it.[38]

Two defences of Mill against Plato's criticisms might be tried: (1) People with Calliclean views should be allowed to express them as much as they like, and they should not be penalized, legally or non-legally, for their opinions. But they should not be allowed to act on them. The proper function of the state is to regulate behaviour, not to encourage one or another set of beliefs or values. (2) These views should be discouraged by all appropriate methods of education and formation of opinion. Toleration should be restricted to cases where it does not undermine the moral foundations of the community.

The first defence has some support in *On Liberty*, where Mill attacks not only legal persecution but also "merely social intolerance" of deviant opinions.[39] In this passage he is thinking especially of the disapproving attitude that some people take towards agnostics and atheists; "it is the opinions men entertain, and the feelings they cherish, respecting those who disown the beliefs they deem important which makes this country not a place of mental freedom." Mill deplores the inhibiting effects of these disapproving attitudes even when they do not go as far as legal persecution. In taking this view, he seems to endorse the liberal view that requires the state – and, speaking more broadly, the public – to be neutral about views, as opposed to behaviour.

The second defence has some support in Mill's assumption that we are free to use non-legal sanctions against "defect of prudence or personal dignity".[40] These sanctions include 'loss of consideration', the expression of distaste, and standing aloof 'from a person as well as from a thing that displeases us'. Such attitudes, if widely shared and directed against atheists or agnostics, would surely strike Mill as the 'merely social intolerance' that he deplores. If most people took the attitude to atheists that they are permitted to take to habitual drunkards or alcoholics, their attitude would apparently tend to inhibit the profession of atheist views. Mill mentions the report that in the United States

the feeling of the majority, to whom any appearance of a more showy or costly style of living than they can hope to rival is disagreeable, operates as a tolerably effectual sumptuary law, and . . . in many parts of the Union it is really difficult for a person possessing a large income to find any mode of spending it which will not incur popular disapprobation.[41]

While he seems to regard this disapprobation as legitimate in principle (though liable to be mistaken in practice) when it is directed against attitudes or conduct that are held to be undesirable even though (according to Mill) they do no direct harm, he does not seem to think it is legitimate when it is directed against deviant views and their expression. What justifies him in distinguishing these two cases?

Mill might argue that social intolerance ought to be restrained for the sake of encouraging freedom of thought and expression, and that legal and non-legal sanctions ought to be applied only to actions that harm others. Some Greek supporters of oligarchy took the oath "I will bear ill-will to the people[42] and I will devise against it every evil I can".[43] Mill might be taken to claim that the view expressed in the first part of this oath ought to be exempt from legal penalties and social intolerance, while anyone taking action on the second part of the oath ought to be prevented. It is difficult to see, however, how the cultivation of civic sentiment in a democracy could be expected not to result in social intolerance directed against people expressing the sentiments of the first part of this oath. And so Mill's first possible defence of toleration seems difficult to reconcile with his emphasis on civic sentiment.

Mill's second possible defence fits better with his emphasis on the importance of cultivating civic and social sentiment. It does not undermine his argument for the different types of toleration that he advocates, but it makes the application of this argument to particular cases more difficult to decide. In particular, the second defence does not justify the state in taking a neutral attitude to the expression or propagation of beliefs, and it does not assure us that we secure the appropriate tolerance of beliefs and actions simply by leaving them alone if they do not directly harm anyone. Someone's holding or expressing the anti-popular sentiment of the first part of the oligarchic oath does not directly harm anyone,[44] but it may still be a legitimate object of social intolerance.

It is hard to attribute a definite position to Mill, because his example of an opinion that should be free of social intolerance is religious unbelief, an attitude that, in his view, does not conflict with appropriate civic sentiment. It would have been easier to see what he believes if he had considered a clearly 'anti-civic' view such as the first part of the oligarchic oath (or the modern analogues professed by fascists and racists). At any rate, this issue about Athenian and modern democracy and liberty raises an issue about social sentiment and toleration on which Grote and Mill apparently did not agree. In his essay on Coleridge, Mill notices that Coleridge sees the importance of loyalty in the preservation of a society:

its essence is always the same; viz. that there be in the constitution of the State *something* which is settled, something permanent, and not to be called into question; something which, by general agreement, has a right to be where it is, and to be secure against disturbance, whatever else may change.[45]

In considering the various possible objects of loyalty Mill mentions the one he thinks best:

Or finally (and this is the only shape in which the feeling is likely to exist hereafter) it may attach itself to the principles of individual freedom and political and social equality, as realized in institutions which as yet exist nowhere, or exist only in a rudimentary state. But in all political societies which have had a durable existence, there has been some fixed point; something which men agreed in holding sacred; which, wherever freedom of discussion was a recognised principle, it was of course lawful to contest in theory, but which no one could either fear or hope to see shaken in practice; which, in short (except perhaps during some temporary crisis), was in the common estimation placed beyond discussion.[46]

This was one of many aspects of Mill's essays on Bentham and Coleridge that disturbed Grote, who often referred to this passage as evidence of Mill's equivocal attitude to liberty.[47] Grote apparently accepts the first defence of tolerance, advocating neutrality by the state. His dispute with Mill is not about legal toleration, since Mill makes it clear (in 'lawful to contest in theory') that he does not advocate legal restraint of anyone questioning a 'fixed point'. He must apparently take Mill to be advocating collective action to secure the 'fixed points' by the cultivation of civic sentiment, supported by social intolerance.

The difference between Grote and Mill appears clearly in the difference between Grote's description of Athenian democracy and Mill's paraphrase of his description. While Grote emphasizes the necessary restraints on behaviour, Mill emphasizes the positive cultivation of civic sentiment. Mill supports his emphasis by appealing to Grote's approving description of the growth of civic sentiment under democracy. Though he does not allude to the dispute about Mill's approval of Coleridge on loyalty, Mill appeals – quite legitimately – to passages in Grote that support Mill's side of the dispute.[48]

Grote's disapproval of Mill is all the more striking in the light of his recognition, at other places in his history, of the importance of civic sentiment. In describing the role of religious and family feeling in the trial of the generals after Arginusae, Grote remarks that some Athenians had "forgotten their sense of political commonwealth" and "become degraded into exclusively family-men".[49] It is clearly unjust to treat this passage as evidence of "Grote's vendetta against modes of human association other than the ties of citizenship".[50] He is pointing out, quite legitimately, the morally bad effects of allowing family loyalties to overcome a commitment to justice for fellow-citizens. But the case he mentions here – though Mill does not mention it – provides an excellent illustration of the general point that Mill derives from Coleridge and that Grote disapproves of so strongly.

It is unfortunate that Mill and Grote did not pursue their disagreement more openly and in more detail. Their general agreement about the right interpretation of Greek history and political life throws into sharper relief their deep disagreement about the relations between freedom, democracy, and social sentiment. Both of them believe, and for good reasons, that Athens provides the best model of how democracy, loyalty, and individuality might be reconciled and might support each other. But they have different views about the nature of the reconciliation. Mill's views depart from the version of utilitarianism that Grote shared with James Mill; but Mill does not pursue them far enough to make it clear whether he can consistently maintain his own version of utilitarianism, and whether he is entitled to the defence of liberty that he constructs on a utilitarian basis.

V. MILL'S ATTITUDE TO PLATO

Mill was acquainted early in his life with Plato, and his father formed some definite views in him about the philosophical value of some aspects of Plato:

It was about at this period that I read for the first time, some of the most important dialogues of Plato, in particular the Gorgias, the Protagoras, and the Republic. There is no author to whom my father thought himself more indebted for his own mental culture than Plato, or whom he more frequently recommended to young students. I can bear similar testimony in regard to myself.[51]

Mill does not attribute any similarly strong convictions about Aristotle to his father; his interest in Plato was not matched by any corresponding interest in Aristotle.

In this respect Mill's philosophical education differed sharply from the education he would have received at Oxford (as opposed to Cambridge).[52] When Bentham was an undergraduate, he used the textbook called *Ethices Compendium in usum iuventutis academicae*.[53] His references and quotations suggest that it was a fairly uninspired summary of Aristotelian ethics; it certainly did not arouse Bentham's admiration. In 1800 Oxford introduced university-wide public examinations, and in 1807 it introduced an examination *in literis humanioribus*.[54] Aristotle's *Ethics* and Butler constituted most of the moral philosophy in this examination. Though undergraduates read some Plato as early as the 1820s, he did not hold the central place held by Aristotle.[55] When Gladstone sums up what he learned at Oxford, he does not mention Plato:

I have no intention whatever of breaking with the traditions in which I have grown up, which I have learned from Oxford, which I have learned from four writers far beyond any, perhaps all others – Butler, Aristotle, Dante, St Augustine, my four doctors.[56]

The intellectual influences on Mill are sharply different. There is no sign of his ever having paid close attention to Aristotle's *Ethics*,[57] but his interest in Plato lasted throughout his life.

Mill reports that his father taught him to value Plato, and that he fully agrees with his father on this point. The Socratic method of investigation by cross-examination and refutation "even at that age, took such hold of me that it became part of my own mind".[58] When Mill began to publish his translations of Plato in the 1830s, he regarded himself as a pioneer. He remarks that the only available English version was both inaccurate and unintelligible,[59] and that very little about Plato had appeared in English in recent years.

He goes further, however, and suggests that hardly anyone even read Plato:

of the young men who have obtained university honours during the last ten years, we are much misinformed if there be six who had even looked into his [Plato's] writings. . . . The consequence is, that there are, probably, in this kingdom, not so many as a hundred persons who ever *have* read Plato, and not so many as twenty who ever *do*.[60]

When Mill makes this sweeping claim, his aversion to 'the impostor-universities of England' seems to have led him into exaggeration.[61] As we have seen, Oxford undergraduates seem to have read some Plato in the 1820s. In 1841 William Sewell, who had been Whyte's Professor of Moral Philosophy in Oxford, published a book on Plato, incorporating some of his essays and (presumably, to judge by the style) his popular undergraduate lectures from the 1830s.[62] During the same period disciples of Coleridge were lecturing on Plato in Cambridge. Mill may have been misled by somewhat out-of-date views about what was actually being taught and read in the 'impostor-universities'.

Even if Mill had known more about the extent of Platonic studies in England, however, he might not have welcomed it. Several aspects of Sewell's outlook are fairly summarized in his remark:

In England the study of the Greek philosophy has been chiefly confined to the University of Oxford, which providentially has been saved from setting the seal of its sanction to either Paley or Locke; and has adhered firmly to Aristotle as the text-book in her plan of education.[63]

Bentham and James Mill evidently represent the sort of philosophy from which Sewell believed Oxford had been providentially preserved.[64]

Sewell emphasizes the practical, moral aim of all of Plato, his attacks on the sophists, and, more broadly, his opposition to empiricism in epistemology and hedonism in ethics. He stresses the continuity and unity of these aims in all the dialogues, and finds Plato's views most clearly expressed in a group of four dialogues, the *Republic*, *Timaeus*, *Critias*, and *Laws*. On these he comments: "These four form one grand group openly connected together. And there is not a question left unsettled in any one of the former dialogues, which does not find its solution here – a solution unmixed with a particle of doubt."[65] Sewell describes the favourable views that the Christian Fathers take of Plato, and includes a long chapter on the Christian Platonism of Alexandria. Sewell himself was an early supporter of the Tractarians; one might conjecture that the

Tractarian zeal for Patristic studies helped to turn his interest to Plato.[66] His general outlook – philosophical, educational, and theological – would hardly have appealed to Mill.

Mill's failure to mention Platonic studies in Oxford is therefore explicable. It is more difficult to explain his failure to mention the Platonic interests of the Cambridge Coleridgeans. Shortly after publishing his translations of Plato, Mill published his sympathetic essay on Coleridge; for several years before that, he had been on good terms with the Coleridgeans F. D. Maurice and John Sterling.[67] In the 1830s, when Platonic studies had begun to revive in Oxford, they had begun to revive in Cambridge too; Julius Hare and Connop Thirlwall, among others, had begun to lecture on Plato.[68] It is rather remarkable that Mill does not mention the influence of Plato on Coleridge or on those influenced by him.

To explain this omission, it may be relevant to draw attention to the difference between Mill's attitude to Plato and the attitude of some earlier English philosophers. Cudworth and Price appeal especially to Plato's realism and objectivism, in order to attack Hobbes (in Cudworth) and Hutcheson and Hume (in Price). They turn especially to the *Theaetetus* for its discussion and (in their view) refutation of the view that 'nothing is true or false (any more than sweet or sour) in itself, but relatively to the perceiving mind'. This is the view of Protagoras, who also applied it to moral properties. Price finds the same view in Hutcheson and Hume:

> Such is the agreement, in this instance, between the opinions of modern times and those of Socrates's times. Such the tendency of the account of morality I have opposed; and it is astonishing how far some, who have embraced it, have extended it to our other perceptions, and revived, perhaps even exceeded, the wildest doctrines of ancient scepticism.[69]

Cudworth and Price find this defence of objectivism in Plato's argument in the *Euthyphro* against morality as resulting from a divine command, and in his theory of Forms, as well as in the *Theaetetus*. This Platonic line of argument underlies both Cudworth's objections to Hobbes's positivist account of morality and Price's anticipation of Moore's 'open question' argument.

Mill is completely silent about this constructive use of some aspects of Platonic metaphysics and epistemology. Though he warmly endorses Plato's argument as exposing the fundamental unsoundness of 'divine command' theories,[70] he never credits Plato with the argument. None of his writings give the reader any idea of the previous influence of Plato on English moral philosophy. Two reasons for his silence might be suggested. First, the meta-ethical and normative views that Price rests on these Platonic foundations are not attractive to Mill. Secondly, Mill is not disposed to take Plato's positive contributions to philosophy very seriously in general.

The aspect of Plato that Mill praises repeatedly is the Socratic cross-examination:

> The Socratic method, of which the Platonic dialogues are the chief example, is unsurpassed as a discipline for correcting the errors, and clearing up the confusions incident to the *intellectus sibi permissus*, the understanding which has made up all its bundles of associations under the guidance of popular phraseology. The close, searching *elenchus* by which the man of vague generalities is constrained either to express his meaning to himself in definite terms, or to confess that he does not know what he is talking about; the perpetual testing of all general statements by particular instances; the siege in form which is laid to the meaning of large abstract terms, by fixing upon some still larger class-name which includes that and more, and dividing down to the thing sought – marking out its limits and definition by a series of accurately drawn distinctions between it and each of the cognate objects which are successively parted off from it – all this, as an education for precise thinking, is inestimable, and all this, even at that age, took such hold of me that it became part of my own mind.[71]

The positive philosophical doctrines of Plato, by contrast, are, in Mill's view, largely misguided.

One important qualification is needed here. In Mill's view, his father's moral convictions "wholly dissevered from religion, were very much of the character of those of the Greek philosophers".[72] Mill's reading of Plato and Xenophon aroused admiration for the same moral ideal:

> At a somewhat later period the lofty moral standard exhibited in the writings of Plato operated on me with great force. My father's moral inculcations were at all times mainly those of the 'Socratici viri'; justice, temperance (to which he gave a very extended application), veracity, perseverance, readiness to encounter pain and especially labour; regard for the public good; estimation of persons according to their merits, and of things according to their intrinsic usefulness; a life of exertion in contradiction to one of self-indulgent ease and sloth.[73]

Despite his admiration for the moral content of the Platonic dialogues, however, Mill never allows that Plato has any cogent argument for his moral conclusions. In his concluding comment on the *Gorgias* Mill claims that "the reader has now seen the substance of what the greatest moralist of antiquity finds to say in recommendation of a virtuous life".[74] He finds Plato's arguments unsuccessful, not simply because Plato overlooked some good arguments, but because no good argument can be given:

It is impossible, by any arguments, to prove that a life of obedience to duty is preferable, so far as respects the agent himself, to a life of circumspect and conscious selfishness. It will be answered, perhaps, that virtue is the road to happiness, and that 'honesty is the best policy'. Of this celebrated maxim, may we not venture to say, once for all, without hesitation or reserve, that it is not true. The whole experience of mankind runs counter to it.[75]

Mill's arguments for the conclusion that he maintains with such vigour consist in appeals to the familiar fact that virtue and vice are not correlated with the ordinary advantages and disadvantages of life.

These considerations do not justify rejection of the claim that Plato puts forward in the *Gorgias*. Plato is as familiar as Mill is with the facts that Mill adduces. In Plato's view, people who identify their welfare with the ordinary measures of success in life are simply mistaken about where their welfare lies. This may or may not be a promising line of argument, but it is certainly not the one that Mill answers in his discussion of honesty as the best policy.

Mill is not simply criticizing Plato for attempting to show that virtue is in the agent's interest; he believes Plato is wrong to attempt to give reasons for preferring virtue at all:

All valid arguments in favour of virtue, presuppose that we already desire virtue, or desire some of its ends and objects. . . . Those only will go along with Socrates in the preceding dialogue, who already feel that the accordance of their lives and inclinations with some scheme of duty is necessary to their comfort. . . . But no arguments which Plato urges have power to make those love or desire virtue, who do not already: nor is this ever to be effected through the intellect, but through the imagination and the affections.[76]

In this passage Mill seems to raise two objections to Plato: (1) simply accepting an argument to show that virtue deserves to be loved is not enough for loving virtue; (2) no sound argument can be given to show that virtue deserves to be loved. The first objection manifests a disagreement between Mill and Plato (in the *Gorgias*, at any rate) about the connexion between rational conviction and motivation. The second objection is more directly relevant to the cogency of Plato's argument in the *Gorgias*; Mill must maintain the second objection in order to dismiss the argument of the *Gorgias* as brusquely as he does. Perhaps Mill does not sharply distinguish the two objections, but he seems to raise the second as well as the first (in the sentence 'Those only will go along with Socrates . . .').

Mill's convictions about the limits of moral argument help to explain why he believes that the main value of Platonic argument lies in its negative cross-examination of conventional views, and not in its defence of one moral position over another. Perhaps he had convinced himself by close and careful examination of Plato's positive arguments that they were completely unsuccessful; but the reasons he offers suggest some misunderstanding of Plato. The strength of Mill's conviction may perhaps be explained by his antecedent conviction of the pointlessness of Plato's attempted defence of justice.

VI. GROTE ON PLATO

Mill had already held these views about Plato for many years when he read and reviewed Grote's elaborate four-volume study of Plato. Before the book was published, Mill thought Grote was taking too long over it, and that he would not develop his own philosophical views enough: "[Grote] seems to take a length of time only to be warranted by using the opportunity to speak out very plainly on the great subjects – a thing I rather wish than expect he will be found to have done."[77] Grote certainly took a long time, and Mill's hope was indeed disappointed.

Still, Mill's criticisms are rather unfair. Grote had a good reason to take a long time. His book shows wide knowledge not only of Plato and Platonic scholarship, but also of many ancient philosophical texts relevant to the understanding of Plato. Many an unobtrusive footnote contains an interesting and relevant comment or parallel from an ancient source outside Plato. Grote examines Plato closely, in the light of this deep and wide-ranging scholarship, and pursues questions that had not been properly faced.

When A. E. Taylor published his important general study of Plato in 1926, he compared himself with Grote:

If it were not that the remark might sound immodest, I would say that the model I have had before me is Grote's great work. . . . Enjoying neither Grote's superb scholarship nor his freedom from limitations of space, I have perhaps the compensation of freedom from the prejudices of a party. Whatever bias I may have in metaphysics or in politics, I have tried to keep it out of my treatment of Plato.[78]

Taylor is right both to praise Grote and to remark that Grote is not free from the prejudices of a party. It is not clear, however, that freedom from such prejudices is an advantage, or that Grote's work would have been better if he had lacked the prejudices of his particular party. The outlook of James Mill is not the best preparation for a sympathetic exposition of Plato's doctrines, but it is a good preparation for a critical examination of Plato. Since Grote is not at all tempted to believe Plato's conclusions, he is in a good position to identify weaknesses and difficulties in Plato's arguments for them, and to call attention to the valuable aspects of Plato that are independent of his degree of success in formulating or defending specific doctrines. Grote's philosophical position leads him to an important part of the truth about Plato. The modern reader has reason to be grateful for Grote's failure to fulfill Mill's hopes; for Grote would surely have achieved far less if he had given us more of his own philosophical views than he achieved by his concentration on the critical study of Plato and of ancient philosophy in general.

Grote's scholarship and critical intelligence give extensive support to the view that Mill had already formed about Plato's positive philosophical doctrines. In the preface to his translations Mill suggests that it is hopeless to attribute definite positive views to Plato, except on issues of philosophical method. He mentions the apparent conflicts between different dialogues, Plato's failure to appear in his own person, and the frequency of Socrates' displays of irony.[79] As we have seen, this division between the tentative and the definite in Plato is to some extent correlated with Mill's own convictions about what can and cannot be defended by argument.[80] But he is also entitled to point out the obvious difficulties in finding a single consistent body of thought in the Platonic dialogues.

These difficulties emerge still more clearly from two aspects of Grote's discussion of Plato: (1) he affirms the authenticity of all the works in the Platonic corpus that are not specifically marked by ancient critics as doubtful or spurious; and (2) he is sceptical about all attempts to fix a definite order for the dialogues, and so about all attempts to trace Plato's philosophical development.

These two moves reinforce each other and together reinforce Grote's disinclination to attribute a settled body of positive doctrine to Plato. One reason for doubting the authenticity of one of the dialogues or letters is its apparent irreconcilability with the doctrines of the other dialogues. Grote altogether disallows this argument, claiming that it assumes a greater degree of doctrinal unity and system than we have any right to expect. Similarly, he rejects any search for an answer to the objections that the *Parmenides* raises to the theory of Forms, claiming that we ought not to be surprised that Plato raises objections that he does not answer.[81]

Grote's views about the questions of authenticity and development go further than many more recent writers would be willing to go. Many students of Plato are more willing than Grote is to rely on some judgments about philosophical subject matter and quality in deciding about the authenticity of particular dialogues, and many have more confidence in hypotheses about the chronology of the dialogues and about Plato's likely development. Still, Grote's arguments provide a salutary warning against accounts of Plato that lay too little emphasis on those critical and exploratory aspects of the dialogues that, in Grote's and Mill's view, constitute Plato's contribution to philosophy.[82]

Mill claims that he held this view about Plato ever since his first recognition of the value of the Socratic method:

I have felt ever since that the title of Platonist belongs by far better right to those who have been nourished in, and have endeavoured to practise Plato's mode of investigation, than to those who are distinguished only by the adoption of certain dogmatical conclusions, drawn mostly from the least intelligible of his works, and which the character of his mind and writings makes it uncertain whether he himself regarded as anything more than poetic fancies, or philosophic conjectures.[83]

He expresses the same view in his review of Grote, suggesting that Plato really includes two philosophers:

There are thus, independently of minor discrepancies, two complete Platos in Plato – the Sokratist and the Dogmatist – of whom the former is by far the more valuable to mankind, but the latter has obtained from them much the greater honour. And no wonder; for the one was capable of being a useful prop to many a man's moral and religious dogmas, while the other could only clear and invigorate the human understanding.[84]

The main philosophical value that Mill sees in Grote's study of Plato is its emphasis on the independent value of the 'Socratist' in Plato. Grote's own assessment of the comparative value of the negative and the positive elements in Plato agrees with Mill's.

Like Mill, Grote gives us no conception of the extent of Platonic influence in previous English philosophy. When Grote discusses the argument against divine-command ethics in the *Euthyphro*, he never mentions its historical influence and significance in Cudworth and Price (to go back no further).[85] Though he discusses quite fully the philosophical issues about objectivity that are raised in the *Theaetetus*, he says nothing about Price and almost nothing about Cudworth.[86] These omissions are surprising in view of the impressive scope of Grote's classical and philosophical scholarship; perhaps they are to be explained by his unsympathetic attitude to the use that his philosophical predecessors had made of these aspects of Plato. At any rate, if Grote had paid attention to Cudworth and Price, they would hardly have modified his unfavourable view of the constructive aspects of Plato's philosophy.

Grote's neglect of this aspect of Plato is a symptom of one of the gravest errors in his book: his separation of the elenctic method from Plato's positive doctrines. This same separation is marked in Mill's appealing, but basically misguided, picture of the 'two complete Platos'. These views miss the crucial fact that from the earliest dialogues onwards the Platonic Socrates regards elenctic cross-examination as a means of constructive philosophical argument, not only exposing the difficulties in a position or in an interlocutor's defence of it, but arguing at the same time for the Socratic and the Platonic position. We may not agree that Plato is justified in attributing a positive role to Socratic cross-examination, and we may not be persuaded by the particular positive conclusions that he draws from it. But if we do not recognize and examine this role of Socratic *elenchos*, we are missing a central element in Plato's conception of philosophical argument. Because Grote and Mill miss this central element, their estimate of Plato is irreparably flawed.[87]

VII. MILL'S DISAGREEMENTS WITH GROTE

Mill's general agreement with Grote's views should not be taken to betray Mill's lack of independence. We have seen that he had already formed views rather similar to Grote's.[88] He was therefore already sympathetic to Grote's general view, and he was in a position to evaluate it for himself. Moreover, however closely he agrees with Grote's general assessment of Plato, he adds something distinctive to it. One specific example will make this point clearer. Grote believes that Plato is simply misguided in trying to argue that virtue is good for the agent; he takes Plato to have anticipated a long series of moralists whose errors were set right by James Mill.[89] Mill does not dissent from Grote's main criticisms of Plato's argument in the *Gorgias* and the *Republic*.[90] But his tone towards Plato is perceptibly different from Grote's. Grote believes it is simply mistaken and misleading to pretend that virtue, especially justice, is good for the agent. He believes that Glaucon and Adeimantus, followed by James Mill, are right in treating justice as exclusively 'another person's good' (*allotrion agathon*); a virtuous agent benefits, in Grote's view, not from her own justice, but from the just behaviour of other people.[91] Plato's attempt to find some further benefit in being just is, according to Grote, simply a mistake; it betrays the extent to which the preacher in Plato gets the better of the philosopher.[92]

Once again Mill shows himself to be a deviant from strict utilitarian orthodoxy (as James Mill and Grote conceive it). He stops noticeably short of Grote's judgment that Plato's claim about justice and happiness is actually false. We may trace this difference from Grote back to the broader difference that is expressed in Mill's essays on Bentham and Coleridge. Mill explains and criticizes Bentham's attitude to Socrates and Plato as a symptom of a more general intellectual limitation:

Socrates and Plato are spoken of in terms distressing to his [Bentham's] greatest admirers; and the incapacity to appreciate such men, is a fact perfectly in unison with the general habits of Bentham's mind. He had a phrase, expressive of the view he took of all moral speculations to which his method had not been applied, or (which he considered as the same thing) not founded on a recognition of the moral standard; this phrase was 'vague generalities'.[93] Whatever presented itself to him in such a shape, he dismissed as unworthy of notice, or dwelt upon only to denounce as absurd. He did not heed, or rather the nature of his mind prevented it from occurring to him, that these generalities contained the whole unanalysed experience of the human race.[94]

While it would be absurd to accuse Grote of Bentham's philistine attitude towards Socrates and Plato, Mill perhaps sees in Grote some of the same failure to appreciate the aspects of 'the unanalysed experience of the human race' that are captured in some of the positive aspects of Socratic and Platonic ethics. In his view, "there is, indeed, ample justification for the homage which all cultivated ages have rendered to Plato simply as a moralist – as one of the most powerful masters of virtue who have ever appeared among mankind."[95] Mill suggests that Plato's aim of showing "the infinitely superior eligibility of the just life, even if calumniated and persecuted, over the unjust"[96] is after all a correct and appropriate aim for a moralist.

Mill's own moral theory suggests that when he praises Plato as a moral teacher he is not just carried away by momentary enthusiasm. He believes that Bentham's narrowness shows itself in his attitude to the virtuous person's outlook:

Man is never recognized by him as a being capable of pursuing spiritual perfection as an end; of desiring, for its own sake, the conformity of his own character to his standard of excellence, without hope of good or fear of evil from other source than his own consciousness.[97]

This is why Bentham overlooks the aspect of morality that consists in "self-education; the training, by the human being himself, of his affections and will".[98]

In *Utilitarianism* Mill recognizes that a virtuous person chooses virtue for its own sake as a part of happiness.[99] Though (in his view) we originally prefer virtuous action for its resulting pleasure, the relation between virtue and happiness is not always purely external and causal; the development of will and habit produce an attitude to virtue and happiness that cannot be understood if we take the relation between them to be purely external. This attitude is the one that Plato takes to be the correct attitude to justice and happiness, when he sets out to defend the view that justice is to be chosen for its own sake, not for its consequences, but still for the sake of happiness.

Mill endorses this attitude of the virtuous person, when he discusses the growth of moral feelings. In his view, the recognition of interdependence of interests does not simply produce the result that Grote mentions, the recognition that other people's justice benefits me and that my justice tends to encourage them to treat me justly. It also changes my attitude to my own interest:

Not only does all strengthening of social ties, and all healthy growth of society, give to each individual a stronger personal interest in practically consulting the welfare of others, it also leads him to identify his *feelings* more and more with their good, or at least with an even greater degree of practical consideration for it. He comes, as though instinctively, to be conscious of himself as a being who *of course* pays regard to others. The good of others becomes to him a thing naturally and necessarily, to be attended to like any of the physical conditions of our existence.[100]

If moral training is complete and successful, our moral feeling does not present itself as the product of social pressure:

to those who have it [the moral feeling], it possesses all the characters of a natural feeling. It does not present itself to their minds as a superstition of education or a law despotically imposed by the power of society, but as an attribute which it would not be well for them to be without.[101]

If we regard this as an attribute which it would not be well for us to be without, then apparently we must accept something like Plato's conviction about the value of virtue to the virtuous person.

These remarks about the growth of moral feeling help to explain why Mill thinks Grote is missing something in his estimate of Plato. According to Mill, the belief that Plato defends by argument is a belief that the morally educated person ought to have acquired. We ought not, in Mill's view, to finish our moral education with the conviction that our commitment to morality is burdensome and unwelcome from the point of view of our own good, but appropriate and required for the good of society. We ought to reject the complete separation between our own good and the good of others that is implied in the merely dutiful conviction; and if we reject that, we must implicitly accept something like Plato's claim that virtue – in its own right and not simply because of its consequences – is part of our own good.

If we compare the third and fourth chapters of *Utilitarianism* with Mill's early comments (on the *Gorgias*, quoted above) on Plato's attempt to prove that virtue promotes happiness, must we conclude that Mill has changed his mind about whether a successful argument of the sort that Plato sought can be given? He does not say so. He explains how people can come to acquire the belief that virtue is a part of their happiness, and he affirms that it is desirable that they come to acquire this belief, but he does not explain why we should be convinced that the belief is true.

VIII. MILL AND PLATO ON VIRTUE AND HAPPINESS

Let us suppose, then, that Mill accepts Plato's conclusion about the relation between virtue and happiness as true, but he believes that Plato is wrong to suppose that the conclusion can be rationally defended. Mill supposes (on this view) that to agree with Plato we need Coleridgean 'aesthetic culture' rather than Benthamite 'logical culture'. Would this be a reasonable position for Mill to adopt?

We might want to ask why Mill thinks it is legitimate for the Platonic belief to be inculcated by moral education. It may be beneficial to society to inculcate this belief, but if Mill himself cannot give a reason for supposing that the belief is true, he cannot defend himself against the charge that he is advocating the inculcation of a false belief. He can certainly deny this charge, but he cannot – on his own showing – give a good reason for believing that the charge is false.[102]

This issue is sharply raised by Plato's *Gorgias*.[103] Callicles suggests that conventional beliefs about justice are false, and that they reflect the tyranny of the majority. Superior people are indoctrinated until they lose sight of the fact that their own good requires them to violate the rules of conventional justice that require some respect for the interests of others. Mill believes that though Callicles is wrong, no good reason can be given to show why he is wrong.

Perhaps this would not matter so much if the anti-Calliclean view were universally, or nearly universally, held; but this is clearly not so, since such respectable people (from Mill's point of view) as Grote disagree with Mill. Apparently, then, Mill puts himself in a weak position if he accepts Plato's conclusion, but rejects any argument for the conclusion.

Mill's position becomes still more precarious if we try to combine these views on morality with his views on liberty. Part of the point of free thought and discussion is to practise the elenctic method that Mill takes to be Plato's chief contribution to philosophy. Mill believes that elenctic examination will reveal the failure of all arguments in favour of an internal connexion between virtue and the agent's own good. It is difficult, then, to see how the practice of the elenctic method could fail to weaken the commitment to virtue that Mill himself takes to be necessary for complete moral education.

A further question arises if we consider Mill's defence of individuality. It is supposed to be aimed at fuller self-development, "the highest and most harmonious development of his powers to a complete and consistent whole".[104] The expression of individuality is not supposed to be the uncritical satisfaction of whatever tastes or inclinations we happen to have formed, but the expression of some deliberately and critically formed conception of a worthwhile life:

He who chooses his plan for himself employs all his faculties. . . . And these qualities he requires and exercises exactly in proportion as the part of his conduct which he determines according to his own judgment and feelings is a large one.[105]

We would not be giving the appropriate scope to our own judgment and feelings if we did not subject our moral convictions to the sort of reasoning, judgment, and discrimination that Mill advocates. If we examine them critically, then they do not seem to give a good account of themselves, if they involve our acceptance of a conviction (about virtue and the virtuous agent's good) for which we acknowledge that no sound argument can be given.

If Mill has an answer to this question in On Liberty, it perhaps comes in the next chapter, in which he argues that individuals ought to be restrained only from actions that are directly harmful to others. This might suggest that a person's moral convictions are within the area that ought to be left to individual choice. But this is not a satisfactory answer; for Mill himself points out forcefully that it is a mistake to confine moral education to mere behavioural conformity. It looks as though he must advocate the inculcation of the Platonic conviction that he acknowledges to lack any rational support. It is difficult to see how such a conviction could be expected to withstand the sort of critical scrutiny that Mill himself advocates.

Can Mill answer these objections? We might reasonably wonder whether his later work maintains the scepticism that he displays in his early comments about Plato's attempts to argue that virtue promotes happiness. Indeed, we might argue that *Utilitarianism* and *On Liberty* provide the materials of an argument for the Platonic conclusion. The main steps in the argument would be these:

(1) Happiness is a compound whose components are pleasures, understood as activities in which we take pleasure.
(2) Pleasures are to be evaluated by reference to the deliberation of appropriately informed rational agents.
(3) The appropriately informed rational agents are those who pursue the full realization of their capacities as rational agents, and know what activities are required by this full realization.
(4) These rational agents will discover that the virtues constitute the appropriate states of character for the full realization of our capacities as rational agents.

It is difficult to say whether this sort of argument should be regarded (i) as Mill's considered and consistent view, or (ii) as an element in his view that conflicts with other elements, or (iii) as a development of some materials that he provides without himself presenting them in an argument.[106] At any rate, if Mill could defend this argument, he would have shown that the sort of critical scrutiny that should be used to decide what counts as 'the highest and most harmonious' development of a person's powers will vindicate, rather than undermine, the desires and aims that result from our moral convictions. It will turn out, on this view, that the sorts of moral convictions that Mill advocates actually belong to the way of life that expresses the highest and most harmonious development of our powers.

If Mill sets out to show this, he sets out to do what Plato and Aristotle set out to do when they try to defend their conviction that virtue promotes the agent's good. Moreover, some steps in the argument are strikingly similar to Platonic and Aristotelian claims. Mill's claim that virtue is to be chosen for its own sake and as a part of happiness suggests a plausible account of what Plato and Aristotle mean in their claims about virtue and happiness.[107] In arguing that pleasures differ in ethically relevant respects other than their quantity, and that the ethically informed rational agent must choose among them, Mill accepts a view of pleasures and their objects that is developed by Plato in *Republic* IX and the *Philebus*, and by Aristotle in the *Ethics* (especially X:1–5).[108] In claiming that the virtues are a central element in the realization of our capacities as rational agents, Mill helps himself to Plato's and Aristotle's claims about the connexion between the human 'function' (essential activity), practical reason, and virtue.

It is rather surprising that Mill never mentions these connexions between his own arguments and Plato's and Aristotle's, either in his essays on Greek philosophy or in his own ethical works. He does not qualify his rejection of the main argument of the *Republic*, and he mentions the obscurity of the *Philebus* without mentioning what can be learnt from it.[109] He does not point out that if Plato's arguments are as thoroughly misguided as Grote says they are, his own arguments about happiness and virtue must also be rejected.

Why does Mill not acknowledge the extent to which he accepts Platonic arguments as well as Platonic conclusions? It is difficult to believe that he knows the extent of his debt and deliberately conceals it; such concealment would not fit Mill's generous and appreciative attitude to Plato. Probably he is unaware of his debt. Such unawareness might be explained in different, but complementary, ways: (i) Mill is so firmly convinced of the failure of Plato's positive arguments, taken as a whole, that he does not consider carefully the merits of individual arguments or of elements in the Platonic position. (ii) The 'Platonic' line of argument that I have sketched on Mill's behalf is not systematically presented by Mill himself, and so he may not have fully recognized how far he is committed to the acceptance of some Platonic arguments. (iii) He does not explicitly renounce his earlier sceptical view of the prospects for arguments to show that virtue promotes happiness, and so he may not have seen that he needs to qualify his doubts about the prospects for Plato's arguments. (iv) To the extent that Mill accepts the 'Platonic' line of argument, he separates himself from the utilitarianism of James Mill and Grote. His indecision about how far to separate himself from this position may explain some lack of clarity in his presentation of his own argument and in his recognition of its historical sources.

Perhaps this fourth reason is the most instructive. In this area as in several others, Mill is willing to bend or modify some aspect of a more narrowly utilitarian position in order to acknowledge and incorporate some truth that he thinks he sees in the views of his opponents. To this extent he profits from the elenctic examination of opposed positions. His extensive sympathy for other views raises the distrust of a clearer-headed utilitarian such as Sidgwick; for, in Sidgwick's view, Mill's extensive sympathy leads to serious conflicts with fundamental utilitarian principles.[110] In examining Mill and Grote we can see another example to support Sidgwick's general objection. Mill's recognition of what is wrong with Bentham allows him to accept something in Plato that Grote rejects. Once we explore the further difficulties that result for Mill, we can see why his agreement with Plato is more important than it may initially have seemed. In this case Mill has learned something important from his reflexions on Greek philosophy; it would have been even better if he had learned more.

NOTES

1 *Autobiography, CW* I:23–25.
2 The discussion of Sedgwick is in *CW* X:41–45. The St Andrews rectorial address is in *CW*: XXI. Mill discusses Classics at pp. 225–31; see esp. p. 229f on Plato and Aristotle.
3 *CW* XI:37–238.
4 *CW* XI:239–44.
5 These works of Mill are discussed by F. E. Sparshott in his introduction to *CW* XI. I am indebted to Sparshott for much information and for several suggestive remarks. Since his introduction appears in the standard edition of Mill (and the only current edition of these particular

works), I have thought it worthwhile to indicate disagreements with his judgments on some important issues.

6 *CW* XI:xviii; *Autobiography*, *CW* I:207.

7 Bain 1882, 85f.

8 I have certainly not re-read all these volumes of Grote recently. My memory of Grote's Plato and Aristotle is more vivid than my memory of most of the *History*; but I have tried to check my claims about Mill and Grote by reference to the appropriate passages in Grote.

9 Vlastos 1994, 18, refers to Grote as "that great Victorian student of Greek antiquity, whose multivolume *History of Greece* and three-volume *Plato* are, in my opinion, still, all in all, the finest contributions yet made in their respective themes".

10 Letter to Carlyle, 2 Aug. 1833, *CW* XII:170f. Mill's assessment is discussed by Momigliano 1952, 222. Momigliano's doubts about Mill's seriousness are removed by the later letter.

11 Letter to R. B. Fox, 23 Dec. 1840, *CW* XII:453.

12 *CW* XI:79n.

13 *Autobiography*, *CW* I:15. Mitford's history is discussed by Turner 1981, 192–211. G. Grote 1826 is an entertaining critique of Mitford.

14 A large part of Mill's review of an undistinguished book on the life of Socrates (in 1840) consists of a passage from Niebuhr quoted by Thirlwall in a note to his translation of an essay on Socrates by Schleiermacher. Mill quotes the passage as an advertisement for Thirlwall's history and the point of view it expresses: "We cannot help quoting . . . a noble passage of the great historian Niebuhr, in vindication of the Athenian Demos. For the translation of this passage the English public are also indebted to Bishop Thirlwall, whose *History of Greece* is throughout conceived in a kindred spirit" (*CW* XI:242). Thirlwall had the leisure to begin his eight-volume *History of Greece* because he had been compelled to resign his tutorship at Trinity College, Cambridge (after opposing compulsory attendance at chapel), and had the leisure of a country parson. Grote recognizes Thirlwall as the pioneer in overturning Mitford's view of Greek history; see the Preface to G. Grote 1846–56, I:vi. For Mill's estimate of Thirlwall and Grote see *CW* XI:275. See also Turner 1981, 212.

15 Thucydides II. 65.1–4; VI. 24.

16 In rendering Greek proper names into English, Grote rejects the customary Latinizations, preferring 'Sokrates' to 'Socrates'. Mill sometimes follows Grote and sometimes follows custom. I have followed custom and Latinized, except when I quote from Grote and Mill.

17 He refers to Thucydides as "oligarchically inclined" (*CW* XI:322).

18 A favourable assessment is given by Ste Croix 1972, 4: "Still supreme
in many ways is the great *History of Greece* written over a century ago
by George Grote, whose judgment on many historical and philosophical matters is superior to that of most subsequent writers.... Modern
epigraphic, numismatic and archaeological discoveries have not made
Grote's work nearly as out of date as is generally supposed...." The
favourable judgments of Ste Croix and Momigliano (see note 28) should
warn us against accepting the gross underestimate of Grote's *History*
by Sparshott in *CW* XI:xxx.

The evidence not available to Grote for fifth-century Athenian history is of two types: (1) inscriptions, which are especially important for
the history of the Athenian empire (they are used in the full account of
the empire in Meiggs 1972; (2) the Aristotelian *Constitution of Athens*,
whose political judgments would often be welcome to Grote's
opponents.

19 *CW* XI:331–32.

20 G. Grote 1846–56, VI:150.

21 G. Grote 1846–56, VI:232.

22 Grote discusses Thucydides on Cleon at VI:476–80. He mentions the
story that Cleon was responsible for Thucydides' exile, and remarks
that resentment may have affected Thucydides' attitude. He continues:
"But though this sentiment is probably not without influence in dictat-
ing the unaccountable judgment which I have just been criticizing – as
well as other opinions relative to Kleon, on which I shall say more in
a future chapter – I nonetheless look upon that judgment not as peculiar to Thucydides, but as common to him with Nikias and those
whom we must call, for want of a better name, the oligarchical party of
the time at Athens" (VII:480). Though Grote calls Thucydides' unfavourable judgment on Cleon 'unaccountable', as though it were an
isolated lapse from Thucydides' impartiality, he identifies a similar
partiality in Thucydides' favourable remarks on Nicias; see VII:480.
When we compare the remarks on Cleon with those on Nicias, it is
easy to draw the conclusion that they reflect a rather systematic bias in
Thucydides; but Grote himself never explicitly draws this conclusion.

23 See Thucydides I. 75; II. 8.4; II. 63.2; V. 105.1–2.

24 See G. Grote 1846–56, VI:53. Sparshott (*CW* XI:xxxv) suggests that
Mill's "readiness to condone Athenian imperialism" may strike the
modern reader as strange. He refers to Mill's experience in the
East India Company. But while Mill's own experience is no doubt
relevant, it is strange that Sparshott does not even bother to mention
the argument that Grote and Mill present on the basis of the historical
evidence.

25 Grote (1846–56, VI:43–64) discusses the Athenian empire at length. He compares the Athenians' treatment of the empire favourably with British behaviour in India and Ireland.

26 I have discussed Grote's treatment of the sophists, and some of the reactions to it, in Irwin 1995a.

27 *CW* XI:330.

28 Momigliano 1952, 222, says: "What gives Grote's History its almost unique distinction is this combination of passionate moral and political interests, vast learning, and respect for the evidence".

29 *CW* XI:294.

30 See *Autobiography, CW* I:153–59. The relevance of Mill's interest in Coleridge to his comments on Homer is noticed by Sparshott in *CW* XI:xxxi.

31 *CW* XI:320.

32 *CW* XI:321.

33 *CW* XI:324–25. An interesting modern account of these aspects of Athenian political life is given by Ober 1989, esp. chs. 3–4.

34 *CW* XI:436.

35 *On Liberty, CW* XVIII:268f.

36 *CW* XI:319.

37 *CW* XI:327f.

38 See esp. Plato, *Laws* 888d–889c.

39 *On Liberty, CW* XVIII:241.

40 *On Liberty, CW* XVIII:279.

41 *On Liberty, CW* XVIII:286. Perhaps Mill would be relieved to know that showy and costly styles of living are now widely tolerated in the States of the Union.

42 I.e., to the lower classes. The Greek *dēmos*, used here, corresponds (as does the English 'people') both to *populus* and to *plebs* in Latin.

43 Aristotle, *Politics* 1310a8–10. See Newman 1887 for some partial parallels to the oath quoted by Aristotle. Grote comments on this oath, and the extreme attitude it betrays in some Greek oligarchs (1826, 290f).

44 I am allowing, for present purposes, that Mill is entitled to the distinction he draws in chapter IV between behaviour that directly harms others and behaviour that does not.

45 'Coleridge', *CW* X:133f.

46 'Coleridge', *CW* X:134.

47 On Mill's strained relations with Grote see his letter to Fonblanque, 30 Jan. 1838, *CW* XIII:370; Bain 1882, 56, 83, 104, 160; Clarke 1962, 68.

48 Mill quotes a long passage from Grote on Athenian civic sentiment at *CW* XI:325.

49 G. Grote 1846–56, VII:448–49.

50 Turner 1981, 225.

51 *Autobiography, CW* I:25. The influence of James Mill's view of Plato is discussed by John Glucker, in two informative papers (Glucker 1987 and 1996). I regret that I had not seen these papers before I wrote this essay. I am grateful to Julia Annas for mentioning them.

52 Jonathan Barnes (in Stopper 1981) provides some important modifications and supplements to Turner's picture of Platonic and Aristotelian study in Oxford.

53 See Bentham 1983, 137n. 1.

54 See Ward 1965, 12.

55 See Morley 1908, I:38, 48f, 58, 8of; Bill 1973, 21; Stopper 1981, 279. On the dominance of Aristotle and Butler see Liddon 1893, I:30.

56 Letter to Manning, 1865, quoted by Newsome 1961, 15. See also Morley 1908, I:63, 155; Lathbury 1910, II:163f.

57 Not surprisingly, he refers to Aristotle's logical works quite often in *A System of Logic*.

58 *Autobiography, CW* I:25.

59 *CW* XI:42.

60 *CW* XI:40.

61 He does not mention the Scottish universities or Trinity College, Dublin, but generalizes from the two English universities to 'this kingdom' as a whole. The St Andrews rectorial address displays a less Anglocentric attitude; see *CW* XXI:219–22.

62 Sewell is discussed briefly, and rather slightingly, by Turner 1981, 371, 373. See also Ogilvie 1964, 101. The evidence cited by Turner and Ogilvie refutes Sparshott's judgment that "Mill's strictures on the condition of Platonic studies in England at this time . . . appear to be just" (*CW* XI:xxi). Sparshott misleadingly takes the publication of editions of Plato's dialogues as a sufficient index of the 'condition of Platonic studies'.

63 Sewell 1841, 3.

64 Mill's views on Butler are expressed in his discussion of Sedgwick, *CW* X:64.

65 Sewell 1841, 46.

66 Sewell broke with the Tractarians after Newman's *Tract* 90 (which sought to reconcile the Thirty-nine Articles with Roman doctrine). Perhaps it is relevant to mention that Martin Joseph Routh, whom Mill acknowledges as a contributor to the study of Plato, was also a student of the Fathers. He was sympathetic to the Tractarians and admired by them. I do not know of any specific evidence that Routh influenced Sewell. It would be wrong to suggest that interest in Plato was confined

to Oxford Tractarians; R. D. Hampden (on whom see Turner 1981, 268–74), an opponent of the Tractarians, lectured on Plato in the 1820s and 1830s.

67 *Autobiography, CW* I:159–63.
68 See Ogilvie 1964, 102.
69 R. Price 1948, 55.
70 *CW* X:27.
71 *Autobiography, CW* I:25.
72 *Autobiography, CW* I:49.
73 *Autobiography, CW* I:49.
74 *CW* XI:149.
75 *CW* XI:149.
76 *CW* XI:150.
77 Letter to Bain, 15 Oct. 1859, *CW* XV:639f. See also 14 Nov. 1859, *CW* XV:645.
78 A. E. Taylor 1926, viii.
79 *CW* XI:40–42.
80 My previous illustration only considered Mill's views on moral philosophy. Clearly he does not hold a similarly sceptical view on all the philosophical questions discussed by Plato.
81 See G. Grote 1888, 70–72.
82 The non-specialist reader should beware of supposing that Sparshott's ungenerous estimate of Grote's and Mill's treatment of Plato (*CW* XI:xxxix–xli) reflects the outlook of most contemporary students of Plato. He supposes, very strangely, that "in so far as Anglo-American academic orthodoxy is still wedded to one or another form of the 'experience philosophy', the Platonism of Grote and Mill is substantially that still imported to most anglophone undergraduates" (p. xxxix). I doubt whether this was true in 1978 (when the volume of *CW* was published), and it is certainly false now. It is especially misleading to suggest that one can learn from Grote's and Mill's criticisms of Plato only if one shares their philosophical outlook. For a just estimate of one part of Grote's book see White 1981, 267: "I particularly recommend Grote's treatment, which, for all its faults and harshness, seems to me by far the best and most intelligent treatment of the ideas of the *Republic* which I have encountered".
83 *Autobiography, CW* I:25.
84 *CW* XI:415.
85 See G. Grote 1888, I:454.
86 The index to Grote lists a reference to Cudworth only at III:74n; there is a further reference at III:132n. I cannot find any reference to Price, but I have not searched exhaustively. Grote's treatment of Protagoras is

the one major issue on which Mill explicitly (and correctly) disagrees with him; see *CW* XI:426–28.

87 On Grote's view of Socratic method see Vlastos 1991, 4–6; Vlastos 1994, ch. 1. As Vlastos remarks, "fine Platonist though Grote was, in this he had missed the bus and jumped on another going the opposite way". Vlastos, however, accepts an important element in the picture of the 'two Platos'; see Vlastos 1991, ch. 4 (I have disagreed with this in Irwin 1994, ch. 10).

88 We might wonder how much hindsight informs Mill's account in the *Autobiography* of his early views. But his "Notes on Plato" confirm that he held these general views long before he read Grote.

89 G. Grote 1888, IV:105n. Grote's views on these errors are set out more fully in G. Grote 1876, Essays 3 and 5.

90 *CW* XI:416f.

91 G. Grote 1888, IV:128, citing James Mill again.

92 G. Grote 1888, IV:131f.

93 Mill himself uses this phrase in discussing Socratic cross-examination. See the quotation from *CW* I:25 in section V of this chapter.

94 'Bentham', *CW* X:90. For the views that distress Mill see Bentham 1834, 39f; 1983 ed., 135–37.

95 *CW* XI:415.

96 *CW* XI:415.

97 'Bentham', *CW* X:95.

98 'Bentham', *CW* X:98.

99 *Utilitarianism*, *CW* X:235.

100 *Utilitarianism*, *CW* X:231f.

101 *Utilitarianism*, *CW* X:233.

102 This objection is connected with (though not quite the same as) a question raised by George Grote's brother John Grote (a philosopher of quite a different outlook) in his discussion of Mill's views about the virtuous person's attitude to virtue:

Utilitarianism says that the rightness, goodness, valuableness of actions lies only in their conduciveness to happiness, and yet we are told that it is right and conducive to happiness that men should believe in something (virtue to wit) as having a goodness and value in itself, *independent* of its conduciveness of happiness – is not this equivalent to saying, that however true utilitarianism may be, it is not well that men should believe in it and act upon it? (J. Grote 1870, 126)

103 See *Gorgias* 483a–d, 491e–492c. In *Laws* 663d6–664a8 (cited by G. Grote 1888, IV:107) Plato actually suggests that it would be desirable to propagate belief in the benefits of justice even if the belief were false.

104 *On Liberty*, *CW* XVIII:261.

105 *On Liberty, CW* XVIII:262f.
106 The most persuasive arguments for (i) that I know of are presented by Berger 1984, ch. 2, and Brink 1992. I am not entirely persuaded by them, and I lean to (ii) rather than (i).
107 I have discussed Plato's claims in *Republic* II in Irwin 1994, ch. 12. The view I attribute to Plato is similar to the one attributed to Aristotle by Ackrill 1974. A different view of Plato's position is defended by White 1984. The relation between Mill's views and Plato and Aristotle is discussed in White 1995 and Irwin 1995b.
108 Gibbs 1986 explores the similarities between some of Mill's arguments about pleasure and some Platonic and Aristotelian views. He points out (p. 36) that Mill never mentions these similarities.
109 See *CW* XI:418f.
110 See Sidgwick 1907, 93n. 1, 121, 478, 499 n. 1.

13 The reception and early reputation of Mill's political thought

I. INTRODUCTION

Mill would have found it entirely appropriate that, in a collection on his philosophy, attention should be paid to his political writings and to their reception, which itself had a strong political dimension. Mill saw his political ideas as an integral part of his philosophy, and his philosophical battles as also political battles whose outcome had great practical importance. He stated this explicitly in his *Autobiography* in the survey of his aims in writing his principal philosophical books, *A System of Logic* and *An Examination of Sir William Hamilton's Philosophy*. He thought it crucial to set out in the *Logic* the true philosophy, deriving all knowledge from experience, because it was "hardly possible to exaggerate" the practical mischiefs done in morals, politics, and religion by the false philosophy that "truths external to the mind may be known by intuition or consciousness, independently of observation and experience". The latter was "the great intellectual support of false doctrines and bad institutions" because it allowed "every inveterate belief and every intense feeling, of which the origin is not remembered . . . to dispense with the obligation of justifying itself by reason. . . ." "There never was", Mill concludes, "such an instrument devised for consecrating all deep seated prejudices."[1] Not surprisingly, Mill identified "a natural hostility" between the practical reformer and

a philosophy which discourages the explanation of feelings and moral facts by circumstance and association, and prefers to treat them as ultimate

I am grateful to John Skorupski; and to my colleagues Susan Mendus and Jane Rendall for their comments on a draft of this chapter.

elements of human nature; a philosophy which is addicted to holding up favourite doctrines as intuitive truths, and deems intuition to be the voice of Nature and of God, speaking with an authority higher than that of our reason. In particular, I have long felt that the prevailing tendency to regard all the marked distinctions of human character as innate, and in the main indelible, and to ignore the irresistible proofs that by far the greater part of those differences, whether between individuals, races, or sexes, are such as not only might but naturally would be produced by differences in circumstances, is one of the chief hindrances to the rational treatment of great social questions and one of the greatest stumbling blocks to human improvement.[2]

The Intuitionist philosophy which he controverted in the *Logic*, then, had to be undermined in order to upset unthinking acquiescence in whatever opinions and institutions there happened to be, good or bad indifferently, and halt unthinking acceptance of whatever feelings – especially antipathies – one happened to have, whether reasonable or groundless. Mill's intention was to encourage in his readers instead a critical cast of mind, so that feelings, opinions and institutions were subjected to challenge and inspection, and their "justification by reason" demanded. The aim of *On Liberty*, for instance, was "to make the many more accessible to all truth by making them more open minded".[3] The good person, for Mill, "is one who has thought out and can give a rational defense of his (or her) lifestyle and opinions and actions".[4]

In short, Mill sought to exert moral and political influence through his philosophy. Above all, he condemned the Intuitionist philosophy for its political conservatism, for standing in the way of moral and political progress. He claimed that his own philosophy of experience promoted that progress by requiring that all our knowledge be tested by experience, in morality, politics and religion as everywhere else. Acting on this principle in his own writings in these spheres, Mill consistently challenged prejudiced feelings, received opinions and customary practices, and frequently produced radical conclusions.[5]

Considered from this perspective Mill may be seen as primarily a reformer, who undertook his philosophical work in the course of his programme for effecting the improvement of mankind. It is an irony that so many of his contemporaries found him much more persuasive as a philosopher than as a reformer. Mill's reputation rose and fell even in his lifetime. He made his name as a philosopher with the *Logic* (1843), which was immediately recognised as a major contribution. The *Principles of Political Economy* (1948) was equally influential in its field. Both these works had an extensive popular audience, as well as being closely studied at the universities. At Oxford "Mill was a classic, both as a logician and as a political economist, throughout the University, and men reading for Greats were constrained to study him"; while at Cambridge, even though fewer students had to tackle the *Logic* and *Political Economy* for examination purposes, they were as diligently perused.[6] Mill's reputation was at its height in the 1850s and 1860s, particularly at the universities, where his views were adopted by many of the next generation of political leaders and formers of opinion.[7] The impact of his political writings was more patchy; sometimes well received by political radicals, they were highly unpopular in many quarters. Further, some of Mill's specific views were rejected even by many sympathetic readers as "crochets", for example his opposition to the secret ballot and his advocacy of plural voting. When he died and his career was reviewed by his contemporaries, although there was praise for the sincerity, enthusiasm and lucidity of his political writings, especially *On Liberty*, most commentators rested his claim to continuing intellectual fame on the *Logic* and *Political Economy*. Sidgwick rated him "the best philosophical writer – if not the greatest philosopher – whom England has produced since Hume".[8] On the other hand, his public interventions in politics, in his writings and in his parliamentary career, were often seen as lapses revealing unsound ("feminine") judgment and an excess of emotion. As one obituarist put it: "That a man of such wide cultivation and such extraordinary intellectual power should, so to speak, swallow the radical creed whole, was somehow not quite satisfactory. . . . Mr. Mill was regarded as having rather lowered himself by his political action and as having descended too easily from the judgment-seat into the open arena".[9] This emphasis continued for several decades. Even those who reported that they had been deeply influenced by the philosophical position of the *Logic* had reservations of varying degree and number about the political writings and were opposed to certain doctrines in them.[10]

This contrast between Mill's reputation as a philosopher and as a political reformer may at first sight be puzzling, given that he himself considered the two sides of his thought so closely linked. The puzzle is solved partly, of course, by taking account of the varying assumptions and goals of his readers. Those of different political persuasions or religious affiliations, for instance, naturally dismissed some of the conclusions Mill drew. But the source of the puzzle lies partly in Mill himself: not only in the range and richness of his position, but also in the very nature of his philosophy.

In this chapter I concentrate on two of Mill's political tracts, *On Liberty* and *The Subjection of Women*, and survey a sample of the opinion expressed in Britain up to 1900.[11] Thus I deal with only a selection of his controversial political views and reactions to them. Further, I have left aside the complex and unsettled questions of how far in *On Liberty* Mill was stating his own views and how far Harriet Taylor's and how far in *The Subjection of Women* he was influenced by Harriet Taylor and Helen Taylor.[12] These questions cannot be separated totally from the study of the impact of "Mill's" writings, because after his public statements in *On Liberty*, *The Subjection of Women*, and his *Autobiography* of his indebtedness to his wife, they were in the minds of his audience, and sometimes alluded to by commentators. However, widening the survey of Mill's political writings, or taking a particular position on the issues of authorship, would not require significant revision of the conclusions I have reached.

I begin with the reviews of *On Liberty* and *The Subjection of Women*, taking each book in turn and examining the main critical comments made. Then I turn to the reconsideration in 1873, continuing into the following year, occasioned by the appearance of the full and robust critique of Mill's political ideas in James Fitzjames Stephen's *Liberty, Equality, Fraternity* (in March), Mill's death (May), and the publication of his *Autobiography* (November). Finally I discuss the view which developed over the remainder of the century.

II. THE IMMEDIATE RECEPTION OF *ON LIBERTY* AND *THE SUBJECTION OF WOMEN*

On its publication, *On Liberty* was extensively reviewed and discussed. However, as John Rees pointed out in his study of its early critics, it did not instantly achieve the classic status usually attributed to it in the twentieth century but was "more critically received in the journals of the time than we usually tend to allow".[13] Rees found that the criticism was largely hostile: "apart from a few introductory words of praise (and not always these), the reviews follow a similar pattern. They usually make serious reservations about the leading principles or question Mill's application of them".[14]

Many of the points and queries which are familiar from the current literature on *On Liberty* occur in the reviews. For instance, the "one very simple principle" itself, and its main terms, were said to be vague and ambiguous; the distinction between self-regarding and other-regarding action was condemned as inoperable and mistaken; the emphasis placed on the individual was judged excessive, at the expense of society and its proper need to protect itself; liberty was wrongly taken as something negative, whereas it was positive too; and the applications of the principle in the final chapter were highly problematic.[15] Other criticisms related to concerns important at the time. The temperance press attacked Mill – as he had expected – for his strong opposition to their proposals for legal prohibition of the sale of alcohol.[16] There was also very considerable objection to what many held was Mill's unjustifiably low view of Christian morality.[17]

But the commonest, and frequent, criticism was that Mill had exaggerated or misdiagnosed the extent to which conformism was actually stifling, or even threatening, liberty and the development of individuality. Mill seemed to James Fitzjames Stephen "to be distinctly wrong in asserting that, as a matter of fact, originality of character is ceasing to exist".[18] Even Buckle, in by far the most positive, indeed adulatory, reception to *On Liberty*, differed here, holding that "on the whole, individuality is not diminishing, and that so far as we can estimate the future, it is not likely to diminish".[19] Hutton made the point the opening move in his discussion. Agreeing with Mill over some of the facts of recent social change in England, he rejected Mill's conclusion from them, that they indicate increasing despotism of social and political masses over the moral and intellectual freedom of individuals, as "singularly hasty, and utterly unsustained by the premises he lays down". The admitted "process of social assimilations . . . has not contracted, but rather enlarged, the sphere of individual freedom".[20] The tone of the contemporary response is well caught in the entry Macaulay made in his private journal after a brief reading of the book in the Athenaeum: "He is really crying 'Fire!' in Noah's flood".[21] It is worth spending some time on this criticism.

In the light of the critical discussion which *On Liberty* has generated over the past century and a half, it is no surprise that Mill's contemporaries too should have noted the difficulties in defining and applying his principle of liberty. But it surely is a surprise that so many of them resisted outright his interpretation of the conditions for and extent of freedom in English society. How could Mill have been so wrong, one might wonder; or, less contentiously, why did his assessment of the situation differ so much from most people's? His failure to persuade his contemporaries in this area, moreover, is crucially important, because the urgency of his case for his principle of liberty depends upon his diagnosis of the great need for it.[22] I have two observations to make. Mill gave his own explanation in the *Autobiography*. The truth taught in *On Liberty* was "the importance, to man and society, of a large variety in types of character, and of giving full freedom to human nature to expand itself in innumerable and conflicting directions". In 1859, "to superficial observation, [this truth] did not seem to stand much in need of such a lesson", and it was true that social change "has thus far been decidedly favourable to the development of new opinions, and has procured for them a much more unprejudiced hearing". However, he immediately qualified this, arguing that the new openness was "a feature belonging to periods of transition, when old notions and feelings have been unsettled and no new doctrines have yet succeeded to their ascendancy", and people who have given up old beliefs "listen eagerly to new opinions". But a period of transition is "necessarily transitory", and will be followed by the predominance of a new creed, and its domination of society – unless "mankind have by that time become aware that it cannot be exercised without stunting and dwarfing human nature".[23] *On Liberty*, we should remember, seems to have arisen originally from the plan formed by Mill and his wife for his completing a volume of essays containing "the best of what we have to say" before they died (both were seriously ill), "if not in the best form for popular effect, yet in the state of concentrated thought – a sort of mental pemican, which thinkers, when there are any after us, may nourish themselves with

& then dilute for other people".[24] In other words, Mill always intended to address an audience in the future when the period of
transition was over, and "the teachings of the *Liberty* will have their
greatest value".[25] To that extent, the verdict of his contemporaries
was irrelevant: it was superficial, short-sightedly ignoring the
deeper social tendencies hostile to human freedom. Mill was content to be judged by the future.

My second observation is that to some extent the critics were
mistaken, or deceiving themselves, in their dissent from Mill's
analysis of the substance and force of the threats to freedom and the
development of individuality. They had not fully appreciated the
implications of his arguments. This is perhaps because Mill had
moved so cautiously, temperately and decorously in *On Liberty*,
starting off from agreed ideas about religious freedom, sticking to
familiar examples, and often making his points in very general
terms. It was fairly easy for readers to assume that Mill was not
demanding anything which they could not accept: that there already
was in plenty the kind of individuality he proposed, because they
had in mind instances of "individuality" which posed no real problems, and of which they could approve – harmless eccentricity, or
unusual ideas or behaviour but in directions either with which they
could sympathise or to which they were indifferent. Mill did not
parade before them the kind of instance which would have antago-
nised them and revealed to them more clearly how revolutionary
and radical his principle of liberty was. His position in *On Liberty*
followed from that in the *Logic*: all individuals must be free, and
should be encouraged, to consider new opinions and to consult
experience in their own lives, to conduct experiments (note the
word) in living – however unpopular, however much disliked by
other people. We cannot know a priori, and custom cannot tell us,
what is good for us: the only way we can find out is by trying and
seeing; hence the importance of freedom, and the emphasis on
individuality. In urging against Mill the great extent to which
English society was free in this way, his critics tended to forget that
most people, themselves included, have closed minds on many
matters. They exemplified the limits of their imagination when
they failed to reflect that their conception of individuality might be
narrower than Mill's. An outstanding case of this was that what
Mill said about "individuals" and their freedom was intended to

apply to women as well as men, and that the whole position of women in society was meant to be regarded as an open question. Once Mill did make this clear in detail and at length, when *The Subjection of Women* was published a decade later, he met much stiffer resistance. That book, in Morley's words, memorably applied the abstract plea for liberty, and all the arguments supporting it, "to that half of the human race whose individuality has hitherto been blindly and most wastefully repressed".[26] Women too, equally with men, should be free, free to read and discuss and form their own opinions, free to marry or not and equal in marriage, free to work, and allowed equally with men to find out what they could or could not do. That was not the position of women in England in 1869, and the mere suggestion that it should become their position was extreme, and very upsetting and unpopular: no one could meet Mill with a parallel reply to that so often made to *On Liberty*, that in fact women already had all the opportunities he demanded for them. Thus, once Mill put forward a threatening proposal, one requiring people to question seriously the conventions about women, and consequently about marriage and the family, it became clear that the boundaries of freedom were not set as widely as the critics of *On Liberty* had claimed. There might be little or no legal restriction on free expression of opinion, yet there were topics whose serious discussion was effectively precluded by custom and prejudice. *The Subjection of Women* brought to the surface the latent opposition to the doctrines of *On Liberty*.[27]

The Subjection of Women was not, of course, Mill's first announcement of his views about women's position in society. For example, in his pamphlet *Thoughts on Parliamentary Reform* (1859) he proposed to give the vote to educated householders "without distinction of sex – for why should the vote-collector make a distinction where the tax-gatherer makes none?"[28] To this G. C. Brodrick responded in the *Times* that such a "doctrinaire" proposal exemplified "a kind of pedantry which . . . occasionally disfigures Mr. Mill's writings". Such a measure was totally impracticable because it would be unacceptable to most people, and would have to be preceded by their education and conversion: "To base the franchise upon principles half recognised by a few philosophers, but utterly strange to the mass even of educated men, seems to us a complete inversion of the natural order".[29] Mill's reasoning, on the other hand, was presumably that to convert society – so that "the crochet of to-day, the crochet of one generation, becomes the truth of the next and the truism of the one after" – required taking the rights of women seriously, and raising for public debate such matters as truly universal suffrage.[30] In the Westminster campaign, while he did not make a major issue of it, he did explicitly draw attention to his views on extending the franchise to women equally with men.[31] Walter Bagehot commented that "no party, and scarcely any individual politician except himself, holds this theory, and it will be long before it becomes a practical question". By then, Bagehot predicted, stating a standard objection, Mill would have changed his mind once he realised that very few women "would have any political opinions at all, or any *political* preferences for one candidate over another; and that in consequence to give them votes would merely be giving extra votes vicariously to their fathers, their husbands, their masters, their lovers, or their priests".[32] Once in Parliament, Mill presented the first petition to the House of Commons praying that enfranchisement should be without distinction of sex, and spoke to the subject shortly after; he moved an amendment to the Reform Bill to substitute 'person' for 'man', which would have admitted a small but significant number of women to the franchise; he supported reform of the law concerning the property of married women; and he appeared in public to plead the cause of women's suffrage.[33] His activities were not ignored. The *Saturday Review* regarded the idea of women having votes as a philosopher's dream, and the incredulity and laughter which greeted it as decisive: "If an arrangement strikes ninety-nine out of a hundred persons as supremely ludicrous, there is probably some real incongruity in the plan itself". The social position of women should be improved, for instance there should be better education in the higher classes. But there should continue to be a division of labour, with politics – "hardly the highest employment of the human intellect" – left for men.[34] Nonetheless, Mill's advocacy of women's suffrage did make a difference, the *Saturday Review* admitting that "when Mr. Mill makes a legislative proposal, something may probably be said in its defence".[35] It noted that Mill's amendment to the Reform Bill was voted for by a "respectable minority", but iterated that, besides the practical difficulties, the main objection was "the unfitness and impropriety of allowing women an active share in public affairs".

Nature had established irrevocable differences between men and women; custom was based on those; and "as a general rule, it is for men to govern, and the best and wisest women are not the least willing to obey".[36] There was indeed one woman (Margaret Oliphant), claiming to speak on behalf of the mass of women and especially the female leaseholders who would have been enfranchised by Mill's amendment, who had asserted that they did not want the vote, but wished to leave politics to men.[37]

So Mill must have been aware of the strength of the continuing grip of custom on the minds of his contemporaries when in 1869 he decided on a further move in his campaign for women's rights, and published *The Subjection of Women*. This examination of women's "domestic subordination and social disabilities" had been written in 1860–61 but held back until it could carry most political weight, and in particular "stir up the zeal of women themselves".[38] He had been preparing the ground; nonetheless he thought it was "sure to be very bitterly attacked", and he was right.[39] The book did of course receive an enthusiastic welcome from the supporters of women's rights, but the reviews in the major periodicals were predominantly hostile and criticised Mill both on the fundamentals and on the details of his argument. Their tone was usually respectful, with resort to ridicule rare. It was felt that Mill was too rhetorical and too much of an advocate, and not as balanced and fair as he usually was. He was accused of grossly exaggerating the disadvantages of the actual position of women and ignoring the happiness of the lives of the great majority of them. It was universally conceded, however, that the legal position of women was unsatisfactory, in particular as regards married women's property. It was also widely conceded that women should have better opportunities for education, and for entry to the professions. But it was argued that these and other reforms could be made, so that women were treated justly, without instituting the wholesale equality Mill recommended and in particular without interfering with the husband's position. It was noted that Mill's proposal for equality in marriage appeared to imply a freedom of divorce which risked destroying marriage and the family, and which would leave women less secure than they were currently.

Some women strongly opposed the changes Mill was suggesting. Anne Mozley, writing anonymously but hinting strongly that she was a woman, felt insulted by Mill's arrogance and intolerance. He thought he knew better than Englishwomen themselves what they could and should do; he found them conservative, hindering his subversion of society as it now stood, and wanted to eradicate "the feminine element" out of them. "Woman, as she is, is his enemy".[40] Mozley vigorously reasserted that the ideal woman was man's help-mate, that most women saw marriage as their liberty (and were happily and beneficially married), that women were different from men (and needed a different education), and that women were by nature physically weaker than men and could not be equal. She added:

Equality that rests on sufferance ceases to be equality.... The notion is a mere inflation that ends in bluster. Mr Mill's whole line is really that women are not equal to men, but we are to act as if they were. He calls upon the law to defend the weak, which, in truth, is the law's one business; but the fact that they are dependent on law is subversive of the theory of equality.

Women should, as they largely did, have their just claims protected by law: but they had no just claim to full equality, and men justly had certain "privileges founded on their different and stronger organisation".[41] Margaret Oliphant, also writing anonymously but obviously a woman, stressed that in marriage the man and woman were not two parties to a contract but, as the law – for all its present faults, which she readily admitted – grasped, "*are* one person". The woman was weaker than the man, but she was not thereby, as Mill's approach implied, inferior. Rather, "a woman is a woman, and not a lesser edition of man". Woman was not rival to man, "they are two halves of a complete being" and their differences made them a harmonious one. The traditional offices and work of men and women, above all the man's to win their bread and the woman's to minister to him at home and to bear children, were natural and God-given and would not change, resting as they did on "an instinctive law which antedates all legislation, and lies at the very root and beginning of all human affairs."[42] Consequently the idea of a mar-ried woman possessing independent political power ran "counter to the whole theory of married life", and it would be an unnecessary and unjust complication to give two voices to a composite being which was "to all intents and purposes one".[43] Oliphant seems to

perceive in Mill an insulting condescension towards women as they
are, and an undervaluing of their achievements as wives and mothers. If compared directly with men, as she takes Mill to be doing in
his search for equality, women's lives appear deficient and imperfect; but in fact women are different from men and have their own
distinct capacities and occupations (which are at least as important
as men's), and they are already successful and fulfilled as women,
and content.[44]

Mozley and Oliphant presented a clear, full, and argued defence
of much of the status quo. Their main appeal was to the contrast between how appalling Mill theorised the present position of
women must be, and how satisfactory for most women they observed it actually was. Such a reaction, of course, was no more than
Mill had expected. He was deliberately challenging existing attitudes to the relations between men and women. Accordingly, that
much of what he proposed should be rejected out of hand, and the
natural and divine basis of the customary should be reasserted, as it
was by so many reviewers, was simply further evidence of the grip
of custom and feeling on both men and women, on both subjectors
and subjected alike. The immediate reception of *The Subjection of
Women* established that, this time, Mill's diagnosis of the prevalent
mood was correct. The extent of the attack his polemic provoked
was for him an index of its usefulness.[45]

III. THE RECONSIDERATION IN 1873

As already mentioned, there was a major reconsideration of Mill in
1873. So far as *On Liberty* and *The Subjection of Women* are concerned, the catalyst was Stephen's *Liberty, Equality, Fraternity*.[46]
This was very influential, both bringing together and elaborating
many of the earlier criticisms, and stating them colourfully and
energetically (indeed too vigorously for some who, like Henry
Sidgwick, found its style too often "offensively loud and overbear-
ing").[47] Stephen focussed his opposition on a key feature of Mill's
position, and it is that upon which I shall concentrate.

Stephen belonged to the generation which had been greatly influenced by Mill. But he had some doubts and they grew. As he began
to compose the book, he remarked that it was "curious that after
being, so to speak, a devoted disciple and partisan of his up to a

certain point, I should have found it at last impossible to go on with him, but his politics and his morals are not mine at all, though I believe in and admire his logic and his general notions of philosophy."[48] Stephen was quickly able to satisfy himself that it was not really curious at all, but explicable very simply. He, like Mill, believed that a man's philosophy and his political and moral views should be all of a piece; Mill had produced, in his *Logic*, the correct philosophical basis for political and moral opinions; Stephen had, on the basis of his experience of life (and especially of his experience, just finished, of British rule in India), followed that philosophy in formulating the correct political and moral opinions; and since Mill had reached different and therefore incorrect conclusions in politics and morals, it must be because Mill had fallen away from his own philosophy. Early in *Liberty, Equality, Fraternity*, Stephen explained that Mill, "a great man to whom I am in every way deeply indebted", was the only modern author on the subject "with whom I agree sufficiently to differ from him profitably". He immediately added that "up to a certain point I should be proud to describe myself as his disciple, but there is a side of his teaching which is as repugnant as the rest of it is attractive to me, and this side has of late years become by far the most prominent". He set out to explain how he could agree with the principles of the *Logic* and *Political Economy* and simultaneously "dissent in the strongest way from the view of human nature and human affairs" in *On Liberty, Utilitarianism* and *The Subjection of Women*.[49] The key is the philosophy of experience. Stephen was greatly attracted by the appeal to experience on all questions, the reverence for facts and dismissal of sentimentalism, which he found in Bentham's utilitarianism and in Mill's *Logic*.[50] What this implied for political questions, such as the nature and proper extent of liberty, was clear. Liberty, for example, was an element of social life which had its "advantages and disadvantages according to time, place, and circumstance".

There are some acts, opinions, thoughts, and feelings which for various reasons people call good, and others which for other reasons they call bad. They usually wish to promote and encourage the one and to prevent the other. In order to do this they must use promises and threats. I say that the expediency of doing this in any particular case must depend on the circumstances of the case, upon the nature of the act prevented, and the nature of the means by which it can be prevented; and that the attempt to lay down general principles like Mr. Mill's fails. . . .[51]

Stephen, then, accused Mill of dealing with liberty in terms of a principle absolutely barring society from interfering in certain areas of individual life, which was a priori or intuitive. That was a fundamental and damaging philosophical error. Stephen also charged that Mill's distinction between self-regarding and other-regarding action, crucial to his being able to mark off the individual's protected sphere, was fallacious, unfounded and vicious. Furthermore, he claimed that Mill placed the boundary in the wrong place anyway because he always exaggerated the advantages of liberty and underestimated the importance of its disadvantages; Stephen traced the cause of this miscalculation to Mill's having formed too favourable an estimate of human nature. This is the core of Stephen's case. He works it out in detail, contending for example that under certain circumstances society may use coercion for other purposes than self-protection (principally to establish and maintain religion or morality); that freedom of thought and discussion is usually good but not necessarily so; and that the wise minority may be justified in coercing the foolish majority for its own good, and is cowardly if it does not. Thus according to Stephen, when we apply the Benthamite philosophy of experience, and when we confront the realities of our own experience and of history without allowing sentiment to distort the view, we are forced to conclusions very different from those Mill himself reached in his later writings. Stephen felt he had fallen foul of "John Mill in his modern and more humane mood – or, rather, I should say, in his sentimental mood – which makes me feel that he is a deserter from the proper principles of rigidity and ferocity in which he was brought up".[52]

Whether there is a break, or at least a tension, between the Benthamism of Mill's youth and ideas he assimilated and developed later is of course one of the persistent and unresolved debates about his thought. Contemporary critics too were divided over the question, some accepting Stephen's argument and some resisting it. For instance, Sidgwick judged that Stephen had selected the right ground for attacking *Liberty*, because "it is undeniable that in this and some other parts of his works Mill seems to forget the essential limits of the empirical utilitarian method which he avowedly employs". That method yields no absolute practical axioms, "only general rules of a relative and limited validity", so that "in criticising the apparent absoluteness with which Mill's principles are enounced [Stephen's] position is very strong."[53] Sidgwick added, however, that while Mill's arguments were formally inadequate to prove his conclusions, Stephen ignored their substantial force. "*E.g.* if Mill had contented himself with pointing out that by persecuting legally or socially opinions opposed to our own, we deprive ourselves of a most important and valuable guarantee for the truth of our own convictions, viz. that given by the free consensus of experts, I conceive that his position would have been unassailable."[54] This seems to concede to Stephen that Mill did not make out as good a utilitarian case for liberty as he should have done. John Morley, on the other hand, one of Mill's closest disciples at this time, responded to Stephen with an unqualified defence of Mill. Mill's doctrine of liberty "reposes on no principle of abstract right, but like all the rest of its author's opinions, on principles of utility and experience."[55] Stephen failed to see that "the very aim and object of Mr. Mill's essay is to show on utilitarian principles that compulsion in a definite class of cases, the self-regarding parts of conduct namely, and in societies of a certain degree of development, is always bad".[56] Mill argued, on sound utilitarian and empirical grounds, that in those cases the good obtained by employing compulsion could never in fact overbalance the general inconvenience and expense of the compulsion. Stephen never confronted, let alone confuted this. He did not disprove Mill's arguments that leaving men free in the self-regarding sphere had beneficial social consequences, and was valuable to the individual.[57] Nor did Stephen demonstrate that there were no self-regarding acts. "As a matter of observation", Morley wrote, "and for the practical purposes of morality, there are kinds of action whose consequences do not go beyond the doer of them."[58] Mill's division between self-regarding acts and others was not arbitrary, but rested on "observation of their actual consequences". Mill treated self-regarding acts as an important class, "so important as to be carefully and diligently secured by a special principle of liberty", because "observation of the recorded experience of mankind teaches us that the recognition of this independent provision is essential to the richest expansion of human faculty".[59] Morley held, then, that Mill's defence of liberty was entirely drawn from experience, and did not depart from his philosophy in the *Logic*; moreover, Morley considered that Mill generally drew the actual limits of society's interference with the individual in the correct places.[60]

The same issues lie behind Stephen's examination of *The Subjection of Women* in chapter V of *Liberty, Equality, Fraternity*. His own position was that equality was like liberty: it was not an absolute good but sometimes good and sometimes not. Equality was good only when and in so far as it was expedient. He remarked that Mill ought to have acknowledged this, but instead, on Stephen's reading, Mill asserted in *Utilitarianism* "the notion that a presumption is in all cases to be made in favour of equality quite irrespectively of any definite experience of its utility", and in *The Subjection of Women* embraced a "pet opinion" that the social relations between the two sexes should be regulated by a principle of perfect equality.[61] We had to ask, Stephen urged, whether in fact equality in this instance was expedient. He judged that it was not. To apply Mill's doctrine in practice would have been injurious, because it could not be proved that it was expedient that all people should live in society as equals. For there were many inequalities between human beings of sufficient importance to influence the rights and duties which it was expedient to confer upon them. Some of these differences "are so marked and so important that unless human nature is radically changed, we cannot even imagine their removal; and of these the differences of age and sex are the most important".[62] The difference of age was so distinct that even Mill recognised it: and the inequality of sex was as real.

There are some propositions which it is difficult to prove, because they are so plain, and this is one of them. The physical differences between the sexes affect every part of the human body, from the hair of the head to the soles of the feet, from the size and density of the bones to the texture of the brain and the character of the nervous system. . . . men are stronger than women in every shape. They have greater muscular and nervous force, greater intellectual force, greater vigour of character. This general truth, which has been observed under all sorts of circumstances and in every age and country, has also in every age and country led to a division of labour between men and women, the general outline of which is as familiar and as universal as the general outline of the differences between them. There are the facts, and the question is whether the law and public opinion ought to recognise this difference?[63]

Stephen proceeded to illustrate his case that, men and women not being equals, the law and public opinion ought not to treat them as equals. His examples are fascinating, read in the light of later social developments, and emphasise how treacherous are the apparently solid "facts" of human culture and behaviour. First, men and women ought not to be subject to compulsory military service indiscriminately:

> If any one says that they ought, I have no more to say, except that he has got into the region at which argument is useless. But if it is admitted that this ought not to be done, an inequality of treatment founded on a radical inequality between the two sexes is admitted, and if this inequality is once made, where are you to draw the line?[64]

Second, turning to what should be the other great branch of State activity, education:

> Are boys and girls to be educated indiscriminately, and to be instructed in the same things? Are boys to learn to sew, to keep house, and to cook, and girls to play at cricket, to row, and be drilled like boys? I cannot argue with a person who says Yes. A person who says No admits an inequality between the sexes on which education must be founded, and which it must therefore perpetuate and perhaps increase.[65]

Having established to his satisfaction that there is a real inequality of sex, Stephen traced the consequences to "the vital point of the whole question – marriage". The marriage law would have been extremely unjust to women if it had treated them as equal with men, for then the marriage contract, like other partnerships, might have been dissolved at pleasure and this would have made women the slaves of their husbands. The divorced wife was far more likely than the husband to be unattractive to another partner, to be burdened with children, and to be unable to earn a living. The wife was weaker and in the weaker position, and needed to be protected by the law, not treated equally.[66] The corollary was that the government of the family had to be put in the hands of the husband. When husband and wife reached opposite conclusions on questions of common interest, "the wife ought to give way". He was the captain and she his first lieutenant, bound to obey his orders.[67] (Stephen accepted that the "captain's" powers are limited by the law, and that the English law of marriage needed some reform concerning property and violence against women.)[68]

The upshot of Stephen's discussion is that Mill's "pet opinion" is inexpedient because its implementation would subvert indissoluble monogamous marriage and the subordination of the wife to the husband, at the expense of the wife. There were critics happy to support Stephen against Mill in full.[69] Others, however, challenged Stephen's conclusions and his methods of reaching them. Millicent Fawcett, Henry Fawcett's wife and a leading active suffragist, wrote that Stephen's theory was the theory of the common law, with all its failings. The simile of the captain and the management of a vessel she found misleading; the government of a family had a greater resemblance to parliamentary government, where no one person or chamber had absolute authority and the consent of all estates was required. As for the protection which Stephen claimed women obtained in exchange for their subordination to their husbands, she thought women received little and were grossly overcharged for it.[70] Lydia Becker, prominent in the Manchester and national women's suffrage movements, provided a spirited, robust reply to Stephen which is tightly argued point by point. Stephen fallaciously assumed that "the law ought to treat as equals those only who are equals in moral, physical, and intellectual vigour". But that was not how the law treated men; and "if the personal rights of all men are equal in all things that concern their individuality as men, notwithstanding all differences of personal strength and power, logic seems to demand that the personal rights of women and men shall be equal in all that concerns their individuality as human beings, notwithstanding any difference which may exist between them in physical strength".[71] Stephen argued from inequality in age to inequality in sex, but the cases were so different that no conclusions about the expediency of the second could be drawn from that of the first.[72] Stephen proposed that society ought to recognise inequality of sex as the foundation of inequality of rights, giving conscription as an illustration. Should men and women be subjected to it indiscriminately, he asked? But men were not subjected indiscriminately: "the maimed, the blind, the halt, and the aged would be exempt, at least, until all the able-bodied had been called out". Women would have been called on to serve in other ways. Anyway, "it would be as reasonable to say that because men do not hazard their lives in the duties of maternity they ought to be deprived of political rights, as to say that because women are not called upon to run the risk of being shot in the service of the country they are therefore not to be counted as citizens"; leaving aside the fact that "the per centage of women who lose their lives in the dangers incident to them in the profession of marriage exceeds the per centage of soldiers killed in battle".[73] Stephen said that marriage was the vital point of the whole question. It was not. Women were women before they were wives, and it was the rights of women that were vital. "We say that the personal and political rights of unmarried women ought to be equal and similar to those of unmarried men, and that the conditions of the marriage contract ought to be determined by the free consent of both the sexes who are parties to it, and not arbitrarily imposed by one sex on the other by physical force." This would not have entailed that the marriage contract could have been dissolved at pleasure: that would have depended upon the law of the land.[74]

The striking feature of Stephen's attack on *The Subjection of Women* is his failure to follow fully the pattern he himself set in his criticism of Mill's principle of liberty. As before, Stephen insisted that the question must be settled on the basis of experience; but in this instance, the experience appealed to is extremely limited. As the hostile reviewers showed, Stephen was prone to look no further than existing institutions, behaviour, and attitudes, to which he envisaged relatively minor adjustments. He revealed no appreciation whatsoever of the force of Mill's claim at the opening of *The Subjection of Women* that in fact we did not know what women were capable of because they had never tried out their capacities in more than a few directions; nor that, this being so, answers to questions about the position of women are necessarily more open and subject to future developments than those about liberty, where our experience is much more extensive. Indeed Stephen never really admitted how far Mill's argument was empirical and how far its conclusions were provisional. In fact, as Morley argued, *The Subjection of Women* was "the capital illustration" of the application of the modes of reasoning about human character in Mill's *Logic*.[75] Mill refused to accept as natural and unchangeable what could be shown to be the product of circumstance and alterable.

Rather than examining, empirically, possible alternatives, Stephen seems to be attempting to sustain the status quo. He fails to acknowledge how narrow our experience is and that there could be change and new experience to learn from, and he seems all too often to confuse the customary for the natural – the very mistake Mill was warning against. Altogether it looks as if Stephen is promoting a "pet theory" of his own, instead of pursuing the argument in the manner that the philosophy of experience requires. He has not emptied his mind of prejudice, and he never recognises that the answers to these questions about women must be open-ended. In none of this, of course, was he at all unusual. A few others, however, who did treat the issues empirically, claimed that one was led to the same conclusions as Mill; that there is, for instance, a good case resting on experience for giving the suffrage to women.[76]

IV. THE REST OF THE NINETEENTH CENTURY[77]

There is very little to report about *The Subjection of Women* in this period. It was highly regarded in the women's suffrage movement as a compendium of key arguments, and was kept in print in both Britain and America. Mill had helped to make women's issues prominent, and much was achieved, particularly over married women's property rights (1870, 1882) and in steadily opening higher education and the professions to women. Women ratepayers gained the vote in municipal elections (1869), and could vote and stand for the new school boards (1870). But repeated attempts to have the parliamentary suffrage extended to women, Mill's prime objective, failed: possibly, as Packe claims, Mill's campaign was near success and would have succeeded had he "lived a few years longer".[78] Support on this issue declined, especially after the failure to make any impact in 1884 when the male franchise was greatly extended, and did not revive until the activities of the militant suffragettes early in the next century.[79] Two of Mill's keenest and most steadfast co-workers for women's suffrage died, Cairnes in 1875 and Henry Fawcett in 1884. Among the generation of intellectuals which had been so influenced by Mill in their youth, and who agreed with him on so many matters, most declined to follow him over women's suffrage. Some rejected his position outright; some supported it in principle, but thought that other reforms, such as opening up higher education to women, should come first – reversing Mill's own order of priorities.[80] Even Morley decided in 1885 he would not continue to vote in the House of Commons for female suffrage.[81] In the academic literature, there is little discussion of women's issues and little mention of *The Subjection of Women*. Perhaps this is because the reforms which had been achieved made these matters less urgent; or perhaps this is another measure of how far the hold of customary assumptions continued over the public and many intellectuals alike.

Though *The Subjection of Women* was relatively neglected in this period, *On Liberty* continued to be much debated. Two related trends are discernible: Mill's idea of liberty is increasingly seen as too negative and, at the same time, the case for greater state action is argued. Both appear in T. H. Green and others in the British Idealist tradition he helped to create.

Green was of that generation of university men so strongly influenced by Mill. Green, however, whilst he was a radical Liberal and shared many of Mill's views in practical politics, in philosophy adopted much from Kant and Hegel, and distanced himself from some of Mill's doctrines in ethics and in logic.[82] As regards liberty he treated Mill's position in *On Liberty* as needing revision. Mill had written, for example: "The only freedom which deserves the name, is that of pursuing our own good in our own way, so long as we do not attempt to deprive others of theirs, or impede their efforts to obtain it".[83] This was inadequate from Green's point of view, first because it stressed the individual's autonomy of choice but said nothing about the moral worth of what he or she might choose to do, and second because it emphasised the individual's freedom to be left alone at the cost of the duty to help others achieve their freedom. One was barred from harming others, but not instructed to help them. Green, on the other hand, argued that real freedom consisted in pursuing the right objects, and that one had a duty to take positive steps, including government action, to liberate other people's powers by giving them the opportunity for real freedom too. Freedom had to be understood not in individual terms, but as what the members of a society could achieve cooperatively.

In a famous popular lecture in 1881, Green noted that recent and proposed Liberal social legislation covering working conditions, sanitation and education limited the supposed inherent right of every man to do what he liked with what he considered his own.

Such legislation restricted the kind of individual freedom from government interference which Liberals, including Mill, had long fought to protect and extend. Yet in Green's view, such interference could be justified in the name of freedom itself:

... freedom, rightly understood, is the greatest of blessings; ... its attainment is the true end of all our effort as citizens. But ... we should consider carefully what we mean by it. We do not mean merely freedom from restraint and compulsion. We do not mean merely freedom to do as we like irrespectively of what it is that we like. We do not mean a freedom that can be enjoyed by one man or one set of men at the cost of a loss of freedom to others. ... we mean a positive power or capacity of doing or enjoying something worth doing or enjoying, and that, too, something which we do or enjoy in common with others. We mean by it a power which each man exercises through the help or security given him by his fellow-men, and which he in turn helps to secure for them. When we measure the progress of a society by its growth in freedom, we measure it by the increasing development and exercise *on the whole* of those powers of contributing to social good with which we believe the members of the society to be endowed; in short, by the greater power on the part of the citizens as a body to make the most and best of themselves. Thus, though of course there can be no freedom among men who act not willingly but under compulsion, yet on the other hand the mere removal of compulsion, the mere enabling a man to do as he likes, is in itself no contribution to true freedom.[84]

Green's "true freedom", "the full exercise of the faculties with which man is endowed", might be read as a version of Mill's goal of the development of human individuality and diversity. Nonetheless, Green can be seen as amending Mill in several ways here: freedom is given substantive content and is not simply the absence of restraint, the exercise of freedom is social and not simply individual, and the state is given an important role in providing universally the conditions and opportunities for the attainment of freedom. One instance of the last, one Green thought especially urgent, was legal restriction of the liquor trade in order to protect men, women and children from the damage done by drunkenness. He presented this as a case of limiting the (negative) freedom of contract of traders in the interest of the positive freedom of all. Although he did not name Mill, he perhaps had him in mind when he said, a generation after *On Liberty*:

It used to be the fashion to look on drunkenness as a vice which was the concern only of the person who fell into it, so long as it did not lead him to commit an assault on his neighbours. No thoughtful man any longer looks on it in this way. We know that . . . the excessive drinking of one man means an injury to others in health, purse, and capability, to which no limits can be placed. Drunkenness in the head of a family means, as a rule, the impoverishment and degradation of all members of the family; and the presence of a drink-shop at the corner of a street means, as a rule, the drunkenness of a certain number of heads of families in that street. . . . Here, then, is a wide-spreading social evil, to which society may, if it will, by a restraining law, to a great extent, rid itself, to the infinite enhancement of the positive freedom enjoyed by its members.[85]

Green, like Mill, appealed to experience: he made his case here on grounds of expediency. But at the same time, Green's emphasis on the positive and social nature of freedom made him more sympathetic to extending state action than Mill had been in the final chapter of On Liberty. This side of Green was developed by his pupils and followers, who made the contrast with Mill starkly and greatly in Green's favour.

For example, in Bernard Bosanquet's Philosophical Theory of the State (1899), a book widely read well into the twentieth century, there is a full, albeit complicated, statement of the interpretation of Mill's On Liberty which the British Idealists built up. Bosanquet took Mill, along with Bentham and Spencer, as leading examples of the narrow political philosophy which he was trying to displace in favour of Green's.[86] As Bosanquet saw it, Mill followed Bentham in thinking that law was contrary to liberty, that every infraction of liberty caused pain, that liberty was the absence of restraint, and that the individual and law were fundamentally hostile to one another. As a result, Mill "treats the central life of the individual as something to be carefully fenced round against the impact of social forces".[87] Mill misconceived individuality as lying in "a sort of inner self, to be cherished by enclosing it, as it were, in an impervious globe"; whereas it was plain to Bosanquet that individuality, "the fulness of life and completeness of development which Mill so justly appreciates", was really "nourished and evoked by the varied play of relations and obligations in society".[88] The distinction between self-regarding and other-regarding action receives special attention. Bosanquet objected that if it was pressed, Mill's distinction "excludes individuality from every act of life that has an important social bearing"; and that it was arbitrary as a practical criterion because, every act being both self- and other-regarding, which aspect was fastened on in a particular case was "a matter of mood and momentary urgency". The distinction Mill was attempting to describe was "practically recognised by every society", but it could not be made in Mill's terms. It should rather be drawn in terms Green had used: Mill was really after the distinction between actions where it was crucial that they be done for the right moral motive, so that they should not be subject to legal coercion, and actions whose performance was so important to society that they should be legally enforced, even if then not done for the right moral motive.[89] Bosanquet agreed with Mill that morality or religion should not be enforced by law and penalty, but thought that Mill's confused distinction led him both to object to state intervention which was justified because it maintained an external condition of good life, and to propose coercive interference in cases where it risked thwarting that life. The true criterion was "the nature of what coercive authority is and is not able to do towards the promotion of good life".[90] This was Green's basic position, that the state may act to expand people's "positive freedom", and it opened up greater possibilities for legislation and government action. Rather than law being a restriction of the individual's freedom, law had a moral purpose and was ruled out only when legal interference would have been morally counterproductive. If the state could act to promote positive freedom without causing moral damage, then it was permitted to act even if that involved infringing negative freedom.

The British Idealists shared a view of where the faults of *On Liberty* lay. Often they selected for attack the same points as earlier critics. But by now a new political philosophy has emerged, which has developed its own explanation of where and why Mill goes wrong in *On Liberty*. It is that Mill failed to free himself from the atomic individualism of Bentham. He failed to reach the truths the British Idealists emphasised, that the self was social, that individual and society were interdependent, and that the state had a major role in creating the conditions for its members to be free. Many aspects of these allegations against Mill are, of course, contentious. Further, in retrospect, we may be less struck by the differences than by the similarities and continuities between the British Idealists' political thought and Mill's. We may judge that, keen to distinguish their approach as new, they tended to exaggerate their disagreements with Mill. There are many respects in which Mill and the British Idealists are close. For example, Mill did in fact have a positive view of what the life of the individual should be, though in *On Liberty* he expressed it in terms of "individuality" and "development" rather than "freedom".[91] He allowed exceptions to laissez-faire and advocated some extensions of government action.[92] He was well aware of the individual's need for society, and the power of socialisation in forming individuals.[93] Green, on the other hand, was as opposed as Mill to excessive centralisation of government power, and as protective of the self-reliance of individuals.[94] Politically, Green too was an advanced Liberal and shared most of Mill's views on practical issues, displaying the same concern for all members of society, not excepting women.[95] Green and the other British Idealists always acknowledged the great contributions to political reform and social improvement achieved by Bentham and Mill.[96] In political thought, Mill and the British Idealists are two overlapping and intertwining strands in the tradition of liberalism; and Idealist views do not so much replace Mill's ideas as complement and extend them.[97]

V. CONCLUSION

In looking back to the original reception and early reputation of Mill's political ideas, some adjustment of our own perspective is needed in order to make sense of them. This requires some effort on our part. Mill is close enough in time for us easily to assume that his problems and his answers to them are not too dissimilar from ours and that we have immediate access to them. But it is not quite like that. There have been changes, and it requires some exercise of historical imagination to recapture some of Mill's concerns. Similarly, in estimating Mill's reputation we have to take account not only of Mill's ideas but also of the varying expectations of his successors, who revised his reputation in the light of their own concerns.

Mill saw himself, and was seen by others, as addressing public debates and contributing to political activity. He was, in the term Stephan Collini has recently elucidated so fully, a "public moralist".[98] We should bear in mind that there was then no separate, and isolated, profession of "philosophy" and "moral and political theory": the rise of philosophy as a distinct academic discipline began to occur only in the last years of Mill's life. He was in the thick of public debate – and not just during his brief spell as a member of Parliament – and his writings were read as contributions to it, not as detached scholarly treatises. It follows that his merits were judged partly by political and ideological criteria, and that his reputation was bound to reflect that.

Mill's reputation has fluctuated, declining after his death and through the first half of the twentieth century, but rising steadily and strongly since. It can be expected to continue to fluctuate. Just as every philosopher is "the son of his times", so is every critic. Any philosopher's writings are liable to be viewed from many different perspectives by later critics and valued differently. But in Mill's case, two further factors make his reputation volatile. In the first place, there is his ability to keep his mind open to a great range of ideas, and his ambition to combine and harmonise them. He seems to have persisted throughout his life in the attempt to "weave anew" the "fabric" of his thought as he dropped or revised old ideas and incorporated new ones.[99] This has led to charges of eclecticism and inconsistency. But the process of extension and amalgamation can also be seen as one of Mill's great strengths: his system of ideas is particularly rich and many-hued. Either way, because his thought contains numerous elements, the chances of his reputation falling in and out of favour have been increased. In the second place, many of Mill's conclusions, especially in morals and politics, were bound to be challenged just because his was a philosophy of experience. He had to expect that both contemporaries and later thinkers might not agree with him. Morality was always, for Mill, a *progressive* body of doctrine:

According to the theory of utility . . . the question, what is our duty, is as open to discussion as any other question. Moral doctrines are not more to be received without evidence, nor to be sifted less carefully, than any other doctrines. An appeal lies, as on all other subjects, from a received opinion, however generally entertained, to the decisions of cultivated reason. The weakness of human intellect, and all the other infirmities of our nature, are considered to interfere as much with the rectitude of our judgments on morality, as on any other of our concerns; and changes as great are antici-pated in our opinions on that subject, as on every other, both from the progress of intelligence, from more authentic and enlarged experience, and from alterations in the condition of the human race, requiring altered rules of conduct.[100]

His empirical philosophy exposed all established moral and political doctrines to the cold blast of analysis and criticism. But if that led to their dismissal, his philosophy could not provide substitutes which were fixed and final. What Mill's philosophy does establish is a presumption in favour of free enquiry, and the legitimacy and necessity of submitting any institution or belief to critical scrutiny. However, just because of the empirical dimension to such scrutiny, the answers one reaches about the right institutions and beliefs are never settled but always remain open. Disagreements at that level are only what one should expect. They indicate no failure of Mill's philosophy but on the contrary exemplify its health and vitality.

NOTES

1 *CW* I:233.

2 *CW* I:269–70.

3 Letter to Alexander Bain, 6 August 1859, *CW* XV:631. Custom and feeling as obstacles to reform are persistent themes in Mill: see e.g. "Whewell on Moral Philosophy" (1852), *CW* X:194–95; *On Liberty*, *CW* XVII:220–21; and *Subjection of Women*, *CW* XVIII:261–63.

4 H. S. Jones 1992, 288.

5 For treatments of Mill's philosophy which connect it with his moral and political thought, see e.g. Ryan 1974, chs. 3 & 4; and Skorupski 1989, ch. 1, esp. sections 4–8.

6 The Rev. Charles Crowden, undergraduate at Lincoln College in 1856–59, reported in Hirst 1927, I:22; Fawcett 1873, 74–75.

7 On the great extent of Mill's influence at Oxford and Cambridge, see the evidence of Sidgwick 1873a, 193; Fawcett 1873, 74–80; Anon. 1873, 638–39; Morley 1873a, 102–03; [L. Stephen] 1873, 382; L. Stephen 1885, 24 and 102; L. Stephen 1903, 71–77; and Dicey 1905, 386, 428 & 432.

8 Sidgwick 1873a, 193.

9 [L. Stephen] 1873, 382. Similarly, Anon. 1873, 639; [Cowell] 1873, 298–301; and [Hayward] 1873, 663–64 & 675–81.

10 See the examples given in Collini 1989, pp. 45–48. Henry Fawcett was one of Mill's most ardent and consistent disciples (see L. Stephen 1885, 24, 97, 102–03 and 134), but even he dissented on several important points in economics and politics (pp. 47–48).

11 The initial impact of the *Principles of Political Economy* has been fully studied, including attention to Mill's aims, his target audience, and the background of the commentators, by Marchi 1974; and the early reception of *Utilitarianism* is discussed by Schneewind 1976 and, in a somewhat different version, in Schneewind 1977, 174–88.

12 These matters have been discussed recently in J. E. Jacobs 1994, Mendus 1994, A. Robson 1991, and Robson and Robson 1994.

13 Rees 1985, 79; ch. III discusses the reception of *On Liberty* in the periodical and pamphlet literature up to 1872. A number of the items surveyed by Rees are conveniently reprinted, together with some later appraisals (in periodicals up to 1883), in Pyle 1994; the editor provides a helpful analysis of the contemporary political issues and perennial philosophical issues discussed by the critics. Two of the anonymous items in Pyle's collection can be identified: the reviewer in *The Athenaeum*, 26 February 1859, is given as Augustus de Morgan by Marchand 1941, 363; and the reviews in *The Saturday Review*, 12 and 19 February 1873, are claimed for James Fitzjames Stephen by L. Stephen 1895, 314. On the reception of *On Liberty* more generally, as well as in the reviews, see Himmelfarb 1974, 162–65 & 284–301.

14 Rees 1985, 80.

15 See the reviews, 1859–60, reprinted by Pyle 1994, and the analysis by Rees 1985.

16 See Rees 1985, 94; and Nicholson 1990, 181–4.

17 Rees 1985, 101–03.

18 [J. F. Stephen] 1859, 16; see pp. 15–20.

19 Buckle 1859, 57; see generally pp. 53–59.

20 [Hutton] 1859, 82–83; see generally pp. 81–90.

21 Quoted by Himmelfarb 1974, 163. For other challenges to Mill on this point, see Anon. 1860, 186–91; [Church] 1860, 215–20 & 243–44; and the citations in Rees 1985, 84–87. Himmelfarb 1974, 145–68, examines the extent of social conformism in Mill's England, and suggests that the evidence supports the critics' assessment rather than Mill's.

22 Rees 1985, 83–84.

23 *CW* I:259–60.

24 Mill to Harriet Mill, 29 Jan. 1854, *CW* XIV:141–42. See too Mill to Harriet Mill, 7 Feb. [1854] and 7 Feb. [1855], *CW* XIV:152 & 320.

25 *Autobiography, CW* I:260.

26 Morley 1874, 153.

27 The closeness of the themes of the two books is brought out well by Himmelfarb 1974, ch. VII passim. "For Mill the central problem was the individual: how to give to the individual woman the same degree of

liberty enjoyed by the individual man, how to make more complete individuals of both women and men" (p. 174).

28 *CW* XIX:328. See *Considerations on Representative Government* (1861), *CW* XIX:479–81, for a clear statement of Mill's case that the suffrage should be distributed with "no account of difference of sex".

29 Brodrick 1859, 143–44. Brodrick was an "advanced" Liberal, one of the "university liberals" discussed in Harvie 1976, and generally sympathetic with Mill's politics.

30 The quotation is from his first speech of his Westminster candidacy, 3 July 1865, *CW* XXVIII:16–17.

31 See the letter to Beal [17 April 1865] published in the press, *CW* XVI:1032, and speeches to the electors of Westminster, 5 and 8 July 1865, *CW* XXVIII:21 & 39.

32 [Bagehot] 1865, 542–43.

33 *CW* XXVIII:91–93, 151–62, 283–86, 373–80, 386–91 & 402–07. For women's issues and movements in this period, including Mill's role, see Rover 1967; Packe 1954, 492–503; Himmelfarb 1974, ch. VIII; Rendall 1985, 284–91 & 307–20; Kent 1987; Tulloch 1989, 103–16; Rendall 1994; and especially Kinzer, Robson and Robson 1992, ch. 4. Victorian feminists themselves varied in their view of Mill's tactics, not all finding him as central and advanced as did Millicent Fawcett, who herself departed from Mill on some points: see Caine 1992, 32–42, 94, 152, 219–21 & 225–27.

34 Anon. 1866, 715–16.

35 Anon. 1867a, 385.

36 Anon. 1867b, 648.

37 Oliphant 1866. Prolific novelist and popular biographer, Mrs Oliphant was married in 1852 and widowed in 1859. She wrote extensively for *Blackwood's*. The details, complexities and later development of her views on women are discussed in M. Williams 1986, ch. 7; M. Williams 1995; and Jay 1995, chs. 2 & 3.

38 Letter to Bain, 14 July 1869, *CW* XVII:1623–24; quotation from letter to Cairnes, 9 April 1869, *CW* XVII:1587. For other explanations of the timing of the book, see Robson and Robson 1994, xxix.

39 Letter to Cairnes, 9 April 1869, *CW* XVII:1587. The survey which follows is based on the following selection: [Amos (?)] 1870, Anon. 1869a, Anon. 1869b, Anon. 1869c, Cobbe 1869, [Dixon] 1869, [James] 1869, Kingsley 1869, [Maurice] 1869, [Mozley] 1869, [Oliphant] 1869, [Rands] 1870, and H. Taylor 1870; many of these are reprinted, together with related material, in Pyle 1995, whose introduction separates out what was at issue between Mill and his critics. Amos, Cobbe, and

Kingsley are wholehearted supporters of Mill and the cause of women's suffrage; Maurice is sympathetic but feels Mill weakens his case by overstating it. The *Fortnightly Review*, edited by John Morley, carried a very brief Critical Notice describing *The Subjection of Women* as "the book of the past month" and saying that "probably no other contribution of Mr. Mill's to social speculation is marked by so far-reaching, exalted, and courageous a kind of wisdom" (July 1869, p. 119). A discussion in a subsequent number was promised, but none appeared.

40 [Mozley] 1869, 90. Mozley, an author, contributed to the *Saturday Review* between 1861 and 1877 (only her articles of 1861–64 have been identified). She was unmarried.

41 [Mozley] 1869, 99–100.

42 [Oliphant] 1869, 118—22.

43 [Oliphant] 1869, 126. Oliphant conceded she could find no reason for refusing the franchise to the exceptional women, becoming more influential, to whom Mill's arguments really applied, and who alone could benefit – "the class of highly cultivated, able, mature, unmarried women who have never themselves undergone the natural experiences of their sex, and really feel themselves in the position to compete with men, without fear or favour. . . . [T]hey are, without doubt, intellectually superior to the ordinary mass of women, and still more certainly are much more like men" (p. 128; see pp. 128–30).

44 [Oliphant] 1869, 119–20; and especially [Oliphant] 1866, 371–79.

45 See letter to Cairnes, 9 April 1869, *CW* XVII:1587.

46 For accounts of the book, see L. Stephen 1895, ch. V, section II; Colaiaco 1983, ch. 7 (pp. 162–66 on the contemporary response to it); and K. J. M. Smith 1988, ch. 7 (pp. 203–09 on the contemporary response).

47 Sidgwick 1873b, 292.

48 Letter of 1 May 1872, quoted in Colaiaco 1983, 124.

49 J. F. Stephen 1873, 53–54.

50 See L. Stephen 1895, 122–23, 182–83, 193, 205–06, 275 & 308; Colaiaco 1983, 50–01, 61–62 & 89–90; K. J. M. Smith 1988, 44–46; and Nicholson 1990, 154. When in 1872 Stephen was revising the Indian laws of evidence, he based his introduction on the principles of evidence on the principles of induction and deduction of the *Logic*: and he sent the proofs to Mill for his comments (O'Grady 1987, 8).

51 J. F. Stephen 1873, 53 & 28–29 (the latter is from the Preface to the second edition).

52 Letter, quoted in L. Stephen 1895, 308.

53 Sidgwick 1873b, 293. Dicey (1905) writes that Stephen provides "a vehement criticism of Mill from the point of view of the older utilitarians, and certainly shows that Mill had diverged considerably from Bentham" (p. 427, n. 1; for his account of the "double aspect" of Mill, i.e. his Benthamism and his deviation from it, see pp. 422–31). On Dicey's and other "Individualists" view of Mill as the corruptor of the true interpretation of Benthamism, see Taylor 1992, 37–46.

54 Sidgwick 1873b, 293.

55 Morley 1873b, 277.

56 Morley 1873b, 282–83. Stephen retorted bluntly in the second edition: "That this was Mr. Mill's 'very aim and object', I saw, I think, as distinctly as Mr. Morley himself. My book is meant to show that he did not attain his object...." (J. F. Stephen 1873, 29).

57 Morley 1873b, 282–89.

58 Morley 1873b, 293.

59 Morley 1873b, 294.

60 An interesting empirical argument that in modern civilisations complete freedom of thought and expression has in fact become an essential condition of development and therefore of promoting happiness is given in L. Stephen 1883. This reinforces Mill against Fitzjames Stephen. I have discussed the question whether Mill takes an a priori or an empiricist view of liberty in Nicholson (1990), 140–57 (especially 150–53) & 181–85, agreeing with Morley against Stephen.

61 J. F. Stephen 1873, 185. Dicey (1905) agreed: "John Mill was throughout his life the ardent advocate of the political equality of the sexes, but ... though honestly basing all his political views on the principle of utility, entertained, though unconsciously, a sentiment in favour of equality which belongs to the school rather of Rousseau than of Bentham" (p. 160, n. 3).

62 J. F. Stephen 1873, 192.

63 J. F. Stephen 1873, 193–94.

64 J. F. Stephen 1873, 194. Women as soldiers were one of Mill's passing examples in The Subjection of Women, CW XXI:270.

65 J. F. Stephen 1873, 194.

66 J. F. Stephen 1873, 195–96.

67 J. F. Stephen 1873, 196–98.

68 J. F. Stephen 1873, 198.

69 See e.g. [Cowell] 1873.

70 M. Fawcett 1873. Stephen disdainfully dismisses her: J. F. Stephen 1873, 205, note to the second edition. For the Fawcetts' activity in women's causes, see Rubinstein 1989.

71 Becker 1874, 225. Stephen ignored, or did not see, her critique. On Becker see A. Kelly 1992.

72 Becker 1874, 225–28.

73 Becker 1874, 228–29. Becker is equally sharp with Stephen's illustration of education, and handles him as roughly as he does his opponents; see pp. 229–32.

74 Becker 1874, 232–35.

75 Morley 1874, 153. For a recent statement of the empirical dimension of Mill's position, see Robson and Robson 1994, xxxii–iii.

76 E.g. Cairnes 1874. He was responding to G. Smith 1874, a particularly intemperate and full parade of the prejudices of the time, by a Liberal who had withdrawn his support from Mill on this point.

77 For a more general survey of Mill's reputation in the period 1873–1933, see Collini 1991, ch. 8, tracing his passage "from dangerous partisan to national possession".

78 Packe 1954, 500–01. Kinzer, Robson and Robson 1992 write that Mill's "contribution to the women's movement" generally "cannot be overestimated" (p. 148).

79 For details, see Rover 1967.

80 For Mill's priorities, see the letter (dictated by Helen Taylor) to Florence Nightingale, 31 Dec. 1867, *CW* XVI:1343–46. Of the "University Liberals", who were at one with Mill over the 1867 Reform Bill's extension of the male franchise, Bryce, Dicey, Frederick Harrison and Leslie Stephen all opposed giving the suffrage to women: see B. Harrison 1978; and Annan 1984, 109–10. They did, however, support higher education for women. Sidgwick would have given the franchise to self-supporting unmarried women and widows: Sidgwick 1891, 384–87. Sidgwick played a leading part in opening university education to women at Cambridge: Sidgwick and Sidgwick 1906.

81 Hirst 1927, II:255–56.

82 See Nicholson 1990, 62–63 & 189–90.

83 *On Liberty*, *CW* XVIII:226.

84 T. H. Green 1881, 199. Green's view of freedom is highly contentious in some respects; for instance some argue that a negative view of freedom – such as Mill's is taken to be – captures what freedom is, and deny that Green's "positive" freedom is freedom at all. For an account of Green on freedom, and discussion, see Nicholson 1990, Study IV.

85 T. H. Green 1881, 210. Green's and Mill's views on the drink question are compared in Nicholson 1990, 177–85.

86 Bosanquet 1899, especially ch. III & ch. IV, section 1.

87 Bosanquet 1899, 56.

88 Bosanquet 1899, 57.

89 Bosanquet 1899, 60. Bosanquet elaborates the distinction and puts it to work in ch. VIII, "Nature of the End of the State and Consequent Limit of State Action", explicitly citing T. H. Green's discussion (1886, sections 10–18). For Green on the proper extent of state intervention, see Nicholson 1990, 157–97.

90 Bosanquet 1899, 61–65, quotation on p. 62.

91 *On Liberty, CW* XVIII:305–06. In the *Logic*, as John Skorupski has pointed out to me, Mill makes "moral freedom" part of his ideal of character; see *CW* VIII:841.

92 *Principles of Political Economy, CW* III:936–71; and *On Liberty, CW* XVIII:301–05.

93 See e.g. *On Liberty, CW* XVIII:224–25, 230, 282 & 302. Indeed the principal problem addressed in the book might be described thus: given that every individual must live in society, how can the huge power of society to mould its individual members be controlled and limited rationally, so that they can make their own characters (*Logic, CW* VIII:839–43) and develop freely as individuals? Or in the terms in which I have presented Mill in this essay, how to ensure that individuals are able to appraise critically their own feelings and the institutions and opinions of their society?

94 T. H. Green 1881, 194, 202–03 & 211–12.

95 Nicholson 1990, Study V passim. On Green and women, see Anderson 1991.

96 Nicholson 1990, 248, n. 54.

97 For comparisons of Mill's and Green's political thought, including their relation to liberalism, see Sabine 1973, ch. 33 passim; Bellamy 1992; Gaus 1983, passim; Greenleaf 1983, ch. 4; Nicholson 1990, 111 and Study V passim; and Skorupski 1993a, 94–99.

98 Collini 1991, especially ch. 4 on Mill's career as a partisan polemicist and activist in the last fifteen years of his life.

99 For this very strong and suggestive metaphor, revealing Mill's ambition to construct a comprehensive and unified system of ideas, see *Autobiography, CW* I:163–65, also 259.

100 "Sedgwick's Discourse" (1835), *CW* X:74.

14 Mill in a liberal landscape

Mill's essay *On Liberty* had both the good and the ill fortune to become a "classic" on first publication. The immediate success of the book, dedicated as it was to preserving the memory of Harriet Taylor, could only gratify its author. Yet its friends and foes alike fell upon it with such enthusiasm that the essay itself has ever since been hard to see for the smoke of battle.[1] *That* it is a liberal manifesto is clear beyond doubt; *what* the liberalism is that it defends and *how* it defends it remain matters of controversy. Given the lucidity of Mill's prose and the seeming simplicity and transparency of his arguments, this is astonishing; ought we not to know by now whether the essay's main target is the hold of Christianity on the Victorian mind[2] or rather the hold of a monolithic public opinion of whatever kind; whether its intellectual basis lies in utility as Mill claimed or in a covert appeal to natural right; whether the ideal of individual moral and intellectual autonomy is supposed to animate everyone, or only an elite; and so indefinitely on?

The account of Mill's essay I offer here does not settle these issues. My account is neither conclusive nor comprehensive, nor will it resolve very many of the problems that Mill's readers have had with the essay. My argumentative aim is to emphasise the difficulties a late twentieth-century reader will have with Mill's liberalism, and to mark quite sharply its differences from many contemporary – that is, late twentieth-century – liberalisms. I therefore begin with a sketch of Mill's argument, then say something about the context of Mill's discussion, that is, about whom the essay was aimed at, negatively and positively; I conclude by contrasting Mill's liberalism with the liberalisms of John Rawls and Isaiah Berlin, in order to bring out some of the ways in which Mill was and was not a pluralist, did and did not attend to "the separateness of persons," did and did not espouse a fully-fledged teleological and ideal conception of the autonomous individual.[3] I make no secret of my preference for Mill's ambitious and comprehensive theory over Rawls's more limited and defensive (latterly a narrowly "political") liberalism, nor of my uncertainty about quite what to say about Mill's seeming blindness to the attractions of colourful but illiberal cultural alternatives – such as that presented by the Indian subcontinent, whose political affairs he directed.[4] There is much in Mill's essay that I do not discuss here, but I have tried to avoid repeating what I have written elsewhere and what others have (to my mind at any rate) dealt with adequately.[5] It is in the nature of "classics" that their students are exhausted before they are.

I

Mill's essay was conceived in 1854 when he discovered that he and Harriet were suffering from consumption, and might well die in the near future. It was to be part of the "mental pemican" that they would leave to thinkers "if there should be any" after themselves.[6] The absurdity of their fears for the wholesale collapse of British intellectual life has often been commented on, and the kindest gloss on it is that no two people who had waited to be married as long as they had should be chided for excessive gloom when they so soon afterwards discovered that their long-deferred happiness was to be snatched away.[7] *On Liberty* was conceived at a time when Mill was for the first time contemplating a long essay on Comte, his intention in part being to counter the excessively favourable impression that his use of Comte's work in *A System of Logic* had created. Mill abandoned the Comte essay for the rest of the 1850s (it eventually appeared in 1865), but *On Liberty* has the marks of Mill's ambivalence about Comte all over it.[8] On the one hand, Mill thought highly of Comte's appreciation of the need for a scientific reorganisation of social and economic life; on the other, Mill condemned Comte's version of that project as "liberticide." On the one hand, Comte saw deeply into the need for some kind of moral system to play the role in individual lives that Christianity had formerly played; on the other, Comte's version of the religion of humanity "could have been written by no man who had ever laughed."[9] On the one hand, Comte understood that as society became increasingly complex, the bonds of duty must tie us ever more tightly to one another; on the other he wholly failed to see that unless we lived for ourselves as well as for others, nothing would be worth living for, nothing would exist for which it was worth doing our duty. Of course, Mill had many other writers in mind. *On Liberty*'s famous epigraph invokes von Humboldt and the German concern for *Bildung*;[10] the historical sociology of democratic culture on which Mill relied to explain the nature of the threat to liberty posed by that culture was lifted bodily from Tocqueville's *Democracy in America*. But the intellectual and political vision that Mill was anxious to check is one that his friends and colleagues found tempting – not just the "soft" despotism in the form that Tocqueville feared, but that of a benevolent bureaucracy also.

Like that of *Utilitarianism*, the argument of Mill's essay is not so much familiar as notorious. Mill writes that "The object of this Essay is to assert one very simple principle, as entitled to govern absolutely the dealings of society with the individual in the way of compulsion and control. . . ."[11] Commentators have complained about Mill's appeal to one very *simple* principle; they have said that little in human life is simple, and the question of when to interfere with each other's liberty is not part of that little. This complaint may be mistaken; simple principles are often complicated to apply – a planning minister or his civil servants may be required not to withhold consent "unreasonably" when a citizen applies for permission to build a house or a garage, but that simple requirement leads to complicated lawsuits. Mill's simple principle is that we may coerce others into doing what they do not choose to do only for the sake of self-defence, and by extension to make them perform a small number of good offices (such as giving evidence in a court of law) required if others are not to be harmed by their inaction. It *is* a simple principle, however complicated it may be to apply.

Mill was less interested in employing the principle to restrain coercion by single individuals than to restrain the coercive actions of groups. It is not the fear that we shall individually assault or incarcerate others when we ought not that motivated him, but the fear that we shall collectively gang up on eccentric individuals when we ought not. The fear is based on two things. The first and more obvious is Tocqueville's observation that Americans had less freedom of thought and speech than one might suppose from their constitutional arrangements; Americans were notably bad at thinking for themselves, and were vulnerable to the desire to think like everyone else and to the desire that everyone else should think like them.[12] The second and less obvious is an idea that Mill picked up from the Saint-Simonians during the late 1820s and early 1830s. This is the view that the progress of modern civilisation is a movement away from individual genius and towards action *en masse*.[13] Mill largely relied on the first thought. It was a corollary to the view of the history of democracy that he had come to, partly under Tocqueville's tutelage, but quite largely independently of that influence. The ordinary people of a country like Britain had successfully altered the balance of power between themselves and their rulers, until the country was in practice, though not in constitutional principle, democratic; but they had not noticed that in fending off the tyranny of monarchs and aristocrats, they rendered themselves vulnerable to a different and more insidious tyranny, the tyranny of all collectively over each individually.

The insidiousness of this tyranny was not only that "self-government" often meant in practice the government of each by all the rest, but that this was a soft, constant social pressure for conformity rather than a visible political tyranny. The consequence was that they tyrannised over themselves as well as over each other:

reflecting persons perceived that when society is itself the tyrant – society collectively, over the separate individuals who compose it – its means of tyrannizing are not restricted to the acts which it may do by the hands of its political functionaries. Society can and does execute its own mandates: and if it issues wrong mandates instead of right, or any mandates at all in things with which it ought not to meddle, it practises a social tyranny more formidable than many kinds of political oppression, since, though not usually upheld by such extreme penalties, it leaves fewer means of escape, penetrating much more deeply into the details of life, and enslaving the soul itself.[14]

There was nothing to be done about the movement towards political democracy. It was a movement that Mill thought inevitable, and like Tocqueville Mill thought it was on balance morally desirable on the grounds of justice and liberty alike. All the same, a new view of liberty was needed to counter the threat posed by the tendency of the public to suppose that once its mind was made up, dissentients should defer to public opinion. Mill's "very simple principle" was intended to provide part of that counter. Individuals must acknowledge the right of society to coerce them out of behaviour that harmed other people, that violated their rights, that damaged their legitimate interests; over all else, each individual remained sovereign.

Critics have complained, not only that Mill's principle was too simple, but that he had no business offering it as an "absolute" principle. Mill himself was aware that it was dangerous for a utilitarian to offer any other principle than utility as "entitled to govern absolutely" the dealings of society with its members. Utilitarians prided themselves on having reduced morality to principle: ethics had been rationalised when the principle of utility justified the everyday morality that utilitarians accepted and the non-everyday morality with which they wished to improve everyday morality. The status of any other principle was thus a delicate matter. Mill was ready with his answer. The individual's sovereignty over him- or herself was not based on natural right; it was derived from utility. It was absolute not in the sense that the liberty principle is "ultimate," but in the sense that it is exceptionless. This claim, however, raised another difficulty. The impetus to the writing of *On Liberty* was to protect freedom from the assaults of illiberal do-gooders – as it were an advance warning against the "bourgeois, benevolent and bureaucratic" Sidney and Beatrice Webb when they should arrive on the scene, and perhaps a warning against his own good friend Edwin Chadwick, with his enthusiasm for Prussian efficiency. This supposed a conflict between the pursuit of freedom and the pursuit of the general welfare; but Mill proposed to defend freedom in terms of its contribution to the general welfare.

In essence, the rest of *On Liberty* spelled out the way in which the principle of *no coercion save to prevent harm to others* promoted utility. The first step was to point out that the utility involved had to be taken "in its largest sense": it was the utility of "man as a progressive being" that was at stake, not only the bread-and-butter utility of man as a consumer, with fixed tastes and desires.[15] Giving a persuasive account of what the utility of such a person was based on, as most critics have seen, forms the substance of the work.[16] It is worth noting that Mill's expansive conception of the utility of a progressive being rested on a sober basis. In terms of recent discussion, Mill's liberalism is "perfectionist" in the sense that it proposes an ideal way of life; in the sense in which his contemporaries would have understood such terms, it was more nearly "anti-perfectionist" inasmuch as it repudiated the idea that the state or society generally had a right to *make* individuals conform to some existing ideal of good character. In any case, Mill's concern for individual liberty rested both on a doctrine of self-protection and on a doctrine of self-development. We have two great needs that rights protect: the first and most basic is for security, and the second is for room to expand and flourish according to our own conception of what that entails.[17] In *Utilitarianism*, Mill went on to explain the achievement of security as the province of *justice*, and to tie the notion of justice to the notion of rights. Our interest in security has the character of a right that must be protected against threats from other persons.

Although Mill was not a functionalist, he plainly thought that organised human society and its legal and political arrangements existed in order to provide each individual with a collective defence against such threats. One of the ways in which the principle of no coercion save to prevent harm to others is glossed by Mill, therefore, is to include the right of society to make each of us bear our share of the burden of sustaining the institutions that provide collective security. The refusal to give evidence at a trial is not a matter of our making a legitimate decision to withhold a kindness to the person whom that evidence would help, but a threat to the arrangements on which everyone's security depends, and so a case of harm to others; we may therefore be coerced into giving evidence:

There are also many positive acts for the benefit of others which he may rightfully be compelled to perform; such as, to give evidence in a court of justice; to bear his fair share in the common defence, or in any other joint work necessary to the interest of the society of which he enjoys the protection; and to perform certain acts of individual beneficence, such as saving a fellow-creature's life, or interposing to protect the defenceless against ill-usage, things which whenever it is obviously a man's duty to do, he may rightfully be made responsible to society for not doing. A person may cause evil to others not only by his actions but by his inaction, and in either case he is justly accountable to them for the injury. The latter case, it is true, requires a much more cautious exercise of compulsion than the former. To make any one answerable for doing evil to others, is the rule; to make him answerable for not preventing evil, is, comparatively speaking, the exception. Yet there are many cases clear enough and grave enough to justify that exception.[18]

Mill's argument that rights are to be elucidated in this way remains contentious; it was, and is, a bold move to defend the right to liberty as something other than a *natural* right. Consider, for example, the relationship between Mill's views and those of such recent writers as H. L. A. Hart and Robert Nozick. Mill's view that the limits of our liberty are to be understood by reference to the purpose of our living in society is squarely at odds with Nozick's natural-rights-based view. And while Mill's view that we may be made to bear our fair share of the burdens of maintaining society is on all fours with the natural-rights-based views of H. L. A. Hart, Mill's argument reaches that conclusion more directly than does Hart's.[19] Hart explained our obligation to obey the law by arguing that a society may coerce others into doing their fair share to sustain institutions from which they derive the same benefits as those they help. This was intended to explain how someone who enjoyed a natural right to "maximum equal liberty" may still be under an obligation to obey the laws of his or her community, including laws that impose obligations of the sort discussed by Mill.

Nozick's response to Hart's argument was to argue that if we have a right to equal liberty, it is only our own consent that can give others the right to demand such positive assistance as our giving evidence in a law court.[20] Merely being part of a community in which we benefit from the assistance of others is not enough to generate obligations of "fair play." It might be true that it would be *good* of us to return something for the benefits we received, but it would violate nobody's rights if we did not. Mill would surely have concluded that this and similar disputes among rights theorists showed the superiority of his utilitarianism. He relied on a simpler thought: that society is a mutual aid system designed to protect our fundamental interests; we are born into society, not into a state of nature, and within that society we are obliged to sustain the protective system from which we benefit. Everything then hinges on explaining our fundamental interests as persuasively as possible.

Mill appears in much of *On Liberty* to take it for granted that his readers will understand the principle of no coercion save to prevent harm to others in much the same way as himself. That is, there is no very elaborate discussion of what constitutes harm; and, as Jeremy Waldron has argued, there seems every reason to believe that at least *some* sorts of distress – such as being startled to discover that our neighbour is not a Trinitarian Christian, or that she is not heterosexual, say – would have been counted by Mill as positively good for us and not in the least "harmful."[21] The confidence in the transparency of the concept of harm on which his argument relied meant that Mill argued in a way that bypasses much of the argument of recent years. Two common arguments against his position he hardly bothered to rebut except in passing. One, made popular thirty-five years ago by Lord Devlin, is that if society is to defend each of us against assault, robbery, breach of contract, and so on, it will also be necessary for society to defend a common morality covering all aspects of social and individual, or all aspects of public and private, life.[22] James Fitzjames Stephen had produced during Mill's own lifetime a related but by no means identical argument; Stephen's crude utilitarianism implied that we should beat good behaviour into people whenever the policy offers sufficient prospect of success. Utilitarianism is therefore not a basis for, but at odds with, Mill's self-abnegating doctrine. Stephen prided himself on his roughness, as his nickname "the Gruffian" suggests,[23] but the argument is far from easy to defeat. Stephen in particular was opposed to the idea that freedom was as important to the utility of "man as a progressive being" as Mill supposed; but the problem posed by a "no holds barred" consequentialism of the sort he represented is quite general. One of its implications, for instance, is that if Mill thought that a taste for liberty was an element in a good character, he ought to have been ready to beat a taste for liberty into the recalcitrant, too.

Devlin's view was not so much a dismissal of Mill's concern with freedom as the claim that a plausible account of Mill's harm principle would license the defence of a collective morality. Devlin thought, at a time when most of public opinion was against him, that the Victorian laws against homosexual acts between consenting adults ought to be abolished. This, however, was not because they infringed liberty in the abstract, but because they violated a concern for privacy and for intimate relationships that was inherent in existing British moral attitudes. To set up an abstract test of the kind Mill proposed was to invite the unravelling of social cohesion. The reply implicit in Mill's essay would, however, answer both Devlin and Stephen. In essence, it is that the facts are against his critics. *Some* common morality must be generally enforced, and its features are just those that Mill suggests; but there is no reason to believe that a failure to secure uniformity of belief on disputed conceptions of the good life will bring about any harm other than whatever discomfort is attendant on being required to think for ourselves. Conversely, there is good reason to suppose that trying to enforce more than the basic morality Mill had in mind would result in the damage that *On Liberty* laments.

It is sometimes suggested that a utilitarian defence of liberty is a non-starter; utilitarianism would license any degree of interference that gave enough pleasure to the majority. If people *want* to believe in a shared morality, the majority has a right to have a common morality enforced, on the utilitarian basis that the enforcement will provide pleasure to the majority. Mill's response to this vulgar but not implausible argument was offered glancingly, in several places, and in three instalments. One was an appeal to the intuitive idea that any claim that others should behave as I wish *just because* I wish them to do so, has no merit. Mill knew that nobody *avowed* such a view. The buried premise of Mill's argument against it therefore was that where enough moral discord existed to excite the desire for uniformity, the demand that others should do anything in particular for the sake of a "shared morality" is tantamount to the claim that they should think like me and act like me, because I want them to. This is what Mill denounced as his contemporaries' belief that their "likings and dislikings" should be a universal guide.[24] The second was sketched in the previous paragraph: the content of the "common morality" that any society must enforce was essentially limited to the defence of each of its members against a limited range of harms, and the enforcement of the common rules of interaction that made life more prosperous and more rationally controllable – the morality that underlies the making and keeping of contracts, the doing of jury duty, recognising the obligation to go to work and earn a living, and so on. Any greater uniformity would do more harm than good. The third was essentially an elaboration of the conception of "more harm" that was involved in such a response; that elaboration supplied the bulk of the positive argument of *On Liberty*. Mill denied that enforcing uniformity would be a good bargain in utilitarian terms; the entire essay was an argument to that effect, since it was an argument against yielding to the desire for uniformity of sentiment, whether for its own sake or for the sake of the general welfare.

Mill's concluding admonition to beware of creating a society whose animating spirit has been sacrificed to the perfection of a bureaucratic machine summed up Mill's underlying theme: a society of what Tocqueville had called "industrious sheep" was the only alternative to the lively and flexible (and emotionally uncomfortable) society that Mill was arguing for. It is a famous peroration:

The worth of a State, in the long run, is the worth of the individuals composing it; and a State which postpones the interests of their mental expansion and elevation, to a little more of administrative skill, or of that semblance of it which practice gives, in the details of business; a State which dwarfs its men, in order that they may be more docile instruments in its hands even for beneficial purposes – will find that with small men no great thing can really be accomplished; and that the perfection of machinery to which it has sacrificed everything, will in the end avail it nothing, for want of the vital power which, in order that the machine might work more smoothly, it has preferred to banish.[25]

Some of Mill's elaborations of what follows from his very simple principle have become justly famous. Others have languished in an unwarranted obscurity, among them his insistence that it was no illicit interference with liberty for the state to demand that young people who proposed to marry should demonstrate that they had the means and the intention to look after the probable children of their union;[26] others, such as his insistence that the state should on no account take a large part in the provision of education, have been much less attended to than one might have expected, perhaps because modern liberals both British and American take public education for granted, while enthusiasts for the privatisation of education have not generally been Millian liberals in other respects.[27] In the contemporary United States, enthusiasts for "home schooling" are overwhelmingly concerned to keep their children at home in order to indoctrinate them in creationism or some other quirk of fundamentalist Protestantism; they are not natural allies of Mill. It is a matter for regret that commentators have been so eager to assimilate Mill's ideas to those of mainstream twentieth-century liberalism that they have not seen what a very awkward ally of twentieth-century liberals he is.

The same cross purposes have been visible in much subsequent commentary on Mill's defence of an almost absolute freedom of speech. Characteristically, attention has been divided between two different modern concerns. On the one hand, Mill's insistence that such a freedom is the best route to the discovery of the truth has been subjected to some anxious scrutiny in the light of a more sceptical view of the lessons of the history of science, while on the other his view that speech was intrinsically not a source of harm to others has been scrutinised equally anxiously in the light of American First Amendment jurisprudence and both British and American obscenity law. What emerges most clearly, however, is that Mill's concern with truth has more to do with religious "truth" than scientific truth, and that he had almost nothing to say about indecency and nothing at all to say about pornography. Mill's arguments are interesting just because his concerns were so unlike the concerns of recent theorists.

It is perhaps more surprising that Mill not only has little or nothing to say about sexual freedom, but nothing to say about the concept of privacy, the basis of most modern arguments. This is, I think, a real defect in his treatment of the subject. For one thing, it is because we mind so much about privacy and about the near-sanctity of intimate relationships that we flinch from Mill's insistence that society should impose financial requirements on people intending to marry and have children. Again, many of us would think that the same considerations were a powerful argument for abolishing penal laws against homosexuality – and that even if some harm were to be done by their abolition the argument that their enforcement was an outrage against privacy would be a powerful argument in the other direction. For Mill's own purposes, a simpler case sufficed. He drew a distinction that good sense requires, between arguments from decency and arguments from harm, and left it at that. The distinction is simple enough and best illustrated by an imaginary example. A married couple having sexual intercourse in Piccadilly Circus in broad daylight engage in an indecent act, but not one that violates any obligation they owe to one another. Conversely, an adulterous liaison may be objectionable because it violates the trust that the injured spouses had placed in their errant partners, but if conducted discreetly, it could not be condemned as indecent. Decency is essentially a matter of obtruding offensive displays upon others. A moment's thought about our insistence on the privacy of defecation shows plainly how often decency is not concerned with the *moral* content of acts that nobody has ever suggested are immoral in themselves, but is concerned with the fact that they would be indecent if done obtrusively in public:

Again, there are many acts which, being directly injurious only to the agents themselves, ought not to be legally interdicted, but which, if done publicly, are a violation of good manners, and coming thus within the category of offences against others, may rightfully be prohibited. Of this kind are offences against decency; on which it is unnecessary to dwell, the rather as they are only connected indirectly with our subject, the objection to publicity being equally strong in the case of many actions not in themselves condemnable, nor supposed to be so.[28]

One might regret that Mill so cavalierly waves away arguments about decency, but he had other fish to fry. Most of Mill's argument about freedom of thought and speech had two aims. The first was to establish that freedom was an essential condition for discovering truth; the second was to elaborate an account of what sort of truth he had in mind. Much of the argument was negative, in the sense that many of Mill's arguments were devoted to repudiating familiar arguments against freedom. Thus Mill denied that the defence of free speech amounted to the acceptance of the war of all against all; he thought himself entitled to the conventional distinction between mere speech and incitement, as in his famous claim that we must be free to publish the opinion that corn dealers are thieves but not to put it on a placard and wave it at an angry mob outside a corn dealer's house: "An opinion that corn-dealers are starvers of the poor, or that private property is robbery, ought to be unmolested when simply circulated through the press, but may justly incur punishment when delivered orally to an excited mob assembled before the house of a corn-dealer, or when handed about among the same mob in the form of a placard."[29] Some critics have affected not to see the point, but a brief consideration of the abolition of slavery enforces it well enough. Slave owners ought not to own slaves: their property is simply illicit. Nonetheless, private citizens ought to try to abolish slavery by peaceful means if at all possible. John Brown was rightly hanged for murder, even though slavery was an atrocity and he was an abolitionist.

More interestingly, at least in the sense that his seeming espousal of a "proto-Popperian" position was in some tension with his usual inductivist views, Mill argued that truth was internally related to controvertibility. The only ground we have for believing in the truth of what we believe is that it has been or can be exposed to attempted refutation and that it has survived or will survive it. To believe something, properly speaking, is to understand what would contro-vert one's belief in it, and to have confidence in that belief's ability to withstand test. This appears to be Mill in proto-Popperian mode rather than Mill the inductivist. Yet even here, Mill's interest did not lie where Popper's lay. Mill did not offer an empirical claim to the effect that scientific progress depends on an intellectual regime of "conjecture and refutation."[30] What he put forward was a strongly *normative* conception of belief that entailed among other things that most of what we describe as our "beliefs" are not so much "believed" as acquiesced in. Much the greater part of Mill's chapter on freedom of thought was concerned with religion; as this might suggest, Mill's concern was with strong conviction and lively belief, and much of his argument was an argument for trying to maximise the liveliness of our beliefs. A mere recording machine could pick up and reiterate the ideas of others, and might by coincidence reiterate the truth; a human mind might do much more.[31] The question how far Mill's conception of the self allowed him to appeal as unself-consciously as he did to the importance of making our beliefs "our own" is a difficult and underexplored one, but that is what animates his argument. It is one of many arguments in the essay that rests upon a "positive" conception of liberty.[32] Mental freedom is a form of positive possession of our ideas.

The argument is plainly more persuasive when applied to moral and religious beliefs than when applied to scientific ideas. This is yet another field in which Mill's argument was directed not towards our anxieties but towards his own. We have become used to the arguments of T. S. Kuhn and Paul Feyerabend, who have claimed that scientific truth is established in a more coercive and non-consensual fashion than previous philosophers of science supposed. So far from making bold conjectures and accepting painful refutations, scientists habitually preserve orthodoxies and run dissenters out of the lab.[33] But Mill was not interested in what made science "special," nor in discussing the difference between establishing low-level facts and high-level theories. He was interested in the degree of conviction with which people held their beliefs about the ends of life. Unless they were in the habit of arguing for their views, they were not in full command of them: "However unwillingly a person who has a strong opinion may admit the possibility that his opinion may be false, he ought to be moved by the consideration that however true it may be, if it is not fully, frequently, and fearlessly discussed, it will be held as a dead dogma, not a living truth."[34]

When we turn to the argument for freedom of action in the forming of our own plans of life, the considerations Mill adduces remain within the same framework. In part Mill was concerned to deny that society was in the condition of an armed camp where everyone must devote all their efforts to the well-being of their fellow creatures. There were emergency situations in which individual claims to freedom had to be more or less denied, but everyday life was not such a situation. A man on sentry duty might be shot for falling asleep; in everyday life, we may choose our own bedtimes. A sentry might be shot for drunkenness on watch; in everyday life, we may generally drink as we like. The rationale for the distinction is the familiar one; we are answerable for the predictable harm we cause others: "No person ought to be punished simply for being drunk; but a soldier or a policeman should be punished for being drunk on duty. Whenever, in short, there is definite damage, or a definite risk of damage, either to an individual or to the public, the case is taken out of the province of liberty, and placed in that of morality or law."[35]

Mill was particularly concerned to deny that a proper concern for the moral welfare of our fellows must take the form of censoring their thoughts and inclinations. This is a feature of his argument that has received less attention than it deserves. He drew a very careful distinction between coercive and uncoercive means of altering other people's behaviour, and was anxious to insist that where coercion was illicit, non-coercive measures might well be appropriate. Mill knew that he was vulnerable to the objection that *On*

Liberty put forward a doctrine of ethical laissez-faire that encouraged pure self-centredness and an unconcern with the well-being of others – and he duly denied in several places that he was doing anything of the sort.

It would be a great misunderstanding of this doctrine to suppose that it is one of selfish indifference, which pretends that human beings have no business with each other's conduct in life, and that they should not concern themselves about the well-doing or well-being of one another, unless their own interest is involved. Instead of any diminution, there is need of a great increase of disinterested exertion to promote the good of others.

He was eager to point out that it was absurd to suppose that the choice lay between indifference on the one hand and force on the other. "But disinterested benevolence can find other instruments to persuade people to their good, than whips and scourges, either of the literal or the metaphorical sort."[36] This is an echo of Locke's sardonic observation in his *Letter on Toleration* that we can concern ourselves with other people's spiritual welfare without throwing them in jail or burning them at the stake.

Mill argued that we must think of ways of non-coercively encouraging other people's highest aspirations, carefully distinguishing between even the most strenuous exhortation on the one hand and punishment on the other; we may, and we should, tell other people exactly what we think of their behaviour in matters that reflect on their character. If we deplore their drinking, we should say so. If we think their literary tastes are vulgar, we should say so. Ordinary standards of politeness militate against this, but so much the worse for ordinary notions of politeness.

Though doing no wrong to any one, a person may so act as to compel us to judge him, and feel to him, as a fool, or as a being of an inferior order: and since this judgment and feeling are a fact which he would prefer to avoid, it is doing him a service to warn him of it beforehand, as of any other disagreeable consequence to which he exposes himself. It would be well, indeed, if this good office were much more freely rendered than the common notions of politeness at present permit, and if one person could honestly point out to another that he thinks him in fault, without being considered unmannerly or presuming.[37]

Himmelfarb quite rightly notices that Mill himself was quicker to object to other people taking a non-punitive interest in his conduct than this passage supposes he ought to have been.[38] But this does not in itself impugn the distinction. Punishment involved penalties that were organised either overtly and institutionally by the legal system, or covertly and unconsciously by the operations of a censorious and collective public opinion. Penalties were intended as threats before the event and as retribution after; they involved visiting their target with evil.

Mill's contemporaries were puzzled by his insistence on the difference between penalties strictly speaking and the accidental misfortunes that might befall us as a result of differences in taste. To Mill it was of the greatest importance because he saw moral coercion as the opinion-based shadow or background of legal coercion. In a democratic *society*, even in the absence of a democratic political system, public opinion was an organised force. Mill absorbed Tocqueville's conviction that what made the force so impressive was its silent and unobtrusive quality; where physical penalties aroused resistance in the person punished, the penalties of opinion worked in his soul. He might, indeed, become his own mental jailer.[39]

Mill's argument in *On Liberty* was deliberately repetitive. He was laying siege to a frame of mind that he thought permeated English society, and he set about driving it from one position after another. He also believed that few people had thought about the problems he had identified, and thus that it was particularly difficult to make the argument he wished to make.[40] This was not always in the interest of extending freedom. It was sometimes, and quite startlingly, in the interest of restricting it. Too few critics attend to the fact that Mill was not attacking only the habit of interfering with harmless conduct. He was equally concerned to attack the absence of rational and publicly understood principle that allowed harmful conduct to flourish unchecked while harmless conduct was repressed. "I have already observed that, owing to the absence of any recognised general principles, liberty is often granted where it should be withheld, as well as withheld where it should be granted," wrote Mill in the context of his claim that society took too little interest in the improvidence and fecklessness with which young people contracted marriage and brought children into the world without having any idea how they were to be reared and educated.[41] His argument was squarely in line with the basic principles underlying *On Liberty*; to produce children who could not be brought up properly was a double offence, once against the wretched children, and secondly against society at large:

It still remains unrecognised, that to bring a child into existence without a fair prospect of being able, not only to provide food for its body, but instruction and training for its mind, is a moral crime, both against the unfortunate offspring and against society; and that if the parent does not fulfil this obligation, the State ought to see it fulfilled, at the charge, as far as possible, of the parent.[42]

To throw unproductive extra bodies onto the labour market was an anti-social act.

Mill's unconcern with twentieth-century anxieties about privacy and intimacy is a striking feature of his bleakly high-principled acceptance of restrictions on marriage as well as on the parents' rights over their children.

To undertake this responsibility – to bestow a life which may be either a curse or a blessing – unless the being on whom it is to be bestowed will have at least the ordinary chances of a desirable existence, is a crime against that being. And in a country either over-peopled or threatened with being so, to produce children, beyond a very small number, with the effect of reducing the reward of labour by their competition, is a serious offence against all who live by the remuneration of their labour. The laws which, in many countries on the Continent, forbid marriage unless the parties can show that they have the means of supporting a family, do not exceed the legitimate powers of the State: and whether such laws be expedient or not (a question mainly dependent on local circumstances and feelings), they are not objectionable as violations of liberty.[43]

Mill was perhaps unwise to make so few concessions to the popular feeling that even where there are good prudential reasons not to marry, the impulsiveness of youth must be given some leeway. It appears to be an emotional blind spot that led him to pay so little attention to the more elaborate sentiment that intimate relationships are so valuable that we should make more room for them than narrowly prudential arguments can provide. At all events, it may have been such austere moments that gave him his reputation as an "intellectual iceberg."

The concluding chapter of "applications" added little to the argument of *On Liberty* in the narrow sense, but much to one's sense of

what Mill was after. He faced difficulties familiar to later generations. One awkward question was whether it was right to prevent
people getting together to do collectively what they had an individual right to do; running a brothel would be an example – for
fornication is not illegal or to be repressed by the collective censo-
riousness that he described as the "penalties of opinion"; but one
might wish to prevent people living off immoral earnings or trading
in sexual services. The same thought applies to gambling houses;
one might not object to individuals getting together in an informal
fashion to gamble, but still fear the effects of gambling dens.[44] Mill's
approach generally concentrated on detaching genuine offences
from their non-punishable causes. A man who gambled away his
family's housekeeping money was to be blamed, and if necessary
forced to look after his family; but he ought not to be treated worse
than if he had spent the housekeeping money on failed attempts to
invent electric lighting. Still, Mill also understood the problem of
attractive nuisances, and he hesitated to put his name to the principle that what a person is allowed to do another person must be
allowed to advise him to do.[45]

Mill also reminded his readers of a view that he made rather more
of in his *Principles of Political Economy* and *Representative Government*. There he argued that just as private individuals may ex-
hort and encourage where they may not coerce, so governments may
take a position on matters where they may neither forbid nor require any particular line of conduct. Moreover, governments may
act on such views when they consider how to distribute the burden
of taxation. Mill was ferociously opposed to temperance agitation,
partly because temperance reformers claimed that drinkers violated
their "social rights," and Mill thought the appeal to social rights
tyrannical. Yet he was ready to agree that while governments were
not entitled to tax alcoholic drink at a level designed to stop its
consumption, they were entitled to put a tax on alcoholic drink
rather than on tea or bread; supposing the tax to be necessary at all,
its incidence would be less damaging if it fell on drink than if it fell
on tea or bread.[46]

II

The question at whom and at what Mill aimed the weapons of *On
Liberty* has partially been answered by this sketch of the argument.

There were several distinct targets of his attack, and a brief list may fix our thoughts. At its vaguest but most encompassing, the target was the mid-Victorian middle-class conception of respectability, and the stifling effect it had on individuals whose lives were circumscribed by its demands. Mill and Mrs. Taylor were, in their own eyes, victims of its effects. Mill sometimes suggested that England was uniquely blighted by this, as it were, mass fear of and mass imposition of public disapproval of the unusual. To Pasquale Villari, he wrote that his essay "n'a guère de valoir que pour l'Angleterre."[47] This was hardly his considered view, but he was convinced that Italy and France were less socially repressive even when they were more politically repressive than Britain.

The largest target was the democratic disposition of mind deplored by Tocqueville in *Democracy in America*. To the extent that Tocqueville had been an accurate observer of opinion in the United States and a not absurdly over-anxious spectator of the march of democracy in France, Mill's essay must have had some purchase both in France and in the United States, as well as in England. The democratic frame of mind was an elusive prey, but exceedingly important to Mill. The distinction between true and false democracy was one that he continually recast; by the time of *On Liberty*, the most salient distinction lay between genuine self-government and the tyranny of the majority. Self-government certainly embraced most of the goals that professed democrats sought, including a chance for the ordinary person to exercise an influence on government by way of the ballot box and other devices; but for Mill it also had to embrace such character-improving devices as the requirement that everyone must play some part in actively managing the affairs of his or her own community, whether in jury service, or serving on parish councils, or in some novel way.[48]

The more urgent point, however, was to escape the tyranny of the majority. Following Tocqueville, Mill thought that the everyday understanding of democracy was insufficiently attentive to the difference between ruling oneself and being dominated by everyone else. It had been one of Mill's complaints against Bentham years before that Bentham had failed to make this necessary distinction; Mill agreed that it was progress to curtail the unbridled power of the former ruling classes, but it was not much progress if all it did was give unchecked power to "the majority."[49] What one might call the democratic frame of mind was the belief that there was something special about the opinion of the majority once the majority had settled on it, something over and above the mere fact that it happened to be the opinion of more than half the people in question. This majoritarian superstition was a peculiarly American vice, but it had more than a little in common with the passion for respectability that drove the English middle classes. That is, both were examples of the habit of thinking that if "everyone" believed something or other, it was faintly improper for an individual to doubt it.

Although there is little solid evidence to rest such a case on, it is not implausible to think that the passion with which Mill wrote *On Liberty* owed much to his antipathy to this deadly conjunction of the forces of respectability and the inevitable march of democracy. Paradoxically, the anti-liberal pressure of public opinion was increased by a factor that one might have thought would work in the opposite direction. Mill was almost as depressed by his contemporaries' inability to recognise intellectual authority where it was appropriate as by their readiness to defer to mere feelings that were not entitled to authority at all. It was the honour of the ordinary man that he could be led to embrace great things with his eyes open.[50] Nonetheless, he had to be led. He could not do all the work of self-development himself. Mill distinguished as sharply as he knew how between the pressure of the "likings and dislikings" of mass opinion and the persuasive force of insights and arguments that could sustain a rational scrutiny and a dispassionate assessment. One must not exaggerate the role of *rational* assessment in the acceptance of the insights generated by the outstanding individuals on whom Mill relied; to the extent that Mill has poets and social critics such as Goethe or Wordsworth in mind, some of their authority must be ascribed to the *affective* force of their insights. The point remains that Mill passionately wished his countrymen to acknowledge *some* form of intellectual, moral, and spiritual authority, one they could acknowledge freely and intelligently; if they were to do so, they must also understand how different such an acknowledgment is from mere subservience to social pressure.[51]

Behind this thought lay Mill's lifelong complaint against the influence of intuitionist philosophy. Intuitionism in any form was committed to the claim that indubitability was the mark of truth, and that there were many truths about the world, both scientific and ethical, that we knew because when we scrutinised them we were convinced that they *could not be* false. Mill was never particularly careful to make the intuitionist case as plausible as it might be made, but he understood well enough that intuitionism did not set out to guarantee large numbers of particular truths by appealing to their indubitability. The object of intuitionism was to guarantee principles and generalisations, such as the principle that every event has a cause, or the law of the conservation of matter, or the priority of the right over the good. Mill thought the doctrine was superstitious in whatever form it was presented. It was, he said, the great support of conservative doctrines and attitudes, and encouraged mankind to believe that any conviction which they held sufficiently strongly was warranted.[52] Since people were all too inclined to swallow whatever local orthodoxy they encountered and to regard it as revealed truth, the object of philosophy ought to be to unsettle this passion for certainty rather than to pander to it.

The difficulty that faced the would-be unsettler was not only that people find challenges to their ideas more or less painful, but that many people had been taught not to obtrude their own ideas upon others. This was where Mill's antipathy to Christian ethics became significant. It was not that he wished to destroy the existing clergy to replace them with a Coleridgean "clerisy." He did hope for the growth of a Coleridgean clerisy, but he had little anti-clerical animus. Nor was Mill eager to see Christianity as a social force in British life destroyed before it had been improved; in France, he thought, it was too late to rescue Christianity from the damage done to it by both the church and the anti-clerical, but in Britain, it was possible to revive it. Nonetheless, *On Liberty* was more committed than were Mill's more conciliatory discussions of Christianity to reducing the influence of the Calvinist view of the self.

The target of Mill's assault was self-abnegation.[53] He contrasted Christian self-abnegation with pagan self-assertion, the latter being a force capable of working great evil, but also of doing great good. "Pagan" was perhaps two sweeping a category; neither Plato nor Aristotle were theorists of the will to power, and the Stoic doctrine of *apatheia* taught something very like self-abnegation as the route to freedom. Mill, of course, was mostly concerned to attack the effects of Calvinism; it, he thought, had rendered its adherents timid, fearful of their own desires, and unambitious. Critics have, quite rightly, complained that Mill's association of Calvinism with weakness of will does an injustice to the many striking conjunctions of Calvinist allegiance and stiff-necked intransigence that we find both in fact and in fiction. Mill is not wholly without resources in his own defence, for it is certainly true that Calvinism denounced "self-will," and its characteristic view of education was that the first step was to break the child's wilful ways. Even John Locke's relatively benign and "child-centred" views on education insist that the beginnings of instruction lie in breaking the child's will. In any event, one can forgive Mill for following Machiavelli in praising "pagan self-assertion" to the detriment of the Christian ideal of self-abnegation. In gross at any rate that contrast holds up perfectly well.

We can now begin to see why *On Liberty* seemed to so many readers to be a root-and-branch assault on the English society of its day. For the truth is that it was such. Protestant self-abnegation was a poor foundation for Humboldtian *Bildung*; questioning received opinion was not something that came naturally to people brought up on a middle-class Protestantism. The peculiarly English conviction that scepticism was both wicked and unrespectable was likely to deaden such flickerings of independence as might occur. If they were then further stifled by the prevalence of intuitionist ideas about the irrefutability of commonplace moral and political convictions, the prospects of intellectual and cultural independence were slender indeed. As if this were not enough, Mill knew that there were many reasons of a wholly unsuperstitious kind why individuality would be hard to preserve in an industrial society. Such a society required more complicated forms of cooperation and collaboration than its agrarian predecessors; people would live closer and closer together, and therefore had to be more careful of each other's interests. In matters from sewerage to lighting, transport, and much else, they would need to make collective provision for their needs. Society would thus have to become more *organized*, more of a consciously organic whole. If this was not to bring the tyranny of the majority – or the tyranny of the benevolent, bourgeois, and bureaucratic Fabians or Comtists – a different social psychology must prevail. This could only be built on a positive enthusiasm for variety, eccentricity, novelty, strenuousness, self-overcoming. These were virtues more obviously at home in the writings of Goethe, whose work he knew well, and Nietzsche, whose work he never encountered, than in those of Bentham and James Mill.

III

The view I ascribe to Mill is, evidently, a view of liberty that is teleological, consequentialist, and genuinely, if awkwardly, utilitarian. It falls, because of its attention to the ideal perfection of individual character, within the class of what are today called perfectionist theories, even though Mill's contemporaries would have noticed that Mill had stolen the clothes of the anti-utilitarian moral theorists of his day in arguing so emphatically that a concern for individual perfection was a utilitarian concern. Being comprehensive, teleological, even ambiguously perfectionist, it stands in sharp contrast to later contractualist theories, such as that offered by both of John Rawls's accounts of the basis of a liberal society. Less obviously, it is also at odds, though less simply as well as less obviously, with the pluralist liberalism of Isaiah Berlin's *Two Concepts of Liberty*, and, for the matter of that with the Idealist liberalism of T. H. Green and the pragmatist liberalism of John Dewey.[54] Now that we are tolerably clear about what Mill believed, it is easier to understand why *On Liberty* relates so awkwardly to its successors. What follows is not a comprehensive account of Mill's later admirers, critics, and rivals, but an attempt to extract particular points of contrast for our more local purposes. I begin with the contrast between Mill and Rawls, since this is so striking, then say something about the role of pluralism in Mill's work, then say a little more about the communitarian and anti-communitarian aspects of his liberalism to sharpen our sense of how Mill's ideas were and were not assimilable within the Idealist-pragmatist tradition.

The contrast between Mill's defence of liberalism and John Rawls's rests on what is now a commonplace, though the implications of that commonplace for discussions of liberalism are perhaps less well understood. Rawls has insisted, particularly in his recent *Political Liberalism*, that liberals must not try to impose a "comprehensive moral doctrine" on their society, but only to establish terms on which persons who hold a plurality of different comprehensive views can live with one another.[55] The reasoning behind this fastidiousness is complicated but persuasive. In part it rests on the plausible thought that social stability is easier to achieve if we do not thrust contentious moral and religious ideals upon people unwilling to receive them. It is a central element in Rawls's liberalism that the "strains of commitment" should not threaten the social order, and it seems obvious enough that we would feel less committed to a social order that espouses moral values we disapprove of.[56] In part, however, it rests on a moral value that goes to the heart of Rawls's view of the basis of liberal politics. This is the idea of the inviolability of the individual.[57] An important element of that inviolability is the inviolability of the individual conscience. Such considerations give each person a right not to live under institutional arrangements that violate his or her conscience. A constraint on anyone claiming such a right is that their conscience must not be so "unreasonable" that they impose unfair burdens on others; the difficulty – perhaps greater in theory than in practice – is to give an account of what it is to have "reasonable" conscientious scruples on which secular liberals, secular conservatives, religious conservatives, and religious liberals can agree.[58] This, however, is one of the things that a constant attention to fairness may cope with, although my own belief is that it will not, and that the ground of consensus must be sought in a prior agreement on the facts of social life and the consequences of change, rather than in a principled abstention from taking them into account.

The details of Rawls's developed theory are not our concern. The contrast with Mill is. Rawls begins with a conception of society as *essentially* a contractual arrangement between individuals; the considerations on which we have just focussed reflect the view that society is, for purposes of moral discussion, best understood as an agreement on terms by individuals concerned to preserve the central core of their interests. Almost all of Rawls's differences from Mill follow from Rawls's contractualist beginnings. So, for example, the "strains of commitment" interpreted as strains upon our consciences are not a simple sociological fact; people feel them only when they have a particular conception of themselves, one in which their conscientious scruples play an important part. It is arguable that late twentieth-century Americans have retained much of their seventeenth-century Puritan prickliness, and that this is therefore a proper starting point for an account of liberalism in the United

States. Mill, to the contrary, thought that the problem in Victorian England was to rouse people to understand that their convictions were something that they could revise in the light of the evidence and their other convictions. Individuals were under too little strain of commitment rather than too much. They either stood pat on the deliverances of conscience or took the majority opinion as they encountered it as definitive of what any rational person could believe.

Someone who resisted armchair sociological speculation of this sort might say that it is an obvious *moral* truth that we should start from some such principle as the inviolability of the individual conscience, no matter what the degree of local fastidiousness. But Mill would have resisted the claim that we should *start* with such a principle. This is not to deny that we should take the principle seriously; Mill took it very seriously. Yet we may still believe that it is not a foundational principle, but a derivative one. It is certainly a central element in liberal morality; but we should think of it as a principle that becomes increasingly important in the collective life of "man as a progressive being." Just as freedom becomes an essential element in the welfare of an individual with a strong sense of his or her own individuality and a commitment to self-development, so the passionate attachment to following our own consciences that is expressed in the claim of inviolability would spring up in a liberal society – though it might well spring up in others as well.[59]

Whether we begin from Mill's position or Rawls's makes a great difference to what one supposes that liberal project is, even though it makes less difference to how that project should be pursued. Rawls writes as though the liberal project is to create a society of individuals whose primary commitments are to their own private well-being on the one hand and to their own consciences on the other. Given that view of the opening situation, what liberalism must be "about" is the task of finding fair terms of social cooperation among individuals who are willing to respect others' rights on condition that their own are equally respected.[60] It is not surprising that this results in the thought that justice is the first of all social virtues; nor is it surprising that the liberal commitment to freedom emerges as a branch of the liberal commitment to justice. This is why Ronald Dworkin, explicitly explicating liberalism as understood by Rawls, explains liberalism in terms of the right to equal concern and respect.[61] To Mill and his disciples that must seem wrong. Certainly *some* freedoms will be protected by the attempt to secure justice; the utilitarian account of justice as concerned above all with security implies that freedom of movement, personal safety, and no doubt many freedoms of speech and association should be secured to individuals. But Mill's liberalism is centred on Mill's account of what freedom is and why it matters; and part of that argument is an argument against an excessive concern with security.

Rawls's subsequent account of the implications for international law of his theory of justice as fairness is worth glancing at for its implications for *domestic* politics. Rawls raises a question that Mill's notorious essay "A Few Thoughts on Non-Intervention" had raised a hundred and thirty years before; when and on what grounds may an outside power violate the sovereignty of other nations?[62] Rawls has recently argued that any society that does not violate the fundamental rights of its population should be immune to intervention from other societies for the sake of whatever economic, social, religious, or moral principles those other societies may have in mind. This is the natural counterpart to his insistence in *Political Liberalism* that social groups which do not violate the fundamental rights of their members are entitled to immunity within a single society. This provides the basis of what Rawls calls a "reasonable" pluralism. We are now faced with two possibilities. The first is that we can give a non-liberal account of fundamental rights: a just society is one in which no group attempts to impose its view of the world on any other, though everyone stands ready to aid persons whose fundamental rights are violated, either by members of their own or any other social group. The assumption would be that protection from assault, deliberate starvation, acute emotional deprivation, and so on, are fundamental rights, but that nobody has a "right to be free." If they did, then it would in principle be possible for outsiders to police the groups to which they belong in order to make sure that that right had not been violated. The second possibility is that we explain fundamental rights in terms of liberal values and so give society at large the right to police constituent groups within our own society, and to police other societies where we can do it, in order to impose a liberal world view. Rawls plainly wants to avoid the second position, but he may in the process have abandoned too much of what traditional liberalism seeks to achieve, for it looks as though the pluralism he accepts could embrace a society in which every cultural allegiance was to illiberal values, so long as no group's members acted aggressively towards any other's, and members who wished to leave a particular group (or country) could do so. Whether such a situation is stable over the long run is debatable; one might think that any group ready to allow its members to exit would adopt more liberal values over time, or conversely that any group of a thoroughgoing illiberalism would soon refuse to allow its members to exit freely. Whether it is a form of liberalism at all is also debatable.

Still, our concern is rather with what Mill's liberalism amounts to in contrast. It is an awkward consequence of Mill's consequentialism that *in principle* it licenses liberals to promote the growth of freedom by all means whatever. Mill himself denied that any society had a right to civilise another by brute force,[63] but it is not obvious why he thought so, nor that he was consistent in so thinking. What liberals want is the greatest possible expansion of the values of individuality, open-mindedness, and self-criticism; as a good consequentialist Mill cannot escape the thought that we may contemplate coercive means to such an end. We may suppose that there are all sorts of good reasons for not trying to force liberation on unwilling adults. The case of India was offered as an explicit exception to the general rule against paternalism, in much the same spirit as Elizabethan England and the Russia of Peter the Great. Still, conservative religious groups such as the Hassidic Jews who follow the Lubavicher Rabbi or the Amish farmers of Pennsylvania who surely do no harm to anyone except (arguably) themselves and their children, may think that relying on Mill's judgment as to when the rest of the human race has reached "the maturity of their faculties" is a dangerous business.[64] Moreover, Mill's emphasis on protecting children from the neglect or ill-treatment of their parents, together with his feminism, would give them reason to fear that they will be prevented from doing what they very much wish to do – that is, from isolating their children from the secular currents of the wider society. More interestingly, perhaps, they may find their marital relations held up to unkind scrutiny, too, since the considerations that suggest we should liberate children from their parents also suggest that we should curtail the authority of husbands over wives.

Mill expressly repudiated this view of the consequences of his doctrines. Writing of the Mormon practice of polygamy, he observed:

No one has a deeper disapprobation than I have of this Mormon institution; both for other reasons, and because, far from being in any way countenanced by the principle of liberty, it is a direct infraction of that principle, being a mere rivetting of the chains of one half of the community, and an emancipation of the other from reciprocity of obligation towards them. Still, it must be remembered that this relation is as much voluntary on the part of the women concerned in it, and who may be deemed the sufferers by it, as is the case with any other form of the marriage institution; and however surprising this fact may appear, it has its explanation in the common ideas and customs of the world, which teaching women to think marriage the one thing needful, make it intelligible that many a woman should prefer being one of several wives, to not being a wife at all. Other countries are not asked to recognise such unions, or release any portion of their inhabitants from their own laws on the score of Mormonite opinions. But when the dissentients have conceded to the hostile sentiments of others, far more than could justly be demanded; when they have left the countries to which their doctrines were unacceptable, and established themselves in a remote corner of the earth, which they have been the first to render habitable to human beings; it is difficult to see on what principles but those of tyranny they can be prevented from living there under what laws they please, provided they commit no aggression on other nations, and allow perfect freedom of departure to those who are dissatisfied with their ways.[65]

That is about as unequivocal a statement of the non-interventionist view as one could wish. It is one that puts Mill squarely on the same side as the Rawls of *Political Liberalism*.

But Mill was not exactly of one mind. He opened the flood gates himself by remarking in so casual a fashion that until mankind is capable of improvement by rational discussion, they had better be dragged down the path of progress by Akhbar, Charlemagne, Elizabeth I, or Peter the Great – and doubtless by the East India Company.[66] He was eager to insist that in countries such as Britain and the United States the time had long since arrived when everyone was to be presumed amenable to rational persuasion. Nonetheless, he was quite right to raise the possibility of what I have elsewhere called "compulsory liberation." The thought behind compulsory liberation is not that we ought to tour the world looking for people to emancipate, by brute force if necessary. Mill did not hold liberal-Kiplingesque views about the white man's burden being to rescue his fellow man from immemorial torpor. It was, rather, the thought that if we found ourselves for whatever reason in a position where we had to act, we should not flinch from forcing liberal values on those we could affect.

The positive argument for compulsory liberation is thus no more elaborate than the suggestion that if we *can* force people into the liberal fold, we may. For Rawls, and for liberals who think like him, the rights of individuals and peoples rule out such a suggestion from the beginning. In a utilitarian perspective, the question turns on the grounds, which were provided by Mill but not much addressed by him, for not engaging in intra- or international wars of cultural liberation. There are four that can be extracted from *On Liberty* without violence to the text and its spirit. The first is essentially prudential; the second is a recognition of the importance of family and social loyalties; the third hinges on the good of *self*-development; the last on the (possibly) intrinsic value of variety and plurality. The first and second close the gap between Mill and Rawls on matters of practice while leaving them at odds over principle; the third closes both the principled and the practical gap between Mill and Idealists such as Green and pragmatists such as Dewey, while the last raises some awkward questions about both Mill's liberalism and that of Isaiah Berlin.

Mill's position is that a government may espouse but not enforce what Rawls calls a comprehensive theory of the good life. The liberal view that I have so far ascribed to Mill amounts to the thought that it is a legitimate object of social policy to bring into existence as many autonomous, self-critical, public-spirited men and women as possible. There are two things to be noticed about this view. The first is that Mill treats governments as if they are individuals writ large; individuals can advocate moral visions without imposing them on others, and in Mill's eyes governments can do so, too. This view animates his distinction between the coercive and the educative roles of government in the discussion of government action in his *Principles of Political Economy*.[67] For all its merits, it may embody a mistake. One might say that governments are *essentially* the bearers of authority, so that their advocacy cannot be on all fours with that of individuals. Their resources, too, are greater than those of any individual; they must be tempted, as individuals are not, to employ increased resources to bear down opposition or disbelief. (In some contexts, such as that of the contemporary United States, of course, the argument would run in the other direction – that government is so unpopular, and its agents have so little moral authority, that they would do better not to espouse any particular good cause lest they give it the kiss of death.)

It might be said, in the spirit of Robert Nozick's *Anarchy, State and Utopia*, that governments do not own the resources they employ in the way individuals do; if I choose to spend my money on publishing views that others do not share, that's my business, but a government's resources are really the taxpayers' resources, government action is more like my spending your money to advocate views that I hold and you detest. This last point Mill would have had little difficulty with. That governments drew upon the labour of their subjects he acknowledged; that their subjects had a natural proprietorship over their incomes and resources of the kind this argument presupposes, he denied. The previous objections he seemed not to consider with the seriousness they deserved.

If Mill regarded governments as endowed with the same right to press a moral case as anyone else, he also saw that there were many reasons for them to tread very gently. For one thing, Mill was well aware that governments are intrinsically clumsy. Where individuals might cajole, charm, seduce, and woo others into an acceptance of a new world view, governments were all too likely to arouse their resentment and antagonism. As Mill tartly observed, one argument against the public enforcement of *any* moral view was that when governments interfered in private life they were overwhelmingly likely to do so in the wrong place.[68] This would be one prudential argument against unrestricted interference. All the same, Mill's view was not Rawls's. Rawls's *Political Liberalism* proposes that liberals should reassure the devout that they will not be put under pressure, but Mill merely proposes that liberal governments should act delicately.

Consider an example where the difference between them might make a difference. The famous U.S. Supreme Court decision in *Wisconsin* v. *Yoder* established that the Amish were exempt from the requirement to send their children to school beyond the eighth grade. One view of this decision might be that it was rightly decided as the result of a "balancing act" between different policy considerations. A society that values religious commitment *and* an educated work force may have to trade the one against the other; in this case, however, the Supreme Court rightly held that the Amish were unlikely to let their children become unemployed whatever their acquaintance with formal education, and that the balance thus tilted towards allowing the Amish to withdraw their children from school at fourteen.[69] One can imagine Mill agreeing: truth aside, passionate religious conviction is valuable, and deserves protection. Family ties deserve some consideration, too, and governments ought not to interfere where all members of the family appear to be in agreement. Once again, this is not Rawls's view. Rawls's grounds for agreeing with the Court rest on the idea that an insistence on children being educated to the age of eighteen imposes a comprehensive secular liberal view of the good life on a group that does not share it.

However, one might think – and Mill might have thought – that the case was wrongly decided. On one liberal understanding of the interests of the child in this case, it was a violation of the interests of the child to allow the parents to withdraw him from school. The child's interests "as a progressive being" lay in preserving an open mind until the end of adolescence. If the Amish cannot preserve their hold over their young people without preventing them from learning whatever an American high school might teach them after the age of fourteen, they have no business trying to preserve their way of life at all. The crucial question is not the rights of the parents, but the interests of the child. Quite what follows then is obscure. On one view, the Millian ought to be moved by the changes between nineteenth- and twentieth-century society to extend Mill's insistence on the duty of parents to fit their offspring for the society in which they will later live – and thus insist that young Yoder remain at school. On another, young Yoder's chief obligation in later life is to be self-supporting and not a drain on other people's resources, and his parents have done enough to ensure that he can do that. Had the boy wanted to go to school, his parents might be made to let him do so. If not, not.

One might suppose that Mill's position ought to have been something like this: liberal consequentialism does not license attempts to bully the Amish parents into changing their minds about their own lives. Any such attempt would surely be counterproductive, ineffective, and therefore pointless.[70] The adult Amish's beliefs harm only the adult Amish (if they are restrained from hobbling their children's acquaintance with the outside world), and this puts them squarely into the class of the self-regarding actions that are protected from coercive intereference. Children are another matter. They are, *ex hypothesi*, susceptible to something other than rational persuasion. They are, from the liberal perspective, to be protected against youthful indoctrination that makes them incapable of freedom as adults.

It is thus good liberal policy to insist that they go to school until eighteen, painful though that is for their parents. The principle that parents may not inhibit the development of freedom in their offspring has far-reaching consequences. Many of them are quite at odds with the practice of American governments and perhaps at odds with a principled adherence to the separation of church and state. A liberal government might insist that parochial and religious schools teach comparative religion alongside whatever particular faith animated their founders and the parents of the children they teach, in order that the children should at least know what the world has to offer. Since liberalism is distinguished from other comprehensive views by its attachment to criticism, there can be no question of protecting *it* from criticism in such classes, but the classes themselves would be justified as a means of allowing children to decide for themselves when they reach the age of reason what view of the world to adopt.

Given the resistance such policies would surely arouse, it is easy to see how Mill and Rawls might end by advocating similar but not identical policies in practice. Mill's sensitivity to the imprudence of more than modestly aggressive policies to favour a liberal perspective would yield the same results as Rawls's principled forbearance. However, there may be unaggressive possibilities that a Millian liberal would seize and a Rawlsian liberal would have to forego. Consider the potentialities of a national broadcasting service, or the educational possibilities latent within a national health service. Mill's liberalism would encourage us to make the most of them; Rawls's view that the state ought to be neutral as between competing conceptions of the good life would apparently require us to forego such opportunities.

A more principled argument against an energetic state frequently employed by Mill will lead us from Mill's differences with John Rawls to his differences with his Idealist and pragmatist successors. Mill suggests in support of his "no coercion save in self-defence" rule that it matters very much that we come to our mature view of ourselves by self-chosen paths. This means, among other things, that if *per impossibile* there were a pill that we could swallow in order to make ourselves good Millian liberals, we probably ought not to swallow it, and if we concluded that we ought to swallow it, we should do so with regret. This provides another reason for non-coercion when dealing with adults. We might go to the length of *nagging* couch potatoes – perhaps by showing public service advertisements during the intervals of televised football games to suggest that they should engage in strenuous rethinking about their lives – but that is about it. The reason is not that individuals possess an inviolability that entitles them *not* to be badgered and harassed, but that one of the goods of the pursuit of individual autonomy is precisely that it is *our own* pursuit.

The fact that this yields a requirement of liberal self-restraint similar to that produced by the principle of individual inviolability may tempt some critics to think that this shows what others have said, that Mill relies much more heavily on a natural rights view of liberty than he is willing to admit. The better gloss is that talk of rights is a shorthand; the deeper considerations are those of social prudence and individual self-development. "No coercion except in self-defence" summarises the liberal's calculation of where the arguments for and against coercive liberation come down. To talk of rights, said Mill, was to talk of important interests, and an important individual interest that reinforces the prudential arguments for a restrained policy is an interest in self-development.

This suggests how Mill's liberalism relates to that of an Idealist like Green or a pragmatist like Dewey. Mill, Green, and Dewey held surprisingly similar views on individual development in spite of their very different metaphysical – or in Dewey's case anti-metaphysical – convictions. I do not deny that Green thought of the self with which we ultimately identify as Godlike or even God, nor that Dewey turned away from Green's moral philosophy in the early 1890s because Green separated the empirical selves of individuals too sharply from the Self that was the reality behind the universe as a whole.[71] I only want to emphasise the importance to all three of the idea that we become who we are by creating a self that we regard as "ours." It is because we want people to identify strongly with the views and aspirations that they think of as constituting their own identity that we mind that they arrive at their allegiances by an autonomous route. Unlike the prudential argument that coercion causes pain and resentment, or the "balancing" argument that asks us to set family and local loyalties in the scale against the value of liberty, this is a genuinely liberal argument for restraint in the pursuit of liberal goals.

Where Mill and later liberals of a Greenian or Deweyan stripe differ more sharply is in their understanding of the relations of individuals and their communities. Mill was in several senses of the term a "communitarian liberal." He thought social philosophy should begin by contemplating human beings not in a state of nature or behind a veil of ignorance, but immersed in their social setting. He shared neither the ontology of Hobbes and Locke nor the methodological convictions of Rawls. Mill had no doubt that it was an important truth that we grow up in communities of different kinds, and form our ideas and ideals in the course of learning to live with others. He thought that most of us find it difficult to imagine ourselves outside the social settings in which we move; and he wanted to create a *society* of liberals, not a collection of liberal monads.[72] All this he shared with Green and Dewey, and with most people who have not acquired some strong theoretical reason for thinking differently.

Nonetheless, Mill was not a communitarian in at least two further ways, and these set him sharply apart from Green and Dewey. Because Mill was an empiricist and a naturalist, he thought of individuals as only partially socialized creatures. Idealists and pragmatists were disinclined to stress the way in which embodied beings like ourselves were to some degree at the mercy of psycho-physiological forces over which we have limited and quite slowly developed authority. One might say that this was Mill's non-theological acknowledgment of the concept of original sin. In Green the idea of original sin was replaced by his emphasis on the distance that remains between empirical selves and the universal self that is God; Dewey deplored any talk of original sin whatever. While Mill did not believe in the theology of original sin, he believed in a good deal of the psychology and sociology it implied. But not all of our unsocial and unsocialised promptings were to be treated with caution. Many were beneficial. We might light on new visions of the world and new ideals of human happiness. Once these visions were understood, they could be imparted to our fellows with some hope of acceptance by them. Until then, however, we might have to stand by them at the price of social isolation. Mill thus wanted to encourage a degree of separation from our social attachments to which Dewey and Green would have been hostile. I have always thought Mill was right and they were wrong.

When assessing the merits of one or other interpretation of liberalism, we inevitably balance different liberal aspirations against one another. Which liberalism we find most congenial is a matter of emphasising one aspiration rather than another. It is time to take account of one last aspiration. Mill dedicates *On Liberty* to "the absolute and essential importance of human development in its richest diversity."[73] It is thus a treatise on a form of pluralism. Yet Mill was quite clear that ways of life had no right to exist unmolested simply because they added variety to the human landscape. The British were not invited into India, but the East India Company's government of India transformed Indian life very drastically, and Mill justified this intervention as a means of development.[74] Mill was not in the usual sense an imperialist. He had no particular enthusiasm for imperial projects, and thought that once the British had given the Indian subcontinent the tools of self-government, their next task was to go home and leave the Indians to work out their own destiny. Still, Mill had no doubt that until that time arrived the East India Company was acting in the best interests of the Indian people and ought to continue doing so. There was little room in Mill's mind for the thought that what he saw as the superstitious, indolent, and intermittently violent life of the Indian subcontinent was to be enjoyed as one more variant on the theme of a diverse and contradictory human nature. Comparison with one distinguished twentieth-century pluralist, Isaiah Berlin, may sharpen the point. Berlin is a moral pluralist, and one of the grounds he offers for placing a high value on negative liberty is that there are many different acceptable ways of life, and negative liberty allows them to coexist. Mill in contrast was committed to the view that there is in principle a "right answer" to every moral question; since the British know what the Indians do not, and are in a position to make the right answer stick, they had better do so.

This is a very different outlook from that which holds that one community has no right to civilise another against its will, which was set out by Kant.[75] But it is also at odds with the principle of no coercion except in self-defence, a principle that has sometimes been taken as coextensive with Mill's "very simple principle." But "no coercion except in self-defence" is not identical with "no coercion save to prevent harm to other"; the first places a constraint on *who* may engage in coercion that the second does not. The first implies that a fitting reply to the suggestion that the British might properly try to teach nineteenth-century Indians how to become good Victorian liberals would be that it was none of their business, since the Indians were doing the *British* no harm. The second is less restrictive; if we thought that the Indians were doing "harm" to their children, their neighbours, or whomever else, we might decide it was our business – that is, that it was the business of anyone who could act to prevent the harm in question. A direct appeal to the utilitarian backing of the entire essay is even less restrictive; Mill was clear enough that paternalism was justified *if* the facts warranted it. The anxiety that the moral hyperactivism implicit in utilitarianism induces in many critics is only exacerbated by the suggestion that "we" – whoever "we" are – occupy a morally privileged position from whose height we can decide the fate of the less privileged. Obviously, one form of pluralism is sustained by the counterclaim that there are no right answers in ethics, and that nobody can occupy that privileged position in virtue of having that answer.

To a degree Mill weakened the force of the claim that there were right answers to moral problems by suggesting that even though the "right answer" was right for utilitarian reasons, it was delivered by the judgment of a suitably sensitive critic, and not by any very simple utilitarian algorithm.[76] This might imply that there could be several incompatible "right answers" to a given question, an idea not as odd as it sounds: the paintings of Monet and Cézanne provide right but different answers to the question of how to render a landscape for late nineteenth-century sensibilities. If one thinks of ultimate moral questions as having much in common with, and perhaps even as being identical with, aesthetic questions about the shape of a life, it is not foolish to think that discussion of the ends of life will result in plural answers.

Pluralism and liberalism – at any rate, some liberalisms – are thus awkward allies. One form of pluralism, indeed, is consistent with thoroughgoing illiberalism, namely the form in which an overarching, unconstitutional, undemocratic, and anything-but-liberal political authority allows specified social groups to handle the affairs of their own members. The Ottoman Empire was not a liberal enterprise, but operated after such a fashion. Another form is liberal, in the sense that it amounts to the creation of a peace treaty between groups, in order to give each group the freedom to conduct its life as it chooses; but the establishment of a peace treaty does not secure the prevalence of liberal values outside anything other than the political realm, nor does it secure to group members more freedom than their group cares to grant. A pluralism of this kind might be consistent with the Roman Catholic church being able to visit heretics with sanctions, perhaps to deprive them of their livelihoods, so long as the church does not attempt to control the lives of non-Catholics and does not prevent members leaving the church. The Dutch state is more liberal than most, yet it financially aids Catholic universities that can dismiss theologians whose doctrines they dislike.

Such a peace treaty presupposes a liberal state in the background, since that allows members of the church to leave without suffering civil disabilities. A theocratic state, as opposed to a liberal state, might tolerate more diversity than we would suppose likely, but would not offer legal guarantees of this kind. One view of the transformation of the Catholic church in the United States is that it has been forced to become more liberal, and to be more liberal than it is elsewhere, precisely because its members are guaranteed an unsanctioned exit. The theory put forward in John Rawls's *Political Liberalism* is liberal in this fashion; the requirement that they do not violate the human rights of their members constrains the authority any group can exercise over its members. But the theory is not comprehensively liberal; there is no suggestion that the group should be urged or encouraged to adopt liberal conceptions of authority or liberal arrangements for its internal government. Catholics may not chase after their departed members to do them ill, but they may violate equal opportunity in recruiting for the priesthood, and impose burdens that liberals would disapprove of: they are not obliged to accept women as candidates for the priesthood, and they can impose the requirement of celibacy.

The moment of truth for a pluralist comes when he is asked whether he is happy to see a great variety of non-liberal ways of life flourish for the sake of variety, or whether he really wishes to see only a variety of liberal ways of life even if the result is less variety than there would be by admitting non-liberal ways of life. Mill ducked that question by insisting that as things stood, we had too much to lose by curtailing anything but grossly illiberal ways of life; we knew too little about what would in the end suit human beings to be justified in curbing all but the most approved liberal ways of life. Isaiah Berlin's liberalism causes his critics some difficulty because Berlin's pluralism is straightforward and his liberalism therefore not; Berlin would rather see vivid, non-liberal ways of life flourish than see them suppressed for the sake of the spread of liberal principles. The question, then, is not whether there are non-liberal forms of moral and political pluralism, but whether liberalism entails pluralism at all, and whether Mill believed that it did.

Mill thought it entailed one kind of pluralism, about which he and Berlin agree. We have no definitive, unchallengeable answer to the question of what the good life consists in, and we must allow experiment to winnow out the mistakes and refine the better answers. There is one kind of pluralism over which Mill and Berlin disagree. Mill thought that in the last resort a rational morality reduced to a single principle, and Berlin dissents. Berlin is, and Mill was not, an ethical pluralist. Berlin holds the common sense view that freedom is one thing and happiness another; Mill argued that the search for freedom was a search for happiness.[77] What is left standing is two puzzles. The first is whether Mill thought that answers to the question How shall we live? would eventually converge and so eliminate diversity; the second whether Mill thought that irrespective of the answer to that question, sheer variety was something to be valued for its own sake. We know that Berlin's answer to the two questions is no and yes – that answers to How shall I live? do not converge, and that variety is intrinsically worth preserving.

I do not know the answer to my question. It is possible that Mill was not of one mind about the answer; it is possible that he never put the questions to himself in quite the form I have given them, and so never confronted ambiguities in his own views; it is possible that he had a clear but complicated view, and never found an occasion to spell it out. The difficulty it makes for his liberalism is simple enough to describe. Mill argues, against liberticide theorists like Comte, that we do not know enough about human well-being to warrant us in trumping individual choices except to prevent harm to others. This suggests that Mill may have thought that *if* we knew enough about human welfare, we might trump misguided choices on paternalist grounds, so that in the end science trumps liberty. But he might equally have thought that *if* we were ever to reach the point where that was in principle a live possibility, it would not be in practice a live possibility, because nobody would simultaneously be sufficiently in their right mind to be a claimant to the usual liberties and yet so perverse as manifestly that is to say, *really* manifestly – to act against their own interests.

Mill's arguments always revealed traces of his attraction to and scepticism of the Saint-Simonian and Comtist view of the transition from the present critical phase of history to the organic phase that will end it. By the time he wrote *On Liberty*, he had lost the enthusiasm visible in early essays such as *The Spirit of the Age*. Even in the 1860s, however, Mill seems to have thought that something like the Saint-Simonian view of history might be true, but that the Saint-Simonians generally, and Comte particularly, were much better at explaining why the critical phase had been going strong for eight centuries than why we should expect it to end within the next thirty-five years.[78] In other words, the arguments for freedom and experiment in *On Liberty* might be superseded by the discovery of the ultimate truth about how we should live, but that discovery and its universal, uncoerced acceptance would be several centuries off, and therefore not an option worth discussing now. A further difficulty, however, is that Mill relied on the analogies between scientific and moral progress and at the same time resisted them. Thus Comte scorned the idea of free speech on the grounds that there was no free speech in science. Mill acknowledged that the authority of the properly trained was, in science, very great; but he also noted that a scientific consensus was not maintained by coercion, and then suggested that moral debate was anyway not on all fours with debate about findings in chemistry. So, it appears that the response to Comte was first to deny that there was no place for free speech in science, and second to deny that moral progress was sufficiently like scientific progress to sustain any argument like Comte's.

I am inclined to believe that Mill held the following view. There *is* an answer to the question what ways of life best suit human beings; it is not a unitary answer, because human nature varies a good deal from one person to another, and therefore yields diverse answers – though these are answers that have a common form, since they will be answers about what conduces to the long-term well-being of the people in question. To reach those answers, we need experiments in living because human nature is exceedingly ill-understood. What we see is the manifestations of human nature as it has been socialised in a variety of ways, of which many are inimical to human flourishing. Mill argued more continuously in *The Subjection of Women* than in *On Liberty* that we have little idea of what we might achieve if we adjusted the ways we socialise the young so as to enable them to live more flourishing and self-actualised existences thereafter, but the thought plainly sustains *On Liberty*, too.[79] Women might be the most immediate benefi-ciaries of a deeper understanding of how far the interaction of socialisation and human nature distorts or hides the possibility of new forms of happiness, but humankind generally would be the ultimate beneficiaries of such an understanding. Hence Mill's never-realised hopes for the science of ethology.

Human nature is malleable, and as we work on our own charac-ters, so we open up some indeterminacy in the answer to the ques-tion of how best to live. We do not only come to be better at pursuing happiness, we change our view of what happiness is. We can also change our own characters so as to be better able to live by the views we come to. Mill, as I have argued elsewhere, suggested that the answer to ultimate questions about what sort of happiness to pursue lay in the realm of aesthetic judgment.[80] Aesthetic judg-ment has a tendency not to converge in any very straightforward way; it is, in that sense, the antithesis of scientific judgment. Mill is hard to interpret because he wanted both to emphasise the place of scientific rationality and to leave space for aesthetic judgment in determining the ends of life. The experimental life would, if this is a proper interpretation of Mill, have a tendency to settle some questions while opening up others. It would thus promote and destroy pluralism at the same time.

How much pluralism does this yield? It yields as many distinctive and therefore different lives as there are different people; it does not yield as many different political systems as there are human communities. There are many common tasks that governments must perform, and any society concerned with efficiency will have them performed in the same way. It does not yield an infinity of cultural options (in the anthropological sense of "cultural"), since many cultures now visible will vanish, because they rest on superstitious beliefs that cannot withstand inspection. In other senses of "cultural" it yields room for infinite variety; there is no sign that the number of available musical, sculptural, literary, and other aesthetic *formulae* will soon diminish, and no sign that we shall soon settle down to repetitively re-creating works of art to a single pattern. Since Mill's borrowings from von Humboldt and Goethe imply that aesthetic invention is the model of experiments in living, we should have no fear that Mill's liberalism is likely to reduce the number of available cultural options to one. Mill's pluralism remains less hospitable to non-liberal and illiberal ways of life than Berlin's pluralism, though perhaps not very much less hospitable. The reason why the gap may not be as great as one would imagine at first sight is that vivid, fully-realised lives for the sake of which Mill, like Berlin, defends freedom, may also be realised in non-liberal settings. Where they are, the liberal will face a familiar transition problem: how much of the vividness and commitment can be kept when beliefs and attitudes change in a liberal direction? It is every moderniser's question. That Mill was more inclined than Berlin to sacrifice vivid traditional societies to less vivid modern ones goes without saying. That he was wrong to make that choice is a more contentious claim. It is also one that there is no space to discuss any further.

NOTES

1 See the interesting collection of the first reviews of *On Liberty* assembled in Pyle 1994.

2 As Joseph Hamburger (1991) is the latest of a long line of critics to argue.

3 On the "separateness of persons," see Rawls 1971, 27; my discussion of utilitarianism in Ryan 1970, 227–29, made a similar though not identical point.

4 On Mill's career in the service of the East India Company, see Zastoupil 1994 and Moir 1990.

5 For instance, I pay no attention to the difficulty of giving an account of the concept of "harm," since I can add nothing to the discussion by Joel Feinberg (1984), and I am content to endorse Jeremy Waldron's (1987) insistence that Mill would have counted the mental discomfort caused when our prejudices are shaken not as a harm but as good for us.

6 *Later Letters*, CW XIV:141.

7 For those in search of something sharper, Himmelfarb 1973 offers a notably unkind account of the conception, purposes, content, and effects of the book.

8 J. M. Robson's Textual Introduction to *CW* X gives a complete account of the writing of *Auguste Comte and Positivism*; Mill was deterred from tackling Comte in 1854 by his own antipathy to Harriet Martineau, whose recent translations and commentaries would have been the ostensible occasion for his *compte rendu*, and even more by Harriet Taylor's antipathy to Mrs. Martineau. See *CW* X:cxxix–cxxxii.

9 *Comte and Positivism*, CWX:343.

10 " 'The grand, leading principle, towards which every argument unfolded in these pages directly converges, is the absolute and essential importance of human development in its richest diversity.' – WILHELM VON HUMBOLDT: *Sphere and Duties of Government.*" On Liberty, CW XVIII:215.

11 *On Liberty*, CW XVIII:225.

12 Tocqueville 1994.

13 "Civilization," *CW* XVIII:121.

14 *On Liberty*, CW XVIII:219.

15 "It is proper to state that I forego any advantage which could be derived to my argument from the idea of abstract right, as a thing independent of utility. I regard utility as the ultimate appeal on all ethical questions; but it must be utility in the largest sense, grounded on the permanent interests of man as a progressive being. Those interests, I contend, authorize the subjection of individual spontaneity to external control, only in respect to those actions of each, which concern the interest of other people." *CW* XVIII:224.

16 See, for instance, Gray 1983.

17 See Gray 1983 for a book-length elaboration of that claim, and *Utilitarianism*, *CW* X:250–51, for Mill's explanation of rights.

18 *CW* XVIII:224, cf. 276.

19 Hart 1955.

20 Nozick 1974, 92–93.

21 Waldron 1987.

22 Devlin 1965.

23 He acquired it as a result of the savagery of his reviews in the *Saturday Review*; it was bestowed on him by his friends, who admired his prose but winced for his victims' sensibilities.

24 *On Liberty, CW* XVIII:222.

25 *CW* XVIII:308.

26 *CW* XVIII:302–04.

27 *CW* XVIII:302.

28 *CW* XVIII:296.

29 *CW* XVIII:260.

30 Popper 1974 is, perhaps surprisingly, not the classic source for the doctrine that science progresses by the process of making hypotheses and testing them against the evidence; Popper 1954, first published in German in 1937, is that.

31 *CW* XVIII:245.

32 For the distinction between "negative" and "positive" liberty see Berlin 1969.

33 Kuhn 1962; Feyerabend 1975; Musgrave et al. 1970.

34 *CW* XVIII:245.

35 *CW* XVIII:281.

36 *CW* XVIII:276.

37 *CW* XVIII:277.

38 Himmelfarb 1974:49–51.

39 Tocqueville 1994, I:264; *CW* XVIII:219.

40 *CW* XVIII:226.

41 *CW* XVIII:302–04.

42 *CW* XVIII:302.

43 *CW* XVIII:304.

44 *CW* XVIII:296.

45 *CW* XVIII:296.

46 *CW* XVIII:297.

47 *Later Letters, CW* X:550; see also his letters to Theodore Gomperz and Arnold Ruge in which he suggests that the essay is less needed in Germany "than here." *CW* X:539, 598.

48 *Representative Government, CW* XIX:411–12.

49 "Bentham," *CW* X:106–08.

50 *On Liberty, CW* XVIII:268.

51 *CW* XVIII:267–68.

52 *Autobiography, CW* I:270.

53 *On Liberty, CW* XVIII:254.

54 For a representative selection: Berlin 1969, Green 1874, and Dewey 1935.

55 Rawls 1993a, xvi–xvii, 154–57.

56 Rawls 1993a, xviii–xix, 134–44.

57 See, for instance, the discussion of liberty of conscience in Rawls 1971, 205–11.

58 See Rawls 1933a, 48–62; there is already a substantial critical literature.

59 Raz 1983 hints at such possibilities; the argument of Wollheim 1979, 253–69, would provide yet another route.

60 Rawls 1971, 3–7.

61 Dworkin 1981a.

62 "A Few Thoughts on Non-Intervention," *CW* XXI:109–24.

63 *On Liberty, CW* XVIII:290.

64 *CW* XVIII:224.

65 *CW* XVIII:290.

66 *CW* XVIII:224.

67 *Principles of Political Economy, CW* III:799–804.

68 *On Liberty, CW* XVIII:283.

69 *Wisconsin* v. *Yoder*, 406 US, 205, 92 S. Ct. 1526 (1972).

70 This is partly a prudential argument against such measures, not an argument from high principle; and the moral principle in question is simple utilitarianism – the misery caused is not justified by the good achieved.

71 See Ryan 1995, ch. 3; and for a much longer and more detailed account Rockefeller, 76–124.

72 Cf. C. Taylor 1989; *Utilitarianism, CW* X:230; *On Liberty, CW* XVIII:220.

73 *CW* XVIII:215. See n. 10 of this chapter.

74 *Memorandum of the Improvements in the Administration of india during the Last Thirty Years, CW* XXX:91–160.

75 "Perpetual Peace," in *Kant's Political Writings*, ed. H. B. Reiss (Cambridge University Press, 1974).

76 *Utilitarianism, CW* X:211.

77 See, for instance, "Two Concepts of Liberty," in Berlin 1969.

78 *Comte and Positivism, CW* X:325–26.

79 *Subjection of Women, CW* XXI:259–340; *On Liberty, CW* XVIII:260.

80 Ryan 1970, chs. XII–XIII.

Guide to further reading

BIOGRAPHICAL AND GENERAL

Packe 1954 is a comprehensive and readable biography, but not philosophically reliable. Bain 1882 is an early biography and criticism which is still well worth reading. Britton 1953 has an interesting biographical chapter. Hayek 1951 presents the relationship between Mill and Harriet Taylor through their letters.

Ryan 1974 is a study of Mill's thought as a whole; Ryan 1988 and Skorupski 1989 are general studies of his philosophy. Harrison 1996 provides a usefully succinct and clear outline of recent interpretations of Mill's philosophy. Donagan 1971 is a perceptive discussion of Mill's prose.

SOCIAL AND INTELLECTUAL CONTEXT

Mandelbaum 1971 locates themes in Mill's thought in the larger context of nineteenth-century philosophy. For Mill's place in nineteenth-century philosophy and politics, seen from a variety of angles, see Alexander 1965; Collini 1991; Collini, Winch and Burrow 1983; Dicey 1905; Duncan 1973; Hamburger 1961; Kahan 1992; Kinzer, Robson and Robson 1992; Okin 1979; Robson 1968; Schneewind 1977; Skorupski 1993a; W. Thomas 1979; Zastoupil 1994.

LOGIC AND METAPHYSICS

In comparison to the wealth of commentary on Mill's ethics and politics, discussion of his logic and metaphysics is still thin. Much remains to be done. Scarre 1989 and Skorupski 1989 provide general accounts of this side of Mill's thought.

On general metaphysical issues Alan Ryan's 'Introduction' to *CW* IX (*An Examination of Sir William Hamilton's Philosophy*) provides a useful starting point. Price 1926–27 discusses Mill's phenomenalism. On Mill's view of religion see Carr 1962.

In philosophy of science, mathematics and logic the contributions of Jackson 1937–38, 1941a & 1941b have an honourably pioneering place among accurate reassessments of Mill's thought. Buchdahl 1971 discusses the debate between Whewell and Mill on the hypothetical method. Mackie 1974 is a masterly study and development of Mill's 'methods of experimental inquiry'. Kessler 1980 and Kitcher 1980a, 1983, are good on Mill's philosophy of arithmetic. De Jong 1982 is an informative study of Mill's semantics.

MORAL AND POLITICAL PHILOSOPHY

Here the secondary literature on Mill is vast, and the following selection represents no more than a sample of well-known or recent work. A valuably comprehensive survey of Mill's moral and political thought is provided by Berger 1984. The most recent general study of *Utilitarianism* is Crisp 1997. Some particular topics follow.

Justice, right, duty and obligation. Perhaps the most important development in understanding nineteenth-century utilitarianism over the last few decades has been the light commentators have thrown on the role these notions play in Bentham and Mill. The structure of Mill's political theory, the connexion between his social philosophy and his Ricardian political economy, and the continuities with his philosophic Radical inheritance now stand out more clearly. For Bentham's treatment of these concepts see Kelly 1990. For the way in which Bentham's treatment fits into his general conception of meaning, see R. Harrison 1983. A discussion which covers both Bentham and Mill is Rosen 1987.

A pioneering article on the interpretation of Mill's utilitarianism was that of Urmson 1953, from which the discussion of 'act-utilitarianism' and 'rule-utilitarianism' largely grew. On this see also Mabbott 1956; Brown 1973, 1974; Sumner 1979; Gray 1983; Berger 1984; Crisp 1997. An important series of interpretative articles by Lyons on Mill's treatment of rights, justice and morality is collected in Lyons 1994. See also Brown 1972, 1982; Berger 1984, ch. 4; Riley forthcoming. On the definition of 'moral' and Mill's 'art of life', see Ryan 1974, p. 104ff; Berger 1984, pp. 105–20; Skorupski 1993b.

The 'proof' of the principle of utility: Seth 1908; Hall 1949; Kretzman 1958; Mandelbaum 1968b; Stocker 1969; Dryer's introduction to *CW* X 1969; West 1972, 1982; Skorupski 1989, ch. 9.

Mill's concept of happiness or well-being, including his notion of 'higher pleasures': West 1976; Gibbs 1986; Hoag 1986, 1987; Donner 1991; Long 1992; Sumner 1992; Riley 1993.

Virtue, and Mill's relation to 'republicanism': Semmel 1984; Burrow 1988; H. S. Jones 1992; Kahan 1992, ch. 4.

Liberty: Radcliff 1966; Berlin 1969; Wollheim 1973; G. Williams 1976; Ten 1980; Gray 1983, 1996; Berger 1984, ch. 5; Rees 1985; Sartorius 1975; Honderich 1974, 1982; Skorupski 1989, ch. 10; Pyle 1994.

Democracy and socialism: Duncan 1973; Thompson 1976; Arneson 1979; Sarvasy 1985.

The rights of women: Annas 1977; Okin 1979; Goldstein 1980; Urbinati 1991; Hekman 1992; Donner 1993; Mendus 1994; Pyle 1995.

ECONOMICS, PSYCHOLOGY, SOCIAL SCIENCE

For discussion of Mill's treatment of history and the moral sciences, see Mandelbaum 1971. On his abortive project to write a treatise on 'ethology', Feuer 1976. On psychology: Wilson 1990. On economics: Stigler 1965; Schwartz 1972; Marchi 1974; Hollander 1985, 1989; V. R. Smith 1985.

Bibliography

Where the author's name appears in square brackets, the work was originally published anonymously. Attributions of authorship were provided by Peter Nicholson and taken from Walter E. Houghton et al., eds., *The Wellesley Index to Victorian Periodicals* (Toronto: University of Toronto Press and London: Routledge & Kegan Paul, 1969–89), except where indicated.

I am grateful to Elizabeth Brake for assistance in preparing the bibliography and to the School of Philosophical and Anthropological Studies of the University of St Andrews for awarding me a grant to cover her costs.

Ackelsberg, Martha, and Shanley, Mary L. 1996. "Privacy, Publicity, and Power: A Feminist Rethinking of the Public–Private Distinction." In Christine di Stefano and Nancy Hirschmann, eds., *Revisioning the Political*. Boulder, Colo.: Westview Press.

Ackrill, J. L. 1974. "Aristotle on Eudaimonia." *Proceedings of the British Academy* 60: 339–59. Reprinted in A. O. Rorty, ed., *Essays on Aristotle's Ethics*. Berkeley: University of California Press, 1980.

Addis, L. 1968. "The Individual and the Marxist Theory of History." In Brodbeck 1968c, 317–35.

1975. *The Logic of Society*. Minneapolis: University of Minnesota Press.

Alexander, Edward. 1965. *Matthew Arnold and John Stuart Mill*. London: Routledge and Kegan Paul.

[Amos, Sheldon W. (?)]. 1870. "The Subjection of Women." *Westminster Review* 37. Reprinted in Pyle 1995, 142–73.

Anderson, Olive. 1991. "The Feminism of T. H. Green: A Late-Victorian Success Story?" *History of Political Thought* 12: 671–93.

Annan, Noel. 1984. *Leslie Stephen: The Godless Victorian*. Chicago: University of Chicago Press.

544

Annas, Julia. 1977. "Mill and the Subjection of Women." *Philosophy* 52: 179–94.

Anon. 1694. "A System of Logic, Ratiocinative and Inductive, by John Stuart Mill." *Athenaeum*: 501–03.

   1860. "*On Liberty.* By John Stuart Mill." *British Quarterly Review* 31. Reprinted in Pyle 1994, 184–209.

   1866. "Women's Rights." *The Saturday Review* (June 16): 715–16.

   1867a. "Female Suffrage." *The Saturday Review* (March 30): 385–86.

   1867b. "Female Suffrage." *The Saturday Review* (May 25): 647–48.

   1869a. "The Subjection of Women." *The Saturday Review* (June 19). Reprinted in Pyle 1995, 37–45.

   1869b. "J. S. Mill on *The Subjection of Women.*" *Meliora* 12: 207–19.

   1869c. *An Answer to Mr. John Stuart Mill's "Subjection of Women".* London: Darton.

   1873. "Mr. Mill." *The Saturday Review* (May 17): 638–639.

Arneson, Richard J. 1979. "Mill's Doubts about Freedom under Socialism." In Cooper, Nielsen and Patten 1979.

Arnold, Matthew. 1993. *Culture and Anarchy and other writings.* Cambridge: Cambridge University Press.

Arrow, K. J., and Hahn, F. H. 1971. *General Competitive Analysis.* San Francisco and Edinburgh: Holden-Day.

Atkinson, R. F. 1957. "J. S. Mill's 'Proof' of the Principle of Utility." *Philosophy* 32.

Ayer, A. J. 1940. *The Foundations of Empirical Knowledge.* London: Macmillan.

   1954. "Phenomenalism." In *Philosophical Essays.* London: Macmillan.

   1964. "The A Priori." Reprinted from *Language, Truth, and Logic.* In Benacerraf and Putnam 1964, 289–301.

Badhwar, Meera Kapur, ed. 1993. *Friendship: A Philosophical Reader.* Ithaca: Cornell University Press.

[Bagehot, Walter]. 1865. "Mr. Mill's Address to the Electors of Westminster." *The Economist* (April 29). Reprinted in N. St J. Stevas, ed., *The Collected Works of Walter Bagehot,* vol. 3. London: The Economist, 1968.

Bain, Alexander. 1882, 1993. *John Stuart Mill: a Criticism.* London: Longmans, 1882. Reprinted, Bristol: Thoemmes Press, 1993.

   1901. *Autobiography.* London: Longmans.

Balfour, Arthur James. 1915. *Theism and Humanism.* London: Hodder and Stoughton.

Baumgardt, David. 1952, 1966. *Bentham and the Ethics of Today.* Princeton: Princeton University Press, 1952. Reprinted, New York: Octagon Books, 1966.

Baumol, W. J. 1982. "Contestable Markets: An Uprising in the Theory of Industry Structure." *American Economic Review* 72: 1–15.

Baumol, W. J., and Becker, G. 1952. "The Classical Monetary Theory: The Outcome of the Discussion." *Economica* 19: 355–76.

Baumol, W. J., Panzar, J. C., and Willig, R. D. 1982. *Contestable Markets and the Theory of Industry Structure*. San Diego: Harcourt, Brace, Jovanovich.

  1986. "On the Theory of Perfectly Contestable Markets." In J. E. Stiglitz and G. F. Mathewson, eds., *New Developments in the Analysis of Market Structure*. Cambridge: MIT Press.

Beauvoir, Simone de. 1974. *The Second Sex*. Trans. H. M. Parshley. New York: Random House, Vintage Books.

Becker, Lydia E. 1874. "Liberty, Equality, Fraternity. A Reply to Mr. Fitzjames Stephen's Strictures on Mr. J. S. Mill's *Subjection of Women*." *Women's Suffrage Journal*. Reprinted in Jane Lewis, ed., *Before the Vote Was Won: Arguments For and Against Women's Suffrage*, pp. 223–40. New York: Routledge and Kegan Paul, 1987.

Beiser, Frederick C. 1987. *The Fate of Reason: German Philosophy from Kant to Fichte*. Cambridge, Mass.: Harvard University Press.

Bellamy, Richard. 1992. "T. H. Green, J. S. Mill, and Isaiah Berlin on the Nature of Liberty and Liberalism." In H. Gross and R. Harrison, eds., *Jurisprudence: Cambridge Essays*, pp. 257–85. Oxford: Clarendon.

Benacerraf, Paul. 1973. "Mathematical Truth." In Benacerraf and Putnam 1983, 403–20. First published in *Journal of Philosophy* 70 (1973): 661–79.

Benacerraf, Paul, and Putnam, H., eds. 1964. *Philosophy of Mathematics*, 1st ed. Oxford: Blackwell.

  1983. *Philosophy of Mathematics*, 2d ed. Cambridge: Cambridge University Press.

Bennett, J. 1971. *Locke, Berkeley, Hume: Central Themes*. Oxford: Clarendon.

Bentham, Jeremy. 1834, 1983. *Deontology*. Ed. J. Bowring. 2 vols. London: Longman, 1834. Reprinted, ed. A. Goldworth, Oxford: Clarendon, 1983.

  1962. *The Works of Jeremy Bentham*. Ed. John Bowring. 10 vols. New York: Russell and Russell.

  1970. *The Collected Works of Jeremy Bentham: An Introduction to the Principles of Morals and Legislation*. Ed. J. H. Burns and H. L. A. Hart. London: Athlone Press.

Berger, Fred. 1984. *Happiness, Justice, and Freedom: The Moral and Political Philosophy of John Stuart Mill*. Berkeley: University of California Press.

  1985. "Reply to Professor Skorupski." *Philosophical Books* 26: 202–07.

Bergmann, Gustav. 1957. *Philosophy of Science*. Madison, Wis.: University of Wisconsin Press.

Berkeley, G. 1962. *Principles of Human Knowledge and Other Writings*. Ed. G. J. Warnock. London: Fontana.

Berlin, Isaiah. 1958. *Two Concepts of Liberty*. Oxford: Clarendon. Also in Berlin 1969.

1969. *Four Essays on Liberty*, London: Oxford University Press.

Bill, E. G. W. 1973. *University Reform in Nineteenth-century Oxford*. Oxford: Clarendon.

Blackstone, William. 1765–69. *Commentaries on the Laws of England*. 4 vols. Oxford: Clarendon.

Bladen, V. 1965. "Introduction to Mill's *Political Economy*." In J. S. Mill, *CW* II.

Bloor, David. 1974. *Knowledge and Social Imagery*. London: Routledge.

Boolos, George. 1971. "The Iterative Conception of Set." *Journal of Philosophy* 68: 215–31.

Boring, E. G. 1957. *History of Experimental Psychology*, 2d ed. New York: Appleton-Century-Crofts.

Bosanquet, Bernard. 1899, 1923. *The Philosophical Theory of the State*, 4th ed. London: Macmillan, 1923. First published 1899.

Bradley, F. H. 1876, 1962. *Ethical Studies*, 2d ed. Oxford: Oxford University Press, 1962. First published 1876.

Brandt, Richard B. 1979. *A Theory of the Good and of the Right*. Oxford: Clarendon.

1992. *Morality, Utilitarianism, and Rights*. Cambridge: Cambridge University Press.

Brink, David O. 1992. "Mill's Deliberative Utilitarianism." *Philosophy and Public Affairs* 21: 67–103.

Britton, Karl. 1953. *John Stuart Mill*. Penguin. Reprinted, New York: Dover, 1969.

Brodbeck, M. 1968a. "Explanation, Prediction, and 'Imperfect' Knowledge." In Brodbeck 1968c, 363–97.

1968b. "Methodological Individualisms." In Brodbeck 1968c, 280–303.

ed. 1968c. *Readings in the Philosophy of the Social Sciences*. New York: Macmillan.

Brodrick, George C. 1859. "Principles of Parliamentary Reform." *The Times*. Reprinted in Brodrick, *Political Studies*, pp. 139–53. London: Kegan Paul, 1879.

Bronaugh, Richard. 1974. "The Utility of Quality: An Understanding of Mill." *Canadian Journal of Philosophy* 4: 317–25.

Brouwer, L. E. J. 1975. *Collected Works*, vol. 1. Amsterdam: North-Holland.

Brown, D. G. 1972. "Mill on Liberty and Morality." *Philosophical Review* 81: 133–58.

1973. "What is Mill's Principle of Utility?" *Canadian Journal of Philosophy* 3: 1–12.

1974. "Mill's Act-Utilitarianism." *Philosophical Quarterly* 24: 67–68.

1978. "Mill on Harm to Others' Interests." *Political Studies* 26: 395–99.

1982. "Mill's Criterion of Wrong Conduct." *Dialogue* 21: 27–44.

Buchdahl, G. 1971. "Inductivist *versus* Deductivist Approaches in the Philosophy of Science as Illustrated by some Controversies between Whewell and Mill." *Monist* 55: 343–67.

Buckle, Henry Thomas. 1859. "Mill on Liberty." *Fraser's Magazine*. Reprinted in Pyle 1994, 25–80.

Burge, Tyler. 1977. "A Theory of Aggregates." *Nous* 11: 97–117.

Burns, J. H. 1968. "J. S. Mill and Democracy, 1829–1861." In Schneewind 1968.

1976. "The Light of Reason: Philosophical History in the Two Mills." In Robson and Laine 1976, 3–20.

Burrow, J. W. 1988. *Whigs and Liberals: Continuity and Change in English Political Thought.* Oxford: Clarendon.

Butts, Robert E., ed. 1968. *William Whewell's Philosophy of Scientific Method.* Pittsburgh: University of Pittsburgh Press.

Caine, Barbara. 1992. *Victorian Feminists.* Oxford: Oxford University Press.

Cairnes, J. E. 1874. "Woman Suffrage. – A Reply." *Macmillan's Magazine* 30. Reprinted in Pyle 1995, 286–300.

Call, W. M. W. 1875. "John Stuart Mill's Three Essays on Religion." *Westminster Review* 47: 1–28.

Campbell, Keith. 1974. "One Form of Scepticism about Induction." In R. G. Swinburne, ed., *The Justification of Induction.* London: Oxford University Press.

Carnap, Rudolf. 1963. "Intellectual Autobiography." In P. Schilpp, ed., *The Philosophy of Rudolf Carnap.* La Salle, Ill.: Open Court.

1967. *The Logical Structure of the World.* Berkeley: University of California Press.

Carr, Robert. 1962. "The Religious Thought of John Stuart Mill: A Study in Religious Scepticism." *Journal of the History of Ideas* 23: 475–95.

Carrithers, Michael. 1992. *Why Humans Have Cultures.* Oxford: Oxford University Press.

Cartwright, (Major) John. 1817. *A Bill of Rights and Liberties; or, An Act for a Constitutional Reform of Parliament.* London: Printed by John M'Creery and sold by Effingham Wilson.

Cass, D. 1965. "Optimum Growth in an Aggregative Model of Capital Accumulation." *Review of Economic Studies* 32: 233–40.

Casullo, Albert. 1988. "Revisability, Reliabilism, and A Priori Knowledge." *Philosophy and Phenomenological Research* 49: 187–213.

Chihara, Charles. 1990. *Constructibility and Mathematical Existence.* Oxford: Oxford University Press.

Chipman, John S. 1965. "A Survey of the Theory of International Trade: Part 1, The Classical Theory." *Econometrica* 33: 477–519.

1979. "Mill's 'Superstructure': How Well Does it Stand Up?" *History of Political Economy* 11: 477–500.

[Church, R. W.] 1860. "Mill on Liberty." *Bentley's Quarterly Review.* Reprinted in Pyle 1994, 210–54.

Clarke, M. L. 1962. *George Grote.* London: Athlone Press.

Cobbe, Frances Power. 1869. "The Subjection of Women." *Theological Review* 6. Reprinted in Pyle 1995, 54–74.

Colaiaco, James A. 1983. *James Fitzjames Stephen and the Crisis of Victorian Thought.* London: Macmillan.

Coleridge, S. T. 1934. *S. T. Coleridge's Treatise on Method.* Reprinted in Alice D. Cooper, ed., *Encyclopædia Metropolitana.* London: Constable and Son.

Collini, Stefan. 1977. "Liberalism and the Legacy of Mill." *Historical Journal* 20.

1989. "'Manly Fellows': Fawcett, Stephen and the Liberal Temper." In Lawrence Goldman, ed., *The Blind Victorian: Henry Fawcett and British Liberalism,* pp. 41–59. Cambridge: Cambridge University Press.

1991. *Public Moralists, Political Thought and Intellectual Life in Great Britain 1850–1930.* Oxford: Clarendon.

Collini, Stefan, Winch, Donald, and Burrow, John. 1983. *That Noble Science of Politics: A Study in Nineteenth-century Intellectual History.* Cambridge: Cambridge University Press.

Cooper, Neil. 1969. "Mill's 'Proof' of the Principle of Utility." *Mind* 78: 278–79.

Cooper, Wesley E., Nielsen, Kai, and Patten, Steven C., eds. 1979. *New Essays on John Stuart Mill and Utilitarianism. Canadian Journal of Philosophy,* supplementary volume 5. Guelph.

[Cowell, Herbert]. 1873. "Liberty, Equality, Fraternity: Mr John Stuart Mill." *Blackwood's Edinburgh Magazine.* Reprinted in Pyle 1994, 298–320.

Cowling, Maurice. 1963. *Mill and Liberalism.* Cambridge: Cambridge University Press.

Craig, E. 1987. *The Mind of God and the Works of Man.* Oxford: Clarendon.

Crisp, Roger. 1997. *A Guidebook to J. S. Mill's "Utilitarianism."* London: Routledge.

Cunliffe, Christopher, ed. 1992. *Joseph Butler's Moral and Religious Thought: Tercentenary Essays.* Oxford: Clarendon.

Cupples, B. 1972. "A Defence of the Received Interpretation of J. S. Mill." *Australian Journal of Philosophy* 50: 131–37.

Curry, H. B. 1964. "Remarks on the Definition and Nature of Mathematics." In Benacerraf and Putnam 1964, 152–56.

CW. See Mill, John Stuart.

Dahl, N. O. 1973. "Is Mill's Hedonism Inconsistent?" *American Philosophical Quarterly*, Monograph 7.

de Jong, William Remmelt. 1982. *The Semantics of John Stuart Mill*. Dordrecht: D. Reidel.

Devlin, Patrick. 1958, 1965. "The Enforcement of Morals." *Maccabean Lecture in Jurisprudence*. Reprinted, London: Oxford University Press, 1965.

Dewey, John. 1935. *Liberalism and Social Action*. New York: G. P. Putnam's Sons.

Dicey, A. V. 1905, 1914. *Lectures on the Relation between Law & Public Opinion in England during the Nineteenth Century*. London: Macmillan, 1905. 2d ed.: 1914.

di Stefano, Christine. 1989. "Re-reading J. S. Mill: Interpolations from the (M)other World." In M. Barr and R. Feldstein, eds., *Discontented Discourses*. Urbana: University of Illinois Press.

    1991. *Configurations of Masculinity*. Ithaca: Cornell University Press.

[Dixon, William Hepworth]. 1869. "*The Subjection of Women* by John Stuart Mill." *The Athenaeum* (June 19). Reprinted in Pyle 1995, 46–53 (identified by Marchand 1941, 366).

Donagan, Alan. 1971. "Victorian Philosophical Prose: J. S. Mill and F. H. Bradley." In S. P. Rosenbaum, ed., *English Literature and British Philosophy*. Chicago: University of Chicago Press.

Donner, Wendy. 1983. "John Stuart Mill's Concept of Utility." *Dialogue* 22: 479–94.

    1987. "Mill on Liberty of Self-Development." *Dialogue* 26: 227–37.

    1989. "Gray's Autonomy: In Defence of Mill." In Guy Lafrance, ed., *Ethics and Basic Rights*, pp. 117–30. Ottawa: University of Ottawa Press.

    1991. *The Liberal Self: John Stuart Mill's Moral and Political Philosophy*. Ithaca: Cornell University Press.

    1993. "John Stuart Mill's Liberal Feminism." *Philosophical Studies* 69: 155–66.

Downie, R. S. 1966. "Mill on Pleasure and Self-Development." *Philosophical Quarterly* 16: 69–71.

Dummett, Michael. 1978. *Elements of Intuitionism*. Oxford: Oxford University Press.

1991a. *Frege: Philosophy of Mathematics.* Cambridge, Mass.: Harvard University Press.

1991b. *The Logical Basis of Metaphysics.* Cambridge, Mass.: Harvard University Press.

Duncan, Graeme. 1973. *Marx and Mill: Two Views of Social Conflict and Social Harmony.* Cambridge: Cambridge University Press.

Dworkin, Ronald. 1977. *Taking Rights Seriously.* Cambridge, Mass.: Harvard University Press.

1981a. "Liberalism." In Stuart Hampshire, ed., *Public and Private Morality.* Cambridge: Cambridge University Press.

1981b. "What is Equality? Parts I & II." *Philosophy and Public Affairs* 10: 185–246, 283–345.

1987a. "What is Equality? Part III." *Iowa Law Review* 73: 1–54.

1987b. "What is Equality? Part IV." *University of San Francisco Law Review* 22: 1–30.

1991. "Foundations of Liberal Equality." In S. McMurrin, ed., *The Tanner Lectures*, vol. XI, pp. 1–119. Cambridge: Cambridge University Press.

Ebenstein, L. 1985. "Mill's Theory of Utility." *Philosophy* 60: 539–43.

Edwards, Rem. 1979. *Pleasures and Pains: A Theory of Qualitative Hedonism.* Ithaca: Cornell University Press.

Eisenstein, Zillah. 1981. *The Radical Future of Liberal Feminism.* New York: Longman.

Elshtain, Jean Bethke. 1981. *Public Man, Private Woman.* Princeton: Princeton University Press.

Fawcett, Henry. 1873. "His Influence at the Universities." In H. R. Fox Bourne, ed., *John Stuart Mill: Notices of His Life and Works*, pp. 74–80. London: Dallow. Boston: James R. Osgood.

Fawcett, Millicent Garrett. 1873. "Mr Fitzjames Stephen on the Position of Women." *Examiner.* Reprinted as a pamphlet. London: Macmillan.

Feinberg, Joel. 1984. *Harm To Others: Moral Limits of Criminal Law*, vol. 1. New York: Oxford University Press.

Feuer, L. S. 1976. "John Stuart Mill as Sociologist: The Unwritten Ethology." In Robson and Laine 1976, 86–110.

Feyerabend, Paul. 1975. *Against Method.* London: New Left Books.

Filipiuk, M. 1991. "John Stuart Mill and France." In Laine 1991.

Fisher, E. O. 1992. "Sustained Growth in the Model of Overlapping Generations." *Journal of Economic Theory* 58: 77–92.

Fogelin, R. 1985. *Hume's Scepticism in the "Treatise of Human Nature."* London: Routledge.

Forbes, Duncan. 1951. "James Mill and India." *Cambridge Journal* (October): 19–53.

Forget, Evelyn. 1990. "John Stuart Mill's Business Cycle." *History of Political Economy* 22: 629–40.

Frege, Gottlob. 1884, 1950. *The Foundations of Arithmetic*. Trans. J. L. Austin. Oxford: Blackwell, 1950. First published as *Die Grundlagen der Arithmetik*, 1884.

1893, 1964. *The Basic Laws of Arithmetic*. Trans. Montgomery Furth. Berkeley: University of California Press, 1964. First published as *Die Grundgesetze der Arithmetik*, vol. 1. Jena: Verlag Hermann Pohle, 1893.

Freud, Sigmund. 1985. *The Future of an Illusion*. Reprinted in *Civilization, Society and Religion*, vol. 12 of the Pelican Freud Library. Harmondsworth, Middlesex: Penguin Books.

Friedman, Michael. 1992. *Kant and the Exact Sciences*. Cambridge, Mass.: Harvard University Press.

Friedman, R. 1966. "A New Exploration of Mill's Essay *On Liberty*." *Political Studies* 14: 281–304.

Garnett, Jane. 1992. "Bishop Butler and the *Zeitgeist*: Butler and the Development of Christian Moral Philosophy in Victorian Britain." In Cunliffe 1992, 63–96.

Gaus, Gerald F. 1983. *The Modern Liberal Theory of Man*. London: Croom Helm. New York: St. Martin's Press.

Gibbs, B. R. 1986. "Higher and Lower Pleasures." *Philosophy* 61: 31–59.

Glucker, John. 1987. "Plato in England: the nineteenth century and after." In H. Funke, ed., *Utopie und Tradition*, pp. 149–210. Königshausen: Neumann.

1996. "The two Platos of Victorian Britain." In K. A. Algira, P. W. van der Horst, and D. T. Ruina, eds., *Polyhistor: Studies in the History and Historigraphy of Ancient Philosophy*, pp. 385–406. Leiden: Brill.

Gödel, Kurt. 1964. "What is Cantor's Continuum Problem?" In Benacerraf and Putnam 1964, 258–73.

Goldman, L. 1983. "The Origins of British 'Social Science': Political Economy, Natural Science and Statistics." *Historical Journal* 26: 587–616.

Goldstein, Leslie F. 1980. "Mill and Marx on Women's Liberation." *Journal of the History of Philosophy* 18: 319–34.

Gray, John. 1983. *Mill on Liberty: A Defence*. London: Routledge and Kegan Paul. Rev. ed., 1996.

1989. *Liberalisms*. London: Routledge.

1993. *Post-Liberalism, Studies in Political Thought*. London: Routledge.

1995. *Isaiah Berlin*. London: Harper Collins.

Gray, John, and Smith, G. W., eds. 1991. *J. S. Mill's "On Liberty" in Focus*. New York: Routledge.

Green, Michele. 1989. "Sympathy and Self-Interest: The Crisis in Mill's Mental History." *Utilitas*: 259–77.

Green, Thomas Hill. 1881. *Liberal Legislation and Freedom of Contract: A Lecture*. Reprinted in Harris and Morrow 1986, pp. 194–212.

1886. *Lectures on the Principles of Political Obligation*. Reprinted in Harris and Morrow 1986, 13–193.

1890. *The Logic of J. S. Mill*. In R. L. Nettleship, ed., *Works of Thomas Hill Green*. London: Longmans.

Greenleaf, W. H. 1983. *The British Political Tradition*, vol. 2: *The Ideological Heritage*. London: Methuen.

Griffin, James. 1986. *Well-Being: Its Meaning, Measurement and Moral Importance*. Oxford: Clarendon.

Griffin, N. 1972. "A Note on Mr Cooper's Reconstruction of Mill's 'Proof.'" *Mind* 81: 142–43.

Grote, G. 1826. "The Institutions of the Ancient Greeks." *Westminster Review* 5: 269–331.

1846–56. *A History of Greece*. 12 vols. London: John Murray.

1876. *Fragments on Ethical Subjects*. Ed. A. Bain. London: John Murray.

1888. *Plato and the other Companions of Socrates*, new ed. 4 vols. London: John Murray.

Grote, J. 1870. *An Examination of the Utilitarian Philosophy*. Ed. J. B. Mayor. Cambridge: Cambridge University Press.

Hall, Everett M. 1949. "The 'Proof' of Utility in Bentham and Mill." *Ethics* 60: 1–18.

Hamburger, J. 1961. *Intellectuals in Politics: John Stuart Mill and the Philosophic Radicals*. New Haven: Yale University Press.

1991. "Religion and 'On Liberty.'" In Michael Laine, ed., *A Cultivated Mind: Essays on J. S. Mill Presented to John M. Robson*, pp. 139–81. Toronto: University of Toronto Press.

Hamilton, A. 1990. "Ernst Mach and the Elimination of Subjectivity." *Ratio* 3, 2: 117–35.

1992. "Carnap's *Aufbau* and the Legacy of Neutral Monism." In D. Bell and W. Vossenkuhl, eds., *Science and Subjectivity*. Berlin: Akademie Verlag.

1995. "A New Look at Personal Identity." In *Philosophical Quarterly* 5: 332–49.

Hamilton, W. 1865. *Lectures on Metaphysics*, vol. 1. Edinburgh: Blackwood.

1866. *Discussions on Philosophy and Literature*. Edinburgh: Blackwood.

Hare, R. M. 1981. *Moral Thinking*. Oxford: Clarendon.

Harman, Gilbert. 1967. "Quine on Meaning and Existence I." *Review of Metaphysics* 31: 124–51.

Harris, Paul, and Morrow, John, eds. 1986. *T. H. Green: Lectures on the Principles of Political Obligation and Other Writings*. Cambridge: Cambridge University Press.

Harrison, Brian. 1978. *Separate Spheres: The Opposition to Women's Suffrage in Britain*. London: Croom Helm.

Harrison, J. 1975. "The Right, the Just and Expedient in Mill's *Utilitarianism*." In T. Penelhum and Roger Shiner, eds., *New Essays in the History of Philosophy. Canadian Journal of Philosophy*, supplementary vol. 1.

Harrison, Ross. 1983. *Bentham*. London: Routledge.

1996. "Bentham, Mill and Sidgwick." In Nicholas Bunnin and E. P. Tsui-James, eds., *The Blackwell Companion to Philosophy*, pp. 627–42. Oxford: Blackwell.

Harsanyi, John C. 1977a. *Rational Behavior and Bargaining Equilibrium in Games and Social Situations*. Cambridge: Cambridge University Press.

1977b. "Morality and the Theory of Rational Behaviour." *Social Research* 44: 623–56.

1992. "Game and Decision Theoretic Models in Ethics." In R. Aumann and S. Hart, eds., *Handbook of Game Theory*, vol. I, pp. 669–701. Amsterdam.

Hart, H. L. A. 1955. "Are There Any Natural Rights?" *Philosophical Review* 64: 175–91.

Harvie, Christopher. 1976. *The Lights of Liberalism: University Liberals and the Challenge of Democracy 1860–86*. London: Allen Lane.

Hayek, F. A. 1951. *John Stuart Mill and Harriet Taylor: Their Friendship and Subsequent Marriage*. London: Routledge.

[Hayward, Abraham]. 1873. "John Stuart Mill." *Fraser's Magazine*, n.s. 8: 663–81.

Hearns, S. J. 1992. "Was Mill a Moral Scientist?" *Philosophy* 67: 81–101.

Hegel, G. W. F. 1931. *The Phenomenology of Mind*. Trans. J. B. Baillie. London: George Allen and Unwin. New York: Humanities Press. First published 1807.

Hekman, S. 1992. "John Stuart Mill's *The Subjection of Women*: The Foundation of Liberal Feminism." *History of European Ideas* 15.

Held, Virginia. 1993. *Feminist Morality: Transforming Culture, Society, and Politics*. Chicago: University of Chicago Press.

Hempel, C. G. 1964. "On the Nature of Mathematical Truth." In Benacerraf and Putnam 1964, 366–81.

Hepburn, Ronald. 1965. "Questions about the Meaning of Life." *Religious Studies* 1: 125–40.

Heyting, Arend. 1956. *Intuitionism: An Introduction*. Amsterdam: North-Holland.

Himmelfarb, Gertrude. 1974. *On Liberty and Liberalism: The Case of John Stuart Mill*. New York: Knopf.

Hirsch, Gordon D. 1975. "Organic Imagery and 'On Liberty.'" *Mill News Letter* 10, 2: 3–13.

Hirst, F. W. 1927. *The Early Life and Letters of John Morley*. London: Macmillan.

Hoag, Robert W. 1986. "Happiness and Freedom: Recent Work on John Stuart Mill." *Philosophy and Public Affairs* 15, 2: 188–99.

   1987. "Mill's Conception of Happiness as an Inclusive End." *Journal of the History of Philosophy* 25: 417–31.

   1992. "J. S. Mill's Language of Pleasures." *Utilitas* 4, 2: 247–78.

Holcolme, Lee. 1983. *Wives and Property: Reform of the Married Women's Property Law in Nineteenth-Century England*. Toronto: University of Toronto Press.

Hollander, Samuel. 1976. "Ricardianism, J. S. Mill, and the Neo-classical Challenge." In Robson and Laine 1976, 67–85.

   1985. *The Economics of J. S. Mill*. 2 vols. Toronto: University of Toronto Press.

   1989. "John Stuart Mill as Economic Theorist." In J. Eatwell, M. Milgate, and P. Newman, eds., *The New Palgrave: A Dictionary of Economics*, vol. 3, pp. 471–76. London: Macmillan.

Honderich, Ted. 1974. "The Worth of J. S. Mill on Liberty." *Political Studies* 22: 463–780.

   1982. "*On Liberty* and Morality – Dependent Harms." *Political Studies* 30: 504–14.

Hopkins, James. 1973. "Visual Geometry." *Philosophical Review* 82: 3–34.

Humboldt, Wilhelm von. 1996. *The Sphere and Duties of Government*. Trans. Joseph Coulthard. Bristol: Thoemmes Press.

Hume, D. 1973. *A Treatise of Human Nature*. Ed. L. Selby-Bigge. Oxford: Clarendon.

[Hutton, R. H.] 1859. "Mill on Liberty." *The National Review*. Reprinted in Pyle 1994, 81–117.

Irwin, T. H. 1994. *Plato's Ethics*. Oxford: Clarendon.

   1995a. "Plato's Objections to the Sophists." In C. A. Powell, ed., *The Greek World*. London: Routledge.

   1995b. "Prudence and Morality in Greek Ethics." *Ethics* 105, 2: 284–95.

Jackson, Reginald. 1937–38. "Mill's Joint Method," Parts I and II. *Mind* 46: 417–36; 47: 1–17.

   1941a. *An Examination of the Deductive Logic of John Stuart Mill*. London: Oxford University Press.

   1941b. "Mill's Treatment of Geometry." In J. B. Schneewind, ed., *Mill*, pp. 84–110. New York: Anchor, 1968. First published in *Mind*, 1941.

Jacobs, Harriet. 1987. *Incidents in the Life of a Slave Girl, Written by Herself*. Ed. Jean Fagan Yellin. Cambridge, Mass.: Harvard University Press. First published 1861.

Jacobs, Jo Ellen. 1994. "'The Lot of Gifted Ladies is Hard': A Study of Harriet Taylor Mill Criticism." *Hypatia* 9: 132–62.

[James, William]. 1869. "*Women's Suffrage*, by Horace Bushnell and *The Subjection of Women*, by John Stuart Mill." *North American Review*. Reprinted in James, *Essays, Comments, and Reviews*, pp. 246–56. Cambridge, Mass.: Harvard University Press, 1987.

   1950. *The Principles of Psychology*, vol. 1. New York: Dover.

Jay, Elisabeth. 1995. *Mrs Oliphant: "A Fiction to Herself": A Literary Life*. Oxford: Clarendon.

Jevons, W. S. 1877. "John Stuart Mill's Philosophy Tested." *Westminster Review*. Published in 4 parts: "On Geometrical Reasoning," December 1877, 167–82; "On Resemblance," January 1878, 256–75; "Experimental Methods," April 1878, 88–99; "Utilitarianism," November 1879, 521–38. Reprinted in R. Adamson and H. Jevons, eds., *Pure Logic and other Minor Works*, pp. 199–229. London: Macmillan, 1890.

Jones, Hardy. 1978. "Mill's Argument for the Principle of Utility." *Philosophy and Phenomenological Research* 38: 338–54.

Jones, H. S. 1992. "John Stuart Mill as Moralist." *Journal of the History of Ideas* 53: 287–308.

Jones, Jacqueline. 1985. *Labor of Love, Labor of Sorrow: Black Women, Work, and the Family from Slavery to the Present*. New York: Basic Books.

Jones, L. E., and Manuelli, R. E. 1990. "A Convex Model of Equilibrium Growth: Theory and Policy Implications." *Journal of Political Economy* 98: 1008–38.

   1992. "Finite Lifetimes and Growth." *Journal of Economic Theory* 58: 171–97.

Jones, Richard. 1831. *An Essay on the Distribution of Wealth and on the Sources of Taxation, Part 1: Rent*. London: John Murray.

   1859. *Literary Remains*. London: John Murray.

Kahan, Alan S. 1992. *Aristocratic Liberalism: The Social and Political Thought of Jacob Burckhardt, John Stuart Mill, and Alexis de Tocqueville*. Oxford: Oxford University Press.

Kelly, Audrey. 1992. *Lydia Becker and the Cause*. Lancaster, England: University of Lancaster Centre for North-West Regional Studies.

Kelly, P. J. 1990. *Utilitarianism and Distributive Justice: Jeremy Bentham and the Civil Law*. Oxford: Clarendon.

Kemp-Smith, Norman. 1941. *The Philosophy of David Hume*. London: Macmillan.

Kent, Susan Kingley. 1987. *Sex and Suffrage in Britain, 1860–1914*. Princeton: Princeton University Press.

Kessler, Glenn. 1980. "Frege, Mill, and the Foundations of Arithmetic." *Journal of Philosophy* 77: 65–79.

Keynes, J. M. 1963. *A Treatise on Probability*. London: Macmillan. First published 1921.

Kim, Jaegwon. 1982. "The Role of Perception in A Priori Knowledge." *Philosophical Studies* 40: 339–54.

Kingsley, Charles. 1869. "Women and Politics." *Macmillan's Magazine*. Reprinted as a pamphlet. London: London National Society for Women's Suffrage.

Kinzer, Bruce L., Robson, Ann P., and Robson, John M. 1992. *A Moralist In and Out of Parliament: John Stuart Mill at Westminster 1865–1868*. Toronto: University of Toronto Press.

Kitcher, Philip. 1975. "Kant and the Foundations of Mathematics." *Philosophical Review* 84: 23–50.

1979. "Frege's Epistemology." *Philosophical Review* 88: 235–62.

1980a. "Arithmetic for the Millian." *Philosophical Studies* 37: 215–36.

1980b. "A Priori Knowledge." *Philosophical Review* 89: 3–23.

1981. "How Kant Almost Wrote 'Two Dogmas of Empiricism' and Why He Didn't." *Philosophical Topics* 12: 217–49.

1983. *The Nature of Mathematical Knowledge*. New York: Oxford University Press.

1992. "The Naturalists Return." *Philosophical Review* 101: 53–114.

1993a. *The Advancement of Science*. New York: Oxford University Press.

1993b. "Knowledge, Society and History." *Canadian Journal of Philosophy* 23: 155–78.

1994. "Contrasting Conceptions of Social Epistemology." In F. Schmitt, ed., *Social Epistemology*, pp. 111–34. New York: Rowman and Allanheld.

1996. "Aprioristic Yearnings: Reflections on Michael Friedman's Kant." *Erkenntnis*, 44: 397–416.

Kleining, J. 1970. "The Fourth Chapter of Mill's *Utilitarianism*." *Australian Journal of Philosophy* 48: 197–205.

Kretzman, N. 1958. "Desire as Proof of Desirability." *Philosophical Quarterly* 8: 246–58.

Krouse, Richard W. 1982. "Patriarchal Liberalism and Beyond: From John Stuart Mill to Harriet Taylor." In Jean Bethke Elshtain, ed., *The Family in Political Thought*, pp. 145–72. Amherst: University of Massachusetts Press.

Kuhn, T. S. 1962. *The Structure of Scientific Revolutions*. Chicago: University of Chicago Press.

Kupperman, J. 1978. "Do we desire only pleasure?" *Philosophical Studies* 34: 451–54.

Ladenson, Robert F. 1977. "Mill's Conception of Individuality." *Social Theory and Practice* 4: 167–82.

Laine, M., ed. 1991. *A Cultivated Mind.* Toronto: University of Toronto Press.

Lathbury, D. C., ed. 1910. *Correspondence on Church and Religion of W. E. Gladstone.* 2 vols. London: John Murray.

Laudan, Larry. 1981. *Science and Hypothesis.* Dordrecht: Reidel.

Lévi-Strauss, Claude. 1967. *Structural Anthropology.* Trans. C. Jacobson and B. G. Schoepf. Garden City, N.Y.: Doubleday (Anchor).

1969. *The Elementary Structures of Kinship*, 2d ed. Trans. J. H. Bell, J. R. von Sturmer, and R. Needham. Boston: Beacon.

Lewis, D. 1973. *Counterfactuals.* Oxford: Blackwell.

Liddon, H. P. 1893. *Life of E. B. Pusey.* 4 vols. London: Longman.

Lively, J., and Rees, J., eds. 1978. *Utilitarian Logic and Politics.* London: Oxford University Press.

Lloyd, T. 1991. "Mill and the East India Company." In Laine 1991.

Locke, John. 1988. *Two Treatises of Government.* Ed. Peter Laslett. New York: Mentor Books. First published 1690.

Long, Roderick T. 1992. "Mill's Higher Pleasures and the Choice of Character." *Utilitas* 4, 2: 279–97.

Lukes, Steven. 1978. "The Underdetermination of Theories by Data." *Proceedings of the Aristotelian Society*, supplementary vol. 52.

Lyons, David. 1965. *Forms and Limits of Utilitarianism.* Oxford: Clarendon.

1994. *Rights, Welfare, and Mill's Moral Theory.* Oxford: Clarendon.

Mabbott, J. D. 1956. "Interpretations of Mill's *Utilitarianism.*" *Philosophical Quarterly* 66: 115–20.

Macaulay, T. B. 1978. "Mill's Essay on Government: Utilitarian Logic and Politics." Reprinted in Lively and Rees 1978.

McCloskey, H. J. 1970. "Liberty of Expression: Its Grounds and Limits," Part I. *Inquiry* 13: 219–37.

1971. *John Stuart Mill: A Critical Study.* London: Macmillan.

Mach, E. 1959. *The Analysis of Sensations.* New York: Dover.

MacIntyre, Alasdair. 1981. *After Virtue: A Study in Moral Theory.* London: Duckworth.

Mackie, J. L. 1955. "Evil and Omnipotence." *Mind* 64: 200–12.

1974. "Mill's Methods of Induction." In J. L. Mackie, *The Cement of the Universe.* Oxford: Oxford University Press.

1975. "Causes and Conditions." In E. Sosa, ed., *Causation and Conditionals.* London: Oxford University Press.

Maclaurin, Colin. 1742. *Treatise on Fluxions*. 2 vols. Edinburgh: T. W. and T. Ruddimans.

Madden, E. H. 1962. *Philosophical Problems of Psychology*. New York: Odyssey Press.

Maddy, Penelope. 1990. *Realism in Mathematics*. Oxford: Oxford University Press.

Mandelbaum, M. 1968a. "On Interpreting Mill's *Utilitarianism*." *Journal of the History of Philosophy* 6: 35–46.

  1968b. "Two Moot Issues in Mill's Utilitarianism." In Schneewind 1968, 206–33.

  1971. *History, Man and Reason*. London: Johns Hopkins University Press.

Marchand, Leslie A. 1941. *The Athenaeum: A Mirror of Victorian Culture*. Chapel Hill: University of North Carolina Press.

Marchi, N. B. de. 1974. "The Success of Mill's *Principles*." *History of Political Economy* 6: 119–57.

Marshall, J. 1973. "The Proof of Utility and Equity in Mill's *Utilitarianism*." *Canadian Journal of Philosophy* 3: 13–26.

Martin, R. 1972. "A Defence of Mill's Qualitative Hedonism." *Philosophy* 47: 140–51.

[Maurice, C. E.] 1869. "*The Subjection of Women*, by John Stuart Mill." *Contemporary Review* 11: 618–21.

Meiggs, R. 1972. *The Athenian Empire*. Oxford: Clarendon.

Mendus, Susan. 1994. "John Stuart Mill and Harriet Taylor on Women and Marriage." *Utilitas* 6: 287–99.

Mill, James. 1829, 1869. *An Analysis of the Phenomena of the Human Mind*. 2 vols. 1st ed., 1829. 2d ed., 1869, ed. John Stuart Mill. London: Longmans, Green and Dyer. Reprinted, New York: Augustus M. Kelly, 1967.

  1978. "An Essay on Government." Reprinted in Lively and Rees 1978.

Mill, John Stuart. 1963–91. *The Collected Works of John Stuart Mill* (cited as *CW*). Gen. ed. John M. Robson. 33 vols. Toronto: University of Toronto Press.

Millar, Alan. 1988. "Following Nature." *Philosophical Quarterly* 38: 165–85.

  1992. "Butler on God and Human Nature." In Cunliffe 1992, 293–315.

Miller, Harlan B., and Williams, William H., eds. 1982. *The Limits of Utilitarianism*. Minneapolis: University of Minnesota Press.

Mitchell, D. 1970. "Mill's Theory of Value." *Theoria* 36.

Moir, Martin. 1990. "Introduction" to *Writings on India*. In J. S. Mill, *CW* XXX.

Momigliano, A. D. 1952. "George Grote and the Study of Greek History." In *Contributo alla Storia degli Studi Classici*. Rome, 1955. First published as inaugural lecture. London: University College, 1952.

Mondadori, Fabrizio, and Morton, Adam. 1976. "Modal Realism: The Poisoned Pawn." *Philosophical Review* 85: 3–20.

Monro, D. H. 1970. "Liberty of Expression: Its Grounds and Limits," Part II. *Inquiry* 13: 238–53.

Montaigne, Michel de. 1976. "Of Friendship." *The Complete Essays of Montaigne*, 135–144. Trans. Donald M. Frame. Stanford: Stanford University Press.

Moore, R. J. 1983. "John Stuart Mill at India House." *Historical Studies* 20: 497–519.

Morley, John. 1873a. "The Death of Mr. Mill." *Fortnightly Review*. Reprinted in Stansky 1970, 101–10.

1873b. "Mr. Mill's Doctrine of Liberty." *Fortnightly Review*. Reprinted in Pyle 1994, 271–97.

1874. "Mr. Mill's Autobiography." *Fortnightly Review*. Reprinted in Stansky 1970, 139–63.

1908. *Life of Gladstone*. 2 vols. London: Macmillan.

Moser, S. 1963. "A Comment on Mill's Argument for Utilitarianism." *Inquiry* 6: 308–18.

Mounce, H. 1994. "The Philosophy of the Conditioned." *Philosophical Quarterly* 44: 174–89.

[Mozley, Anne]. 1869. "Mr Mill on the Subjection of Women." *Blackwood's Magazine* 106. Reprinted in Pyle 1995, 89–108.

Mueller, Iris. 1956. *John Stuart Mill and French Thought*. Urbana: University of Illinois Press.

Musgrave, Alan, et al., eds. 1970. *Criticism and the Growth of Knowledge. Proceedings of the International Colloquium in the Philosophy of Science*, vol. 4. London: Cambridge University Press.

Nakhnikian, G. 1951. "Value and Obligation in Mill." *Ethics* 62: 33–40.

Nedelsky, Jennifer. 1989. "Reconceiving Autonomy: Sources, Thoughts and Possibilities." *Yale Journal of Law and Feminism* 1: 7–36.

1990. "Law Boundaries, and the Bounded Self." *Representations* 30: 67–89.

Negishi, T. 1989. *History of Economic Theory*. Amsterdam: North-Holland.

Newman, W. L. 1887–1902. *The Politics of Aristotle*. 4 vols. Oxford: Clarendon.

Newsome, D. 1961. *Godliness and Good Learning*. London: J. Murray.

Nicholson, Peter P. 1990. *The Political Philosophy of the British Idealists: Selected Studies*. Cambridge: Cambridge University Press.

Noonan, H. 1989. *Personal Identity*. London: Routledge.

Nozick, Robert. 1974. *Anarchy, State and Utopia*. New York: Basic Books.

Ober, J. 1989. *Mass and Elite in Democratic Athens*. Princeton: Princeton University Press.

Ogilvie, R. M. 1964. *Latin and Greek*. Latest ed., Harmondsworth, Middlesex: Penguin Books, 1980.

O'Grady, Jean. 1987. "Mill and Fitzjames Stephen: Personal Notes." *Mill News Letter* 22, 1: 2–9.

Okin, Susan M. 1979. *Women in Western Political Philosophy*. Princeton: Princeton University Press.

    1989. *Justice and Gender*. New York: Basic Books.

[Oliphant, Margaret]. 1866. "The Great Unrepresented." *Fraser's Magazine* 100: 367–79.

    1869. "Mill on 'The Subjection of Women.'" *Edinburgh Review* 130. Reprinted in Pyle 1995, 109–41.

Olsen, Frances E. 1985. "The Myth of State Intervention in the Family." *University of Michigan Journal of Law Reform* 18: 835–64.

Packe, Michael St. John. 1954. *The Life of John Stuart Mill*. London: Secker and Warburg.

Parsons, Charles. 1964. "Infinity and Kant's Conception of the 'Possibility of Experience.'" *Philosophical Review* 73: 183–97.

    1986. Review of Kitcher 1983. *Philosophical Review* 95: 129–37.

Pattison, M. 1865. "J. S. Mill on Hamilton." *The Reader* 5 (May 20).

Peacocke, C. 1992. *A Study of Concepts*. Cambridge, Mass.: MIT Press.

Pears, D. 1990. *Hume's System*. Oxford: Oxford University Press.

Pitcher, G. 1977. *Berkeley*. London: Routledge.

Popper, Karl. 1950. *The Open Society and Its Enemies*. Princeton: Princeton University Press.

    1954, 1959. *The Logic of Scientific Discovery*. London: Hutchinson. Originally published as *Logik der Forschung*, 1934.

    1961. *The Poverty of Historicism*. London: Routledge and Kegan Paul.

    1974. *Conjectures and Refutations*. London: Routledge and Kegan Paul.

Postema, G. J. 1986. *Bentham and the Common Law Tradition*. Oxford: Clarendon.

Price, H. H. 1926–27. "Mill's View of the External World." *Proceedings of the Aristotelian Society* 27: 109–40.

Price, R. 1948. *Review of the Principal Questions in Morals*. Ed. D. D. Raphael. Oxford: Clarendon. First published 1787.

Prior, A. 1976. *The Doctrine of Propositions and Terms*. Ed. P. Geach and A. Kenny. London: Duckworth.

Putnam, Hilary. 1983. "Mathematics without Foundations." Reprinted in Benacerraf and Putnam 1983, 295–311.

Pyle, Andrew, ed. 1994. *Liberty: Contemporary Responses to John Stuart Mill*. Bristol: Thoemmes Press.

    1995. *The Subjection of Women: Contemporary Responses to John Stuart Mill*. Bristol: Thoemmes Press.

562   Bibliography

Quine, W. V. 1963. *From a Logical Point of View*. New York: Harper and Row.

1966. *The Ways of Paradox*. New York: Random House.

Radcliff, Peter, ed. 1966. *Limits of Liberty: Studies of Mill's On Liberty*. Belmont, Calif.: Wadsworth.

[Rands, W. B.] 1870. "The Subjection of Women." *Contemporary Review* 14. Reprinted in Pyle 1995, 207–22.

Raphael, D. D. 1955. "Fallacies in and about Mill's *Utilitarianism*." *Philosophy* 30: 344–57.

1994. "J. S. Mill's Proof of the Principle of Utility." *Utilitas* 6: 55–63.

Rawls, John. 1955. "Two Concepts of Rules." *Philosophical Review* 64 (January): 3–32.

1971. *A Theory of Justice*. Cambridge, Mass.: Harvard University Press. Oxford: Oxford University Press.

1993a. *Political Liberalism*. New York: Columbia University Press.

1993b. "The Law of Peoples." In Susan Hurley, ed., *Amnesty Lectures on Human Rights*. New York.

Raz, Joseph. 1983. *The Morality of Freedom*. Oxford: Clarendon.

Rees, John C. 1960. "A Re-Reading of Mill on Liberty." *Political Studies* 8: 113–29. Reprinted with a new postscript in Radcliff 1966.

1985. *John Stuart Mill's "On Liberty."* Ed. G. L. Williams. Oxford: Clarendon.

Regon, Milton C. 1993. *Family Law and the Pursuit of Intimacy*. New York: New York University Press.

Reid, T. 1872. *Essays on the Intellectual Powers of Man*. In Sir W. Hamilton, ed., *The Works of Thomas Reid DD*. Edinburgh: McClachlan and Stewart. (First published in 1785.)

Reiss, Erna. 1934. *Rights and Duties of Englishwomen*. Manchester: Sheratt and Hughes.

Rendall, Jane. 1985. *The Origins of Modern Feminism: Women in Britain, France and the United States 1780–1860*. Basingstoke: Macmillan.

1994. "Citizenship, Culture and Civilization: The Languages of British Suffragists, 1866–1874." In Caroline Daly and Melanie Nolan, eds., *Suffrage and Beyond: International Feminist Perspectives*, pp. 127–50. Auckland: Auckland University Press.

Ricardo, D. 1951. *On the Principles of the Political Economy of Taxation*, vol. 1 of P. Sraffa, ed., *Works and Correspondence of David Ricardo*. London: Cambridge University Press. (This is a reprint of the third edition of 1821.)

Riley, Jonathan. 1988. *Liberal Utilitarianism: Social Choice Theory and J. S. Mill's Philosophy*. Cambridge: Cambridge University Press.

1989. "Justice Under Capitalism." In J. Chapman and J. R. Pennock, eds.,

Markets and Justice: NOMOS 31: 122–62. New York: New York University Press.

1991a. "One Very Simple Principle." *Utilitas* 3: 1–35.

1991b. "Individuality, Custom and Progress." *Utilitas* 5: 217–44.

1993. "On Quantities and Qualities of Pleasure." *Utilitas* 5: 291–300.

forthcoming. *Security of Rights: A Liberal Utilitarian Theory of Justice.*

Ring, Jennifer. 1985. "Mill's *The Subjection of Women*: The Methodological Limits of Liberal Feminism." *Review of Politics* 47: 27–44.

1991. *Modern Political Theory and Contemporary Feminism.* Albany: State University of New York Press.

Robson, Ann P. 1991. "Mill's Second Prize in the Lottery of Life." In Michael Laine, ed., *A Cultivated Mind: Essays on J. S. Mill Presented to John M. Robson*, pp. 215–41. Toronto: University of Toronto Press.

Robson, Ann P., and Robson, John M., eds. 1994. *Sexual Equality: Writings by John Stuart Mill, Harriet Taylor Mill, and Helen Taylor.* Toronto: University of Toronto Press.

Robson, John M. 1966. "Harriet Taylor and John Stuart Mill: Artist and Scientist." *Queen's Quarterly* 73: 167–86.

1968. *The Improvement of Mankind: The Social and Political Thought of John Stuart Mill.* Toronto: University of Toronto Press. London: Routledge and Kegan Paul.

1976a. "Rational Animals and Others." In Robson and Laine 1976, 143–60.

1976b. "Thoughts on Social Change and Political Accommodation in Victorian Britain." In Josef L. Altholz, ed., *The Art and Mind of Victorian England*, pp. 78–93. Minneapolis: University of Minnesota Press.

Robson, John M., and Laine, Michael, eds. 1976. *James and John Stuart Mill: Papers of the Centenary Conference.* Toronto: University of Toronto Press.

Rockefeller, Steven. 1991. *Religious Faith and Democratic Humanism.* New York: Colombia University Press.

Romer, Paul. 1986. "Increasing Returns and Long-Run Growth." *Journal of Political Economy* 94: 1002–37.

Rosen, Fred. 1983. *Jeremy Bentham and Repesentative Democracy.* Oxford: Clarendon.

1987. "Bentham and Mill on Liberty and Justice." In F. Rosen and G. Feaver, eds., *Lives, Liberties, and the Public Good*, pp. 121–38. London: St. Martin's Press.

Rossi, A. S. 1970. "Sentiment and Intellect: The Story of John Stuart Mill and Harriet Taylor." In J. S. Mill and H. T. Mill, *Essays on Sex Equality.* Ed. A. S. Rossi. Chicago: University of Chicago Press.

Rover, Constance. 1967. *Women's Suffrage and Party Politics in Britain 1866–1914*. London: Routledge & Kegan Paul. Toronto: University of Toronto Press.

Royce, J. 1882. "Mind and Reality." *Mind* 7: 30–54.

Rubinstein, David. 1989. "Victorian Feminists: Henry and Millicent Garrett Fawcett." In Lawrence Goldman, ed., *The Blind Victorian: Henry Fawcett and British Liberalism*, pp. 71–87. Cambridge: Cambridge University Press.

Ruskin, John. 1902–12. *Works*. Eds. E. T. Cook and A. D. C. Wedderburn. 39 vols. London: G. Allen.

Russell, Bertrand. 1951, 1968. "John Stuart Mill." In Bertrand Russell, *Portraits from Memory*. New York: Simon and Schuster, 1951. Reprinted in Schneewind 1968, 1–21.

1956. *Principles of Mathematics*, 2d ed. London: Allen and Unwin.

1963. *Mysticism and Logic*. London: Allen and Unwin.

1972. *Our Knowledge of the External World*. London: Allen and Unwin.

1975. *Why I Am Not a Christian*. London: Routledge.

Ryan, Alan. 1966. "Mill and the Naturalistic Fallacy." *Mind* 75: 422–25.

1970, 1988. *The Philosophy of John Stuart Mill*. London: Macmillan, 1970. 2d ed., New York: Macmillan, 1988.

1974. *J. S. Mill*. London: Routledge and Kegan Paul.

1985. Review of Berger 1984. *Times Higher Education Supplement*, 29 March.

1995. *John Dewey and the High Tide of American Liberalism*. New York: Norton.

Sabine, George H. 1973. *A History of Political Theory*, 4th ed. Revised by Thomas Landon Thorson. Hinsdale, Ill.: Dryden Press.

Sartorius, Rolf E. 1975. *Individual Conduct and Social Norms*. Belmont, Calif.: Wadsworth.

Sarvasy, Wendy. 1985. "A Reconsideration of the Development and Structure of John Stuart Mill's Socialism." *Western Political Quarterly* 38: 312–33.

Scarre, Geoffrey. 1983. "Was Mill Really Concerned with Hume's Problem of Induction?" *The Mill Newsletter* 18: 6–23.

1989. *Logic and Reality in the Philosophy of John Stuart Mill*. Dordrecht: Kluwer.

Schlick, M. 1974. *General Theory of Knowledge*. La Salle, Ill.: Open Court.

1981. "Positivism and Realism." In O. Hanfling, ed., *Essential Readings in Logical Positivism*. Oxford: Blackwell.

Schneewind, J. B., ed. 1968. *Mill: A Collection of Critical Essays*. Garden City, N. Y.: Doubleday. London: Macmillan.

1976. "Concerning some Criticisms of Mill's Utilitarianism, 1861–76." In Robson and Laine 1976, 35–54.

1977. *Sidgwick's Ethics and Victorian Moral Philosophy.* Oxford: Clarendon.

Schochet, Gordon. 1975. *Patriarchalism in Political Thought.* New York: Basic Books.

Schwartz, Pedro. 1972. *The New Political Economy of J. S. Mill* (English translation). London: Weidenfeld and Nicholson.

Schwartz, Robert. 1995. "Is Mathematical Competence Innate?" *Philosophy of Science* 62: 227–40.

Semmel, Bernard. 1984. *John Stuart Mill and the Pursuit of Virtue.* New Haven: Yale University Press.

Sen, Amartya, and Williams, Bernard, eds. 1982. *Utilitarianism and Beyond.* Cambridge: Cambridge University Press.

Seth, James. 1908. "The Alleged Fallacies in Mill's Utilitarianism." *Philosophical Review* 17: 468–72.

Sewell, W. 1841. *Introduction to the Dialogues of Plato.* London: Oxford University Press.

Sextus Empiricus. 1933. *Outlines of Pyrrhonism.* In *Works.* Trans. R. G. Bury. London: Loeb Classical Library.

Shanley, Mary L. 1981. "Marital Slavery and Friendship: John Stuart Mill's *The Subjection of Women.*" *Political Theory* 9: 229–47.

1989. *Feminism, Marriage and the Law in Victorian England.* Princeton: Princeton University Press.

Shapiro, J. Selwyn. 1943. "John Stuart Mill, Pioneer of Democratic Liberalism in England." *Journal of the History of Ideas* 4: 127–60.

Sharpless, F. Parvin. 1967. *The Literary Criticism of John Stuart Mill.* The Hague: Mouton.

Sidgwick, Arthur, and Sidgwick, Eleanor Mildred. 1906. *Henry Sidgwick: A Memoir.* London: Macmillan.

Sidgwick, Henry. 1873a. "John Stuart Mill." *The Academy* 4 (May 15): 193.

1873b. "'Liberty, Equality, Fraternity.' By James Fitzjames Stephen." *The Academy* 4 (August 1): 292–94.

1882. "Incoherence of Empirical Philosophy." *Mind* 7: 533–43.

1891. *The Elements of Politics,* 4th ed. London: Macmillan.

1907. *Methods of Ethics,* 7th ed. London: Macmillan. First published 1901.

Skorupski, John. 1985. "The Parts of Happiness." *Philosophical Books* 26: 193–202.

1989. *John Stuart Mill.* London: Routledge.

1990–91. "The Legacy of Modernism." *Proceedings of the Aristotelian Society* 91: 1–19.

1993a. *English-Language Philosophy 1750–1945.* Oxford: Oxford University Press.

1993b. "The Definition of Morality." In A. Phillips Griffiths, ed., *Ethics: Philosophy Supplement* 35: 121–44. Cambridge: Cambridge University Press.

1997. "The Ethical Content of Liberal Law." In J. Tasioulas, ed., *Law, Values And Social Practices.* Aldershot: Dartmouth Publishing.

Smart, J. J. C. 1982. "An Outline of a System of Utilitarian Ethics." In J. J. C. Smart and B. Williams, eds., *Utilitarianism: For and Against.* Cambridge: Cambridge University Press.

Smith, Adam. 1904. *The Wealth of Nations.* Ed. Edwin Cannan. New York: Random House.

Smith, Goldwin. 1874. "Female Suffrage." *Macmillan's Magazine* 30. Reprinted in Pyle 1995, 266–85.

Smith, K. J. M. 1988. *James Fitzjames Stephen: Portrait of a Victorian Rationalist.* Cambridge: Cambridge University Press.

Smith, V. R. 1985. "John Stuart Mill's Famous Distinction Between Production and Distribution." *Economics and Philosophy* 1: 267–84.

Solow, R. M. 1956. "A Contribution to the Theory of Economic Growth." *Quarterly Journal of Economics* 70: 65–94.

Sosa, Ernest. 1969. "Mill's Utilitarianism." In James M. Smith and Ernest Sosa, eds., *Mill's Utilitarianism.* Belmont, Calif.: Wadsworth.

Spence, G. W. 1968. "The Psychology behind J. S. Mill's 'Proof.'" *Philosophy* 43: 18–28.

Stansky, Peter, ed. 1970. *John Morley: Nineteenth-Century Essays Selected with an Introduction.* Chicago: University of Chicago Press.

Ste Croix, G. E. M. de. 1972. *Origins of the Peloponnesian War.* London: Duckworth.

[Stephen, James Fitzjames]. 1859. "Mr. Mill on Political Liberty." *Saturday Review.* Reprinted in Pyle 1994, 6–24 (identified by L. Stephen 1895, 314).

Stephen, James Fitzjames. 1873, 1967. *Liberty, Equality, Fraternity.* 2d ed., London: Smith, Elder, 1874. Reprinted, ed. R. J. White, Cambridge: Cambridge University Press, 1967.

[Stephen, Leslie]. 1873. "The Late Stuart Mill." *The Nation* 414: 382–83.

Stephen, Leslie. 1883. "The Suppression of Poisonous Opinions." *The Nineteenth Century.* Reprinted in Pyle 1994, 409–43.

1885. *Life of Henry Fawcett.* London: Smith, Elder.

1895. *The Life of Sir James Fitzjames Stephen.* London: Smith, Elder.

1903. *National Review.* Reprinted in *Some Early Impressions*, pp. 52–96. London: Hogarth Press, 1924.

Stewart, Dugald. 1814. *Elements of the Philosophy of the Human Mind*, vol. 2. Edinburgh: Constable. London: Cadell and Davies.

1854–58. *Collected Works.* Ed. Sir W. Hamilton. London: Hamilton, Adams. Edinburgh: Constable.

Stigler, George J. 1965. "The Nature and Role of Originality in Scientific Progress." In George Stigler, *Essays in the History of Economics*. Chicago: University of Chicago Press. Also in *Economica* 1955.

    1976. "The Scientific Uses of Scientific Biography." In Robson and Laine 1976, 55–66.

Stocker, M. 1969. "Mill on Desire and Desirability." *Journal of the History of Philosophy* 7: 199–201.

Stokes, E. 1959. *The English Utilitarians and India*. Oxford: Oxford University Press.

Stopper, M. R. 1981. "Greek Philosophy and the Victorians." *Phronesis* 26: 267–85.

Stove, D. 1993. "The Subjection of John Stuart Mill." *Philosophy* 68: 5–13.

Strasser, M. 1984. "Mill and the Utility of Liberty." *Philosophical Quarterly* 34: 63–68.

Street, Charles Larrabee. 1926. *Individualism and Individuality in the Philosophy of John Stuart Mill*. Milwaukee: Moreland.

Sumner, L. W. 1974. "More Light on the Later Mill." *Philosophical Review* 83: 504–27.

    1979. "The Good and the Right." In Cooper, Nielsen, and Patten 1979, 99–114.

    1987. *The Moral Foundation of Rights*. Oxford: Clarendon.

    1992. "Welfare, Happiness, and Pleasure." *Utilitas* 4: 199–206.

Sweet, William. 1995. "Law and Liberty in J. S. Mill and Bernard Bosanquet." In Y. Hudson and W. C. Peden, eds., *The Social Power of Ideas*, pp. 361–85. Lewiston: Edwin Mellen Press.

Taylor, A. E. 1926. *Plato: The Man and his Work*. London: Constable.

Taylor, Charles. 1989. *Sources of the Self*. Cambridge: Cambridge University Press.

Taylor, Sir Henry. 1870. "Mr. Mill on the Subjection of Women." *Fraser's Magazine* 1. Reprinted in Pyle 1995, 174–206.

Taylor, M. W. 1992. *Men versus the State: Herbert Spencer and Late Victorian Individualism*. Oxford: Clarendon.

Ten, C. L. 1980. *Mill on Liberty*. Oxford: Oxford University Press.

Thomas, David Lloyd. 1983. "Rights, Consequences, and Mill on Liberty." In A. Phillips Griffiths, ed., *Of Liberty*. Cambridge: Cambridge University Press.

Thomas, William. 1979. "John Stuart Mill and the Crisis of Benthamism." In William Thomas, *The Philosophical Radicals*. Oxford: Oxford University Press.

    1985. *Mill*. Oxford: Oxford University Press.

Thompson, Dennis F. 1976. *John Stuart Mill and Representative Government*. Princeton: Princeton University Press.

Tocqueville, Alexis de. 1994. *Democracy in America*. London: Dent (Everyman Library).

Tronto, Joan. 1993. *Moral Boundaries: A Political Argument for an Ethic of Care*. New York: Routledge.

Tulloch, Gail. 1989. *Mill and Sexual Equality*. Hemel Hempstead: Harvester Wheatsheaf. Boulder, Colo.: Lynne Rienner.

Turner, F. M. 1981. *The Greek Heritage in Victorian Britain*. New Haven: Yale University Press.

Urbinati, Nadia. 1991. "John Stuart Mill on Androgyny and Ideal Marriage." *Political Theory* 19: 626–48.

Urmson, J. O. 1953. "The Interpretation of the Moral Philosophy of J. S. Mill." *Philosophical Quarterly* 3: 33–39.

Vlastos, G. 1991. *Socrates*. Cambridge: Cambridge University Press. Ithaca: Cornell University Press.

   1994. *Socratic Studies*. Cambridge: Cambridge University Press.

Waldron, J. 1987. "Mill and the Value of Moral Distress." *Political Studies* 35: 410–23.

Walsh, H. T. 1962. "Whewell and Mill on Induction." *Philosophy of Science* 29: 279–84.

Ward, W. R. 1965. *Victorian Oxford*. London: Frank Cass.

West, Henry R. 1972. "Reconstructing Mill's 'Proof' of the Principle of Utility." *Mind* 81: 256–57.

   1975. "Mill's Naturalism." *Journal of Value Inquiry* 9: 67–69.

   1976. "Mill's Qualitative Hedonism." *Philosophy* 51: 97–101.

   1982. "Mill's 'Proof' and the Principle of Utility." In Miller and Williams 1982, 23–34.

Whewell, William. 1829. "Mathematical Exposition of Some Doctrines of Political Economy." *Transactions of the Cambridge Philosophical Society* 1829, 1831, and 1850. Reprinted as *On the Mathematical Exposition of Some Doctrines of Political Economy*. London: Gregg International Publishers, 1968.

   1831. Review of Richard Jones's *Essay on the Distribution of Wealth and on the Sources of Taxation*, Part 1: Rent. *British Critic* series 4, 10: 41–61.

   1845. *The Elements of Morality, including Polity*. New York: Harper.

   1847. *The Philosophy of the Inductive Sciences*, new ed. 2 vols. London: John W. Parker.

   1849. *Of Induction, with Especial reference to Mr. J. Stuart Mill's System of Logic*. London: Parker. Reprinted as "Mr. Mill's Logic" in Butts 1968.

   1858a. *History of Scientific Ideas: Being the First Part of the Philosophy of the Inductive Sciences*, 3rd ed. 2 vols. London: Parker and Son.

1858b. *Novum Organum Renovatum: Being the Second Part of the Philosophy of the Inductive Sciences*, 3rd ed. London: Parker and Son.

1859. "Prefatory Note" to R. Jones 1859.

1862. *Six Lectures on Political Economy*. Cambridge: Cambridge University Press.

White, N. P. 1981. *A Companion to Plato's Republic*. Oxford: Blackwell.

1984. "The Classification of Goods in Plato's *Republic*." *Journal of the History of Philosophy* 22: 393–421.

1995. "Conflicting Parts of Happiness in Aristotle's *Ethics*." *Ethics* 105: 258–83.

Williams, Bernard. 1982. "A Critique of Utilitarianism." In J. J. C. Smart and B. Williams, eds., *Utilitarianism: For and Against*. Cambridge: Cambridge University Press.

Williams, G. 1976. "Mill's Principle of Liberty." *Political Studies* 24: 132–40.

Williams, Merryn. 1986. *Margaret Oliphant: A Critical Biography*. New York: St. Martin's Press.

1995. "Feminist or Antifeminist? Oliphant and the Woman Question." In D. J. Trela, ed., *Margaret Oliphant: Critical Essays on a Gentle Subversive*. Susquehanna: Susquehanna University Press. London: Selinsgrove and Associated University Presses.

Wilson, F. 1983. "Mill's 'Proof' of Utility and the Composition of Causes." *Journal of Business Ethics* 2: 135–58.

1985. *Explanation, Causation and Deduction*. Dordrecht, Holland: D. Reidel.

1986. *Laws and Other Worlds*. Dordrecht, Holland: D. Reidel.

1989. "William Wordsworth and the Culture of Science." *Centennial Review* 33: 322–92.

1990. *Psychological Analysis and the Philosophy of John Stuart Mill*. Toronto: University of Toronto Press.

1991a. *Empiricism and Darwin's Science*. Dordrecht, Holland: Kluwer.

1991b. "Mill and Comte on the Method of Introspection." *Journal for the History of Behavioral Sciences* 27: 107–29.

Winkler, K. 1989. *Berkeley: An Interpretation*. Oxford: Clarendon.

Wittgenstein, Ludwig. 1953. *Philosophical Investigations*. Trans. and ed. E. Anscombe and R. Rhees. Oxford: Blackwell.

Wolff, R. P. 1968. *The Poverty of Liberalism*. Boston: Beacon Press.

Wollheim, R. 1973. "John Stuart Mill and the Limits of State Action." *Social Research* 40.

1979. "John Stuart Mill and Isaiah Berlin." In Alan Ryan, ed., *The Idea of Freedom*, pp. 253–70. Oxford: Oxford University Press.

Woods, T. 1961. *Poetry and Philosophy: A Study in the Thought of John Stuart Mill*. London: Hutchinson.

Wright, G. H. von. 1957. *The Logical Problem of Induction*, 2d ed. Oxford: Blackwell.

Wright, T. R. 1986. *The Religion of Humanity: The Impact of Comtean Positivism on Victorian Britain.* Cambridge: Cambridge University Press.

Wynn, Karen. 1992a. "Addition and Subtraction by Human Infants." *Nature* 358: 749–50.

　1992b. "Evidence against Empirical Accounts of the Origins of Numerical Knowledge." *Mind and Language* 7: 315–32.

Zastoupil, Lynn. 1988. "J. S. Mill and India." *Victorian Studies* 32: 31–54.

　1994. *John Stuart Mill and India.* Stanford: Stanford University Press.

Zerilli, Linda M. G. 1994. *Signifying Women: Culture and Chaos in Rousseau, Burke, and Mill.* Ithaca: Cornell University Press.

Index

571